England's Shipwreck Heritage
From logboats to U-boats

England's Shipwreck Heritage

From logboats to U-boats

Serena Cant
with a contribution by Alison James

ENGLISH HERITAGE

Published by English Heritage, The Engine House, Fire Fly Avenue, Swindon SN2 2EH
www.english-heritage.org.uk
English Heritage is the Government's statutory adviser on all aspects of the historic environment.

© English Heritage 2013

The views expressed in this book are those of the authors and not necessarily those
of English Heritage.

Images (except as otherwise shown) © English Heritage or © Crown copyright.EH.
Maps © Crown copyright and database right 2013. All rights reserved. Ordnance Survey licence
number 100024900.

First published 2013

ISBN 978–1-84802–044–3

Product code 51529

British Library Cataloguing in Publication data
A CIP catalogue record for this book is available from the British Library.

Application for the reproduction of images should be made to English Heritage. Every effort has
been made to trace the copyright holders and we apologise in advance for any unintentional
omissions, which we would be pleased to correct in any subsequent edition of this book.

For more information about English Heritage images, contact Archives Research Services,
The Engine House, Fire Fly Avenue, Swindon SN2 2EH; telephone (01793) 414600.

Brought to publication by René Rodgers and Sarah Enticknap, Publishing, English Heritage

Typeset in 9.5 on 10.75 point Charter

Edited by Jeremy Toynbee
Indexed by Caroline Jones
Designed by Francis & Partners
Printed in UK by Butler Tanner & Dennis Ltd.

CONTENTS

Introduction vii

Notes on the text xii

1 The hazards of the natural environment 1

2 Ships at war 51

3 The vagaries of human nature 115

4 The transport of people and goods around the world 149

5 Solving mysteries 189

6 How does it all come together? What is left to find out? 235

Appendix 245

Notes 249

Bibliography 267

Acknowledgements 275

Index 277

In memory of my mother,
who did not live to see me finish this book

INTRODUCTION

We have fed our sea for a thousand years
And she calls us, still unfed,
Tho' there's never a wave of all her waves
But marks our English dead …
We must feed our sea for a thousand years
For that is our doom and pride,
As it was when they sailed with the *Golden Hind*
Or the wreck that struck last tide,
Or the wreck that lies on the spouting reef,
Where the ghastly blue lights flare …

(Rudyard Kipling, 'The song of the dead')

Shipwrecks are historical monuments like any other, and yet completely different. Embedded deep in the human psyche, shipwrecks are woven into religion and myth, based on all-too-real experiences: Noah's Ark came to rest on Mount Ararat, a stranding that subverted the usual outcome to stand as a sign of survival; Odysseus' shipwrecks and his travails upon the sea form the core of the *Odyssey*; Jesus calmed the waves as a storm arose, while his disciple St Paul came ashore on Malta; the sagas of Iceland tell of shipwreck among the cold waters of the North, and, of course, the more recent wreck of the *Titanic*, a real-life event, has acquired quasi-mythological status.

In real life, shipwrecks stand as a testament to heroic achievement in overcoming an alien environment with few resources, which we in the 21st century can only admire. The shores of England and her territorial waters are littered with shipwrecks, as are her estuaries, rivers, lakes, and canals. Shipwreck remains may become designated sites, in a process akin to the listing of buildings; like Iron Age hillforts and timber-framed houses, they are intimately connected with the environment in which they are found. Ultimately, however, it is the nature of their relationship with that environment which turns them into monuments, in an unsuccessful battle with wind and waves, with severe weather and natural hazards, with sandbanks, offshore rocks and cliffs, or man-made entities such as piers and harbours.

Other causes may conspire to wreck a vessel, such as warfare or human error, but it is the contact with the environment that finally causes the loss of a ship as she founders at sea or is dashed against cliffs. The way that a ship becomes a historical monument in the context of its landscape is also different: the events – usually – of a single night rather than the careful, patient construction of a cathedral or a palace over many years or even decades.

The stories presented in this book are threefold: the history of wreck events themselves, in their diversity and range; their relationships with terrestrial monuments; and the story behind the research involved in identifying wreck remains and documented wrecks not currently associated with any remains. It is not intended to be an exhaustive account of all wrecks in England covered by heritage protection legislation, although many feature in the book. Rather the aim is to show ship remains and documentary research in their common context and to showcase, at a crossroads of Europe, the fascination of shipwreck archaeology. The shipwrecks which litter the North Sea, English Channel, Bristol Channel and Irish Sea coastlines of England are an English heritage – and an international one. Vessels from northern and eastern Europe must pass through the English Channel on their way out to southern and western Europe and across the Atlantic, and vice versa. Thus it is that a variety of ships of all nations, and from times before the concepts of modern nationalities, have met their end in English waters. At the time of writing, over 37,000 shipwrecks are known to have occurred in English waters, of which some 6,000 are represented by wreck sites, identified to a greater or lesser degree (Figs I and II).

Researching wrecks is a challenge involving a number of disciplines other than archaeology. Linguistic skills not only encompass languages but also documentary research into areas as diverse as obscure saints, national flags and emblems, other alphabets, medieval wreck law,

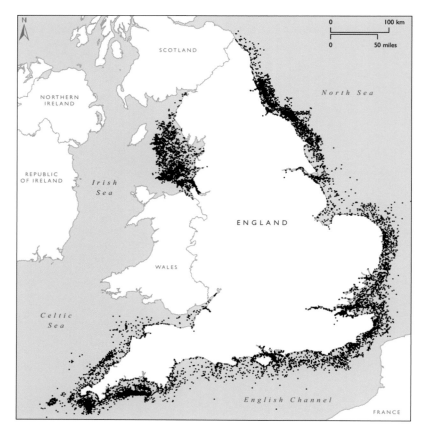

Fig I
*Distribution map of all
shipwrecks documented
around the coast of England
on the NRHE database,
at the time of writing.
There is no sector of the
English coastline which is
entirely free of shipwrecks,
though concentrations
appear particularly dense on
the approaches to Liverpool
on the north-west coast,
on the south Cornish coast,
along Kent and the Thames
Estuary, and off the
north-east coast near
Newcastle-upon-Tyne,
with noticeably fewer
wrecks documented on the
Bristol Channel coastline or
in the Wash.*

early state papers, place-name history, naval and military history, economic history, industrial history, gun founding, manorial law, meteorology, literary works and the development of journalism. One early journalist was Daniel Defoe, who was clearly fascinated by shipwrecks: although *Robinson Crusoe* was a fictional work (albeit one based on real-life events), Defoe put together a sober journalistic anthology based on eyewitness accounts of the Great Storm of 1703, the worst recorded storm in British history. Defoe was not the only author who referred to shipwrecks: shipwrecks, real or based on real events, are embedded in the history of English literature, from Shakespeare to Gerard Manley Hopkins, and art, from the paintings of the Dutch masters of the Golden Age who recorded the Anglo-Dutch wars of the 17th century, to the works of Turner (Fig III). All these, whether based on truth, fiction, or somewhere in between, are as valuable as more official records in shedding useful light on 'what really happened'.

Given the number of potentially useful disciplines involved, extracting meaningful shipwreck data from contemporary sources often requires lateral thinking and the ability to read between the lines. Sources with a less

obvious maritime connection can be exceedingly useful. The value of personal diaries and church burial registers is immediately apparent: their counterparts the tangible artefacts of ordnance recovered from the sea and reused as street furniture, or grave markers in churchyards on the coast. Less obvious may be cathedral building accounts, the 'hue and cry' (the 18th-century equivalent of televised appeals for information on crimes) or the obituaries of women who died of grief following the loss at sea of husbands, brothers and sons, whose stories are otherwise lost to us. Unsurprisingly, the *New York Times* is an important source for the losses of emigrant ships of all nationalities and of vessels with North American connections.

A complete database of shipping losses, even for so restricted an area as the English coastline and the national limit of territorial waters up to 12 miles out to sea is impossible. From earliest times vessels have miscarried out of sight of land or of any other vessel which could come to their assistance and so were never recorded, even in literate times. There are many reports of vessels overdue, and thus presumed lost, on a voyage passing the English coastline. A significant proportion of these will have been actually lost within English waters, but they remain a mystery, as do the losses of vessels between one English port and another. At best they can only be ascribed to the North Sea or the English Channel. As far as written evidence goes, the further back in time, the less survives, and what remains may be inherently unreliable: propaganda claims that more ships had been sunk on the opposing side are common to both Anglo-Saxon and Second World War records of shipping losses. Many wrecks, however, must have occurred before the concept of making literate records existed in the British Isles (or elsewhere). Remains of wrecks dating from the Bronze Age, Iron Age and Roman period, evidence of early trading activity: yet even the Romans, masters of literacy, have left little record of shipwrecks off this north-western corner of their Empire, only reachable by sea.

Many more wrecks are recorded during the medieval period, although many have been lost twice over, once during the wreck event itself and again through the loss of any subsequent documentation. Medieval shipwreck remains are scarce, and are far outweighed by the number of documented wrecks, yet these in turn are so patchy that it is clear many have been lost to us. Those documented wrecks are thus doubly important as indicators of the archaeological potential from the Middle Ages. There is, in fact, a serious bias in surviving documentary evidence towards official records, filtered through 'what happened next' and the consequent disputes over theft and rights to wreck – concentrating on the goods, over which all parties squabbled, from the king and landowners who wanted their share of the goods, and the merchants who demanded restitution, down to the poorest peasant, who appropriated and concealed cargoes. In such documents the information which appears most important archaeologically, the circumstances of loss and what happened to the hull, is frequently overlooked.

This already selective evidence was further winnowed through haphazard preservation: destroyed through time or discarded as of little interest, while details of ecclesiastical rights in the matter of wreck were deliberately destroyed during the Dissolution of the Monasteries (1539). The introduction in the late 1600s of local and national newspapers, most of which carried shipping news as a matter of course, went some way towards preserving records of far greater numbers of wrecks. For the early modern period, therefore, our knowledge is more comprehensive (though not exhaustive) and the documented wrecks provide extremely useful contexts for the significant numbers of located remains dating from the 16th century onwards.

The reliance on journalistic sources throws up its own issues, of course, some of which are explored in this book, including variant accounts of the same wreck and dependence on contemporary editorial policies. One paper may retain ship names in the original language, another may translate them for their readership. The deceptively English-sounding *Two Brothers*, for example, may be matched with the *Deux Frères* of Le Havre through common details. The principal source, of course, was the specialist marine press, as exemplified by *Lloyd's List*, which was established in 1734, and continues to publish shipping news and details of losses today. Yet six years of wrecks are lost to us since the earliest extant issues date from 1740.

Early *Lloyd's* reports are terse, brief and to the point, with local newspapers providing fuller, but sometimes less reliable, accounts of the wreck event. With the invention of the telegraph in the 19th century, *Lloyd's* was able to publish hour-by-hour accounts of a wreck's disintegration and the progress of the rescue of the crew and recovery of the cargo, or otherwise. Victorian newspapers published lengthy and

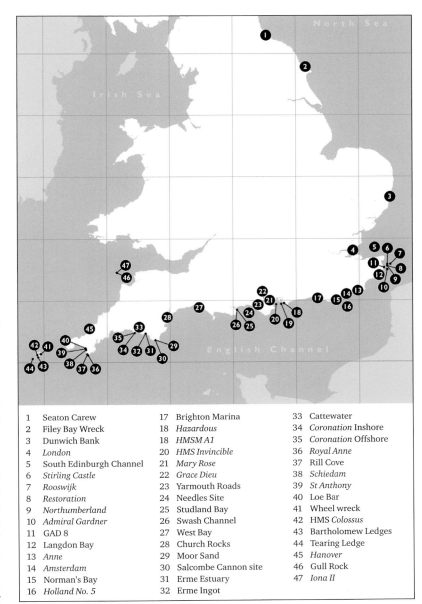

1	Seaton Carew	17	Brighton Marina	33	Cattewater
2	Filey Bay Wreck	18	*Hazardous*	34	*Coronation* Inshore
3	Dunwich Bank	18	*HMSM A1*	35	*Coronation* Offshore
4	*London*	20	*HMS Invincible*	36	*Royal Anne*
5	South Edinburgh Channel	21	*Mary Rose*	37	Rill Cove
6	*Stirling Castle*	22	*Grace Dieu*	38	*Schiedam*
7	*Rooswijk*	23	Yarmouth Roads	39	*St Anthony*
8	*Restoration*	24	Needles Site	40	Loe Bar
9	*Northumberland*	25	Studland Bay	41	Wheel wreck
10	*Admiral Gardner*	26	Swash Channel	42	HMS *Colossus*
11	GAD 8	27	West Bay	43	Bartholomew Ledges
12	Langdon Bay	28	Church Rocks	44	Tearing Ledge
13	*Anne*	29	Moor Sand	45	*Hanover*
14	*Amsterdam*	30	Salcombe Cannon site	46	Gull Rock
15	Norman's Bay	31	Erme Estuary	47	*Iona II*
16	Holland No. 5	32	Erme Ingot		

melodramatic accounts of events in which crew members were 'hurried into eternity' as their vessel broke up. These had their counterpoint in the factual, statistical and analytical records incorporating all relevant data provided from by the Board of Trade in their *Casualty Returns* from the mid-19th century onwards.

There were earlier official accounts, of course. Sixteenth-century state papers, as well as Admiralty papers and newspaper accounts of hearings and courts-martial from the 17th century onwards, concentrated on warship losses by whatever cause. Naturally the frequent wars with France and Scotland during the Middle Ages, the attacks of the Spanish Armada,

Fig II
Distribution map of designated shipwrecks.

Fig III
J M W Turner, The
Shipwreck, *exhibited 1805.*
Fishing boats cautiously
approach a boat carrying
survivors of a ship which has
capsized in the background,
with substantial wreckage on
a sea 'mountains high', to use
a contemporary phrase, in the
foreground. The fishermen can
use their oars to draw the craft
to them, or push it away to
avoid collision and capsize.
Sketches dating back to
1799 reveal Turner's plans
for this subject, unrelated to
a specific incident, although
viewers would undoubtedly
have recalled the recent
tragedy of the Earl of
Abergavenny *off the Bill of*
Portland (February 1805),
lost under not dissimilar
circumstances.
(© Tate, London 2011)

the Anglo-Dutch wars of the 17th century, the resumption of war with France during the Revolutionary and Napoleonic Wars, and both World Wars accounted for the losses of many warships and auxiliary vessels. Neutral and mercantile vessels might also fall victim to warships and privateers, and during the 20th century they succumbed to aerial bombardment, submarine attack and mines. During the same period, new types of craft turned into wrecks – aircraft, submarines, landing craft, aircraft carriers – in line with the advances in technology and the demands of 20th-century warfare. Unsurprisingly, 20th-century sources are the richest in detail, and not only because they are closer in time to our own, nor because the two World Wars accounted for a significant number of wrecks during the century, but because record-keeping in itself became more detailed. *Lloyd's* kept a record of all mercantile losses to war causes during both World Wars, which were supplemented by official government statistics, secret charts and logs from survivors, witnesses, escorts and attacking vessels, all in the

government domain. Photographic evidence also played its part in times of peace as well as war.

Reports of wrecks from the 16th century onwards are therefore more likely to be matched with surviving vessel remains on the foreshore and on the seabed, assisted particularly by the presence of distinctive cargoes and armament. Unsurprisingly many wreck sites are well-documented losses of warships, such as the site of the *Mary Rose*, Henry VIII's great warship, lost in the Solent in 1545. Some sites are precisely identified in both position and vessel name, for example, the designated wreck of the Dutch East Indiaman *Amsterdam*, lost at Hastings in 1749; clues for other vessels may be more ambiguous, so that a probable identity may emerge, but remain contentious in the absence of a breakthrough. A good example is the wreck site known as the possible remains of the English warship the *Resolution*, of 1703: she may instead be the remains of a Dutch vessel of slightly earlier date.

Just as greater numbers of, and more detailed,

sources survive from the 20th century, so also do wrecks of this era form a greater proportion of known wrecks on the seabed. Their remains survive, not only because of their relatively recent date, but also their method of construction, with iron and steel hulls, which do not disintegrate in sea water, where the timber wrecks of earlier periods are more likely to do so. The dimensions and building details of these wrecks often survive in the records of the building yards of Newcastle-upon-Tyne, Sunderland, Glasgow, Workington, Liverpool and Belfast, but identification becomes more difficult where there are clusters of vessels of similar size and date, all carrying a coal cargo and all blown apart by torpedoes or mines, distorting, flattening and scattering them beyond their known dimensions. In such cases the researcher or diver must look for other clues.

Wreck events and associated wreck remains differ in another important respect from terrestrial monuments: the human cost (Fig IV). The event which turns a ship into a monument often results in great loss of life or acts of heroic altruism. This is the story not only of shipping losses, but the clues which have uncovered the events and matched them to vessel remains where possible, in all their range and diversity, lost to the weather and to the natural environment; to the fortunes of war, and to human faults of poor navigation, greed and incompetence and to faulty design. Whether lost on the 'Great Ship-Swallower' (the Goodwin Sands off Dover), the chalk stacks of the Needles, the Farne Islands and the jagged rocks of Cornwall and the Isles of Scilly, the variety of locales is matched by the craft and their cargoes: medieval merchantmen and French privateers, hospital ships and U-boats, East Indiamen and Liberty Ships, slavers and convict ships, sailing vessels and paddle-steamers, ironclads and concrete ships, great ocean liners to small fishing vessels of localised type. These are in turn matched by the diversity of their fates across time in England's territorial seas. Although there are common themes of extreme weather conditions, navigational error, warfare and piracy, or simply unfortunate and almost incredible chains of circumstance, there are almost constant variations and more stories than can be told in a book of this kind. There are always suggestions of new wrecks, new causes of wreck and new finds, tantalising hints which have so far not been matched to particular records. Shipwrecks provide the key not only to unlocking England's maritime past, but to placing that past in its global context, and exploring its links with terrestrial archaeology, a story that continues in exploring our maritime heritage today.

Fig IV
In a rare composition by the noted architectural photography firm Bedford Lemere, who normally specialised in ship portraits focusing on architectural features, a group of visitors sit on the deck of the newly built Aquitania *in 1913, ostentatiously flanked by a lifeboat and a lifebelt. This group illustrates the cultural impact of the recent loss of the* Titanic *in 1912, not least on the shipowners who commissioned these photographs. (BL22725/001)*

NOTES ON THE TEXT

This book has been designed to be interactive so that the reader can directly access English Heritage's National Record for the Historic Environment (NRHE) via the PastScape website for further details of any given shipwreck. Each wreck referred to in the text has a unique monument reference number, quoted in the endnotes, which can be entered in the advanced search under Monument Number to bring up the relevant record on PastScape; all wrecks are also searchable by name using the basic search. The reader will then be able to see full details of each individual wreck site, or to use the PastScape 'Contact Us' page to add to the database with further information. All monument numbers are correct at the time of writing and, where wreck remains have been definitively identified, are stable. However, English Heritage maintains a dynamic database, and occasionally, as more information comes to light on particular wreck sites, identifications and/or reference numbers may change. Should this happen, the wrecks concerned will remain accessible by name searches under the new monument number.

Registration for PastScape is a quick, easy and free way to search around 400,000 database records: please go to www.pastscape.org.uk.

The numbers of shipwrecks designated under the Protection of Wrecks Act 1973 were likewise correct at the time of going to press, but may be revised in the future with new discoveries. Up-to-date information may be accessed on the National Heritage List for England, http://www.english-heritage.org.uk/professional/protection/process/national-heritage-list-for-england.

Prior to the introduction of the Gregorian Calendar in England in 1752, the Julian Calendar was in use, although much of Continental Europe had already adopted the Gregorian Calendar. Contemporary English sources refer to the Julian Calendar as Old Style (OS) and the Gregorian as New Style (NS). This has its implications for shipwreck research, which are discussed more fully at various points in the book. Essentially, the Old Style calendar was adrift from the New Style calendar by 10 days in the 17th century and 11 in the 18th century, so that English sources may vary from one another and from contemporary Continental sources using New Style. The English custom of beginning the official New Year on 25 March also prevailed prior to 1752, when it was brought into line with the beginning of the calendar year. Therefore, dates between 1 January and 24 March, inclusive, within contemporary Old Style sources are normally dated the previous year: thus 1 January 1639 Old Style would be 1 January 1640 New Style and only on 25 March would the two styles agree in expressing the year as 1640. Where I have discussed these issues, I have followed the custom of clarifying all dates with (OS) and (NS) respectively. Finally, although *Lloyd's List* ceased referring to ships as 'she' in 2002, the Royal and US Navies continue to do so. This historic convention has been followed throughout this book for consistency with the numerous contemporary sources which all use 'she'.

The hazards of the natural environment

Introduction

Weather and the natural environment are the two principal hazards facing any vessel at sea: the former may cause the wreck of a ship in an area not otherwise particularly notable for dangers to navigation, while maritime obstructions may cause vessels to be lost even in a flat calm. The combination of the two has frequently been lethal around the coast of England with the notoriously variable weather conditions thought of as 'typically British'. The concentration of shipwrecks in English territorial waters is high, for the very location of the British Isles as a whole at the western edge of Europe has historically attracted a great deal of passing seaborne trade involving other lands, as well as ships bound to and from English ports. In terms of the English coastline, the 'right angle' of the southern and eastern coasts face Continental Europe across the North Sea and the English Channel, while the western coastline favours the remainder of the British Isles: a strategically important location, looking out both to the Atlantic and Ireland, and towards southern Europe, the Mediterranean and Africa.

The geological formation of the English coastline is also exceptionally varied (Fig 1.1), from Cornwall's rocky shores facing the Atlantic, to the beaches of Northumberland; the flat shingle banks of Chesil in Dorset and Spurn Point off the Humber; the chalk stacks of the Needles and the cliffs of Dover; remote islands such as the Isles of Scilly and the Farne Islands; the busy estuaries with dangerous mudflats of the Severn, Thames and Humber, leading to equally busy ports; notorious sandbanks out to sea such as Haisborough off the coast of Norfolk; stretches of treacherous sand trapping unwary ships entering the Tyne and Mersey; and forbidding cliffs of rock or chalk on the Channel coasts. Danger lies in close proximity to safety, for many of these features lie close to harbours,

ports and havens of refuge, just as, for example, the Goodwin Sands lies between the sailor and the port of Dover or the safe anchorage of the Downs in the confines of the narrow Straits of Dover. Even today this is one of the busiest shipping channels in the world, warranting 24-hour radio and radar surveillance governed by regulations which have legal force on both sides of the Channel.[1]

The following are just a few of the most evocatively named shipping hazards in English waters, worthy of a full book in themselves: the isolated rock hazards of Wolf Rock off Land's End, or the Eddystone with its waters swirling around granite rocks, guarding Plymouth Sound.[2] The names of the Tearing Ledge reef in the Isles of Scilly, the Knivestone among the Farne Islands, and the Needles off the Isle of Wight suggest what might happen to ships coming to grief in those locations, as do the Black Middens, the black rocks at the entrance to North Shields, appearing to imply that a ship

Fig 1.1a
As seen from the air looking south-west over the Isles of Scilly, there is an excellent view of the submerged rocks and the breakers which swirl around these islands. White Island lies in the foreground, with the larger island of St Martin's just beyond. These two islands alone have accounted for their fair share of wrecks among nearly 800 documented as having come to grief among the Isles of Scilly as a whole. (23893/12 SV9217/1)

Fig 1.1b (right)
Land's End, the most
westerly point of the English
mainland, has seen over
245 recorded shipwrecks
associated with the
immediate vicinity, though
others have occurred on the
Peal Rocks, seen to the left of
the picture, and the Armed
Knight, to the right, and still
further wrecks have taken
place in the neighbouring
bays and coves. How many
more went down unseen
over the centuries?
(23680/30)

Fig 1.1c (below left)
The power of the sea can be
seen to good effect in this
view looking south-west
from Handfast Point, with
Old Harry Rock nearest the
viewer: the spectacular
erosion by the sea of the
chalk cliffs gives the
impression of a giant
snacking upon the coastline.
The detached pillars seen at
background left are the
remains of collapsed arches.
Both Handfast Point and
Studland Bay to the north-
west (on the right of the
image) have been associated
with wrecks since at least the
Tudor period, including the
early 16th-century Studland
Bay wreck.
(23703/22)

Fig 1.1d (far right)
Coastal plain,
Northumberland, looking
south from Holy Island
towards Gulle Point.
(17862/04 NU1241/16)

unlucky enough to strand thereupon would be pounded to smithereens in the Tyne like so much rubbish (as was in fact the fate of so many ships entering or leaving Shields).

The dangers posed by these hazards were increased by the typical prevailing winds around the coast of England. One fatal effect was becoming 'embayed on a lee shore', that is, unable to get off a beach against a wind from the seaward. The ship would then be pounded by the wind and waves on the beach, an archetypal wrecking process along the southern coasts of England with their prevailing winds from the same direction. Colliers delivering their cargo of coal on the beaches of Sussex were particularly

vulnerable to this process: if the wind shifted and blew hard enough, these vessels could be driven so far up the beach that they ended up 'high and dry' and a continuing spell of severe weather might mean that such vessels broke up altogether.

Regular storms, especially typical of the winter season, were interspersed with more extreme weather events, which were more violent even than the storm of October 1987, the most severe in living memory. Even minor, localised, storms could inflict great damage at a time when shipping, fishing and the navy were major sources of employment. At the time when more detailed records started to be kept,

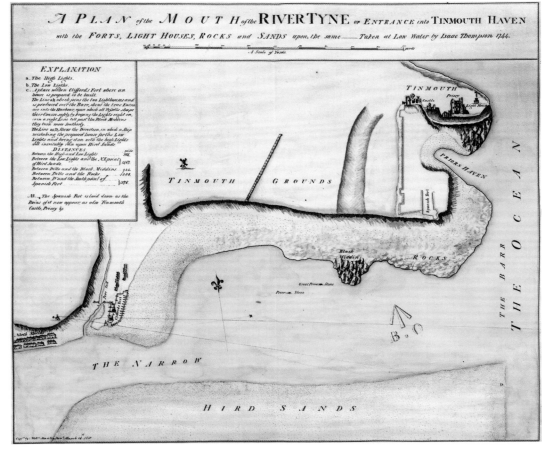

Fig 1.1e (above)
An excellent example of longshore drift by which sediment has been deposited at an angle to the coastline, to form the narrow arm of Spurn Point half-barring the entrance to the Humber Estuary, bringing in its wake some 200 recorded wrecks.
(DP139801)

Fig 1.1f (left)
A Plan of the Mouth of the River Tyne or Entrance into Tinmouth Haven, with the Forts, Light House, Rocks and Sands upon the same – taken at Low Water by Isaac Thompson 1744. *This chart, once in the possession of the Admiralty, as shown by the 'broad arrow' stamp, depicts the 'Hird Sands' and 'Black Middins' as an 18th-century Scylla and Charybdis, ready to trap the unwary on either side of 'The Narrows'.*
(MP_TYN0006)

Northern Europe was still in the grip of the 'Little Ice Age' so winters were generally much colder than they have been since the 20th century, with prolonged periods of snow and ice; there were 'Titanic' events in England too. These extreme events have a fascination all their own in the light of topical concerns over the effects of climate change, and the vagaries of the British weather continue to have their impact on wrecks even today.

Early extreme weather events

Extreme weather events have always caused great loss of life at sea, but were not generally recorded with any level of detail until the 17th century when the printing press made newspapers and their capacity to disseminate news both rapidly and cheaply possible. Although recognisable 'newes-papers' appeared from the 1620s onwards, in such a turbulent century they understandably focused on political issues, both domestic and foreign. Only later in the century would shipping news be included in any great level of detail. Even then, warship losses were more likely to be covered than mercantile vessels, unless the vessel was richly laden or there were extraordinary circumstances

attached to its loss. The *London Gazette* was published from 1665 onwards; in the early 18th century regional newspapers began to appear, such as the *Newcastle Courant*, founded in 1711, and *Lloyd's List*, dedicated to commercial and shipping news, dates back to the 1730s.

For a wider audience less able to subscribe regularly to a newspaper, individual pamphlets, rushed to press to keep them topical, were more affordable. Single-issue in both senses of the phrase, they appeared once only, devoted to one particular event. Essentially mementoes, their nearest modern equivalents are newspaper souvenir supplements covering notable events. In the late 16th and 17th centuries these pamphlets or broadsheets covered a wide variety of topics, including storms and floods, and form a principal source of information on early 17th-century wrecks. They described the effects on land and sea, to underline repentance in the face of sudden floods seen as instruments of divine wrath, dealing death and destruction.

As an example of a startling environmental event, the overflow of the Severn in 1607 was clearly exceptional: both the English and Welsh shores were inundated to a considerable distance inland, with great loss of life (Fig 1.2). There is some debate about whether these inundations

Fig 1.2
Aerial photograph of February 1953 showing flooded housing at Jaywick Sands, near Clacton, Essex, following a storm surge on the East Coast and Thames Estuary, giving some impression of how the 1607 Bristol Channel 'tsunami' and other early flooding events might have looked. (AFL03/Aerofilms/A48271)

were the result of a 'tsunami' triggered by an undersea earthquake, or a storm surge, possibly exacerbated by a tidal bore.[3] A number of pamphlets covered the effects on either side of the Bristol Channel, which were also noted in contemporary chronicles and diaries. The effects on land took precedence over those at sea, where danger was a matter of course. However, given the severity of the flooding, it is surprising that only one potential wreck event has been extracted from the surviving literature relating to 1607, especially as reference was made to wrecks during similar earlier events. One 1607 pamphlet directly compares one flood event with another, the inundations of 1570 'in the last Queens raigne',[4] including a list of some 50 wrecks on the east coast of England, but without any similar list for the more recent event. Remarkably, the names of ship owners, and specific locations of loss in 1570, recalled 40 years later, suggest either that the writer was personally familiar with those events, or had access to original documents (still extant in his time, but since lost). Perhaps he even quoted them verbatim. He reported, for example, that on the coast of Norfolk, 'a greate Hulk loden with Oyle and Pitch, was lost at Worry Sand,[5] and about XX [twenty] men lost therein and XXX [thirty] saved by the Hulk boat'.

The lack of a 'wrecks list' for the 1607 flood may indicate several possibilities: that there were genuinely few losses; that the wrecks concerned did not make it into print because they were of small fishing boats or coasters (such vessels being routinely ignored even at a later date); or that details were not to hand at the time of writing, for the profitability of a topical souvenir took precedence over detail. The 1570 account, the earliest known item of this kind, suggests that the formula of describing the twin destruction of ships and 'cattell' was established early on and was much imitated during the following century for subsequent flood events, such as one on the east coast of England in 1671.[6]

An expanded edition of the 1607 pamphlet later that year,[7] includes a 'Gentleman's letter' from North Devon, which is the source for the only known possible wreck resulting from the storm, at Appledore (Fig 1.3) on the North Devon coast. This and the pamphlet's title, '… with other reports of accidents that were not before discouered …', strongly suggests that details of shipping losses were not yet available at the time of printing. A third edition was probably planned, since the letter was included with the comment 'And let this suffice thee (good Reader) at this time, for a tast[e] of more newes …', but this was either never printed or is

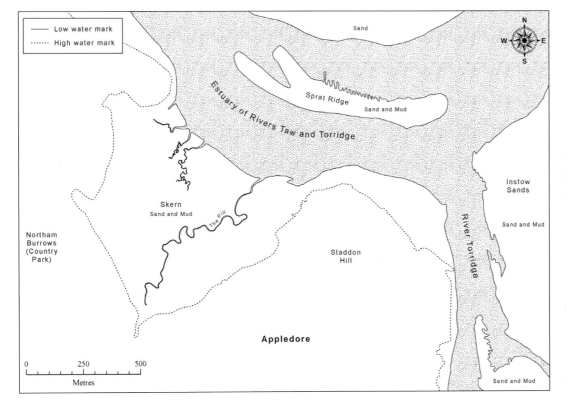

Fig 1.3
Location map showing the present-day low- and high-water marks in the vicinity of Appledore. The marshlands at the entrance to the River Torridge are so extensive that it is difficult to say precisely where the victim was driven ashore among the marshes, except that her position was exceptionally far inshore: 'beyond flight-shotte of all water mark' suggests that she may have come ashore at or beyond the typical shot of an arrow from a bow, perhaps 300 yards or so inshore.

no longer extant, raising the tantalising possibility that more details of the effects on shipping have been lost to us. The effects on the locality were certainly dire:

> A ship of some three score tunne, being ready to hoise [hoist] saile, and being well-laden, was driven by the breach of this tempest up into a marrish [marsh] ground, some flight-shotte beyond all water-mark, and is likely never to be brought back againe.[8]

> … in the year 1607 it [Barnstaple] suffered a kind of inundation … from the ocean so high swelling, that it subverted houses, drowned beasts, and destroyed people, of whom some, to save their lives, were constrained from their upper rooms to take boat and be gone.[9]

Whether a 'tsunami' or storm surge, it seems unlikely the Appledore vessel was the only shipping victim. As the powerful flood funnelled its way up the Severn estuary, it seems plausible that the same tide capable of destroying houses several miles inland must also have forced several ships from their anchors and deposited them above the high-water mark. But for the Appledore vessel, we might never have been aware of the potential impact of the flood on shipping.[10]

A century later, the Great Storm of 1703 (Fig 1.4) struck as regional journalism was beginning to take off, freed from the worst excesses of state control and censorship. The *London Gazette* was the principal newspaper source for the effects of the storm, but this event also illustrates the growing power of the press in other respects. The term 'correspondent' to indicate a professional journalist derives from the contemporary practice of printing letters from individuals, not necessarily edited for length, veracity or date, some of whom became regular contributors. It is arguable that 1703 marks the transition of journalism into a professional activity, when Daniel Defoe, author of *Robinson Crusoe*, advertised in the *London Gazette* for eyewitness accounts of the storm. Like its predecessors, the pamphlets and broadsheets, the resulting book, *The Storm*, which appeared in 1704, came out quickly enough to remain topical and thus to sell well. In a sense, it is a much more sophisticated version of these

Fig 1.4
England's Great Storm. *Contemporary engraving alluding to the loss of Rear-Admiral Beaumont of the flagship* Mary *on the Goodwin Sands. Despite the specific title the engraving is an imaginative composite view of the devastation wreaked by this storm, since two coastlines are visible with a prominent rock in the foreground. Several vessels, including men of war and some smaller ships, are seen in various stages of foundering.*
(© Fotomas/TopFoto)

little souvenir sheets, maintaining some of the same formulae.[11]

Defoe retained an interpretation of the magnitude of the storm event as a manifestation of divine wrath, and included a balanced account of the effects felt on both land and sea. In other ways his approach was radical and innovative, with a new sense of editorial responsibility. Advertising for information from witnesses was a much more sophisticated, interactive approach to a major event, shaping material sent in by others – much as today major television broadcasters will show 'user-generated' mobile phone footage sent in by eyewitnesses on site anywhere in the world. He also prefaced his material with a perceptive introduction analysing the meteorological conditions prior to the storm and explaining its extraordinary impact: he noted the possibility that the storm could have been the tail-end of an Atlantic hurricane. The 'user-generated' content was then edited for veracity and credibility and shaped to provide a coherent and reflective account of events.

The storm blew from south-west to west-south-west, and was strong enough for eyewitness accounts to reach Defoe 'from a ship blown out of the Downs to Norway', a distance of over 700 miles. It affected vessels of all types, and, like the later 'Great Storm' of 1987, it principally affected the southern area of England. A comparison with the rest of the year adds context to the catastrophic human cost of the storm, in which at least 1,400 to 1,800 lives were lost in English waters.[12] Out of all the 104 recorded wrecks for the year 1703, 98 were a direct result of this one storm alone, although it is scarcely credible that there were only 6 other wrecks in English waters during the remainder of 1703. Rather, we should say that the 1703 event was noteworthy enough to leave significant traces in the surviving historical record, while the other wreck events may have been much more localised and less devastating in their effects.

Thirteen out of these 98 wrecks were warships. A number of other warships were either severely damaged or reported prematurely as 'lost', for example, the *Litchfield Prize*, which was recovered and eventually sold out of service in 1706. They illustrate a common principle of wreck research: the loss of life does not correlate to the loss of a vessel. A high death toll does not necessarily imply that the vessel itself was lost (the *Canterbury* storeship lost most or all of her crew, but may have been recovered and sold); conversely, a ship may be totally lost under circumstances that permitted the preservation of the crew (for example, the *Resolution*, from which none of the 221 crew were lost). Five out of the 13 warships have been relocated, a significant enough proportion in itself (*Eagle, Northumberland, Resolution, Restoration* and *Stirling Castle*), but very unusual for a single weather event of this antiquity. All, with the exception of the *Eagle*, are designated: in other words, this one storm accounts for almost 6 per cent of the total number of designated wreck sites in the UK.[13]

Defoe's excellent eye for the editorial organisation of the material he received is particularly well displayed in a wreck event[14] described in letters scattered throughout the book from three different witnesses, that of a ship laden with tin blown out of the Helford River in Cornwall all the way to the Isle of Wight. Two of these accounts came from the Cornish end of this extraordinary voyage, and the third from the other end, the Isle of Wight. All three bring out different aspects of the wreck, so that taken together they form a credible and coherent narrative, particularly as the aftermath of that incident is also recorded. Certainly unique in Defoe's own work, it is also virtually unique for the early 18th century to combine three accounts from different sources for the same, non-warship, wreck, and as exceptional as the strange wreck event itself. The journey from Helford to the Isle of Wight, under favourable weather conditions, would normally have taken at least 24 hours, but took half that time, in a journey tense with vividly recalled drama:

> I presume you never heard before, nor hope may never hear again of a ship that was blown from her anchors out of Helford Haven to the isle of Wight, in less than eight hours, viz. the ship lay in Helford Haven about two leagues and a half westward of Falmouth, being laden with tin, which was taken on board from Guague Wharf ... About eight o'clock in the evening before the storm begun, the said commander and mate came on board and ordered the crew that he left on board, which was but one man and two boys; that if the wind should chance to blow hard (which he had some apprehension of) to carry out the small bower anchor, and moor the ship by two anchors, and gave them some other orders, and his mate and he went ashoar ... bout nine a clock the wind began to blow ... it continued blowing harder and harder at West North West, at last the ship began

Fig 1.5 (opposite) Abraham Hondius' view of the Thames during the Frost Fair of 1677 is seen from the watermen's stairs, depicting watermen adapting their trade to escorting people across the surface of the ice instead of ferrying customers across the river. Their boats seem to be icebound: the blocks of ice look curiously boat-shaped, as if the ice has formed around them with gaps between. which appear to parallel the natural gap between moored vessels. The block to the extreme right seems to be prow-shaped: some of these boats may well have been crushed in the ice which constantly broke up and reformed in the tidal Thames, and in so doing increased pressures at different points in any given vessel's hull. As shown by later written records concerning similar losses, it is likely that smaller boats such as these were the most vulnerable to ice, causing them to sink when the thaw came.
(© Museum of London)

to drive … Between eleven and twelve a clock the wind came about west and by south in a most terrible and violent manner … she was drove from all her anchors, and about twelve a clock drove out of the harbour without anchor or cable, nor so much as a boat left in case they could put into any harbour. In dreadful condition the ship drove out clear of the rocks to sea, where the man with the two boys consulted what to do, at last resolved to keep her far enough to sea, for fear of Deadman's Head, being a point of land between Falmouth and Plimouth, the latter of which places they designed to run her in if possible, to save their lives; the next morning in this frighted condition they steered her clear of the land (to the best of their skill) sometimes almost under water, and sometimes a top … but instead of getting into Plymouth next day as intended … the next morning they saw land, which proved to be Peverel Point … so that they were in a worse consternation than before, for overrunning their designed port by seven a clock, they found themselves off the Isle of Wight; where they consulted again what to do to save their lives, one of the boys was for running her into the Downs, but that was objected against, by reason they had no anchors nor boat, and the storm blowing off shore in the Downs, they should be blown on the unfortunate Goodwin Sands and lost. Now comes the last consultation for their lives, there was one of the boys said he had been in a certain creek in the Isle of Wight, where between the rocks he believed there was room enough to run the ship and save their lives, and desired to have the helm from the man, and he would venture to steer the ship into the said place, which he according did, where there was only just room between rock and rock for the ship to come in, where she gave one blow or two against the rocks, and sunk immediately, but the man and two boys jumpt ashore, and all the lading being tin was saved (and for their conduct and the risk they run) they were all very well gratified, and the merchants well satisfied.[15]

The 'unfortunate Goodwin Sands' reappeared in *The Storm* and in the *London Gazette* as the wreck site for the *Northumberland, Stirling Castle, Mary* and *Restoration*. Simply because they were warships, each loss was described at great length and in dramatic detail, even though details were somewhat garbled and perhaps exaggerated in the confusion of lost shipping in such a small area. For example, one man was miraculously saved out of the *Mary*, being washed onto another vessel (either the *Northumberland* or the *Stirling Castle*) before she too went down, and finally being rescued by a local boat.

Defoe's 1704 work seems to have influenced the popular souvenir pamphlets into including more detail. A single sheet with a lengthy title begins in the old style: *England's Second Warning: Being a further and more particular Account of the great Damage done both by Sea and Land, by the late amazing Storm and Tempest that happened on Saturday the 11th of August 1705* … before proudly promising … *a true List of the Names and Numbers of the Merchant Ships, and other Vessels, that were Cast-a-way at Portsmouth, Plymouth and other Harbours* … .[16]

True to its word, the pamphlet names five laden colliers, the *Weazel, Dainty Cruiser, Happy Merchant, Goodhope* and *Swallow* as 'intirely loss' at Shields.[17] We therefore know their cargo, and since Shields was chiefly concerned with coal export, we may deduce that the lost ships were outward-bound. As they were among 50 ships 'forced from their anchors', it seems they were lying just offshore, and it is likely that they were driven ashore, because their names could be read and ascertained. The names of the other vessels may not have been included, being disregarded because less substantial, or because they were forced ashore further north or south along the same stretch of coastline, or blown out to sea. Because the intelligence from Shields was committed to press before further news came in from outlying areas, it seems likely that as the lost vessels were laden with their cargo they would have been off the Tyne rather than moored at the quaysides or in dock. The wind direction is nowhere explicitly stated, but as the storm seems to have affected the southern and eastern coasts, judging by reports from Plymouth, Portsmouth, London, Harwich and Shields, it may have been easterly. The wind may, of course, have varied tremendously within this area, but it would have be consistent with driving vessels off the Tyne onto the east coast of England, perhaps on the Herd Sand, near the roadstead to Shields.

Similar pamphlets likewise recorded the 'Frost Fairs' of London, when the Thames froze over, pedestrians and traffic could pass from one side to the other, and stalls were set up on the ice. The dates of known Frost Fairs, the first being in 1309 or 1408,[18] and the last in 1814, are roughly coincident with the descent of the 'Little Ice Age', when average temperatures appear to have consistently been lower than in the early medieval period (the 'Medieval Warm Period') or since. These Frost Fairs regularly coincided with the loss of vessels to the ice in the Thames and thus provide a context for the sometimes terse entries in contemporary sources. The earliest known wreck which appears in the documentary record and coincides with a known Frost Fair can be dated to 1709, while the freezing over of the Thames in the last weeks of 1739 and first weeks of 1740 accounted for at least eight losses, probably more.[19]

However, there is possible visual evidence of wrecks in the ice in the Thames from an earlier period as shown in scenes of the frozen Thames painted in 1677 and 1683 by Abraham Hondius, a Dutch artist living in London, combining the Dutch tradition of winter landscapes with a journalistic record of events (Fig 1.5), and other artists. Was ice damage an explanation for the loss of the late 17th-century Blackfriars Ship II? Was she damaged so as to sink at her moorings, or was she damaged and brought up ashore, or, as a shallow-draught barge, could she have been swamped in the subsequent thaw (Fig 1.6)?[20]

In 1709 the East India Company made representations to the Customs Commissioners who refused to allow their ship *Rochester* to proceed above Woolwich, despite having safely arrived 'after many hazards'. Citing examples of damage already done, they protested against 'the danger the cargo is under by the severity of the weather, which is daily growing on them, several ships having been cut to pieces and sunk by the late frost.'[21] The winter of 1739–40 was particularly destructive: at Limehouse Hole, a laden collier sank by a collision with ice;[22] while several boats were 'driven from their fastenings above bridge near Shoreditch and stav'd to pieces by the large flakes of ice that were brought down by the tide' (Fig 1.7).[23]

In 1739/40 the principal victim was the *Elliot*,[24] 'bulged' (bilged, that is, the ship's bottom, or bilge, was holed) by the ice, on her arrival from Zakinthos with currants and oil. The bilging of a ship would not necessarily indicate that she was beyond repair; however, initial reports of hopes of saving the cargo, valued at over £9,000 (over £1m today),[25] imply that the vessel herself was beyond repair; this appears to be confirmed in the vocabulary used to translate the news from London, using the French word *échoui* (modern *échoué*, in this context 'lost' or 'ruined').[26] All these descriptions suggest a manner of loss more common to Arctic, Baltic or Antarctic waters, of vessels being crushed by the ice, like Shackleton's *Endurance* in 1915/16. It emerged shortly afterwards that the cargo was 'entirely ruined',[27] with a subtext perhaps that the vessel herself was also irrecoverable. Furthermore, the long cold spell

Fig 1.6
The Blackfriars Ship II, the second of a number of ships found in the area, was located in 1969 and is shown here in the course of excavation.
(© Peter Marsden)

is likely to have frustrated any efforts to recover the ship, particularly if snow froze on the vessel's structure and rigging, placing further stress on the hull, a common feature of shipping difficulties in more northerly latitudes.

The Tyne and the Wear also regularly froze over in the late 18th and early 19th centuries, normally freezing in different years from the Thames, although 1785 was a 'freeze year' in both north and south. Like the barges in the Thames, the Tyne's small coal keels were the most vulnerable to being crushed as the ice formed, while collisions with blocks of ice were also frequent. Meltwater posed an additional problem, since it could carry away smaller vessels and smash them against the Tyne Bridge or drive them out to sea. In 1809 the thaw affected both the Tyne and Wear, compared with the severe flooding after rain seen in 1771:

> Last Sunday morning exhibited a scene of confusion and distress among the ships in Shields harbour, such as has not been seen since Nov. 1771 … The ice broke up in the Tyne on Saturday night, and descended down to Shields early on Sunday morning, carrying whole tiers of ships from their moorings. Neither posts, anchors, cables or chains, could bear the pressure … Thirty sail of ships were scattered on the Herd Sand and Black-midding Rocks … they were mostly got off … A Humber Keel was sunk on the Herd Sand.

The *Hope*, a loaden collier, was dashed to pieces on the Blackmiddings. At Sunderland, considerable damage was done on Sunday morning, by the fresh coming down the Wear. Upwards of 20 keels were driven out to sea; one of them is sunk in the Roads [ie Sunderland Roads].[28]

Lloyd's List attributed losses at Shields in this incident not to flooding but to 'the late gales' countrywide,[29] suggesting that the wind had given extra impetus to the meltwater: south coast ports reported the conditions as 'tremendous gale from the WSW'. Paragraphs from more northerly ports do not specify the wind direction, but it must have blown from the same quarter, since it would have driven shipping east out to sea from the Wear as described. Similarly, a wind from that quarter would have driven the *Hope* onto the Black Middens on the northern bank of the Tyne, suggesting that she was moored in the middle of the Tyne or at South Shields.

Artificial waterways, narrower and without a natural current or tidal flow, could also freeze over quite severely, and as more canals were built, there were more opportunities for wrecks to occur. In 1824, the *Hannah*,[30] a 'small, fragile coal-vessel' was no match for the frozen conditions of the recently opened Carlisle Canal, and sank after being 'cut through by the ice'.[31] Damage caused by exceptional ice conditions

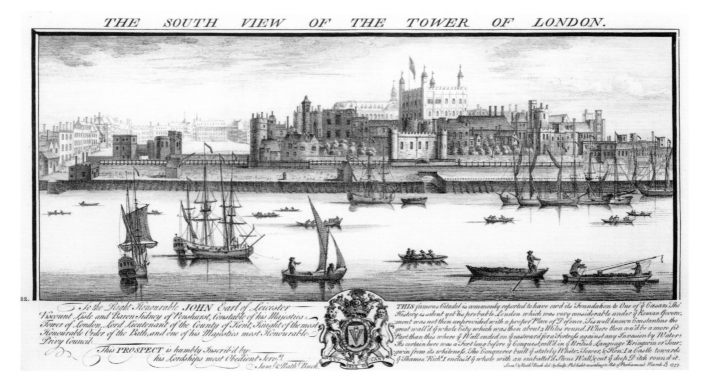

occurred off the coast of north-east England as late as 18 January 1841, which conditions accounted for several wrecks. It was said to be one 'of the heaviest disasters that ever befell the shipping of the river Wear'.

For some time previous the river had been frozen over in various places above Sunderland harbour. The frost continued until Saturday the 16th, when a thaw commenced, the wind being then from S to SW. On that and the following day great quantities of rain fell, by which the river was much swollen and the ice loosened before any considerable portion of it had time to be dissolved with the thaw; the consequence was, that several floating fields of ice were carried down the river, at succeeding intervals, during the ebb tides of Saturday and Sunday, until it arrived at … the high end of Sunderland harbour, where the progress of the ice was stopped. On Sunday afternoon the Wear above Sunderland bridge presented one sheet of ice, as far as the eye could reach … very soon the rain came down in torrents; the river rose rapidly, and the pressure of the ice, urged on by the flood, carried away some ships … about midnight, large pieces, several inches in thickness, that had covered the river some miles above, were observed to be floating down past Hylton … This continued till about four in the morning, when the barrier of ice formed below Pallion yielded to the increasing pressure of the water, and the mingled torrent

rushing down with irresistible force, tore away whole tiers of ships from their moorings …[32]

One victim of this disaster was the collier brig *Newby*, outward-bound for Bordeaux with Sunderland's archetypal export of coal. She was picturesquely described as lying 'on her broadside at the mouth of the harbour, heaving and lurching in the waves, and at intervals spouting out water like a huge whale', being just one of about a dozen larger ships which were forced out of the river Wear, while about 30 coal keels, and an unknown number of harbour craft were also lost.[33]

Fascinating in themselves for climatological reasons, original reports of weather events, whether a storm which made national news or an event of local significance, have a particular resonance in filling out gaps in the record of shipwrecks around the country, especially in river contexts, which have traditionally received less attention than accidents at sea. They provide a sense of scale in understanding the shipping of the period, the large numbers of ships lost in any single event allowing us to visualise the even greater number afloat at any one time, but they also serve as a reminder that even Britain's typically temperate climate has historically taken on the characteristics of other climate zones around the world – the hurricanes and ice zones.

Fig 1.7
The South View of the Tower of London, *Samuel and Nathaniel Buck, 1737. This 18th century 'prospect' illustrates a variety of small craft plying the river and passing the larger vessels at anchor. Variously sailed, rowed, or punted, they appear to be ferries or small cargo vessels and are probably typical of the craft which were lost in the severe winter of 1739–40.* (N070831)

1824: 'A most tremendous gale'

If Defoe's approach to the reporting of the Great Storm in 1703 was radical, the year 1824 marks another great step forward in the reporting of the effects of major weather events. Aside from the major storms there were numerous, more localised storms which dispatched individual ships or groups of vessels. However, unlike the early pamphlet mementoes of storms and floods, newspapers tended to divorce maritime news from the weather news inland with which it was, in fact, intimately associated. Wrecks were rarely placed in a wider context, a problem exacerbated by the local focus of the regional press.

Generally, news of accidents at sea were confined to the 'Shipping Intelligence'[34] columns, unless particularly newsworthy on account either of the severity of the storm or the nature of the ships lost (or both), in which case it was felt that they deserved a column or columns all to themselves. Whether incorporated in the 'Shipping Intelligence', or in dedicated columns, wreck items were normally dissociated from columns describing the effects of severe weather inland, often in greater detail but listed under news for individual towns on a different page. Even specialist publications dedicated to maritime news, such as *Lloyd's List*, usually said very little to place wreck news in the nationwide context other than a few terse words on wind direction where it was known, or the vague clichés of 'a most violent gale of wind', and 'the sea mountains high'.

Additionally, it was not unusual for letters containing wreck news to be printed up in the order they arrived from different correspondents, so that news concerning the same wreck would be separated by several paragraphs or even pages. The tendency for partial information concerning a given wreck event is never more clear than when this occurs, since one report may give the stricken vessel's name, and another her voyage details. Sometimes this makes it difficult to identify such differing reports as the same vessel without the presence of a detail common to both, and it also makes ascertaining exact numbers difficult.

A more sophisticated journalism began to emerge in the early 19th century: the events of late 1824 illustrate this shift towards greater detail. In that year alone, there were over 300 distinct wreck events throughout the country, which, given 293 wrecks in 1823, does not

appear unusual.[35] However, early 1824 was unusually benign, with only six documented losses: virtually all that year's wrecks occurred during four major storms during the period from October to December,[36] which saw regular spells of stormy weather with very high winds. That year broke the usual pattern of shipwrecks being more evenly distributed throughout the winter months from October to March, with smaller numbers during the summer months. That only 179 losses were recorded in 1825 shows how unusual the events of 1824 were.

The first storm was reported in *Lloyd's List* on 15 October, referring to gales from the 10 to the 12 October: 'A most violent gale of wind from NNE to SE commenced on Sunday night, and continued until Tuesday'.[37] As might be expected, a wind from an easterly direction principally affected the North Sea, littering the north-east coast of England from Northumberland to Humberside with stranded wrecks. Not only was the wind at its most powerful along this stretch of coastline, but being from the east it would be expected to drive vessels in the English Channel away from the coast with fewer strandings. Thus this one storm alone, concentrated in the relatively restricted area of the north-east coast, accounted for approximately 90 vessels, nearly one-third of the reported wrecks for the year in England.[38]

Not that the English Channel escaped unscathed that autumn. A 'severe gale' reported on 18 November at Gravesend, seems to have affected much of the country on the same day, but with the known loss of only two vessels which made their way into press reports.[39] It was the forerunner of a much more devastating gale the following week along the English Channel coasts, which resulted in 60 known losses of larger vessels: as so often, the smaller vessels were generally overlooked, except, perhaps, in snippets in the regional press. On the face of it, this third storm was less spectacular than the first in October, but in addition to the ships lost, the numbers of those damaged was exceptionally high. The printers at *Lloyd's List* were kept busy typesetting all the news as it came in from all over the country (Fig 1.8). From port after port along the southern coasts, details of the impact emerged: as in October, the wind direction suggested where the damage onshore would be greatest. Individual letters from 'correspondents' covering the events as they unfolded over several days, were printed under each port heading, but were collated far

LLOYD'S LIST.

No. 5963] LONDON, FRIDAY, NOVEMBER 26, 1824. [*PRICE* £1 10s *per Annum.*

Printed by W. PHILLIPS, George-yard, Lombard-street.

Prices of Stocks.	Wednesd.	Thursday	Friday
Bank Stock	—	231½ 3¾	232½
3 per Cent. Reduced	95 4⅛ 5	94¾ ⅞ ⅝	94½ ¾
3 per Cent. Consols	95⅝ ¾	95½ ⅝ ⅜	95¼ ½
3½ per Cent.	—	101¼ 1	—
Ditto...... Reduced	101⅜ ½ ⅜	—	101¼ ⅛
4 per Cent. Assented	—	—	—
4 per Cent. 1822	108⅛ ¼	108⅛	108⅛ ⅜
Bank Long Annuities	23⅛ 3/16	23⅛ ¼	23 1/16 3
Imperial 3 per Cent. Ann.	—	—	—
Irish 5 per Cent.	—	—	—
India Stock	—	—	—
Ditto Bonds	98 9	98	98
South Sea Stock	—	—	—
Old Annuities	—	—	—
New Ditto	—	—	—
Exchequer Bills, .. £1000	54 5	54 5	57
Ditto ... 500	53	—	56
Small	—	—	—
Bank for Opening	—	—	—
Consols for Account	95⅝ ¾	96 5¾	96 5¾

Course of Exchange This Day.

Amsterdam ...... *C.F.*	12 1	
Ditto, at Sight	11 18	
Rotterdam	12 2	
Antwerp	12 2	
Hamburgh	36 10	
Altona	36 11	
Paris, 3 Day's Sight	25 15	
Ditto	25 45	
Bordeaux	25 45	
Frankfort on the Main	151½	
Petersburg 9 3 U.	—Berlin 7 10	
Vienna ...... *Eff. flo.*	10 2	
Trieste ...... *D°*	10 2	
Madrid ... 36	Cadiz ... 35¼	
Bilboa.... 35¼	Barcelona 35	
Seville.... 35¼	Gibraltar 31.	
Leghorn .. 48¼	Genoa ... 44½	
Venice. 27 0	Malta ...	
Naples	38¼	
Palermo	per oz. 115½	
Lisbon.... 50½	Oporto . 50¼	
Rio Janeiro 47¾	Bahia...49	
Dublin 9½	Cork 9½ per Cent.	

Mails From	Wednesd. arr.	Wednesd. due	Thursday arr.	Thursday due	Friday arr.	Friday due
Dublin	1	—	1	—	1	—
Waterford	1	—	—	1	2	—
Donnaghadee	—	1	2	—	—	1
Guernsey & Jersey	—	1	—	1	—	2
Gothenburg	—	2	—	2	—	2
Hamburgh	—	6	—	6	—	6
Holland	—	—	—	—	—	1
Flanders	—	—	—	—	1	—
France	—	—	1	—	—	—
Lisbon	—	—	—	—	—	—
Mediterranean	1	—	—	—	—	—
America	—	1	—	1	—	1
Leeward Islands	—	—	—	—	—	—
Jamaica	—	—	—	—	—	—
Brazils	—	—	—	—	—	—
Buenos Ayres	—	—	—	—	—	—

	£	s.	d.	
Portugal Gold, in Coin	0	0	0	per Oz.
Foreign Gold, in Bars	3	17	9	per Oz.
New Doubloons	0	0	0	per Oz.
New Dollars	0	4	10¼	per Oz.
Silver in Bars, Standard	0	5	0½	per Oz.

THE MARINE LIST.

A most tremendous Gale at about SSW. was experienced on Monday night, and throughout the whole of Tuesday; and it continued to blow on Tuesday night and Wednesday morning. — The following Accounts have already been received of Losses and Accidents on different parts of the Coast.—

Whitstable, 24th Nov.

"The Alpha, Tyrer, from Youghall to London, has put in here with loss of her rudder, an anchor and cable, and leaky."

Margate, Nov. 23d.

"A brig was discovered at daylight this morning, on shore on Margate Sand, and shortly afterwards went to pieces. Fears are entertained respecting the Crew.—It still continues to blow heavily from the S. and W."

——— 25th Nov.

"A topmast, painted white at the heel and head, and part of a yard, painted white at the yard-arm, with a gaff, also painted white, have been brought in to-day from the wreck of the Brig on Margate Sand, which is stated to have sunk in 7 fathoms, on the outer part of the sand."

Broadstairs, 24th Nov.

"The Amity, —, from London to Penzance, after running against the Pier at Ramsgate, is driven on shore here. Cargo landed without much injury. The Vessel is much damaged."

Ramsgate, 23d Nov.

"The Cornelia, Sypkes, from Batavia to Amsterdam, is on shore at the back of the East Pier, with loss of anchors, cables, rudder, and four feet water in her hold.—The Harmony, Voss, from Memel to Topsham, cut her cable, struck the Pier, carried away bowsprit, stove her bows, and filled with water in the Harbour.—6 P.M. blowing a violent Gale from the SSW."

——— 24th Nov.

"The Cornelia, Sypkes, filled last night's tide; her mainmast has been cut away, and part of her cargo is discharged in a damaged condition; she is so far swaddled in the sand, that there are little hopes of her being got off. — The Harmony, Voss, whose larboard bow and stern were stove in, has been lightened, and will be got into the Basin next tide. She must discharge to repair. The Henrietta Louisa, Christmas, sprung a leak during the Gale of yesterday, and makes so much water that she must discharge her cargo to repair."

——— 24th Nov.

"The Mevagissey, Andrews, from London to Smyrna, was driven from her anchor in Dungeness Roads yesterday; brought up in the Downs with the second, where her cable parted, and she went on shore on Sandwich Flats, floated off with loss of rudder, and in attempting Broadstairs, got on shore to the northward, where she now lies, making but little water. Cargo discharging, and it is expected she will be carried into harbor next tide."

Ramsgate 25th Nov.

"The Cornelia, Sipkes, is become a total wreck. Cargo landing when the water is off. The Mevagissey has been brought in here."

Deal, Nov. 23d.

"It blew hard last night from the SSW. and this day increased to a complete Hurricane. The Belina, Craig, from London for Grenada, got on shore on the Goodwin Sand early this morning, and is totally lost; the First Officer and twelve Seamen drowned; the Captain, Second Officer, three Seamen, and a Boy, saved by the Deal Boatmen, who took them off some pieces of the floating wreck, in an exhausted state, being unable from the tremendous sea, to approach the Ship within a cable's length.—½ past 6, P.M. Wind W. blows very hard."

Dover, 23d Nov.

"It has blown tremendously the whole of the day, with a very heavy sea."

——— 25th Nov

"The Resolution, from Bordeaux to Antwerp, has been seen to the Westward, with loss of mainmast, anchor, cables, sails, and rigging, and in charge of some pilots. Just before dark, a large vessel was discovered to westward in a very damaged state, with a boat attending her. She appears to be either a Ship or a large Brig, with only her foremast standing."

Hastings, 23d Nov.

"The Sloop Providence of Chichester, timber laden, is on shore near here, and it is feared will go to pieces next tide."

Newhaven, 24th Nov.

"The Vrow Alida, Kremer, from Bordeaux to Rotterdam, put in here this day; she was struck by a sea off the Wight, and thrown on her beam ends, and carried away her mizen mast. Part of the cargo damaged."

Littlehampton, 23d Nov.

"We have had a most tremendous gale all night, and the tide is as high as it has been known for many years."

——— 24th Nov.

"The Hazard, Beale, from Bordeaux to London, was driven on shore yesterday to the westward of this harbor, but it is expected she will be got off and brought in here."

Portsmouth, 23d Nov.

"During the whole of last night and up to this time (7 p.m.) we have had one of the most severe Gales from the SSE to SW. ever remembered here. The Victory, Finney, from Bengal to London, is on shore on Blockhouse Beach; the Shipley transport, bound to Valparaiso, is on shore on SouthSea Beach; the Admiral Berkeley transport, bound to Cape Coast Castle, is on shore near the Hospital, with masts gone and bilged; the Madras, ——, for Madras, is on shore in Stokes Bay; the Lady Arabella, Renner, for Carthagena, run into the Harbour, and is on the East Mud; the Comore carefully than in the 18th century, and arranged in date order. In effect, they were the early 19th century equivalent of real-time and continuously updated television and Internet news.

Many letters from each port began with hopeful enough accounts of vessels thought only to be damaged but repairable. As the gale continued, further reports came in, printed in the same or subsequent issues, detailing the disintegration of those ships, weakened by their stranding and now battered by the combination of wind and tide. The fate of the *Cornelia*,[40] homeward-bound from Batavia (now Jakarta, Indonesia) to Amsterdam, was typical. In the first of three letters from Ramsgate, dated 23 November, she lay behind the East Pier with 'four feet water in her hold'. This letter concluded with an account of the wind still continuing at 6 pm as a violent gale from the south-south-west. A second report from the following day, the 24th, was much more pessimistic in its outlook, the *Cornelia* having filled with water during the previous night's high tide. Part of her cargo had been taken out damaged, and the prognosis was gloomy: 'she is so far swaddled in the sand that there are little hopes of her being got off'. On the 25th loss of her hull was confirmed, although the cargo was being landed 'when the water is off', that is, when the tide was out.

Similarly, the Swedish brig *Christina*,[41] bound from Cadiz for Gothenburg, was embayed by the south-westerly wind, which drove her towards the north-eastern shore of Christchurch Bay. She was driven into the mouth of Bec[k]ton Bunny (a 'bunny' in Hampshire, like the 'chines' of the Dorset, Hampshire and Isle of Wight coasts, is a ravine down to the sea, created by a stream). One man was lost, for the violence of the gale had broken both his legs and he was unable to save himself from being washed overboard. The cargo was destroyed, but otherwise the news was more hopeful than that of the *Cornelia*: 'every effort is making to save the hull and stores'.[42]

The final major gale of the season, which again caused significant damage to shipping, was that of 21 to 25 December. On 21 December it was reported from Deal that 'it came on to blow very strong from SSW to WSW', while the wind conditions were reported on the 22nd at Falmouth as 'WSW – a tremendous gale'.[43] These conditions had little effect on the south coast, but on the north-eastern coastline the gale

backed to the north-east and continued blowing until Christmas Day, with much more severe casualties. Fifteen ships were lost on the 22nd, one on the 23rd, and two more near Hartlepool on Christmas Day.

The loss of the *Isabella*[44] on 22 December amply illustrates the magnitude of this last storm of 1824 along the North Sea coastline. Bound from St Petersburg on a 'northabout' course to Greenock on the west coast of Scotland, with naval stores of iron and hemp, she was blown off course by the gale from the north-east and was driven ashore far to the south near Warkworth in Northumberland. Her position just north of the pier suggests that the master had tried to steer her into the harbour to save his vessel, but the gale forced him ashore just short of his target. On this occasion there were no casualties, apart from that of a Preventive Service watchman who perished from the cold in the course of his duties, as he guarded the wreckage to prevent looting: the Northumberland coast on a winter's night was no place to be without shelter.

Even by the standards of *Lloyd's List*, a specialist maritime publication, to devote an entire issue to a single storm in November 1824 reflected the magnitude of the event: this comprehensive coverage was as newsworthy in its own right as the storm itself. According to one Dutch newspaper, 'the last issue of Lloyd's was filled with three full pages of reports of ships known to be wrecked',[45] which hints at an important point obvious to most contemporary observers: that, conversely, there would be an unknown number of other victims. In those days without radar, telegraph or any modern communications device, the numbers of ships lost unseen and unreported were incalculable and could only be guessed at. For every storm in which wrecks were recorded, crew were rescued or their demise at least witnessed by others, an unknown number of vessels were driven off the coast to founder at sea, their wreckage washed ashore with no identifying features, perhaps mingled with that of others which had shared the same unhappy fate, and often far from the place where they had gone down.

The archaeological potential of these storms therefore remains, to a large extent, unquantifiable, but in modern times we have an advantage denied to our forebears with the increasing numbers of newspaper archives placed online and which can be accessed and directly compared via digital media. The gap can therefore be partially filled in by further research in local newspapers for the affected counties targeting known wreck events, depending on the emphasis given to maritime news by each source. Additionally, further research in foreign-language newspapers may reveal, for example, foreign vessels which went missing in English waters on the relevant dates, and which may well be candidates for inclusion in the casualties of these storms. This advantage enables us to overcome an inherent bias in the historical record which was previously all but insurmountable: the vexed question of the survival of documentary evidence.

By comparison, the wrecks attributable to the 'Great Storm' which struck the north-east coast of England in November 1901 were more accurately recorded, not least because literacy levels were greater. Better communications in port (telegraph) and a greater number of organisations concerned with safety and the protection of commerce and navigation (harbour boards, lifeboat organisations, coastguard, Lloyd's agents, Receiver of Wreck) ensured more accurate reporting systems; the initial news and the subsequent official investigations (Board of Trade Inquiries and Casualty Returns) would be disseminated more widely through the media; the supporting bureaucracy as well as the wide-spread press interest ensured that more of this material survives. This was the natural outcome of having a dedicated marine publication, and its consequent ability to innovate in compiling comparative data into a single issue. For the first time ever, in November 1824, an in-depth analysis of a single nationwide storm event was possible.

'A very dangerous flat and fatal'

To the skilled navigator a natural hazard within the marine environment by itself need not present much difficulty under normal conditions, but when allied with unfavourable weather conditions, a sandbank, rock or cliff becomes a lethal presence. Nowhere is this more true than the Goodwin Sands off the coast of Kent, one of the world's most notorious shipping hazards. Over 800 wrecks have been recorded on the Goodwin Sands, either through the documentary evidence, or through the existence of wreck remains, whether or not they have been identified. Over one-half of these were of foreign origin, with a great number which disappeared without leaving behind any identifying trace of name or nationality.[46] The story of the sands is one of a remarkable geological formation literally on a collision course with human activity, its brooding presence off the coast of Kent having an untold human dimension.

This notoriety was well established by the Middle Ages. The very presence of the Roman lighthouse at Dover suggests that the peril existed on the sands nearby in Roman times, although to date no shipwrecks corresponding to that period have been found. The first secure mention of a ship specifically said to have been lost on those particular sands dates from 1371, when *Le Nicholas* was 'imperilled and broken' on 'Godewynsonde' en route from Bayonne to London with wine and iron (Fig 1.9).[47] By the latter part of the 16th century the Goodwins began to make a regular appearance in historical or topographical accounts,[48] coinciding with the emergence of these literary genres. It may also have coincided, though this is difficult to prove, with a historical spike in the number of wrecks on the sands, perhaps owing to storm surges altering the regular tidal patterns, and it certainly seems to have led to regular calls for a light to avoid the hazard. It was just at this period, in 1580, Gawen Smith made a proposal for a beacon that was both warning light and tower of refuge, 'able to receive and preserve 30 or 40 persons at least'.[49] Sir John Coke, writing in 1623, said:

> but as to the proposed light on the Godwin Sands, understands that the Hollanders have suffered great wrecks for want of it, and offer liberally towards it.[50]

Dutch concerns were understandable, for at least 29 of their ships are known to have been lost on the Sands during the 17th century, to reach a peak of 72 in the 18th century. Indeed, at least one 'Hollander' was lost annually on the Goodwins between 1616 and 1620, an important consideration when the Dutch were the world's leading maritime nation.[51] During the reign of Charles II, proposals to erect a lighthouse were still under lively discussion, as Captain John Poyntz enthusiastically recommended a lighthouse and castle on the Goodwins to Samuel Pepys, with the intention of making 'the sands a firm islands above high water mark' but these remained a dream until the more practical suggestion of a lightship was installed in 1793.[52]

It was also at this time that the Goodwin Sands became embedded in the popular consciousness as an archetype of the ship's

Fig 1.9
We lack much detail as to exactly how Le Nicholas, *the first recorded victim of the 'Great Ship Swallower' in 1371, was 'imperilled and broken at Godewynsonde'. This reconstruction is based on the few details available in the original records, fleshed out by later accounts of sailing vessels meeting the same fate and 20th-century photographs showing the sands partially exposed at low water. Sails ripped and torn,* Le Nicholas *has become unmanageable and so cannot avoid the infamous Goodwins: 'imperilled'. She has struck during flood tide and the crew have jettisoned some of the cargo in a failed attempt to lighten and refloat the ship before the ebb. They have now realised that, as the tide goes out, the exposed sands will begin to suck in and crush the vessel ('broken') which is beginning to settle by the stern, and are now abandoning ship. More cargo was 'thrown ashore' by the sea as the vessel broke up, but the mariners 'landed in safety'.*

graveyard. Living and working by the Thames in London, Shakespeare must surely have frequently heard the news of vessels which had miscarried on the Goodwin Sands, perhaps from ships safely arrived in port whose crews had seen the plight of other ships in company. Evidence for shipwrecks on the Goodwins during his years as a playwright is patchy, owing to the survival or otherwise of contemporary sources, but when he wrote the *Merchant of Venice*, thought to date from the mid to late 1590s, he may have had in mind the losses of the *Red Lion* of London and the *Golden Lion* of Middelburg, Zeeland, in late 1592, of a Dutch vessel lost in January 1594 or of the English privateer *Pegasus* in 1598.[53] Given the numbers of ships of different nationalities which suffered on these notorious sandbanks, there was nothing implausible about Shakespeare's Venetian characters having heard of the Goodwin Sands:

Salanio: Now, what news on the Rialto?
Salarino: Why, yet it lives there unchecked that Antonio hath a ship of rich lading wrack'd on the narrow seas; the Goodwins, I think they call the place, a very dangerous flat and fatal, where the carcasses of many a tall ship lie buried, as they say, if my gossip Report be an honest woman of her word.[54]

Shakespeare in fact encapsulates the enduring danger of the Goodwin Sands – where since his time many more 'tall ships' have been buried – and its location in the Narrow Seas. At the time 'Narrow Seas' could refer to any sea separating England from her neighbours, but was also used more strictly to refer to the Straits of Dover. Whether bound from Flanders with cloth for England or Spain, or from the Baltic with deals, barrel staves and tar, Setubal in Portugal with salt for Stockholm, or Bordeaux with wine and claret for England and Germany, all traffic between northern and eastern Europe on the one hand and southern and western Europe on the other was funnelled through the narrowest gap between England and France, where the waters of the English Channel and southern North Sea met and mingled.

This in part was what made the Goodwin Sands so dangerous: a concentration of vessels as northbound and southbound traffic passed one another, not to mention traffic from east to west and west to east between England and France. The Downs to the west of the Goodwin Sands formed a natural deep water anchorage opposite Deal where individual ships, mercantile convoys or naval fleets could await a fair wind for their onward passage. The Goodwins sheltered the Downs to the east, unless the wind began to blow hard from the west or south-west. Any ships at anchor in the Downs were then immediately at risk of being driven straight onto the Goodwins. Naturally, vessels from the coasts of north-western Continental Europe and from the Baltic were also potentially vulnerable as they headed south; a wind from the north-east was favourable for the English Channel, but left them exposed to the Goodwins before reaching the safety of the Downs.

Geographically the Goodwin Sands lie orientated north-east to south-west, the northernmost point of the North Sand Head now lying approximately opposite Ramsgate, while the tip of the South Sand Head is almost as far south as to lie opposite Dover. The sands are bisected by the Kellett Gut, a shallow channel which has appeared, disappeared and reappeared over the centuries. The movement of the Kellett Gut reflects the wider mobility of the entire formation: the dangerous location of the Goodwin Sands is compounded by their shifting nature, influenced by tidal and weather streams, and by their composition, consisting of sand 25m deep over a chalk platform. The upper layers of sand are highly mobile above, but more compacted below; however, the nature of the surface sand can alter and become denser or looser under particular tidal conditions. This can in its turn make the Goodwins dangerously unpredictable: one can also see why the imagery of the Goodwins as a swallower of ships arose, and when wrecks reappear, it is as if the sea has spat them out.

The mobility of the Goodwin Sands is likely to be behind the well-known legend of the *Lady Luvibund*, purportedly the ghost of a vessel lost on the sands in 1748, which is said to reappear once every 50 years. According to the legend, one of the crew, jealous of the captain who had married his sweetheart, deliberately drove the ship onto the sands, drowning them all. It would seem logical that the known phenomenon of the Goodwin Sands, covering and recovering wreck sites on a regular basis as a result of sand wave migration,[55] has led to a folk memory, perhaps, of just such an event being worked up as the basis for a dramatic story. The story of the *Lady Luvibund* is untraced before the 20th century and remains unsubstantiated in any contemporary source.[56] Certainly roughly 50 years elapsed between a 1921 sighting of the *U-48*, lost in the First World War in 1917,[57] and her apparent reappearance in 1973. *U-48* is not the only vessel to have come to light in this way, for the *Stirling Castle* has also disappeared and reappeared.[58] Thus, whatever remains of a sailing vessel seen on one such occasion may have inspired this eerie modern myth.

The shifting nature of the sands has another aspect which would repay further investigation, even tempered by the ever-present question of the survival of documentary evidence. Just as the sands ebb and flow with the tide, so too do the numbers of wrecks. Little reliable data is available prior to the late 1740s or so, when newspapers ensured that knowledge of Goodwins wrecks was disseminated into the public domain. Between 1747 and 1847, at least two wrecks seem to have occurred yearly on the Goodwins, with the exception of 1756, 1759, 1767, 1778 and 1806.[59] In some years there appear to be particularly high numbers of wrecks, which may have come about as a direct result of storms. They may also be indirectly related to previous storm activity through alterations in the extent, shape and height of the sands, the tidal patterns associated with them, and the extent or disappearance of safe channels, catching even crews familiar with the sands unawares. Other notable rises in the numbers of wrecks could occur because of errors in navigational charts, since early charts of the

Goodwin Sands lacked detail and accuracy (Figs 1.10 and 1.11).

The Goodwin Sands will almost certainly throw up new wrecks of interest as they shift and resettle, particularly as they continued to claim ships and lives well into the late 20th century. Even many of these more recent wrecks have disappeared into the maw of the sands. Something of the order of nearly 800 wrecks have been documented on the Goodwin Sands

Fig 1.10 (right)
A true and lively description of his Ma.sties Roade the Downes … sheweing how commodious & necessary a new haven to Sandwich would be for his Ma.sties service … and preserveing many hundreds of his subiects lives, ships and goods in tyme of fowle weather …
A chart by Robert Jager, c 1640/1, the Goodwin Sands looming large to the east. They are drawn extremely schematically and almost symmetrically, so much so that, even given the dynamic nature of the Sands, it is perhaps fortunate that the chart was not intended to be used for navigation.
(The National Archives: ref. MPF 1/278)

Fig 1.11 (below right)
The Goodwin Sands are depicted somewhat differently a century later on this Plan of the Coast of Kent from Ramsgate to Rye *from 1740. How much this is due to the sands shifting, and how much to a conventionalised representation of the sands, is unclear. The relationship of the North and South Sand Heads to one another is more accurate, and the areas shown as drying at low water correspond more or less to the shallowest areas today, but the Swatch appears to be orientated horizontally, rather than the north-east to south-west orientation of the present-day Kellett Gut.*
(J010166)

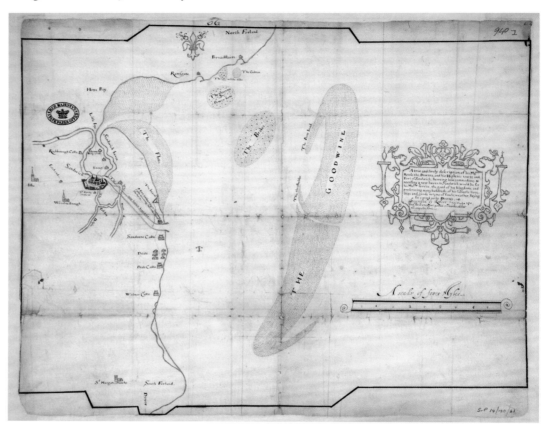

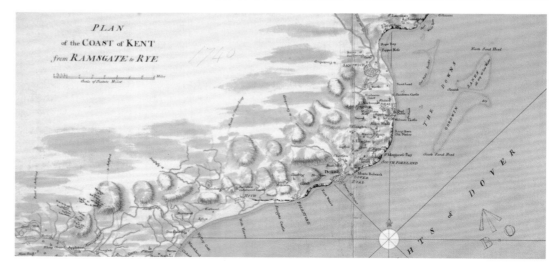

up to and including the 20th century, outnumbering the sites of known vessel remains by over 10 to 1. Not all of these sites have been matched definitively with a documented wreck (or indeed with any wreck), so that the archaeological potential of the Goodwins remains enormous. The area's potential for preservation is equally great because of the dominance of fine-grained sediments.[60] One particular group of more recent wrecks incorporates the East Goodwin and South Goodwin lightships, both sunk by German bombers in 1940. Despite this relatively recent date, the former was only positively identified in 2006, the latter plotted but not confirmed as the wreck of the lightship.[61] The successor to the South Goodwin lightship then capsized in a severe storm in 1954, with only one survivor. Despite contemporary aerial photographs and film footage of the vessel sinking into the sand, her position today remains unknown and uncharted by the United Kingdom Hydrographic Office (UKHO).[62]

The notoriety of the Goodwin Sands has thus historically run deep in English culture: like scattered flotsam picked up far from the site of a wreck, and put to use in the built environment, the connections between Goodwins wrecks and the Kent coast are sometimes hard to uncover. They can, however, be seen in the development of a way of life which endured for centuries and preserved in written evidence left by figures from all walks of life. This evidence begins with the local boatmen who made their living from the Goodwin Sands, whose activities were recorded as early as the 17th century, but which must have originated at a much earlier date, given the history of wrecks on the Sands. They belonged to Dover, Deal, Walmer and Ramsgate, all towns which sat directly opposite the Sands. Even in the early 17th century, however, there were accusations that the 'salvage' of wrecked goods and materials exceeded the bounds of propriety, which must have added to the Dutch concerns about the dangers of the sands at this period. There was a complaint 'against the Deal boatmen, for bursting open the merchants' packs, and opening them' in 1616, which involved two Dutch vessels, while another complaint concerning an English ship in 1621 claimed 'the boatmen insisted on taking up more lead than the master wished'. Nevertheless there was also great admiration of their talents: in 1619 the Ramsgate boatmen managed to get one of two ships, belonging to Hoorn, off the Goodwins, no mean feat.[63]

The assiduity of a later generation of these hardy local men resulted in the salvage in 1825 of a considerable quantity of goods from the East Indiaman *Ogle Castle*, though parts of her cargo and hull were driven on shore as far afield as Rotterdam, Ostend and Vlissingen (Flushing), and landed there. The 'boatmen' of the Deal coastline worked not only as salvors, but also as the saviours and rescuers of stricken passengers and crew. One Deal boatman spoke of his distress at being unable to save anyone from the wreck to members of the government watching from the shore, the Earl of Liverpool and George Canning:

> His Lordship asked me if there were any female passengers on board, and I told him I could not tell. His Lordship said we had a great deal of trouble: I said, yes, my Lord, but not the pleasure of saving the crew.[64]

Another figure whose involvement in the local boatmen's culture may at first seem surprising was Augustus Welby Northmore Pugin, the Gothic Revival architect, who resided at Ramsgate and left testimony to several wrecks during the 1840s and 1850s (Fig 1.12). He noted, for example, the loss of the *Royal Adelaide* steamer in heavy weather off Margate in his diaries in 1850; she fired signals of distress on the Tongue Sand but in the rough conditions no one else could approach to render assistance, so that as she broke up over 200 passengers lost their lives.[65] For the boatmen to be unable to approach to give assistance to the *Royal Adelaide*, conditions must have been atrocious, for they were well-known for their fearlessness.[66]

Someone of Pugin's social and professional

Fig 1.12
View of the Grade I listed house at The Grange, Ramsgate, Kent and adjoining chapel built by the devout Catholic architect Augustus Welby Northmore Pugin for himself in 1843/4, and from which his diaries show that he witnessed several wrecks. Up until his death in the house on 14 September 1852, the house overlooked more than 40 wrecks, the majority on the Goodwin Sands: the pressure of his work and his indefatigable travelling meant that his personal involvement in the salvage of the Royal Adelaide *and the* Gazelle *was probably the exception, rather than the norm.*
(BB43/01211)

standing might have been expected to be a mere witness and a bystander to wrecks, noting them in his diary. Surprisingly, as the owner of a lugger, the *Caroline*, he was actively involved in salvaging material from wrecks on the Goodwin Sands, like many poorer men. Pugin's involvement with salvage seems at odds with his respectable architectural career, but it was an extra source of income and his journals provide a unique outsider's insight into the boatmen's way of life and the ferocity of the conditions under which they sometimes worked.

The wreck of the *Gazelle*, from Sydney, later in 1850, netted him 18 tons of tallow, for which salvage payments went some way to easing his financial situation. The *Gazelle* was lost in a gale which blew up from south-south-west on 25 November, which also threatened the church next to his home, St Augustine of England, Ramsgate.[67] As the scaffolding around the tower threatened to collapse, 'as if every moment was the last', Pugin's diaries illustrate the severity of the storm in which all hands on the *Gazelle* perished. It also raises the intriguing question of just what Pugin did salvage from his other forays in *Caroline*, the names of the ships with which he was associated in this way, whether he made use of any of any salvaged materials in his own home or elsewhere, or whether any souvenirs came into his personal possession by legitimate purchase or donation.

In this way the Goodwin Sands have both international and localised significance at the gateway to the Continent, and can be regarded as a geological phenomenon having a cultural impact far beyond a mere navigational hazard: they led to the creation of one of the few surviving Roman lighthouses in the world, acquired a fearsome reputation at home and abroad, became embedded in the canon of the most famous playwright in the English language, touched the lives of well-known 19th-century figures, and fostered a way of life on the Kent coast which endured for centuries (Fig 1.13).

Fig 1.13 This RAF view reveals the 'footprints' of the Goodwin Sands and Downs. The sands are dynamic, but even allowing for movements over the intervening centuries they reveal the inaccuracies of the earlier charts. They lie opposite Deal, which witnessed many distress signals and launched local shallow-draught boats capable of skimming over the sands to the rescue. The Times reported that following a storm in 1809 'a most distressing scene presented itself to the spectators from Deal. Three large ships were seen on the Goodwin Sands with only their fore masts standing, hoisting signals of distress, and the sea dashing over them mountains high.' (Apollo, 891466; Admiral Gardner, 1082122; and Britannia, 1229926). (RAF Photography RAF/D/1322/0041 6 October 1959)

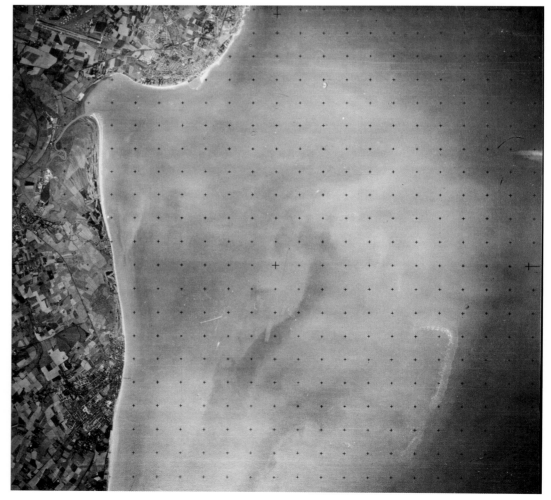

Rooswijk and *Stirling Castle*: two Goodwin Sands wrecks

It is useful to turn the spotlight on two victims of different storm conditions in the same location: comparing contemporary accounts sheds light on the wrecking processes involved for each vessel, and demonstrates that, although wrecked in the same area, the different weather and tidal conditions caused the vessels to disappear in different ways, and have since continued to have an impact on their remains. The first event was, of course, the Great Storm of 1703, which swept in from the south-west, and the second 36 years later, in 1739, which came in from the opposite quarter, the north-east: two different, but equally fearsome, combinations of weather and a threatening natural environment which both produced major disasters and swallowed up two of the principal ships of their time.

The 1739 victim was the *Rooswijk*[68] (also appearing variously in contemporary sources as *Rooswyck* and *Croeswijk*), an outward-bound Dutch East Indiaman, which was wrecked among the Goodwin Sands. She was unfortunate enough to run into a storm the day after leaving the Texel for the Dutch East Indies. The gale came howling in with a sudden drop in temperature, the effects being felt throughout the North Sea, especially on the south-eastern coasts of England. She was, in a sense, wrecked before she even set out: much as the Concorde airliner was timetabled to arrive in New York before the time of her departure from London or Paris, owing to the time difference across the Atlantic, the *Rooswijk* was wrecked on 30 December 1739, after her departure on 8 January 1740. The discrepancy can be explained by continued use of the Julian ('Old Style' [OS]) calendar at this time in England, 11 days behind the Gregorian ('New Style' [NS]) calendar already in use by the Dutch but not adopted in England until 1752.

The *Rooswijk* belonged to the Amsterdam Chamber of the Vereenigde Oost-Indische Compagnie, VOC for short, otherwise known as the Dutch East India Company in English. For ships whose home ports opened onto the Zuider Zee ('Southern Sea') rather than the North Sea coast, the 'Texel' was the traditional outbound assembly point: not the island of the same name dividing the Zuider Zee from the North Sea proper, but the roadstead to the south of the island in the Zuider Zee, leading to Marsdiep,

which, as its name suggests, was a suitable deep water channel. On 29 December 1739/8 January 1740, therefore, the *Rooswijk* set sail, laden with passengers, coin, bullion and a general cargo, including copper, stone and sabre blades for Batavia. This was her second voyage, having returned from a similar 21-month round trip in July 1739. Dutch East Indiamen were built to withstand these long voyages, typically of 18 months to 3 years, hence their name: *retourschepen*, or 'return ships'.

On the very same day English newspapers reported the beginning of a 'violent storm of wind',[69] which was concentrated on the south-eastern counties, principally between Kent and Norfolk, but one Dutch source noted wreckage cast ashore as far north as Newcastle-upon-Tyne[70] (Fig 1.14). This storm is therefore likely to have also affected the Dutch coast, since a gale at east-north-east was also noted as far to the east as Copenhagen on 31 December.[71] The range and extent of this storm appears comparable to the storm surge which caused widespread flooding in both England and Holland in 1953.[72] In 1739, as in 1953, the Thames Estuary was particularly badly affected, since 'the coast from Essex to Margate is strowed with wrecks, among whom are several colliers'.[73] The extensive damage of the scattered wreckage reported by the Dutch was computed at over £100,000 (or over £12.5m today).[74] The *Rooswijk* was bound south-west to the English Channel via the Straits of Dover on this first leg of her long journey. On such a course the east-north-

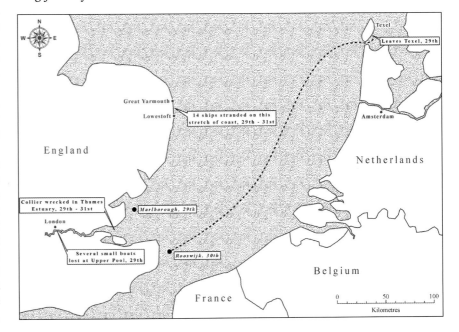

Fig 1.14
The Rooswijk's *doomed voyage in the context of other wrecks reported on the English coast at the same time.*

east wind was set fair for her departure from the Texel: it is hard to believe that she would have left the shelter of the Texel in dangerous conditions. Perhaps, if she had been waiting some time there for the first fair wind, her captain and crew may have been willing to risk their first opportunity to leave.

They may have proceeded at first for a number of hours, perhaps overnight, under reasonably favourable conditions. It is difficult to know how much their arrival next day off the Goodwin Sands, a distance of nearly 200 miles, can be attributed to making good speed with a fair wind, or to the gale driving her onwards with increasing loss of control. Perhaps the weather worsened before the *Rooswijk* had scarcely left the Netherlands out of sight, since another report, from Burnham-on-Crouch in Essex, stated that the *Marlborough* sloop was driven from her anchors onto the Whitaker Spit 'by contrary winds' on the same day of the *Rooswijk*'s departure.[75] The *Marlborough* had been ordered to proceed north to Great Yarmouth on Christmas Day; at this point the wind is likely to have blown from a westerly quarter, favourable for the *Marlborough*'s voyage, but keeping the *Rooswijk* windbound in the Texel. Conversely, a fair wind for the *Rooswijk* would have turned into 'contrary winds' for the *Marlborough* sailing in the opposite direction.

The *Marlborough*'s fate illustrates the predicament in which the crew of the *Rooswijk* now found themselves, since the cold was added to the already perilous mix of the violent storm and dangerous sandbanks. The Whitaker Spit is a well-known shipping hazard, although less notorious than the Goodwin Sands: in fact the loss of the *Marlborough* and two other vessels in this storm[76] is the first documented account specifically detailing losses upon the Whitaker. This is not to say that there were no earlier wrecks on the Whitaker, since historical records pertaining to losses in the Thames Estuary tend to be rather vague, frequently little more than 'lost in the Swin' (the Swin Channel at the mouth of the Thames). The *Marlborough* beat upon the Whitaker for three days:

> before the crew could get on shore: one man perished by the severity of the weather, the rest are all blister'd and swell'd with the frost in such a manner that they are not able to move.[77]

The 'severity of the weather' extended far inland, so much so that 'large flakes of ice were brought down by the tide' into the Thames 'above bridge

near Shoreditch', possibly in the vicinity of the Pool of London. In fact this was one of the winters in which the ice developed sufficiently for a Frost Fair to take place upon the Thames.[78] The wind and ice together were especially lethal for the numerous small craft which plied the capital's river, and which were 'stav'd to pieces' as they were driven into the ice.[79] Further north, and at the latitude of the Netherlands, 14 vessels were driven ashore between Great Yarmouth and Lowestoft alone.[80]

Under such circumstances the *Rooswijk* stood little chance. The gale drove her onto the north-eastern end of the Goodwin Sands, where she must have been beaten to pieces. Given the documented severity of the weather, the storm was likely to have been accompanied by snow, reducing visibility ahead considerably and making it even more difficult to spot danger in the broken water whipped up by the storm over the sands, until it was too late. The Goodwin Sands were far more lethal than the Whitaker Spit on which the *Marlborough* was lost, and the *Rooswijk* disintegrated quickly, suggesting that she pounded heavily on the sands. She was seen from Deal on the morning of 30 December (according to a letter which appeared in the London press the following day),[81] but by the afternoon she had disappeared with all her crew, thought to have numbered over 200 persons, including her master, Daniel Ronzieres. The bleak words 'this afternoon it was reported to be lost, and all her crew', even hint that the atrocious weather veiled the final disintegration of the vessel from those on shore, but the weather must have cleared sufficiently by the early December sunset for her disappearance to be noted on the same day. The *Rooswijk* was dispatched by the sea in a matter of hours, but the gale continued unabated for a further two days, so that as a natural consequence, stray wreckage and miscarried letters were all that came ashore, rather than any significant structural frames of the ship. Hendrik Hop, a VOC representative in England, was no better informed than anyone else, for his letter home on the 12 January (2 January English/Old Style) contained substantially the same information as could be gleaned from English newspapers, suggesting that little or nothing else had been found over the previous few days.

> They write from Deal, that there are several Pieces of Wreck frequently taken up at that Place, and a great many Packets of Letters, all of them directed to Batavia.[82]

Given the widespread freeze, and the struggles of the men in the *Marlborough* to the north, it seems likely that the problems of running aground were compounded by the winter conditions. The *Rooswijk* may have struck too quickly for the crew to save themselves by lightening the vessel: jettisoning cargo, cannon, masts and rigging. Under more favourable weather conditions, this was a reasonable course to take to 'get her off'. In a tempest it was a calculated risk to cut down the masts and rigging, which might otherwise have saved the *Rooswijk*, but the physical stresses on the ship in such wintry conditions were enormous. Frozen spray or snow clinging to her sails would both have weighed her down further and made her far less responsive to any attempts to manoeuvre her off the sands: her timbers would have been creaking under the pressure of water freezing to them. The dead weight of ice may even have contributed to the demise of the vessel as she beat against the edge of the sandbank.[83] As the

ship pounded on the sands and began to break up, her masts are likely to have 'gone by the board', that is, fallen overboard, as part of the process of disintegration (a nautical phrase still in common currency, though not now in its original context). The crew of the *Marlborough*, although suffering from what we would now recognise as hypothermia, were more fortunate since their vessel held together sufficiently over the three days of the gale for them to get ashore when it finally blew itself out. By contrast, anyone who did not drown as the *Rooswijk* 'went to pieces' (another common phrase now used in a figurative sense, for a failure of nerve in a difficult situation) is likely to have died of hypothermia on board the vessel or in the water.

No more was heard of the *Rooswijk* until 2004 when she appears to have finally been relocated: the debris trail of the site suggests wreck remains scattered over a larger area than her dimensions as built, consistent with a vessel breaking up rapidly *in situ* (Fig 1.15). Large numbers of 4lb

Fig 1.15
Plan of one of the three co-ordinates investigated by Wessex Archaeology, showing the fragmentary nature of the Rooswijk *wreck. The inset shows two other plotted co-ordinates, illustrating the widely dispersed nature of the wreck site.*
(© Crown copyright. Data collected and processed by Wessex Archaeology)

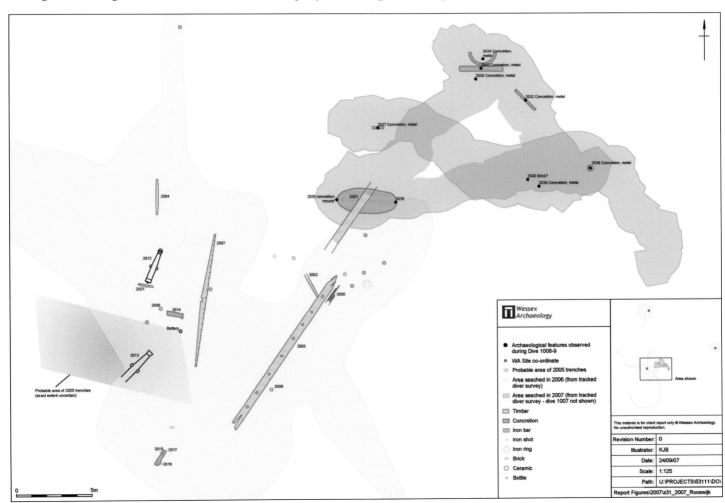

silver bars bearing the VOC monogram logo of the Dutch East India Company were found nearby, from which the nature of the wreck site could be easily recognised, and also consistent with her known cargo (Fig 1.16). Her marks suggested the Amsterdam chamber of the VOC, to which the *Rooswijk* was known to have belonged. Coinage dated to 1737/8 was recovered from the site, again pointing towards the *Rooswijk* and excluding two other VOC ships, the *Loosdrecht* and *Meermond*, lost on the Goodwins in 1736. These two, also Amsterdam ships, would otherwise have also been candidates for the identification of the wreck.[84]

The *Loosdrecht* and *Meermond* were also outward-bound, unfortunate enough to be passing the Goodwin Sands in the aftermath of a storm surge event datable to 16 February 1736, when an exceptionally high tide was recorded in the Thames.[85] The *Loosdrecht* and *Meermond*, in company with the *Buis*, struck the Goodwins on 19 February: the *Buis* was fortunate enough to be 'got off' again but was unable to put to sea again for three months. All three vessels had attempted to depart from the Netherlands on the 12th, but put back to shelter in the Texel between the 13th and 18th. By the 18th the danger was felt sufficiently past to proceed once more on

voyage: the convoy's arrival off the Goodwin Sands on the 19th suggests that the time it took the *Rooswijk* to sail from the Texel to as far south as the Goodwins was not unusual under reasonably normal weather conditions. It is likely that the storm surge had had some impact on the configuration of the Goodwin Sands. The commanders of all three ships had sailed over the Goodwins at least once before, so it seems they traversed shoals where they remembered clear water on previous occasions, trapping them in the maw of the sands. The Goodwins were not, of course, the only sands which could catch the unwary in this way: in the early 19th century the *Swift* was the victim of a 'new shoal' which had appeared south-west of the Dudgeon lightship.[86] If, despite previous experience, ships' captains could still run aground on the Goodwin Sands, this suggests that an inexperienced captain was in even graver danger, for *Rooswijk* was Ronzieres' first, and in the event last, command of an East Indiaman.

A fourth Dutch East Indiaman, the *Oostereem*, laden with silver, was also lost on the Goodwins in 1783, but the recovery of her cargo at the time appears to preclude that vessel and to point definitively towards the *Rooswijk*.[87] Like her predecessors, she was outward-bound, and it

Fig 1.16
These silver bars are among the number recovered from the wreck of the Rooswijk *and presented to the then Dutch Finance Minister. They display the monogram VOC logo surmounted by A for Amsterdam, one of the six chambers of the VOC, over a hitherto unidentified assay mark enclosing a goat. A simple but effective logo: the V, which stands for Vereenigde ('united'), is interlinked with O and C. They are relatively small, being 15.3cm × 4cm × 3.7cm. Over 500 were found on the site and demonstrate the great demand for bullion silver which could be easily melted down for jewellery and coinage in the Asian markets, making it a profitable outward-bound cargo. (© Zeeuws Maritiem MuZEEum, Vlissingen)*

may be that there is an additional pattern of navigational error which can be discerned here: she was the last Dutch East Indiaman to be lost on the Goodwin Sands, although not the last to be wrecked in English waters.[88]

Why did so many Dutch East Indiamen risk storm and shipwreck in the wintry waters of northern Europe, with more unsettled weather, temperatures at a lower extreme and a higher likelihood of poor visibility (rain, snow and fog)? The answer lies in the need to take advantage of trade winds and specific currents further south in the less familiar waters of the Atlantic coast off Africa, round the Cape of Good Hope into the Southern Ocean and into the Indian Ocean, where they had to time their arrival and departure outside the monsoon seasons where possible. Failure to do so could leave ships port-bound, or engaged during the off-season in the Indian Ocean trade rather than making a profitable return to Europe. Presumably the risks of the winter season in the more familiar waters of Northern Europe were considered an acceptable trade-off for the riches brought from China, India and Indonesia. Statistically, however, the wrecks of outward-bound Dutch East Indiamen far outnumber those of homeward-bound ships in English waters by 9 to 1.[89]

The finding of the *Rooswijk* was as dramatic as her end. The location and identification of the site, a coup in itself, was accompanied by the equally rare identification of an owner with an interest in the wreck founded on a historical basis. Any wreck material found within UK territorial waters (that is, to the 12-mile limit of UK territorial waters), or recovered from waters outside the UK and brought within UK territorial waters, must by law be reported to the Receiver of Wreck. The Receiver then assigns a *droit* ('right') to the material and attempts to establish whether there is a legal heir to the original owners of any wreck. If no heir can be found, which in the case of medieval or earlier mercantile wrecks is clearly impossible, then the salvors may be entitled to retain their finds, although where possible they are encouraged to donate them to an appropriate museum. In this case, the VOC's rights had passed to the modern Dutch state, represented by the then Junior Minister of Finance, Joop Wijn, who received part of the recovered silver in December 2005 in a ceremony aboard the Netherlands Royal Navy frigate *De Ruyter* in Plymouth. A number of items from the wreck have been donated to the MuZEEum, Vlissingen, where they were undergoing conservation and research at the time of writing. Small arms, candleholders and even part of a propelling pencil were recovered from the site, giving an insight into life on board (Fig 1.17).[90]

The wreck has not yet yielded up all her secrets: the drama of a single afternoon in December 1739 will take many years to piece

Fig 1.17
Gold ring recovered from the Rooswijk wreck.
(© Mark Dunkley)

together. The two questions below have only been partially answered, but at this stage the answer is conjectural. The foremost question is why the vessel broke up so quickly when she was a well-built *retourschip* designed to withstand a number of marine environments over a lengthy voyage, and relatively new. The intervening months between her maiden round trip and the second departure would have been sufficient time to careen her (beach and lay a vessel on her side for examination, cleaning and repair) and make her ready for her next voyage. The second question is why she broke up at all in these conditions. By all accounts, the fatal storm – vicious, wintry and squally though it was – pales into insignificance beside the Great Storm of 1703, 36 years earlier, in which a number of English warships, such as the *Stirling Castle*, were also lost on the Goodwin Sands.

The *Stirling Castle* was recognised in 1979, when the sands, in one of their periodical movements, uncovered her gun deck, virtually intact, with the guns still in a reasonably ordered sequence.[91] The ultimate fate and resting place of the *Rooswijk* and the *Stirling Castle* was the same, but the wrecking process entirely different. Why was it so different for these two vessels, each a representative of a type at the forefront of the development of ship technology, and of fairly similar dimensions? The *Stirling Castle* was, at 1,059 tons builders' measurement, somewhat larger than the *Rooswijk* at 850 tons; both were also, of course, armed. All East Indiamen were defensively armed to protect both crew and cargo, while the *Stirling Castle*, as a Third Rate ship of the line, mounted 70 guns; the largest and best armed vessels were known as First Rates, and so on, down to the smallest ships of the line, the Sixth Rates, hence the expression which remains current today, 'first rate', to indicate something of the best quality. The *Stirling Castle* was therefore a fairly substantial vessel.

The direction and power of the wind during each event inevitably affected the manner of loss. The *Rooswijk* was driven south-west, more or less on her intended course, by a north-easterly wind, and seems to have struck the Goodwin Sands roughly at the first possible point of contact, at their north-eastern tip. By contrast, the *Stirling Castle* was driven out of her anchorage in the Downs in the opposite direction, by a south-westerly hurricane force wind. According to a contemporary eyewitness, a survivor from a ship in the Downs blown up to

Norway, the *Stirling Castle* was driven helpless before the storm. Unlike the crew of the *Rooswijk*, the men on board the *Stirling Castle* clearly had time to help themselves by cutting away their masts, even though this meant that she was no longer navigable. Her sails were no longer filling with the wind and the combined weight of the masts, rigging and sails was gone, giving them a slender chance of escaping the sands for which they were headed:

> By four-a-clock we miss'd the *Mary* and the *Northumberland*, who rid not far from us, and found they were driven from their anchors; but what became of them, God knows, and soon after a large man of war came driving down upon us, all her masts gone, and in a dreadful condition … she drove at last so near us, that I was just going to order the mate to cut away, when it pleas'd God the ship … which we found to be the *Sterling Castle*, drove clear off us, not two ship's lengths to the leeward.

> It was a sight full of terrible particulars, to see a ship of eighty [*sic*] guns and about six hundred men in that dismal case; she had cut away all her masts, the men were all in the confusions of death and despair; she had neither anchor, nor cable, nor boat to help her; the sea breaking over her in a terrible manner, that sometimes she seem'd all under water; and they knew, as well as we that saw her, that they drove by the tempest directly for the Goodwin, where they could expect nothing but destruction: the cries of the men, and the firing their guns, one by one, every half minute for help, terrified us in such a manner, that I think we were half dead with the horror of it.[92]

The *Stirling Castle* was effectively swamped: she struck the sands in a position more or less due east from the Downs ('directly for the Goodwin') and then foundered, displacing the sand below as she settled, as if settling into a bog. Like the *Rooswijk*, the *Stirling Castle* struck as soon as she made contact with the Goodwin Sands: it was relatively unusual for ships to 'beat over' this sandbank sufficiently to escape, although a fortunate few made it under the right circumstances or the assistance of other vessels. The eyewitness accounts of the wreck and her reasonably coherent structure when found would therefore appear to be a classic case of the Goodwin Sands in action as the 'Great Ship Swallower' before the *Stirling Castle* was more or less 'regurgitated' in 1979 in losing the covering of sand which had protected her for so long.

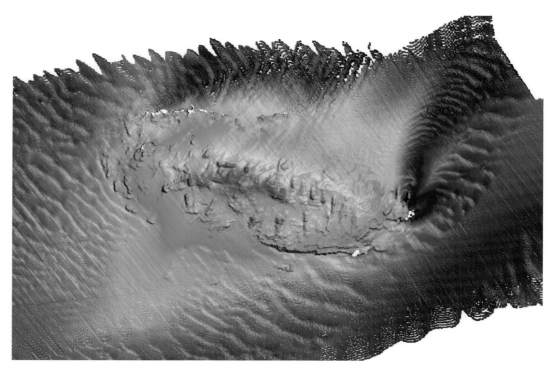

Fig 1.18
Multibeam data for the
site of the *Stirling Castle*
showing the cannon
recognisably disposed
around the wreck site,
in an area of clear
sandwaves indicating
the dynamism of the
surrounding seabed.
(© Crown copyright. Data
collected by University of
St Andrews and processed by
Wessex Archaeology)

The *Stirling Castle*'s dimensions and guns revealed her for what she was: a Third Rate man of war (Fig 1.18). Recovered artefacts such as guns and a ship's bell with the 'broad arrow' mark characteristic of British naval-issue property confirmed this hypothesis (*see* Fig 1.1f, for example). Several personal items with the marks I I and I B, at a time when I and J were interchangeable in writing and printing, suggest that they belonged respectively to the captain, John Johnson, and first mate, James Beverly, thus confirming her identity virtually straight away.[93] Other items illuminating shipboard life were also recovered, making the *Stirling Castle*, like the *Rooswijk*, something of a time capsule of her period. (Fig 1.19).

The difference between this more or less intact warship and the *Rooswijk*'s scattered remains may also in part be because of the varying nature of the Goodwin Sands. Generally speaking, wrecks in the area surrounding the *Rooswijk* appear to be characteristically well broken up, even those of more recent date, consistent with the high mobility of the sand in the Kellett Gut area. This suggests that wrecks in this vicinity are particularly subject to attrition by sandwave action. The Kellett Gut lies immediately to the south of the North Sand Head, which seems to be the pivot for the rotation of the Goodwin Sands in an anti-clockwise direction against the prevailing

Fig 1.19
Candlestick recovered from
the Stirling Castle *wreck*
in 1999.
(© Crown copyright.
Photograph taken by
Archaeological Diving Unit)

clockwise tidal conditions.[94] The northernmost part of the sandbank illustrates this neatly by curling to the north-west in a pattern resembling the hook of a clothes hanger. Additionally, the Kellett Gut seems to have a historical pattern of appearing and disappearing, which may account for the *Loosdrecht* and *Meermond* disaster of 1736 in the unexpected disappearance of a previously safe channel, whether silted up following a storm surge or not.

The exposure of the *Stirling Castle* since 1979 has inevitably led to the site's decay: she was uncovered and recovered a number of times between 1979 and 2012 by forces similar to those operating on the area where the *Rooswijk* now lies, some 4 miles eastward. The *Stirling Castle* is no longer being supported from underneath by a firm sand bottom, while sand continues to pile in from above, exposing and recovering different areas each time and creating pressures which displace the timbers of the hull. As a result the vessel's structure is no longer as intact or coherent as it was until 1979.

These forces make it difficult to identify wreck sites on the Goodwins – hidden by physical sands as well as the sands of time. These two examples have been recognised for what they were by their status as among the most important ships of their time: the *Rooswijk* as a Dutch East Indiaman, pushing the boundaries of both trade and shipbuilding innovation, and the *Stirling Castle* as a Third Rate ship of the line of the English Navy. Both were significant enough for their origins and demise to be documented in contemporary sources. Other vessels on the Goodwins were less fortunate and their story can only be pieced together with difficulty, making identification among the many ships' remains on the sands that much more uncertain. This uncertainty is typical of the Goodwins: as mentioned above, not even the tragic loss of the South Goodwin lightship, in the Kellett Gut, can be charted today (*see* p. 19).[95]

The direct comparison of wrecks in a given area can be extended beyond the *Rooswijk* and *Stirling Castle*. As we have already seen, the discussion of what happened to the *Rooswijk* illuminates what happened to other Dutch East Indiamen also wrecked at other dates on the Goodwin Sands, but it also happens to add a further dimension to wrecks on the same sands, which occurred more or less at exactly the same time. For example, we know that the *Adventure* grounded on the Goodwins on 21 December 1739. A number of letters in French in a Dutch newspaper dated 26 January 1740 (NS) contain the news that the *Adventure* had been recovered and brought into Margate for repair. (This, incidentally, illustrates the ever-present problem of the haphazard survival of contemporary evidence, otherwise we would not have known of the *Adventure*'s recovery.[96]) The storm suggests that the *Adventure* must have been recovered by 30 December since, being already in a perilous position, she would otherwise inevitably have been lost together with the *Rooswijk*.

Looking at wrecks in relation to one another and to the marine environment permits us to appreciate them as an intrinsic feature of the landscape which forms their final resting place, rather than looking at the relationship of landscape and wreck in purely accidental 'cause and effect' terms. An old phrase for shipwreck, 'to set up shop on the Goodwin Sands', first came into being as an ironical comment on the numerous cargoes scattered in the sea as the ships carrying them perished on the sands, but it also accidentally reveals a truth about the nature of shipwrecks on these sandbanks and elsewhere. A shipwreck is as much a historical monument, albeit with its foundations literally on shifting sands, as any ruined abbey or derelict castle. An understanding of the site formation processes already undergone by surviving wreck remains could potentially become a valuable tool in suggesting strategies for the management of similar wreck sites, whether or not they are ultimately protected under heritage protection legislation, as these two vessels have been. In the case of shipwrecks in sites which are difficult to access, as on the Goodwin Sands, these tools become even more valuable.

Threading the Needles

One of the most recognisable and picturesque of all maritime hazards in English coastal waters, visible on land as well as at sea, is the site known as the Needles, where the westernmost tip of the Isle of Wight tapers out into the sea, leaving a dotted line of three chalk stacks. There were originally four such stacks: one, also known as 'Lot's Wife' from the biblical figure who looked back and was turned into a pillar of salt, was certainly recorded in 1646 by a visiting Dutch artist associated with the circle of Rembrandt.[97] According to island folklore, this pillar is said to have collapsed entirely in or by 1764 but the exact date remains unclear and is unsupported by, for example, any corresponding shipping losses which might have occurred during a storm of sufficient magnitude to finally force its wholesale collapse.[98]

The loss of this pillar left a gap between the innermost and centre stacks of the three now remaining, none particularly needle-like in appearance, but jagged and sharp enough to suggest that 'Needles' is not entirely a misnomer (Fig 1.20). The danger they pose is exacerbated by their location at the entrance to the Solent from the west, and by the tidal race (as the name implies, a strong, rapid current contending with underwater obstructions or constrictions in a particular area) leading off the Needles: a lethal combination, presenting a dilemma for ships caught in a storm in the English Channel off the Isle of Wight. Should they stand out to sea and attempt to weather the storm, risking foundering in deep water with no one in sight to assist or even record their loss; or navigate the very narrow passage between the Wight and Hampshire coasts, running the risk of being caught up in the tidal race and being smashed onto the Needles, to gain the shelter of the Solent and its safe anchorages on either shore?

Either way, the decision was likely to prove fatal – over 150 vessels have been recorded as being lost 'off the Isle of Wight', and another 50 or so in a scarcely more specific location, 'on the back of the Isle of Wight', that is, on the south coast of the island.[99] The earliest known wreck certainly associated with the Needles is that of an Italian carrack lost in a tempest on 'les Nedeles' in 1409, while inbound for Southampton.[100] Over the centuries the Needles have claimed other victims which now lie close to the chalk stacks or in Alum Bay to the north and Scratchells Bay to the south. One of the more recent victims was the Greek SS *Varvassi*,[101] lost in 1947 on the outermost edge of the Needles: like her predecessor in 1409, she was bound for Southampton and carrying wine among

Fig 1.20
The Needles lighthouse seen from the south-east. Outcrops of rock can be seen just below the surface and the broken water stretching away to the north tells its own tale of underwater danger. (© Peter Clark. Source English Heritage)

Fig 1.21
Early aerial view of the
Needles from 1920 in which
Alum Bay, resting place of
the Vliegende Draak, *can be*
seen to the north of the
Needles (left in photograph),
and Scratchells Bay to the
south. Both bays have seen
a number of wrecks: at least
five known wrecks are
documented in Scratchells
Bay, among them the
English Fifth Rate ship of the
line Looe *in 1705 (899248)*
and the Scottish schooner
Irex in 1890 (805267).
(EPW000479/Aerofilms)

a general cargo. The *Varvassi* remains well broken *in situ*, but still significant enough to pose a hazard in her own right, particularly during the annual Round Island Race when yachts continue to run aground in the shallows over her remains; the wreck of the *Teamwork* from 1983 is also charted in the same area, although not necessarily caused by that of the *Varvassi*.[102]

Among the many wrecks associated with the Needles are two specific pairs of vessels: the first pair illustrates the problems posed by rounding the Needles from the westward in storm conditions, and the second the potential for wrecks to accumulate in a given area associated with a shipping hazard and, like the *Varvassi*, compound the problems associated with that hazard.

The first pair of wrecks involved came from a convoy of Dutch East Indiamen which left the Texel on 12 October 1627.[103] In that fleet there

were seven ships, comprising the *Nassau, Terschelling, Vlieland, Wieringen, Prins Willem, Vliegende Draak* (or *Draek*) and *Kampen*, bound for India or Indonesia. They voyaged into a storm in the English Channel, which scattered the fleet. The *Terschelling, Prins Willem, Vliegende Draak* and *Kampen* attempted to run for shelter by actually undertaking the risky manoeuvre known as 'threading the Needles', making their way between two of the chalk stacks: the gaps would have been narrower than today since the fourth stack was still extant. The smallest ship, the *Terschelling*, of 80 tons, naturally made her way through, as did, surprisingly, the largest of the four, the *Prins Willem*, of 500 tons. The two ships in between, the *Kampen* and the *Vliegende Draak*, at 300 and 320 tons, respectively, were those which came to grief.[104]

The *Kampen* failed to even make the gap and smashed broadside on to the outermost rocks,

where she now lies today; the *Vliegende Draak* failed to live up to her name, the 'Flying Dragon'. She did indeed manage to squeeze in through the gap, but in doing so her bottom was holed and making water, so that her crew were forced to beach her in Alum Bay, to the north-east (Fig 1.21). The news first reached Portsmouth on 17 October[105] that 'two Dutch East Indiamen outward-bound were cast away near the Needles'. A less accurate report of three vessels lost reached Southampton the next day, computing their combined tonnage as 1,600 tons. This suggests that information had reached Southampton from several different witnesses, whose somewhat conflicting reports were difficult to reconcile. No doubt the knowledge of the quantities of rich goods involved also led to a natural tendency to exaggerate the scale of the disaster. Doubtless correctly, however, this second report noted 'many women and children' on board.[106] Perhaps surprisingly, in view of the danger involved, there was no loss of life, and all the crew and passengers from both ships, whether women, children, soldiers or sailors, were able to continue their passage on the other vessels. The *Prins Willem* and *Nassau* arrived in Jakarta on 22 June 1628, while the *Vlieland*, *Terschelling* and *Wieringen* came to Pulicat in June and July 1628.[107]

While the remainder of the fleet continued on their voyage, efforts were being made to recover material from the wrecked ships. By February 1628, despite the intervention of the winter, a certain amount of the cargo was evidently saved, since the High Court of the Admiralty ordered the restitution of goods saved 'from the *Green Dragon* and *Champen*' [sic] to the Dutch East India Company.[108] The prime mover of the recovery efforts was Jacob Johnson, a diver of Dutch origin residing at Dover. By 17 August 1628, he had recovered 2,360 *reales* (unit of Spanish currency in widespread trading use by other nationalities: 8 *reales* formed a Spanish dollar, the so-called 'piece of eight'). Apart from the currency, Johnson also brought up 5 'pieces of ordnance', 101 lead pigs and 9 anchors from the two wrecks, according to inventories and an invoice presented by Johnson in order to claim his share of the salvage.[109] He was evidently a specialist in recovering valuable materials – guns and precious metals – from similar wrecks, since he had previously been involved in bringing up 43 guns from the wreck of the English East Indiaman *Moon* off Dover in 1625/6; furthermore, on the back of his success with the

Vliegende Draak and *Kampen*, he petitioned to be permitted to recover material from a Spanish ship which had been lost off the Lizard in 1619.[110]

Johnson's involvement illustrates how wreck sites may become associated with one another in less direct ways than being wrecked in the same location. The *Moon*, *Kampen* and *Vliegende Draak* shared the distinction of being dived by the same man, who was attracted by their common cargoes. All three may have had other common features, the most obvious being the depths at which it was possible for Johnson to dive. Further examination of Johnson's involvement in diving these particular sites and his working methods may reveal patterns which could enable not only the site of the *Vliegende Draak*, but also those of the *Moon* and the Spanish cargo vessel, to be identified; none have been recognised despite having been recorded and dived at the time of loss.[111]

Also on the Needles and close west of the *Kampen* lie the remains of two Royal Navy vessels, HMS *Assurance* and HMS *Pomone*,[112] lost 58 years apart in 1753 and in 1811, respectively, but in the same area (Fig 1.22). The coincidences between the two continue: both vessels were Fifth Rates (small warships, mostly frigates). Both carried important passengers returning home from their posts: the governor of Jamaica aboard the *Assurance*, the British ambassador to Persia on the *Pomone*. The coincidences which surrounded the circumstances of loss have made a fuller

Fig 1.22
Diver examining the anchor of HMS Pomone *off the Needles, the fluke still recognisable despite seaweed cover.*
(© Hampshire and Wight Trust for Maritime Archaeology)

interpretation of the sites difficult: they comprise two vessels of fairly similar design and size, lost reasonably close in date. Both struck on Goose Rock and now lie intertwined to some extent in very shallow depths between 1m and 4m. Within the designated site no structural remains of the *Pomone* survive, although outside the area some of her hull timbers remain, increasing the difficulties of interpreting the site. It seems that the *Pomone* jammed between Goose Rock and Lighthouse Rock upon a raised section of rock (which, however, is submerged), known as the Saddle, working her way into three different positions.[113]

Some of the guns have been clearly assigned to one or the other vessel, while some damaged copper plating can only belong to the later *Pomone*, since copper sheathing had not been introduced on Royal Navy ships during the *Assurance*'s period of service. Such sheathing protected the lower hulls of vessels from marine life – boring worms and weeds – all of which structurally weakened ships' timbers, necessitating regular careening (beaching at high tide to expose the bottom) for maintenance and repair. That the sheathing belonged to the *Pomone* was confirmed by its markings, the 'broad arrow' which marked naval property, a 'C' for Chatham Dockyard and a date of December 1804, all of which are consistent with the *Pomone*.[114]

The intrusion of other materials into a wreck site, or 'contamination', also increases the difficulty of interpreting the archaeological remains. These may come from later wrecks on the same site; from modern vessels fouling the site by dragging or losing anchors and nets; from cargo and cannon jettisoned from other ships in difficulties at the same site, but not lost. Interpretation of the site has been made more difficult still by the fact that in or around 1850 a schooner also struck Goose Rock. This intruder into the site of the *Assurance* and *Pomone* was the *Dream*,[115] whose bell was retrieved by divers, while stone ballast blocks or cargo thought to be from the *Anglo-Saxon*, lost in 1879, have also been noted in the same area; the wrecking process for the *Anglo-Saxon* closely parallels that of the *Pomone*.[116]

Yet the *Assurance* and *Pomone* are themselves apparent intruders into an even earlier site, for a number of Roman coins dating to around AD 280 have also been found in the area, suggesting a Roman shipwreck, perhaps from an invasion fleet sent against the usurping Emperor Carausius in AD 289.[117] This suggests that in the intervening 2,000 years between the likely Roman shipwreck and the loss of the *Assurance*, other ships may well have come to grief in the identical area. More is likely to be discovered, not only concerning the vessels whose physical remains or associated artefacts are known to lie in this site, but to identify what, if any, other vessels from this intervening period may be turned up in documentary evidence for the same area. A concentration of shipwrecks over 2,000 years apart in the same rocky area may seem incredible, but the intervening history of Southampton as a trading port and *de facto* naval base in the Middle Ages, and the strategic location of the Isle of Wight effectively at the mid-point of the southern coastline of England, have permitted such coincidences. Concentrations of wrecks at particular historical periods, and not others (in other words, historical 'spikes') would appear to be less likely in rocky environments than in dynamic and shifting environments, such as the Goodwin Sands, which change shape and pattern from time to time and are therefore more likely to pose an especial threat at some times, but not others.

As we saw at the beginning of the chapter, a high number of wrecks are recorded only at a vague distance or bearing from the Isle of Wight. The same is true of the Needles, and among these may be further candidates in or around Goose Rock whose remains may now be admixed with those of the *Assurance/Pomone* site or remain to be discovered in the many gullies which comprise much of the site. Much of the artefact material was washed into these gullies during the wrecking event, and subsequently; perhaps the same could be true of the hitherto undiscovered wrecks recorded in documentary evidence, as having been lost in the immediate vicinity of the Needles, especially those which are said to have specifically been lost 'upon' or 'in' the Needles. Characteristically, little remains of the hulls in this particular location. Artefact scatters may still remain in the gullies, for example, from an Amsterdam merchantman 'wrecked upon the Needles' in 1668, or a 'French banker, laden with fish' which 'run on the rocks coming in at the Needles', was 'now past all hopes of getting off again' in 1697.[118]

In this respect – the variety of potential wreck sites over a long period of time – the Needles site most closely resembles another designated site, the Salcombe Cannon site, which has an equally dramatic date range: a mid-17th-century wreck site characterised by its cannon, overlying a Middle Bronze Age site identified by its jewellery and weapons.[119] The presence of these two wrecks separated by a wide time span in the same network of gullies is, perhaps, more likely to exclude other wrecks than those at the foot of Goose Rock in the Needles, a well-known hazard in a historically busy shipping lane, always busier during rough weather as ships ran for shelter in the Solent. The Moor Sand site, another Bronze Age site near to the Salcombe Cannon site, however, also shows that in some respects this area resembles the Needles as a shipping hazard (in this case underwater) where the Needles break the surface (Fig 1.23). It is also always possible that the presence of one wreck leads to another as vessels in the course of navigation strike an existing wreck in the open sea, or that an existing wreck will compound their difficulties.[120] In more modern times, the sequence of events in the busy shipping lane of the Straits of Dover exemplifies this phenomenon: in 1971 the collision between the *Texaco Caribbean* and the *Paracas* off Folkestone led to the loss of the former; in short succession the *Brandenburg* and the *Niki* then struck the *Texaco Caribbean* and also sank.[121]

The two pairs of Needles wrecks, the *Kampen* and *Vliegende Draak*, and the *Assurance* and *Pomone* illustrate two of the most common ways for vessels to be associated with one another in terms of wreck events. The first pair shows how two vessels in company can be lost in either the same event or at the same location, or both, without necessarily being each responsible for the loss of the other; while the second illustrates how vessels lost many years apart may nevertheless end up associated through their location, and point to a site which has a propensity to attract wrecks and which may lead to the discovery of further wrecks from artefact evidence, if nothing else.

Fig 1.23
Magnetometer survey of the overlapping designated Salcombe Cannon and Moor Sands sites, clearly showing the rocky fissures that characterise the local seabed. Marine magnetometer surveys reveal the presence of ferrous (iron) material in the natural environment: the black lines represent the tracks of the magnetometer and the iron material from the 17th century site coincides with one of the tracks over a gully.
(© Crown copyright. Data collected by University of St Andrews and processed by Wessex Archaeology)

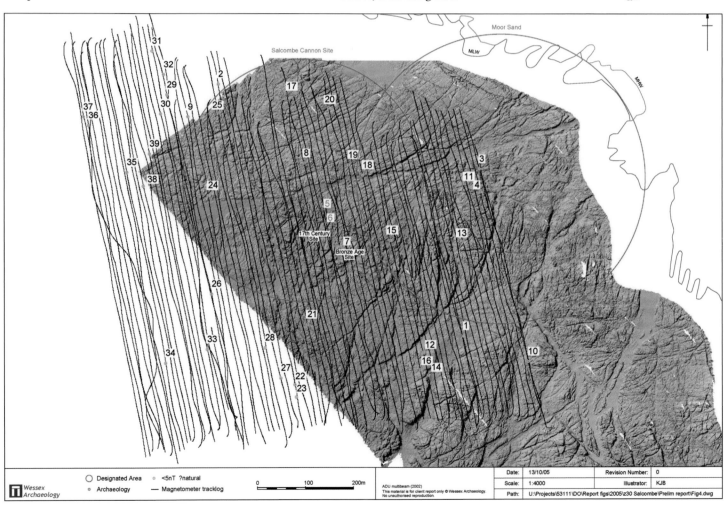

Cornwall's rocky coves

No county is as rich in shipwreck heritage as Cornwall, from Bude Bay (Fig 1.24) in the extreme north-east of the county via Land's End (Fig 1.25) and the Lizard peninsula (Fig 1.26) to the River Tamar in the south-east and entrance to Plymouth (Fig 1.27) which forms the natural county boundary with Devon, and all along the coastline passing uncounted rocks among which innumerable vessels have come to grief. It is almost invidious to single out any particular stretch of Cornwall's long coastline, whose coves knit sea and land together, and whose offlying islands and rocks extend the county outwards to the sea.

Some 4,500 shipwrecks overall are recorded for the county, of which some 12.75 per cent are sites, identified or otherwise.[122] Investigation throws up some surprises. Wrecks on the

Fig 1.24 (right)
Chapel Rock, Bude, whose outer face was struck in 1853 by the smack Margaret (905571), while attempting to enter the harbour, causing her to sink. (BB98/02035)

Fig 1.25 (below)
The forbidding rocks of Land's End at the extremity of mainland England, looking north from Dr Syntax's Head. (BB98/02428)

Longships rocks off Land's End, were sparsely documented until the 19th century, and even for the Land's End itself were not regularly reported until the 18th century. There are occasional exceptions, particularly among the medieval accounts of the Duchy of Cornwall, which took an interest in 'wreck of sea' and preserves records from the late 13th and early to mid-14th centuries otherwise now lost to us.[123] The origin of 'wrack of timber and other raff cast a-land in Whitsonbay and other places about the Land's End' 'oftentimes seen' during the 16th century by one witness is obscure. Some of this material is likely to have come from ships which smashed into Land's End, but the tides may have carried wreckage from the Scilly Isles or further afield in the Atlantic to the extremities of Cornwall.[124]

However, records for Wolf Rock go back to

at least the 14th century when the *Gabriell* was lost on 'les Wolves' in 1394,[125] with a handful being recorded in the 1700s and numbers picking up exponentially in the 1800s. A similar pattern is observable for the Eddystone Rock, despite being a persistent obstruction on the approaches to Plymouth and significant enough

to warrant the building of its lighthouse from as early as 1698: only a handful of documented wrecks appear to antedate the first Eddystone lighthouse.[126]

These gaps in the records owe much to the remoteness of Cornwall from the centre of power in London and the inaccessibility of its

Fig 1.26
Close up of the rocks on the south-eastern tip of the Lizard peninsula.
(© Andrew Wyngard)

Fig 1.27
Aerial view of the Citadel at Plymouth, showing Plymouth Sound, the anchorage in Cattewater and Sutton Pool.
(N090635)

coastline, so that wreck cargoes and materials were often difficult to retrieve. The medieval Duchy of Cornwall records documenting a keen royal interest in profiting from wrecks, no matter how remote from the seat of power, are a notable exception. Even so, it is quite startling that, despite its associations with the Arthurian legend and its 13th-century castle, Tintagel Head only came to prominence as a shipwreck site in the 19th century. Here, as elsewhere in Cornwall, the haphazard survival of evidence and the remoteness of the location itself has masked the full story of Tintagel as a place where ships were lost. The earliest known account of a shipwreck nearby post-dates the castle, being from the 14th century, and the intervening history of Tintagel as a wreck site remains obscure, for the next known wreck dates from 1811.[127] Traces of Romano-British and early post-Roman occupation suggest a site of fairly extensive trading activity as revealed by archaeological deposits of imported pottery, suggesting that there may also have been wrecks from this period of Tintagel's history. Roman or early modern vessels alike may well have been wrecked just as they came into, or left, the small natural harbour (Fig 1.28). The fate of the ironically named *Narrow Escape* with her cargo of local Delabole slate, caught by a ground swell in 1826 and dashed to pieces against the rocks, suggests the kind of wrecking pattern which must have happened here.[128]

Pendennis and St Mawes castles, overlooking Falmouth and the Carrick Roads, on the English Channel coastline of Cornwall, would have provided a good view of shipping – which, after all, was the reason for their existence – and consequently of any marine accidents for several miles around (Fig 1.29). Yet even from the primary port of Falmouth few wrecks antedating the 19th century are known, with a scattering from the 18th, in contrast to the much earlier and more consistent reports from Deal, overlooking the Straits of Dover, for example.

An extensive document left by one John Penheleg in 1580, recording shipwrecks throughout Cornwall from the early 1500s to 1580, partially fills this chronological gap. The Penheleg manuscript relies largely on the memory of elderly men and has a bias inherent in the purpose of its creation, justifying claims to wreck made by the local landowners, the Arundell family.[129] This may mean that corroboration of the same event by different witnesses involved coaching. It is also entirely possible that different events with similar outcomes in roughly the same locale were conflated by these elderly witnesses after so many years. Nevertheless, the attention to detail is significant, sometimes with single, relatively small, items of wreckage being reported, and tying in with events in the wider world, such as war with France. Sometimes the Penheleg manuscript reports a cluster of wrecks from specific locations, such as Basset's Cove, for

Fig 1.28 (below)
A 19th-century view looking south-west from Barras Nose towards the small stretch of beach serving as Tintagel Haven and a natural harbour. Although the ship is merely beached, not wrecked, this view illustrates the area's archaeological potential for shipwreck: narrow, obstructed by rocks, and surrounded by high cliffs if wind and tide prevented entry into the haven.
(OP04890)

Fig 1.29 (right)
Aerial view of Pendennis Point looking north-east towards the Carrick Roads, which has seen wrecks as diverse as those of a possible cargo vessel laden with butter from Ireland in the late 1560s (1463354) to the 20th-century freighter Mitera Marigo *in 1959 (1520133).*
(NMR_18513_19)

which five wrecks were reported in the 1560s and 1570s.[130] This does not necessarily indicate that Basset's Cove was any more dangerous in the late 16th century than at later periods, but instead alerts us to the distortion of the archaeological potential by showing us what may potentially be missing from the documentary evidence of later periods.

The earliest wreck report in the manuscript goes back to 1515/16, when a 76-year-old man recalled a 'wrack' of a vessel laden with Irish hides and textiles between Lelant and Carbis Bay during the 6th year of Henry VIII's reign, and thus between 21 April 1515 and 20 April 1516. If true, the memory must have stayed with him all his life, since at 76 when the manuscript was written in 1580 he would have been a child in 1515/16.

Harry Angwyne, also 76, recalled the loss of a specific type of vessel, a hulk, in 1531/2, and located it to 'Senar Clyffe by Innyall Chappell', that is, Gurnard's Head, to the south west of Zennor, where a ruined chapel still stands today.[131] These more specific details appear credibly based on personal witness in adulthood, offering a level of detail rare in eyewitness wreck reports even at later periods. He recalled the loss of the crew, the lading of the vessel (salt) and the salvage of her materials. He was backed up by four even older witnesses, the eldest 84, who also all recalled that a boat from the hulk had fetched up in one of the nearby narrow cliff clefts known as 'zawns' in Cornish dialect, 'Savyn Dolle' or Zawn Duel (Fig 1.30).[132] The hulk was typical of Northern Europe, possibly Scandinavia; her cargo of salt was a typical return cargo for such ships homeward-bound from southern France or Iberia. It seems that she had possibly been blown off course, missing the entrance to the English Channel. Perhaps her name had been forgotten in the intervening years, or had never been discovered since she is likely to have broken up quickly and the crew were all dead.

As a case study the short stretch of coastline running north-west to south-east between Porthleven and Mullion to the south gives a true flavour of Cornwall's shipwrecks in its variety of topography – the sand bank of Loe Bar to the north and to the south coves, cliffs and rocks (Fig 1.31) – as well as a melange of ship types, nationalities, documented wrecks and surviving archaeology, and manner of loss. The diversity of wrecks in the area is well illustrated by high concentrations of designated wreck sites and other, well-known sites. From the Loe Bar alone three high-status vessels have been found. One is the *St Anthony* wreck, a Portuguese carrack

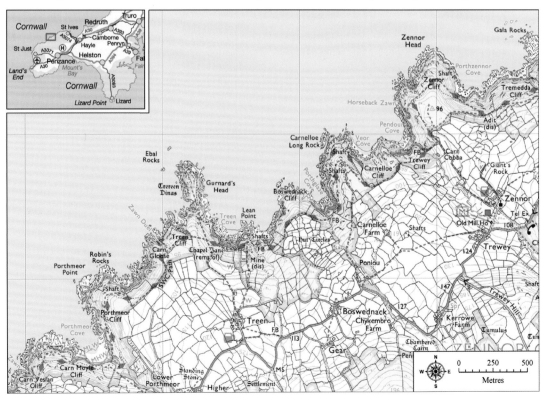

Fig 1.30
Despite Harry Angwyne's very specific memories from 1531–2, 'Senar Cliffe by Innyall Chapel' is difficult to pinpoint precisely, given the numerous coves and cliffs between Zennor and Gurnard's Head. Did he mean that the vessel was lost at Zennor, or at Gurnard's Head, or that the vessel was lost on the Zennor, that is, eastern, side of Gurnard's Head. To the west lies the very small fissure of Zawn Duel where the equally small ship's boat was found.

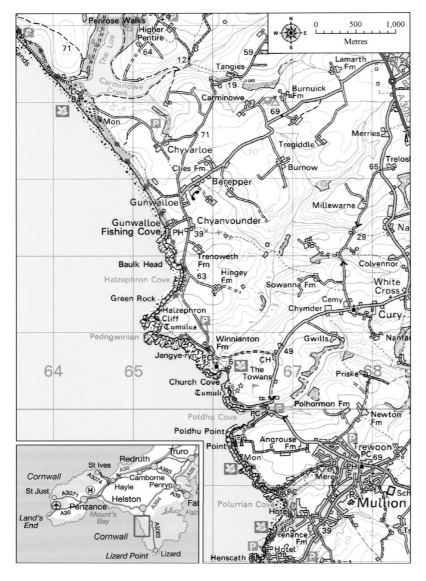

Fig 1.31
Location map of the 6km stretch of coastline between Gunwalloe and Loe Bar, illustrating its varied landscape with a common wreck archaeology in the light of its position on the north-western side of the Lizard.

other into a hollow of the Rock. As soon as the Tide was out they descended with no small danger to the Sands.

It seems that these 'defenceless wretches' had one further ordeal to undergo before being rescued by the local landowner – from the hands of 'two country Fellows' who tried to rob them.

The next major wreck to strike the Loe Bar and whose remains survive nearby was HMS *Anson*, which struck on 29 December 1807, four days out from Falmouth.[135] *Anson* was involved in the blockade of Brest, France's principal naval port, by which the English fleet pinned the French in harbour, unable to inflict damage on English shipping and English interests in the Channel or elsewhere. This was an arduous and tedious 'cruize' in the teeth of the regular Channel gales which whipped up from the west, and every so often individual members of the blockading fleet would return to England to revictual or for repairs. Having replenished her stores, *Anson* slipped out of Falmouth but met with contrary winds pushing her back towards the English coast: there was nothing for it but to run for home again. Land was sighted and *Anson*'s crew attempted to clear what they believed was the Lizard, but was in fact Land's End to the west. As they scudded with the wind towards Mount's Bay they were well and truly embayed, unable to clear the land. The consequences of being unable to stand out far enough to sea became frighteningly clear. As the vessel broke up, her masts crashed overboard, 'through the assistance of which, by the aid and blessing of a merciful and kind Providence, about 250 were saved from a watery grave.'[136]

Halzephron and Jangye-Ryn to the south of Loe Bar appear to have seen – or caused – the loss of a number of similarly substantial ships: the earliest apparently a Spanish ship homeward-bound to Spain from the West Indies and Vera Cruz, intercepted by the Earl of Cumberland during his cruise to the Azores in 1589 and sent to England. She was lost at 'Als Efferne' together with all her rich lading, of hides, cochineal, sugar and silver. The loss of this rich prize was advanced to support the case for a lighthouse on the Lizard in the early 17th century: 'the shipwreck for want of it [a lighthouse] of a Spanish prize, value 100,000 *l* [£100,000], sent home by the Earl of Cumberland in 1589'.[137]

In 1669 the *San Salvador* was lost between Poldhu Cove and Gunwalloe Church Cove: iron cannon found at Jangye-Ryn are thought to

bound from Lisbon to Antwerp lost in 1527 with a mixed general cargo (Fig 1.32), which was said to have included high-status items such as tapestries, musical instruments and a set of horse harness, as well as more mundane cargoes of pitch and tar.[133] The eponymous Loe Bar wreck is thought to be the remains of an English East Indiaman, the *President*, lost in dramatic circumstances in 1684, homeward-bound with textiles, spices, peppers and other goods. A contemporary pamphlet vividly brought to life the terrors of the two survivors:[134]

> These two persons sate on the fore-part of the Ship while the hinder-parts were broken, seeing most of their companies drowned, before they quitted their Station … Smith and Harshfield very hardly preserving themselves by wedging each

represent the remains of the *San Salvador*. The Dollar Wreck also at Jangye-Ryn with which the *San Salvador* is often associated has been traced to the 1770s.[138] Coins have regularly turned up from both sites: from the *San Salvador*, pieces of eight (eight-*real* coins, or Spanish dollars), and the eponymous dollars from the other wreck. These finds were so well known that in the 19th century there were several attempts to recover the cargo, all of which ended in failure.

Also nearby is the *Schiedam*, a vessel whose history was one of adventure: it seems only fitting that she came to grief on a coastline with a cluster of significant wrecks.[139] She began service as a *fluit* to the Dutch East India Company, a career which ended when she was captured by the Barbary corsairs off Gibraltar in 1683. She was then retaken, not by the Dutch, but by the English, who sent her for Cadiz and took her into the service of the Royal Navy as a transport vessel. Returning to England in April 1684 with captured guns and stores, she met her end by driving ashore at Jangye-Ryn during a gale.

Turning from identified wreck sites to recorded casualties, the wrecks involved might have been less spectacular but are still interestingly varied. The *Hercules* of New York came ashore at Gunwalloe Church Cove in 1795 with barrel staves, potash, tar and a valuable import of deerskins among the cargo plundered, and the German galliot *Neutralist* taking wine, vinegar and sugar from La Rochelle to Norway likewise in 1823.[140] The year 1862 was a particularly bad year for strandings in this area: first the *Auguste Padre* of Trieste came ashore at Poldhu Cove on 31 January, followed in December by the French *L'Union*, and, a week later, by the Truro schooner *Arwenack*, laden with copper ore from Devoran for Swansea.[141] A local newspaper disdainfully noted that the four survivors from *Auguste Padre* 'knew neither

French nor German … they appear to be illiterate common seamen and exceedingly dull' although, more kindly, the correspondent added 'or exhausted from perilous adventure'.[142] It seems extraordinarily 'dull' not to realise that, as they had already discovered the wreck belonged to Trieste, the survivors might instead have spoken Italian or Slovene! After the loss of the *Arwenack*, the same newspaper noted the location of all three wrecks in relation to one another:

> the place where the wreck [*Arwenack*] came on shore is about 2 miles from where *L'Union* was wrecked on the previous Saturday, and about one mile from where the Italian barque *Padre* was lost.[143]

Why did so many ships come to grief in this area in particular? It is impossible to say for absolutely certain, without the full data on each ship and on the tide, current, wind and the weather conditions which all contributed to each loss, but some common themes emerge among the better-known wrecks, which had all endured long voyages. It is highly likely, for example, that the Earl of Cumberland's prize was in a fairly distressed condition, a contemporary trans-Atlantic voyage from Vera Cruz to the Azores being a matter of some weeks at best: her subsequent capture and navigation by a crew unfamiliar with the vessel would not have helped matters. The *Schiedam*, too, was a captured vessel; the Dollar Wreck, with her cargo a worldwide trading currency, suggests that she was at the end of a long voyage, and the *Anson* had been battered by Channel gales, not only on her final voyage, but on her recent 'cruize' off Brest. The lot of the *President* East Indiaman in 1684 was one of hardship throughout the homeward-bound voyage: the survivors noted that they 'met with extraordinary rough weather' and when only three days' sail from England, the wind backed to the north-east and drove them out to sea

Fig 1.32
Strap end recovered from the wreck of the Portuguese carrack St Anthony *off Gunwalloe.*
(DP084338)

again, the wind 'still in their teeth'.[144] Distance, damage and crew debility had their part to play, but this was only true for a certain number of vessels.

A significant clue to the concentration of losses on these few miles of coastline lies in the word 'weather', in a sense subtly different from making reference to atmospheric conditions – though weather conditions naturally played their part in any wreck event. A ship may, of course, 'weather' or pass safely through a storm, but an allied meaning is to 'weather a point', to pass a point or headland in safety. The Loe Bar to Mullion area we have just been considering is located on the western side of the Lizard, the most southerly point of mainland England, where it is subject to the prevailing winds in the Channel and its western approaches, which blow from the south-west. The situation was summed up in the words of a 17th-century writer familiar with Cornwall, Narcissus Luttrell: 'Not being able to weather the Lizard Point because of the strong south west wind.'[145]

The contrary winds which had buffeted the *President* for so long would have torn her sails, strained her masts and rigging, caused her to spring one or more leaks, and exhausted her crew. When the wind finally set fair for England, blowing from the opposite quarter, from the south-west rather than the north-east, the distressed *President* probably became unmanageable in running before the wind, since everything on which skilful navigation depended, sails, rigging and rudder, were most likely all damaged – with the result that she was blown before the wind and her crew were unable to 'weather the Lizard', as with so many other ships before and since. A contemporary description of the loss of the *Royal Anne Galley*, also a designated wreck, upon the Stags at the Lizard in 1721,[146] suggests what is likely to have happened to the *President* as the wind strengthened:

> Thursday the 9th, at four in the afternoon, they made the land, about five leagues off, which they took to be the Lizard, wind at WSW, blowing fresh, they had two reefs in their topsails. They then tacked to the southward, and lay by with the foretopsail to the mast, courses balled up, intending to bear away for Plymouth, it being like to be bad weather. They lay by till 12 at night and (the captain being upon deck) they bore away, and steer'd NE with their two topsails reeft, a fresh gale.[147]

These prevailing winds meant that this single stretch of coastline was by no means unique in Cornwall, and serves only as a very brief case study: similar studies could be carried out for the whole of Mount's Bay or at the Lizard itself, where the *Royal Anne* came to grief, and elsewhere throughout Cornwall. As ships were driven off course to the north and into the Bristol Channel, or struck on the southern coasts, the irresistible force of the prevailing south-westerlies, strengthening to gale force, met Cornwall's immovable granite coastline: wind and rocks were the twin but inevitable hazards for anyone criss-crossing Europe north to south or east to west. No wonder the western entrance to the English Channel was called 'the chops of the Channel': the Channel seen as a yawning jaw, and Cornwall's rocks its teeth.

What happens to maritime archaeology remains

What happens after the wreck event?

A wrecking event can be regarded as 'the beginning of the end' for, even after settling on the seabed, the wrecking process continues: complete disintegration may follow within a short time, or continue over centuries or millennia, depending not only on the wreck's materials but also on the seabed environment, local tidal forces – and human intervention. Despite appearances, a wrecking event is rarely a single, violent, calamitous shock but instead triggers a sequence of events in which a vessel may be lost: 'cause' and 'effect', as when she strikes rocks or springs a leak at sea and sinks afterwards.

In many cases, the 'post-wreck event' or site formation processes for sunken vessels may mirror the wrecking event processes for stranded vessels, since they come to rest in typical foreshore environments – sand, shingle, silt, mud, rocks – but which happen to be submerged. In other words, though the original manner of loss differs, the eventual effects as the environment eats away at the vessel will be similar. Paddling barefoot on the fringes of the tide brings home the power of the waves in action, even on a calm day with a little swell. The sea stirs up and washes sand over the paddling feet, dragging it back again with the receding waves and at the same time scouring beach sand away from underneath. Exactly the same process occurs in the vicinity of an offshore wreck site, particularly one in a very dynamic and mobile environment. Strong tides and currents may force the wreck to pivot within a certain area, effectively hollowing out or 'scouring' a pit into which she will eventually wholly or partially collapse. The depth and location of the scour will translate into stresses on the ship's frame elsewhere, typically amidships, where the vessel will be in danger of 'breaking her back', exactly the same thing which may happen above water (*see* Fig 3.6).

The fate of the outward-bound *St Andrew* on the sands of Taylor's Bank off Liverpool in 1840 is characteristic: 'lying with her back broke'. The same is true of the *Richard Montgomery* who also broke her back just over a century later on the edge of Sheerness Middle Sand in the Thames as the floating support of the water ebbed out underneath her at low tide.[148] The fate of these two vessels in the intertidal zone points to what can happen to sunken ships under scouring conditions. Usually one of two things then happens: the vessel may 'hog' the sands, leaving her fast amidships but one or both ends unsupported where the sand has been scoured out; or the reverse position, where she 'sags', her ends settled at the edge of a scour pit leaving her unsupported amidships. Scour for-

mation is often, by its very nature, an ongoing process, but occasionally it is reversible, depending on the surrounding environment and human action. For example, the scour pits of the tanker *Arinia*, mined off Southend-on-Sea, Essex, in 1940, were examined in 1949 after dispersal and seen to be filling up again.[149]

In predominantly sandy and silty environments the wreck becomes the nucleus for an accumulation of sand, or 'wreck mound'. This acts as a protective layer, such as those over the *Admiral Gardner* and *Stirling Castle* on the Goodwin Sands, and the *Mary Rose* in the Solent (Fig 1.33).[150] Such environments are often very mobile, as in the Goodwin Sands, where wreck mounds may be periodically or regularly covered and uncovered by sand. The *Northumberland*, also on the Goodwins, was seen to be less exposed in 2009 than in 2008: most of the timbers observed by archaeological divers in 2008 had been re-covered by sand.[151] Storm action also inevitably plays its part in eroding the protective mound layer: this same process is more visible when hitherto hidden wrecks on the foreshore are exposed, as in the case of the two wrecks found at Seaton Carew and Littlehampton. Tantalising hints of up to three others may remain on the shore at Praa Sands, south Cornwall, which can be covered by up to 4m of sand, but from which coins have

Fig 1.33
Not all of the Mary Rose *has been raised. A multibeam image from 2005 shows a distinct wreck mound covering surviving undersea remains, believed to be a section of the port bow: these surviving remains ensure the continued designation of the wreck site despite the raising of much of the structure in 1982. (© Crown copyright. Data collected by University of St Andrews and processed by Wessex Archaeology)*

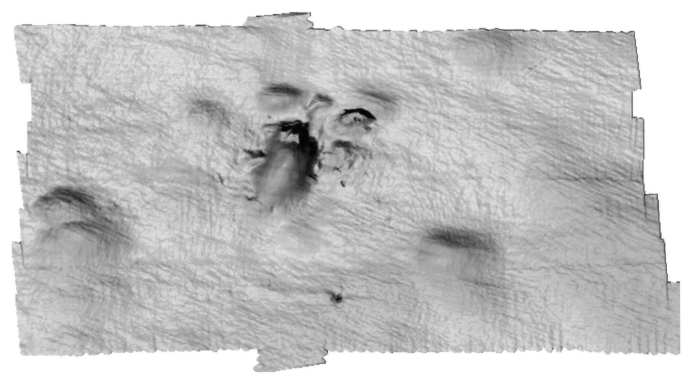

Fig 1.34
Undulating boulder eroded by the waves around Praa Sands, Cornwall, showing the dynamism of an environment where the surrounding sand levels may be scoured away. (AA086637)

Fig 1.35
A view down the keel and ribs of the Norwegian barque Nornen *(1003025) which came to grief in 1897 on Berrow beach, Somerset, bound from Bristol for the United States. Full of water even as the tide recedes, she is now a prominent wreck stranded in the inter-tidal zone, but RAF aerial photographs from the Second World War show no sign of the wreck, suggesting that she was buried in this dynamic sand environment. (MF99/0746/)*

occasionally been recovered when the sand level drops (Fig 1.34). Similar processes are repeated on beaches the length and breadth of the country (Fig 1.35).[152] These processes also make it very difficult to understand just how many wrecks there may be at a site or sites: this issue is, of course, compounded underwater.

It may take some time for protective mounds to form, as in the case of the *Royal George*, which sank in the Solent in 1782, and remained a constant danger to navigation for the next 50 years or so. By the time of her rediscovery in 1965, she was buried under a well-defined mound layer 3m thick, which clearly gave away the presence of a significant wreck site and appears to have been the result of almost two

hundred years' accumulation of sand and silt. The mound prevented both further structural disintegration through the external forces of wave action and storm disturbance, and fouling of the wreck by fishing nets or anchors, which might otherwise have damaged both the existing wreck and the surface vessel casting their gear.[153]

This process may also occur on the shore, where a wreck may be filled from within (as well as covered with an overburden of sand). The VOC ship *Amsterdam*, beached at Bulverhythe in 1749, 10 years after the loss of the *Rooswijk*, exemplifies this phenomenon.[154] She is exceptionally well-preserved, with two-thirds of her hull structure surviving: even so, this site illustrates the negative as well as the positive impacts of sand cover. Her hull remains relatively coherent, but the sand and sediment above have forced the ship to settle under her own mass, effectively burying her in the sand. Only the tips of jagged timbers resembling a fossilised jaw of teeth (Fig 1.36a) betray her presence. Scouring is also visible at the stern (Fig 1.36b). Though her presence has been known locally for centuries, disturbance and damage by a mechanical excavator in 1984 prompted investigations into her identity. At the same time a protective U-shaped cofferdam was placed around the seaward end of the wreck to prevent sand crushing the wreck during excavation. Since then, the excavation process has largely concentrated on removing the deposits in and around the wreck and on strengthening the hull in so doing.

Internal build-up of sediment will also cause vessels in deep water to collapse. In the case of the Dutch steamship *Edam II* which foundered after a collision en route from New York for Rotterdam in 1895, approximately 13 miles off Bigbury Bay, Devon, the local seabed environment, prone to sandwaves (the deposit of large quantities of sand in patterns, caused by strong tidal action) has compounded the initial damage caused by the collision, leaving her partially buried. Also off south Devon lie the remains of the *Ambassador*, lost in 1891, upright but silted up sufficiently to force the collapse of the structure.[155]

Another aspect of the power of external forces on stranded vessels can be seen in the many reports of the sea 'making a clean breach' over a ship. The word 'breach' contains within itself both cause and effect: the physical action of the waves 'breaking over' the vessel and the consequential structural disintegration.

Fig 1.36a
Outline of timbers from the
Amsterdam *protruding*
above the sand level.
(DP14008)

Fig 1.36b
Amsterdam *seen to be*
sinking towards the stern
into her own scour in
the sand.
(© Crown copyright.
Photograph taken by
Archaeological Diving Unit)

Daniel Defoe illustrates this dual impact in *Robinson Crusoe* (1719): 'we all knew that when the boat came near the shore she would be dashed in a thousand pieces by the breach of the sea'. Usage in 1815 was also in this sense:

> On Friday morning, about 7 o'clock, the lime-sloop *Thomas*, of Sunderland, Michael Readman, master, in running for Whitby harbour, was struck by the heavy breach of a sea, which carried away her mast, and turned her bottom upwards.[156]

Even where a ship is lost upon a sandbank the final position of loss may very well not be at the point of impact, but some distance away on the same feature. A ship could 'bump over' a sandbank before arriving at her final resting place, whence her crew were unable to extricate her before the ebb left her 'high and dry'. In such cases it is easy to see how scattered 'debris fields' of wreckage, consisting of fragmentary timbers or scatters of cargo or even a separate section of wreck structure, can be formed some distance from the principal wreck site. A debris field trails between more substantial sections at the *Rooswijk* site, consistent with a wreck event involving a point of initial impact and the site where the vessel finally disappeared into the sands (*see* inset to Fig 1.15). It is also consistent with contemporary reports of scattered wreckage and mail being picked up at sea.

'Going to pieces' suggests the breach of the hull and release of some or all of the cargo, dispersing wreckage over a wide area. Frequently, after a storm, fragmentary wreckage driven ashore in a specific area would be the only indication of lost shipping, the number and identity of the lost ships often unknown. This report from 1780, following a storm from north-north-west, was typical:

> We hear from Cleveland in Yorkshire, that in the late storm … several dead bodies, and a great quantity of wreck, were cast ashore on that coast.[157]

Besides submerged debris fields or wreckage washed up on a nearby shoreline, scattered wreckage often had an international dimension. When the English East Indiaman *Ogle Castle* struck the Goodwin Sands at 6.30 am on 3 November 1825 in a gale at west-south-west she was observed to break up at noon with the loss of all hands. Her cargo was picked up not only at Dover and Margate in the immediate aftermath of the wreck, but ten days afterwards a report came in from Ostend: '5 leagues [15 miles] to the NE of this port the sea was covered with goods, making for the North Sea',[158] the first of many such reports over the ensuing weeks as the wreckage washed ashore on the coasts of France, Belgium and the Netherlands.

The impact with the seabed, as well as continuing dynamic undersea action during a storm, could similarly release cargo from the holds. November 1821 saw the stranding of the German brig *Hoffnung* on the Goodwin Sands in a 'tremendous sea' in strong south-westerly gales. The gales increased with the flood tide, when the waves 'broke over the wreck and plunged the whole of the crew … into a watery grave'. Those on board included members of a rescue party of local boatmen, one of whom was fortunate enough to be able to cling on to a detached portion of wreckage and remain afloat for two days before being taken up. This revealed that the *Hoffnung* was already breaking up before she sank. Otherwise 'not a vestige was to be seen'; the vessel must have disintegrated further rather than being simply entombed by the 'Great Ship Swallower', for several days later some packets of her cargo were taken up.[159]

Disintegration of this kind on sandbanks and rocks in the marine environment can be read as a 'submerged stranding'. In both cases a ship's hull and bottom will take a pounding, but the process can naturally be accelerated out to sea, and especially upon a rock or group of rocks. The hull is subjected to similar forces whether on the shore or resting on the seabed, except that on the seabed the turbulent marine environment will magnify the stresses on the vessel both inside and out rather than simply crashing against the external hull. Countless wrecks were 'stoved to pieces' among rocks close inshore or far offshore, like the *Royal Anne Galley* on the Stags off Cornwall in 1721 or the collier which went 'immediately to pieces' on the Spanish Battery Rocks near Shields harbour in 1806.

The anonymous 'Wheel Wreck' from the 19th century is a good illustration of 'what happens next' to a wreck under these circumstances, lying as it does on a rocky seabed environment 300m south of Little Ganinick, Isles of Scilly – a continuation of the surface rocks characterising the islands' landscape. Little ship structure survives for a relatively recent wreck event of late 19th-century date (Fig 1.37). No timber hull remains have been located but her cargo of metal mining equipment, including the drive wheels for which this wreck is currently named, has survived and suggests that it originated as an export cargo from the Cornish mining industry, and thus is particularly significant in terms of its connections with an industrial landscape inscribed as a World Heritage Site.[160]

Inevitably the older the wreck, the greater the likelihood that the original hull has either disappeared or remains only in a very fragmentary state. The best chance of recognising such ship remains therefore lies through identifying surviving cargo scatters of non-organic items which do not deteriorate as readily as organic timbers: amphorae from Roman wrecks, tin and coins, for example. In this case a rocky seabed may act as a preservation mechanism, since cargo scatters may be especially well preserved in the shelter of rock gullies, as in the case of the Salcombe wreck.[161] We may compare this process with the remains of the 7th-century Sutton Hoo ship burial:[162] when excavated, it was found that the timber had leached away in the acid soil, leaving behind a perfect ghost image of her construction, but her 'cargo' of grave goods had survived. The Salcombe example serves to underline just how fragmentary our knowledge of such wrecks is, for we have very little or no contemporary written evidence to go on, and the extent of the potential archaeology is therefore very poorly understood.

Unsurprisingly, because of their organic origin, timber hulls may be subject to a number of different processes. The sea's power will erode the stoutest of exposed oak timbers, a process naturally accelerated if the ship is already well broken up (Fig 1.38). Other environmental factors are also at work, mirroring ongoing processes during the vessel's service afloat. Both timber and metal remains are subject to biological formations which will in the first place alter their appearance: mussel or kelp colonies naturally obscure wreck remains, so that characteristic features which may help to identify the ship involved are difficult to see.

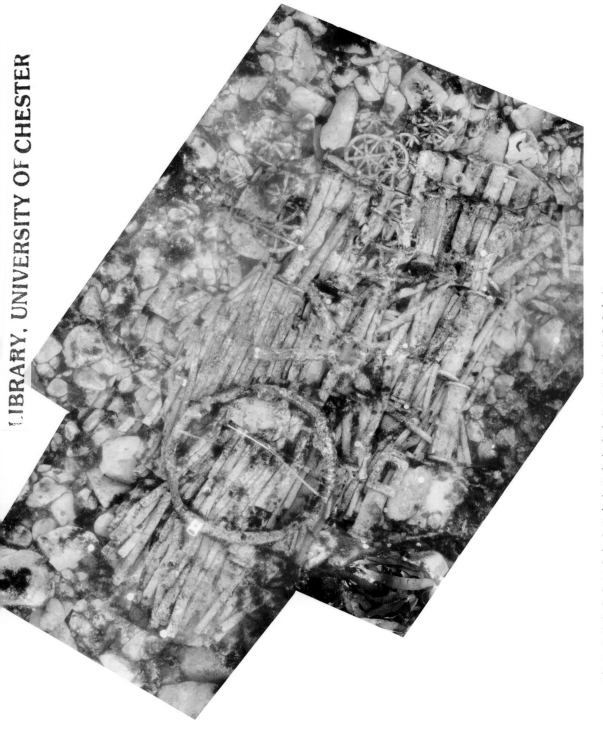

Fig 1.37
A discrete and coherent cargo mound of mining equipment, overlain with the wheels of different sizes which have given a working name to this otherwise unidentified wreck.
The orderliness of the mound is all the more astonishing given the apparent lack of surviving ship structure, which suggests that the vessel broke up on impact with the seabed, releasing the cargo.
A wheel rim can be seen to the south-west: like a starfish, its spokes are spread-eagled across the centre of the mound.
The remainder of the cargo comprises boiler tubes and eight-spoked sheave wheels, and a rectangular clack valve, all associated with the Cornish mining industry.
(© Crown copyright.
Photograph taken by
Wessex Archaeology)

Biological colonisation has both positive and negative effects, depending on the vessel's construction. For metal structures, a dense carpet of mussels may act as a protective barrier between seawater and the wreck structure, helping to slow down corrosion processes. Conversely, mussels may in their turn attract bacteria which can accelerate the decay of organic timber remains, weakening the remaining hull structure.[163] This is, in effect, a variation of the same processes which normally weakened the bottom structure of a wooden sailing vessel during her life afloat. It may indeed have been a contributory factor to a number of wreck events, namely, fouling by barnacle colonisation and the boring action of the teredo worm, hence the constant need for cleaning and repair after long voyages (Fig 1.39). The introduction of copper hull sheathing from the late 18th century onwards had the aim of preventing biofouling of the vessel and the consequent structural damage and deterioration in vessel performance and speed through 'drag'.

Iron and steel vessels, like artefacts of the same material found in the ground, are naturally subject to intense corrosion when fully submerged. Clearly this is the most significant process attacking vessels of metal construction. Like biofouling, rust is a process affecting vessels when in service afloat, historically involving

a constant battle to prevent its spread.[164] Wrecks of metal hulls react to the seabed environment in a somewhat different way from timber wrecks. Their construction material naturally facilitated their greater size, which in turn influences the survival of the wreck itself on the seabed. Their relatively recent date is a major factor in their survival: when found, most 20th-

Fig 1.38c
This is a good example of a coherent wreck structure which has been preserved by the sand cover now being eroded away, in turn exposing the timbers to erosion. They are also heavily colonised by a variety of seaweeds. The remains of this vessel, thought to be a merchantman built of timbers felled after 1585, possibly in Germany or the Netherlands, and now lying off Dorset, are designated under the Protection of Wrecks Act 1973. (© Crown copyright. Photograph taken by Wessex Archaeology)

century steel wrecks still retain a reasonably coherent vessel shape (depending on the manner of loss, especially where compromised by damage from war causes) despite obvious areas of corrosion and concretion.[165] These processes remain ongoing and are likely to accelerate in the long term, judging by the effects of similar processes upon older artefacts retrieved from the seabed, eg cannon. It seems that wreckage sheltered within a depression will corrode less quickly than an exposed wreck 'proud' of the seabed and that areas or artefacts standing on the deck will similarly corrode more quickly than less elevated areas with more

Fig 1.39
Remains of a 25m-long vessel, which survives on the foreshore at Cleethorpes, seen from the seaward end (1532568). Its location in the inter-tidal zone has permitted colonisation by Ulva-species seaweed and illustrates something of the post-wreck marine colonisation process. Characteristically bright green, this species flourishes in the inter-tidal zone, rapidly colonising wrecks and groynes. (Photograph reproduced courtesy of Hugh Winfield, North East Lincolnshire Council)

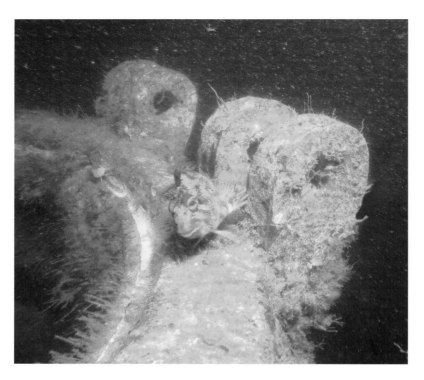

Fig 1.40
A tompot blenny, a typical
species for the English
Channel coast, peers
inquisitively at the
photographer recording the
missing conning tower hatch
of HMSM A1, an example
of vandalism which has
permitted increasing
environmental damage to
this designated wreck site.
(© Crown copyright.
Photograph taken by Wessex
Archaeology)

displaying the effects of 250 years of immersion (Fig 1.41). The retention of this material for examination and publication was rare in 1779, and rarer still its early description of the concretion process:

> partly covered with a thick incrustation … formed of shells, mixed with gravel and sand, and rendered as hard as a rock; which is a proof that a species of petrifaction is continually going on, at the bottom of the sea, on our coasts.[170]

A similar find from Norfolk, a cannon discovered 'almost wholly encrusted with an earthy or rocky substance' on Blakeney beach in 1835, was believed to have been lost over a century earlier. It may have been lost more recently than that, since the closest known match is the *Harmony* privateer which came ashore in the area in 1783.[171] That these artefacts were recorded at all is remarkable enough given the fledgling nature of archaeology at the time: from the marine environment it is even more remarkable. These examples serve to show how little we know of what was recovered in the past and how there is still more to discover about how artefacts are preserved or degrade in the wreck environment (Fig 1.42).

The accidents of human intervention form another layer in the continuing evolution of wreck sites and inadvertently do much to obscure their history. The cycle of ballast material from extraction to dumping adds further layers of complexity to wreck interpretation. To take the loading and the discharge of ballast material first, its presence can narrow down a wreck's departure point, as with the wrecks at Studland Bay and West Bay, both in Dorset, which contain stones located to the Spanish Basque region, and south-western England or northern France, respectively.[172] Often, however, the context of ballast material from other ships may make matters more difficult. For example, it remains debatable whether coins from Tynemouth come from a Roman-era wreck or from ballast material originating elsewhere and dumped by colliers returning in ballast to the Tyne before their next journey south.[173] If the latter, it is even conceivable that they may be wreck material removed from somewhere else or not be wreck material at all, a reminder that the archaeological potential of the seabed has been unquantifiably but often inadvertently compromised. It also raises the question of how far this discharge of ballast material has

environmental protection.[166] Thus wrecks from the First and Second World Wars may eventually degrade far more significantly than is apparent at the time of writing. Interference with wreck sites from this period will also accelerate corrosion decay (Fig 1.40).

The earliest iron wrecks located thus far in English waters date from approximately 160 years ago, for example, the *Marshall*, *Nile* and *Faith*, steamers all lost in the mid-1850s. As might be expected the *Nile* has suffered significant degradation, being described as 'extremely rotten' by the 1970s.[167] Likewise, the remains of the paddle steamer *Lelia*, lost on her maiden voyage in Liverpool Bay in 1865, are heavily compromised by her steel construction, which was a novelty at the time. This new material is thought to have been of poor quality with inclusions (contamination products incorporated during the steel-making process), which have naturally affected the corrosion rate.[168]

The condition of cannon and cannonballs retrieved from centuries-long submersion, all within concretion, from four sites at Gull Rock (Lundy), Gull Stream (Goodwin Sands), Kingswear Castle and Salcombe Castle (both in Devon) provides a parallel for the decay of metal structures.[169] The Gull Stream site is particularly interesting since it pertains to a brass cannon trawled up in 1779, believed at the time to be 400 years old, but datable to the 1520s and

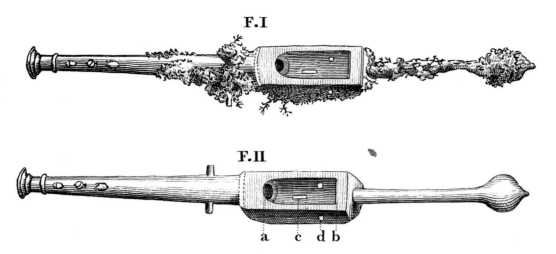

F.I

F.II

a   c   d b

Fig 1.41
The original text describing
this plate depicting an early
16th-century cannon
retrieved from the Gull
Stream, Goodwin Sands,
in 1775, explained:
'fig I. represents the
appearance it now has, with
shells, and pieces of rock,
and corallines adhering to
it.' The iron part of the
cannon has clearly been
eaten away by corrosion,
while the brass section was
less affected by its long
immersion, with the
additions of areas of
concretion ('pieces of rock')
and marine growths
('corallines'), among them
a prominent tube worm shell
pointing downwards.
Figure II represents
a reconstruction view.
(Archaeologia, 1779, vol. V,
plate XII, facing 149: Society
of Antiquaries of London)

obscured wreck sites in the vicinity. In its turn, the historical extraction of ballast material, particularly sand or stones, has probably also disturbed wreck sites in ways that we are only now coming to understand through modern reporting processes.

One of the main themes in this chapter has been the way environmental processes both threaten and preserve wreck sites. Paradox is a central feature of maritime archaeology. Aggregate extraction has historically threatened archaeological sites: judging by the numbers of dredgers which were themselves wrecked, the offshore extraction of stone and aggregate material became increasingly common from the mid 19th century onwards. For example, the *Saucy Jack* and *Ruby* were lost in similar circumstances while dredging in the vicinity of the West Rocks off Harwich in 1844 and 1846, but they were small smacks which were set to work as dredgers, rather than purpose-built vessels.[174] Systematic dredging occurred from the 1880s onwards in areas still prime grounds for aggregate extraction, in the English Channel, off Norfolk, and so on. It is thus difficult to assess just how much extracted material has been lost through crushing, or returned to a different context by being dumped overboard in a different location. However, since 2005 the aggregate industry has helped to rectify this situation through the adoption of the British Marine Aggregate Producers' Association (BMAPA) protocol in which dredged finds, which may be anything from mammoth tusks to aircraft, are reported to, and recorded by, English Heritage and the Receiver of Wreck.[175] In this way aggregate extraction is now becoming a force for recovering the past.

Fishing and trawling activities are inextricably linked with wrecks, sometimes literally so, with positive and negative impacts on wreck archaeology. Wrecks create new habitats which attract fish as well as other fauna and flora, so that an established wreck may harbour commercially viable fish or shellfish species. Fishermen may report the presence of 'fasteners' which snag their nets, which sometimes leads to the identification of a named wreck site, of which the most spectacular example, is, of course, the *Mary Rose*.[176] More often these reports simply suggest the *presence* of a wreck (or even a natural feature). Snagging and dragging of nets have the potential to damage the structure of the hull or any remaining superstructure on the vessel, as well

Fig 1.42
The cascabel or non-muzzle
end of a 16th- to
17th-century bronze
muzzle-loading cannon
associated with the West Bay
wreck off Dorset. Despite
corrosion and colonisation
by marine life the radial
petal design of the cascabel
is clearly discernible and
appears consistent with
greater sand cover over the
wreck until relatively
recently, acting as a
preservation mechanism.
(© Crown copyright.
Photograph taken by Wessex
Archaeology)

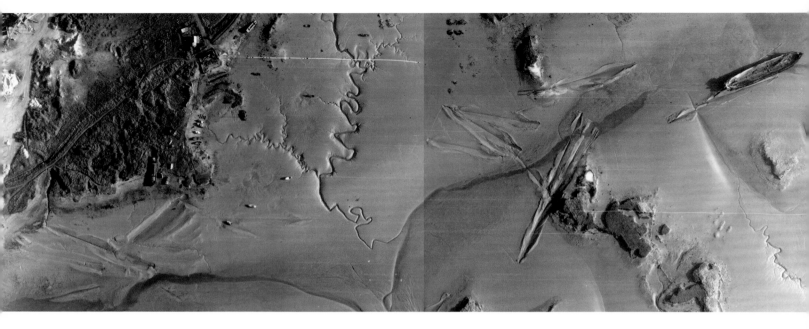

Fig 1.43
Local tidal and current
systems may also affect
wreck sites and make them
difficult to find, a process
which is poorly understood
and on the seabed is
exceptionally difficult
to illustrate. However,
this mosaic of two RAF
photographs taken on the
same day in 1952 show the
migration trajectory of an
abandoned hulk first seen in
the 1950s. Lying in the
inter-tidal zone, the vessel
continued to migrate
south-east for a number
of years. By 1973 she was
pulled up in the position
where she now lies
disappearing under
a silt layer.
(RAF Photography.
Composite of RAF 58/856
4176 24-APR-1952 and RAF
58/856 4177 24-APR-1952)

as introducing intrusive material to the wreck site if the snagging is significant enough to lose the net to the wreck, detrimental both to the fishing vessels and to the wreck archaeology alike. In contrast, this material can also be interpreted as adding a further archaeological 'layer' to a wreck site: for example, First World War wrecks in the North Sea had a significant impact on trawlers as they lost increasingly large, sophisticated and expensive, fishing gear, which, if found, could prove to be a 'snapshot in time'.[177] (Fig 2.23 shows how severely the fishing grounds were compromised by the war.)

As with the aggregate industry, to what extent has trawling since the late 18th century affected wreck sites (and other archaeological features) existing before that period? This is especially significant in terms of North Sea archaeology, with the remains of an inhabited land bridge dating from the time before Britain became separated from the Continent; this former land bridge is known as 'Doggerland' after its last remnant, the Dogger Bank in the middle of the North Sea. A Mesolithic bone harpoon, dating from approximately 4,000 to 10,000 years ago, evidence of human hunting activity, was trawled up off the Norfolk coast in 1931: a rare reported and extant find for the time (though similar material has since turned up in the BMAPA reports).[178] Understandably,

fish took priority in trawler holds, so that historically curios were simply jettisoned overboard, and, because any given trawl would cover a wide area, it was difficult to pinpoint the location from which an artefact had come, suggesting that much archaeological material from wrecks and otherwise may have been returned to the sea far from their point of origin. It is hoped that the Fishing Protocol for Archaeological Discoveries, launched in 2012 by English Heritage, will help to reveal the archaeological interdependence of fishing and wrecks.[179]

Human intervention can be seen in some respects as representing the final stage in the evolution of wreck sites, not least by illegal diving activity involving the removal of significant archaeological material from its proper context, often material which could lead to the identification of a given wreck site. The spectacular recovery of vessels such as the *Mary Rose* is a rarity, so that in general terms investigation of vessel remains and 'preservation by recording', is the feasible option for most sites (though this may have to be decided on a case-by-case basis). It is certain, however, that whatever decisions are taken, the wrecking process is ongoing: long, slow and continuing, centuries or millennia after the original wrecking event (Fig 1.43).

2

Ships at war

Introduction

Warships were naturally lost to weather and natural hazards like any other ship, but deliberate human intervention through naval engagements – battles or skirmishes – could equally bring about significant vessel losses. The presence of naval vessels may sometimes appear to overshadow the loss of other craft in the documentary and archaeological record, owing to their association with power in the form of the monarchy or the state, and involvement in events of major international significance. They thus leave more of a trail in the historical record than purely mercantile vessels. Before the late 17th century extant accounts of shipwreck are largely skewed towards noting the losses of war vessels. After that time, the location of warship losses is also generally recorded with more certainty than for other ships, owing to better record keeping on board and arising from subsequent courts martial and inquiries; greater interest from shore; and greater efforts expended in recovery of the vessel or guns to avoid the expense of replacements. Inevitably, also, shipboard cannon are among the most recognisable of all shipwreck artefacts.

The contemporary importance of these vessels thus emphasises their historic value. All these factors lead to the high number of designated warship remains, approximately one-half of all designated wrecks in English waters. Others appear to represent armed cargo vessels, the earliest of which may also, or instead, have had a warship function. Of the handful not directly warships or armed cargo vessels, one may have been a privateer (the Filey Bay site, suggested as the remains of the American privateer *Bonhomme Richard*); another was lost in support of war (*Iona II*, said to have been acting as a gun-runner for the Confederate side in the American Civil War).

Only two appear to have been merchantmen operating in peacetime, without needing to defend their cargoes: the Seaton Carew wreck site and the Wheel Wreck site, both 19th-century vessels.[1]

The story of warship wrecks is the story of technological evolution, being intertwined throughout with the use of, and attacks on, commercial shipping. Early records are sparse and vague. Despite dedicated naval building programmes from the 13th century onwards, the names and fates of most of the resulting ships remain obscure. Other 'King's Ships', cargo vessels requisitioned by the Crown and modified for regular naval use, or merchantmen simply listed as being available for war, if needed, also remain little documented. The diversification of hull types according to function evolved only slowly, hence the difficulty in definitively distinguishing between warships and armed cargo vessels (Fig 2.1).

Greater size and increased manoeuvrability were generally the few features which distinguished medieval warships from their 'civilian' counterparts, but vessels of civilian origin have been lost at later periods in a naval role along the English coastline. In the 17th century Dutch East Indiamen were requisitioned to fight the English, their existing armament, for the protection of their valuable cargoes, making them fit for purpose. Likewise, the trawlers of the two World Wars, urgently fitted up with single guns and minesweeping cables, made an important contribution. Both will be discussed in more detail in this chapter. The wartime flexibility of civilian ships was seen as late as 1982 when the *QE2* liner became a troopship during the Falklands War.

One other form of civilian ship in military use is worthy of mention. The lives lost on homeward-bound 'transports', as troopships were known, can be seen as the forgotten final casualties of the American War of Independence,

Fig 2.1
Two well-preserved late medieval bench ends themselves preserve the memory of medieval sailing ships. Both are from villages within a few miles of the coast: (left) St Mary's, Bishop's Lydeard, Somerset, showing an early 16th-century ship (BB36/01288); (right) All Saints, East Budleigh, Devon, depicting a 16th-century armed vessel, pierced with gunports: armed merchant or warship? (BB68/07222)

or theatres of war during the Napoleonic Wars, particularly in the Peninsular campaigns.[2] Some transport wrecks show the shifting alliances of the time, such as the loss of HMS *Espion* in 1799 on the Goodwin Sands while carrying Russian troops from Den Helder in the Netherlands (*Espion* herself was an former French warship captured off Cork in 1794). The Anglo-Russian invasion of Den Helder in 1799 appeared to result in an inordinately high casualty rate, with four transports, both outward and homeward bound, being lost in a single week off Great Yarmouth.[3] Other transport wrecks impact on regimental histories, such as the loss of troops from the 79th Regiment of Scotch Highlanders (79th Regiment of Foot or Cameronian Volunteers) off Harwich in 1807. From this last wreck many drowned, hampered by their knapsacks which 'constrained' their arms. The father who saved his child by getting hold of its petticoats between his teeth revealed that some troops were accompanied by their families.[4] Other transports lost with troops of German origin display the close links between the British Crown and Germany through the House of Hanover: Hanoverian troops were lost in 1803 on the Goodwin Sands, and men of the German Legion in two separate wrecks of 1807.[5]

Other than Caesar's invasion fleets of 55 and 54 BC (treated more fully in Chapter 5), the earliest mentions of warship losses surface during the Anglo-Saxon period. Aethelhelm is said to have led the Saxons into a naval battle against the Danes, but the entry in the *Anglo-Saxon Chronicle* is brief, the date ambiguous (either AD 837 or 840) and the outcome unclear: no certain losses are known.[6] More certainly, and appropriately, given his traditional status as the 'father of the English navy', more detail on warship losses emerges during the reign of King Alfred. In AD 877, 120 Danish galleys were apparently sunk off Swanage after concluding a treaty with Alfred, almost certainly an exaggerated account of an actual incident (Fig 2.2).[7] In AD 896 two more war galleys, whose sailors were too weakened from a battle with the Saxons to be able to weather a storm, ran ashore on the coast of Sussex.[8]

Throughout the early medieval period and well into the Middle Ages warships were a means to a land-based end, disgorging troops for battle ashore or carrying out hostile 'piratical' raids. Conversely, reflections of terrestrial warfare, such as hand-to-hand combat, endured well into the 19th century. Given these operational tactics, earlier warship losses were largely caused by environmental hazards or poor landing tactics, whereas later seaborne combat and gun action increasingly sent combatant ships to the bottom. Towards the end of the

Fig 2.2
According to several versions of the Anglo-Saxon Chronicle, *Guthrum's Danish fleet was caught in a storm off Swanage in AD 877 and wrecked: it is unclear whether the pursuing English were also caught in the same storm.*

medieval period, ship-to-ship combat became more frequent, but the objectives were frequently to capture, not sink, enemy vessels, which were more useful afloat than sunk.

Detailed accounts of sea battles emerge from the late 16th century onwards and coincide with the evolution of the ship itself as an offensive weapon: new ships bristling with guns, and older vessels primed to act as fireships as required (as in the case of the forces prepared to counter the Spanish Armada in 1588). Technological innovation coincided with an evolution in personnel strategy: ships carried vast numbers of men, dedicated either to crewing and navigation, or to combat. Soldiers aboard naval vessels were effectively marines, though they were not known by this name until the 17th century and were not organised on anything other than an ad hoc basis until the 18th century. The *Mary Rose* was crewed in this way, with the consequent huge loss of life when she sank.[9]

Administrative records for the construction and manning of these ships has left a greater trail in the documentary record, while naval encounters and the attendant preparations also find their way into official papers (for example, the *Calendar of State Papers Domestic*). Accounts for the combat with the Armada in 1588 are reasonably full and detailed, as are those for the three Anglo-Dutch wars in the 17th century,

including the diaries of Pepys and Evelyn. War journalism, in the form of both pictures and newspaper records, was on the rise, as was the apparatus of the state which has left behind many official 17th-century documents pertaining to naval bureaucracy. Even so, chronological gaps in shipwreck records remain, such as during the Civil War and Interregnum (1642–60), when domestic upheaval took precedence over maritime matters, the First Anglo-Dutch War of 1652–4 notwithstanding.

Private warships, or 'privateers' increasingly complemented 'official' naval actions from the 16th century onwards by capturing commercial shipping belonging to enemy nations. Following on from the adventures of Raleigh and Drake, privateers could be engaged as 'letters of marque', named for the letters they carried with them granting official sanction for intercepting, capturing or destroying enemy shipping. Captured merchantmen became 'prizes' to be sold or taken into the service of the capturing navy. They were sent for the nearest appropriate port, usually with a 'half-and-half' crew, directed by the capturing ship, but leaving the management of the ship to those familiar with her. Inevitably, prizes were lost because their crews were unfamiliar with the coastlines to which they were directed. Perhaps they did not always understand the language in which their orders were given. Such mismanagement led to the loss of several high-profile captures. The Spanish *Nympha Americana* was wrecked near Crowlink, Sussex, in 1747 after being captured mid-Atlantic en route from Cadiz for Veracruz, to the very great disappointment of the authorities, for she was said to have been insured for 'above 100,000 *l*' [£100,000] in London. Other lost prizes included a French East Indiaman off the Mersey in December 1778 or January 1779, 'the most valuable prize yet taken', and the Dutch *Zeelilie* off the Isles of Scilly in 1795, sent for London with a large consignment of porcelain.[10]

After the Napoleonic Wars the Royal Navy only lost ships en route to, or engaged in, supporting the expansionist aims of empire as there was no call to defend home waters. During the 19th century and early 20th century the replacement of sail by steam and the arrival of the ironclads marked not only design and technological innovation but also advances in ship safety and battle tactics. They also led to new types of wrecks and new ways in which ships could be wrecked: practicality overrode sentimentality, for the decommissioning process could lead to the gradual downgrading of a warship. The route to the end could be extremely convoluted: the brig sloop HMS *Beagle* was already on her second incarnation as a survey vessel when she circumnavigated the globe with Charles Darwin aboard in the 1830s. She was then laid up for some time at Woolwich before transferring to the Coastguard Service, undertaking an anti-smuggling function off the coast of Essex. In 1870 she was sold for breaking up, but may have instead been abandoned to rot. A vessel of similar dimensions has been located on the Essex mudflats and is undergoing tests to prove her identity.[11] Similarly, another obsolete warship, HMS *Eurydice*, by this time over 40 years old, underwent a long, slow decline before meeting a violent end. Formerly a Sixth Rate ship of the line, she was converted into a training ship and capsized in a sudden snow squall in March 1878 off the Isle of Wight while returning from a training voyage to Bermuda, with enormous loss of life among the cadets on board.[12]

Unusually, and fittingly, HMS *Implacable* was 'buried at sea' with full military honours in 1949: the costs of maintenance and restoration for this venerable warship were too great for a post-war austerity Britain. A long history stretching back to Trafalgar, where, as *Duguay-Trouin*, she had served on the French side before being captured by the English, and had, like *Eurydice*, dwindled to a training ship, came to an end when she was towed out to mid-Channel and sunk, bearing the two flags under which she had served, the Union Jack and the Tricolore, saluted by witnesses from both the Royal and French navies.[13]

Others were deliberately sunk or 'scuttled' as gunnery targets, for example, the old sailing frigate HMS *Hussar* off the Shoebury firing range in 1861, or the surrendered German battlecruiser SMS *Baden*, sunk after being expended as a gunnery target off St Catherine's Deep, Isle of Wight, in 1921.[14] What remained of the Imperial German Navy after the First World War was divided up among the allies as part of the war reparations to prevent Germany forging ahead with another arms race. Historically, the surrendered German High Seas Fleet has received most attention for its dramatic scuttling in Scapa Flow, Scotland, in 1919, but other German warships and submarines were also surrendered to the British. Not all were scuttled, but instead a surprisingly common fate awaited a score or so of German warships: they frequently broke their tow ropes and foundered en route to the breakers, so that the sea effectively did the job for which the Admiralty had commissioned the breaker's yards (Fig 2.3).[15]

Scuttling had historically been responsible for the loss of a number of warships at the end of their service, not necessarily at sea: *Augustine* in 1665, *Richard and John* in 1692 and the *Play Prize*, a former French warship, in 1697, were sunk as foundations for dockyard or breakwater works at Harwich, so that they found a continuing use in another form.[16] The practice of scuttling obsolete warships continues up to the present day, but for different purposes: HMS *Scylla* was sunk in 2004 to create an artificial diving reef quickly colonised by maritime fauna.[17]

Early submarines were notoriously prone to failure and also vulnerable in exercise manoeuvres: with underwater detection technology still primitive, they succumbed to collisions by conventional warships also on exercises (HM Submarine *L24*, 1924 or *M2*, 1932) or fell into the path of commercial vessels (HM Submarine *M1*, 1925).[18] The end of HM Submarine *H52* was perhaps the most spectacular wreck of a decommissioned submarine and is covered in more detail later in this chapter.

The exponential growth of the British shipbuilding industry in the 19th and early 20th centuries was fuelled by demand from home and abroad, with a ready export market among the newer nation-states. West-facing Liverpool, with its ties to the Americas, became a specialist in the American and Latin American markets with gunboats specially adapted for particular situations and conditions on the other side of the Atlantic. Two interesting wrecks barely made it off the stocks before they sank. One was the *Iona II*, the other the *Lelia*,[19] both products of the paddle steamer era. *Lelia* was a very early example of a steel-hulled vessel at a time when iron dominated shipbuilding (*Iona II* was iron-built); iron would only give way to steel in the late 19th century. This alone made *Lelia* a significantly interesting vessel, but she was also commissioned at a pivotal point in history as a Confederate blockade runner during the American Civil War. She left her nominal home port of Liverpool on her maiden voyage bound for Bermuda with a general cargo including coal on 14 January 1865, as cover for her true purpose in running to Wilmington, North Carolina. She was never even to see the waters of the Atlantic, for she was swamped and foundered in Liverpool Bay. Likewise the *Iona II* foundered off Lundy on her maiden voyage out of the Clyde, which also sold ships destined for the American market, in dense fog in early 1864.

Iona II was also involved in blockade running, while the *Thomas Lawrence*[20] was laden with a cargo of obsolete guns when she was lost following a collision in the Channel south of Hastings in 1862. As her destination was Cap Haitien, it seems likely that her cargo was sold cheaply to insurgents in Haiti rather than destined for the Civil War, but this cluster of wrecks is a tangible connection with the turmoil on the American continent in the 1860s.

Another warship destined for South America managed to get somewhat further from Liverpool before sinking: the *Loreto*, a river gunboat destined for Peru via the Amazon, which was lost north-west of the Isles of Scilly in 1903.[21] Her intended function provides the clue to her loss: as a river gunboat she had a shallow draught designed for the Amazon, which rendered her unsafe in heavy Atlantic swells. Sailing her direct from Liverpool to Peru across the ocean and down the Amazon would have been a great technical feat. The safer but much more laborious alternative of transporting vessels in kit form for onward shipment from Peru's Pacific coast by llama across the Andes was discounted. This precedent was established as early as 1862 when the *Yavari* and *Yapura* had been transported in this way to Lake Titicaca,[22] although undoubtedly lack of direct river access and the remoteness of the region influenced the 'kit form' decision for these vessels. The onward

Fig 2.3
Remains of a U-boat surrendered following the First World War, lying in Stoke Saltings, on the north coast of Kent. Her identity is not confirmed but she may be UB-122 which broke tow en route for breaking in 1921 (900735), presumably at Chatham. Interestingly, in subsequent years at least one barge was abandoned next to the disintegrating U-boat, thought to be the remains of the Swale *(1538287), although another barge may have been sited for some time in this location.*
(27196/27 19-AUG-2011)

Fig 2.4
Hospital ships were not immune from attack during the First World War. Besides the Anglia, *mined off Folkestone in 1915,* Donegal *and* Warilda *were torpedoed by U-boats in the English Channel, and* Rewa *and* Glenart Castle *in the Bristol Channel, contrary to the Hague Convention (1907), causing international outrage. Here the* Gloucester Castle *is seen sinking after being torpedoed on the night of 30/31 March 1917, ferrying war wounded from Le Havre to Southampton. She was refloated, repaired, and returned to peacetime service, but was torpedoed off Africa during the Second World War. (*Anglia, *901788;* Donegal, *1917, wreck event, 1440061, and possible remains, 767226;* Warilda, *1918, wreck event, 903629, possible remains, 1482340 and 1482391;* Rewa, *1918, 1442427, and* Glenart Castle, *1917, 1440147)*
(© Charles Pulman Collection)

transit and consequent build in situ, however, took years, so that it is easy to understand why the apparent 'short cut' of sailing her fully built was so appealing. Equally understandably, most underwriters regarded the voyage as prohibitively expensive to insure, but she was eventually insured for the then considerable sum of £12,000 (approximately £1m today).[23] In the event, their fears were to prove well founded.

Both World Wars were deadly to the mercantile marine as well as the belligerent navies, bringing into play the developing technologies of the torpedo and the mine, which made a naval and commercial blockade of Britain not only possible, but also alarmingly effective. The aim was to sink as many ships as possible, rather than the previous aim of capture and integration into the other side's naval force, rendering the old prize rules obsolete: the impact upon civilian shipping was greater than ever before. Mines in particular struck irrespective of nationality, vessel type or size. In the early months of the Second World War, the Danish *Canada,* therefore neutral at that point in the conflict, preferred to leave the Humber independently for Copenhagen without a convoy.[24] She struck a mine less than 2 miles out to sea. At over 11,000 tons she was significant enough to pose an additional navigational hazard in her own right, to the very great annoyance of the British authorities, now faced with a dangerous rescue operation within a minefield that risked further casualties. Stray mines continued to claim victims following both World Wars, and were posted as post-war 'war losses' in the war casualty

record books kept by Lloyd's, not least among the minesweepers.[25]

Perhaps the most surprising aspect of wrecks in time of war is the ratio of military to civilian losses. Despite their contemporary strategic importance and historical links from the modern perspective, wrecks of military origin, including aircraft, account for just under 4 per cent of the documented shipwrecks in English waters. Many of these naval wrecks were, however, not lost in wartime, but by accident or on exercises, or scuttled when obsolete, as discussed above. By contrast, twice as many civilian ships (some 8 per cent) were direct victims of warfare, sunk by gunfire, mine or torpedo, captured and sunk by privateers, or simply lost through being in the wrong place at the wrong time, caught up in events beyond their control (Fig 2.4).[26] The useful life of a vessel might well have been a long one: even when no longer on active service a warship could well have been lost as a training ship or as a storeship, prison or 'receiving ship' hulk, and, arguably, was more predisposed towards loss through age-induced structural weaknesses. Where a warship reached the end of her useful career, not necessarily without incident (for most warships had colourful lifespans), but without incident leading to a loss event, her normal fate was to be sold out of service and broken up. Thus warship wreck sites outnumber examples preserved ashore. The wreck event may be seen as a form of accidental preservation, all the more important because obsolescence was a natural result of continuing improvements to warship design and offensive technologies.

From the early Middle Ages to the early 17th century

> In this year Ealdorman Wulfheard fought at Southampton … And the same year Ealdorman Aethelhelm with the people of Dorset fought against the Danish army at Portland, and for a long time he put the enemy to flight; and the Danes had the possession of the battle-field and killed the ealdorman.[27]

It is known that in AD 840 (or 837, according to some versions) a battle of some kind took place between the men of Wessex and the Vikings. Was it a land or sea battle? Typical of the raids carried out by the Vikings, Danes and Norsemen, in which ships disgorged fighting men for land battle, it was probably an amphibious assault, which seems to be confirmed by the location at the Bill of Portland, an effective strategy both for landing and moving troops quickly, and in retreating equally rapidly if defeated. On this occasion, the Danes appear to have won the day, as they did 150 years later at the Battle of Maldon in AD 991.

Even though our principal source for the Battle of Maldon is a poem, the Vikings' winning strategy sounds suspiciously similar to Portland. At first the defending English appeared to have the upper hand against the invaders, until they were lured onto ground more favourable to the attackers, whereupon the English were overwhelmed and their leader killed. This neatly illustrates the dual problems posed by surviving documents: they were written in hindsight, not necessarily contemporaneously to the events they portray; and they share common descriptive formulae which may not accurately reflect the true sequence of events.

These issues, coupled with problems of ambiguity as to who did what to whom, make it very difficult for us to identify whether any ships were lost in these early medieval actions between Saxons and Danes: for example, whether, even if fighting took place on land, ships on either side were captured and hacked to pieces or torched to put them out of action, damaged beyond repair in the fighting or stranded in such a position that they could not be refloated. During a combat at Thanet in AD 853, 'many men on both sides were killed and drowned',[28] suggesting that some part at least of this battle took place at sea. In autumn AD 895 the English blockaded the Lea north of London, cutting the overwintering Danish camp off from the river.

This had little impact on the Danes' mobility, as they simply marched overland instead. 'The English men from London fetched the ships, and broke up all which they could not bring away, and brought to London those which were serviceable',[29] suggesting that, perhaps, some ships had been damaged by autumn weather, and were then broken up and put completely out of use by the English.

The following year marked a turning point in the war of attrition between the English and Danes. AD 896 is the year popularly supposed to be the foundation of the English navy, when King Alfred had 'long ships' built to counter the Danish threat. Nine of these new ships entered service that summer, pitted against the six Danish ships raiding the southern coast as far afield as Devon from a base on the Isle of Wight. The English then blockaded what appears to have been the Hamble estuary from seaward. Once more, the English appeared to be winning at first, but then ships on both sides went aground in the estuary, and the battle continued on foot. The tide then literally turned in favour of the Danes, whose ships floated off first (perhaps because they were smaller than Alfred's new ships, specifically said to be twice as long), giving them a head start in rowing out of the estuary, but their pursuers caught up with them somewhere on the coast of Sussex:

> They were then so wounded that they could not row past Sussex, but the sea cast two of them onto the land, and the men were brought to Winchester to the king, and he ordered them to be hanged. And the men who were on the one ship reached East Anglia greatly wounded.[30]

The *Anglo-Saxon Chronicle* then continues nonchalantly: 'That same summer no fewer than 20 ships, men and all, perished along the south coast'. This laconic entry raises a number of intriguing possibilities, for so few wrecks are recorded in the *Chronicle*. Perhaps the '20 ships' were victims of the raiding parties suppressed by Alfred, but out of context; perhaps the chronicler was reinforcing the English victory in scouring the seas of Danish raiders; or perhaps the weather was exceptionally unseasonal that summer.

The context may tend towards the last hypothesis. It follows on from the account of the sea 'casting' two of the ships onto the land, suggesting both that the marines had to contend with the elements as well as their injuries, and that the loss of the 20 ships was a separate event or sequence of events unconnected with the battle. The choice of the word 'perished' suggests that the agent of destruction was elemental, rather than human, particularly since all the crews were also lost at the same time. For 20 vessels to be lost with all hands along the southern coasts in a single summer suggests at least one event of adverse weather, in which some or all of the vessels foundered at sea (had they run aground, as with the Danish ships driven ashore the preceding year, the mortality rate is likely to have been much lower).

Although stories of sea battles may have been told to chroniclers by eyewitnesses or participants, it was often well after the event. The particular audience intended by the author lent bias to his account, and he is likely to have had little or no experience or understanding of the sea, compounding the errors of recall with second-hand transcription and confused or inaccurate detail. This lack of seafaring knowledge may even have led medieval chroniclers to miss a trick by overlooking particular details which would in fact have served their propaganda or partisan purpose very well.

This is the case with the attack now known as the Battle of Winchelsea or Battle of Les Espagnols sur Mer, in 1350, which has come down to us in the words of the chronicler Froissart and the minor poet Laurence Minot. The battle's alternative name reveals its

Fig 2.5
Reconstruction based on the highly literary description of Edward III's orders to the master of the Cog Thomas *to ram his Castilian opponent: 'steer for that ship, for I want to joust with her', showing the shock of the collision between the two ships. Some accounts state that the* Cog Thomas *was sunk in the battle, others that she limped home with damage, the usual outcome for the ramming vessel in such a confrontation. The mainmast of the anonymous Castilian ship has shivered and is about to come crashing down.*

protagonists' aim to intercept and challenge a fleet of Castilian ships returning home from Flanders.

Froissart is a principal source for the events of the battle. He tells us that two ships commanded by Edward III and his son the Black Prince, the *Cog Thomas* and the *Bylbawe* respectively, foundered after ramming enemy vessels. This appears to be untrue: no less a person than Edward III's clerk of ships recorded that both royal vessels limped back to London after the action, calling Froissart's reliability into question.[31] According to Froissart, the enemy lost 14 ships while the numbers of lost Castilian vessels have been placed as high as 24.[32] Froissart as a courtier depicts the battle in the evocative terms of chivalry: the King orders the master of the *Cog Thomas* to 'steer for that ship, for I want to joust with her' (Fig 2.5), as if the *Cog Thomas* were a war horse thundering down upon her opponent. By this date bowsprits were a well-established feature of ship constructions: an early 14th century illuminated manuscript depicts close combat between cogs with very prominent bowsprits, the one chasing the other. Bowsprits, of course, were not offensive weapons, but the visual parallel with a pair of opposing tournament lances was clearly not lost on Froissart.

In this context the Castilians may have lost their ships to surrender or capture as well as destruction in battle, so Froissart's choice of words does not enlighten us much further. Laurence Minot's narrative poem, while lacking specific detail, seems to confirm that some of the Castilian fleet were sunk:

> Thare kindles thi care; kene men shall the kepe
> And do the dye on a day, and domp in the depe[33]

> (You kindle your grief; brave men shall stay you
> And cause you to die and be dumped in the deep)

What can we reconstruct of this sequence of events, and uncover of the potential archaeology? Ramming another ship was a risky strategy, but would not have been attempted had the ramming ship been more at risk than its intended victim. (Indeed, in 1373, a vessel of Zeeland was said to have been deliberately struck by one of her compatriots in the North Sea, somewhere between the Tees and London, perhaps acting out a personal dispute on the high seas – which itself illustrates that cargo vessels could act with belligerent intent towards one another, in a form of piracy.[34])

Instead Froissart concerns himself more with doing honour to the personal bravery and leadership of the King and the Black Prince, than with a narrative of the battle as such. His personal connection to Edward III, in the service of his queen, Philippa of Hainault, and the standards of medieval kingship at a time when kings were expected to lead their men into battle leads him to omit key statistics of the outcome. The most we can say is that 2 at least of the 14 Spanish ships were actually sunk, possibly more. The *Cog Thomas* and the *Bylbawe* were severely damaged, so it is plausible that their victims may have sunk – ramming vessels were less at risk of sinking than the ships on the receiving end, subjected to the full forces of a deliberate collision and normally left to sink. Consummate courtier he may have been, but Froissart frustratingly appeared unaware of the propaganda value of naming the Spanish ships sunk as a result of the action at Winchelsea, which would have, from a modern perspective, done even greater honour to Edward III. Thus both the actual outcome and the potential archaeology of the sunken ships remain difficult to quantify.

The English and Spanish met again in 1588 in circumstances now almost legendary, but which left relatively few casualties: the coming of the Armada. Those ships lost on the coast of England went down not dramatically in battle but in the anti-climax of its aftermath. As the Spanish fleet skirmished its way through the English Channel, with the smaller and nimbler English fleet snapping at their heels, there was an explosion on board the carrack *San Salvador*[35] on 21 July, disabling her enough to be captured by the English, who towed her to Weymouth, where she was stripped of her armament. The *San Salvador* remained at Weymouth for some months, but foundered under tow to Portsmouth in November. In the meantime the two fleets finally closed battle on the coast of France at Gravelines, on 29 July. A southerly gale then impelled the Spanish fleet 'northabout', dispersing them around the coasts of Scotland and Ireland, wrecking several en route. Virtually the last casualty of this deadly detour within British waters was one of the stragglers in the fleet. The support vessel and hospital ship *San Pedro Mayor*[36] had survived the combined perils of autumn gales and the Western Isles of Scotland, which claimed so many of her compatriots, and had rounded the rocky coasts of Devon. Now, with her course set for home and to the south, she came to grief at Hope Cove in Devon. It was the second accident for some of those on board, who had been picked up from the *San Salvador*. Of lesser account than some of the great warships, the *San Pedro Mayor* nevertheless presented an attractive target both for the local inhabitants, who looted the vessel, and for the government in London, who demanded the names and rank of all on board in order to demand a ransom.[37]

At Gravelines the English had famously made use of fireships to scatter the Armada, an ancient technique that came to the fore in the 17th century in accounting for a number of wrecks. Fireships were particularly lethal in the days of wooden ships with yards of flapping canvas sails manipulated by ropes, all of which were exceedingly combustible matter. It was a strategy only rendered obsolete by the advances in shipbuilding technology in the 19th century, as hulls were sheathed in copper and sail gave way to steam. No combatant fleet would, of course, expend their most useful vessels as fireships, not even under the most exigent of circumstances, but fireships played a role, along with victuallers and other support vessels. Those warships which were obsolete in terms of seaworthiness or technology could retain some semblance of usefulness as fireships. Similarly obsolete mercantile vessels could be bought up for the same purpose. As need arose, they could be filled with combustible material and set alight to drift and cause panic among the opposing fleet.

The first fireships recorded in an action in English waters in the course of the 17th century were expended in an extraordinary action known as the Battle of the Downs in 1639.[38] For all that it took place so close to the coast of Kent, no English warship participated in the battle, although the Admiral for the Guard of the Narrow Seas, Sir John Pennington, and his fleet kept a wary eye on the proceedings (Fig 2.6). Instead the encounter took place between England's enemy from 1588, the Spanish, and a new maritime power which would occupy England's naval forces for the next 30 years or so, the Dutch. The backdrop to this action was the struggle of the secessionist Seven Provinces of the Netherlands for independence from the rule of Hapsburg Spain during the Eighty Years' War which was only to end in 1648. Pennington sent urgent dispatches to London, as did Theophilus Howard, 2nd Earl of Suffolk.[39] Pennington took a neutral stance by default, since he could not be induced to join in on either

Fig 2.6
Anonymous 17th-century painting of the three castles strategically placed to overlook shipping at this point of the Kent coast, looking north-east. Walmer lies in the foreground, Deal to centre left, with the turrets of Sandown beyond. All three, as shown in the picture, overlook the safe anchorage and roadstead of the Downs with the Goodwin Sands lying invisibly on the horizon. Wrecks on the Sands were spotted from all three castles and the painting is almost contemporary with the Battle of the Downs in 1639, for which they provided an excellent vantage point to report shipping losses. (J920039)

side,[40] but in truth while Charles I was debating which side to support, Pennington could do little but wait for orders from his king. The sea-fog cannot have helped the situation: any intervention might well have escalated into a risky three-cornered conflict.

During the battle the English were able to do little more than fire warning shots, and attempt to harry the combatants out of their territory. As it happened, they were not the only neutrals discomfited by this clash: in his running commentary on the action, the Earl of Suffolk made passing reference to six Lübeckers who had been run on shore; this seems to have been within sight of Deal, since he was watching the battle from Deal Castle.[41] These appear to have been a group of merchantmen which had either been driven ashore, or deliberately beached themselves, to escape the heat of battle, in what was normally a safe anchorage and gathering place for vessels of all nationalities awaiting a fair wind for their passage north or south.

Both sides appear to have expended fireships: two Spanish ships were fired under the lee of

Walmer Castle.[42] In the melee, no one was quite sure how many Spanish ships had been lost: Pennington was sharply rebuked for the confusion and lack of detail in his dispatches and the hapless Lübeckers seem to have been forgotten in the confusion. In the aftermath of the battle, the English could do little more than try to prevent looting of the ships on shore, for warships were not immune to the depredations of local communities. It is almost certain that some of the ships, which might otherwise have been saved, were broken up by locals in this way.[43]

The events of 1639 ushered in a new chapter in warfare, pivoting around the English Channel. Rather than sporadic and irregular engagements at sea, the English now locked horns with a determined enemy capable of sustaining long-term action across the sea: neither the 'old enemy', France, nor the might of the Spanish Armada, but the self-confident and powerful Dutch who were eyeing up naval control of the North Sea and the English Channel as a means of securing their commercial power.

The Anglo-Dutch wars: a landscape of war

> Fifteen sail were the Dutchmen bold,
> Duncan he had but two;
> But he anchored them fast where the Texel shoaled
> And his colours aloft he flew.
> 'I've taken the depth to a fathom,' he cried,
> 'And I'll sink with a right good will,
> For I know when we're all of us under the tide,
> My flag will be fluttering still.'

> Henry Newbolt, 'Admirals All' (1897)

The Dutch show of force at the Battle of the Downs in 1639 preceded the Anglo-Dutch wars of the mid-17th century, which showcased the Netherlands' up-to-date navy, commercial dominance and a willingness to deploy their navy to protect their commercial power. In the years either side of 1650, the English Commonwealth under Oliver Cromwell and the United Provinces of the Netherlands in fact had much in common. In many ways their political landscapes mirrored one another. The United Provinces had just concluded the Eighty Years' War (in 1648) to become a Protestant republic independent of Spanish Hapsburg (and Catholic) control, the nucleus of the modern state of the Netherlands. On the other side of the North Sea, the country was reeling from the regicide of Charles I in 1649, having become under Puritan rule a *de facto* republic of the Commonwealth.

Instead of being natural allies, however, the geopolitical location of the two countries, facing one another across the North Sea, was both the trigger and the stage for a bitter rivalry which exploded in the three Anglo-Dutch wars which followed in the latter half of the 17th century. [44] The North Sea became a landscape of war that reached around the coasts of Europe, from Norway to the Mediterranean, involving both harassment of mercantile convoys and slugging it out in classical naval engagements. In all three wars the fighting was concentrated on the coasts where each nation faced the other, for whoever dominated the North Sea coasts would also control shipping and therefore trade within Europe and onwards further afield, particularly to the East Indies.

The Anglo-Dutch wars have a fairly low profile in English history, overshadowed by the other events of a turbulent century at home: the Civil War and beheading of Charles I, the dour Commonwealth and the welcome Restoration, the Great Plague of 1665, Great Fire of 1666 and the 'Glorious Revolution' of 1688 are all much better known. Yet in the mid-17th century Dutch persistence surpassed even the traditional and recurrent enmity with that other neighbour across the Channel, France. In just 6 years of warfare, from 1652–4, 1665–7 and 1672–4 (Fig 2.7), approximately 85 ships from both sides were lost in battle, and there may have been more, for less significant losses were overlooked

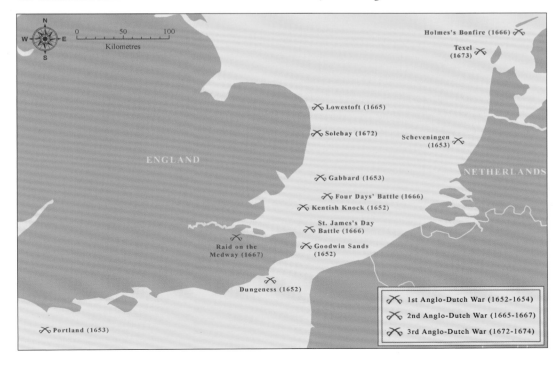

Fig 2.7

Approximate battle locations of the three Anglo-Dutch wars: as can be seen, the Dutch carried the war to the English coast. Precise locations are unclear and may have ranged anywhere up to 40 miles off the coast.

61

Fig 2.8 (opposite)
Battle of Lowestoft.
This pen and ink drawing commemorates the Battle of Lowestoft of 3 June 1665 during the Second Anglo-Dutch War, which was witnessed by Willem van de Velde the Elder, who has included himself sketching away in the galliot in the left foreground. The action swirls around the Eendracht, *seen just after she has blown up: a pall of smoke billows away and blends with the smoke from firing guns elsewhere amongst the fierce press of battle. As a bird's eye view the battle scene is a composite and cannot have been witnessed in its entirety by the artist, and it is likely that this particular version was created from memory many years later. (PAH 3901 © National Maritime Museum, Greenwich, London)*

in favour of more spectacular losses and captures. The Anglo-Dutch wars delineate a landscape of war defined by the opposing coastal boundaries of the combatant nations, and thus fought in within a fairly specific theatre of war, and characterised by the use of broadside engagements, the widespread use of fireships and the scuttling of blockships.

Complexity and confusion characterised both the domestic and international political landscape of the time and have in their turn left their mark upon the outcomes of each naval encounter. Samuel Pepys' famous diary illustrates how political intrigue and rumour could colour perceptions of the conduct of individual commanders and captains,[45] while varying accounts had to be pieced together as combatants returned or dispatched news. It is arguable that, given the numbers involved, the confusion of noise and smoke, the weather and the tides, and multitasking in both fighting an enemy and controlling a vessel, few of the participants were really able to have a good overview of events outside those to which they were immediate witnesses. The outcome was also, naturally, coloured by nationalistic sentiment on both sides and was frequently so unclear that both sides claimed victory. The line of battle stretched out over several miles and for the duration the combatants would manoeuvre 'up' or 'down' channel, attempting to obtain the weather gage (a more favourable position windward of the opposition). All these factors make it difficult to arrive at an accurate tally of the ships involved, and in some cases, their names: a difficulty exacerbated by the hurried requisitioning as fireships of mercantile ships near the end of their useful lives at sea, a development of the medieval practice of calling upon merchantmen at need.

The Anglo-Dutch wars began with a trivial incident, which escalated into battle. The Dutch, already irritated by the impact of the Navigation Act 1650, found English demands for foreign vessels to salute the English flag outmoded and arrogant, and refused to comply. These demands were rooted in England's 'sovereignty of the seas' as claimed by medieval kings, implicitly resurrected by Charles I's naming his principal warship *Sovereign of the Seas*.[46] This policy, ironically, was continued by Cromwell, whose intransigence led to the first action of the First Anglo-Dutch War, the Battle of the Goodwin Sands, on 19 May 1652. On this occasion, an English squadron under Admiral Blake left Rye Bay to investigate a Dutch fleet lying off the South Sand Head of the Goodwin Sands, meeting with a second English squadron at anchor in the Downs. At first the Dutch appeared to withdraw to 'avoid the dispute of the flag', but then altered their course: as Blake put it, 'we lay by and put ourselves into a fighting posture, judging they had a resolution to engage'. Captain Lawson of the *Fairfax* was forced to abandon a captured ship in a sinking condition, since her mainmast was 'shot by the board', that is, shot through and fallen overboard, and 'much water in the hold made Captain Lawson's men to forsake her'.[47] This version of events tallies with the fate of the Dutch *Sint Maria*, which was captured and abandoned, but which, according to some accounts, may have managed to make her way back to Dutch waters, so it may refer to another vessel lost both in this melee and to posterity.[48]

This incident illustrates the need to examine the language of the original documents very closely; 'forsaking' a vessel implies that no-one remained aboard, but, in this case, she was abandoned by a prize crew. Either part of her original Dutch crew were still aboard; she was reboarded by the Dutch after abandonment; or other Dutch vessels took her in tow and kept her going until they arrived in home waters, although it is at this point the vessel disappears from the accounts. Possibly she was, in the insurance terms used by a later age, a 'constructive total loss', that is, not worth the cost of repair, and perhaps left to sink outside English waters.

The Battle of the Goodwin Sands led to the formal commencement of hostilities in July 1652. A number of fairly spontaneous engagements along the southern coastline of England thereafter set the scene for all three wars. In August 1652 a French prize, captured 2 years previously, was expended off Plymouth against a Dutch fleet convoying a group of merchantmen down Channel.[49] In October, the Dutch lost four vessels at the Battle of the Kentish Knock, including the *Burgh van Alkmaar*,[50] of 30 guns, which exploded just off the Goodwin Sands. The name of the battle reflects the first sighting of the fleet off the North Foreland near the Kentish Knock, but it ranged towards the Goodwin Sands. A contemporary print shows four ships sinking beneath the waves, tallying with the number of known losses. A matter of weeks later, in November, English fortunes were reversed at the Battle of

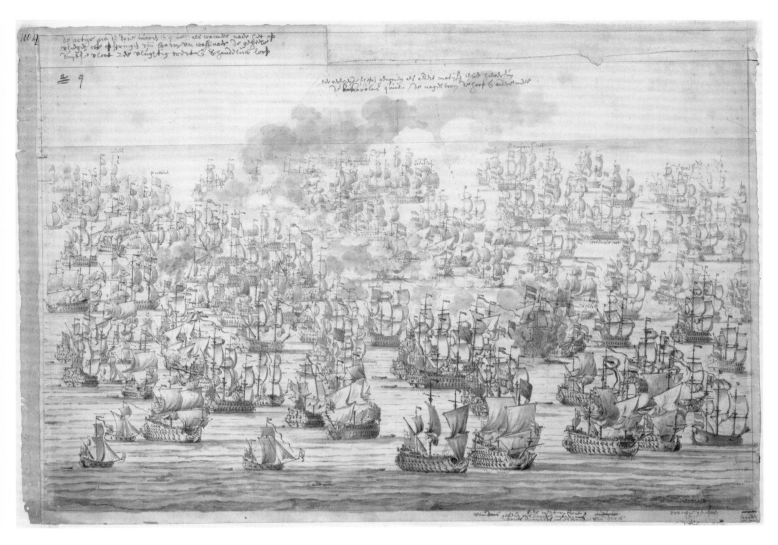

Dungeness.[51] The Battle of Portland, the so-called 'Three Days' Battle' in February/March 1653,[52] was a much more serious incident: the English lost one ship, the Dutch lost three, including the hulk *Engel Gabriel*[53] which was captured and scuttled as the action ranged towards the Isle of Wight.

As varied as the fortunes of the principal combatants were the types of vessels involved and battle tactics employed, illustrated by the outbreak of the Second Anglo-Dutch War from 1665 to 1667. The events of this second war were hugely dramatic, but have been overshadowed by an accident of history which saw even more momentous events at home: they took place against the backdrop of the Great Plague of London in 1665, and the Great Fire in 1666. As in 1652–4, the principal actions took place on the English coast, in the summer months when conditions for joining battle were optimum.

The two sides clashed in the first action of this renewed war at the Battle of Lowestoft in June 1665 (Fig 2.8). As Defoe put it in his novelized account, probably based on his uncle's journals:

> We indeed had a hot war with the Dutch that year, and one very great engagement at sea in which the Dutch were worsted, but we lost a great many men and some ships.[54]

English losses comprised two expended fireships, the *Dolphin* and *Fame*,[55] agreeing with accounts that two groups of Dutch vessels were fired by the English. This seems to have been more along the lines of taking advantage of an opportunity provided by the confusion of a sea battle, rather than a deliberate strategy, but the story attached to the two groups so fired appears suspiciously symmetrical. Both involved three Dutch vessels in a mixed group of merchantmen and warships embroiled in a collision. On the one hand the two purpose-built warships *Prins Maurits* and *Utrecht* (or *Stad Utrecht*) became caught up with the hired *Koevorden*; the other group comprised the warship *Ter Goes*, the hired *Zwanenburg* and the requisitioned East Indiaman *Maarsseveen*.[56] East Indiamen, bristling with ordnance to defend themselves and their extremely valuable cargoes against the constant risk of capture and piracy, were a natural choice for wartime requisition. The *Maarsseveen* was not the only East Indiaman to sink at Lowestoft: the *Oranje* also caught fire after contact with a fireship, which naturally triggered off an explosion in her gunpowder, after which she sank.[57] Elsewhere in the battle the opposing flagships *Eendracht* and *Royal Charles* were engaged in direct combat. *Royal Charles*, a Civil War ship, pointedly renamed on the Restoration

from her original Cromwellian name of *Naseby*, emerged the victor on this occasion as a shot from her landed in *Eendracht*'s magazine and blew her to smithereens.[58]

Cannonballs dredged up from the North Sea off Suffolk are likely to be evidence either of this battle or of the Battle of Solebay in 1672 during the Third Anglo-Dutch War, or even of both (Fig 2.9), since there seem to be two distinct clusters of finds.[59] It is difficult to confirm which, however, since sea warfare was highly mobile and dependent on the line of battle, in turn depending on the winds and tides, so that as the battle raged the combatants are likely to have slipped in and out of English territorial waters as we now understand them (12 miles offshore). In the same battle, a ship may be lost within territorial waters, but another ship well outside. Any individual battle of the Anglo-Dutch wars therefore reflects the landscape of the wars in microcosm, strung out across the North Sea.

The following summer two battles took place in quick succession: the Four Days' Battle off the approaches to the Thames (1 to 4 June [OS]), and the St James's Day Battle (25 July [OS]), off the North Foreland. Apart from the intentional casualties of five fireships expended on the English side, during the Four Days' Battle losses were equal at four warships on each side. The Dutch *Duivenvoorde* and *Hof van Zeeland*[60] fell victim not to English fireships, but to a variation on the same theme, the fire shot, which easily ignited the sails and rigging. Though losses occurred on both sides, the majority of the casualties were Dutch-built, for several were prizes which had been taken at the Battle of Lowestoft the previous year, and incorporated into the English navy, like the *Black Spread Eagle*,[61] formerly *Groeningen*. The English ship *Resolution*[62] was severely disabled by gun action during the St James's Day Battle. Her foremast was shot away, not necessarily fatal in itself, but, seeing an enemy ship in difficulties, the Dutch sent over a fireship[63] to grapple with her. Both vessels exploded in the middle of the duel as the fire spread to the magazines in the *Resolution*.

The most dramatic incident of the Second Anglo-Dutch War, and arguably of all the Anglo-Dutch wars, was the audacious raid on the Medway in June 1667 (Fig 2.10). Repairs to a great part of the English navy, and the standing down of many of the crews, left the country wide open to a seaborne attack. An obvious and easily accessible target for the Dutch was the Thames,

Fig 2.9
Location map of cannonball finds, showing significant clusters consistent with the engagements off Lowestoft (1665) and Sole Bay (1672). Many of these were found in dredging for aggregates and reported to English Heritage through the BMAPA (British Marine Aggregate Producers Association) Protocol.

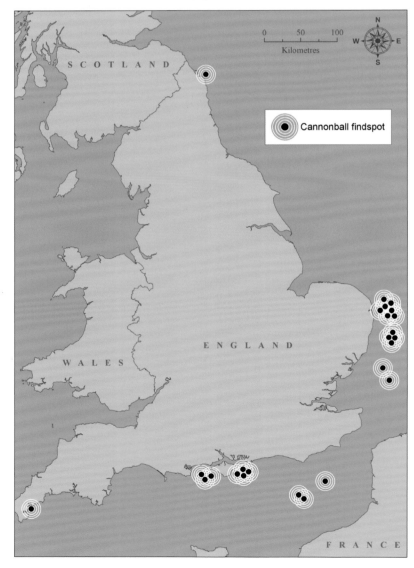

and the naval yard at Chatham in particular, but this was exactly what was least expected by anyone in England (despite rumours to the contrary leaking out of the spy network). On 9 June 1667 [OS] a Dutch fleet sailed as far up as Sheerness, burning the fort as they went. The situation was dramatic, and desperate: other forts at Upnor and Chatham were in peril, and London was also under threat from a second Dutch squadron sailing up the Thames Estuary. The response was to scuttle a number of older prizes and merchant vessels on the Mussel Bank to act as blockships forming a chain across the Medway to stop the Dutch from passing and to protect the valuable dockyard at Chatham: Pepys, besides being a diarist, was a naval administrator and was involved in the pressing of fireships for service. Pepys hurried to Gravesend where he noted that 'the Dutch are fallen down from the Hope and Shell-haven as low as Sheernesse, and we do plainly at this time hear the guns play.'[64] The *John and Sarah* was a typical example of one of the eight ships whose names we know which was 'pressed' as a fireship: a merchantman nearing the end of her useful life, and thus suitable to be expended.[65] She was set on fire, but not defensively: instead she was sunk as part of the Medway chain, and was fired by the Dutch as they broke through. Pepys' contemporary, and fellow diarist, John Evelyn, described the situation at Chatham even more eloquently:

> but here I beheld that sad spectacle, namely more than halfe of that gallant bulwark of the King-dome miserably shatterd, hardly a Vessell intire, but appearing rather so many wracks and hulls, so cruely had the Dutch mangled us: when the losse of the *Prince* (that gallant Vessell) had ben a losse to be universaly deplor'd, none knowing for what reason we first ingagd in this ungratefull warr: we lost besids 9 or 10 more, and neere 600 men slaine, and 1100 wounded 2000 Prisoners, to balance which perhaps we might destroy 18 or 20 of the Enemies ships and 7 or 800 poore men.[66]

The Dutch failed to press home their advantage and inexplicably turned back from London. The drama of the raid simply fizzled out in an anti-climax, but at the very least it could have resulted in a significant battle for the capital, as Pepys himself feared. Nevertheless, the Dutch actions were a severe blow to national pride, not least in the capture of the emblematic *Royal Charles*, which had sunk the *Eendracht* two years earlier. The *Royal Charles* is one of the few surviving tangible remains of the Anglo-Dutch

wars for her counter-stern remains on display in the Rijksmuseum in Amsterdam: despite the proximity to the shore of the defensive chain, very little identifiable remains have as yet been recovered in the Medway.[67]

War broke out for a third time in 1672, with an action off Southwold that has become known as the Battle of Solebay, and a new development: the French sent a squadron to the battle on the English side (Fig 2.11). Most of the casualties were the inevitable fireships, which were expended with such frequency during these wars. The English boasted that they had not only captured a fireship but 'forced them [the Dutch] to spend most of the rest, without doing us any damage'.[68] The confirmed casualties among the fireships seemed to have been two on the English side and at least two on the Dutch side; another English fireship ignited prematurely by a stray shot and two more were sunk by cannon fire.[69] The Dutch ship *Josua* of 52 or 54 guns was captured but 'afterwards sunk being Leaky.'[70]

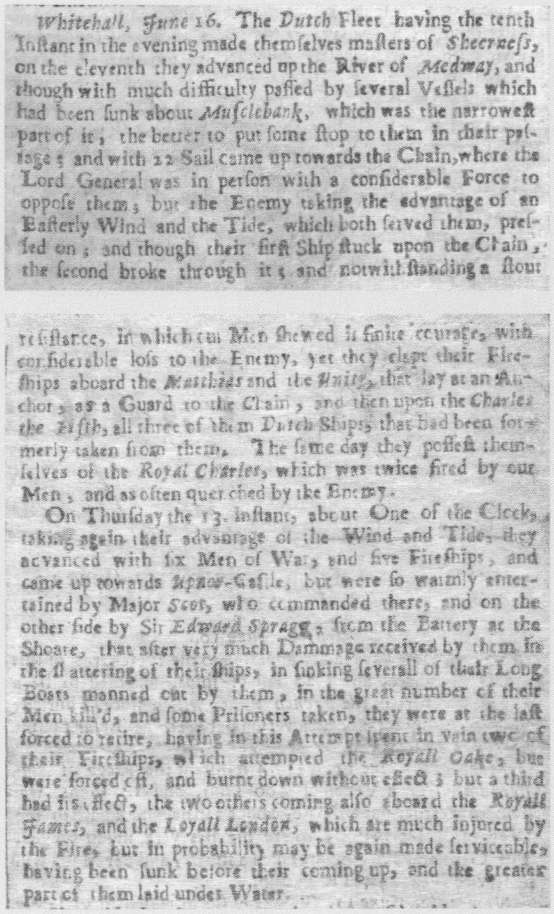

Fig 2.10
The London Gazette, *founded in 1665, is the oldest continuously-published periodical in English history, still printed today as an official journal of public record (indeed it is where notices of honours, for example, are 'gazetted'). In the 17th century, however, published twice a week, it was a news source. The excerpt illustrated describes in vivid detail the audacious raid on the Medway and its lack of follow-through: 'Since this they have not made any considerable Attempt.' (*London Gazette, *Thursday 13 June to Monday 17 June 1667, no. 165, 2. Image courtesy The British Library)*

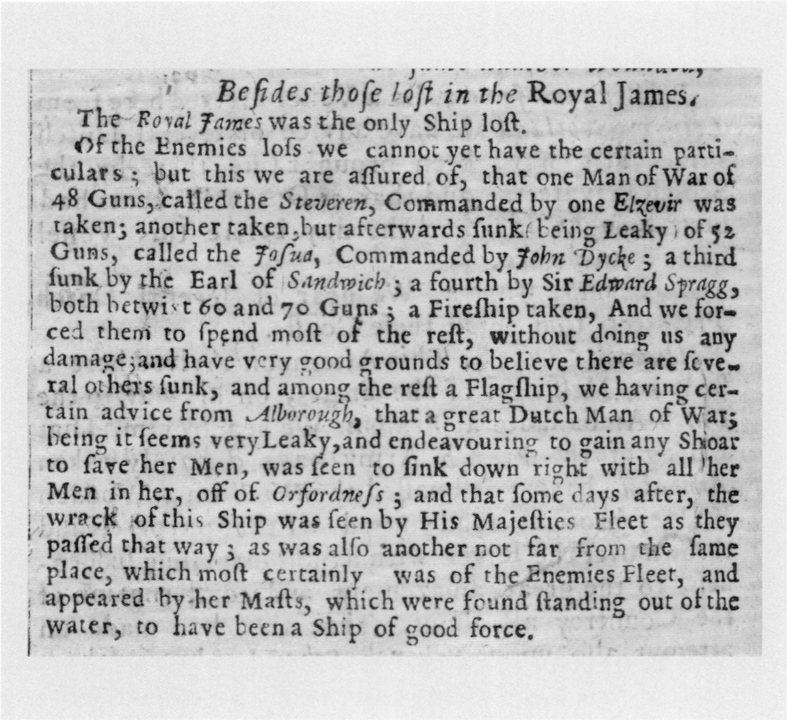

Befides thofe loft in the Royal James.
The *Royal James* was the only Ship loft.
Of the Enemies lofs we cannot yet have the certain particulars; but this we are affured of, that one Man of War of 48 Guns, called the *Steveren*, Commanded by one *Elzevir* was taken; another taken, but afterwards funk (being Leaky) of 52 Guns, called the *Jofua*, Commanded by *John Dycke*; a third funk by the Earl of *Sandwich*; a fourth by Sir *Edward Spragg*, both betwixt 60 and 70 Guns; a Firefhip taken, And we forced them to fpend moft of the reft, without doing us any damage; and have very good grounds to believe there are feveral others funk, and among the reft a Flagfhip, we having certain advice from *Alborough*, that a great Dutch Man of War; being it feems very Leaky, and endeavouring to gain any Shoar to fave her Men, was feen to fink down right with all her Men in her, off of *Orfordnefs*; and that fome days after, the wrack of this Ship was feen by His Majefties Fleet as they paffed that way; as was alfo another not far from the fame place, which moft certainly was of the Enemies Fleet, and appeared by her Mafts, which were found ftanding out of the water, to have been a Ship of good force.

Fig 2.11
The two ships described as sunk – the Josua *and the ship sunk by the Earl of Sandwich in the* Royal James *– would appear to tally with the two ships seen off Orfordness. (It is very common for wrecks to be reported twice in the same publication from different sources.) The location suggests that the battle ranged at least 10 to 15 miles south of Sole Bay. (*London Gazette, *Thursday 6 June to Monday 10 June 1672, no. 684, 2. Image courtesy Bodleian Library)*

The principal casualty, however, was the *Royal James*, a new vessel which became the victim both of one of the Dutch fireships and of the cannon fire which spewed from the encircling Dutch ships. Over the years a number of remains on the seabed have been suggested as possibly the remains of the *Royal James*, but so far nothing has been located that appears consistent with a First Rate ship of the line having burnt to the waterline.[71] Nevertheless this is the only 'capital ship' directly associated with the wars which has been investigated in any way: the only other archaeological remains from this period are those of the *London*, which blew up at the Nore in 1665 just prior to war breaking out and so was not lost in action.[72]

As explained earlier, the Anglo-Dutch wars were oddly inconclusive, both in political outcomes and in losses: first one side, then the other, had the advantage, matching one another battle by battle, loss for loss, yet this lack of resolution has also possibly contributed to the lack of archaeological evidence for the battles despite their seminal importance. This was the point at which the ascendancy of the Dutch navy waned and the star of the Royal Navy began to rise, but it seems that the tumult at home obscured the rise of the Royal Navy among the English public. Most of the battles during the three wars were fought closer to the English

coast than to the Dutch, yet the wars have not lapsed into obscurity in the Netherlands, in part because the 17th century, the Golden Age of Dutch art, and the era of Hals, Vermeer and Rembrandt, is well studied.

Dutch confidence in their maritime trade – and the prosperity arising from it – had already encouraged the emergence of the Dutch seascape as an artistic genre. It could be said that the Anglo-Dutch wars saw the zenith of the seascape in furnishing suitably dramatic and topical subjects. Willem van de Velde the Elder became the pre-eminent marine artist, regularly incorporating himself sitting in a boat, in the thick of battle, making the sketches which he and his son, Willem van de Velde the Younger, would later work up into full-scale canvases. War artist and war journalist combined, his works, often recreated long after the event from the original sketches, are perhaps more neutral than most and less confused than many contemporary written accounts, although they too may not be completely accurate in some respects (*see* Fig 2.8). The two van de Veldes recorded the First and Second Anglo-Dutch Wars as commissions for Dutch patrons; however, the Third was recorded for Charles II of England. Charles was not intrinsically hostile to the Netherlands, having spent much of his time in exile there, and was happy to welcome Dutch economic refugees to England in 1672; the Dutch economy had suffered from previous wars, culminating in 1672, the *Rampjaar*, 'Year of Disasters'. Among the refugees were the two van de Veldes who had scarcely settled at Greenwich before becoming involved in recording the Battle of Solebay in May 1672 for their new patron.

As journalists they were innovative, and the extent of surviving eyewitness accounts beyond 'official sources' displays the increasing democratization which, in one way or another, was so much the cause of political upheaval at home during the 17th century. Pepys' and Evelyn's diaries demonstrate the legacy of middle-class literacy, and the impact of the very new print media (in the form of the *London Gazette*) was profound. From the 21st-century perspective of constant exposure to electronic and televisual mass media, it is difficult for us to realise just how much of a novelty it was to read regular 'updates' during the threat of an invasion, for example. Contemporary journalism had, of course, its limitations and biases, as it does today, but for us combining personal accounts and news media with the drier material of state papers permits a more rounded account of events. In another example of the increasing democratization of the era, the *London Gazette* is, for example, the only source which pays attention to the losses of the 'long boats' as well as to the fighting ships, sunk by gunfire from Upnor Castle, where Major Scot 'warmly entertained' them, and gives us a better understanding of the potential archaeological landscape of the Chatham chain.[73]

All this is in stark contrast to the low profile of the Anglo-Dutch wars as a whole in English historical studies, despite occurring at a point in history when more information, from more sources, was available than ever before. Developments at home, particularly the Civil War and Commonwealth, simply eclipsed them in the national narrative. The internal preoccupations of the Civil War were so great that, in its turn, it eclipsed records of shipping losses in English waters: for the period from 1642 to 1651, the dates usually assigned to the Civil War proper, only 19 wrecks have hitherto been extracted from contemporary records, of which approximately one-half were directly connected to the war in some way.[74] Mercantile losses seem to have been largely ignored and cannot be explained away solely by the lack of surviving documents or by a downturn in trade arising out of the war: tempests and accidents will still have occurred. In the 10 years preceding the Civil War (1632–41) there were 112 wrecks, and 71 in the subsequent 10 years (1652–61). The lower figure for the latter period probably reflects a continuing preoccupation with domestic political issues during the Interregnum, since they are primarily inflated by the victims of the First Anglo-Dutch War.[75] The period 1662–71 saw a sharp jump to 297 recorded shipwrecks: even though the 67 or so confirmed losses of the Second Anglo-Dutch War are included in this figure, the additional 230 records demonstrate that the national gaze was looking beyond purely political events.[76] The gap in the maritime record for the Civil War period is therefore noticeably marked, as is the lack of actual maritime archaeological evidence for the Anglo-Dutch wars themselves: a distinct contrast with the surviving evidence of the Civil War in terrestrial landscapes, which remains with us today in the form of battlefields, destroyed buildings and scars on the urban landscape, and with the commemoration of the Anglo-Dutch wars in the Netherlands today.

Privateering

The demarcation line between 'official' and 'private' warships has historically never been particularly clear-cut. If there was little distinction in form between a mercantile ship and a warship during the Middle Ages, enabling the former to be requisitioned at need, commerce raiding was regarded as equally as acceptable a form of warfare as naval engagements proper between warships. This opened the way for private warships fitted out by individuals or organisations to take on enemy commercial vessels or warships.

The Middle Ages set the tone for a long history of privateering by English ships and in English waters. This had its roots in the law of 'marque and reprisal' which permitted shipowners who had been robbed by citizens of one country in peacetime and failed to find legal satisfaction to seize goods and ships at sea belonging to the offending nation. Privateering could, and did, degenerate into piratical harassment of foreign mercantile ships – regardless of the initial provocation, or whether their two nations were officially at war. The official sanction implied by the law of marque and reprisal permitted a diplomatic blind eye to be turned to misdeeds, but all too frequently it led to serious diplomatic incidents. In 1325, or possibly earlier, a foreign ship was attacked by East Anglian men: ironically, in view of the Dunkirkers' later fame as privateers, the victim in this case belonged to Dunkirk:

> complaint by Jordan Clokeman of Dunkirk, Flanders, that John Warde of Colcestre, John Galod, John son of Roger Belch of Colcestre, and others, entered his ship called *La Pilegrym* on the sea coast at Corton, co. Suffolk, carried away goods, assaulted the mariners in the said ship, so that for fear he and the said mariners fled from the ship and left it without guard, whereby it was wrecked.[77]

Though Henry VIII had encouraged privateering activity by a proclamation of 1544,[78] the best-known 16th-century privateers were Sir Francis Drake and Sir Walter Raleigh who sailed the 'Spanish Main' during the reign of Elizabeth I (1558–1603). Drake famously received a 'letter of marque' from Elizabeth I, a commission authorising an armed vessel to search, seize or destroy the shipping of a hostile nation, in this case Spanish shipping. From the commission itself it was but a short step to the ship executing such a commission being known as a 'letter of marque'.

The term was used interchangeably with 'privateer', implying warships funded privately by wealthy individuals or, increasingly in the 18th century, groups of shareholders or town guilds, who regarded it as their patriotic duty to fund the building of such ships, which thereby acquired a semi-official function. They aimed to capture rather than sink enemy shipping in order to disrupt trade and enrich themselves and their country thereby. Captured ships and their goods became lawful prizes and could be 'condemned' and sold to be taken into the service of the capturing nation as commercial vessels, as privateers for the 'other side' or into the navy, depending on their original status. The prize money was distributed among the crew or crews responsible for the capture, enriching even ordinary seamen with quite significant sums.[79]

The heyday of privateering was in the 17th and 18th centuries and has left a distinctive legacy of archaeological evidence, in the form of cannon which remain even where the organic remains of a wooden hull have been scattered, degraded or covered by sand. Like their 'official' warship counterparts, privateers were well armed, but the natural corollary was that cargo vessels were forced to carry arms commensurate to their size to fight off capture where at all possible.

Though English ships preyed upon those of other countries in both home waters and overseas, in their turn they succumbed to Continental privateers in Channel and North Sea waters, and distance from the Mediterranean could not prevent the activity of the most ruthless privateers of the time, the 'Sallee Rovers' or the 'Barbary Corsairs' operating out of Salé in Morocco or the 'Barbary coast' in general (modern Morocco, Algeria, Tunisia and Libya). Stories of their depredations against the shipping of all European nations abounded: they were much feared since they enslaved their captives, some of whom were put to work in Mediterranean rowing galleys. Religious differences fuelled the fear, but not all corsair commanders were of North African Islamic origin: indeed, two of the most notorious corsairs of the time were European, the Englishman Francis Verney and the Dutchman Jan Janszoon, who both 'turned Turk' and converted to Islam, the latter taking the name of Murat Reis. This fear of the Sallee Rover or Barbary Corsair entered popular culture: early in Defoe's novel of the same name Robinson Crusoe escapes from a Sallee Rover.

The Salcombe Cannon designated wreck site

Fig 2.12
Heavily concreted and well covered with marine life, the muzzle of this gun located at the Salcombe Cannon site nevertheless remains easily identifiable for what it is. (© Crown copyright. Photograph taken by Wessex Archaeology)

has been interpreted as a typical corsair vessel, a xebec of the mid-17th century, consistent with the period when the Barbary corsairs raided the southern English coasts (Fig 2.12). In April 1625, for example, the Mayor of Plymouth complained to the Council of State, that 'Certain Turks, Moors and Dutchmen of Sallee, in Barbary, lie on our coasts, spoiling such as they are able to master.' In the same incident 'a Dartmouth ship and three Cornish fisher boats' were taken, 'even in the mouth of the harbour' at Plymouth. Further letters from Plymouth later the same year note the corsairs' continuing presence on the coast.[80] Objects of Dutch origin have been located among the assemblages retrieved from the Salcombe wreck, leaving the 'corsair' interpretation open to debate, but in the light of Jan Janszoon's example and the 'Dutchmen' who featured in the raid in 1625, a Dutch presence among the crew of a corsair becomes more plausible. Indeed, the Dutchmen, familiar with northern waters, may have been behind the increasingly daring raids as the corsairs extended their reach into the waters as far north as Iceland, where in 1627 a number of Icelanders were captured and enslaved.[81] With this reputation, no wonder even the wreck of a corsair just off Penzance in 1760 caused fear and alarm, even though the active period for the corsairs in English waters was long past:

> London, October 2. An express has been received from Mount's Bay, that between the 26th and 27th ult. an Algerine Chebeck, of 20 guns, and full of men, was driven ashore by a strong southerly wind, and entirely lost; 170 of the crew got on shore, which terribly affrighted the country people. It is 25 years since an Algerine cruizer was in any of our ports in England.[82]

The ingenuity of the corsairs' crews and captains in undertaking these raids so far north is remarkable. Their single lateen (triangular) sail suitable for the Mediterranean with its lower tidal range, placed them at a considerable disadvantage in the violent waters of the Atlantic and the English Channel. One corsair vessel was even wrecked in the service of the Royal Navy. Armed originally with 34 guns, and captured from the Algerians in the Mediterranean in 1664, the English fireship *Fountain*, was ironically burnt by accident during the Battle of Solebay in 1672.[83]

Notwithstanding their fearsome reputation, records of wrecked xebecs are proportionate to the irregularity of their raids on the English coast. The depredations of Dutch, Flemish and French privateers, however, were much more frequent and unsurprising, with a corresponding number of wreck sites. The Dutch were, of course, a constant irritation for the English throughout the 17th century, using privateering as another weapon to gain supremacy over their main rivals, but it was the French privateers who were to become the most prolific raiders against English commerce in English waters.

French privateering, whether official, unofficial or connived at, was fairly constant and persistent from the Middle Ages onwards. Even in peacetime, privateers might put out from Dunkirk to harass English shipping (so much so, that 'Dunkirker' became the generic name for a French privateer from the 16th century onwards; the privateers of Ostend were almost as notorious).[84] Dunkirker shipwrecks are recorded from the 1620s onwards. Historically, 60 per cent of all privateer wrecks in English waters were French.[85] French harassment of English shipping reached its peak in the late 18th and early 19th centuries and became a constant of life at sea, especially during the Revolutionary and Napoleonic Wars.

The tit-for-tat as ships were taken and retaken was virtually continuous and extensively chronicled by *Lloyd's List*, since clearly such activities were a source of concern for the merchants whose goods were at risk. Ships could change nationalities as fast as they were taken and retaken. An English 10-gun naval ketch, the *Scarborough*, was captured by the French in 1694. Her new owners put her to use as a privateer, rearming her to 12 guns, and sent her to prowl her former home waters. On 10 December, 1696, she was intercepted by the *Plymouth*, and sent for Plymouth or Falmouth, but was, like so many captured privateers sent for a port with which the crew were unfamiliar: 'forced on shore near this harbour [Falmouth] and lost, but the men saved: 'tis said she was the *Narborough* [sic] ketch formerly taken from us' (Fig 2.13).[86]

It was a patriotic duty to defend your ship as far as possible, since an attack on British commerce represented a strike at the country itself through her prosperity, a duty taken very seriously indeed by the masters of Tyneside colliers. During this era, most colliers, small as they were (200 to 400 tons), seem to have been defensively armed, and could occasionally overpower and capture French lugger privateers.

Sometimes incidents inspired real pride at home, particularly on Tyneside, which celebrated the hardiness of its seamen against apparently insuperable odds in what may be exaggerated feats. In 1797, it was reported that the *Providence* collier of Shields had engaged the *Courageux* of Dunkirk in Hollesley Bay, off Suffolk. They were reasonably evenly matched in terms of armament: the *Providence* had two carriage guns while the *Courageux* had a single carriage gun, four swivels and 'abundance of small arms'[87] (Fig 2.14). It appears that the *Providence*, unusually, went on the offensive immediately she encountered the Dunkirker: instead of fighting her opponent off once an attack had been launched, her captain hailed the French captain and 'fired direct into him, which shot three holes into her fore lug-sails, and three holes into his hull between wind and water'.

Seeing the determination of his opponent, the French captain surrendered and 'politely delivered his sword, and two pistols from his side'. The damaged French vessel was taken in tow but foundered in the Wash in a gale the following day.

The tale which emerged of the way the Sunderland collier *Joseph and Hannah* fought back in 1798 was even more extraordinary, and the odds greater. It seems that she might have been the smallest and slowest ship in a convoy out of Portsmouth, easy prey for a fast and manoeuvrable French lugger privateer: in an engagement, the *Joseph and Hannah* looked likely to come off worse. Appearances were deceptive:

The privateer ordered the JOSEPH AND HANNAH to strike, which he not complying with, fired into

Fig 2.13 (right)
Swedish-designed 6-pounder cannon on a reproduction wooden sea carriage, datable to around 1650, and retrieved from the seabed by Gull Rock, off Nare Head, to the east of Falmouth. In date and location, it ties in well with the French privateer, formerly the English naval ketch Scarborough *or* Narborough, *lost 'east of Falmouth' in 1696, to which this gun is therefore now attributed. (Scarborough wreck event, 1225833, site of cannon find 1549573.) The cannon is now on display at Pendennis Castle, not far from where it was found. (DP140864)*

Fig 2.14 (below right)
A relatively small-bore but effective 2½-pounder cannon of a type used on smaller vessels to protect their cargoes, dredged up from the Carrick Roads by an oyster boat in 1932. As the circumstances of the find are now no longer clear, it is uncertain whether the cannon came from a shipwreck, or was cast overboard or lost from a vessel in bad weather (site of cannon find, 1549589). Nevertheless it is a tangible artefact from the age of privateering, representing the 'other face' of privateering, the requirement for self-defence, dating from about 1720, and like the larger 6-pounder, also on display at Pendennis Castle. (DP140863)

him instantly; the collier returned the fire, with only two small swivels and one four-pounder, and did some execution. Unfortunately it blew so hard that they could not get the priming to lay on the touch hole of the swivels, which rendered them useless. By some contrivance they covered the four-pounder with a sail, in order to keep it clear of the wind. While this was doing the privateer ran along-side, when one of the collier's men coming up with a red hot poker, in order to fire the gun, seeing one man in the act of boarding, immediately ran the red hot poker into his mouth, and tumbled him into the sea, where he met his fate. By this time the collier had swung with his bowsprit across the enemy, and his main-chains catching hold of her, being clinker-built, the sheathing gave way, and tore her in such a manner, that in a few minutes, she parted in two, and went with her crew to the bottom, before any assistance could be given. The captain of the collier was at the time laid on his back steering the ship, and only two men assisting on deck, as the others had been wounded in the action. The privateer mounted 8 guns, and had 45 men on board. The collier only 5 men and boys.[88]

Though the defence by the *Joseph and Hannah*'s crew was undoubtedly what would, in contemporary parlance, have been described as 'stout', the fate of the French lugger owed more to accident than to design. It also demonstrates that advances in ship safety, in terms of coppering the hull, could instead be extremely hazardous in fighting at close quarters, perhaps because the coppering had been poorly attached or had worked loose in places.

Against this backdrop of virtually continuous depredations by privateers for the best part of two centuries, two remarkable incidents were to take place: the loss of the vessel currently known as the Norman's Bay wreck site on the Sussex coast, an area easily accessible from the French coast and therefore prone to being infested by privateers, and the extraordinary loss of an American privateer in the aftermath of the War of Independence – not on the western coasts of England, which might have been the more obvious target, but the eastern.

The Norman's Bay wreck: is it a warship?

In 2005 the chance find of a large anchor and guns by divers attempting to free a lobster pot just off Norman's Bay in East Sussex led to the involvement of the Shipwreck Heritage Centre

at Hastings and of English Heritage. It seemed at first that the search for the *Resolution*, an English Third Rate warship lost in the Great Storm of 1703[89] was finally over: diving revealed 40-odd guns, all apparently muzzle-loading weapons of cast iron, a strong indication that the wreck was most likely to be the remains of a warship. The wreck site was accordingly designated in the following year (Fig 2.15).

As with so many wreck sites in general, and those of the 17th and 18th centuries in particular, the identity of the vessel is not so clear-cut as it might first appear. The guns are an important element of the mystery, but so, too, are the timbers. A number of samples were cut from a restricted area of the timbers (so may not be representative of the wreck as a whole). They appear consistent with known chronologies of timbers of German or Dutch origin in a date range before 1659,[90] and therefore probably less of a match with the English warship *Resolution* than with any one of a number of Dutch warships lost during the Battle of Beachy Head off the same stretch of coastline in 1690. This battle, part of the Nine Years' War, pitted a combined Anglo-Dutch fleet against their mutual enemy, the French. This was, in fact, the same battle, in which another English Third Rate, the *Anne*, was lost on the Pett Level near Rye, also in Sussex; she was deliberately beached and then scuttled by burning to prevent her capture, and is now also a designated wreck site.[91]

The *Anne* was lost as the English and Dutch allies fought a rearguard action, withdrawing in a tactical retreat towards the Nore in the Thames Estuary against the onward press of the French fleet. As might be expected, the ensuing events gave rise to conflicting reports, but it seems that the *Anne* was not the only vessel from the allied fleet which was beached and burned either by her own crew or by the pursuing French. An ambiguous item from the French-language *Nouvelles d'Amsterdam* (the choice of language reveals the target market as a sophisticated international political and mercantile readership, rather than reflecting national affiliation) describes something of the immediate aftermath of the Battle:

On mande de Hasting, que 2 vaisseaux de guerre Hollandois y étoient arrivés pour se faire radouber, aïant été fort maltraités, mais que quelques navires de guerre François les aïant suivis jusqu'à la Rade, les autres s'étoient resolus de brûler leurs vaisseaux plutôt que de les laisser prendre, et après s'être tous sauvés a terre, ils y avoient mises feu.

Fig 2.15
Site plan of the Norman's Bay wreck, showing the cannon which led to the identification of the vessel as a warship. They have largely heeled to the east of the site, consistent either with the deliberate careening of the vessel as salvaged, or with a wrecking event.
(© Crown copyright. Data collected and processed by Wessex Archaeology)

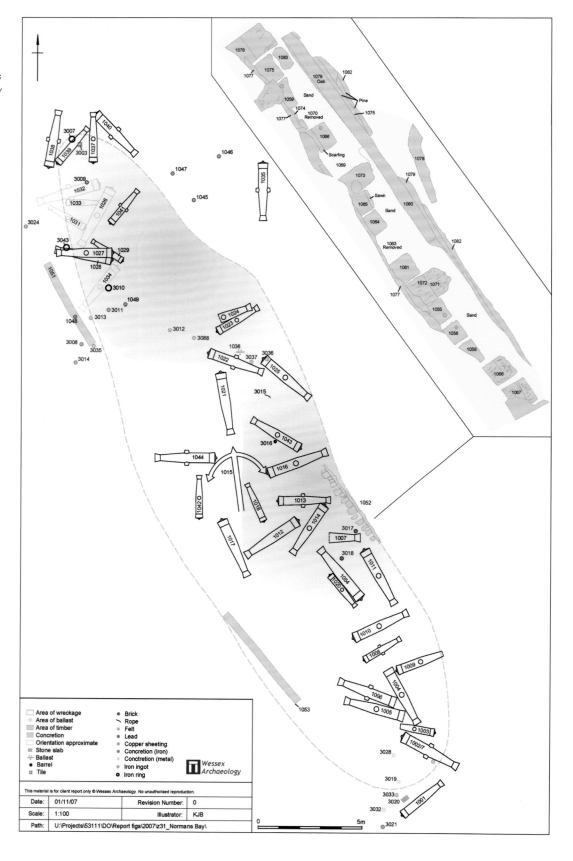

They write from Hastings, that two Dutch men of war arrived there to refit, having suffered greatly, but since several French warships had followed them towards the Roads, the others resolved to burn their ships rather than allow them to be taken, and after all escaping to land, they set fire to them.[92]

Who were these 'others' – and how many of them were there? It seems to refer to a third group of ships, also Dutch, but tellingly it does not quite tally with English or French versions of events. An English report noted that 'two Dutch vessels were burnt by the French in Pevensey Bay', while 'two more were ashore on the White Rocks at Hastings, in which town the Dutch landed 250 wounded'.[93] It seems odd that the wounded Dutch national pride did not seek to specify or minimise the numbers involved, and shift the blame onto the enemy, as in the English accounts. Perhaps information had not yet come to hand in the Netherlands at the time of writing, or had only arrived in a confused form. As it stands, the account in the *Nouvelles d'Amsterdam* appears very pessimistic. Almost certainly some Dutch commanders scuttled their own vessels rather than permit them to be captured, but this was not necessarily true of all the ships involved, and some may well have been captured, then burnt, by the French. The French did indeed claim greater numbers of losses on the Dutch side, but Philippe de Villette-Mursay, commander of one of the French squadrons at the battle, recalled in his memoirs that the Dutch set fire to their own ships:

Celle [l'armée] des ennemis était fort affaiblie ; je fus détaché le lendemain pour aller à la côte d'Angleterre faire brûler 9 ou 10 vaisseaux qui avaient été obligés d'y échouer. Ils se brûlèrent eux-mêmes, l'un après l'autre, à mesure que j'en approchais.

The enemy forces were greatly weakened: I detached myself [from the squadron] for the coast of England to burn 9 or 10 ships which had been forced to run ashore. They were set on fire by their own crews, one after another, as I approached each one.[94]

One ship at least, the *Vriesland*,[95] of 64 guns, was certainly captured and burnt by the French *Souverain* and is therefore a good candidate for one of the vessels burnt in Pevensey, and hence for the wreck site in Norman's Bay. The locations and fates of the remainder are less clear: the *Elswout, Maagd van Enkhuizen, Tholen* and *Wapen van Utrecht* are also known to have been lost. All had more guns than have so far been located at the Norman's Bay wreck site, which also makes their candidacy plausible, since some guns may have been cast overboard or salvaged from the wreckage at the time. The presence of more guns than the known armament would make the identification of the wreck with any of these ships difficult but would not entirely rule it out, since ordnance was also carried as ballast (or freighted as cargo).[96]

These were not the only Dutch ships lost in the Battle of Beachy Head and its aftermath, however: the final tally of Dutch ships lost seems to have been seven overall, as at least two others were lost as the fleet straggled back towards the Thames. Two or three of the losses quoted by Villette-Mursay thus remain unaccounted for. Some of these seven may have been fired east of the battle site, since the *Nouvelles d'Amsterdam* suggests that other ships still at sea beached their vessels on realising that the French were in pursuit. It is possible that the final two vessels making up the seven Dutch losses are included in Villette-Mursay's tally, suggesting that they were also lost on the Sussex coast. Alternatively, two further ships may have fled to be beached further east, not necessarily in eastern Sussex, which would then match the numbers quoted by Villette-Mursay. The potential area of loss is large: anywhere between Sussex and the safety of the Nore in the Thames. At present it is therefore somewhat unclear as to whether the named vessels were lost nearer to the site of the battle, or in the retreat: it is equally likely that the identity of the Norman's Bay wreck site is to be found among the vessels whose names are not currently known, rather than those whose identity certainly appears in the historical record.

It is not difficult to see why the situation with regard to the possible Dutch identity of the Norman's Bay wreck site is opaque. Confusion and conflicting versions of events, obstacles for the modern historian, are completely understandable at times of war or in the aftermath of a storm. There might be several ships wrecked in close proximity to one another, and current weather conditions might lead the crew of other vessels to be uncertain about what they actually saw, in addition to the discrepancies apparent between all three nations in this case. Naval crews additionally were keen to exonerate themselves from charges of desertion or negligence at the inevitable court martial, and salvors were ready to make excuses as to their lack of progress.

William Boswell, writing five weeks after the loss of the *Resolution* on 1 January 1704, to the Navy Board, said that French privateers had burnt the vessel 'down to ye ballast, and ye upperworks to a strake under ye lower wale: her masts is all confound: I am now endeavouring to save ye iron'.[97] Other commentators have previously noted that this appears to contradict the work of a contractor who careened her to salvage the masts and yards,[98] but this need not necessarily be the case. The significant detail lies in mentioning the masts at all: if they had been salvaged, what were they doing at or near the wreck site for the French to burn the vessel and destroy the masts? Did the French come along during the salvage?

The masts were, in Boswell's words, 'confound', that is to say, either 'destroyed' or 'confused', according to two possible contemporary meanings. If the vessel was upright when burnt down to the ballast, and to a strake (that is, horizontal plank forming the side of the ship) below the lower wale (a strake stronger and thicker than the others, forming a ridge on the side of the ship) it seems likely that the masts were 'confound' in the sense of 'destroyed'. However, could the ship have been attacked and fired during a pause in the salvage process, while lying on her broadside? In that case, she may have been fired on one side only with some remains on the underside. The masts, perhaps then under water, may still have been saved, if damaged, or left in a 'confound', ie confused, state. This, then, might explain the equally confused state of the guns as found.

The *Resolution* was built in 1667, and rebuilt in 1698 at Chatham. Could some of the timber used have been of Dutch origin, perhaps from Dutch prizes captured earlier in the century during the three Anglo-Dutch wars? This is a trail that could possibly be followed since in the 1690s, there was considerable activity with past prizes. Several were sunk as breakwaters or foundations at various naval ports, when they were no longer seaworthy or useful; for example, the *Play Prize*, a captured French warship, at Harwich in 1697,[99] or the Dutch prize *Wapen van Rotterdam*, hulked in 1675 as the *Arms of Rotterdam* in English service and broken up in 1703.[100] Their materials may well have been salved and used in other ships as necessary. The twin strands of dendrochronological analysis from further samples elsewhere at the Norman's Bay site, and archival research on the rebuilding of the *Resolution*, may shed some light on the matter.

In attempting to solve the mystery of the wreck site's identity there are two related impediments in the documentary evidence: as so often, the casual way in which the location of the wreck is discussed in contemporary reports compounds the difficulties posed by the gaps in surviving records. From the 18th century or earlier, locations of loss are cited vaguely at best (with some notable exceptions), even when dealing with the fate of warships or notable cargo vessels, which would undoubtedly be the subject of attempts to salve or raise the vessel. For these it is more likely that some discussion of a wreck's position would find its way into correspondence, official records and accounts in print, but this is by no means universal, and details often little more than 'near' or 'off' a given place. For lesser vessels the details may be even less explicit, that is, if the vessels were reported at all. Often the site given as 'near' a place turns out to be at a considerable distance: in 1808, for example, it emerged that a wreck reported as 'near Whitby' was lost some 30 miles away at Speeton Cliffs in Filey Bay.[101] When investigating a newly discovered wreck site, there is therefore a case to be made for routinely searching wreck reports associated with a wider area during the relevant period (even if only for elimination purposes).

In this case, the date range and likely origin of the timber samples suggests a useful starting point of German or Dutch vessels, wrecked on the coastline of Sussex, at roughly the same period as the *Resolution* and the Dutch warships, but not immediately associated with the vicinity of Norman's Bay. Taking the date of the timbers as a *terminus post quem*, looking further along the coastline suggests a number of possible wrecks against which the present wreck site at Norman's Bay can be measured.

If the wreck is not the *Resolution*, what is she? All the potential alternative candidates had some connection with privateering, the practice of capturing mercantile ships belonging to the enemy as prizes in time of war, to disrupt their commerce. In theory, privateering activity was only to be undertaken between belligerents during wartime. In practice it often spilled into outright piracy, attacking the ships of other nations which were not involved, or continuing to harass the erstwhile enemy's ships after peace had been made. The modern axiom that 'one man's freedom fighter is another man's terrorist' could equally well have existed during the age of privateering as: 'one man's privateer is another man's pirate', which seems to have been how the Spanish had seen the exploits of Sir Francis Drake against their ships during the 16th century.

One remote possibility was the *Orange Tree* English fireship which caught fire 'near Rye' in 1673.[102] Purchased in 1672, her name, associated with the ruling Dutch House of Orange, suggests a possible Dutch origin, perhaps as a mercantile prize, captured in the then current Anglo-Dutch war (1672–4) or the previous war of 1665–7. It was an unlikely name for an English ship, for William of Orange and his wife Mary were yet to be installed on the throne and establish the British connection with the House of Orange. As already noted with the *Wapen van Rotterdam*, Dutch prizes were usually given English names which were a literal rendition of the original.[103] Since, however, fireships were essentially weapons in themselves, and lightly armed, typically with four to eight guns, this seems to rule out the *Orange Tree*. However, she shared a common fate with the other major candidates for the Norman's Bay wreck: in a curious and rather ironic twist of fate, she caught fire by accident rather than by being expended in battle.

A more promising candidate might be the Dutch ship *St Christopher*[104] which stranded, again 'near Rye', in 1697, while carrying 'Holland and Hamburg linen and guns'; she had been taken by the French, and retaken by the Dutch, only to be lost on the coast of England. Her nationality is a likely guide to the origin of her timbers (assuming she had not been captured or purchased on an earlier occasion) and the cargo included guns. However, again, much, if not all, of the cargo appears to have been salvaged, and brought to Rye, ruling her out perhaps on the grounds of supposed proximity to Rye as well as the recovery of the guns.[105] Nevertheless, the wreck of this vessel reminds us that it is worthwhile exploring the possibility of guns carried as cargo rather than as active armament in seeking to find a match for a given wreck site.

A third vessel which stranded near Beachy Head at more or less the right period was the *Sarah* or *Saragh* galley, a German cargo vessel lost in 1709. However, her cargo was wine and she is not explicitly stated to have been armed. In any case, while merchantmen were often defensively armed, particularly at periods of international tension or outright warfare, their armament was minimal compared to active warships or even the privateers to which they were so vulnerable.[106]

A fourth possibility lies in a wreck datable to 1667, when a ship was 'cast away' near Pevensey. We may be able to make a case for her origins, for she was lost at the same time, and reported in the same letter, as three 'Ostenders' at Dungeness, perhaps suggesting by association that the Pevensey ship was part of the same fleet or convoy, and by extension possibly also an Ostender.[107] Wine was saved from the three Ostenders at Dungeness. Many Ostenders operated as regular cargo vessels, as other contemporary Ostender wrecks demonstrate. Not all were so legitimate: putting aside the possibility of use by the crew, the wine could have been a cargo used to deepen cover as a regular merchantman by a privateer, or part of a plundered cargo.

Valuable though it was, the wine is likely to have been only part of the reason why these vessels turn up in surviving correspondence from the *State Papers Domestic*, since the Ostenders enjoyed a certain contemporary notoriety, with their counterparts from Dunkirk and Vlissingen (Flushing). The typical formulae of such high-level correspondence lend some credence to the suggestion that the fourth vessel was also an Ostender. During the 16th and 17th centuries, with some exception, official correspondence focused on important losses (domestic warships and East Indiamen); wrecks of ships which posed a threat to national security (foreign warships and privateers); or those whose salvage would contribute greatly to the royal and national coffers (richly laden merchantmen of any nationality). A fourth group was lesser wrecks with the potential to cause an embarrassing diplomatic incident, as in the case of a Scottish ship stranded upon the coast of Durham in 1534.[108] The Ostenders clearly fall into the second group, since they, like 'Dunkirkers', loomed large in the popular consciousness. Thomas Shadwell's play, *The Libertine* (1675), for example, mentions 'Ostend privateers', while the English envoy to Portugal complained in 1663 from Lisbon that they 'rob all ships without distinction',[109] suggesting that they were operating not so much as privateers in support of a specific wartime target as out-and-out commerce raiders.

The supposed Ostender's date of loss also brings her much more closely into line with the date of the wreck timbers as analysed. While the life of a ship could be extended by rebuilding and refitting, such interventions diminish the likelihood of surviving materials of earlier date (although materials could certainly be recycled from other ships). In broad terms, therefore, there is a greater chance that a ship lost in 1667 contained, or was largely built from, timbers with a *terminus ante quem* of 1659, than would have been the case for ships lost around 1690 or later, but this is a consideration rather than a rule.[110]

Most privateers of the period were less well armed than their counterparts in 'official' warfare (typically from 4 to 26 guns: some had more), so that this alone may rule out the 'Ostender' when considered against the site's 40-odd guns, even though it would appear to be a good match for the dendrochronology in date and probable origin, and for the archival sources in the location given at the time of loss.[111]

This re-examination of the evidence suggests that no single known wreck seems to fit the profile of the remains perfectly. The other candidates do, however, reveal an intense level of privateer activity at a time of almost continuous warfare and shifting allegiances. The Third Anglo-Dutch War (1672–5) over-lapped with the Franco-Dutch War 1672–8; the Nine Years' War or War of the Grand Alliance (1688–97), in which England and the Netherlands joined forces with their mutual former enemy, Spain, and the Holy Roman Empire, against French expansion, culminating eventually in the War of the Spanish Succession, 1701–14.

Reviewing and eliminating other possible contemporary wrecks in the general area of Norman's Bay (other possible wrecks currently undiscovered in historical records notwith-standing) circumstantially strengthens the case for the remains being one of the two principal groups of candidates originally considered for the wreck site, that is, either the *Resolution* or one of the Dutch warships lost in the Battle of Beachy Head in 1690. Discovery of charred timbers for sampling among the wreck site is likely to exclude other possibilities at this stage rather than positively identify a particular candidate (charred timbers remain identifiable after being waterlogged for a considerable period of time).[112]

Whichever one of the two possible candidates it is, the coincidence of the final manner of loss indicates that they form part of a landscape informed by privateering activity along the southern coasts of England during the late 17th and early 18th centuries. Privateers and their victims formed a significant minority of contemporary wrecks in and around the Sussex coast. Out of 166 wrecks for the period 1670–1720 on the coast of Kent, 6 privateers were wrecked, while 5 ships were lost as they fell victim to the depredations of the privateers. For the neighbouring county of Sussex, the proportion of ships for the same period directly sunk by privateers or lost as they attempted to escape, rises to 8 privateer victims out of 26 wrecks, or 30 per cent of wrecks; but these statistics over a 50-year period suggest a considerable degree of under-reporting.[113] Most of the privateer victims were chased ashore (an effective strategy in the vicinity of the Goodwin Sands in particular). Whether they were stranded and subject to the attrition of the natural environment, or whether they were burnt by their crew to prevent them falling into the hands of the enemy, they were as effectively put out of action and lost to their owners as if they had been captured, burnt or sunk in direct battle.

Dendrochronological analysis is therefore a starting point for the profiling of a wreck site by comparison with the documentary evidence for other wrecks which brings up specific characteristics of a specific location at a given period. We can say, for example, that priva-teering operations had specific consequences. A contemporary wreck on the coast of Sussex is very likely to have been deliberately run ashore as a means of escape, and thereafter scuttled by burning (whether by her own crew or by the enemy). This form of 'archival profiling' has revealed a diverse and disparate landscape of war in which the Norman's Bay wreck, whatever its identity, almost certainly played a part, whether officially, as a warship, or semi-offi-cially, as a privateer. It can almost certainly be used in other maritime contexts, for example, looking at characteristic national groups passing a particular stretch of coastline, or for examining wrecks likely to be the potential victims of a particular, localised, storm in a particular county. Many groups of wrecks, such as French warships, remain poorly understood since the focus has been on their history, service and the events in which they participated, rather than those in which they were lost. Profiling of such groups by context of loss in a particular landscape may yet reveal the true identity of the Norman's Bay wreck.

The *Bonhomme Richard* and the father of the American Navy

The date: Thursday 23rd September, 1779. The place: the North Sea, some distance off Flamborough Head. The target: a group of English merchantmen being convoyed home from the Baltic. The weapon: the *Bonhomme Richard*.[114]

As a former East Indiaman, the *Bonhomme Richard* followed in the wake of the *Maarsseveen* and the *Oranje* East Indiamen, requisitioned by the Dutch Navy for the Anglo-Dutch wars in the 17th century, and had originally been the French Indiaman *Duc de Duras*. Despite her new name, also in French, she was now an American vessel, converted into a warship, or, as the British would have regarded her, as a privateer. Her name came from Benjamin Franklin's pen-name ('le Bonhomme Richard') in the French translation of his annual *Poor Richard's Almanack*. At the time Franklin was the American ambassador to France: the former *Duc de Duras* was donated by the French authorities to the Americans, perceived by the French as an ally after the War of Independence against the British: both had common cause in the harassment of British shipping. The *Bonhomme Richard* was commanded by John Paul Jones, of Scottish extraction, but a colonist who turned against the country of his birth in favour of his adopted home.

His aim was to strike at British shipping, both mercantile and naval, and he was an experienced transatlantic sailor. The former *Duc de Duras*' chief advantage was being well-suited to the rigours of transatlantic travel – East Indiamen were, after all, built to endure long voyages – but as a ship of war she left something to be desired: she was already quite old, and was not the swift sailer desirable in outmanoeuvring potential victims. Jones left Lorient in France, sailing northabout via Ireland to Scotland; spreading alarm as he went: he was, for example, reported off Whitehaven on 7 September, his passage being marked by accounts of ships scuttled or captured, including the sloop *Johns*, captured between Greenock and Shetland.[115] By late September, with his little squadron of French ships (*Pallas, Vengeance, Cerf and Alliance*), crewed principally but not exclusively by Frenchmen, he was harassing British shipping in the North Sea from Scotland to the Humber. His principal target was the collier trade: according to a witness on board *Bonhomme Richard*, a Shields man who had been taken in the *Hawk* letter of marque and was taken on board 'in the hope of gaining his liberty', Jones had captured several colliers off Scotland, disposing of them through scuttling them near Whitby and cruising the Yorkshire coasts for several days, since he was sighted off Scarborough on Monday 20th having 'taken, sunk and burnt' several vessels.[116]

It is unclear whether the colliers taken in Scotland and sunk off Whitby and the burning and sinking of several vessels off Scarborough on the 20th relate to the same incident, or represent two separate attacks.[117] In any case, Jones was contemplating a third assault on colliers near the Humber, as a prelude to his most audacious attack plan yet – for the convoy he hoped to intercept represented an indirect strike at the heart of the Royal Navy. He was keen to pursue this plan despite the continuous rumbles of insubordination on board, which was to play an interesting part in what happened next. The forests of the Baltic were the Navy's principal source of hemp for ropemaking; deals for shipbuilding and general purposes; and logs prepared and exported as masts. The escorts – the Fifth Rate HMS *Serapis* and the armed merchantman *Countess of Scarborough* were small – but *Serapis*, at 44 guns, was more than a match for the larger *Bonhomme Richard*, at around 40 guns, not only outgunning her but also having been built specifically as a warship, and therefore much more manoeuvrable under battle conditions. The omens were not good for the *Richard*, and things continued to go from bad to worse. What followed was a nautical game of chess which grew increasingly desperate, an inside-out game in which the convoy, which so easily could have been pawns to be captured, became multiple kings and queens to be protected at all costs.

The convoy was seen heading south by *Vengeance*, which signalled *Bonhomme Richard*, while the scattered American squadron was lying off Flamborough Head, at approximately 2 pm, and Jones accordingly made the first move to cut the convoy off from the safety of their onward destination, with 'English colours flying'. Despite this attempt at disguise, she had been recognised along the coast: the commander of the *Serapis*, Captain Richard Pearson, had been advised of Jones' squadron by dispatches from a boat when lying off Scarborough earlier that day, but the 'van of the convoy kept their wind, with all sail stretching out to the southward from under Flamborough Head'.[118] The next move was made by the *Serapis*, who signalled in her turn the ships under her convoy to scatter to the northward, which they accordingly did, most to Scarborough or Shields, and two, bravely, to Hull. In Jones' words, 'the trade took refuge under the cannon of Scarborough Castle'.[119] As the *Richard* approached, Pearson hailed her and asked 'what ship it was': hearing only 'evasive' answers he threatened them with gunfire. The response of the *Richard* was to open fire (Fig 2.16).

The 'Severe Engagement' which ensued took place between Flamborough Head and Scarborough according to contemporary commentators from Hull: accounts from Scarborough place the location at approximately 'three or four leagues from our Castle' (9 to 12 miles) and the local inhabitants were able to 'hear every gun that was fired'. A first-hand account serialised in an English newspaper in 1802, from a manuscript by Jones, places the action 'two leagues [6 miles] distant from the coast of England'.[120]

The action zig-zagged nearer the shores of Yorkshire as the *Serapis* and *Countess of Scarborough* in their turn stood in for the shore, screening their convoy moving to the north, and Jones again moved to 'cut off the enemy' from the land[121] but this sent a confusing signal to his consorts, who immediately believed that the insubordination which had dogged the voyage since the outset had finally broken out into outright mutiny – which would have been unsurprising, since the Shields man was not the only prisoner of war on board. Other crews and individuals had also been made prisoner as the *Richard* had pillaged her way around the British Isles. These men would have had an understandable reluctance to carry out orders against their home fleet. Under this misapprehension, the *Pallas* and *Alliance* hung back, and so it was that the *Bonhomme Richard* moved to engage the *Serapis* by herself:

> I accordingly began the engagement at 7 o'clock at night, within pistol-shot of the *Serapis*, and sustained the brunt of it for nearly a whole hour at that distance, exposed, not only to her fire, but also to that of the *Countess of Scarborough*, which raked the *Richard*, by means of the broadsides she fired into her stern.[122]

At least two of the six 18-pounders, heavier artillery than the majority of the Richard's armament, comprising 12-pounders, 'burst at the commencement of the action', further demoralising the crew, and forcing Jones to undertake desperate measures: in his letter to Benjamin Franklin, he suggested that he was intending to ram the *Serapis*, but instead 'the enemy's bowsprit came over to the *Bon homme* [sic] *Richard*'s poop by the mizen mast, and I made both ships fast together in that situation'. The ships were now closer than within pistol-shot: 'the cannon of each ship touching the opponent's side', but by now Jones was aware

that the *Richard* was 'in imminent danger of going to the bottom', having received 'sundry eighteen pounds shot below the water and leaked very much'.[123] The mutiny imagined by the *Pallas* and the *Alliance* now became a reality as one by one three of his crew attempted to strike his colours, preferring to be taken prisoner rather than to go down with their vessel, which they assumed to be on the point of sinking. The prisoners who later bore witness to what had passed on board, and were therefore somewhat biased, suggested that Jones had shot all three dead – a circumstance that Jones omitted or glossed over in both his accounts, although he noted the timidity of his gunner, carpenter and master-at-arms in their attempts to strike. A further disaster struck as the *Alliance* at last came up to engage – raking both the *Bonhomme Richard* and the *Serapis* with her broadside, an instance of 'friendly fire' which was repeated:

On this I and several other persons begged for God's sake that they would cease firing, and send a few men on board of us, but he disobeyed, and fired another broadside as he passed along; after which he kept at a respectful distance, and too great care not to expose himself during the remainder of the action, without receiving a single shot, or having a man wounded during the whole engagement.[124]

Pearson's chronology is broadly similar but he gives a slightly different version of events:

[H]e backed his Topsails, and dropped upon our Quarter within Pistol Shot, then filled again, put his Helm a-weather, and run us on Board upon our Weather Quarter, and attempted to board us, but being repulsed, he sheered off; upon which I backed our Top sails, in order to get Square with him again, which, as soon as he observed, he then filled, put his Helm a-weather, and laid us athwart hawse; his Mizen shrouds took our Jib Boom, which hung him for some time, till it at last gave Way, and we dropt along-side of each other, Head and Stern, when the Fluke of our spare Anchor hooking his Quarter, we became so close Fore and Aft, that the Muzzles of our Guns touched each others Sides. In this position we engaged from Half past Eight till Half past Ten, during which Time, from the great Quantity and Variety of combustible Matters which they threw in upon our Decks, Chains and in short into every Part of the Ship, we were on Fire in different Parts of the Ship, and it was with the greatest Difficulty and Exertion imaginable at Times that we were able to get it extinguished. At the same Time the largest of the two Frigates kept sailing round us the whole

Action, and raking us Fore and Aft ... At Ten o'Clock they called for Quarters from the ship alongside, and said they had struck: Hearing this, I called upon the Captain to know if they had struck, or if he asked for Quarters; but no answer being made, after repeating my Words two or three Times, I called for the Boarders ... they discovered a superior Number laying under Cover with Pikes in their Hands ... on which our People retreated instantly into our own Ship, and returned to their Guns again till Half past Ten, when the Frigate coming across our Stern, and pouring her Broadside into us again, without our being able to bring a Gun to bear on her, I found it in vain, and in short, impracticable, from the Situation we were in, to stand out any longer... I therefore struck ... On my going on Board the *Bon Homme Richard*, I found her in the greatest Distress; her Quarters and Counter on the Lower Deck intirely drove in, and the Whole of her Lower Deck Guns dismounted; she was also on fire in two Places, and six or seven Feet Water in her Hold, which kept increasing upon them all Night, and the next Day, till they were obliged to quit her, and she sunk, with a great Number of her wounded People on Board her. She had 306 Men killed and wounded in the Action.[125]

Nathaniel Fanning, Jones' midshipman, later recorded the end of the *Bonhomme Richard* in his own memoirs:

Captain Jones desired me ... to remain where I then was, take three hands with me, and return on board of the *Good Man Richard*: for said he, I have left in such a part of her cabin, naming the place, sundry valuable papers, and you must go back and get them ... I was quite sensible it was a kind of forlorn Don Quixote undertaking.

I therefore made sail upon my little bark ... the wind then blew a fresh gale, and there was at the time a pretty bad sea running. I say, I shaped my course for the poor old ship, which was then about a mile from the *Serapis* ... Arriving alongside of the *Good Man Richard*, under her guns, we found her lying nearly head to the wind, with her top-sails aback, and the water running in and out at her lower deck ports: we shot along under her stern, where we were becalmed. I now ordered the oars to be got out, as I found by her motion, and by her being nearly under water, that she was on the point of sinking; this somewhat staggered me, and I ordered my men who were with me to pull at the oars with all their might. Finding our situation very dangerous, we got off about four rods[126] from her, when she fetched a heavy pitch into a sea and a heavy roll, and disappeared instantaneously, being about two ours after we

Fig 2.16 (opposite)
Defence of Captain Pearson in Serapis, *23rd September, 1779. Engraving of the action between the* Bonhomme Richard *(seen to port, with the American flag) and the* Serapis *engaging her to starboard, each pouring broadsides into the other at close quarters. The image closely follows contemporary reports that a member of Jones' crew was making to strike the flag in an act of surrender, while* Bonhomme Richard's *consorts* Pallas *and* Vengeance *hold back, engaging the* Serapis' *consorts rather than coming to the assistance of the* Bonhomme Richard *in engaging the* Serapis. *In the far distance the convoy await the outcome and their fate. Both* Bonhomme Richard *and* Serapis *are severely disabled,* Bonhomme Richard's *masts and rigging largely shot away, to which the floating wreckage in the foreground bears witness, with tattered holes in her remaining sails, echoed by the gaps in the clouds in a dramatic composition. Even so, before his own ship sank John Paul Jones was able to capture the similarly disabled* Serapis *and make good his escape.*
(PAG 8868 © National Maritime Museum, Greenwich, London)

had taken possession of the *Serapis*. The suction occasioned by this, together with the agitation of the waters, was so great that it was perhaps a minute before we could be certain whether we were above or under the water.[127]

In the wake of the sinking Thomas Berry, the Shields man and six other men made good their escape in a boat to Filey, whence Berry made his depositions before a magistrate. Jones snatched victory from the jaws of defeat, and took command of the *Serapis*, herself scarcely able to remain afloat. Her main mast had gone by the board and as the wind increased, the captive ship was tempest-tossed in the North Sea for several days, before reaching the relative physical safety of the Texel, irritating the British sufficiently to be one of the factors contributing towards the Fourth and last Anglo-Dutch War, which broke out the following year. There is also a sequel to the fate of the *Johns*, which narrowly escaped becoming a wreck herself:

> The sloop *Johns*, Capt. Alex M'Dougall, belonging to Greenock, in her passage from thence to Shetland, was taken by Paul Jones, who put three of his people on board her, with orders to carry her to France; but they not knowing the Channel, ran in directly for the Bar of Padstow, where the pilots went out to her assistance, and with difficulty boarded her, and brought her safe in to harbour, and saved her from being wrecked.[128]

Understandably there has since been considerable interest in finding the remains of the vessel. In recent years the first of the 'find sites' said to be the *Bonhomme Richard* resurfaced in 1975 when fishing nets were cleared from some 'large planking', the site then being visited by the Government Diving Contractor in 1996, 2002 and 2003. The site is described as a mass of large wooden ship timbers with areas where the framing remains intact, and a large section of coherent structure some 7m by 3m; however, no guns have been found on the site, one factor which has so far precluded its definitive identification as the remains of Jones' ship. Visibility in the area is generally poor with strong tides: the wreck is heavily obscured by sediment. Few conclusions can be drawn other than that the site is widely scattered and may cover a larger area than that initially observed or surveyed.[129] English Heritage and the site licensee continue to investigate the designated site, for the time being simply known as the *Filey Bay* site. Private individuals and organisations have also searched for other sites in the general vicinity, again without success in positively identifying the remains of the *Richard*, but research by all parties remains ongoing.[130]

So what will the *Bonhomme Richard* look like when eventually found, and where will she be found? The fight took place somewhere north of Flamborough Head and somewhere south of Scarborough, between 6 to 12 miles offshore. As with all sea battles, the action was not static, being carried onward by the press of sail and the tide, but the close entanglement of the two vessels will have slowed down their progress. Her final resting place will have been not the site of the battle, but the spot to which she had drifted after spending some 36 hours in a sinking state in a strengthening breeze, which made it impossible for the *Richard* to reach a friendly port before she sank: the nearest ports, on the English side, would have afforded him nothing but a hostile welcome. She is likely to be identified by her cannon of French origin, which will be set within concretions, but at least two – Jones later said all – of his six 18-pounders had burst so that two cannon, if not more, bearing evidence of having been shattered, are likely to remain *in situ*. According to Captain Pearson's report, her guns were 'dismounted' and so are therefore likely to be more scattered than is usual with the disposition of guns upon the seabed: they may, perhaps, all be found rolled to one end of the remains. Finally, the remains will almost certainly be charred in several places, as noted by both Jones and Pearson: a mystery likely to be solved predominantly by dendrochronological sampling from several locations among the wreck remains.

John Paul Jones ushered in an era of almost constant privateering which was to continue on and off for the next 35 years, but which saw a particularly intense period in the late 1770s and early 1780s as American, French and Dutch ships all joined in attacks on British ships, yet Jones' raid was the most audacious of them all. The engagement between *Bonhomme Richard* and *Serapis* is so swashbuckling that it could almost pass for a film and has passed into legend. Part of that legend includes the retort made by Jones to Captain Pearson's demand that he strike his flag: 'I have not yet begun to fight!' Though the archaeological evidence so far has not yielded up the definitive remains of the *Richard*, contemporary accounts do not record his defiance in such terms – nor did Jones himself. There seem to be as many variants of his actual words as reports of the action. He told Franklin shortly after the battle that he answered the Captain 'in the most determined negative', but did not outline the language he used. Captain Pearson recalled no answer to his demand to strike or to ask for quarter, which appears credible both as an act of defiance in itself and as the response of a harassed commander who was attempting to hold together his ship, quell mutiny and organise the few resources he had left in order to continue the fight. This is the view purveyed by Jones' later manuscript:

The Captain, on hearing the gunner express his wishes to surrender, in consequence of his suppos-ing that we were sinking, instantly addressed himself to me, and exclaimed, 'Do you ask for quarter? Do you ask for quarter?' I was so occupied at this period, in serving the three cannon in the forecastle, that I remained totally ignorant of what had occurred on deck. I replied, however, 'I do not dream of surrendering, for I am determined to make you strike!'

Fanning, his midshipman, allows him a much longer answer, which seems more biased towards expounding a point of view than the words of someone who must surely have been unwilling to spare many words:

'If you have,' said they, 'why don't you haul down your pendant;' as they saw our ensign was gone. 'Ay, ay,' said Jones, 'we'll do that when we can fight no longer, but we shall see yours come down the first; for you must know, that Yankees do not haul down their colours until they are fairly beaten.'[131]

Contemporary English newspapers, which understandably did not view Jones favourably, painted his words in belligerent language, but these few words seem to be short and to the point, and may be the most credible, despite their inherent bias:

[T]he captain of the *Serapis*, who was so near him as to be audible, called out to him to strike, or he must infallibly go to the bottom. Jones replied with an oath, 'I may sink, but I'll be d—d if I strike.'[132]

The truth may never be known, at the distance of over 230 years: in the heat of the battle, with flames crackling, men shouting, confusion and cannonade, the noise of the pumps, both ships creaking and groaning with the strain of leaks and masts about to give way, the flapping of the sails, it is a wonder that Pearson's demand to surrender was heard at all, never mind intelligibly answered.

The battlefield of the North Sea: the sweepers, the colliers and the Scandinavians

The enduring images of the First World War are those of 'Flanders fields' in which a whole generation of young men on both sides was mown down in the mud of the trenches, but an equally important, if not more important, war was taking place at sea. It was a clash of two empires, two navies and two technologies. The British and German navies met at the last major classical sea battle ever to take place, in 1916 at Jutland in the North Sea, in which iron battleships from both sides converged on a point at sea to engage one another. As the course of the First World War showed, however, classical sea battles were, even then, on the way out. As an island nation, dependent as much upon her merchant as well as fighting navy, Great Britain was uniquely vulnerable to being starved of both food and essential supplies by the minefields sown around her coasts and by the raiding U-boats which picked off her ships one by one (Fig 2.17). The toll in men and ships was high, and continued to mount until the implementation of the convoy strategy in 1917.

Fighting a war at sea under these circum-stances demanded versatility on the part of both men and ships. The North Sea was the most dangerous front, for it was the common frontier between the belligerents, a battlefield ranging for hundreds of miles for the entire duration of the war, and claiming untold victims. It was a war of displacement, in which seamen and ships found themselves in unusual roles and locations, for Britain's resources, the largest navy and the largest shipbuilding industry in the world, were simply unable to keep up with sustained maritime losses. This is the story of the war from 1914 to 1918 in the North Sea: the men and ships that swept up the mines; the colliers that continued to run the coal through the swept channels to London, the south coast and abroad; and the Norwegian and Danish ships which filled the ranks of the colliers as they succumbed to mines, despite the best efforts of the sweepers, and torpedoes, which could strike anywhere, swept channels or not.

At the very beginning of the First World War the demands on the Royal Navy were recognised as so great that the purpose-built warships alone could not meet Great Britain's offensive and defensive needs at sea. Auxiliaries were required

as patrol vessels and as minesweepers, the dangers being apparent from the very outset of the war. There was, for example, the famous incident in which the German fleet shelled the north-eastern coastal towns of Scarborough, Whitby and Hartlepool on 16 December 1914, partly as cover for the minelaying operations in which the German light cruiser *Kolberg* was also engaged: Whitby Abbey was hit by *Kolberg* in the shelling and the west front badly damaged (Fig 2.18), while the barracks in Scarborough Castle were destroyed by the battle cruisers *Derfflinger* and *Von der Tann*.[133] Within a week at least six ships had fallen victim to the minefield, including two sweepers:

a round, black object suddenly appeared in a swirl of water astern of, and between, the *Skipjack* and *Gossamer*. It was followed immediately by another. There could be no doubt what they were. Each had four long, black horns – German mines … The *Skipjack* was quite close to the trawlers when the stillness of the morning was rudely shattered by the thudding boom of a heavy explosion. A column of white water mingled with greyish smoke leapt out of the calm sea. It was as high as a church spire, and seemed to hang for a moment in mid-air before curling over to fall sizzling and hissing back to the surface in the

midst of a blackened area dotted with the silver bodies of dead fish. The detonations continued, one after the other. Within five minutes eighteen mines were swept up … The *Kolberg*'s cargo had been very thickly sown. Never afterwards throughout the whole period of the war were mines discovered in such profusion, or so close together.[134]

One of the ships ensnared in the minefield was the *Boston*,[135] which had left Norway with a typical export cargo of wood and paper from Drammen for London on 18 December 1914. Conditions on her departure were heavy seas with a gale at south-west, in other words, a contrary wind for a voyage heading in that same direction. Having made very slow progress, she passed safely by the Farne Islands 3 days later,[136] heading instead for man-made danger: at 4 am on 22 December she struck one of *Kolberg*'s mines laid on 16 December.

The December raid was perhaps the most notorious incident of the war in what became known as the 'Scarborough minefield', but it was not the first North Sea incident, since even from the outbreak of hostilities mines had been sown to attack shipping on England's vital eastern coast: outside territorial waters HMS *Amphion* became the first British victim of hostilities when a mine claimed her on 5 August 1914. The first victims of a field of 194 mines dropped by the minelayer *Albatros* on 26 August 1914, only a few weeks into the war, were sunk very shortly afterwards. With the added element of surprise at this early stage of the war, the toll was higher even than the raid on the Yorkshire coast. One by one six vessels were blown up, the first being the Icelandic trawler *Skuli Fógeti*, homeward-bound for Iceland from Grimsby, caught 25 to 30 miles off the Tyne at approximately 10 pm on the 26th with the loss of some of her crew. Within 24 hours an eclectic mixture of other ships followed her to the deep within the same minefield: the English fishing drifter *Barley Rig*; the Norwegian collier *Gottfried* bound to Blyth in ballast to pick up coal, the Danish schooner *Gaea*, and the British trawlers *Crathie* and

Thomas W Irvine.[137] The fates of the *Skuli Fógeti*, *Gottfried* and *Gaea*, all neutrals, caused outrage at home and abroad. War at sea suddenly appeared all the more sinister: the mines had been not only within Britain's territorial sea (then within 3 nautical miles from the shore and seen as a 'legitimate' offensive target) but much further offshore, and the potential for indiscriminate slaughter of non-belligerents frighteningly realised.

As it happened, the sad little group of ships lost on 26 and 27 August 1914 set the tone for the rest of the war on the North Sea front, with the involvement of colliers, fishing vessels and Scandinavian ships. The need to fight fire with fire was immediately evident, and trawlers were called upon to protect their own under the Admiralty flag. (Indeed many trawling fleets

Fig 2.18
(a) West wall of Whitby Abbey prior to the German bombardment in 1914;
(b) the extent of the damage immediately afterwards; with further collapse evident in (c). Note particularly the exposure (b) and collapse (c) of the stairs to the left of the great west window, still intact in (a).
(AL 0976/014/01 (a); AL 0976/015/01 (b); and AL 0976/016/01 (c))

saw distinguished service, particularly the distinctively named Sleight fleet of Grimsby: *Rado*, *Recepto*, *Remarko*, *Remindo* and *Resono* were all lost on clearance operations during the course of the war.[138]) The *Barley Rig* was still fishing, but the *Crathie* and *Thomas W Irvine* had already slipped into their wartime role as minesweeper-trawlers, like so many of their

colleagues. Small, averaging approximately 200 to 350 tons, they were ideal for the dangerous work of minesweeping. The minesweeper-trawlers were normally commanded by a naval or RNVR (Royal Naval Volunteer Reserve) officer, often supplemented by other RNVR volunteers and gunners, but usually incorporating their peacetime fishing complement

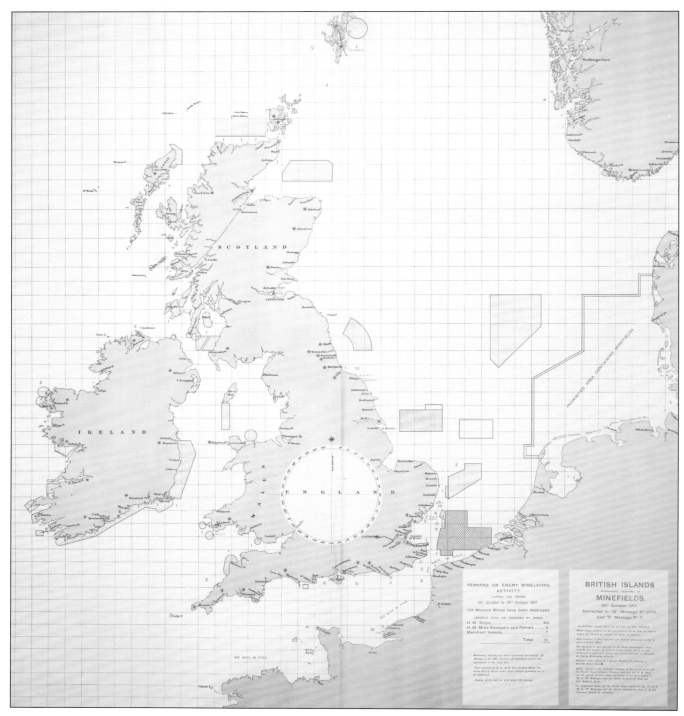

who were intimately acquainted with their hunting grounds, except that this time they were hunting mines, not fish. In the same way these ships of civilian appearance, appeared in official lists of warship losses, identified by the prefix HMS or HMT (His Majesty's Trawler) both used fairly interchangeably.[139] They were robust, suited to heavy weather, had a fairly shallow draft, vital for the task of minesweeping, and were able to substitute cutting wire for their trawl nets. In fact, they were so successful at their task that the Admiralty placed orders with specialist trawler shipyards for 'Admiralty pattern' trawlers.

Minesweepers typically worked in three pairs abreast, a cutting wire suspended between each pair, in order to clear as wide a 'swept channel' as possible to allow shipping to pass in both directions without running the risk of contact with mines. The work was done between tides – high tide made mines dangerously invisible; at low water the risk of contact was greater. At all states of the tide, smallish vessels with shallow draft were less at risk of accidentally detonating the mines they were attempting to make safe. As each pair passed by either side of a mine, their wires cut through the fixing cables, sending them to the surface, whereupon the ships' crews would render them safe in a form of 'controlled explosion' by shelling them with gunfire.

This work was tedious, monotonous and repetitive, requiring the crews to hold their nerve on a regular basis: as fast as the minefields were sown, they were swept, and as fast as they were swept, fresh fields were laid down, necessitating the publication of up-to-date charts monthly or fortnightly for fishermen, merchantmen and the Navy, showing the locations of the most recently swept or identified fields (Fig 2.19).[140] All around the British Isles many minesweeper crews sacrificed themselves so that others would not share the same fate, but the North Sea coast bore the brunt of losses with more than twice as many minesweeper losses as on all the other areas of the English coastline put together. The North Sea was where mines were most thickly sown, principally targeting the colliers which 'kept the home fires burning'. The Grimsby trawlers *Alberta* and *Orcades* were typical, continuing to work the familiar waters off the Humber as paired 'sweeping mates'. On 14 April, 1916, the *Alberta* was blown up while sweeping mines laid by *UC-7*; as her sweeping mate *Orcades* steamed to the rescue of the survivors, she too was blown up.[141] Few

were lost to causes other than their own minesweeping duties, with the exception of HM Trawlers *Elise* and *Lochiel*, which were both torpedoed, and three others which were involved in collisions, not with mines, but with other vessels, unsurprising given the nature of their work.[142]

Despite the dangers, many requisitioned trawlers made it through the war unscathed and some were even to survive another period of arduous duty in the Second World War. Their efforts kept the principal trade and convoy routes open in the significant danger area of the 'Scarborough minefield' (although in fact it extended much further). Mines in this area were continually replenished right up to the end of the war, since they covered a well-used shipping channel used for domestic coasting and international traffic alike. At least 52 vessels were blown up by mines in this general area during the war.[143] This same large stretch of the North Sea was also a fertile hunting ground for the U-boats to expend their torpedoes on merchant shipping. Vital though the minesweepers were, there was little they could do to prevent the sinister undersea track of a torpedo snaking its way towards its victim, an event which became all too familiar, with 118 known torpedo victims in exactly the same area.[144]

The Scarborough minefield, upon which so many sweepers concentrated their efforts, was designed to lie right in the middle of the principal coal route between Newcastle-upon-Tyne and London (although other minefields further south along the route were also a significant threat). The U-boat war was taking a heavy toll on shipping and this was well-known at a high level, even though news of sinkings was suppressed through heavy press censorship. Given the contemporary extent of the rail

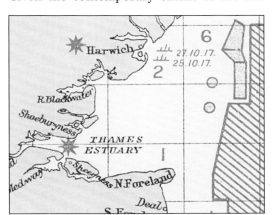

Fig 2.19a (opposite) Example of an Admiralty minefield chart issued on 29 October 1917. These secret charts were issued fortnightly to mariners, showing the locations of minefields and losses in each period, tracking the extents of both offensive (German) and defensive (British) minefields. The wreck symbols show dated losses to mines: those off Yorkshire for 21 and 27 October represent the tug Bunty *(978622) and the collier* Lady Helen *(909171). (Admiralty Chart X74 no. 346, for 15 to 29 October 1917, United Kingdom Hydrographic Office, Taunton)*

Fig 2.19b (left) Detail view of the approaches to the Thames charting both minefields and losses. The hired trawlers HMS Vitality *(1487719) and HMS* Strymon *(1541035) are charted with the dates 20 and 27 October, lost in sweeping the heavily mined area off the Essex/Suffolk coast, which also claimed the collier* Wearside *(wreck event, 901537; possible remains, 908120) on 25 October. All were lost outside the principal minefields: the red numbers represent mines swept up outside the main fields. Whether deliberately placed or having broken free, these stray mines thus represented a very real danger in the swept channels. (Admiralty Chart X74 no. 346, for 15 to 29 October 1917, United Kingdom Hydrographic Office, Taunton)*

network which was less exposed to any airborne threat than it was to become in the Second World War, it seems surprising that coal for home consumption was still predominantly sent by sea and that little was done to increase the inland circulation of coal.

There were three principal reasons for freighting coal by sea. The industry was innately conservative, and heavily dependent on a long-established infrastructure arising in turn out of private ownership patterns. The process of extraction and transportation to the dock and onwards by ship was often entirely in the hands of the traditional colliery magnates such as the Marquesses of Londonderry, who exploited the coalfields around the port of Seaham, itself developed in the 19th century to serve the coalfields. Industries dependent upon coal also favoured a seamless approach between extraction, transportation and consumption. This might mean, for example, contracting to buy up the output of a particular colliery and owning or chartering a fleet to deliver the coal to their plants, as the London-based Gas Light and Coke Co. did. The fragmented nature of the railway companies prior to their amalgamation as the 'Big Four' in 1923[145] also prevented the railways taking on a greater share of the market in freighting coal, particularly as freight lines ran from the coalfields to ports instead of to depots for onward despatch to inland destinations.

To remedy this situation the railways were rationalised to a certain extent during the First World War, dividing the country up into regions within which coal could be transported locally. This saved on the consumption of coal during transportation, since coal was required to fuel the steam propulsion of both trains and ships, and avoided long hauls to market. Further rationalisation was hampered by the colliery owners, who had 400,000 railway wagons in private ownership, and were disinclined to 'pool their wagons, so as to avoid the extensive running of part-full or empty wagons'.[146] The net result was that the collier ships remained the most efficient way to transport coal over long distances.

There were other factors involved in the maritime transport of coal. Bunker coal, that is, coal to fill the steamships' fuel bunkers, was clearly more efficiently sent by sea. The coal-exporting ports of Shields, Sunderland and Seaham had easy access to nearby reserves of bunker coal, but all other ports at home and abroad which did not have the benefit of being sited near coalfields also required fuel supplies. Additionally, the war caused the export market for British coal from all sources to expand dramatically. For one thing, coal was a vital part of the war effort in France, fuelling as it did, for example, every stage in the repatriation of wounded soldiers: stoking the engines of the steam locomotives hauling the ambulance trains to the French Channel ports, and bunkering the ships which made the cross-Channel run with their vulnerable cargo. Coal was still required for normal internal consumption in France and Belgium. There, however, coalfields were in or near the war zones, so that supplies from the affected areas to the domestic market dried up: British coal thus filled the gap.

The sharp rise in shipping losses to war causes reflects a corresponding rise in cross-Channel coal traffic during the First World War: the number of ships lost during the war itself far exceeded those in the previous four years (1909–13) or during the 4 years following (1919–23). Before the war – and in the years afterwards – the Welsh valley ports had specialised in the export of coal to France, but wartime export patterns changed dramatically in the effort to keep France supplied with coal. These changes resulted in diversification. Scottish, Tyneside, Yorkshire and Lancashire coal ports began to send coal to French ports hitherto dominated by coal from the Welsh valleys. Interesting localised patterns of export began to emerge: for example, for a brief period, Ellesmere Port and Runcorn on the north-west coast pressed sailing vessels – schooners and barges – into exporting coal to France, as part of a wider war pattern in which even tugs were requisitioned as Admiralty colliers, such was the pressure on the coal trade.[147] Five out of the seven known wrecks of 'sailing colliers' were lost to the same U-boat on the same day on 10 September 1917 – a significant cluster of wrecks linked in time and date of loss as they were in their contribution to the war effort from the Mersey and Cheshire ports. After November 1917 no further losses of 'acting colliers' from these ports were recorded.[148]

Taken as a whole, colliers can be seen to be a substantial discernible group in the landscape of war (indeed, collier losses were likewise to become a highly significant feature of the Second World War). The few days between 5 and 8 February 1917 illustrate the impact of the war upon the North Sea coal trade route, in which a small group of wrecks is typical and representative of the larger-scale war at sea (Fig 2.20). The first victim was the *Hurstwood*, claimed 6 miles north-east of Whitby by a torpedo from *UB-34* on 5 February 1917. She was a British ship of 1,229 tons, northbound to the Tyne in ballast, owned by Cory Colliers Ltd, whose business was the Newcastle to London coal trade. Cory was typical of the numerous specialist coal shipping companies which suffered from the U-boat war, losing 10 ships in English territorial waters over the course of the war, the majority off the Yorkshire coast.[149] Another Cory collier lost near Whitby was the *Brentwood*, of 1,192 tons, like *Hurstwood* built by S P Austin and Son Ltd of Sunderland: she had been torpedoed in the same area, some 4 miles east-north-east of Whitby, just a few weeks earlier, on 12 January 1917. Like her sister ship, the *Brentwood* was bound from London for the Tyne in ballast. With this level of coincidental detail, it is unsurprising that there was until recently some confusion as to which wreck was which.[150]

This confusion extends beyond those of sister ships understandably difficult to tell apart, given the large numbers of colliers and ships of typical collier dimensions lost off the coast of Yorkshire. The war damage typical of these wrecks also tends to partially or wholly obliterate distinguishing features. An excellent example concerns two other victims of *UB-34* which were both torpedoed two days after the *Hurstwood*, on 7 February 1917. The *Corsican Prince*, of 2,776 tons, bound from Dundee for Dunkirk with timber, was struck 3 miles east of Whitby, being holed through her No. 3 hold. The *Saint Ninian* nearby, of 3,026 tons, bound from Algeria to Hartlepool with pyrites, steamed to her assistance, sending a boat to take off survivors, but was in her turn torpedoed without warning. The men in the boat from the *Saint Ninian* could only shout helplessly as they spotted the U-boat training her periscope upon their ship, yet their act of altruism in setting out to the rescue may well have saved their own lives, for the *Saint Ninian* went down in minutes with half of her remaining crew. Given their similar dimensions, loss in the same incident and the 'fog of war' which must have affected the survivors' recall, the situation with regard to the identification of the remains of the *Corsican Prince* and the *Saint Ninian* is even more complex than that of the sister ships *Hurstwood* and *Brentwood*.

Instead both vessels have, at various times, been associated with different sites in the

Fig 2.20
A rare aerial photograph of an unidentified vessel seen from astern as she sinks after being torpedoed, about 1917–18. She is listing to starboard, awash fore and aft. Her single gun, mounted at the stern, was the standard self-defence for a merchantman of the First World War.
(© Charles Pulman collection)

vicinity. The remains of the *Corsican Prince* have to date not been definitively identified in terms of a named bell or other unique artefact, although the present site contains timber, consistent with her known cargo. A number of different candidates for this vessel have been proposed over the years.[151] The first candidate for the *Corsican Prince* is now considered to be the possible remains of the collier *Membland*, which disappeared between the Humber and the Tyne in 1915.[152] The site now believed to be the *Corsican Prince* was formerly suggested as the remains of yet another collier, the *Lanthorn*, dispatched by a torpedo in May 1917.[153] In the same way, the remains of the *Saint Ninian* were formerly attributed to a site now definitively identified from her bell as the *London*, located 4 miles east-north-east of Whitby, and torpedoed on 23 June 1918, en route from Methil for London with jute, coal and a general cargo; the site of the *London* is within a mile or so of the site where the *Saint Ninian* was reported to have gone down.[154] Like the site of the *Corsican Prince*, the remains now thought to represent the wreck of the *Saint Ninian* had originally been assigned a different identity, again that of a collier lost in the same area – the remains of the *Moorlands*.[155]

This, therefore, is a landscape of war characterised by understandable confusion at the time and subsequently, and only recently, becoming more fully understood generally through diver trips. Divers who make a thorough visual inspection of distinctive features or report to the authorities items unique to a particular wreck, such as maker's plates or a bell, will often prompt not only a reattribution of that site, but as a consequence the further reattribution of other sites in the area (for example, tracking down any alternative locations for a former candidate for a shipwreck site). In this way it can be seen to be not at all unusual for a single item brought up and declared to the Receiver of Wreck to prompt the revision of up to 20 further wreck sites by both English Heritage and the UKHO, who chart the wrecks, illustrating the importance of close liaison between all three bodies.

This particular group of wrecks, closely resembling one another, is also a symbol of the pressure exerted by the U-boat campaign upon the coal trade. Returning to the events of February 1917, by 8 February, another U-boat, the *UC-39*, was also now operating in similar territory to *UB-34*, off the southern Yorkshire coastline. The previous day she had dispatched the Norwegian *Hans Kinck* near the Noord Hinder light vessel off the Dutch coast. On the 8th her first victim was the British *Hanna Larsen*, sunk 20 miles east of Spurn Head.[156] Ironically, as her name might suggest, the *Hanna Larsen* had originally been a German ship: on the outbreak of hostilities she was detained as a prize vessel at Southampton. Along with a number of her compatriots also impounded in British ports on the declaration of war, in 1915 she was put into the service of the East Coast coal trade. This was intended to ease the 'short supply of tonnage, the delays in port, and the consequent difficulty of getting coals into London', with some utility companies reporting that they had only 10 days' stockpiles of coal remaining.[157]

The master and another member of the *Hanna Larsen*'s crew were taken prisoner and *UC-39* then moved on to her next victim, the Norwegian *Ida*.[158] As with so many wartime incidents, the sequence of events as they afterwards unfolded is not wholly clear: *UC-39* may have been disturbed by HMS *Thrasher* in the act of attacking the *Ida* or another vessel in a position reported as 15 miles south-east of Flamborough Head. According to *UC-39*'s crew, they had despatched the *Ida* and were attacking another ship, the *Hornsey*, when *Thrasher* intervened, but *Thrasher*'s intervention appears to have saved *Hornsey* from going the same way as *Hanna Larsen* and *Ida*.[159] Other versions of the event state instead that *Thrasher* intervened during the attack on the *Ida*. A wreck has been located in the approximate position given at the time of loss of the *Ida*, but at the time of writing nothing has come to light to confirm the identity of the remains at this position.

UC-39 attempted to dive, but a depth charge from *Thrasher* disabled her sufficiently to blow away the engine room hatch lid, causing her to fill with water. As she was forced to surface, *Thrasher* began shelling her, unaware of the British prisoners aboard. A human detail, perhaps romanticised, emerges in accounts of the *Hanna Larsen*'s master being forced to wave a white handkerchief to attract attention and avoid being killed with his captors. He and the chief engineer were undoubtedly in great peril of either going down with the listing submarine, or of being shot by what was, from their point of view, 'friendly fire'. Fortunately both men were picked up, along with the surviving crew of *UC-39*, by the *Thrasher*. *UC-39* sank in a position 8.5 miles south-east of Flamborough Head, her propeller now being on display in Bridlington Harbour Museum (the serial number on the propeller confirms the identity of the remains at this site).[160]

In several other respects the coal trade changed. Exports to Norway and Denmark also began to rise after the declaration of hostilities, since the war cut them off from German supplies: the Scandinavians were to be crucial to the continuing battle to get coal supplies through the North Sea minefields to London. They were at home in North Sea conditions and were a well-established and significant presence on the east coast, as illustrated by their appearance in the incidents discussed above: Norwegian *Gottfried* and Danish *Gaea* in 1914, and Norwegian *Ida* in 1917. The annual gift of a Christmas tree from Oslo to Trafalgar Square in London has its origins in Norwegian gratitude for British support of occupied Norway during the Second World War, but the wartime links between the two countries go back to the First World War. Indeed, Britain had great cause to be grateful to the many Norwegian seamen who risked their lives for British coal (Fig 2.21), though their involvement came about as much because of British pressure as through growing anti-German sentiment in Norway. The result was that Norway became Britain's 'Neutral Ally'.[161]

The net losses of shipping to the sustained assault on merchant vessels outstripped the combined production of the British shipyards of Belfast, Glasgow, Liverpool, Shields and Sunderland. As if this were not bad enough, the difficulty of obtaining raw materials for shipbuilding under war conditions, exacerbated by the lack of a convoy system until 1917, meant that Britain had to look elsewhere for replacement ships. The Scandinavian shipping trade looked likely to provide one solution (concrete ships, using less conventional raw materials, were another such solution to this pressing need).[162] On the other side of the equation, despite their well-publicised neutrality, Norwegian ships were also being lost to such an extent that in 1916 the Norges *Rede-forbund* (Norwegian Shipowners' Association) petitioned the Admiralty for a solution, since they had continued to trade with both sides since the outbreak of war. Norwegian neutrality extended to finding markets for their fish in Germany, to which the British authorities took great exception, and which was solved by the British paying more for the fish and by placing a coal blockade on Norway. However, the Germans targeted Norwegian ships with their torpedoes for continuing to trade with Britain. Norway lodged repeated official protests and the sufferings of her seamen caused great sympathy and outrage in the rest of the world, but sinkings of Norwegian ships continued. As the *New York Times* commented towards the end of the war regarding the sinking of the Norwegian barque *Eglinton*:

> In the interest of her mercantile marine, Germany has long made a practice of sinking neutral ships. To the ships and sailors of Norway she has given

particular attention … Without notice, the submarine opens fire on the unprotected bark, shoots away the rigging and sails, breaks the tackle of a lifeboat which the sailors are lowering … They succeed in getting a raft into the water … The sea is choppy, the wind is high. The submarine cruises around the raft and her commander watches the nine hapless sailors. He decides, evidently, that the conditions of wind and water will probably make the sinking 'traceless' without any more bother on his part … Delirious, and just on the edge of death, after drifting nine days on the raft, the sole survivor is picked up by a patrol.[163]

The British were at first reluctant to institute convoys for friendly – but neutral – Norway: however, to put this into context, British merchantmen at this stage of the war were also unprotected by escort or convoy. In any case joining a convoy gave neutrals little protection, since by doing so they were *de facto* perceived to have aligned themselves with the escorting power.

These continuing sinkings and the resumption of unrestricted submarine warfare by Germany in 1917 in an area completely surrounding Great

Fig 2.21
Minebøssen (*'Mine Weapons'*), Sofus Madsen, 1921. Quayside memorial in Bergen to the Norwegian seamen who died in the First World War. The bronze relief by the Bergen-born sculptor Sofus Madsen depicts a drowned sailor and is surmounted by a First World War sea mine, which originally acted as a collection box. It represents the common heritage of the North Sea coasts in war and in peace, for in Britain to this day sea mines are reused as collecting boxes for the Shipwrecked Mariners' Society.
(© Andrew Wyngard)

Britain, and reaching up to the Norwegian coast, tipped Norway into becoming the 'neutral ally'. With a proper convoy system Britain could protect her shipping and take neutrals under her protection, favouring the new arrangements which were now being made. In general terms, the Scandinavian countries were suffering from the German blockade of the North Sea. Norway, lacking mainland coal reserves, and suffering from a severe winter,[164] and Denmark, surrounded by the sea, her sole land border with belligerent Germany, were respectively in need of fuel and foodstuffs. The loan of Scandinavian vessels to Britain in return for coal and food exports (250,000 tons of coal monthly to Norway, for example) under what was termed the 'Tonnage Agreement' thus benefited both parties.[165] Britain gained extra ships and guaranteed overseas markets, with the extra cost of underwriting the war risk insurance: official statistics for Danish losses are particularly detailed and show that there was a war risks insurance scheme for Danish ships administered wholly or partly by British underwriters.[166] These official loans were in addition to the regular charter of Norwegian ships for the domestic and French coal markets which had risen sharply since the beginning of the war. In total just over 250 Norwegian vessels were to be lost in English waters during the course of the war, and 43 Danish, almost equally split between the North Sea domestic and Channel overseas routes. Many chartered or 'requisitioned' Norwegian vessels had, in any case, been built as colliers and seem to have reverted to their former roles: the Norwegian *Borgund I* and *Barmston* had originally been colliers belonging to Newcastle and Sunderland, respectively.[167]

As the owners of the British trawler fleets had done, by making over their vessels to the British shipping controller, a number of Scandinavian

shipowners, whether owners of single ships or magnates with large fleets, specialists in modern steamships or in sailing vessels, sent their ships over into British service. Among them were names which remain familiar to the British public in the 21st century, although in slightly different contexts. One major Norwegian contributor was the company of Fred. Olsen (Fig 2.22), now best known as a cruise line, but the parent firm also continues to operate an international cargo arm, which in the early 20th century was their principal business. Fred. Olsen were to lose just over one-half their fleet of 44 ships during the war, 12 of which went down in English waters.[168] A major Danish contributor to the fleet assembled by the Shipping Controller was Det Forenede Dampskibsselskab (the United Steamship Company, the ferry line better known today by its acronym DFDS).[169] DFDS lost four ships in English waters during the war, although only one of these was under the control of the Shipping Controller at the time, the *Algarve*, lost 15 miles west-south-west of Portland, Dorset, while returning in ballast to Swansea from Rouen.[170] She was operating on a known colliery route and was almost certainly returning to pick up more coal.

Under the Shipping Controller, all British mercantile ships were nationalised in all but name, and their operations co-ordinated and streamlined to keep up the momentum of trade. They supplied civilians at home and troops abroad, and distributed raw materials, finished goods, and vital foodstuffs between allies and trading partners. The adopted Scandinavian ships naturally came within the shipping controller's remit, and like their British counterparts were placed in the hands of British fleet managers to become part of this 'national' fleet. In a clear signal, however, that the change

Fig 2.22
Bamse is seen in the safety of an unidentified but crowded harbour during the First World War. As was, and remains, standard, she displays the house flag of her owners, the Fred. Olsen line, on her funnel. The desperate measures adopted by Norway to advertise her neutral status to enemy periscopes can be seen all over the vessel: Bamse's name and nationality in large white letters amidships, flanked by two Norwegian flags, while another Norwegian flag is painted aft. A painting of Bør shows a similar protective scheme, but with an extra national flag forward. Bamse was requisitioned by the British Shipping Controller in 1917, so the photograph is likely to have been taken around 1916. She was torpedoed under the British flag while en route from Rouen for Swansea in ballast in 1918 to pick up a cargo of coal. (© and by kind permission of Fred. Olsen and Co.)

of control was not intended to be permanent, their Norwegian or Danish names and their original crews, although supplemented by British crewmen, masters and/or gunners, were retained, with the intention of reverting to their original ownership on the cessation of hostilities.

Otherwise, for the duration of the war, these vessels were regarded as British to all intents and purposes: they appeared in the official publication *British Vessels Lost at Sea 1914–18* and were listed as British in *Lloyd's War Losses of the First World War*, a handwritten register of all British, Allied and neutral losses of mercantile vessels to submarines, mines and battleships. In effect, the Norwegian presence in the British mercantile fleet was a forerunner both of the *Nortraships* (the Norwegian Shipping and Trade Mission) which administered the Norwegian fleet from Allied and neutral ports in the Allied cause after the fall of Norway in 1940, and of the Lend-Lease agreement between the United States and Britain during the Second World War.

Norwegian ships were diverted away from their traditional North Sea routes on which they had voyaged early in the war, towards 'less exposed routes', hence their increasing presence on the Wales to Normandy route from 1917 onwards,[171] which suited both the increasingly important export trade to France and the need to 'spread the risk' among Britain's coal ports. Even if the 'less exposed' Channel route was more favourable for the Norwegians, it nevertheless proved a graveyard for Fred. Olsen ships: in March 1918 *Borgå* sank off Dorset after being torpedoed by *U-55*, while bound from Swansea for Rouen with coal; *Bamse* was torpedoed 6 weeks later on the same route by *UB-80*. In August 1918, *Bretagne* was sunk by a collision off Hope's Nose, south Devon, rather than being a victim of enemy action.[172] Other Fred. Olsen ships were either lost in British service outside English territorial waters (and thus outside the remit of this book) or had been lost in English waters carrying British cargoes earlier in the war while still flying the Norwegian flag: among the latter group were *Bob*, *Bonheur*, *Bør*, *Borgny*, *Borgsten*, *Boston*, *Brabant* and *Brisk*.[173]

If, at the beginning of the war, the indiscriminate way in which seamines struck at neutrals and civilian vessels caused widespread shock and outrage, the end of the war showed that seamines could have unexpected repercussions well beyond the cessation of hostilities. Today we are familiar with the effects of landmines persisting well after the conflicts in which they have been indiscriminately sown: for example, after decades of civil war in Angola and during the Falklands War of 1982. The same effects were known at sea after both World Wars: inevitably some mines escaped sweeping after the cessation of hostilities, claiming victims until some years after both conflicts. Lloyd's records show that 174 ships were lost to mines up to 1925 despite the best efforts of the 'International Mine Clearance Committee' which issued regular updated 'Mine Notices to Mariners'.[174] Fred. Olsen's *Bonheur* was one of the unlucky vessels so lost on 23 December 1918: a new motorised vessel, she was bound from Oslo to Hull and on to South America in a resumption of peacetime trade when she was struck by a mine between 12 and 23 miles off the Northumberland coast.[175] Likewise the trawler *Strathord*, ironically a minesweeper during the conflict, was lost to a mine off Yorkshire in 1920, one of the last victims of the 'Scarborough minefield'.[176]

This section has been largely, but not wholly, concerned with the war in the North Sea. All three sets of stories, the contributions of the trawlers, colliers and the Scandinavian vessels to the war, are very little known outside their particular communities, and with the passage of time have become even less so, but they each formed an important link in the chain which ultimately led to Allied victory. In the North Sea a mercantile fleet of diverse composition was pitted against a common enemy, the U-boat, in a counterpoint to the single clash of two mighty navies at Jutland in 1916: it was a long-running battle which ranged the length and breadth of the North Sea, and beyond, fought by ships whose primary peacetime role was very different. The minelaying campaign similarly extended the boundaries of marine warfare, beyond national territorial limits, striking at belligerents and neutrals, civilian merchant ships and warships without distinction, and even extended the war at sea beyond the formal cessation of hostilities. In fighting back, the British also extended the bounds of what was possible, by finding new and imaginative uses for civilian ships to supplement both their naval and mercantile fleets and to prevent their trade and their civilian population from being starved out by the enemy. The end result was a North Sea charted as 'littered with wrecks' (Fig 2.23) for many years afterwards, the marine equivalent of the vast rows of headstones commemorating the dead of 'Flanders fields'.

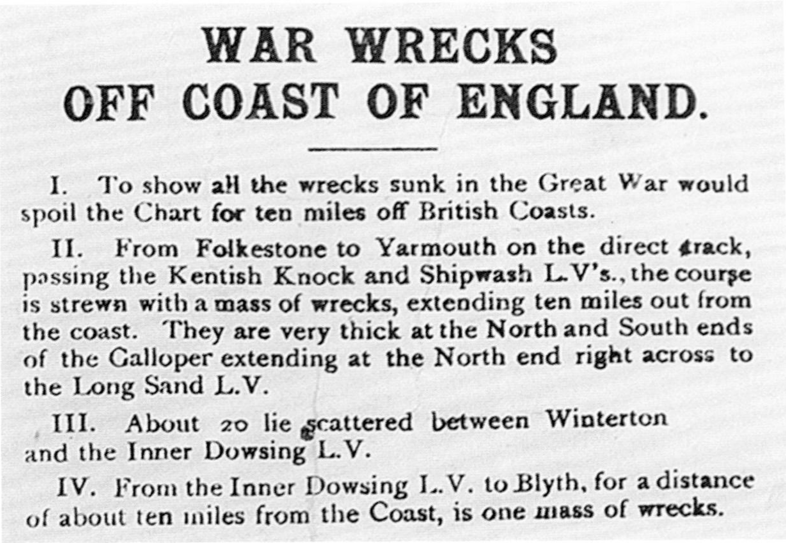

WAR WRECKS OFF COAST OF ENGLAND.

I. To show all the wrecks sunk in the Great War would spoil the Chart for ten miles off British Coasts.

II. From Folkestone to Yarmouth on the direct track, passing the Kentish Knock and Shipwash L.V's., the course is strewn with a mass of wrecks, extending ten miles out from the coast. They are very thick at the North and South ends of the Galloper extending at the North end right across to the Long Sand L.V.

III. About 20 lie scattered between Winterton and the Inner Dowsing L.V.

IV. From the Inner Dowsing L.V. to Blyth, for a distance of about ten miles from the Coast, is one mass of wrecks.

Fig 2.23
Detail from fishing chart published in 1938 showing the continuing socio-economic impact on fishermen, who were in danger of losing their increasingly sophisticated trawl gear on First World War wrecks. The description 'for ten miles off British coasts' tallies closely with the modus operandi of minelayers and U-boats, operating on the convoy routes and in inshore waters. (Close's Fishermen's Chart of the North Sea, compiled by A Close, London, corrected to Nov. 1938 by kind permission of Octopus Publishing. Photograph courtesy of the United Kingdom Hydrographic Office)

The *War Knight*: a tragedy of war

The landscape of war is affected by the strategic and operational decisions taken in the light of events in the vicinity. Thus an attack on a single vessel cannot be seen in isolation but as part of a sequence of events taking place in a wider theatre of war, and even accidents at sea could often be directly attributable to wartime conditions: all these factors combined to magnify the tragedy of the *War Knight* during the First World War.

The story of this ill-fated vessel taps into all aspects of the war at sea, beginning with her name, a reflection of the conditions under which she was built and in which she was designed to operate. British mercantile ships with the prefix *War* were Standard Ships built to the same design for the Shipping Controller under the Emergency Shipbuilding Programme, to counteract heavy maritime losses. Effectively they were products of wartime exigencies. A number of these vessels, like the *War Knight*, were in turn to add to the grim statistics, following to the bottom the ships they were designed to replace.[177]

In the early hours of 24 March 1918 the *War Knight* was proceeding in convoy HN53 off the Channel coast, en route from Philadelphia to London (Fig 2.24). The convoy comprised 16 merchantmen, with an escort of 7 British warships, 6 destroyers, including HMS *Garland*, *Pasley* and *Syringa*, and a sloop.[178] It was an international contingent, mostly American and British ships, with one French refrigerator ship and a Norwegian ship requisitioned for Britain

virtually on the stocks at Sunderland; she nevertheless retained her planned Norwegian name, the *Mirlo*. The merchantmen were conventional cargo vessels and oilers or tankers (terms used interchangeably in those days) with crucial supplies of food and fuel oil. The *War Knight* was one of these oilers, laden with naphtha, another, the American *O B Jennings*, with benzine. The convoy was proceeding in zig-zag formation, a synchronised movement of ships at regular intervals across their main heading to make it difficult for enemy torpedoes to find their mark. They were nevertheless all aiming for their appointed rendezvous off St Catherine's Point on the southern coast of the Isle of Wight, when a new escort would take over.

In order to fully understand the wreck, the sequence of events from the early evening of the 23rd should be taken into account, for until that point the entire convoy had proceeded on its long voyage, disturbed only by the sea, and not the war. The convoy had had a 'rough and exciting voyage, which had set the nerves of our crew on edge' according to an officer of the *O B Jennings*.[179] Entering the Channel, however, things changed: and as they heard *Chattahoochee* and *Madame Midas* being torpedoed in the western Channel early on the 23rd, the convoy's nervousness increased. From 1800 or 1830 – itself a sign of the incipient confusion – no two survivors' accounts agree in all points, which played a major part in the tragedy about to unfold.

Around this time the ships then altered their course slightly more to the starboard than planned, in order to keep clear of mines to their port flank: HMS *New Dawn*, a requisitioned British drifter, had already fallen victim to this minefield 3.5 miles south-south-west of the Needles earlier the same day.[180] At 2300 the convoy returned to a course bearing 'N 71° E', but the escorts were further unnerved by hearing a distress call some distance south-east at 2354. It was identified by Commander Blackwood of HMS *Syringa* as proceeding from the *Seguya*, and by Lt Fegan of HMS *Garland* as the *Segoya* (in fact the *Sequoya*, a British tanker torpedoed en route from Rouen for Avonmouth in ballast: she was, however, only damaged and managed to make her own way to Southampton for repairs).[181] At 0030 a suspected torpedo flash was seen much closer south-east, followed by another distress call in French 10 or 20 minutes later, identified as coming from the French

destroyer *Enseign Roux*. (This call remains unexplained, since the *Enseign Roux* seems not to have been attacked.) The convoy then remained on a north-north-east bearing until the decision was taken at 0200 to change course.

Wartime conditions naturally hampered the change of course. Convoys zig-zagged at prearranged intervals of differing lengths, in order to further confuse the enemy, thereby obviating the need for signalling and ensuring that the group kept good order on the same course: a form of stately synchronised swimming. Though the merchants naturally took orders from their escorts, one was always selected to act as 'Commodore', guiding the rest. They kept their station and executed any movements in relation to the Commodore, which, in this case, was the *Mirlo*. Any other change of course required signalling, which was difficult since both lights and wireless telegraphy would give away their position by sight or sound to the U-boats now presumed to be prowling in the vicinity after the flashes and noises heard to the south-east.

At 0200 therefore HMS *Syringa* ordered the other escorts on the flanks to tell the convoy to alter course 'S 82° E' at 0215, by the time-consuming use of a loudhailer. Visibility was difficult: only minimal lighting was permitted at night, and there was a slight haze. As Lt Fegan of HMS *Garland* acknowledged, the dazzle camouflage destined to prevent the enemy from seeing a ship's true outline and thus get an accurate position fix on her bearing to torpedo her, also made it difficult for ships in company

to discern each other. The group was already losing its cohesion: Lt Fegan reported that they appeared to be 'getting straggled and the columns mixed up together'. The escorts were now attempting to round up their remaining charges, ordering them to 'close the Commodore', keep their station in closer proximity to the Commodore ship, an instruction which was to prove crucial as events unfolded. As the Cunarder *Valacia* challenged HMS *Garland*, demanding to know her identity before obeying orders, she further delayed the message being passed on among the rest of the convoy.

To the *Garland*'s horror, at 0230 two of the centre oilers, the *Aungban* and the *O B Jennings*, were seen to be leading other vessels north-west rather than on a south-easterly course, as ordered. The master of the *O B Jennings* explained afterwards that he was told to stop zig-zagging pending further orders from the Commodore, but the *Mirlo*, notwithstanding her capacity as Commodore, had already disappeared. At 0200 he was then given orders to steer north-west to close the Commodore. The ships steering north-west were bearing down on HMS *Garland*, who had to starboard her helm to avoid being run down before she could catch up with the leading oiler.

She was too late: disaster struck off the Isle of Wight. The *O B Jennings* and the *Aungban*, on the starboard flank, turning north-west, blew two warning blasts as the *Kia Ora* and the *War Knight*, on the port flank, turned south-east, the *War Knight* also signalling a warning. The *O B Jennings* attempted to alter her course further

Fig 2.24
A rare aerial photograph taken in 1917 or 1918 of a large mercantile convoy, approximately 30-strong, with two or three other vessels in the distance in the process, perhaps, of joining or leaving the convoy, or simply happening to be sailing in the same direction. The potential for collision is also apparent in the close formation within the centre of the convoy. Some of the leading vessels, like those in the War Knight*'s convoy, are in dazzle camouflage. (© Charles Pulman collection)*

westward to port, while those on board the *War Knight* attempted to turn to starboard, although there were differing eyewitness descriptions of the two ships' movements. Collision between the two oilers was now inevitable, and *War Knight* struck the *O B Jennings* 'practically at right-angles abreast the bridge, starboard side.' Equally inevitably, there was a devastating explosion. Lt Fegan's sober account stated that the cargo of benzine in *O B Jennings'* No. 2 hold caught alight and:

> the burning oil running out on the wake completely surrounded the *War Knight*, and within 15 seconds the latter was ablaze fore and aft. Unfortunately she had no weigh left to carry her clear of the oil pool or more lives might have been saved.

The officer from *O B Jennings* quoted in the *New York Times* attributed the disaster first to the 'exceptionally rough trip' then to a clash of steel on steel:

> As a result, the churning of the bulk oil we carried had created a tremendous amount of gas. When the *War Knight* hit us there was an instant explosion, caused no doubt by a spark from the impact of the steel setting the gas on fire. Immediately there was a roar of flame spouting out of the hole in the *O B Jennings*'s side, which all but enveloped the Britisher. I learned afterwards that thirty-six of her crew of about fifty were on deck at the time, and they must have been almost instantly incinerated.

Such was the intensity of the flames that the few survivors from the *War Knight* owed their lives to taking shelter in an alleyway where the flames could not engulf them, according to one survivor. Statements were taken in hospital before some of these survivors succumbed to their burns. The two burning vessels were a danger to the rest of the convoy, not just because approaching them was hazardous, but also because they illuminated the other ships sufficiently to expose them to the enemy submarine they believed to be in the vicinity, and which they now believed had torpedoed one of their group. It took a while for the rest of the convoy to realise that they had witnessed an accident rather than an act of war, with one of the escorts, HMS *Pasley*, making preparations to depth-charge the supposed enemy. A gunner from HMS *Oberon* only realised that there were two ships on fire as they neared the stricken vessels: the fireball had seemed to him to coalesce into a single ship. All the remaining merchantmen 'with one accord

increased to full speed. It appeared to be a hopeless task to get them together again', according to Commander Blackwood of HMS *Syringa*. The *New York Times* again took up the story:

> We drifted apart and one of the destroyers by which we were convoyed managed to get a line to her and was towing her *toward*[182] the beach, when in some manner the burning ship drifted onto a mine field and she blew up. The case oil with which she was loaded took fire and completed her destruction. We had our own safety to look after. The burning naphtha had poured out into the sea, and it would have been folly to launch lifeboats. It was then that the destroyers showed their resourcefulness, for they dashed through the burning oil, bumped along side of us and we jumped to their decks in safety. We lost only one man, a seaman named Shea, who was either burned, or fell overboard and drowned. The *O B Jennings*, being a menace to other ships, the destroyers proceeded to sink her, which they did with a number of shots fired into her hold. She settled until her decks were level with the water, extinguishing the flames, and afterward she was taken in tow and beached. She probably is not a total loss.

It seems, then, that the *War Knight* strayed, as the *New Dawn* had, into the very same minefield laid by *UC-17* that the whole convoy was so desperately trying to avoid. This was not quite the end, however, for either *O B Jennings* or the *War Knight*. *O B Jennings* was raised and repaired, only to be torpedoed on 4 August 1918 en route from Plymouth for Newport News. *War Knight* was towed into Watcombe Bay, where she was also scuttled by gunfire (Figs 2.25 and 2.26).

In one respect the fate of the *War Knight* is unusual. Many ships, of course, often undergo more than one cause of loss, but to be lost under this particular combination of circumstances is exceptional: collision and fire from another vessel's cargo; an explosion of her own cargo; a further explosion in striking a mine; and being scuttled by deliberate friendly fire. The mine was a direct war cause, but there were other 'war risk' factors in play. This caused some problems with insurers, the shipping managers, Furness, Withy and Co., pointing out that their vessel was a war loss, since the lack of lights and the impracticality of oilers emptying their gas collecting chambers while in convoy was a direct result of the war situation. They sued the Standard Oil Company, owners of *O B Jennings*, for US$5m damages, although the Admiralty Court found them not responsible for the loss.[183] However, the owners of *Ardgantock*, a cargo vessel requisitioned to carry a government cargo of navigational buoys (itself intended for war operations) which was involved in a collision with HMS *Tartar*, successfully claimed the loss on their vessel as a war risk, since the collision was directly attributable to Admiralty orders to navigate without lights and to the *Tartar*'s direct engagement on patrol, hunting a submarine known to be active in the area, at the time.[184]

In other respects, the loss of the *War Knight* is a very typical event for the First World War, particularly this phase of the war, with the institution of the convoy system in 1917 and the almost simultaneous introduction of dazzle painting. The number of events contributing to the loss mark the *War Knight* out as more than a 'dot' joined to other dots in a landscape of war. The very scale of the First World War meant that convoy passed convoy at sea, criss-crossing one another with men, munitions and supplies, and that incidents in one convoy were witnessed or heard by other convoys, affecting the decisions taken for the survival of their own group. That night there was also one further event in a different convoy which added to the frantic chaos and made the work of the escorts more difficult: another collision was heard to the

Fig 2.25
Given the vicissitudes of a prolonged wrecking event, and the tides and storms of the subsequent 90 years, today War Knight *is understandably a well-broken wreck. (© and by kind permission of Michael Pitts)*

Fig 2.26
In this view the distinctive spirals of the War Knight's *steam turbine engine are visible, an innovation for mercantile vessels brought about by the War Standard design. (© and by kind permission of Michael Pitts)*

Table 2.1
First World War collisions resulting in vessel losses compared with those in peacetime 1913 and 1919

Year	Collisions with unknown vessels	Collisions in convoy (1917/18 only)	All other collisions
1913	1		27
1914	1		31
1915	3		38
1916	5		32
1917	5	1	57
1918	8	5	60
1919	1		13

north-east at 0427. This was also a collision in convoy, this time between the cargo vessel *Petingaudet* and the troopship *Warilda*. The outcome of that incident was far happier, with neither ship being lost: both were repaired, although *Warilda* would also be lost later in the war.[185]

In general, collisions regularly caused peacetime losses, particularly at 'pinch points' in busy major rivers such as the Thames, Humber and Mersey, and such losses continued regardless during the war. However, there is a sharp spike for the 'convoy years' of 1917 and 1918, followed by a dramatic fall on the return of peace. As can be seen from Table 2.1, collisions were almost inevitable given the proximity of the vessels travelling together. However, collisions out of convoy also occurred under the constraints of using minimal lighting, as shown by the collision between *M Lloyd Morris* and *Møhlenpris* in January 1917, blamed on the lights of the former being 'very low, because it was the experience on that evening that more than one ship was sailing without any lights because of the submarine danger'.[186] On that occasion the *M Lloyd Morris* was the victim. The *Møhlenpris* would be lost to a torpedo three months later: like the *O B Jennings* and the *Warilda* she demonstrates another feature of the First World War at sea, the fact that many ships were involved in more than one incident. Moreover, under these circumstances, the same figure also illustrates a surge in the cases where the identity of the colliding vessel was unknown at the time of the incident and had to be worked out from damage reports or records of missing ships.

The *War Knight*'s position of loss was itself influenced by wartime conditions, being at a key point in the English Channel where one escorting group handed over a convoy to the next escort in the chain stationed off St Catherine's Point, which was the intended rendezvous for her

convoy. In that respect the disastrous collision between the *Darro* and the *Mendi*,[187] resulting in heavy loss of life from troops of the South African Native Labour Corps aboard the *Mendi*, which now lies some 6 miles off St Catherine's, has much in common with the *War Knight*. This was also a collision in convoy at a strategic 'pinch point' in the Channel, in foggy conditions accompanied by a blackout, with similarly tragic consequences. Table 2.2 illustrates an even greater spike in losses attributable to all causes – war or otherwise – this time in relation to geographic location, off the Isle of Wight, more or less at the mid-point of the English Channel. Here Atlantic convoys criss-crossed one another, eastbound ships peeling off for their respective English or French destinations, westbound ships returning to the United States for cargo or troops, while hospital ships, troopships, supply ships and colliers made rapid, but no less deadly or dangerous, runs north-south across the Channel.

A single loss such as that of the *War Knight* symbolises a landscape of war in which every sound and movement was a potential threat, a psychological environment in which the physical marine landscape was full of unseen danger. Physically, every single operational strategy made a contribution to the loss of *War Knight*: the dazzle camouflage; the zig-zagging; the convoy system; the minimal lighting and wireless contact. All this was recognised in the subsequent enquiry, as was the psychological stress, but the stress can be seen, perhaps, to have played a greater part in the loss than was acknowledged at the time.

The combat stress engendered by the nightmare of the trenches in the First World War is well known: but the pressures on the men of the mercantile navy were enormous. Nervous and on edge, the conduct of those on board all the vessels in company caused delay and suspicion, indecision and incomprehension, all

Table 2.2
First World War losses off the Isle of Wight compared with peacetime losses 1913 and 1919

Year	Number of ships lost
1913	1
1914	3
1915	4
1916	11
1917	34
1918	31
1919	2

affecting the decisions taken that night and all of which contributed to the scale of the accident and its consequences. The mutual protection of convoy and the reassurance of dazzle painting, wartime initiatives which were instituted together, turned out in this case to be counter-productive. From a 21st-century perspective, we might also question the wisdom of grouping together tankers in a single convoy, yet this was a wartime necessity in terms of mutual protection and pushing through necessary supplies. As a decision it was ultimately fatal.

Under false colours

The U-boats of the First World War did not have things all their own way: occasionally the hunters became the hunted, as the captains and crews of the Q-ships pitted their wits against the U-boat crews. Ships that were not what they seemed countered the peril which lurked unseen beneath the waves: the 'rag-tag and bobtail' of the seas.[188] The small size of fishing vessels, colliers, tramp steamers and even sailing vessels, gave them their advantage in this deception. Initially they were a less attractive torpedo target, giving them a potentially higher capacity for survival after being attacked, for torpedoes were generally not 'wasted' on smaller vessels or sailing vessels where shelling or gunfire were capable of sinking the victim. The Q-ships, officially known as 'Special Service Ships', had two secret weapons: first, literally, secret guns hidden behind a partially collapsible structure which presented to all external appearances the superstructure or deck cargo of an otherwise conventional and unexceptionable merchantman (Fig 2.27); second, their holds were filled with cork or Canadian spruce deal for buoyancy in the event of being fired on, or torpedoed. The cargo was stowed carefully and bolted in so that it could not float out through any holes.

It took three months to refit the former conventional collier of 732 tons as HMS *Stock Force*.[189] The *modus operandi* of the Q-ship was to pose as a lone merchantman, taking a chance on a solo voyage without company or convoy, then, after attracting the attention of a U-boat, keeping up the pretence under gunfire, or worse. The crew had to hold their nerve, sending out a 'panic party' to keep up the deception by seeming to abandon the vessel. To this end only a certain number of the crew were ever

Fig 2.27
'Gun dropped': the hidden gun emerges from the hatch: note the cover structure and the dropped side.
(From Q-Boat Adventures, Harold Auten, VC, Herbert Jenkins, London, 1919: by kind permission of Hutchinson Books)

permitted to remain on view, in the dress of merchant seamen (Figs 2.28 and 2.29): extra numbers above with the normal complement of a tramp steamer would have aroused suspicion. If the worst happened all the crew were provided with a cover story that the extra men were the crew of a mined steamer who had been picked up and everyone had to learn the story off by heart so that no one would forget their 'lines' (Fig 2.30) and they were even required to use mercantile, not naval, jargon at all times. The 'panic party' was drilled and rehearsed to hold their nerve and run back and forth

gathering essentials such as food, to attract the attention of the submarine.

The moment the ship was struck by a torpedo proved the worth of the hidden deal cargo. It was there not only to help preserve the lives of the crew remaining aboard, but also to keep their ship afloat so that the U-boat would be lured towards the apparently abandoned vessel to pick up confidential papers and anything else of value, and bring her within firing range. This was the moment of difficulty, for the concealed guns could only be brought to bear in certain positions. Once the U-boat was within range,

Fig 2.28
Crew of Stock Force *in their naval uniform; many were former merchant seamen. Auten deliberately chose a black cook (back row, third from left) from the port of Bristol, since he wanted the Q-ship to conform as closely as possible to merchant ship norms. Auten knew he had found the right man when he discovered that the man had survived being torpedoed on three previous occasions.*
(From Q-Boat Adventures, *Harold Auten, VC, Herbert Jenkins, London, 1919: by kind permission of Hutchinson Books)*

Fig 2.29
The same crew dressed as merchant seamen, complete with dog: a cat was also on board Stock Force. *The crew had to play a role, and play it well: they not only had to look, but behave and talk, like merchant seamen.*
(From Q-Boat Adventures, *Harold Auten, VC, Herbert Jenkins, London, 1919: by kind permission of Hutchinson Books)*

however, the pretence was dropped, as were the false sides, and the apparently innocuous steamer would turn on her enemy, revealing her guns and running up the naval White Ensign in what would often be a duel to the death.

Q-ships entered the war from 1914, and first came to prominence after an incident involving the *Baralong* Q-ship in 1915, in which the commander shot dead survivors from a sinking U-boat, provoking German protests. The Allies considered the torpedoing of neutrals and undefended ships to be similarly indefensible, and continued the use of 'mystery ships' for the duration. Their numbers grew as the submarine threat intensified, but this increase in numbers did not lead to increasing success. As the war progressed, they lost the element of surprise: U-boats were more inclined to treat apparently abandoned steamers with greater circumspection.

Q-ship losses were therefore relatively high for the numbers of enemy submarines sunk,[190] even though they operated in all the naval theatres of war. They did, however, have a certain deterrent value that remains unquantifiable, since, of course, a prevented attack would leave no trace. Similarly, a torpedo against a Q-ship which could defend herself was one less against an Allied or neutral vessel which was, at best, defensively armed. During the war, the following Q-ships were lost off the coast of England: *Kent County*, a former drifter, off the Cross Sand, Norfolk, 1916; ex-mercantile *Penshurst*, in the Bristol Channel, 1917; trawler *Brown Mouse*, 1918; and collier *Stock Force*, 1918.[191] Others were lost in the North Sea, Atlantic and Mediterranean.

Stock Force was one of the most famous of these Q-ships, the subject of a book by her commander, Lt Commander Harold Auten, VC, and of a British 'docudrama' film of 1928. The film highlights the various strategies employed to counter the U-boat threat: escorted convoys, razzle-dazzle camouflage,[192] defensive minefields, and the new hydrophone technology, before introducing the Q-ships, the most audacious strategy of all. In some places genuine documentary footage of the First World War, such as a full convoy in razzle-dazzle, too difficult and costly to re-enact and the eventual surrender of surviving U-boats at Harwich at the end of the war, has been spliced with the filmed re-enactment.

The climax of the film centres on the events of 30 July, 1918, when a battle between *Stock Force* and a U-boat took place. By this time unrestricted submarine warfare was in place, so that the 'mystery ship' faced an even greater peril: *Stock Force* is identified as 'being the right size for a torpedo'.[193] In real life she was sighted approximately 25 miles off Start Point by a U-boat and the film dramatises the operations of a Q-ship from the moment the characteristic torpedo trail is shown ripping through the water towards the apparently lone collier. The dialogue flashes up: 'Get your panic party away. Tell 'em

Fig 2.30
The Board of Lies: part of the deadly play-acting aboard a Q-Ship involved being able to tell a consistent and plausible story to account for the greater numbers of crew than would be expected aboard a normal collier and to that end the crew had to commit the contents of this board to memory: the board on the left relates to the lost vessel, the one on the right the 'back-story' to their own ship. The cover story was that they had picked up the crew of a lost vessel, which was always mined, never torpedoed, for U-boats in contact with one another would attempt to verify the story of torpedoed vessels, and see who had claimed the 'kill', whereas, with German minefields known to lie in the approaches to the Bristol Channel at the position given on the board to the left, the story of a mined vessel was completely credible and less traceable. (From Q-Boat Adventures, Harold Auten, VC, Herbert Jenkins, London, 1919: by kind permission of Hutchinson Books)

to act their heads off.' The 'panic party' is seen lowering the boat and appearing to abandon ship, complete with the detail of a black cat being handed down into the boat, for the original *Stock Force* had indeed had a black cat aboard who survived the explosion. In the film the German submarine approaches cautiously, fearing a trap of the kind which was about to unfold, but lulled into security by her victim beginning to 'settle by the stern'.[194] The crew staying behind were reprising their roles of 10 years earlier, from the commander, played by Harold Auten himself, down to the gunners. After playing their part of merchant seamen for months on end, unsurprisingly they put on a convincing show both during the incident and on film. All are shown hiding, waiting for the U-boat to come within range: when she does, Auten commands his men to open fire from the hitherto hidden guns.

In the film, the enemy vessel is repeatedly fired upon, a hit upon her conning tower intercut with scenes of the crew in the rowing-boat cheering wildly upon a choppy sea, while a final blast to the bows of the vessel sends her to the bottom. Whether the original attacker was *U-98*, as originally identified, or *UB-80* as later suggested, she limped home to Germany disabled and was surrendered at the end of the war. The two vessels' respective fates have been swapped over and the demise of *Stock Force* is not shown. The facts were not allowed to get in the way of a good story: rather than being historically accurate, the *Stock Force* in the film symbolises all the Q-ships and their adventures, capturing the feel of the U-boat campaign and the counter-campaigns very well.[195] The crew were picked up by a torpedo boat. As Auten put it:

> A minute or so afterwards the poor little *Stock Force* sank to her last home. She had been torpedoed 27 miles from the shore, and it was particularly hard to have got her almost within sight of land – the shore was only eight miles away – and then to lose her.[196]

A site lying some 7 or so miles south-west of the Bolt Tail is now considered to be potentially the remains of the *Stock Force*, relatively close to Auten's own reading of his position when his ship sank.[197]

> [T]he torpedo had hit direct on the second water-tight bulkhead, forcing it clean the other side of the ship. The forward end of the bridge went entirely, and all I recollected was going up in the air, and coming down to find myself under the chart-table … The whole fore-deck was bent, the derricks were blown overboard, and up went an awful shower of flotation planks, unexploded 12-pounder shells and debris caused by the explosion. The lot came down again with an awful clatter.[198]

Auten describes a '40 foot hole in the little ship': her counter-attack on the U-boat was her own undoing, for the firing disturbed her trim, the water gained on them and the inevitable could no longer be delayed, despite their efforts.

In the film there may have been other factors at play besides artistic licence in showing the sinking of the submarine rather than the *Stock Force*. The ship playing the part of *Stock Force* was evidently a vessel hired for the occasion (some scenes appear to be studio shots). Only a certain number of vessels could be expended in the making of the film, and after so many war losses, it was clearly impractical to purchase and sink a collier to represent the *Stock Force*. As far as the U-boat was concerned, the surrender in 1918 was the key to the issues facing the film-makers: the surrendered submarines were either scrapped or had gone to the French navy by 1923,[199] so that a substitute was required. Fittingly, for a film whose subject was subterfuge and masquerade, the film makers obtained a coup in finding an acceptable stand-in for the various U-boats portrayed in the film. This was the obsolete Royal Navy submarine *H52*, seen principally in silhouette, where she could pass for a U-boat despite being much smaller, though her distinctive conning tower, characteristic of a British H-class submarine, was quite different from that of a U-boat.

H52 was sold out of service in November 1927. On 3 January 1928, she was shelled and sunk in a re-enactment of the *Stock Force*'s counter-attack on her U-boat attacker, approximately a mile west of the Eddystone, where she now remains, an extraordinary example of a ship sunk for entertainment purposes. A report on the wreck site points out that her bows are broken off with a debris scatter slightly detached from the main part of the vessel, consistent with the filmed explosion which sank her.[200] The story of the film *Q-ships*, then, embraces the evolution of new technologies which were almost exact contemporaries: submarines and films, seen at a point when both were becoming increasingly sophisticated. Developments in submarine technology had made *H52* obsolete, so that she was available for purchase and sacrificed for the demands of film-making, a novel form of the purchase and scrapping which was, and remains, the usual fate for a Royal Navy vessel at the end of her career.

H52 was not the only vessel expended in this way during the film, for a schooner was shattered to smithereens by explosives in March 1928, off the Bill of Portland, Dorset, in a re-enactment of the typical depredations of the U-boats against sailing vessels, such as the scuttling of the Norwegian barque *Falls of Afton* in 1917 off Wolf Rock.[201] This was the *Amy*,[202] shown under full sail, her hull brightly painted in monochrome stripes emphasising the sweep of her lines, as a paean to the last days of sail. Following two explosions in quick succession, after three previous failed attempts, a shot of an expanse of floating timber is clearly filmed from a boat making its way through the wreckage. This is likely to be the boat that took away the naval ratings and film crew who had laid the explosives: the last explosion was almost too successful and blazing timbers fell on their boat as they rowed away. Nevertheless the burning hull did not sink immediately and drifted for some hours until the destroyer *Salmon* sank her with shellfire.[203] In 1928 there was less concern for health and safety than there would be today, and there were no heritage preservation or protection concerns for such vessels despite the fact that the wreck record shows the dwindling stock of wooden sailing craft.[204] During the interwar period wooden sailing ships were in the minority of reported wrecks, with only 10 per cent being schooners.[205]

Understandably, the wreck site can be no more than the suspected site of the *Amy*, for very little remains at what is thought to be her last resting place. The loss of the *Amy* is the most extraordinary moment of an extraordinary film, in which the crew play themselves playing a role, and liberties are taken with the order of events (the *Stock Force* does not sink in the film although she was the real victim) though it is based on the recollections of those involved and the details down to amusing incidents included by Harold Auten in his book are not comic inventions on the part of the film-makers but based on real events, and stand-in vessels undergo a genuine wrecking process. There was only a short overlap between the age of sail and the age of film, particularly since the First World War itself had already accounted for the majority of the surviving sailing ships of this period, so that, at no other time in history has it been possible to film the end of a ship under full sail from start to finish. The *Amy* remains a unique wreck, recorded at a moment when the old world of the sailing vessel and the modern world of documentary film-making coincided.[206]

Dunkirk and D-Day

> Nevertheless, our thankfulness at the escape of our Army and so many men, whose loved ones have passed through an agonizing week, must not blind us to the fact that what has happened in France and Belgium is a colossal military disaster.
>
> Winston Churchill, 4 June 1940

> Our task in conjunction with the Merchant Navies of the United Nations, and supported by the Allied Air Forces, is to carry the Allied Expeditionary Force to the Continent, to establish it there in a secure bridgehead and to build it up and maintain it at a rate which will outmatch that of the enemy.
>
> Admiral Sir Bertram Ramsay, Allied Naval Commander-in-Chief, 31 May 1944

So far in this book we have looked at battle engagements and the sporadic and widespread nature of commerce raiding through the centuries, from privateers to the sudden attacks on ships in the First World War. There are two particular groups or sub-sets of Second World War wrecks which can be said to have something in common with both groups, but are nevertheless particularly distinct from both: like the first group, they are linked by a specific event, and like the second, they were subject to random attack. They were lost in two of the pivotal operations of the Second World War, 4 years apart: the first group were lost in May–June 1940, in Operation Dynamo, the evacuation of the British Expeditionary Force and other Allied troops from Dunkirk. The second event leading to multiple vessel losses was a flow in the reverse direction as the tide of the war turned and Operation Neptune, the assault phase of Operation Overlord began and the invasion force tasked with liberating Europe set out from the beaches of Britain. The date for the D-Day landings on the beaches of Normandy was set as 6th June 1944, and from then onwards the flow of ships and aircraft in support of the Normandy landings was constant. During both operations the principal losses were naturally on the French coast, respectively off Dunkirk and off the beaches of Normandy, and therefore outside the scope of this book but it serves as a reminder that maritime landscapes of war are no respecter of the political boundaries over which they were fought. However, losses did occur in English waters, homeward-bound, as the ships retreated from Dunkirk in 1940; and outward-bound, as they set out from the south coast in 1944.

The losses of late May and early June 1940 reflect the varied composition of the ships comprising the evacuation fleet, and include representatives of the famous 'little ships' of all kinds which supported the much larger vessels in taking off as many people as they could – pleasure boats, fishing vessels, lifeboats, ships' lifeboats and barges among them. Not all were British – 'little ships' (and larger vessels) from France, Belgium and the Netherlands also volunteered, while Norwegian and Polish cargo vessels and warships also participated in the evacuation, which was co-ordinated from Dover Castle (Fig 2.31). Every single vessel, whether warship or 'little ship', ran the gauntlet not only of the ever-present threat of mines and torpedoes, but also of enemy bombardment from the air and from the shore: added to the mix was the sheer crowding of this, the narrowest point

of the English Channel, with ships shuttling in both directions, providing conditions ripe for collision even without the attendant 'fog of war' in which the fleet found itself under attack from all directions – from above, below and on all sides. The Goodwin Sands, the most notorious hazard in English waters, blocked the way home. Numbers have regularly been placed as high as almost one-third of the fleet: for example, around 200 out of 693, not necessarily including all the smaller auxiliary vessels such as ships' boats and tenders.[207] Recent research suggests that the number of actual losses, not including auxiliaries, was lower, a view which can be borne out in the official statistics which suggest that approximately 65 British vessels, naval and mercantile, large and small, were lost in various locations in the English Channel.[208]

Surprisingly few ships were lost overall, or even in English waters, given the nature of the fleet. The numbers of 'little ships' involved might well have compounded the disaster of the retreat to Dunkirk: the threats of swamping, capsize, collision and friendly fire, were only too real. Many were completely unfamiliar with the waters of the Channel: the *Massey Shaw* fire tender, based on the River Thames, and the

Fig 2.31
Anti-Aircraft Operations Room, Wartime Tunnels, Dover Castle. With bombardment from shore batteries on the Calais side and enemy aircraft, minefields, the operations of E-boats and U-boats, the attacks on both shipping and aircraft, it was little wonder that the Straits of Dover became known as Hellfire Corner.
(DP093287)

cockle boats, known as 'bawleys' of Leigh-on-Sea and Southend-on-Sea had never even left the Thames before. The wooden bawleys in particular looked alarmingly vulnerable but were praised for their 'exemplary' conduct, running the gauntlet of constant enemy fire from all quarters. All but one of these bawleys, however, returned safely.[209] The little ships did have a number of advantages over the larger vessels: they were capable of manoeuvring close inshore where they were able to act as tenders to the larger vessels, and they were at less risk of setting off magnetic mines with their shallower draught, although this did not grant them immunity from that particular peril. Most of the British ships in the fleet built of iron or steel had already undergone a 'degaussing' programme to neutralise the threat posed by magnetic mines, but an emergency programme also took place to degauss as many other ships as possible. Charts were also rapidly printed up to assist the crews in navigating the sandbanks which littered the seas between Dunkirk and safety, in both French and British waters, although the burning fires and constant sound of bombardment were an obvious landmark.

There was also another major logistical problem for the fleet, the provision of safe swept channels, codenamed X, Y and Z (Fig 2.32), avoiding the known minefields. Wreck casualties in these already overcrowded and narrow

channels could not be permitted to obstruct or jeopardise an already precarious operation. *Brighton Belle*, a south coast paddle steamer and excursion vessel, had already been converted for war service when she was requisitioned for Dunkirk (Fig 2.33). On 28 May, she was under attack from above when she met danger from below, as she struck a portion of a wreck around the Gull Light buoy. Quite possibly this was the wreck of the *Brendonia*, which stranded in bad weather on 11 September 1939, or of *Bravore*, mined as recently as 24 April 1940, an extraordinary example of a wreck-on-wreck collision under the most unfortunate of circumstances.[210] Fortunately only one life was lost, as the crew and troops aboard were taken up by other vessels, but it certainly illustrates the point that natural hazards, and the accretions of

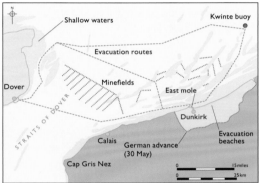
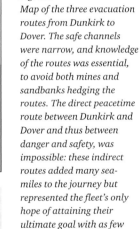

Fig 2.32
Map of the three evacuation routes from Dunkirk to Dover. The safe channels were narrow, and knowledge of the routes was essential, to avoid both mines and sandbanks hedging the routes. The direct peacetime route between Dunkirk and Dover and thus between danger and safety, was impossible: these indirect routes added many sea-miles to the journey but represented the fleet's only hope of attaining their ultimate goal with as few casualties as possible.

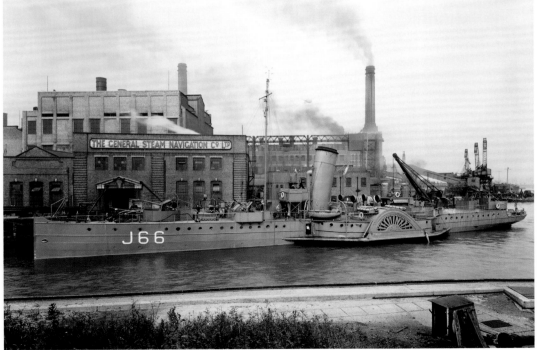

Fig 2.33
The paddle steamer
Plinlimmon (ex. Cambrai) *was hired by the Ministry of War Transport in 1939. She is shown here in battleship grey in 1940, perhaps taken just before or after her participation in the Dunkirk evacuation, with a full complement of anti-aircraft guns, and her naval pennant number of J66 prominently displayed. Like* Brighton Belle, *as a passenger paddler with a shallow draught, she was ideal for minesweeping duties. (CC80/00195)*

wrecks around them, do not cease to be lethal in time of war, but can compound the difficulties of navigating under extreme circumstances. However, the loss of the *Brighton Belle* was unique among the ships returning from Dunkirk in not being due to war causes.

One of the British 'little ships' lost in home waters was HMS *Amulree*, a pleasure yacht. As a steamer she was suitable for war service on harbour defence duties, and so, like most requisitioned vessels of both World Wars, was classed as an 'Admiralty Vessel' and qualified for the HMS prefix. Entries in official accounts were terse: 'sunk in collision, Dover Straits'. The real story emerged after the war: in the evening of 31 May she was ordered to turn back to nurse a crippled yacht, the *Ankh*, to Dover. Other damaged yachts attached themselves to HMS *Amulree* and *Ankh*. The only undamaged vessel of this group was now, effectively, their escort, yet, in the chaos, she would be the one to sink. As a victim of mistaken identity she foundered in the Gull Stream, west of the Goodwin Sands, after being rammed and sunk by a British destroyer, HMS *Vimy*, while *Ankh* arrived safely at Dover at 0815 on 1 June. *Vimy* was on high alert, having spotted a suspected U-boat lurking on the 31st, whereupon she 'commenced to hunt'. The commodore-in-chief at Sheerness expressed his ire at the unfortunate consequences of this 'friendly fire' in the restrained language of the time:

> a matter for regret that this vessel was diverted from the very valuable work which she was performing in towing out pontoons from the beaches, to carry out a seemingly minor administrative duty which indirectly resulted in her being rammed and sunk by a British destroyer in the Downs.[211]

HMS *Comfort* was another requisitioned ship, formerly a drifter, in service as a dan-layer (vessel used to lay 'dan' buoys marking swept channels, or, conversely, the extent of minefields). She was 'rammed and sunk by accident off Dover' which also masks the full extent of the incident. Having picked up survivors from the torpedoed destroyer HMS *Wakeful* off Dunkirk, while homeward-bound she rushed to the assistance of a second torpedoed destroyer, HMS *Grafton*, in the very early hours of 29 May, just after 0250. As she circled to pick up survivors she was mistaken by both the stricken vessel and HMS *Lydd* for the attacking E-boat, which was partially blamed on the fact that she was 'darkened' and so, by inference, her identity was unclear. Both opened fire before the *Lydd* rammed the supposed E-boat, sinking her at around 0307 that morning. As survivors attempted to get on board, they were repulsed by rifle fire under the impression that they formed an enemy boarding party, so that it was some time before the error was discovered, by which time all but five men of the combined *Comfort/Wakeful* complement had died, drowned or been gunned down. Only one man survived out of the *Comfort*, four from the *Wakeful*, including Commander R L Fisher, the captain of the *Wakeful*. He was swept overboard as the explosion from the *Grafton* swamped the *Comfort*; the latter attempted to throw him a rope but the gunfire from the *Lydd* prevented them picking him up. He was left swimming until he was picked up at 0515 by the Norwegian SS *Hird*, an almost accidental part of the fleet, for after Norway fell in April 1940 she was unable to complete her intended voyage and was diverted to discharge her cargo at Dunkirk, at the most difficult time in the history of that port. She remained in Dunkirk awaiting orders and a new cargo as bombs rained down on the docks and sank the lighters which would have otherwise loaded her new cargo. Eventually the orders came to proceed out of Dunkirk as a troopship in the evacuation, where she picked up Commander Fisher and other survivors in the water, for which her master was awarded the *Krigskorset* (the Norwegian War Cross).[212]

The final ship to fall victim to the perils of the Dunkirk evacuation in home waters was the *Emile Deschamps*, a French merchantman converted to a minesweeper, which was sunk by a mine on 4 June, and is known to lie north-east of the North Foreland, having missed her seamarks in fog: she is regarded as the final casualty of Operation Dynamo. Her fate, therefore, differs from that of *Amulree* and *Comfort* in not being a victim of 'friendly fire'. The events aboard the *Emile Deschamps* were recalled by a ship's doctor, Hervé Cras, who later became a maritime historian under the pen-name Jacques Mordal. He recalled a sense of foreboding as the minesweeper nudged her way out of Dunkirk on her final run, laden with 500 personnel, including the survivors of the French torpedo-boat destroyer *Jaguar*, which had been torpedoed off Dunkirk. Unlike the British ships she had not been degaussed. His sense of foreboding grew as the survivors from *Jaguar* stood up to salute their erstwhile vessel, only to hear a stern command to sit down, lest they capsize the overladen ship. *Emile Deschamps* made her way carefully to the English coast, but a fog forced her to anchor for the night, for fear either of straying into a minefield or of coming into contact with another vulnerable vessel laden with troops and being party to a tragic accident. At dawn they realised that they were lost, and signalled other French ships in the vicinity, but these proved to be just as lost as they were. A ship laden with troops was seen to be moving towards what afterwards proved to be the mouth of the Thames, and the French ships swung behind her in single file, but then *Emile Deschamps* struck a mine, with huge loss of life (approximately four-fifths of those on board). Some of the survivors, including Hervé Cras, were taken off by the *Massey Shaw* and other ships nearby: many of the dead were to wash ashore on the Continent two or three months later, carried by the tides to the coasts of Holland and Germany. Others are commemorated on the memorial to French sailors killed in action, at Pointe Saint-Mathieu, France.[213]

An operation on this scale required the assistance of reconnaissance aircraft and of covering aircraft to chase away the Bf109s which harassed the convoys. Avro Ansons *N5065* and *N9919* were lost off Ramsgate on 29 May 1940 returning from reconnaissance missions. Of the covering aircraft, two were Bristol Blenheim bombers *L9481* and *R3630*, which were, in their turn, chased by Bf109s and shot down over the Goodwin Sands on 1 June 1940. The sole survivor was the observer of *L9481* who miraculously survived the hail of bullets which killed his pilot and rear gunner. He was forced to seize control of the aircraft and glide to a nearby armed trawler to port, where he was picked up and put ashore at Ramsgate.[214]

The casualties from Dunkirk therefore reflect the variety of ships and aircraft involved and the evolution of the technology of war. The subterranean stealth of mines and U-boats were familiar from the First World War, but the capacity of airborne forces to deal death and destruction, or to provide cover for naval movements, was only now beginning to be realised, and in the same way aircraft losses at sea became a natural adjunct to seaborne operations. There are likewise certain wreck types which can obviously only be associated with the D-Day landings. Cargo vessels took part and were lost 'On His Majesty's Service', in support of the landings, such as the *Sambut*, which sunk in the Straits of Dover when she was hit by shells from a shore battery at Calais, causing explosions of her ammunition and petrol cargo, and killing many of the troops on board, also destined for Normandy.[215] For an ambitious amphibious operation it was necessarily largely a flotilla of amphibious craft which set out for Normandy, which therefore characterises the losses tied to this historical event. Among these were the various portions of pontoon, destined for the formation of the Mulberry Harbour temporary beachhead landing site, or landing craft of various kinds, intended to discharge personnel, vehicles and artillery, and smaller landing craft on arrival. Many of these were lost as they set out for the invasion, capsizing and foundering while under tow (bridge section) or under their own propulsion (landing craft) on the southern coasts of England.

Even though D-Day is relatively recent history and thus well supported by documentary evidence, including official papers, eyewitness accounts and photographs, there is still scope for new discoveries to be made, for the urgency of the situation at the time and the associations made afterwards have tended to mask the extent of losses in territorial waters. Official secrecy was a necessity at the time and meant that information as to the place of loss was not readily available for the amphibious craft, simply citing the name of the operation or that the vessel was lost in 'Home Waters'. A systematic analysis of all the war reports for D-Day – and the subsequent days – is likely to raise awareness of the true number and location of these amphibious wrecks involved, but at present they are rarely analysed without the 'prompt' of actual remains.

In location, a group of wrecks off Bracklesham Bay, Sussex, is typical of the wrecks in this landscape of war, on the English Channel coast facing France. In 2008 a group of tanks and bulldozers which had long been rumoured to have been lost during the D-Day landings were investigated. They had traditionally been associated with another area of D-Day wreckage lying close to the west, a section of a 'Whale' bridge which had sunk while under tow for the Normandy Beaches to form part of the Mulberry Harbour. The vehicles had generally been assumed to have fallen off the bridge section either because it was in difficulties or they had slid off and caused the bridge to overturn as a result.[216] However, the bridge section was incapable of supporting the combined weight of all four vehicles found – two tanks and two bulldozers. It would have been easy to assume that this simply meant that the bridge section was overloaded and wallowed in the sea to be subsequently lost. However, Alison Mayor and the Southsea Sub-Aqua Club led an investigation into the site combined with documentary research, which led to the reinterpretation of the site. Divers surveyed what was discovered to be a discrete wreck cargo comprising two tanks with a jeep lying between them, and two bulldozers. One tank had turned turtle, broken tracks uppermost; the other was lying on its right side (Fig 2.34). The bulldozers were also keeling over to the right. This suggests they had all slid off the carrying vessel to starboard, the upside-down tank perhaps the first to fall since it had fallen most heavily.

Where had they fallen from, if the nearby Whale Unit was incapable of supporting their weight? The identification of the tanks as Centaurs rather than the Shermans they had expected to find identified their origin as British. From that point their story became much easier to trace, for only 80 Centaurs had been assigned for combat during the Second World War, all of which were designated for D-Day service with the specialist Royal Marines Armoured Support

Group (RMASG), whose records survived, among them noting on 2 June 1944 that the Prime Minister, Winston Churchill, had witnessed their preparations to embark at Gosport.[217] A kedge anchor was found wedged underneath one tank, supporting the view that the cargo originated from a landing craft, so all that was needed now was to find the original craft from which they had come. As with cannon or with cargo cast overboard to lighten a vessel to get her off sand or rocks, the presence of the tanks suggested a craft in difficulties, but not necessarily a wreck site in itself.

Official reports for the movements of the RMASG revealed that they were intended to be among the first waves of troops to embark and land, and that two Centaur tanks had been lost at sea in the late evening of 5 June, or D-Day –1. The loading orders maintained secrecy in a double-blind: the specific landing craft was not named by its pennant number but by a loading table identity number, LTIN 1008, which eventually proved to be that of landing craft tank (armoured) *LCT(A)2428*, which got into difficulties, and broached to (turned sideways), breaking down with a leak on her starboard side and being forced to anchor near the Nab Tower. A survivors' report from the landing craft noted that damage was 'sustained by weather to double bottoms on starboard side aft',[218] entirely

Fig 2.34
Capsized Centaur tank in Bracklesham Bay, tracks uppermost.
(© Martin Davies)

consistent with the disposition of the vehicles aboard, in which the rear tank to the right had fallen most heavily. After taking off the personnel, HM Tug *Jaunty* attempted to take her in tow but the tow failed and the craft capsized, whereupon *Jaunty* sank her by gunfire to prevent her becoming an obstruction to the remainder of the fleet, recalling the attempts to quench the *War Knight* by 'friendly fire'. The association of the Whale Bridge with the tanks and bulldozers site is a more general one in a landscape of war, part of the same fleet setting out for the same event. The exploration of this same landscape of war has helped to identify a hitherto unidentified site (the tanks and bulldozers) and revealed its relationship with a wreck whose existence in home waters was barely suspected and hidden from view among official documents: official post-war statistics simply stated that the vessel was lost during Operation Neptune.

The wrecks in Bracklesham Bay demonstrate that we know very little about the shipwreck remains of the amphibious craft involved in the Normandy landings. Yet this particular landscape of war is associated with shipwrecks far beyond the time of 6 June 1944 and the place of the English Channel coasts on either side. They need not necessarily have been lost during Operation Neptune itself even though they were dedicated to the same operation and objectives: an operation on this scale required a phenomenal commitment in terms of warships and auxiliaries, in preliminary exercises and in continuous support. Pontoons, landing craft and support ships were lost either in preparing for the landings, or in providing reinforcements once the beachhead had been successfully established. Tanks, provisions, personnel and munitions were all required – conveyed by ship and convoyed by covering aircraft. Other ships and landing craft were also lost in the run-up to the invasion, not least in the disaster of Operation Tiger, when two American landing ship tanks (LSTs) *LST507* and *LST531* were torpedoed by a German E-boat in Lyme Bay while undergoing rehearsals for the landings two months later, resulting in heavy loss of life.[219] Post-invasion, but still lost in the ongoing Operation Neptune, were the *LST921* and landing craft infantry (large) *LCI(L)99* which foundered off Hartland Point in August 1944 after being torpedoed in convoy destined for Normandy, or two landing craft (mechanised) lost overboard from the American ship *John L Manson* in Mount's Bay: unlike *LCT(A)2428*

from which the tanks were lost on this occasion the 'mother ship' was not lost.[220] In the case of Dunkirk or of D-Day, each wreck can be described as being lost within the theatre of war with which they were directly associated: to a lesser extent this is also true of the wrecks which took place on preliminary operations such as *Exercise Tiger*. In some cases landing craft were wrecked *between* theatres of war, as in the case of those returning from the landings in Sicily and being made ready for the Normandy landings the following year.

Appropriately enough, Hervé Cras, survivor of the *Emile Deschamps*, considered that the withdrawal from Dunkirk planted the seeds of D-Day: if a flotilla could successfully evacuate hundreds of thousands of men, under the shadow of defeat, then, under more opportune conditions, why not send over a similar flotilla in the reverse direction when the time was right to seize victory? Dunkirk, in his view, was but a trial for D-Day, and in that respect, the two events are linked. They are also linked in a different way, in the monuments they have left behind: the ships, aircraft and smaller craft which remain even as the numbers of those involved dwindle and the events begin to pass out of living memory. From D-Day the two underwater Centaur tanks are the sole known representatives of their kind from a maritime context: two others are known and are both used as war memorials in Normandy, one alongside Pegasus Bridge itself. The wrecks off the Channel coasts therefore reflect a common heritage of war, both in the international composition of the fleets involved on both occasions, and in the location of the wrecks, scattered across the Channel from shore to shore.

Under the sea and from the sky

> … this little world,
> This precious stone set in the silver sea,
> Which serves it in the office of a wall,
> Or as a moat defensive to a house …
>
> William Shakespeare, *Richard II*, Act II, Scene 2

Under the sea

Leonardo da Vinci had sketched both a parachute and a diving suit in the early 16th century,[221] but it took until the 20th century for submarines and aeroplanes to dominate warfare, and consequently wrecks protected under the Protection of Military Remains Act 1986, and Protection of Wrecks Act 1973.

Inevitably the history of submarines is one of experimentation and heroic failure as well as operational losses. Various trials of submersible vessels were held between Leonardo's time and the late 19th century, some more successful than others. At first the technology appeared barely viable, for designers continued to work in terms of modifying existing types of vessel rather than designing something radically new. An early account of an experimental submarine comes from Plymouth in 1774, just prior to the American War of Independence. Submarine technology was not yet ready to make a significant contribution to naval warfare (even though the Americans produced their own wooden submersible, the *Turtle*, in 1776).[222]

It seems that one Mr Day, a self-taught carpenter, became obsessed with proving that it was possible to build a vessel capable of sinking and rising at will. He was undaunted by the prospect of proving his theories, perhaps unwisely, for a wager. It is often suggested that he purchased the 50-ton sloop *Maria* for conversion, but a contemporary account of a small purpose-built vessel is perhaps more plausible. He may have based it on the converted Norwich 'market boat' prototype with which he had conducted earlier trials in the Norfolk Broads, not much more than a submersible chamber.[223] His design is said to have incorporated an ingenious mechanism of ballast stones suspended externally from iron rods built into the vessel. Dropping these stones was intended to assist the vessel in returning to the surface.

In late June 1774 Day was towed out in his little vessel to the Cattewater, intending to spend 12 hours at a depth of 17 fathoms (51 feet). Witnesses said, however, that his craft sank very rapidly, and in less than five minutes the water appeared to rise and become disturbed. Mr Day was never seen again, and, from that day to this, neither was the *Maria,* although in recent years at least two diving expeditions have tried to locate her. The disturbance noted on the surface probably reflects the immense water pressure on such a small vessel at such depths and her consequent likely implosion, scattering the wreckage. News of the tragedy rapidly spread, particularly among the Dutch community based at nearby Flushing. An account sent from Plymouth the day after the incident, and published in Dutch, places the experiment at the

Eastern King opposite Drake's Island. Local mariners lamented that no worse place could have been chosen for the experiment and with the benefit of hindsight said that a rope should have been attached to the vessel to pull her up in case of difficulty.[224]

Day's miserable fate obstinately pursuing his ideas prefigured the sheer claustrophobia endured by crews confined in close quarters for weeks or months, an idea permeating popular culture from the 1860s onwards. American Civil War submarines inspired Jules Verne's novel *Twenty Thousand Leagues under the Sea* (1869), a theme continued with the popularity of the book (1973) and film (1981) *Das Boot*, following the adventures of a German submarine crew of the Second World War. This, of course, had its parallel in the sad reality of submarine wrecks.

In Britain, the Reverend George Garrett was a pioneer in submarine development in 1878–9, designing two early submarines which combined practicality with a strong element of religious symbolism. Clearly referencing the Resurrection as a symbol of confidence in their ability to survive submersion, both were named *Resurgam*, Latin for 'I shall rise again.' The earlier *Resurgam* was human-powered and therefore labour-intensive; the later version larger and steam-powered. The second *Resurgam* may have arisen out of the first, but ironically developed difficulties off Rhyl en route to Portsmouth for sea trials and sank to rise no more. Relocation in Welsh territorial waters in 1996 and designation under the Protection of Wrecks Act 1973 has been the sole resurrection for the *Resurgam*.[225] However, British submarine design was to take off with the Holland Class submarines, named after their designer, John Philip Holland. Of these both *Holland No. 1* and *Holland No. 5* sank under tow to be broken up in 1913 and 1912, respectively. *Holland No. 1* was raised from her resting place off the Eddystone 70 years later and is on museum display, while *No. 5* is a designated wreck site off the Royal Sovereign Bank, Sussex.[226]

One practical issue hindering submarine development was that the advantage of striking unseen, whether as a ramming device or as a sophisticated weapons carrier, was also the principal drawback before the development of undersea communications. Prolonged submersion was possible for early 20th-century submarines, but a series of high-profile collisions revealed how vulnerable they were to vessels on the surface. In 1904 the British submarine *A1* was mown down on exercises by the liner *Berwick Castle*, with the loss of all 11 crew.[227] She re-entered service after being raised but suffered an explosion in 1910, and was consequently towed out in 1911 to be expended as a gunnery target off the Isle of Wight. Her fate in some ways resembles those of the contemporary Holland class, but in other ways prefigures the recurrent calamity of civilian vessels blundering into submarine manoeuvres. In 1909 the steamer *Eddystone* became entangled with a convoy of submarines heading in the opposite direction, off Haisborough Light, north Norfolk, sinking the *C11*,[228] and as late as 1925 the *M1* was lost to a collision off Start Point, Devon.[229]

A1 is designated under the Protection of Wrecks Act 1973 for her historical significance as the first British-designed and British-built submarine in the service of the Royal Navy. Though her earlier history involved tragedy there was no loss of life involved in her final sinking. She remains unique for the distance travelled from the initial point of loss off Selsey Bill, such that the Navy was unable to find the wreck. It appears that when she sank *A1* was only partially flooded so that her residual buoyancy permitted her to drift with the tide to her final resting place 5 miles away (Fig 2.35).[230]

Collision with undersea hazards was also a drawback of the contemporary lack of sophisticated navigational equipment: in 1917 the German submarine *U-48* could very easily have escaped Allied bombing and the fouling of a net barrage with some damage. However, being disabled, she could not escape the Goodwin Sands and was lost through stranding.[231] At the same time, if accidental collision caused peacetime tragedy, in wartime deliberate collision was a ruthless tactic to dispatch enemy submarines, sometimes in the very act of attacking a convoy. By ramming and sinking the German *UC-75* off Flamborough Head in 1918, HMS *Fairy* brought to an end an extremely successful run of 58 sinkings and 8 vessels damaged. Normally the ramming vessel survived the collision, since the rammed vessel bore the full brunt of the impact, but this time the *Fairy* herself foundered as a result of the damage sustained in two ramming attempts. Unsurprisingly, therefore, the remains of both vessels have been identified, approximately half a mile apart.[232]

The new submarine technology demanded the development of new counter-measures, and

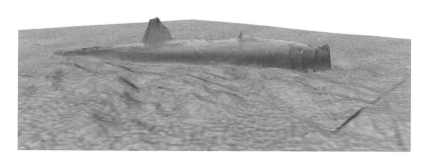

in due course a new manner of loss emerged: sinking by depth charges, cased explosives dropped or shot overboard over the enemy below. The requirement for a 'dropping mine' had been anticipated before the First World War, but not multiple submarine successes such as those of the *UC-75*. The mounting toll of losses to submarines in the Second World War also drove the development of the depth charge as a direct counter-attack measure.[233] At first, depth-charge technology was somewhat crude and necessitated a time lag before the explosion to allow the attacking vessel time to steam out of range so as not to be sunk by her own charges (Fig 2.36). During the Second World War not even aircraft were immune from the dangers of depth charges. In 1942, a Short Sunderland flying boat was forced to ditch into the Bristol Channel off Cornwall, when she dropped her practice depth charges in a suspected minefield which can only have compounded the force of the subsequent explosion.[234] Similarly the Admiralty trawler *Comet* 'disappeared' in an explosion on 30 September 1940.[235] The area was subsequently found to have recently been laid with mines: at only 301 tons the *Comet* was perhaps less able to withstand a huge explosion than a larger vessel, but the depth charges which have been seen scattered around the wreck site tell a story of a loss to external forces compounded by her own armament.

The first submarine successfully depth-charged in English waters seems to have been the *UC-19*, sunk on 6 December 1916, south-west of the Isles of Scilly, by HMS *Ariel*.[236] Her possible remains lie close to the position reported at the time of loss, but this is frequently not the case. Indeed, the fact that the remains are 'possibly' only those of the *UC-19* alerts us to a significant fact about U-boat remains: relatively few wreck sites are identified as

Fig 2.35
Multibeam elevation image of the remains of HMSM A1 showing her distinctive raked conning tower. The vessel remains relatively intact with areas of significant damage at the bows and stern, having settled into the undulating seabed. (© Crown copyright. Data collected by University of St Andrews and processed by Wessex Archaeology)

U-boats. Many wreck sites clearly have a U-boat profile but either only a 'possible' or 'probable' identity, or none at all, nor is it always clear to which war they belong. Consequently, those wrecks definitively identified as particular U-boats are fewer still. This is in part because in the heat of battle the target was not always clearly identified by the attacking vessel, and can mean that the same U-boat was claimed on different dates by different vessels (as was, indeed, the case with *UC-19*, also said to have been lost off Dover on 4 December 1916). Many submarines, however, plunged unseen to their fates, whether through internal failure, or through being caught up in a minefield, sometimes even the mines they had just laid (Fig 2.37).

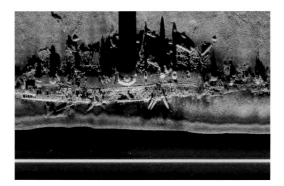

Compared to the First World War, fewer U-boat sites from the Second World War have been recorded in English waters and fewer still have a confirmed identity. During the First World War submarines operated closer inshore and engaged the enemy at closer range than in the Second.[237] Counter-attacks during the Second World War therefore took place at greater depths and further offshore, with less precision. Those U-boats from the Second World War which have been discovered appear to date principally from 1939–40 and 1944–5. At first sight this might be considered to be the result of the success of the U-boat campaign during the middle years of the war, but the situation was inevitably somewhat more complex.[238] During 1942–3, for example, there were no recorded sinkings by U-boats off the English coast, although many ships were sunk by the surface-operating motor torpedo boats known in English as *E-boats* (enemy boats, known in German as *S-boote* or *Schnellboote*). E-boats caused deadly havoc among the convoys for the duration of the war, but appear to have been particularly active in the middle war years as the U-boats turned their periscopes elsewhere.[239] The general lack of U-boats known to have been sunk in English waters is therefore in part directly attributable to the U-boats' worldwide remit.[240]

Another reason that the final resting place of many U-boats, particularly those of the Second World War, remains obscure, is that a last radio contact or other reporting position was frequently far distant from the actual place of loss. To all intents and purposes these U-boats simply disappeared to unknown causes without ever being claimed as a 'kill': accident, mechanical failure, collision, environmental causes or possibly even to mines. Thus the same vessels that coursed invisibly beneath the waves to strike at other shipping could in their turn be lost unseen. This the Allies turned to their own advantage during the latter stages of the War when anti-submarine measures were no longer reactive and defensive but proactive and offensive.

In recent years a number of major finds have been made by specialists, particularly a group of submarines in the Bristol Channel which revealed a secret anti-submarine strategy on the west coast of England. The swept 'War Channels' may have been free of mines, but they could not guarantee immunity from U-boat attacks, with a significant spike in sinkings by U-boats off the coasts of Cornwall and Devon in 1944–5.[241] The tables were turned on the U-boats as minefields were laid off the western coasts deep enough to snare U-boats lurking in the swept channels, without causing an 'own goal' in affecting surface convoys passing overhead. *U-325*, *U-400* and *U-1021* were lost in this way off the coast of Cornwall in the last few months of the Second World War, all containing details which identified them as operational during the latter stages of the war and, thus, crucially, narrowing down the potential pool of identifications in a coup for the researchers who found them.[242] All three typify the problems associated with U-boat identifications, since all were originally thought to have been lost elsewhere: *U-325* in the 'North Atlantic or on the south-west coast of Britain'; *U-400* in the 'North Atlantic, south of Cork'; and *U-1021* off Scotland. These wrecks illustrate particular difficulties in identifying remains on the seabed: since being rediscovered, the proposed identifications for each site have been redistributed within this group, given their common features. *U-1021*, in particular, appears to have been a fairly problematic wreck, and illustrates the difficulty in identifying wreck remains on the seabed.[243] Three separate reports of her last resting place off the Cornish coast have been recorded, two of which have also been suggested as *U-325* and *U-400* instead.[244]

From the sky

The sinking of *UB-115* towards the close of the First World War, on 29 September 1918, exemplifies the development of anti-submarine technology as well as being an example of collaborative effort between aircraft and surface vessels in sinking hostile craft hidden below the surface (Fig 2.38). The value of aerial reconnaissance was proven when oil leaking from *UB-115*, a visible sign of mechanical failure, betrayed her presence to the airship *R29*. The airship signalled to nearby ships and the destroyer HMS *Star* witnessed bombs falling in the vicinity from the airship. *Star* and the trawler HMS *Ouse* led six other vessels to the site of the stricken submarine and proceeded to drop depth charges. Their crews listened in with the newfangled hydrophone equipment which allowed them to hear any signs of undersea activity. Each attempt by *UB-115*'s crew to restart her motors triggered another depth charge attack. At 2.34 pm, as recorded in the *Star*'s log, a sixth depth charge was dropped 'on spot indicated by air ship oil seen coming to surface also air bubbles … 2.51 dropped 7th D. c. on oil patch. Stopped to collect oil and closely examine vicinity'. The crews of all eight vessels, as well as the crew of the airship, were awarded prize bounty money for their role in the destruction of *UB-115*.[245]

R29 exemplifies the patrol and reconnaissance roles to which the Allies devoted their airpower. These roles were also carried out by seaplanes, developed pre-war to be capable of take-off from, and landing on, the sea. Seaplane technology now came into its own, evolving a specialist escort role for shipping convoys, since, unlike conventional seaborne escorts, they could provide a greater range of cover and

Fig 2.38
British Sea Scout Zero SSZ *59 airship descending towards the aft landing deck of HMS* Furious, *converted to an aircraft carrier, some time after April 1918, when the airship was delivered, and illustrating the collaboration between airborne and surface escorts. The cumbersome airship and the clumsily converted cruiser illustrate the potential for a unique nautical accident, which, however, fortunately did not ensue. Note the dazzle camouflage, in port view, making it difficult to make out the details of the ship's structure even at this relatively close range.*
(© Charles Pulman collection)

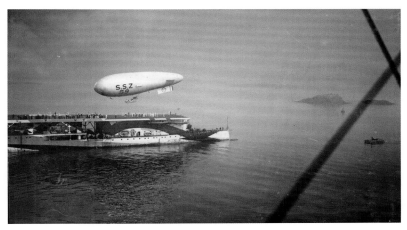

a much speedier response to attack. *The Times* noted that during September 1917 that seaplanes had flown 90,000 miles on patrol, airships 80,000.[246] Hence developments in aircraft and submarine technology led not only to an expansion in the range and capabilities of warfare, but directly pitted aircraft against submarines.

Nevertheless, despite the rise of the 'air ace' in the First World War, of whom the 'Red Baron', Manfred von Richthofen, was the most famous, aerial combat did not characterise the First World War in the same way as it came to define the Second, in particular through the Battle of Britain in 1940. Air technology was still in its infancy, concentrating on the dirigible airships, lumbering, slow and very easily spotted,

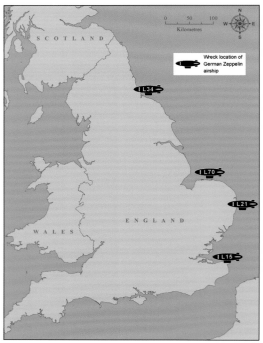

Fig 2.39
Looking somewhat like a beached whale, and giving some impression of a Zeppelin wreck, this unidentified Allied airship is shown downed somewhere off the Channel coasts. Fortunately for the crew, the twisted wreck has not landed on top of them, nor, equally fortunately, has it burst into flames.
(© Charles Pulman collection)

Fig 2.40
As can be seen, Zeppelin losses during the First World War were concentrated on the eastern coasts. Though they penetrated as far inland as London and the Midlands, their limited range constrained them from venturing any further before being forced to turn back.

manoeuvring in the air like great ships at sea, their very name a connection with older maritime technology. On the German side airships filled with hydrogen, lighter than air, were developed by Germany as a terror weapon for bombing raids: these *Zeppelins*, as they were known, had, like the submarines below them, a significant major drawback which contemporary technology could not overcome. In the case of the Zeppelins, anti-aircraft fire simply exposed them to hull breaches which left the hydrogen within extremely vulnerable to exploding in flames. Following raids in 1916 and 1918 several were shot down into the North Sea. The last Zeppelin raid on England was thwarted when the vast bulk of *L70* was easily spotted on a summer's day and intercepted by a fighter biplane, which shot her down in flames off Wells-next-the-Sea with the loss of all on board (Figs 2.39 and 2.40).[247] The Germans were, however, capable of more advanced aerial attack, and a torpedo launched from a seaplane took everyone by surprise in May 1917, including the crew of the *Gena* which sank in the War Channel off Southwold following the attack. Her loss had to be written in the margins in Lloyd's war casualty register, since it did not fit in the pre-printed columns for 'mine', 'submarine' and 'cruiser'. Such attacks remained rare, although at the same time it was noted that British seaplanes were harassing German shipping on the other side of the North Sea.[248]

Although the Second World War was punctuated by a series of events for the duration and was defined by a war on all fronts (in technological as well as geographical terms), it was the invasion of airspace which came to define the war from the British point of view and, later, from a heritage standpoint (the destruction of cities, for example). No wartime event symbolised the struggle for survival more than the Battle of Britain, which is usually viewed in terms of dogfights seen above the south-eastern counties as aircraft rose up from English airfields to intercept German aircraft.[249] Many on both sides plunged into the sea through enemy action, friendly fire, mechanical failure, collision or other accident: from the Battle of Britain alone 126 German and 216 British planes fell into the sea, among them Dornier Do17Z *5K + AR*, which ditched on the Goodwin Sands and 'ground-looped' on impact to end up virtually intact but upside down (Fig 2.41).[250]

The constant need to train up pilots to replace those killed or wounded, as well as to test new aircraft, left its legacy in a number of aircraft lost anywhere between the foreshore and the marine zone – not only the Short Sunderland discussed on p. 109, but also examples such as the British Lockheed Hudson flown by a Canadian crew which ditched half a mile out to sea in the inter-tidal zone at Allonby sands, Cumbria, in 1942, or a Short Stirling heavy bomber which crashed into the Wash off Norfolk on tests in 1943.[251] Figures for aircraft recorded as lost on both sides between 1939 and 1945 currently number some 1,920, of which 1,449 are known to have been lost in the marine or inter-tidal zones.[252] This is in part because no centralised figures were kept of aircraft losses from either air force in English airspace. Once an aircraft was written off there was no further official interest in its fate: those loss lists which exist have been retrospectively compiled and are therefore secondary sources.[253]

Sea versus sky

The interwar arms race demonstrated a fascination with combining the complementary technologies of seaborne and aerial craft. This is reflected in the wreck record, since just under one-half of the aircraft lost in the sea between 1919 and 1938 were seaplanes or flying boats.[254] The technology was so experimental that records of such wrecks preserve the names and types of aircraft which never saw major production, such as the Blackburn Iris flying boat. In 1931 Blackburn Iris *N238* crashed into the sea some hundreds of yards offshore from its base at Mount Batten, Plymouth, and for the lack of a suitable high-speed boat to reach the crew they drowned. One witness was Aircraftsman Shaw, otherwise known as Lawrence of Arabia, who was moved to campaign for high-speed motor launches to rescue the air crew from the sea. Two years later history repeated itself in the same area with the loss of another Blackburn Iris *S1263*, but this time Lawrence was among the rescuers in a motor launch, a significant development in the concept of air-sea rescue.[255]

Rescue of aircraft downed in the sea or of shipwreck victims by air was to be tested further in the war to come and in its turn led to further losses. A Heinkel He 59 seaplane *D-ASAM* belonging to Seenotflug Kommando 3 was lost off Sunderland in 1940, while searching for the crew of a He 115 which had crashed 30 miles off Whitby that same day.[256] Despite its red cross the seaplane's presence close to a British convoy

aroused suspicion, its role was interpreted as reconnaissance rather than rescue, and it was accordingly shot down. Air-sea rescue craft not unnaturally had a knack of being involved in dramatic incidents, none more so than the Short Sunderland flying boat *EJ134* which flew out in 1943 to the Bay of Biscay in a fruitless search for survivors of a downed aircraft which included the English actor Leslie Howard. Eight Junkers Ju 88s came hurtling out of the sky to claim another victim, but the lone *EJ134*'s Australian crew fought them off. Instead of plunging into the Bay of Biscay, they managed to nurse their stricken aircraft for some 400-odd miles back to English airspace, and literally made landfall on Praa Sands, where the tide finished off the aircraft.[257] Other air-sea rescue features which have turned up on the English coast include a German refuge buoy which was located on the seabed off the coast of Sussex in the 1980s: it was characteristic of a type stationed off the coast of France to aid downed Luftwaffe pilots. Either the weather or enemy action must have cut it adrift from station at some point during the war.[258]

For the interwar period the *M2* submarine likewise represented a brave attempt to combine undersea and airborne technology, since she was a First World War submarine modified to carry a Parnall Peto seaplane. In 1932, while out on exercises off the Bill of Portland, she sank through flooding of her aircraft hangar, the exact cause of which has never been determined, but is thought likely to be attributable to the

Fig 2.41
The distinctive shape of the Do17 'Flying Pencil' and of her engines can be seen in this remarkable side scan sonar image, which was made prior to the June 2013 recovery of the wreck. (© Crown copyright. Photograph taken by Wessex Archaeology)

imminent launch of the seaplane, leaving an opening for water to get in. This must surely be an unusual variant of the loss of the early modern warships *Mary Rose* and *Vasa* through water ingress into their open gunports.[259]

The concept of 'mutually assured destruction' or MAD, though associated with the later Cold War nuclear arms race between the communist east and the free market west, is nevertheless appropriate in describing a 1941 incident which sent both combatants to the bottom. HMS *Patia* was a former banana boat built in 1922 and requisitioned in 1940, initially as an ocean boarding vessel, and then marked for conversion into an aircraft catapult vessel. These conversions were a response to a lack of aircraft carriers available as convoy escorts, particularly in the Battle of the Atlantic. A number of merchantmen were converted in this way, either becoming 'fighter catapult ships' like *Patia* if they were taken into direct naval service, or 'catapult armed merchantmen' if they remained in the mercantile service, a fine distinction of role if not of function. Each catapult ship was capable of launching a single fighter to assist in fighting off airborne attack on mercantile convoys. Initially they were fitted with Fairey Fulmar aircraft, but later Hawker Hurricanes, similarly converted for sea warfare as 'Hurricats', were used.[260]

HMS *Patia* was among the first to be converted at South Shields, and on 27 April 1941 was on her maiden voyage post-refit northbound in convoy out of the Tyne. She was attacked off Boulmer, Northumberland, by a German Heinkel He 111 H-5 bomber, *werk nummer* 3677 *1H+MH*, swooping south on a sortie out of her Norwegian base.[261] As *Patia* was bound 'northabout' via Scotland to Belfast to pick up her intended fighter aircraft, she was not fully operational and was unable to send up an aircraft to duel head-on with her attacker. With three 6in 'high-angle' anti-aircraft guns; two 'pom-poms' (naval 2-pounder guns), 2 Hotchkiss machine guns and 3 Harvey rocket projectors, she was not defenceless, however, and returned fire as *1H+MH* passed and repassed overhead. Two bombs dropped on the first pass missed their target, but the accompanying machine-gun fire killed some of the *Patia*'s crew. A second pass seems to have dealt a death blow to *Patia*.[262] Two out of the three bombs found their target, the one between No. 3 hold and the engine room, the other near the bridge on the starboard side. The ship cracked in two even as her anti-aircraft

gunners managed to shoot down the Heinkel, killing two of her five-man crew, while *Patia* lost 39 men from her complement of 70.

As she filled with water *Patia*'s crew abandoned ship and she settled onto the bottom in 63m of water. Her distinctive catapult rails identify her on the seabed,[263] defined under the Protection of Military Remains Act 1986 as a 'protected place', so that she may be dived but cannot be penetrated or disturbed. Still facing her original direction of travel, in turn indicating the rapidity with which she sank, *Patia* lies split in two: the break expands her footprint on the seabed from her original dimensions, typical for a wreck which has undergone a violent explosion. Spent ammunition from her anti-aircraft guns is visible scattered around, although one of the guns has since slipped onto the seabed.

However, the Heinkel's remains have, to date, not been located: regardless of her unknown location and the survival of any of the crew, by default under UK law she is also presumed to be protected under the 1986 Act, since military aircraft are automatically regarded as 'protected places'. Where might the Heinkel be? *1H+MH* flew south to meet the northbound *Patia*, approaching her from starboard, then looping right to attack once more from the port quarter. It was at this point that each sank the other, the Heinkel being forced to ditch into the sea 'close by',[264] consistent with the low angle of attack stressed in accounts of the incident. Possibly *1H+MH* lies to the starboard after her final flight over *Patia*'s decks from the port side. The search area remains wide, however: the area in which the Heinkel must lie is more sparsely populated with identified wreck sites than in many areas of the English North Sea coast and is a relatively unexplored region for wrecks, since the nearest charted wreck lies over a mile away to the south.

Mr Day of the *Maria*, experimenting in an era just before the onset of a major global conflict, could not have foreseen the effects of the technology he was attempting to develop, which spelt the end of the classical sea battle of ship against ship and would result in the potential not only to expand warfare across the world but into new dimensions beneath the waves and in the sky. These new technologies placed shipping losses of the first half of the 20th century firmly in a global context: though they were the result of a domestic battle for survival, the submarines and aircraft lost in English waters form part of a worldwide heritage like no other.

3

The vagaries of human nature

Introduction

Human nature and human error were just as unpredictable as the elements or an enemy materialising out of nowhere, bringing out both the best and the worst in humanity. Heroism and altruism were widely celebrated attributes, even those of animals: the capacity of Newfoundland – and other – dogs as rescuers was regularly recognised, especially the 'sagacious canine perseverance' of one 'much exhausted' which came ashore with the lead line in its mouth from the *Durham Packet* off Norfolk in 1815, enabling rescuers to set up a shore-to-ship rescue apparatus.[1] However, whether by accident or design, human nature could cause or magnify any shipwreck incident. Overloading or carelessly stowing the cargo so that it shifted could lead to a fatal capsize, especially in a gale. In this way, three out of the five crew of a 'deeply loaded' herring boat fell 'sacrifices to the devouring element' off Holy Island in 1812; aboard the *Helsingør* in 1893, the superphosphate consigned from Ghent for Dundee shifted off the Kentish Knock, forcing the crew to abandon ship and row for their lives to the Long Sand light vessel.[2] Some cargoes were, of course, naturally dangerous, as we shall explore later in this chapter, while navigational error could also play its part. Collision was an ever-present danger, especially in fog, but also attributable to keeping an 'improper' lookout. Even worse still was the failure to stop and assist a ship which you had just run down: such assistance was an insurance policy of sorts, with the understanding that another time it could be your own vessel in danger.

Insurance fraud is as old as insurance itself. Although forms of insurance have been recorded since early times, 17th-century trade motivated the development of modern insurance policies. The underwriting of risks at Lloyd's and other coffee-houses led to the emergence of dedicated marine insurance companies,[3] which in turn led to the evolution of insurance fraud and a number of deliberate wrecks, risking lives. Legitimate mercantile interests were often little better. The crew were least in order of importance in countless shipwreck reports: 'part of the cargo and crew saved', or 'the ship went ashore, cargo saved' – but no mention of the crew's fate.

Beaching a vessel at the dead of night to run contraband was dangerous and led directly to the loss of several smuggling vessels, such as a Guernseyman laden with wine, brandy and salt, off the Start in 1726; again, two smuggling cutters with brandy and wine were wrecked among the Isles of Scilly in 1771. Their foes, the 'Preventive' or 'Revenue' men, chased smugglers ashore, fighting fire with fire in the same sort of ships the smugglers preferred, fast cutters or luggers. Occasionally the Revenue ships themselves got into difficulties, the fate of the *Bell* near Porthleven, Cornwall, in 1758, or a lugger off Lytham, Lancashire, in 1802,[4] but, in general, smuggling and wrecking, so often romanticised and thought of hand in hand, play relatively little part in the vast numbers of known wrecks in English waters.

There was, of course, further scope for illegal activity *after* a wreck had taken place which is discussed further in this chapter. The practice of 'wrecking', deliberately luring ships ashore by misleading lights, appears to be rooted more in legend than in fact, though it often occurred accidentally:

On Monday morning, a light brig, named the *Friendship,* of Sunderland, belonging to Mr Hayton, run upon a rock near that place. The cause of the accident was:- The morning being dark, the captain unfortunately mistook a light in one of the houses facing the sea, for the Pier light, and ... made too soon for the harbour; the vessel struck against the new south Pier, and was, by the tide setting strong, driven upon a rock to the southward; – as her bottom is nearly out, she is likely to become a total loss. Many misfortunes of the same kind have happened from lights in the windows of houses fronting the sea.[5]

However, since the Middle Ages, the scavenging of cargo washed ashore has been widely reported, right up to 21st-century events attracting widespread looting.[6] There is a constant refrain of 'swarms' of 'country people', lured by wine, brandy and other cargoes, intent on pillage, with attendant accounts of persons drinking themselves senseless, sometimes to expire 'insensible'. One commentator drily noted:

> The value of the discovery of the stomach pump was lately witnessed in the case of a beachman in this neighbourhood, who had drunk so immoderately of the brandy saved from the NEPTUNES [sic], lately wrecked on the Scroby, that his life was despaired of.[7]

These accounts are of threefold value. At the time, they resulted in tangible improvements in safety: the cumulative impact of accidents at sea inspired practical lifesaving measures and inventions (lighthouses and light vessels, the rocket apparatus, breeches buoy and lifeboat), via scientific investigations into the accurate measurement of longitude, and regulatory commission publications (the *Board of Trade Casualty Returns*) to legislation, all driving down the toll in both ships and lives.[8] They also have great human interest and social history appeal. Finally, incident reports also give evidence for the survival or otherwise of the cargo and of the ship, and may in fact suggest a location, for if all the cargo was stolen or the vessel was completely dismantled it generally confirms the manner of loss (stranding) even though the natural conclusion may be that little or nothing of archaeological value may have been left on the foreshore. This does not rule out the possibility that archaeological evidence in the form of artefacts may be traceable or that ship's timbers may not remain elsewhere in coastal communities, recycled for construction purposes (see Chapter 5 for further discussion of this subject).

Theft in medieval court cases

Within recent memory much of Britain was transfixed in January 2007, when the sinking MSC *Napoli* was beached at Branscombe. The saturation of modern media coverage led to huge numbers of visitors from Britain and Europe descending on the beach to loot items washed ashore from the wreck, ranging from dog food to BMW motorbikes.[9] Many commentators at the time suggested that the looting replicated the plot of *Whisky Galore*,[10] but what few realised was that stealing from wrecked ships has a long and ignoble history, and stretches back in the records of shipwrecks in English waters as far back as the 14th century.

The pious name of the *Navis de Jehsu Christi de Portu* (*Ship of Jesus Christ*, of Oporto), evidently bestowed for its talismanic value,[11] in common with many medieval vessels, afforded no protection when she ran ashore during a storm at Brighstone on the Isle of Wight, en route from Lisbon and Oporto to England (Fig 3.1). The first surviving record for this wreck dates from November 1318, with a commission of *oyer and terminer* ('to hear and to determine'), authorising circuit judges to hold a court for the purpose of a criminal trial. Owing to the haphazard survival of medieval records, and the fact that not all ships are mentioned by name every time they do appear in extant documents, we cannot be sure that the vessel was indeed lost in 1318: it may have been earlier. Prosecutions were hampered by slow communications, and where foreign merchants were involved, matters were dragged out still further. This means that possibly only the richest merchants would mount a case against those who had stolen their goods in a foreign country, and take their appeal to the highest civil authority in the land, that is, the king.

Such a man was Martin de Bek, merchant of Oporto, who tenaciously fought a case against those who stole the cargo out of his ship as 'wreck of sea'; his wealth was clearly what had made his ship so attractive in the first place. In 1321 the 'wares' on the *Jesus Christ* were valued at £5,000 (nearly £3m in terms of the retail price index in 2010, or well over £59m in terms of average earnings).[12] 'Wreck of sea' was their excuse, but the basis of de Bek's case was that under medieval law the ship and her cargo ought not to be declared 'wreck of sea' since 'all on board her had escaped to land'. In other words, if there were survivors, a wrecked vessel was technically not a wreck, even if she went to pieces: only where there were no survivors could a vessel legally be deemed a wreck, since it was then supposed that no legal owner would have survived, since the cargo typically belonged to merchants who would take ship with their cargo. Nor was it a legal requirement for survivors to be human: a dog or a cat sufficed, and continued to do so at least until the 18th century.[13] If a ship was lost with all hands, the wreck reverted to the Crown, thus ensuring looting remained illegal. The situation was regularly complicated in such cases by rights of wreck assigned to local landowners by the Crown or attached to particular manors, estates or monasteries, all vigorously asserting their rights against both Crown and merchant, or against each other.

Over the years de Bek repeatedly named over 40 offenders in his petitions, including 'John, prior of Saresbrok' (Carisbrooke), and men who had crossed the Solent to plunder the vessel in a medieval equivalent of the *Napoli* case. One was Robert le Ysemongere of Winchester, while others crossed from Portsmouth, Christchurch and several from Lymington. The case must have been difficult to prove, owing in part to the isolation of the Isle of Wight, but also to the likely perishable nature of the goods involved. Oporto exports were generally perishable – fruit and wine – as evidenced by other medieval ships

from Portugal which also came to grief on the English coast: figs and grapes (1310, Hove); wine and general cargo (1318, Padstow); fruit, wine and wax (*Seinte Marie*, 1383, Southampton).[14] Any material evidence for the goods claimed by Martin de Bek must long since have disappeared, making his case more difficult.

Yet for nearly 20 years, de Bek persisted in his claim, which was last heard of in 1336, still apparently unresolved. The proceedings were so lengthy that none of those first commissioned in 1318 were still presiding in 1336, although one John de Stonore in 1336 had been involved since 1320, when he had received his first commission of *oyer and terminer*. One can only imagine his feelings on receiving yet another commission to hear the case of 'the ship of Jesus Christ of Portyngall'. The process must have not only become increasingly wearying, but also increasingly difficult to prove, with numbers of accused, witnesses and justices most probably dying in the interval, but de Bek continued to battle on. The case prefigures the fictional satire

Fig 3.1
Reconstruction view of the wreck of the Navis Jehsu Christi de Portu *sometime in the early 14th century, lying on her broadside in Brighstone Bay, looking towards the Needles.*
At low water it would have been relatively easy for the local residents to swarm over the wreck but it also attracted plunderers from Christchurch and Wareham in Dorset, and Lymington, Portsmouth and Winchester in Hampshire.

of *Jarndyce* v *Jarndyce* in Dickens' *Bleak House* (1852–3); de Bek's persistence was exceptional even by the standards of protracted medieval disputes over the right to wreck. *La Welfare* of Dartmouth, lost at Kimmeridge, again naming a lengthy list of alleged plunderers, is perhaps more typical in being traced over 5 years between 1371 and 1376.[15]

The survival of all on board and the wholesale theft of the cargo together suggest that the *Jesus Christ* was driven ashore in the inter-tidal zone, accessible both to the escaping sailors from the seaward end, and to the plunderers intent on despoiling the vessel from the landward direction. She was clearly large enough to attract attention from shipping, which may account for the rapid spread of the news to the opposite shore of the Solent, and as far afield as Winchester. One of the accused, John le Notlye, was a 'spicer', at that time not only a spice-dealer, but an apothecary, suggesting that he would have been interested in the cargo to make up medicinal decoctions and confections. In any case, 'free' fruit and wine would surely have been a welcome addition to the medieval diet for those not wealthy enough to purchase such items for their table.

Even if the case was unresolved by the time the *Jesus Christ* disappeared from the records in 1336, we are still able nearly 700 years later to read between the lines and infer a great deal about what happened to the ship and her cargo. Disappointing as it is that the trail appears to go cold, without Martin de Bek's stubborn persistence, we would have no knowledge of the wreck at all. This particular case illustrates how selective the survival of evidence relating to medieval shipwrecks can be: those which do make it into the historical records tend to be those which were contentious. Wrecks which were straightforward – either where the right to wreck was clear, or the merchants were able to save themselves and protect their cargo – tend not to appear at all.

There were clearly other factors affecting the number of recorded shipwrecks from the Middle Ages which are difficult to quantify in detail – the numbers of ships at sea, their size and construction, the navigational aids used, the trading patterns, the skill and experience of the navigators, the safety of the cargoes: never-theless, it is striking that for the entire medieval period so far only just over 400 wrecks have been recorded in and around the English coastline. Far more wrecks, at over 150, were recorded in the 6 decades following the Dissolution of the Monasteries than for any similar time span over the preceding 5 centuries; the 17th century saw well over 950.[16] The medieval data, already skewed by the mere accident of survival of medieval documents in the first place, is further skewed by the centralised nature of those which do exist (being official, legal, state papers) and by the bias inherent in only making contentious wrecks a matter of record. The lack of a formal inquiry is the exception rather than the rule for the 319 ships known to have been lost between 1250 and 1450; virtually all seem to have been the subject of some kind of dispute requiring the intervention of the authorities.[17] Relatively straightforward wrecks therefore seem to disappear from the record.

The hit and run and the hue and cry

In general the seafaring community was, and remains, happy to assist another vessel in distress, unless the sea or wind conditions prevented them doing so. At the back of their minds was always the knowledge that one day they themselves would be in need of such assistance; those who were forced to bear away to avoid meeting the same fate or to save their own lives often recorded what would today be recognised as 'survivors' guilt'. There were exceptions to this assumed code of conduct, and a degree of complacency could tip over completely into negligent handling of a vessel so as to endanger other ships. Collisions at sea involved, at the very least, damage to property, but could also cause serious loss of life: on these grounds, failing to stop and render assistance during a collision at sea was not only a criminal act, but invited moral censure, in much the same way as a hit-and-run accident involving two cars will invite both prosecution and comment in the press.

Tracing the perpetrators was the first priority and was done via the early 19th-century equivalent of the long-running BBC programme *Crimewatch*, making appeals to the public for information. The 'hue and cry' was of medieval origin, calling attention both to a crime committed and the subsequent need to pursue the criminal, for example by calling out 'Stop thief!' The regular insertion of a formal 'hue and cry' across different newspapers took very

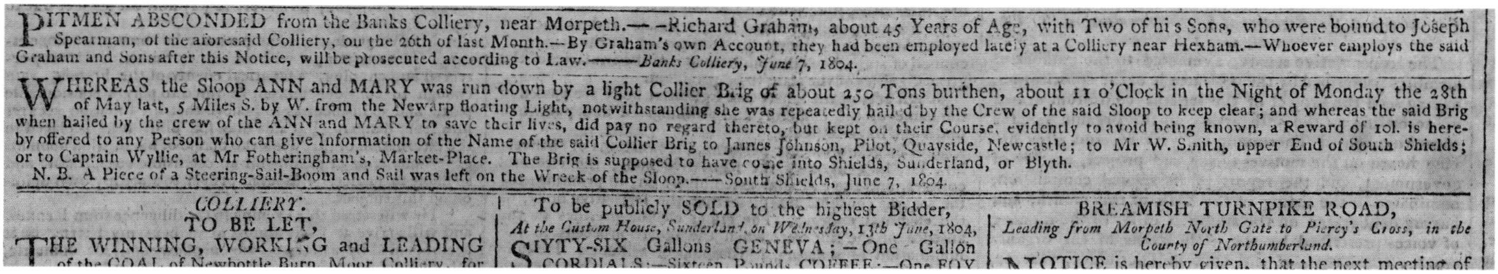

PITMEN ABSCONDED from the Banks Colliery, near Morpeth.——Richard Graham, about 45 Years of Age, with Two of his Sons, who were bound to Joseph Spearman, of the aforesaid Colliery, on the 26th of last Month.—By Graham's own Account, they had been employed lately at a Colliery near Hexham.—Whoever employs the said Graham and Sons after this Notice, will be prosecuted according to Law.——*Banks Colliery, June 7, 1804.*

WHEREAS the Sloop ANN and MARY was run down by a light Collier Brig of about 250 Tons burthen, about 11 o'Clock in the Night of Monday the 28th of May last, 5 Miles S. by W. from the Newarp floating Light, notwithstanding she was repeatedly hail'd by the Crew of the said Sloop to keep clear; and whereas the said Brig when hailed by the crew of the ANN and MARY to save their lives, did pay no regard thereto, but kept on their Course, evidently to avoid being known, a Reward of 10l. is hereby offered to any Person who can give Information of the Name of the said Collier Brig to James Johnson, Pilot, Quayside, Newcastle; to Mr W. Smith, upper End of South Shields; or to Captain Wyllie, at Mr Fotheringham's, Market-Place. The Brig is supposed to have come into Shields, Sunderland, or Blyth. N. B. A Piece of a Steering-Sail-Boom and Sail was left on the Wreck of the Sloop.——*South Shields, June 7, 1804.*

COLLIERY. | To be publicly SOLD to the highest Bidder, | BREAMISH TURNPIKE ROAD,
TO BE LET, | *At the Custom House, Sunderland, on Wednesday, 13th June, 1804,* | *Leading from Morpeth North Gate to Piercy's Cross, in the*
THE WINNING, WORKING and LEADING | SIXTY-SIX Gallons GENEVA;—One Gallon | *County of Northumberland.*
of the COAL of Newbottle Burn Moor Colliery, for | CORDIALS;—Sixteen Pounds COFFEE;—One FOX | NOTICE is hereby given, that the next meeting of

sophisticated advantage of the possibilities offered by the 18th-century mass media: even if many seamen could not read, they could have the news read to them or hear gossip in port. Papers would be carried from port to port, or sent in the post, and the 'hue and cry' would be widely disseminated and reprinted for as long as the offenders were being sought.

Six incidents of this kind were advertised in Tyneside newspapers between 1765 and 1818. The earliest three[18] involved far less detail, perhaps unfortunately in the light of rewards being offered for information leading to identification or prosecution of the offending ship. We can only suspect that the *Fortune*, for example, was southbound with cargo because she was sunk by a 'light' vessel, that is, northbound in ballast: however, formal notices in the 'hue and cry' were much more detailed, enabling the public at large to turn detective, and the later three all establish clear details of the vessel's voyage. In 1804 the *Ann and Mary* was sunk by a Shields collier and almost immediately full details of the accident were published in the 'hue and cry' (Fig 3.2):

> General Hue and Cry. Whereas the ship *Ann and Mary* was run down by a light collier brig of 250 tons burthen, about 11 o'clock in the night of Monday the 28th of May, five miles south by west from the Newarp Floating Light, notwithstanding she [the brig] was repeatedly hailed by the crew of the said sloop to keep clear, and whereas the said brig when hailed by the crew of the *Ann and Mary* to save their lives, did pay no regard thereto, and kept on their course, evidently to avoid being known, a reward of 10l. is hereby offered to any person who can give information of the name of the said collier brig … The brig is supposed to have come in to Shields, Sunderland, or Blyth. NB: A piece of a steering-sail boom and sail was left on the wreck of the sloop. South Shields, June 7, 1804.[19]

Publication in the Newcastle press was clearly intended to alert the readership to two possibilities: since colliers tended to travel in company, there might well have been witnesses to the incident aboard other ships, and that a local ship might very recently have arrived home requiring repair to the missing tackle, for a collier brig encountered in ballast in the North Sea was almost certainly bound north for the Tyneside ports. The level of detail incorporated into the 'hue and cry' permits both an assessment of the damage sustained and the surmise that a portion of the other vessel sank with the *Ann and Mary/Mary Anne*. Additionally, even though the Newarp light vessel was decommissioned in 1990 and her station will have almost certainly shifted according to requirements since the installation of the original light vessel, this description is an extremely important clue as to the location of the wreck. Alerting the public via the 'hue and cry' was evidently a successful strategy, since a prosecution took place, which found for the plaintiffs:

> We formerly noticed that the *Mary Anne* [sic], of Dundee, Wyllie master, was run down and sunk, off Cromer, by a Shields collier, the crew of which, after cutting their vessel clear, inhumanly deserted her, leaving the crew of the *Mary Anne* in the utmost danger. We have now to announce, that ample damages have been awarded against the owners of the Shields vessel.[20]

A similar incident took place 4 years later, in which a Shields collier brig, the *Hope*,[21] was this time the victim, with the loss of all but one of her crew. A 50-guinea reward was offered in the 'hue and cry', with a concluding fulmination: 'Do not such frequent instances of savage inhumanity call loudly for severe punishment?'[22] Fifty guineas appears to have been the standard reward offered for information leading to the identification of offending ships: the same amount was offered for information pertaining to the ship which had run down the *Adventure* or *Endeavour* off Flamborough Head in 1818.[23] The owner of the *Hope* sought damages from the *Mars*, the other vessel involved. The case was heard at the highest level in 1809, in the court

Fig 3.2
Notice on the front page of the Newcastle Courant, *9 June 1804, no.6,661, a fortnight after the incident, showing how seriously the authorities took such cases of 'hit-and-run' accidents. (Newcastle Libraries and Information Service)*

of King's Bench at the Guildhall in London, presided over by the Lord Chief Justice, Lord Ellenborough. The *Mars* was defended by the attorney general. In this case there were impartial witnesses: another *Mary Ann* had been in the vicinity at the time of the accident and rescued the sole survivor from the *Hope*. The mate of the *Mary Ann* gave damning testimony: he heard 'the crew of the *Hope* call three times to the *Mars* when the ships were about a quarter of a mile distant from each other', which was enough for the jury in this case to also find for the plaintiff.[24]

These court cases illustrate that a major strand of detailed documentary evidence for collisions lies in the civic and legal domain, rather than in the straightforward reporting of wrecks in mercantile newspapers, a trend which was to continue until the 20th century. Lives, livelihoods and investments were all at stake – and increasingly large sums of money.

Eighteenth-century insurance fraud

The 18th century was an age of opportunism and of financial scandals (the South Sea Bubble burst in 1720). As Lloyd's Coffee House evolved from a place to meet, drink coffee, read newspapers and exchange mercantile news into the eponymous marine insurance market, shipping register and newspaper (*Lloyd's List*),[25] it also opened up the potential for fraud beyond embezzlement of the cargo (known by the specific term *barratry*). Ship and cargo were normally subject to separate insurance policies, doubling the opportunities for fraud. By exaggerating the true value of the goods and the vessel, the loss of the ship could benefit anyone concerned in the vessel. Barratry was taken to new heights by secretly offloading and selling the cargo prior to deliberately scuttling the vessel, so that masters and merchants stood to gain three times over by the sale of the cargo and successful claims on the underwriters for both cargo and hull.[26]

Martin Creagh, master of the *Friendship*, may have been one such early marine insurance fraudster: it seems that in November 1725 the *Friendship* foundered towards the end of her voyage in the Bristol Channel, homeward-bound with indigo from Bilbao. Suspicions were aroused by the high value of the vessel as insured at Bristol, for the very large sum of £2,600 (approximately £302,000 as at 2010),[27] and by

the fact that Creagh indicated the cargo had gone down with his ship. Further investigation revealed that he had transferred 2000lb of the indigo onto a ship sailing to Carolina, suggesting barratry. Despite this evidence, Creagh was acquitted of 'a felony, in wilfully destroying the said ship' in April 1726.[28] The fact remained that his vessel had gone to the bottom. At least three other cases were considered similarly suspect in the early 18th century, one being a small Dutch ship sunk off Whitehaven in 1751, 'not without suspicion of fraud, there having been a hole in her bottom', and another the *Nightingale*, scuttled and burnt off Lundy around 1753.[29]

A much more spectacular case was that of the *Elizabeth and Martha*,[30] which came to trial at the Old Bailey in June 1752. On one level this was a very sophisticated and complex financial fraud, in which Moses Moravia, John Manoury and Solomon Carolina, were charged with inciting John Misson, the ship's master, 'wilfully to sink her upon the high seas, with intent to defraud several eminent merchants of London, who had made large insurances on that ship';[31] but on another level there was a certain naïveté on the part of the plotters, who seemed to be making it up as they went along. Moravia was an old hand at fraud but perhaps out of his depth when it came to the business of actually sinking a ship.[32]

According to the evidence given at the trial[33] by a merchant, John Wheeler, the vessel was advertised on the Exchange as a 'general ship to carry general goods and passengers', an excellent cover for the scam on the cargo which was about to take place. Loading a miscellaneous cargo would provide an excuse for putting into several ports en route for their final destination of Cork, and allow the conspirators ample opportunity both to maximise their profit by selling what they could, and to sabotage the vessel, without arousing undue suspicion.

A seaman, James Lundin, explained this part of the story further, taking care to blacken Manoury's name in the process: Manoury had first come to his notice while stealing an anchor! Lundin stated that the holds were filled partly with 'good for nothing' dust, 'which we called snuff', and 'brickbats and rubbish'. (*Brickbats* were broken bricks, and thus handy missiles, adopted early on as a metaphor for *criticism*.) They then loaded the ship with genuine miscellaneous goods as cover, including cordage and bales of textiles.

Manoury and Moravia were clearly very resourceful, making use of Carolina's previously unblemished reputation to obtain the insurance on their behalf from Stephen Gyon, an insurance broker. The vessel set sail from Limehouse with a number of passengers, one of whom brought his dogs aboard; Manoury also boarded, as did Moravia, posing as a merchant travelling with his cargo, bound for Cork. He started as he meant to go on, deep in his cover as a merchant, by 'breaking bulk' at Gravesend: that is, selling part of his cargo (stockings) there. Manoury hatched his first plan for disposing of his vessel:

> Manoury said on board I think the safest way to destroy the vessel, and not to endanger our lives, would be to buy some pitch and tar, and get some ignorant man on board, and we will put some nastiness in the pitch pot and say some quantity of pitch near, and she'll take fire, and that will recover the money the same.

This might have been a plausible 'accident' since a number of vessels were burnt while carrying pitch and tar.[34] As agreed they dismissed one hand at Sheerness, taking on another ignorant of the plot. An eventful voyage continued with a little buying and selling here and there, taking on extra ballast at Dover, ostensibly to ensure the ship's stability, but in reality to act as a weight in the execution of the plot, and so on with a fair wind down the Channel. Manoury was all for altering the ship's log to suggest instead an adverse wind at west and north-west, 'for the gentlemen at London (the under-writers) that sit in their white lined chambers, don't know how the wind lies at sea', obviously with an eye to suggesting that the *Elizabeth and Martha* had become distressed during her voyage. The conspirators then put in to Lymington and Cowes to do a little more trading. In his evidence, the ship's carpenter painted the picture of a genuine leak, whereupon they put again into the other side of the Solent, but a slip gave him away as he called Portsmouth 'Plymouth', which suggested that the story was cobbled together. By now Misson was understandably having second thoughts about setting the ship on fire, prompting Manoury to suggest an alternative plan:

> I believe your best method will be to take a crow and go down into the lower Scuttle ... and get the sharpest pointed and heaviest, and endeavour in the after part of the vessel to cut the double of the vessel up, and then to drive the crow plum through, so as to make many holes to let the water in, will do it as well as with an augur [sic].

Despite their rapid overnight progress to the real Plymouth - which suggested that there was nothing wrong with the vessel at all - they pretended otherwise on arrival at port, where they carried out yet another plan. They sailed the ship into the Cattewater at Plymouth, ostensibly to examine her bottom to search for a mythical leak, putting about a story that would cover their tracks by airing prior concerns about the state of the vessel, but it was an opportunity for Misson to bore some holes into the bottom and plug them with 'mop-handles'.

The scene was then set: leaving Plymouth with the wind at east-south-east, they made for a spot approximately 2 or 3 leagues (6 to 9 miles) offshore, and, having ensured that everyone who was not in on the plot was busy about the ship, the makeshift plugs were pulled out, leaving the ship to founder in about quarter of an hour. The gentleman who had embarked with the dogs panicked, offloaded his goods and jumped into the boat, followed by his dogs and the rest of the crew. All aboard were safely landed, and made their way to 'Foy' (Fowey) to 'make protest to a notary-publick'. The chief conspirators, Manoury and Moravia, seemed anxious to demand assurances from the master that he had played his part and the vessel had well and truly sunk: to which he replied that he 'saw her mast-head go under water, and she never will rise again, except the world turns upside down'.

It was after returning to London that Moravia became over-confident and the plot then unravelled. Gyon the broker recalled that 'Mr Moravia came into my compting house and demanded satisfaction for a loss', but he felt that Moravia was overstressing his honesty and this aroused his suspicions. At the trial Moravia and Manoury blamed each other and everyone else but themselves, changing their stories much as they had previously changed their plans for the disposal of the ship. Many of their fellow Jews provided good character references for Carolina, leading to his acquittal, but refused to do so for Manoury. One witness said firmly: 'I have known but little of him of late, nor do I desire to know him.' Moravia and Manoury were found guilty, fined and sentenced to 12 months' imprisonment in Newgate; they were taken out of the prison on two occasions during that time, to be pilloried. It must have been punishment enough to stand in the pillory on a cold December day in 1752, without also undergoing a 'severe pelting from the populace'.[35]

Aside from providing a fascinating insight into crime and punishment in Georgian London, and the willingness of the conspirators to believe in the naïveté of the underwriters, the trial of the three men illuminates a forgotten corner of marine history. Nevertheless, their failure did not deter others from the attempt and similar 'accidents' took place or were suspected into the 19th century.[36] Only a leak could have given a sinking in fair weather an air of plausibility, yet good weather was necessary for maximising the crew's chances of coming out alive and profiting from the incident, even if they had little regard for anyone else. Understandably, a leak in otherwise favourable weather conditions aroused suspicion, though was perfectly possible if the ship was much strained from previous incidents.[37] Nevertheless, no physical harm to anyone ensued and the saga of the inept plotters aboard the *Elizabeth and Martha* provides some light relief among the normally tragic tales of shipwreck. It is also an unusual case. Insurance fraud has occasionally been suggested as the cause of other shipwrecks, but was historically difficult to prove in legal terms. In archaeological terms, very little has been found to betray evidence of such sabotage.[38]

Fire at sea: ships' cats, white elephants and drunken sailors

Paradoxically, one of the greatest enemies of a ship at sea was fire. The surrounding water was little help when virtually every aspect of the construction of a wooden sailing ship was combustible, from her timber hull, caulked with tar or pitch, to her masts, canvas sails and ropes. Cargoes, too, were often flammable: under such circumstances, it was little wonder that incidents fatal to both ship and crew could be started by someone setting off a chain of mishaps culminating in fire.

One of these accidents befell 'one of the finest ships in the coastal trade between London and Gainsborough'[39] as she arrived in the River Trent in 1777 with gunpowder, hemp (for rope-making), rum and porter, all of which were highly combustible cargoes. The accident was caused by a startling concatenation of events:

A hot coal from the cabbin fire falling upon a cat which lay before it, and entangling in her hair, she immediately run into the half-deck, which was nearly full of hemp, and it took fire in such

a manner that the ship's company could not extinguish it, notwithstanding the greatest efforts were used.

As there was twenty barrels of gunpowder on board, they was [sic] obliged to quit the vessel for fear of the consequences. About nine o'clock in the evening she blew up her decks, masts, yards, etc and her bottom immediately sunk, and all her goods were rolled out by the strength of the tide, so that there remains but one puncheon of rum, and two or three barrels of porter.[40]

A common theme was the unfortunate proximity of candles (the only means of lighting available at the time) to flammable goods. The *Marlborough*, belonging to the English East India Company, arrived safely at Blackwall in 1730 after a long voyage from the East Indies. She took fire 'as 'tis said by the snuff of a candle falling among the salt petre, of which there is some hundred bags on board'. The intended meaning of 'some hundreds' turned out to be an understatement, and the quantity of saltpetre was, in fact, the altogether more alarming 12,000 bags.[41] Since the ship was beached at a safe distance from other vessels, collateral damage was mercifully limited, although a nearby house did catch fire. Sadly, one of the victims of the fire was 'a curious white elephant' which 'perished in the flames' after £500 had been offered for it the same day,[42] suggesting that it had been brought back as a speculative cargo, destined either for a menagerie or as a travelling curiosity.

The elephant's near-contemporary Clara the rhinoceros had also survived a similarly arduous voyage from the Dutch East Indies, to become a celebrity in her own right, shown round the courts of Europe. Her portrait was painted on several occasions. Clara's adventures ironically included shipwreck or near-shipwreck, as if captivity, unsuitable diet and lengthy voyages were not enough to threaten the survival of exotic animals from around the globe. The successful outcome in Clara's case increased her interest to visitors from all ranks of society as they came to gawp: a rhino had, for example, died in a shipwreck off Italy in 1516.[43] Shipwreck continued to be a commonplace of animal export or even the transport of animals from place to place: for example, most of the animals from a circus menagerie died when the *Royal Tar* foundered after catching fire off Maine, New England, in 1836. 'Zoo archaeology' is a discipline which has revealed among other things the existence of menageries on British country estates and the presence of non-native animal species in unexpected locations,[44] but so far little or no research has been carried out into the transportation of, or mortality rates among, exotic livestock. The question raises the intriguing possibility that exotic species may turn up in shipwrecks in English waters or that animal remains found in terrestrial locations may be those of creatures which survived the loss of their vessel in English waters (although this latter correlation is likely to be difficult to prove). Certainly less exotic animals died in shipwrecks of all kinds, not just those caused by fire, well into the 20th century. They represented livestock cargoes, animals carried as meat and dairy providers, and those transported in or during wartime. Horses were regularly carried on troop ships in the days of cavalry regiments, and as late as 1941 horses were among the general cargo of the *Somali* when she was bombed and sunk.[45]

Another ship which arrived in London after a lengthy voyage, only to perish, was the West Indiaman *Friendship*, blown up at Lower Hope Point in 1759; the accident was blamed on custom house officers 'searching in the powder room, in which search a spark dropt from the candle',[46] killing both the officers and several visitors who had come aboard to 'congratulate their friends on their safe arrival in England'. A similar incident befell the *Elizabeth* as she entered Falmouth from Montserrat in 1745: three ships' boys went to draw off some rum in the cabin. They carelessly allowed the 'snuff of a candle' to fall, setting alight some grains of gunpowder on the floor. It then 'spread with such rapidity that the vessel was quickly consumed', including her cargo of 80 puncheons of rum.[47] Also at Falmouth, in 1720, plunderers swarming upon a stranded Dutch ship laden with brandy inadvertently set her alight, although she might otherwise 'have been got off':

> the Country People coming so thick, they were obliged to leave her. But some of those plunderers, having drank so much brandy and being busy in the hold with a candle, set fire to the brandy, by which means the ship and cargo were destroyed and two of the ruffians perished in the flames.[48]

Rum and brandy were not the only combustible cargoes, but tobacco, which was, of course, intended to be burnt, was also dangerous if a fire reached the hold, for example, in the case of the *Olive Branch* in 1767.[49] Likewise, when the *Coquille* frigate caught fire in 1798, the fire spread to the *Endeavour* collier brig moored nearby: 'the coals in the bottom of the brig, aground on the bank, were then in a strong body of fire'.[50] However, the indiscriminate use of candles remained a principal cause of loss and was seen as much in the navy as in the mercantile marine. There were a number of incidents at Chatham: in 1682 the Second Rate *Henry* (formerly *Dunbar* in the Cromwellian Navy) caught fire when an aged sailor dropped a lit candle onto some oakum (loose, unpicked fibres of rope).[51]

Similarly, the *Impétueux*, captured from the French in 1794 at the Battle of the 'Glorious First of June' was only to spend a few months in the ownership of the Royal Navy. In August 1794, an accident in Portsmouth harbour prevented her from being renamed and entering British service: following a flood, the powder in her magazine was wet, but remained combustible and was dropped and trodden all over the ship while being offloaded. It might, perhaps, have been less foolish to offload it during the day, rather than by candlelight. The ensuing conflagration following the inevitable dropped candle accounted for 11 lives, but *Impétueux* was cut out of the harbour and beached on nearby mudflats to prevent the spread of the fire to other shipping.[52] Though the cause was never ascertained, in 1796 the Fifth Rate *Amphion* caught fire and blew up in Plymouth, as a result of which landing gunpowder stores before docking the ship was enforced.[53]

Gunpowder explosions were so much feared that, during the Napoleonic wars, when even small colliers were routinely armed for self-defence, false rumours of gunpowder on board the *Norwich Merchant* ablaze on Tyneside were sufficient to prompt a panicked evacuation in 1801, putting the whole quayside and other shipping in jeopardy. Once 'the few cartridges on board had exploded' residents plucked up the courage to return and assisted some factory owners to work a small engine to extinguish the fire, by which time the vessel was 'burnt nearly to the water's edge'.[54]

Fear of the press gangs seeking to impress sailors on merchantmen into naval service ran high during the Revolutionary and Napoleonic wars, inadvertently contributing to the loss of the *Walsingham* or *Washington Packet* in 1799, with the loss of about nine-tenths of her valuable cotton cargo. The ship's cook had:

lost a knife in a private place, formed deep in the cotton for the purpose of concealing the seamen from press gangs; and going down with a candle to look for it the candle dropped from his hand. The cotton immediately took fire, and the place being small and the entrance to it narrow, the thick suffocative smoke that immediately issued from the cotton rendered the carrying down of water impossible.[55]

Fire at sea was something to be feared and was not necessarily extinguished by the surrounding water if it started in or spread below the waterline. Even if the ship's crew were able to escape in the ship's boats, they faced almost certain death in the waves or by starvation unless they were either near land or rescued by a passing vessel. A fire in mid-Atlantic must have been terrifying with the prospect of being adrift for weeks with only a few planks between the

survivors and the might of the Atlantic (Fig 3.3).

In mid-Channel incidents, survivors of fire had a better chance of being picked up by a passing ship or of making landfall before sunburn, madness and starvation took their toll, but even there fire was a terrifying experience. Lightning strikes were a common cause of loss to fire (or could split the vessel asunder, as happened with the *Betsey* off Land's End in 1799).[56] The crew of the brig *Robert Shaw*, of Boston, Massachusetts, struck by lightning off Ushant in 1847, first tried to make 'all sail the ship could carry in order to get her into some port on the English coast', but filling the sails with wind instead literally fanned the flames of the fire. As it took hold, they decided to abandon ship some 40 or 50 miles south of the Bill of Portland. The current carried the burning vessel in the direction of the English coast, where she came ashore as a wreck at Kimmeridge in Dorset, in the opposite direction to her crew who had managed to land safely in France. As for the vessel, only 200 bales of her cotton cargo were saved 'in a damaged state',[57] making her one of the 671 vessels lost in English waters solely by fire or consumed by fire following an explosion.[58]

Lightning strikes could also happen in the safety of harbour: most famously to the *Grace Dieu*, now a designated wreck site, which was laid up in the River Hamble when she caught fire in 1439.[59] In 1809 the *Dwina* caught fire in Grimsby Dock after being struck, and only the first part of her cargo (including liquorice) which had already been unladen, escaped the fire: the rest was consumed, along with the ship.[60]

Inevitably the impact of fire was greatest on vessels constructed of wood: over 530 timber-built ships are recorded as having been lost to fire in English waters. To date only five of these have been located, including the *London*, which caught fire following an explosion.[61] These small numbers are easily explainable. If they caught fire in harbour, they were removed so as not to cause an obstruction, and were subsequently broken up, often leaving few, if any remains. If they caught fire at sea and burnt to the waterline, their remains are minimal, and not easily recognisable, but, undoubtedly, more of this number will join the *London* in coming to light in the future.

Fire at sea: fire and ice

Aside from the problems associated with combustible materials, there were other dangers associated with cargoes, the most obvious issue being overloading. Many vessels were frequently dangerously overloaded by shipowners putting profit before safety. Sailing ships with their tall masts, sitting low in the water and top-heavy with rigging, were prone to heeling over if the cargo shifted in heavy weather, or they were caught in a sudden squall, but overloading also rendered steamships vulnerable. Overloaded ships built of timber were at an increased risk of 'starting', that is, springing a plank, and therefore a leak. Close to shore, this would not matter so much, but in mid-ocean a leak was as terrifying as a fire.

Samuel Plimsoll's famous load line, painted on both sides of the ship's hull, was a late 19th-century refinement of a much older idea: load marks emerged at different times and in different places, including British marks specified by *Lloyd's Register*, but not compulsorily enforced.[62] However, the Merchant Shipping Act 1876 enforced the Plimsoll line for British ships, in order to prevent loss of life at sea in the so-called 'coffin ships', whether steam or sail. Legislation could not eliminate this type of accident altogether, and poor practice continued to endanger lives at sea, exacerbated by the lack of a consistent location for the mark before 1894. One victim of this failure was the *Yanikale*, a Scottish barque of 308 tons gross, laden with 250 tons of iron and 276 of deals from Gavle in Sweden for Gloucester, which foundered off St Ives in 1880. Her voyage since putting into Shields had been dogged by misfortune and leaks, but she struggled south down the North Sea, through the entire length of the English Channel and round the Cornish peninsula before finally succumbing. At the subsequent enquiry it was found that she was not only carrying too much cargo on this voyage, but had been strained by being repeatedly overladen.[63]

Overloading and the shifting of cargo, the first increasing the likelihood of the second, appear to have taken a particularly dangerous turn with the arrival of the railways.[64] As the railways snaked across the country, there were corresponding accidents at sea as railway track and rolling stock were moved around by ship as well as exported overseas. The steam-powered 'iron horse' was to revolutionise land transport, but while steam was also becoming increasingly preferred at sea, early steamships were, like contemporary sailing ships, still constructed of wood; sailing ships still predominated during the first half of the 19th century. The dangers of metal cargo working loose in the hold of a wooden vessel are only too apparent. There were at least 13 such accidents leading to shipping losses in English waters from 1838 to 1859, similar incidents in territorial waters taking place up to 1936.

One particularly noteworthy incident was the loss of the *South Australian* clipper in 1889;[65] having left Cardiff for Rosario (Argentina), the vessel was pitching so much in a heavy gale off Lundy that her cargo of railway track broke adrift and a rail smashed through her side. This, and the vessel's composite construction (a wooden hull laid over iron, rather than timber, framing) led to the wreckage washed ashore on the north coast of Devon being interpreted as the result of a collision between a steamer and a large sailing ship.[66] Other cargo

Fig 3.3 (opposite) The Luxborough Galley *was a slave ship homeward-bound to England with a combustible cargo of sugar and rum, whose crew were cast adrift after a devastating fire in mid-Atlantic in 1727. This scene, one of six in a narrative sequence, shows the vessel 'burnt nearly to the waterline', as the fire consumes her entirely, and emphasises the desolation of the survivors huddled together in the yawl in the loneliness of a vast, empty expanse of ocean. By the time the survivors made landfall a fortnight later, they had dwindled to a handful, resorting to cannibalism to stay alive. (John Cleveley, c 1727. BHC2388 © National Maritime Museum, Greenwich, London)*

shifting incidents were associated with general consignments of iron and other metals: for example, the Sunderland schooner *Betsey* sank in 1859 when her iron freight shifted in a force 8 gale.[67]

Some wrecks were not caused by the cargo *per se*, but simply the quantities involved and the way they were stacked, stored or secured on board: even securely stored cargoes could break loose during severe weather. By contrast flammable materials were inherently dangerous, but of course the dangers would be exacerbated by poor working practices. Before the advent of petroleum products as a principal cargo, one of the most dangerous was *aqua fortis* (Latin,

'strong water', a solution of nitric acid, derived from saltpetre, in water, used for etching). In 1795, before the *Minerva* could leave the Thames for Boston, Massachusetts, with *aqua fortis*, she took fire and had to be scuttled in the river to extinguish the fire (Fig 3.4).[68]

In modern times steel-hulled supertankers are a common sight, crossing the world's oceans with petrol: from this perspective, it is difficult to believe highly flammable cargoes were originally carried in wooden-hulled sailing ships, and even apparently less flammable cargoes posed a hidden risk. Health and safety measures were conspicuously absent (Fig 3.5). In 1797 the American *Indian Chief*,[69] succumbed

Fig 3.4
Not even iron or steel ships could escape the ravages of fire. In 1926 the 50-year-old iron steamer Falcon *(901824) and her cargo of jute and matches caught fire off the Goodwin Sands, bound from Ghent for London. The* Falcon *was taken in tow, but as the fire crept along the tow line, she had to be abandoned, and drove ashore at Langdon Stairs, near Dover where little of her now remains. The Swedish cargo vessel* Vanland *(938428), also laden with matches, burned for a week when she was torpedoed off Runswick Bay in 1917.*
(DP114192)

to fire in Falmouth, as the oil in her typically Cornish export cargo of pilchards for Genoa fed the flames. During the Victorian era, and before the age of the car, the regular transport of petroleum and its derivatives (benzine and naphtha) can be explained by their use in oil lamps and as solvents in the rubber industry and elsewhere. Two accidents in the early 1870s were characteristic: in 1871 an abandoned, or 'derelict', vessel was found at sea south of the Lizard, still with her cargo intact, and towed into Penzance. The cargo consisted of petroleum in barrels marked 'Standard Oil Company, carbon oil, New York and Cleveland, Ohio', which were recovered and put into a Padstow sloop, the *Collina*,[70] for transhipment to Plymouth. Orders were given for all craft to keep clear of the *Collina*, but a Newlyn fishing smack, in ignorance of the embargo intended to prevent just such an accident as was about to occur, moored nearby. The crew went ashore, leaving their vessel unattended. The smack was forced up against

Fig 3.5
A blasted tree stands beside one of the houses extensively damaged in the wake of the explosion of the Tilbury *barge (1525684) on 2 October 1874, as it passed along the Regent's Canal with a miscellaneous cargo bound for the industrial Midlands. Gunpowder, petrol or 'benzoline' and sugar were all stowed on the same 69ft-long barge, each of which was blamed as a contributory factor in the explosion, which occurred just as the* Tilbury *was passing under the Macclesfield Bridge. The bridge itself was severely damaged but rebuilt, and earned the sobriquet 'Blow-up Bridge'. The force of the explosion also sank the barge* Limehouse *(1525705) just behind the* Tilbury *in the five-barge convoy towed by a steam tug, demolished or damaged several houses in the vicinity, including the home of the Victorian artist Sir Lawrence Alma-Tadema, and affected the buildings and the animals of London Zoo. The* Times *of 12 October 1874, noted with relief that the 'immense squares of glass in front of the reptile cages escaped fracture'. The photographers, York and Son, specialised in covering scenes of patriotic interest and noteworthy events. (CC97/00558*

the *Collina* with the tide and in the consequent explosion the ill-fated cargo was involved for a second time in a wreck event, resulting in the *Collina*'s destruction.

The Canadian *Abbie Perkins*,[71] a schooner of only 107 tons gross, blew up at sea in 1873, 10 miles off Bolt Head, south Devon, having safely crossed the Atlantic with her hazardous cargo of naphtha and benzine for London; some of the crew managed to escape into a boat, even though they were badly burnt, and were picked up and landed at nearby Salcombe. Likewise, in 1899, the small ketch *Lady Elizabeth*[72] caught fire shortly after leaving Plymouth for Penzance with a similar cargo. The crew opened the bulkhead with a crowbar, which we would now recognise as feeding the flames with oxygen: unsurprisingly, their efforts to douse the flames with buckets of water were to no avail. On this occasion the crew were able to abandon ship before the inevitable explosion, but not all crews were so fortunate, as the case of the *War Knight* shows,[73] and *War Knight* was by no means the only tanker lost during the First World War. Like *War Knight*, the *Spiraea* was a tanker carrying American petrol, which caught fire while discharging her cargo in the Manchester Ship Canal in 1916. She carried on burning for several days before being towed away for breaking, with over a million gallons of oil said to be a complete loss. Although not attributable to war causes,

the loss of *Spiraea* was still suppressed in the British press as far as practicable but made news in America.[74]

In more recent times oil spills out of stricken vessels, whether they have caught fire or been holed, have been recognised as ecological disasters (for example, the wreck in 1967 of the *Torrey Canyon*,[75] off the Isles of Scilly, with its detrimental impact upon wildlife). A forerunner of this disaster was the loss of the Russian ship *Blesk*, an early purpose-built oil tanker, on the Greystone Ledges in South Devon in fog in 1896.[76] This incident led to an oil spill noted by locals as creeping along the coast, but it was otherwise not as newsworthy as such disasters would be today, for the environmental impact was simply not recognised.

Oil cargoes, including plant and vegetable oils, could conversely be beneficial in time of need: the old saying 'pour oil on troubled waters' has some foundation in truth, a phenomenon recognised as early as Classical times.[77] *In extremis* barrels of oil could be broken open and poured over the side, at one and the same time lightening the distressed vessel and calming the waves through surface tension, optimising the crew's chances of escape (Fig 3.6). As late as 1922 it was noted that the oil leaking out of the *Scandinavia* tanker smoothed the sea when she ran aground on the Bill of Portland.[78] The oil cargo from a 'derelict' brought her to shore in

Fig 3.6
The Royal Fleet Auxiliary Darkdale *sinking after being torpedoed at anchor off St Helena on 22 October 1941. RFA ships as fleet oilers carried large quantities of fuel oil with which to refuel naval ships. The effect of oil on the surface of the water dampening down the waves can be clearly seen. (Photograph © and by kind permission of the Museum of St Helena)*

1637, despite piratical attempts to scuttle her:

> Last night I received news by a Dover man of war of a ship cast on shore at Seaford, and this morning I went thither, where I find a ship, by all likelihoods of Hamburgh, of about 300 tons, which came out of the Straits, and has met with some enemy, which after they had pillaged her of all the rich goods, cut two great holes in the side of the ship to sink her, but being laden with oils it bore the ship, and these winds put her ashore. She first grounded far off at low water, and Seaford boats went aboard and brought ashore various bales of silks. The next high water brought her to the gravel, and various other goods were saved by those of Seaford.[79]

In a similar vein, figures for timber cargoes generally reveal that the most common cause of loss was stranding rather than foundering at sea, since the wood kept the vessel afloat, even with cargoes of denser hardwood such as mahogany.[80] As we would expect from the use of cork as a buoyancy aid by Victorian lifeboatmen, this effect was most marked with a cargo of cork.[81]

Casualties involving the lime trade were common: quicklime reacts vigorously upon contact with water. Stranded vessels, holed upon rocks, would let in water, setting off a chemical reaction, dangerous within the confines of wooden casks aboard wooden sailing vessels. Inevitably, these ships caught fire, and were burnt out, occasionally causing the decks of affected vessels to blow up.[82] The reaction could be triggered not only by water ingress, but also by other factors: in 1766 'a lime sloop took fire about a mile to the southward of Sunderland, occasioned by a coil of new ropes being laid on the lime … she burnt to the keel'.[83] The earliest known loss attributable to a lime cargo dates from 1540,[84] but the most significant group of such losses reveals a constant trading pattern: at least 10 vessels were lost in this way on the coast of Northumberland, carrying lime from Sunderland to Scotland between 1775 and 1829. A description of Monkwearmouth (Sunderland) in 1848 states:

> The chief trade of the port is the exportation of coal and lime, from the collieries and lime-works in the neighbourhood, to Aberdeen, Montrose, Arbroath, and other Scottish ports: of the former, about 30,000 chaldrons annually shipped, and of the latter about 70,000.[85]

The 18th- and 19th-century whalers laden with blubber, chiefly used as a lighting source, were also extremely vulnerable to fire: the *Clapham* of Hull was lost in Greenland in 1815 in this way. At home, the whaler *Newcastle* of Howden Dock caught fire in 1766 in a savage conflagration as she was being readied for her next voyage. Such fires ran the risk of spreading not only to neighbouring ships, but also to adjoining wharves and warehouses. Being outward-bound, it is likely that residues of blubber were ingrained in areas of the ropes, timbers or in the holds, and added fuel to the fire (as we saw in the previous section, ingrained gunpowder residues from the *Impétueux* were sufficient to cause a conflagration).[86] A similar accident befell the *Nautilus*, a Whitby whaler lost in 1795 as she set out on her maiden voyage, although the cause was clearly not combustible residues. The *Nautilus* burnt until noon the next day, when nothing was left except 'a small part of her bottom, filled with ashes, bolts, and the iron hoops of her burnt casks'.[87]

More usually, however, whalers fell victim to ice outside English waters, involved in fatal collisions like the *Titanic*, or crushed in sea ice, like Shackleton's expedition ship *Endurance* in the Antarctic in 1915. However, ice sometimes caused damage from inside. The early 19th century saw demand rise in Britain for ice for food preservation purposes: for domestic consumption, for grocery, fishing and allied industries, and for making ice cream. Ice was initially imported as a natural resource from the northern United States, easily harvestable during the harsh winters there (at once meeting the needs of American agricultural workers unemployed in the winter season and of entrepreneurs seeking cheap labour). Ice then became a return cargo for ships arriving at Boston, Massachusetts, from which they would otherwise have returned empty. Effectively ice was exportable ballast, even to British India, to the Caribbean, and in a 'coals-to-Newcastle' scenario, to the fjords of Chile.[88]

The transatlantic voyage made ice expensive to import into Britain: the long voyage increased the risk of melting and forced up prices. Norway, closer to Britain and with an abundant natural resource, present on the mountains even during the summer, was a cheaper option. Between 1874 and 1911, the zenith of the Norwegian ice trade, no fewer than 44 ice ships were wrecked in English waters with their wet cargo: the demand was such that the Norwegians began to farm ice through artificial lakes on higher ground to supplement their natural resource.[89] The majority of vessels so lost were likewise

Norwegian, although a handful of ships from other nationalities were involved.[90] Most Norwegian ice ships operated out of the ports of Kragerø and Drøbak near Oslo, as well as Oslo itself, as the most convenient port for the British and southern European export trade. The loss of the *August Herman Francke* on the Goodwin Sands in 1886, while en route to San Sebastian, reveals that Norwegian ice, like American ice, travelled lengthy distances.[91]

Despite the shorter North Sea voyage, a quick crossing remained desirable before the ice began to melt, representing both a commercial loss and a danger to the ship herself due to cargo shifting as melting ice blocks began to slip and slide around the vessel.[92] This may have been one of the strains upon the Norwegian wooden barque *Blanche et Marie* which foundered off the Leman Bank off Norfolk in 1877 in a westerly force 8 gale: loose blocks of ice pitching around the vessel in fierce winds were a recipe for springing a leak. No ice vessel wrecks have so far been located: unlike many wrecks it is of course impossible to identify them by their cargo, which will have long ago become part of the sea itself, yet an identifying factor which might still be present on such wreck sites could be their characteristic ice dogs (mechanical 'tongs'), used for loading and unloading the cargo.

Bizarrely, some collier losses were blamed on the spontaneous combustion of the cargo. Spontaneous combustion fascinated the Victorians (Krook dies in this way in Dickens' *Bleak House*, 1852), while a sufficient number of accidents occurred at sea to prompt the foundation of a Royal Commission on the Spontaneous Combustion of Coal at Sea in 1876.[93] The Commission compared, for example, the chemical composition of coal from different seams and veins in an attempt to establish a common trigger for such events, which remained mysterious despite, of course, the purpose of coal, destined to be spent as fuel. The *Sisters*,[94] lost by 'spontaneous combustion' of her coal cargo in the Downs in 1873, must have been one of the recent cases informing the Royal Commission's deliberations. Similar cases arising from other cargoes were sporadically recorded in the *Board of Trade Casualty Returns*: for example, in 1910, the *Ymer*, a Russian barque, burnt to the water's edge and foundered in the River Fal after her cargo of 'organic manure' caught fire.[95]

Such Royal Commissions, and the *Board of Trade Casualty Returns,* which was published from 1856 (following on from its previous incarnation as the *Admiralty Wreck Register* from 1850) and produced annual statistics of wreck events with a breakdown by cause, marked the beginning of a change in social attitudes towards the plight of the ordinary seaman, which culminated in the first high-profile changes of Samuel Plimsoll's act. It became the norm for the Board of Trade to hold inquiries into wreck events, which were published and widely publicised in the press of the day. These inquiries, in addition to the yearly publication of the *Casualty Returns*, sought to draw lessons from preventable accidents and were among the first to inform what we now take for granted as health and safety issues. They were extremely influential abroad, providing the model for other seafaring nations to produce their own statistics and inquiries.[96]

The cargoes of many of these ships are today known as 'legacy wrecks', those which have left a legacy of danger and pollution: munitions (shells, bombs, grenades and torpedoes) can become unstable after decades of immersion in the sea. Oil and other cargoes continue to pollute the sea and pose a danger to divers and to wildlife.

The 'legacy wreck' which causes most concern is the *Richard Montgomery*, known as the 'most dangerous wreck in Britain' and the only wreck in England to be designated under Section II of the Protection of Wrecks Act 1973.[97] While Section I is for wrecks of historical interest, Section II concerns legacy wrecks posing a 'potential danger to life or property'. The *Richard Montgomery* was an American Liberty Ship, which had successfully made her way across the U-boat-infested Atlantic from New York in convoy HX 301, arriving at Liverpool on 8 August 1944 with her cargo of munitions and bombs, destined to support the liberation of France. The *Richard Montgomery* was passed in a kind of seaborne relay race from convoy to convoy 'northabout' around the top of Scotland, from Loch Ewe to Methil in convoy WN 619, then from Methil to Southend-on-Sea in convoy FS 1543, arriving off Southend-on-Sea on 15 August.[98] While awaiting her final convoy on to Cherbourg, she was ordered to anchor immediately off the eastern edge of the Sheerness Middle Sand, to keep her apart from other vessels.

Unfortunately, however, she drifted towards the sands, where she became 'hogged' (though amidships she was supported by sand, her stem and stern were not, which placed great stress on the vessel amidships). At low water, inevitably, therefore, she broke her back (Fig 3.7). Understandably, the Admiralty was at great pains to salvage such a vital cargo, but as the holds began to flood the effort was abandoned half-way through. Nearly 70 years later, she stubbornly remains sandwiched between the Nore Great Ship Anchorage to the north and the Medway Approach Channel to the south in the Thames Estuary, with 1,400 tons of net explosive quantity of material still aboard, her superstructure still visible. She cannot be dispersed or flattened as a navigational hazard by explosives or otherwise; to raise her or cut her up poses an unacceptable risk of explosion, which would have repercussions at sea and on land.

The explosive cargo is likely to remain stable if undisturbed, even as she sinks deeper into the ooze of the Thames Estuary, although sporadic concerns are occasionally raised as to their stability. For more than half a century she has posed an intractable problem which may only be eventually resolved by becoming wholly entombed in the muddy seabed. The condition of the wreck is regularly surveyed using multibeam sonar equipment, safer than the regular inspection by specialist divers which used to take place. Nevertheless, she is actively monitored by 24-hour surveillance by Medway Ports, together with a heavily buoyed exclusion zone, complete with foghorn, to prevent any danger of accidental collision.

The irony is that the *Richard Montgomery* was ordered to anchor where she did because of her cargo, which posed a danger to other ships which were equally vital to the war effort. As a wreck site she is the most dramatic of all the known 'legacy wrecks' in English waters.[99] In a further irony, the most fortunate aspect of the wreck is that she lies upon a sandbank. To some extent her presence mitigates the hazard posed by the sandbank: as ships are warned away from the *Richard Montgomery*, they are also warned off the Sheerness Middle Sand.

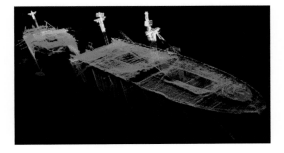

Human error and the human factor

The external factors of marine hazards and warfare may be compounded by decisions taken by the master and crew of a vessel in danger. At its simplest a decision taken to run for shelter or to ride out a storm offshore may mean the difference between life and death, and in time of war the loss of a ship may be as much due to a decision taken by a commanding officer as to the battering received from an enemy – whether by cannonball or torpedo. Even cases of 'friendly fire' arise out of mistaken decisions. However, human factors also affect the outcome when a ship is found to be in jeopardy: panic, indecision or the wrong judgement call can frustrate attempts to get ships to safety or create a chain of circumstances which lead to the loss of a vessel, sometimes in unexpected ways. Human error tends to compound initial factors such as the ship springing a leak or her engines failing – often fatally. Some of the major maritime accidents in British history have been a result of human error, as illustrated by three very well-known naval disasters and a peacetime incident of tragic proportions. Most have been exhaustively chronicled, but remain the subject of conjecture, so bear repetition in this chapter: all involve the difficulty of reconstructing the incident, since the loss of life was so great that witnesses who could have shed light on the disaster were lost with each vessel.

Even today it is generally acknowledged that technology is only as good as the person operating it. How much more is this true of a ship in the waters of the sea or in a river where conditions could fluctuate rapidly? Looking at human error also provides an opportunity to look more at the social composition of the crews and passengers on board stricken ships, simply because accidents at sea provide a window into human nature. These are the wrecks that excited most 'human interest' at the time, and continue to do so today, because in hindsight the tragedies seem so preventable, exciting the compassion of the readership then and now. Most had repercussions for the future of maritime travel as all involved sought to prevent such tragedies from recurring. Sometimes, even, shipwrecks may be a product of the demands of their times: it is impossible to legislate for all possibilities and new types of vessel, new demands, new cargoes and new routes may throw up specific patterns of incidents.

Fig 3.7
'The most dangerous wreck in Britain': The Richard Montgomery *as she now lies, shown by laser scanning and multibeam data in 2009. The white masts represent sections always above water; the break in the hull can be clearly seen. The wreck is regularly surveyed and monitored for the consequences of even the smallest sign of degradation in the hull.*
(© Crown copyright. Courtesy of the Maritime and Coastguard Agency)

Human error may even go right back to the drawing board, because of poor design: missing elements or extraneous features. In the former category was, of course, possibly the most famous wreck of all time, the *Titanic*, which foundered in mid-Atlantic in 1912 with heavy loss of life after collision with an iceberg, poor bulkhead design compounded with her inadequate provision of lifeboats. Also outside English waters, the Swedish *Vasa*, narrowly built and top-heavy with decorative carvings which impeded the ship's functionality, is also a well-known example of design fault, with her gunports sitting so low in the water that it was

almost inevitable she would sink. She foundered in Stockholm harbour on her maiden voyage in 1628, and, like the *Mary Rose*, whose fate and recovery she parallels in many respects, she is now a museum ship and may be visited by the public.[100]

The *Mary Rose* herself sank in 1545 during the Battle of the Solent (Fig 3.8): the parallels with the *Vasa* extend to the manner of loss in many ways, in being a 'top-heavy' capital ship which foundered not far offshore, but many things contributed to the loss of the *Mary Rose* – there was no single overriding cause of loss but instead a lethal combination of design fault and

Fig 3.8
An 18th-century engraving preserves a wall painting at Cowdray House which was lost to fire in 1793. One of a sequence of wall paintings, this shows the Battle of the Solent in 1545, looking south from Portsmouth, during which the Mary Rose *was lost. The canted angles of the mast tops show that the* Mary Rose *has capsized, with a sail floating awkwardly on the surface of the water. A number of crew appear to be calling for help from the boats which have ventured forth to pick up survivors while the battle continues to rage in the background. To the right the English* Great Harry *fires a broadside at the French galleys on the left: her open gunports with a firing gun also sit very low in the water, almost as if mirroring what had happened to the* Mary Rose.
(© Society of Antiquaries of London)

the handling of the ship during the battle. Henry VIII's prized ship heeled over while manoeuvring, sinking with enormous loss of life of both sailors and fighting men: for many years, the cause was considered to be an inrush of water via the open gunports. Since then further theories have been advanced, all of them focusing on different possible elements of human error. The *Mary Rose* was, like the *Vasa*, top-heavy, but for a different reason. She had been refitted in 1528 and rebuilt in 1536–8, increasing her tonnage and armament. The circumstances of the battle fatally exposed the flaws in the rebuild. The decision as to how many personnel to put aboard – both navigational crew and fighting soldiers (effectively marines) – ultimately sealed her fate. Sitting low in the water with her human cargo and her gunports open, the *Mary Rose* was an accident waiting to happen.

> Towards evening the ship *Marry Rose* [sic] of Vice-Admiral Sir George Carew foundered … told by a Fleming among the survivors that when she heeled over with the wind the water entered by the lowest row of gun ports which had been left open after firing.[101]

The most recent research has explored the background to the inrush of water in more detail, with modern techniques permitting dental analysis of some of the recovered human remains. These show that some of the crew grew up in southern Europe around the Mediterranean. Henry VIII is known to have recruited mercenaries from abroad. Could it be, therefore, that their grasp of English was insufficient to understand urgent orders to close the gun ports?[102] This may explain the 'insubordination' attributed to the crew by the vessel's commander, Sir George Carew: it is entirely possible that rather than, or in addition to, language difficulties, battle noise simply prevented the crew hearing orders, an error of omission rather than of commission. However, in more modern times English speakers rapidly learnt to obey orders given in Swedish aboard the Erikson barques,[103] so a lack of training rather than of linguistic competence may have been a factor. Possibly some of the mercenaries or marines were unsure of what to do when all hands were required to carry out orders *in extremis*. The likely inexperience of some of the crew members on an English ship exposes a fundamental weakness of sailing ships with a clear division between the navigational crew and the fighting personnel. Under optimum

conditions, each had a clearly defined role: the 'marines' were trained fighting men who could grapple and board the opposing vessel, while the navigators manoeuvred the ship. Inevitably when things were going badly it was a question of 'all hands on deck' and in a fast-moving wreck event, inexperienced landsmen might well have simply made matters worse, especially with the numbers on board: it seems almost incredible to us that a ship of approximately 700 tons would carry perhaps 500 personnel. Their sheer numbers must have weighted down the ship, but, additionally, and possibly crucially, there were plenty of them to get in the way at a critical moment, particularly if the ship was heeling over.

There are sufficient accounts of passenger behaviour in panic to make this a plausible contributory factor in looking at the fate of the *Mary Rose*. From the behaviour of the passengers aboard small rowing ferries to the *Princess Alice*,[104] stampeding passengers were a danger to themselves and to the safety of the vessel. The natural human tendency to get as far away as possible from danger precipitated capsizes as passengers rushed to one side or the other of a vessel, sometimes even in their desire to assist people in the water. In the case of the *Princess Alice*, overcrowding per se did not cause the final loss of the vessel, though it cannot have helped her to remain afloat once she was struck. The desire to maximise revenue undoubtedly contributed to the high death toll, but this wreck was also very much a product of the conditions of her time.

During the Victorian era, the problems of river traffic were exacerbated by the Industrial Revolution, which not only saw London become one of the world's premier ports, but the transformation from sail to steam, which gathered pace in the latter half of the 19th century. At the same time, rivers, particularly the Thames, were increasingly used as leisure destinations in their own right, with a demand for excursions up and down the Thames – a day out for those who could, perhaps, not afford a holiday (or could not afford the time off work, which, prior to the Holidays with Pay Act 1938, amounted to the same thing). Paddle steamers came into their own as river excursion vessels providing a cheap and cheerful day out for the urban working classes, combining sightseeing and socialising, and remained popular into the late 19th and early 20th centuries, even though by the late 19th century paddle propulsion was outmoded.[105]

The *Princess Alice* was not the first or last excursion steamer tragedy. Similar accidents took place as Lancashire resorts boomed with visitors from the cotton mill towns inland, who took their holidays during 'Wakes weeks'. The *Prince Arthur* sprang a leak off Southport en route from Preston for the Menai Straits in September 1851, and in 1880 the *Columbus* grounded near the North Pier in Blackpool, but was fortunately refloated with the local lifeboat assisting off 133 people.[106]

In 1878 the collision was not only between two vessels, the excursion steamer *Princess Alice* and the steam collier *Bywell Castle*, but also between different worlds, between leisure and commerce: the *Bywell Castle* was leaving the Thames for Newcastle-upon-Tyne in ballast, to pick up coal for Alexandria (Fig 3.9). The result was enormous loss of life, the tragedy compounded by the fact that both the exact numbers of passengers and their identity remain unknown to this day. That the *Princess Alice* was returning after dark from a day trip to Gravesend was cited as a contributory factor to the subsequent accident. The Board of Trade inquiry and the coroners' inquests ran concurrently, with the same witnesses being called at both. It seems that one decision after another contributed to the fatalities as the two vessels came up against each other between Barking Reach and Gallions Reach, at a point where a collision had previously occurred between the *Metis* and the *Wentworth* (though on that occasion neither vessel was lost), ending in a disaster long foreseen. As an editorial in *The Times* noted:

> The wonder, indeed, is not that such an accident should have happened, but rather that it should have been so long escaped. Collisions in the Thames are, as 'Marine Insurance' writes us word, of incessant occurrence.[107]

Indeed, the *Princess Alice* seems to have been a particularly accident-prone vessel, with frequent accusations of collisions and near-misses. There were claims that the *Princess Alice* had narrowly avoided the collision with the Norwegian barque *Ibex* just before the fatal collision, and had on a previous occasion run down a rowing boat.[108]

> Before the boats struck there were cries from one to the other to keep out of the way; but, as usual in such cases, the accident is probably due to a misunderstanding, the one misinterpreting the intention of the other – all the rules of sailing cast to the winds in the moment of peril, each taking the wrong course to avoid each other's blunder, and, like the meeting of two embarrassed pedestrians on the footpath, rushing into each other's bosoms.[109]

Fig 3.9
A collision between worlds and different safety standards: as an excursion steamer crammed full of people leaves the Embankment, lifebelts casually stacked atop one paddle wheel, she encounters a barque with her lifeboats prominently hoisted out on davits. (CC73/00634)

One reason for this tendency of the *Princess Alice* is likely to have been navigational custom. Though the 'rule of the road' applied on the Thames, as at sea, that ships on opposite tacks should pass port side to port side to prevent collision, the state of the tide and the physical geography of the river with its bends and points allowed navigational customs peculiar to the Thames to prevail, such that the *Princess Alice* was accused immediately of 'being out of her proper course'.[110] She seems to have swung to the north in rounding Tripcock Point on the south bank, but then the river curved in the opposite direction, making it difficult to see oncoming traffic in its proper lane hugging the north bank (Fig 3.10). In this way the oncoming *Bywell Castle* was obscured until the two vessels were almost on top of one another, when panic was inevitable. One survivor was George Webb, a naval pensioner and passenger aboard the *Princess Alice*, who put his maritime experience to good use twice over: he kept a cool head and got on board the collier, and remained cool as a witness. His testimony was commended by the Board of Trade inquiry and helped to form its conclusions. He put it baldly: 'Two things caused the collision: the *Princess Alice* starboarding and the *Bywell Castle* porting.'[111]

It was only after examining the turnstile tickets that the London Steamboat Company was able to say that '800 was the lowest estimate'[112] for the number of passengers on board the *Princess Alice*, returning from their pleasant late summer day trip to Gravesend, the type of excursion 'of which the middle and poorer classes of London are very fond': consequently the numbers of dead included 'an extraordinary proportion of women and children'.[113] The ticket collector noted that many tickets admitted two, babes in arms going free. The passenger numbers can only have exacerbated the strain upon the vessel in buckling under the collision, and naturally the main outcome of this particular wreck was its appalling death toll with a final tally of 120 unclaimed and unidentified bodies: bloated by the putrid water, the 'sanitary authorities' were compelled to inter them as soon as possible. One tragic case concerned Londoner Mrs Lee, returning from a stay at Sheerness with her husband and cousin. The Sittingbourne railway disaster of 31 August put her off from returning by rail to London with her family. She boarded the steamer instead – and lost her life. The two

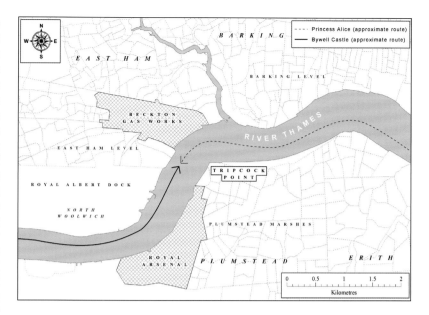

tragedies dominated international headlines for weeks. While the official Board of Trade inquiry was investigating claims that the *Princess Alice* was neither properly maintained nor fit for purpose, journalists were investigating the same claims to sensational effect. The inquiry found upon examination of the wreck that 'there were no signs of straining in the body of the vessel',[114] but a New York writer cast a different slant on the matter.

> The condition of the ill-fated *Princess Alice* revealed its utter unseaworthiness. It was literally broken into three parts. 'My dear sir,' said my companion, who lives on the river in an official capacity, 'these so-called saloon steamers are little better than floating platforms, egg-shells, that must go down on the smallest contact with anything like iron or timber. The London Steam-boat Company ought to be prosecuted. This vessel, with its boasted 30 feet beam, hasn't 20 feet: the breadth is pricked out by planking. It is a mere platform, planked in.'[115]

The Board of Trade inquiry found that the vessel had, in short, too many passengers and not enough lifeboats. In other words, she was overloaded, not so as to contribute directly to the loss of the vessel, but overloaded well beyond the safety of her human cargo. At the time there were no regulations governing the number of lifeboats on board a vessel; by contrast, regulations had just come in for the compulsory use of the load line (the 'Plimsoll line') on British merchant ships, for overloading of cargo could, and did, lead to the loss of vessels.[116]

Fig 3.10
Location map showing the approximate position of loss of the Princess Alice, *based on descriptions of her trajectory and landmarks in relation to the wreck site, namely the Beckton Gasworks and the Royal Arsenal at Woolwich. She swung wide out of her proper course round the sharp bend at Tripcock Point, so that the oncoming* Bywell Castle *was obscured from view until the last possible moment.*

Fig 3.11
Careening a ship in Hove.
*A view of the careening
process on the beach, in
which the bottom is scraped
clean of marine life and any
repairs effected: in the half-
light the figures busily
working with the whole
weight of the ship above
them can just be made out.
Careening was not only
perilous for those working
on the vessel: as the ship's
masts leaning at a severe
angle illustrate, the ship
would also be in peril should
the weather change.
(Jacob Jacobs, about 1846.
© Victoria and Albert
Museum, London)*

The *Princess Alice*, with the loss of her passengers under less than optimum conditions for their survival in the murky and polluted waters of the Thames, thus prefigures the most notorious maritime disaster of all time, that of the *Titanic* in the freezing waters of the North Atlantic in 1912. However, the *Princess Alice* was recovered; her back broken, she was visible midstream, and divers had the grim task of investigating the wreck, recovering the trapped bodies and, eventually, removing the obstruction to navigation. Clearly, though weighed, she was a constructive loss: but this particular incident illustrates that there is not necessarily a correlation between the death toll and the loss of a ship. The *Princess Alice* once more illustrates that, like the ships in the Great Storm of 1703 discussed in Chapter 1, it is possible for all or most of the people aboard to die while the vessel remains intact and can be refloated or salvaged, while conversely the ship may be a total loss but all hands may nevertheless escape, a counterpart to the medieval idea that a vessel was not technically or legally a wreck without the loss of all hands.[117]

Also shocking to modern sensibilities is the loss of the First Rate *Royal George* in 1782 off Spithead:

> having on her last cruize made more water than usual, which had not decreased when she came into harbour, an order was given on Saturday last for her to come into dock; but the carpenter and

other persons, on a strict survey, found it was not more than two feet below the water mark and was supposed to be occasioned by the rubbing off the copper sheathing. It was then resolved, *in order to save time*, to heave her down at Spithead.[118]

The italics are important. Time-saving and corner-cutting measures militated against what we would now regard as 'health and safety'. The copper sheathing was a new line of defence against shipworm and other marine life, and had been introduced within the past few years by Admiral Sir Charles Middleton, Comptroller of the Navy, 1778–94. This innovation was a great stride forward in ship safety, but the coppering was not without its own hazards, not least ingress of water between the sheathing and the hull, but the contemporary practice of fixing the copper sheathing to the hull with iron fastenings caused chemical reactions and the corrosion of the iron fastenings was anyway inevitable. The degradation of the sheathing could therefore cause leaks which seems to have happened in the case of the *Royal George*. 'A number of ships sank suddenly two or three years after they had been coppered, including the famous *Royal George*' so that the ships of the Royal Navy had to be recalled and their iron fastenings replaced with copper versions to prevent future accidents.[119]

Rather than solving the problem, the investigations into the leak precipitated the loss of the vessel. 'Careening', or 'heaving down' a ship for cleaning away marine debris and effecting repairs, was a regular maintenance activity for the wooden sailing fleet, but it also placed great stress on the hull (Fig 3.11). If the vessel had not been coppered, she would still have had to be heeled over to be careened: as it was, she was heeled over at the Spithead anchorage off Portsmouth to inspect her sheathing and discover the site of the leak: her guns were moved to redistribute their weight and facilitate the heel of the vessel. As work proceeded, 'she was ordered to be lowered another streak (strake)'[120] to allow the removal of further sheets of copper, and this seems to have precipitated the disaster. It was a strake too far: according to an eyewitness, 'the ship was heeled beyond all former practice, with all her guns out.'[121] She had clearly reached a tipping point beyond which she could only continue to capsize in the direction in which she had been heeled. Another letter from Portsmouth speculated:

> It is assigned as the principal cause of her going down with that sudden and violent rapidity, that as she lay on her side, her whole tier of water casks, on the opposite side, gave way, and gave her the unfortunate overbalance so much lamented.[122]

Casks contributed to the vessel's capsize – but so did people. The most startling aspect to modern eyes is that there was anyone on board at the time save essential personnel associated with the careening process: that a ship was heeled over with nearly all of her normal crew complement on board, as was stressed by many contemporary sources, seems almost incredible. No accurate figures were had as to how many men were aboard, but it seems that between 850 and 910 people were at their breakfast, and in addition the crew, 'of which the whole was on board'.[123] The final death toll is hard to ascertain since there were, alarmingly, also hundreds of visitors on the ship at the time, and this great press of numbers must have contributed to the existing stresses on the ship's frame in her heeled position.

> as usual on board all ships of war in the harbour, a very large number of women, probably near 400. Of these, the bulk were of the lowest order of prostitutes; but not a few of the wives of the warrant and petty officers. A most poignant scene of anguish and distress was exhibited by a respectable-looking old woman, whose daughter and five children had gone on board the same morning to see their father.[124]

The wreck of the *Royal George* is interesting as much from a social history point of view as any other. Divers were employed on the wreck: one, who returned with a 'dismal' account of the ship, seeing bodies still entombed within the wreck, was black. We know neither his name nor the identity of the correspondent who wrote to the newspapers about him.[125] Where did he come from? Was he a resident of Portsmouth, perhaps attached to the navy in some capacity there? He was in good company, for among his contemporaries were the abolitionist Olaudah Equiano and Francis Barber, later Dr Johnson's servant. Equiano made many voyages both as a slave and as a free man. Barber had joined the HMS *Stag* as a free man. Other names survive from 18th-century muster rolls.[126] In any case, the wreck continued to excite interest then and for many years afterwards (Fig 3.12).

Fig 3.12
Souvenir volume relating to the Royal George, *1842. Shipwrecks have always excited great interest, often for years afterwards, as in the case of the* Royal George, *which became a notorious hazard in the Solent. This pocket souvenir volume brought the history of the wreck up to date, and ran to five editions by 1842, detailing the efforts to disperse her by explosives in the early 1840s. The frontispiece (a) shows the vessel heeling over, and the front matter advertises the binding in timbers from the wreck, presumably retrieved following the dispersal. The front cover is now brittle and broken, whereas the back cover (b) remains intact.*

a
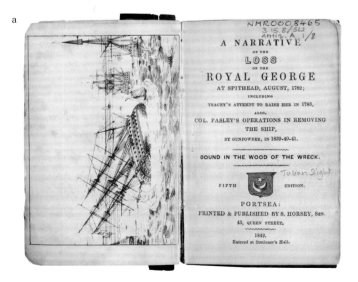

b

The *Association* disaster off the Isles of Scilly in 1707 – which precipitated the Longitude Act 1714 – has its roots in the operational decisions made by the Royal Navy in the Mediterranean, which was at that time the theatre for the War of the Spanish Succession. The Royal Navy was committed to several operations across the western Mediterranean over the summer seasons, including attack, blockade and convoy. The fleets involved were often subject to delays in repair or revictualling which prevented them returning home to English waters before the traditionally unsettled autumn weather closed in. Admiral Sir Cloudesley Shovell was fortunate to escape the Great Storm of November 1703 when he returned from the Mediterranean with his hospital ships.[127] Four years later his luck – and that of his fleet – was to run out in a storm

on 22 October 1707 among the Isles of Scilly, homeward bound to Portsmouth from Toulon and Gibraltar: they were very much off course to the north, believing themselves to be much further to the south, off Ushant. One by one the ships of his fleet smashed into the reefs of the Isles of Scilly in a disaster still unparalleled in the annals of the Royal Navy with the loss of the Second Rate *Association*, the Third Rate *Eagle*, Fourth Rate *Romney* and fireship *Firebrand*.[128] There were a very few survivors from this calamity, in which Sir Cloudesley himself drowned, although two ships of the fleet, the *St George* and the *Phoenix*, survived (Fig 3.13). There is a well-rehearsed tale that an ordinary seaman on board the *Association* challenged their position and was hanged for insubordination, but the story is difficult to credit given

that the preoccupations of the crew were, naturally, with the weather, and the consequent death toll decimating any potential witnesses to such an incident.

The story, however, is one of the psychological effects of collective behaviour, so much a human force for error and evil, and operated within a given ship's crew and between the crews of a fleet or convoy, inducing despair or a wild hope of uncertain safety. In *The Wreck at Sharpnose Point*, covering the wreck of the *Caledonia*,[129] Jeremy Seal speculates that the master of a ship which miraculously survived the same storm on the same stretch of coastline realised that another vessel had local knowledge and decided to follow it to safety. In the confusion and chaos of a storm, split-second decisions would mean the difference between life and death, salvation and despair, and observation of other vessels must have played a large part for good or ill. Deciding to follow another ship under these circumstances was quite a gamble and could well have been an error of judgement rather than a life-saving manoeuvre. There must also have been instances of collective despair in which stupefied crews simply bowed to the inevitable rather than grasping what very slim chances they had left, particularly in the North Sea, where there are few 'harbours of refuge' on that exposed coast. It is clear, however, from the accounts of all three incidents, the *Princess Alice*, the *Royal George* and the loss of the *Association* fleet, that no single decision was necessarily fatal: it was the cumulative effect of one poor decision after another, which led to wreck and disaster.

Monuments to lifesaving

Our brows are bound with spindrift and the weed is on our knees;
Our loins are battered 'neath us by the swinging smoking seas.
From reef and rock and skerry – over headland, ness and voe,
The Coastwise Lights of England watch the ships of England go!
… We bridge across the dark and bid the helmsman have a care,
The flash that, wheeling inland, wakes his sleeping wife to prayer.

(Rudyard Kipling, 'The coastwise lights of England')

Situated where land and water meet, lighthouses and lifeboat stations are the ultimate terrestrial monuments linked to shipwrecks. Lighthouses were built to prevent shipwrecks, and lifeboat stations to launch rescues where shipwrecks could not be prevented. Without lighthouses, the toll in ships and in lives would have been higher, and without the lifeboat stations, higher still. Lighthouses acted (and still act) as locational markers ('seamarks'); as guiding lights into the safety of harbour and haven; and as a warning of notorious sandbanks, reefs and rocks. What can their presence tell us about shipwrecks nearby?

The Roman Pharos at Dover is probably the earliest surviving example of a lighthouse acting as a seamark in England.[130] Though its presence suggests shipwrecks on the Dover approaches, nothing is known for certain about Roman losses. Things changed somewhat in the Middle Ages. In 1313 the *Seinte Marie* or *Blessed Mary* came ashore in Chale Bay en route from Bayonne for Picardy in France and thence to England with her wine cargo,[131] which, as usual, attracted local plunderers. As the wine belonged to the Duchy of Aquitaine, sufficiently influential to leave its mark in the documentary record, it is an unusually well-recorded wreck for the time, since we know the actual date of loss, 'the Sunday after Easter', 22 April 1313. The *Seinte Marie* has also left behind the remains of an oratory-cum-lighthouse with a distinctive 'pepperpot' appearance easily recognised at sea, a light at St Catherine's Point on the Isle of Wight (Fig 3.14). It was somewhere to commemorate the souls of those who perished in the *Seinte Marie*, and other wrecks, as well as to aid the living who might be in similar peril by light and prayer. Now ruined, and replaced by a later lighthouse, but, as a rare example of the few recorded medieval lighthouses, it suggests the scale of the disaster and hints at a possible cumulative effect from previous shipwrecks in the vicinity.

We lack surviving documentary evidence for earlier wrecks close by, but judging by the numbers of other wrecks from as early as 1238[132] recorded elsewhere around the Isle of Wight, the *Seinte Marie* is unlikely to have been an isolated loss off St Catherine's Point in the late 13th to the early 14th centuries. The later lighthouse, still in use, was similarly erected in response to a specific wreck, on the back of previous losses: the *Clarendon*, a stranded West Indiaman which went to pieces in a storm which prevented them from either maintaining an 'offing' from the shore. The crew 'in this critical situation were

Fig 3.13 (opposite)
A First Rate Man of War Driving on a Reef of Rocks, and Foundering in a Gale, George Philip Reinagle, 1826. During his short career George Philip Reinagle, who was a third-generation artist, specialised in marine paintings. This dramatic view is based not on a real-life incident, for there were few First Rates, and fewer still were wrecked under such dramatic circumstances; instead it is a composite, perhaps based on different incidents such as the Association disaster, which involved Second to Fourth Rate ships and a reef of rocks. The painting illustrates a typical wrecking process of grounding and foundering, illuminated by a sudden break in the clouds and a bolt of lightning, suggesting both the speed and fury of the storm. With her sails tattered and torn, and two masts having gone 'by the board', the crew have been unable to keep her from dashing broadside on to the rocks, fatally 'staving in' her hull. Under such circumstances their only – and very slim – hope lies in taking to the boat, which in turn is almost swamped by the waves. (© Royal Albert Memorial Museum, Exeter, Devon /The Bridgeman Art Library)

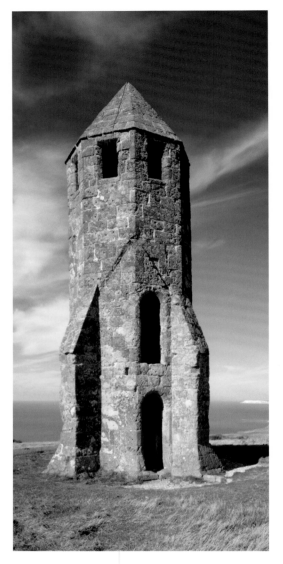

Fig 3.14
The 'Pepperpot' or
St Catherine's Oratory at
St Catherine's Point, Isle of
Wight, looking south-west
to the English Channel and
to the distinctive chalk cliffs
leading up to the Needles.
(K040696)

perfectly at a loss to know what coast they were driving on'.[133]

Other coastal buildings also acted as 'seamarks' and to this day they are marked on paper navigational charts for this purpose, with symbols distinguishing square towers and spires, for example. The mid-12th-century towers at Reculver (Fig 3.15) were a purpose-built seamark, motivated by the near-drowning of an abbess from nearby Davington in a ship wrecked en route from Faversham for Broadstairs.[134] The abbess had the towers built as a monument to her sister, who died in the wreck; they commemorated the original incident and acted as a warning to mariners. Such seamarks also provided useful locators for known wreck hazard sites, even when no longer a feature of the landscape.

From the Humberside coastline comes the name of 'Sister Kirkes' or Sister Churches for the two 11th-century churches at Owthorne[135] and Withernsea just north of the Humber, said to have been built by sisters but also, perhaps, conveying the sense of being 'twin seamarks' (Fig 3.16). Strangely, the account of the *Marie Knyght* 'wrecked by storm off Wythornse' on her passage from Prussia with 'divers goods and merchandise' in 1392, makes no mention of the sister 'Kirkes' or 'Churches' – yet was recorded when both churches were still standing.[136] The name seems to have arisen after Withernsea church was lost to the sea by the mid-15th century. In 1738, a fishing sloop working close inshore was run down off 'Sister Churches', but by this time only one of the 'Sister' churches remained. Perhaps the collapsed church under the sea was regarded as a navigational or fishing hazard and thus still 'present'. Thereafter losses on this shoreline were referenced in relation to the 'Sister Churches'. By the early 19th century Owthorne Church had followed Withernsea Church into the sea, but 'Sister Churches' remained current as late as 1830 when the *Frau Metta* drove ashore, having overshot the entrance to the Humber on her passage from Carolinenziel with rapeseed.[137] Possibly by this time 'Sister Churches' was a convenient shorthand to indicate an area notorious for wrecks, especially as at least 47 have been recorded in the vicinity of Withernsea up to 1900.[138]

Built in response to need or demand, lighthouses and other seamarks flesh out the archaeological potential behind the scanty documentary evidence prior to the early modern period. A harbour light at Winchelsea, Sussex, documented by 1261, indicates not only the town's prosperous maritime trade,[139] but that it was necessary at all suggests that before it was built a number of ships had been in danger of being lost at journey's end. Certainly a ship was wrecked in 1250, one of those whose loss must have prompted the building of the lighthouse. The scant nature of medieval records reveals only three further wrecks so it is difficult to tell if its efficacy as a guiding light improved the harbour – it surely did, but how much?[140] Winchelsea's success contributed to its downfall, as ballast dumped by shipping entering the port encouraged the ongoing process of silt accumulation which eventually led to its decline and present 'inland' location. To date no archaeological evidence of the former 'Old

THE SOUTH VIEW OF RECULVER-ABBY, IN THE COUNTY OF KENT.

Winchelsea' anchorage[141] appears to have been discovered, but it is possible that its presence could be revealed by one of the wrecks, buried under centuries-old silt, which made the guiding light for the harbour so necessary.

Recovery of shipwreck data near other notable lighthouses is similarly difficult. The Eddystone lighthouse, 8 miles south-south-west of the nearest point on the mainland at Rame Head on the approaches to Plymouth, is a good example (Fig 3.17). The first Eddystone lighthouse was erected by the mercantile entrepreneur Henry Winstanley, following the loss of two of his vessels at that location, the *Snowdrop* and the *Constant*, in 1695 or 1696.[142] Only two previous wrecks have so far been discovered in the documentary record for the Eddystone. One was a Spanish prize sent in from Terceira which

'sunk, with much leaking, near the Iddy Stone, a rock that lieth over against Plymouth Sound' in 1589 – yet the earliest known wreck on the Eddystone and thus the earliest citation of the name dates from 1405. From 1405 to 1589, therefore, 184 years of Eddystone wrecks, outside the well-frequented medieval port of Plymouth, and then again from 1589 to 1695/6, appear to have been lost to posterity.[143] The 1405 and 1589 wrecks appear to have been similar in that the 1405 wreck was 'broken' on the rock and widely dispersed, its mast ending up at Rame Head and it sounds suspiciously as if the 1589 wreck, in common with many later vessels lost on the Eddystone, struck, slid off the rock, with a consequent leak sufficiently great for her to founder reasonably close by.[144]

One man's shipping losses cannot have been the sole motivation for the construction of the Eddystone lighthouse, but it was probably the 'tipping point' at which it was felt something had to be done. From the mid-18th century onwards losses to the Eddystone were better recorded – by which time the lighthouse was on its third incarnation. It seems reasonable to assume that the nature of the hazard and the manner of loss differed little between periods lacking surviving records (the medieval and early modern periods) and those where records exist, that is, after the lighthouse was built. It is also possible that vague reports such as that of the *Elizabeth*

*Fig 3.15 (above)
'South View of Reculver' showing the towers, described as 'of great use to Seamen for avoiding Sands & Shelves in the Mouth of the Thames'. The notorious shallows just offshore are heavily buoyed to show the safe channels for passage; just how shallow the water is can be discerned in the broken water surrounding the larger, deeper-draught vessels. The centre vessel seems almost to be 'bumping over' a sandbank.
(J & N Buck, 1735 JO10064)*

*Fig 3.16 (above left)
Commemorative monument at Withernsea, East Yorkshire, to the former 'Sister Kirkes' of Owthorne and Withernsea: the name is preserved not only on this monument, but in numerous shipwreck records up to the 19th century.
(By courtesy of Peter Murphy)*

in 1761, lost between Portland and Plymouth, mask losses to the Eddystone.[145]

There were variables, of course. Some years were subject to more tempests than others,[146] including the famous storm of 1703 which destroyed both lighthouse and nearby shipping; vessels were lost at different states of the tide and current; their tonnage, design and dimensions, and the nature of their voyage, varied from vessel to vessel, and the volume and nature of trade varied from year to year. All of this suggests that the archaeological evidence for shipwrecks in the vicinity of the Eddystone

is likely to be much more widely dispersed than that for Winchelsea where the hazard lay at the entrance to the harbour itself, not least in how far stricken ships managed to proceed before they sank.

The demand was more obvious, because better documented, for the many lighthouses built in the 19th century, of which Trevose Head, north Cornwall, is a good example – and, of course, such steps were required to protect the Victorian growth in shipping and trade. Demand grew for a lighthouse to illuminate this stretch of the Bristol Channel from the early 1800s. When the brig *Star* of Dundee struck near Trevose Head, it was:

> another very striking proof of the great necessity for the speedy erection of the proposed Light-house on Trevose Head, for the want of which many valuable lives and much property are annually lost.[147]

By the time the lighthouse was eventually built in 1847, several more wrecks had taken place along this stretch of coastline, including the *Manly* in 1845, whose 'total loss … will cause everyone who has regard for the lives and property of his fellow man to rejoice the more that a lighthouse is to be immediately erected'.[148]

The case of the Trevose Head lighthouse indicates that lighthouses can both suggest the actual location of loss and a *terminus post quem* for likely archaeological material. In 1850, the survivors from the French chasse-marée *Emile Marie*, which had struck immediately under the lighthouse, stated that they had mistaken it for Lundy light, towards which they were running for shelter. Possibly their charts were not up-to-date following the installation of the lighthouse, hence their mistake, or they were off course, or both, since they were bound from Liverpool to Bordeaux.[149] After another incident when the *Sarah* unfortunately struck in a fog so thick that the crew had not even seen the light, there were no further wrecks in the immediate vicinity, suggesting that the Trevose lighthouse was amply fulfilling its purpose.[150]

Wreck events arising from mistaken lights serve to illuminate just how powerful the function of a seamark or lighthouse actually was. The practice of 'wrecking' through deliberately placing false lights to lure ships into danger instead of safety, by 'wreckers' hoping to plunder the ensuing wreckage, is commonly but erroneously believed to have been widespread. It may well have happened on occasion but primary sources stubbornly refuse to yield such evidence, though, of course, it could well have been hidden at the time, particularly in the more remote areas. However, the term 'wrecker' referred to one plundering a wreck *after* the event (a frequent theme throughout this book); none of the wrecks recorded in the NRHE database refers to wreckers in any other sense but those swarming over a vessel which had already come to grief, that is, without human intervention.[151] Its usage in this sense was attested as early as 1633, when a Portuguese ship 'cast away' on the Isle of Wight was subsequently pillaged by 'wreckers' (*see* p. 162).[152] As late as 1827 'wreckers' were described as 'depradators who generally attend on wrecks'[153] significantly antedating the earliest known usage in 1882 to refer to 'one deliberately luring vessels ashore', by which time the age of the sailing vessel and its attendant dangers were already becoming romanticised, and tales of rocky shores embellished for the nascent tourist industry. However, false lights were sometimes accidentally lit, as noted in Newcastle in 1791 (*see* p. 115).

Lightships or light vessels took the concept of safety a step further, the first being installed at the Nore sandbank just off the deep water anchorage which was a traditional naval assembly point in the Thames, and so much needed, in 1731.[154] By their presence, anchored near the hazard they represented, their 'station', they warned other shipping to keep their distance (Fig 3.18). Sometimes other ships' lights could be mistaken for those of lightships: herring vessels mistaken for the Newarp lights led the *William* and the *Beulah* onto the infamous Haisborough Sands off Great Yarmouth in 1814 and 1817, respectively, mirroring accidents in mistaking lighthouses.[155]

Fig 3.18
Calshot lightship. A distant view of the Calshot lightvessel, sometime in the late 19th century, warning shipping entering Southampton Water off the nearby spit of sand. The light beacon atop the vessel is clearly seen and her lack of propulsion is in stark contrast to the other vessels visible in the photograph. The small shallow-draught craft is able to approach more closely to the lightvessel than the ship carrying the photographer, which remains at a healthy distance from the lightvessel and its associated hazard. (CC39/00486)

Fig 3.19
Life-Boat and Manby
Apparatus Going off to
a Stranded Vessel Making
Signal (Blue Lights) of
Distress. *The shore, bathed in
light, represents safety against
the louring storm offshore as
a lifeboat goes off to a vessel
aground near the end of the
jetty. The ship is barely
discernible in the boiling surf,
despite being quite close
inshore, as was typical for
a Manby rescue, lit up only by
its own distress flares.
The skeleton of a wreck on the
beach suggests that wrecks on
this unnamed coast are only
too common. (J M W Turner,
circa 1831. Given by John
Sheepshanks, 1857. © Victoria
and Albert Museum, London)*

However, lightships themselves could be exceptionally vulnerable: as they lacked any propulsion, they could break adrift in stormy weather. They could not only be wrecked by the very hazard from which they warned other vessels, as in the case of the South Goodwin light vessel in recent times,[156] but also, in moving station, could themselves accidentally lead ships onto the hazard, both of which must have made the crew feel utterly helpless.

Their safety implications, however, extended beyond their presence as hazard lights, for they were able to bear witness to shipping accidents. The Dudgeon Lightship, located well offshore from the Lincolnshire/north Norfolk coasts, was certainly on station by the 1780s and improved the recording of losses in this dangerous area as her crew regularly witnessed the foundering of colliers which might otherwise have disappeared without trace 'between Newcastle and London'.[157] Where appropriate, lightships

also took on survivors from many incidents until a passing vessel could take them off when the weather eased. Equally terrifying was the fact that, unable to raise sail or start an engine, they were unable to take evasive action in the event of a collision. Though lightships all over the country were 'run down', the Dudgeon station was perhaps the most unfortunate, since two separate ships on this station foundered in 1898 and 1902 while in 1940 a later Dudgeon light vessel was bombed (in common with several others at this stage of the Second World War).[158] Steam power was, in itself, a great stride forward in safety terms, since steamships were far less at the mercy of storms. Sailing ships, becalmed when the wind dropped, could drift dangerously, but steamers were able to keep powering on. They were also inherently more stable than sailing vessels in dangerous storms. Other contemporary developments also made a difference. A Captain Manby was inspired to

invent a rocket apparatus (which came to be known as the Manby apparatus) after witnessing HMS *Snipe* in difficulties just off Great Yarmouth in 1807 (Fig 3.19).[159] Designed to communicate with stricken ships fairly close inshore, but difficult to reach, it involved the firing of a mortar with a line attached, in turn enabling a rope to be pulled over and secured, to permit the crew to escape. It was first used in a successful rescue from the *Elizabeth*, also off Great Yarmouth, in 1808, which seems to have slipped past without much publicity.[160] A logical development of this idea was the 'breeches buoy', a contraption consisting of trousers attached to a lifebelt, suspended from a rope pulley system, which successfully saved many mariners who were 'so near and yet so far' from safety.

Elsewhere, though existing boats were dedicated to lifesaving, the first purpose-built lifeboat, based on the coble, came into use at Tynemouth in 1790:

> We hear from Shields, that the boat lately built by Mr Greathead, for the purpose of preserving the crews of ships coming on the Herd Sand, was first tried on Saturday last, and far exceeded the expectations of those who had the most sanguine

hopes of its utility; for, in going off three times, to a vessel then on shore, through a very heavy sea, it scarcely shipt any water, and rendered the crew infinite service.[161]

'Mr Greathead's boat' was adopted elsewhere and in 1802 the crew of the *Sarah* 'owe the preservation of their lives entirely to the admirable life-boat built by Mr H Greathead, and lately sent to Redcar'.[162] The National Institution for the Preservation of Life from Shipwreck was founded in 1824, adopting its present name, the Royal National Lifeboat Institution (RNLI), by 1854. Lifeboat services established outside the RNLI were gradually subsumed into the organisation, with some exceptions which remain independent today, such as the Tynemouth and South Shields Volunteer Life Brigades (Fig 3.20). These two services were set up after a disastrous night in 1864 when four ships were lost at the mouth of the Tyne, a fifth coming to grief the following day as the gale continued.[163] Like the lighthouses, lifeboat stations were placed where the need was greatest, sometimes serving the same locations, as at Tynemouth, Whitby and Dungeness, but often in other danger areas, where lighthouses did not exist or were impractical to build.

Fig 3.20
The South Shields Volunteer Life Brigade Watch House directly overlooks the Herd Sand and the notorious Black Middens to the north, and is still in use, together with the Tynemouth Watch House on the opposite bank: in this view Tynemouth Priory is just visible in the distance on the right.
(BB93/20296)

Lifeboat rescues were – and remain – the very stuff of heroism, volunteer crews putting themselves into the very same conditions endangering the stricken vessel whose crew they were attempting to save. At one and the same time they had to avoid collision with both the hazard which had ensnared the ship, and the ship itself, no easy task in often atrocious conditions and perilous even today.[164] Sadly many lifeboats also succumbed in their efforts to reach 'those in peril of the sea', notably the Southport and St Anne's lifeboats *Eliza Fernley* and *Laura Janet* as they

Fig 3.21
Memorial in Lytham St Anne's to the crewmen of the Lytham lifeboat Laura Janet *who drowned in the* Mexico *disaster, showing the gear worn by Victorian lifeboatmen, a sou'wester hat and a cork jacket for buoyancy. Another memorial exists in Southport dedicated to those who perished in the Southport lifeboat* Eliza Fernley. *(MF99/0626/35)*

strove to reach the German barque *Mexico*, aground on the Horse Bank off Southport in 1886 (Fig 3.21).[165]

Inevitably those manning offshore or 'rock' lighthouses and light vessels as a warning service were forced to take on the role of rescue services at need. The rescue of the survivors from the *Forfarshire* in 1838 in the Farne Islands by Grace Darling, was a contemporary sensation and has passed into quasi-mythology as one of the most famous rescues of all time, pitting a lighthouse keeper's daughter against rock, weather and sea.[166] All the strands of lifesaving discussed in this chapter come together, seen not through the lens of history, but of the way shipwrecks may pass into the wider landscape even if little remains of the vessel – in this case, scattered and almost unidentifiable wreckage off Big Harcar Rock.

The Longstone lighthouse (Fig 3.22) was lit in 1826 after extinguishing the previous light on Brownsman Island, felt to be misleading to mariners. Grace's grandfather, Robert Darling, had been the keeper of Brownsman light and was first on the scene when the *Glasgow Packet* came to grief on the expressively named Knivestone in 1806, establishing a family tradition of rendering assistance in difficult conditions. The men fetching help from the lighthouse in the ship's boat were unable to 'recover', that is, return to, the ship, without Robert's strong guiding hand.[167] The Knivestone, of course, did not go away, and when the *Hero* of Whitby struck upon the same rock in 1817, a local paper fulminated:

> It appears she had struck upon the Naivestone, the outermost rock at the Staples [a local name for the Farne Islands], this was occasioned by the outer lighthouse being placed so far in towards the land, had it been placed on the Longstone, which is a rock nearest the point of danger, perhaps this accident would not have happened.[168]

On the night of 7 September 1838, the *Forfarshire*, bound from Hull for Dundee with passengers and a general cargo, was caught in a storm while sheltering on the lee (landward) side of the Farne Islands, smashing into Big Harcar from the north-west. Huge waves battered lighthouse and ship alike. Its inhabitants snug within, the lighthouse was able to withstand the storm: not so the rapidly disintegrating steamer. It seems that the *Forfarshire* was a victim of negligence and complacency: one survivor said 'he would have given all he possessed to be on shore again', even before she had left the shelter of the Humber estuary, for her boilers were already leaking.[169] Typically for a vessel ashore on the rocks in a vicious storm, the *Forfarshire* had 'broken her back', her stern part being carried away by the sea.

By daylight, when the true extent of the disaster was discernible, only a few survivors remained clinging to what remained of the ship. The weather conditions were far too perilous to mount a rescue from the mainland towards the north-western part of Big Harcar, visible from the lighthouse. Grace and her father William represented the survivors' sole hope of rescue and set out accordingly, despite William's misgivings. They traversed the dangerous half a mile or so to the scene of the wreck in their little rowing coble, an 'instance of heroism and intrepidity on the part of a female unequalled, perhaps, certainly not surpassed, by any on record'[170] taking five people off at the first attempt. Grace kept the coble in position as her father assisted the survivors into the boat. At any time the coble could have been dashed to pieces on Big Harcar, like the big steamer before her.

Grace took charge of the first group at the lighthouse as William returned again to rescue the remainder of the pathetic group still stranded upon the rock.

The Times' led a national wave of adulation: the media storm which succeeded the weather storm ensured Grace's enduring fame even after her early death from the 19th-century scourge of tuberculosis at the age of only 26 in 1842. It was, in fact, a precursor of the media attention which followed the early deaths of film and rock stars in the 20th century and a fitting occasion for the new Poet Laureate, William Wordsworth, to compose a commemorative poem. Ever afterwards, references to later rescues in the same area were carried out not by 'William Darling, Longstone lighthouse keeper' but by 'Grace Darling's father'.[171]

A little scattered wreckage is said to remain just off Big Harcar. The most tangible remains of the wreck remain, however, in the monuments devoted to Grace Darling. In the local museum at Bamburgh the coble she and her father rowed that fateful night remains on display. She was buried in St Aidan's, Bamburgh, where today a monument stands in the churchyard

Fig 3.22
View of the Longstone lighthouse, from which the rescue of the Forfarshire *survivors was launched, and where William Darling remained keeper after his daughter's death. (© Keith Ascough. Source English Heritage)*

Fig 3.23
Memorial to Grace Darling
in the churchyard of
St Aidan's, Bamburgh; the
esteem in which she was held
is reflected in the ornate
Gothic Revival canopy
designed by the pre-eminent
architect working in that
style in the north-east,
Anthony Salvin.
(© Kenneth Robinson.
Source English Heritage)

looking out to sea (Fig 3.23), and she is also commemorated in the Chapel of St Cuthbert, Inner Farne. Yet her most enduring monument is the Longstone lighthouse itself which still stands as a warning to passing shipping, though now automated.

Without lighthouses, the death toll from the sea would have been far higher, and without this particular lighthouse on that particular night in 1838, no-one would have survived the wreck of the *Forfarshire*. Lighthouses, seamarks and lifeboat stations can be understood as the opposite of grave markers and commemorative monuments to disasters, which record the lives lost: they stand as monuments to the many forgotten wrecks to which they owe their own existence, and to the countless lives saved as they stand guard over treacherous rocks and shifting sands. They are the land's answer to the sea, the embodiment of the title of a 1954 film covering an air-sea rescue: *The Sea Shall Not Have Them*.

The transport of people and goods around the world

Introduction

Globalisation is not a new phenomenon: trade has been global, in the sense of trading with the known world, as long as man has had contact with the sea. Pytheas the Greek, from the colony of Massilia, now Marseille, writing in the 4th century BC, appears to provide one of the earliest accounts of trade with Britain, specifically referring to tin mined in Cornwall.[1]

The Erme wreck on the coast of Devon, an offshore site containing tin ingots, may even be contemporary with Pytheas, although its dating remains inconclusive. It is one of an extraordinary collection of three Bronze Age sites on the south Devon coast, hinting at ancient cross-Channel trade links: the artefactual evidence from all three sites points to early contacts in both directions. The ingots at Erme have their closest parallels with similar finds from France.[2] The Moor Sand wreck is datable to approximately the 12th century BC, with objects such as swords and palstave axes, thought to have been made in what is now France; while the adjoining Salcombe Cannon site overlies an assemblage of Middle Bronze Age weapons and amulets which may come from a shipwreck, although no trace of a ship's hull survives at the site (Fig 4.1).[3]

Inland trade routes are as ancient as sea-going routes, if not, perhaps, more so, possibly dating back to the Neolithic, the date attributed to a logboat found in the Cambridgeshire Fenland in 1979.[4] The marshy conditions of the Fens which made the logboat a necessary means of travel have also ensured the survival of a greater concentration of logboats from the Bronze Age than anywhere else in the country, although a well-published collection of sewn boats with sea-going capacity also survives from North Ferriby in East Yorkshire.[5]

The existence of shipwrecks enables us to track the rise and fall of long-standing trade patterns and of specific surges in economic

Fig 4.1
Salcombe Bronze Age shipwreck. Reconstruction of how events might have unfolded during this very early trading shipwreck from which a cargo of amulets and weapons was found. Half the crew use their paddles to try and stave the ship off the rocky shore, while the remainder use their weight to prevent the vessel from capsizing as their fellows lean overboard. Hunched in misery astern, a merchant hugs his valuable cargo of prestigious metalwork.

activities and technological advances: miniaturisation technology in the form of doll's house china which continues to be recovered from the wreck of the *Indian Chief*, lost in the Thames en route to Yokohama in 1881, or the establishment of brand names which are still known today. The *Somali*, bombed off Beadnell Point in 1941, has yielded Heinz food jars, Pond's Cream, and Macleans toothpaste, as well as a general cargo of toy soldiers, golf balls, ringworm ointment and a Bakelite razor, all consigned for the Far East.[6]

Although this chapter will trace the rise and fall of specific trades in detail through their associated shipwrecks, it is worth looking briefly at one particular trade, tobacco. The first known vessel to be wrecked in English waters while carrying tobacco from Virginia in the New World was documented in 1674, the last being the *Paulina* in January 1807.[7] The wreck of the American *Paulina* reflects the shift to American ships in this trade following the Revolutionary Wars. At the same time, public attitudes to the slave trade which underpinned the tobacco plantations in Virginia were changing: the Slave Trade Act was passed in Britain 2 months after the loss of the *Paulina*.

Other trade routes and distribution networks are also revealed: European demand for agricultural fertilizer to feed an ever-increasing population in the late 19th and early 20th centuries saw 34 ships laden with mineral-rich guano from Peru and the Caribbean (including the self-descriptively named Sombrero, or Hat Island) lost in English waters. Guano was not necessarily always of seabird origin: the *Cambrian Princess* and the *Dovenby* were both lost in the early 20th century while carrying seal guano from Islas Lobos de Afuera.[8] Hides and horns from Fray Bentos in Uruguay hint at the by-products of the 19th-century meat processing industry in South America, from which the famous 20th-century brand name for steak and kidney pies derives (Fig 4.2).[9]

These trade routes can also challenge preconceptions: the numerous wrecks of vessels laden with barrels of beef and butter from Ireland on the western coasts of England during the late 17th and 18th centuries illustrate that country's food-exporting capacity prior to the infamous Great Famine caused by potato blight in the 1840s. A typical example was the *Kleine Hendrick*, bound for Hamburg with beef and butter from Cork when she was lost on Exeter Bar in 1765.[10]

These trends can also be seen in internal trade routes with small spikes at particular periods and tied to the industrial development of particular ports, particularly in the case of coal. The number of lost ships is testament to the former significance of the coal trade, in terminal decline in Britain since the 1980s. Ships wrecked in the coal trade form a significant percentage – 14 per cent – of all known shipwrecks of cargo vessels in English territorial waters. At the height of the Industrial Revolution in the 19th century the numbers of colliers lost also reached a peak of 30 per cent of all cargo vessel losses.[11] However, the existence of other industrial features can provide a context for shipping movements, in terms of cargo, or in terms of locating the wreck: the loss of the *Fortitude* in 1785 near the Loftus 'allom-works' is a reminder of the former importance of alum mining on this stretch of the north-east coastline.[12]

The transport of people was a necessary concomitant of the movement of goods: as we shall see later in the chapter the lot of the passenger was not necessarily a happy one. Passenger travel can be subdivided into three broad categories which will be explored later. First, passengers could embark of their own free will, travelling locally or internationally; take goods to market on local ferries; act as 'supercargo', a passenger managing the goods for the owner;

Fig 4.2
Highland Warrior.
Refrigeration plant room, containing sacks of meat on board the Highland Warrior *on her arrival from the River Plate in early 1924, taken by the noted architectural photographer Bedford Lemere. Owned by the Nelson Line, the 'Highland' ships were pioneers in the refrigerated meat trade from South America.*
The Highland Warrior *was to be a victim of the Second World War, torpedoed and sunk off Freetown, West Africa, in 1941.*
(BL26996/06)

or take ship for the colonies either as administrators or to escape poverty, oppression, or famine in Europe. Second, from the 19th century onwards, the concept of the sea as a place of leisure grew, and with it a number of wrecks of yachts and ocean liners, often lavishly appointed. Finally, coercive transportation saw not only the slave trade, but also the establishment of convict transport routes to Virginia from the 17th century onwards (see p. 227), later replaced by the Caribbean and Australia in the 18th and 19th centuries. (Slave trading will be treated separately in Chapter 5: 'How can we identify a ship involved in the slave trade?') However, if few, apparently, cared for the lot of the crews, the passengers were in greater danger still: this chapter traces the tale of ships, crews, cargoes and passengers criss-crossing the earth or simply from one bank of a river to the other, both of which brought them into mortal peril.

East Indiamen

> Six weeks beneath the moving sea
> He lay in slumber quietly;
> Unforced by wind or wave
> To quit the Ship for which he died,
> (All claims of duty satisfied;)
> And there they found him at her side;
> And bore him to the grave.
>
> (William Wordsworth, 'To the daisy', 1805)

In contrast to small, localised forms of vessel, adapted to local tidal conditions and the requirements of the specific cargoes which they normally carried, the long-distance ocean-going vessel needed to be more adaptable, yet remain fit for any purpose. As we have already seen, there were certain characteristics specific to Dutch East India vessels: they were built to be *retourschepen*, 'return ships', and there are a certain number of outcomes shared by the Dutch East Indiamen, namely that they were generally wrecked in English waters while outward- rather than homeward-bound.[13] It seems that the Dutch East Indiamen were greater risk-takers at the outset of their voyages: setting out in the winter or in the teeth of a gale, as in the case of the *Rooswijk*, or attempting to 'thread the Needles', as the *Vliegende Draeck* and *Kampen* did, or attempting the 'northabout' diversion via Scotland (the protected wreck of the *Kennemerland* in Shetland illustrates the dangers of this practice). This discrepancy is less marked among English East Indiamen, with a slight preponderance towards being lost homeward-bound. In 1708 the 'tedious' voyage of the *Albemarle*, returning home from Banten via Rio de Janeiro, may well have contributed to her loss at Polperro (Fig 4.3).[14]

What other features are shared by East Indiamen? The Age of Exploration opened up the world to regular trans-continental trade,

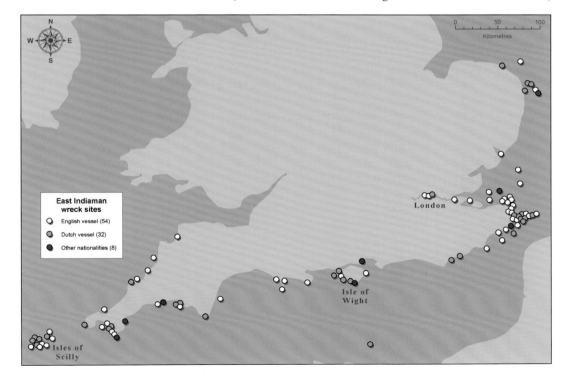

Fig 4.3
Location map showing both historically documented losses and known wreck sites to give an overall picture of East Indiamen lost on the English coast, with the most significant cluster being off Kent.

consolidating contacts and voyages of exploration made during the Middle Ages and after (the voyages of Marco Polo, his father and uncle, to the Far East in the late 13th century; the voyages in the reverse direction by Admiral Zheng He's fleet in 1421; and the arrival of Christopher Columbus in the Americas in 1492). The Portuguese, Dutch and English were quick to capitalise on these new sources of trade wealth, particularly the Eastern spices which were so prized for food flavouring and preservation in Europe. The Portuguese at first had a monopoly, but their union with the Spanish crown, and the beginning of the Seventy Years' War between the Netherlands and their Spanish overlords in 1578 inspired the Dutch to attempt to break Portuguese control of trade with the Far East. The first Dutch East Indiaman was the *Amsterdam* in 1595;[15] the English were quick to follow with the granting of a Royal Charter by Elizabeth I to the 'United Company of the Merchants of England trading to the East Indies in 1600'.

East Indiamen were among the first ships, therefore, to transplant human beings as passengers across continents on a regular basis: merchants for trade, administrators to oversee commerce and relationships with indigenous inhabitants, missionaries to convert the local people to Christianity, and military personnel to protect and enforce the security of Europeans and trade goods. Any or all of these could become colonial settlers: an adventure of the highest degree, psychologically intimidating with the omnipresent threat of shipwreck upon an unknown shore, even when familiar hazards in European waters had been safely passed. The Dutch East India Company (VOC) was pre-eminent for much of the 17th century among its European competitors, the prime source of the wealth that enabled the explosion of painting in the Netherlands, which has since become recognised as the Dutch Golden Age. Without the VOC and the possibilities of patronage afforded by the wealth trickling down to the burgeoning mercantile and middle classes, there may well have been fewer works by Frans Hals, Rembrandt and Vermeer to name but a few artists of the Golden Age (Fig 4.4).

Not all of that wealth reached the Netherlands, and there were disasters from the very inception of the company. The earliest East Indiaman to be wrecked in English waters was not English, but Dutch: the *Maan* (Moon) left Zeeland on 25 March 1598, according to the Gregorian Calendar, in company with the *Zon* (Sun) and the *Langebark* (Long Ship).[16] The *Maan* is said to have capsized at Dover after firing a salute, one of the few ships to have been recorded as lost in the execution of a protocol. By the time of the Armada in 1588, both English and Spanish warships had largely made the transition from a 'fore and aft' arrangement of guns to the broadside (hence 'firing a broadside') although a more limited number of guns would still be installed fore and aft as necessary. By the 1600s the lowering of the topsails was accompanied by the firing of a salute with gunpowder only (not cannonballs), much as today on land the monarch is honoured with a 21-gun salute. Dutch mercantile vessels also saluted their country's own warships as a mark of respect. At the same time the Dutch increasingly resented English claims to sovereignty over the sea, especially at a time when the Dutch seemed to have that honour for themselves in home waters (the North Sea and the Channel) as well as in far-flung oceans: this was to become one of the sticking points leading to the First Anglo-Dutch War. In either case, a peaceable salute required the manœuvring of the vessel stern first with the broadside fired out to sea (rather than towards land or towards the vessel involved, both of which might be perceived as hostile in intention). It may be that in hauling the vessel over to fire her salute the *Maan* was caught by a sudden gust of wind, or the recoil of the guns on one side caused her to heel over, as seems to be suggested by the fact that she capsized.

As the English East India fleet – and its trade – grew there were corresponding losses on the English side. There are few details of the East India vessel lost among the Isles of Scilly in 1619,[17] but some extraordinary details emerged of the passengers on an English East India ship lost near Dover in 1625. Coincidentally, like her Dutch counterpart lost in the same area, she was called the *Moon*.[18] The Governor of the East India Company and Captain Thomas Style (or Styles) wrote to the Secretary of State, Sir John Coke that:

> In their ship the *Moon*, cast away near Dover arrived a Dutchman, who, by his own confession, is one of the judges who gave sentence of death upon the Company's innocent servants at Amboyna.[19]

This was explosive: the rivalry over the spice trade had spilled over into an incident at Ambon in Indonesia, when employees of the English Company were accused of spying, put on trial and executed by the Dutch VOC authorities, known as the 'Amboyna Massacre'. Ill-feeling over the treatment of those killed at Amboyna in March 1623 was to further sour the relationship between the English and Dutch for much of the next century: as an immediately practical measure, naturally the Dutchman was arrested and slung into Dover Castle. We can only surmise that the crew of the vessel and the English authorities were as grimly determined to save

this particular passenger as they were to salvage the guns and the prized pepper cargo which had in part caused the massacre in the first place.[20]

The fate of the passengers often gives us an insight into the wrecking process which we would otherwise lack, although sometimes the language barrier proved an impediment to obtaining a first-hand account. The *Alexander*, lost in 1815, was not an English East India Company ship, but was a 'private' or 'country' ship built, or operating, for a private firm based in India. The term 'East Indiaman' was applied

Fig 4.4
Pieter van den Broecke, *Frans Hals*, c 1633. *There is no mistaking the occupation of the sitter, who worked his way up through the Dutch East India Company (VOC). His weather-beaten appearance and windswept hair mark him out as a seaman, but his finery befits the commander of an East Indiaman, for whom the price of a portrait by his personal friend Frans Hals was well within reach. Painted in 1633, wearing the gold chain presented to him on his retirement, his profession has aged him beyond his 48 years. This was a respectable age for any seaman to reach, and remarkable for someone in the East India service, having survived several arduous voyages to the Far East, including shipwreck in the* Duyfken *near Surat, India, in 1617. (K070101 Kenwood House, the Iveagh Bequest)*

somewhat loosely, a recurrent theme throughout the history of the East India trade.[21] Her background makes her far less traceable in the records: a number of contemporary vessels of that name could potentially be identified as this wreck, but the evidence is harder still to decipher when several variant names also popped up in the contemporary press, notably that of *Abercrombie*, and added to the confusion.[22] There was also the question of language difficulties: the survivors appeared to be four Malays and a Persian lady, none of whom could speak any English.

> Weymouth, March 27 – It has blown a hard gale the whole of yesterday and last night from the SSW and it is with heartfelt regret I inform you of the loss of the *Alexander*, East Indiaman, Captain O-, from Bombay, bound to London. She was driven on shore on the beach during the gale of last night, about two miles west of Portland; and, I am sorry to add, that the captain and all the crew and passengers are lost, except four Lascars and a woman. The ship is gone to pieces; and very little of her cargo can be saved.[23]

Their inability to communicate with their rescuers must have compounded the trauma of their plight, but the pattern of wrecking on Chesil Beach was all too common, being driven by a south-south-west gale directly onto a lee shore, whence the *Alexander* could not escape, and being pounded to pieces. The lack of information from survivors has a natural corollary in that the wreck site has not to date been pinpointed, notwithstanding that the vessel 'went to pieces'. The Dorset coastline was one of the principal wrecking points for English East Indiamen, having also claimed two outward-bound ships, *Halswell* or *Halsewell* in 1786 and the *Earl of Abergavenny* in 1805, both of which have been located.[24] Despite the high death toll in both incidents they were well-documented at the time, and the evidence offered by survivors and salvage attempts on the vessels has ensured that the knowledge of their position has survived. The captain of the *Abergavenny*, John Wordsworth, was the brother of the poet William, and perished; the third mate, Joseph, their cousin, survived.

The *Halsewell* was carrying a number of passengers beside her cargo, including the captain's womenfolk (two daughters and two nieces) and three other young ladies who were among the 'respectable passengers' (Fig 4.5).[25] Usually only the names of those of higher social standing filtered through to contemporary

accounts, although the circumstances of this particular wreck revealed something more about those on board than is often the case. Off the Isle of Wight the *Halsewell* met with the calm before the storm on 2 January 1786, which finally broke later that afternoon with 'very thick weather … and the wind baffling' with freezing snow, followed by a gale at ENE early the next morning. Her crew were obliged to 'cut their cables and run off to sea'. The wind then veered to a 'violent gale of wind to south', and they were obliged to 'carry a press of sail to keep the ship off shore', in order not to share the same fate as the *Alexander*.

Without the details from the survivors, we would be unaware of the distressed state of the *Halsewell* even before she was wrecked. Carrying a press of sail strained the ship, causing a leak by washing in the hawse-plugs. In endeavouring to lighten the ship before she foundered, they cut away the mainmast, which knocked five men overboard as it fell. Later that day the wind abated, but this was not the end of the *Halsewell*'s troubles, for:

> the ship labouring extremely, rolled the fore-top-mast over on the larboard side; in the fall the wreck [i.e. of the mast] went through the fore-sail and tore it to pieces.

The crew now discerned that they were off Berry Head on the Devon coast, and rigged up a 'jury' mast (makeshift mast) in order to return to Portsmouth to refit. Before they could weather Peveril Point to anchor in Studland Bay, the wind turned against them, blowing again from the southward. Trying to prevent being trapped upon a lee shore, they dropped first one anchor, then another, but the vessel 'drove' from her anchors. At about 2 am on Friday 6th, the ship 'struck with such violence as to dash the heads of those who were standing in the cuddy[26] against the deck above them'. The captain remained in the cuddy with his daughters and the other female passengers, endeavouring to reassure them, all the while the ship continuing to beat upon the rocks, which soon 'bulged' or tore a hole in her bottom. One of the survivors, Meriton, also tried to reassure the crew, rousing them from their stupor of horror to save themselves by descending 'on that side of the ship which lay lowest on the rocks'.

There was now nothing to be done but wait for the late daylight of a winter morning to see exactly how, if at all, they could get ashore. In the meantime the officers and 'respectable'

Fig 4.5 (opposite)
The Wreck of the Halsewell, *Indiaman, 1786.*
The unusual angle of the composition depicts the last place of safety within the ship as she breaks up, lurching violently on the rocks. The captain comforts his daughters and nieces, as the other female passengers await their fate in various states of composure, for it was thought impossible for the women to escape in the darkness to the precarious ledge which was their only possible refuge. This pathetic scene is based on the eyewitness accounts of two survivors who are shown to the left just before their own escape. Shortly after they left, the ship fell to pieces as female shrieks were clearly heard: the captain was lost with his vessel and the family he comforted to the last.
(Thomas Stothard, ZBA4537 © National Maritime Museum, Greenwich, London)

passengers had also admitted 'three black women, and two soldiers' wives' into the relative safety of the cuddy. There was little to be done for one of the lady passengers, 'who was in hysteric fits on the floor-deck of the round-house', but the captain rebuked a young gentleman heading for a similar fit of histrionics, by saying that 'though the ship should go to pieces, he would not'.

Meriton owed his survival to going out to investigate the lie of the land, recalling that:

> he perceived a considerable alteration in the appearance of the ship, the sides were visibly giving way, the deck seemed to be lifting, and he discovered other strong symptoms that she could not hold together much longer, he therefore

attempted to go forward to look out, but immediately saw that the ship was separated in the middle, and that the fore part had changed its position, and lay rather farther out towards the sea; and in this emergency, when the next moment might be charged with his fate, he determined to seize the present, and to follow the example of the crew, and the soldiers, who were now quitting the ship in numbers, and making their way to a shore, of which they knew not yet the horrors.

He thus made his way out by means of a spar which almost, but not quite, reached a rock on the shore: he fell and was washed into a cavern. Rogers, another survivor, remained in the cuddy with the captain and the women: he and the captain went out to try their luck, but in the dark 'they could only discover the black face of the

perpendicular rock and not the cavern', so that the captain returned to his family, while Rogers made his way to the same cavern. No sooner had Rogers managed to 'gain the rock', the *Halsewell* broke up in the dark: daylight brought only the realisation of the precarious hand- and foot-holds of those who had managed to get ashore, while they could 'neither be observed by the people from above, as they were completely ingulphed in the cavern and over-hung by the cliff, nor did any part of the wreck remain to point out their probable place of refuge'. As men dropped off their perches, benumbed by cold, the survivors' only hope was thus to creep out to a ledge and thence to scale the steep cliff side to a house called Eastington, whence workmen summoned by the occupier let down ropes to the cavern. Before their ordeal ended, yet more men fell to their deaths, and out of over 240 people on board all told, only 74 lived to tell the tale. All the women died, together with the captain, on board ship, and some survivors were left destitute. One man, a gunsmith by trade, was arrested for burglary in October 1786, and stated in his defence: 'I have not been able to work since I was cast away in the *Halsewell* East Indiaman', yet he had tried for work and was about to take ship for India again in the *King George* Indiaman at the time of his arrest.[27]

Yet still this description of their ordeal pinpoints the locale of the wreck and testifies to the vivid human interest inherent in the transformation of a voyage into a national tragedy and historical monument. Because of their economic and strategic importance in the twin aims of trade and overseas expansion, as much national pride was invested in the East Indiamen as in warships. They made the equivalent of headline news at the time and leave a significant documentary trail which leads to their prominence among protected wrecks: at the time of writing six of the 62 protected wrecks in the UK, are East Indiamen, five in England and one in Scotland, and an 'East Indiaman' identity has also been suggested for another protected wreck, the South Edinburgh Channel site in the Thames, possibly Swedish.[28] There is at least one other Swedish Indiaman which has been recorded but not, so far, located, the *Sophia Magdalena*, and three or four French vessels involved in the same trade, as well as the Dutch vessels already mentioned.[29] The sites of seven other Indiamen are known in English waters, but this remains a small proportion of over 100 known losses of such ships dotted around the English coastline.

These ships must once have been a common sight along the Channel coasts, whether setting out full of hope or returning richly laden. The products they brought from the Far East – from Indonesia, China and India – are so deeply embedded in European culture that most Europeans are barely conscious of their origins and the means by which they came to Europe. The wrecks of these ships are the tangible remains of the trades in spices, such as nutmeg, mace and peppers, which once took 18 months to return to Europe. The trade in tea and coffee, now universal beverages with a weight of tradition behind them, from British 'afternoon tea' in Britain to German *Kaffee und Küche* (coffee and cake), saw the opening of 'coffee houses' where news could be exchanged over the consumption of the fashionable drinks. These coffee houses led, as we have seen, to new commercial concerns – the emergent marine insurance market and a specialist press. Chinese porcelain exports led to cross-cultural fertilisation as Europeans attempted both to imitate the Chinese styles of decoration on their own wares (Delftware, for example), and the manufacture of porcelain itself, first perfected at Meissen in the early 18th century, while European designs were sent out to China to be painted on commissioned sets. Asymmetric Chinese designs were incorporated into fashionable Rococo decoration as *chinoiserie*. Places in India gave their names to textiles, such as calico, imported from Calcutta (now Kolkata), which in turn became exchange cargoes for the transatlantic slave trade. All were transported and transplanted by the East Indiaman, which possibly has had a greater cultural and economic impact than any other form of vessel in world history. The East Indiaman drove globalisation, at the cost of individual lives.

The perils of the passenger: the wreck of the *Deutschland*

> The Liner she's a lady by the paint upon 'er face,
> An' if she meets an accident they call it sore disgrace:
>
> (Rudyard Kipling, 'The liner she's a lady')

There were other dramatic losses besides the *Halsewell*. In a snowstorm on 6 December 1875 the German liner *Deutschland*, outward-bound from Bremen for New York, struck the infamous

Kentish Knock (Fig 4.6), at the entrance to the Thames Estuary.[30] She broke her back and foundered with the loss of about 57 passengers, the conditions which had caused the wreck in the first place also preventing her from being seen from shore, and help being sent. In the immediate aftermath of the wreck the captain also accused passing ships of refusing to answer his signals of distress.

As a liner, a ship purpose-built to run a regular passenger service or 'line' between two fixed intercontinental points, the *Deutschland* was also an emigrant ship and epitomised the outflow from Europe to the United States in search of a better life, predominantly from Central and Eastern Europe and Ireland. The mid-19th to the early 20th centuries were the heyday of the passenger liner: liner wrecks have come to be defined by the loss in the Atlantic of the *Titanic*, following collision with an iceberg, in 1912, which has tended to eclipse other liner tragedies. The *Deutschland* was an earlier instance of such a wreck, part of a cluster of German liners lost in English waters while working the New York route in the 1870s–1880s. The first was the *Schiller* among the Isles of Scilly, also in 1875, followed by the *Pomerania* off Folkestone in 1878, both homeward-bound; the *Mosel* was outward-bound from Bremen for New York with passengers, including emigrants, and mails when she struck Bass Point in Cornwall in 1882. Like the *Deutschland*, she was a Norddeutscher Lloyd ship.[31] Irish passengers formed a significant proportion of the immigrants bound for the United States, but, for geographical reasons, wrecks of Irish vessels bound for North America rarely affected the English coast.[32]

Emigrant ship wrecks naturally had an international dimension: the *Deutschland* was no exception, being extensively reported in English in both *The Times*, as the country concerned with the wreck event, and the *New York Times*, as the port expecting to receive the passengers. To this day the exact number of lives lost remains uncertain, discrepancies in the lists of passengers, of survivors, and of dead and missing persons being compounded by language difficulties.[33] The irony of shipwreck under the circumstances of fleeing poverty and hardship was not lost on contemporary readers. Both innovative poetry and hyperbolic newspaper prose focused on the same core events of the wreck, with sharply differing interpretations.

One follower of the story was the Catholic

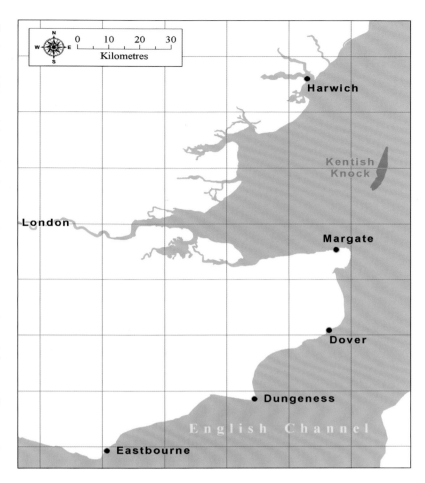

poet Gerard Manley Hopkins who, at the time, was studying to enter the Jesuit order. As the son of a marine insurance specialist, he had a grounding in maritime matters and was attracted to the subject of shipwreck as a religious epiphany. 'The wreck of the *Deutschland*' was not his only shipwreck poem, for, a few years later, he was also moved to write a similar poem on the 'Loss of the *Eurydice*', a training ship which foundered off the Isle of Wight in another snowstorm in March 1878.[34] In both cases the loss of lives excited his pity, leading him to meditate on the spiritual significance of such tragedy – the loss of 'three hundred souls' which were 'precious passing measure / Lads and men her lade and treasure' aboard the *Eurydice*. In the case of the *Deutschland* the story of five nuns, exiled for their beliefs, attracted his attention. He commemorated the event in a highly romanticised version of events, depicting the nuns as heroic martyrs for their faith.[35]

Barbara Hultenschmidt, Henrika Fassbender, Norbeta Reinkobe, Aurea Badzunra and Brigita

Fig 4.6
Location map of the infamous Kentish Knock sandbank, on which over 100 ships are known to have been lost over the centuries. The Kentish Knock lies a considerable distance out to sea, at the seaward end of several parallel rows of sandbanks which stripe their way across the entrance to the Thames, barring the way to London. Harwich and Margate, the nearest ports from which rescue could come, lie respectively 19 miles off the northern tip and 13 miles off the southern tip of the Kentish Knock; the Deutschland *survivors were eventually landed at Harwich, where the inquest took place. One body was washed ashore at Margate.*

Damhorst[36] all came from a convent in Salzkotten (Nordrhein-Westfalen). The twin aims of secularisation and centralised Germanisation of the state under Otto von Bismarck's *Kulturkampf* ('culture struggle') policy were pursued following the formal unification of the separate German states in 1871. Secularisation was seen as essential to internal unity, preventing the geographical divide of religious affiliations from becoming a potential cause of strife. To this day the southern states, including Nordrhein-Westfalen, remain a stronghold of Catholicism in Germany. The doctrine of papal infallibility, issued by the First Vatican Council in 1870, also alarmed Bismarck, who feared undue influence by the Vatican in Germany's internal affairs. Under laws promulgated by Adalbert Falk (the eponymous 'Falk laws') the practice of the Catholic faith was increasingly severely restricted and the five women took ship in the hope of finding the freedom to worship as they wished. As Hopkins saw it, they were called to martyrdom by shipwreck:

> She drove in the dark to leeward,
> She struck – not a reef or a rock
> But the combs of a smother of sand: night drew her
> Dead to the Kentish Knock;
> And she beat the bank down with her bows and
> the ride of her keel:
> The breakers rolled on her beam with ruinous
> shock;
> And canvas and compass, the whorl and the wheel
> Idle for ever to waft her or wind her with, these
> she endured …

> Loathed for a love men knew in them,
> Banned by the land of their birth,
> Rhine refused them. Thames would ruin them;
> Surf, snow, river and earth
> Gnashed: but thou art above, thou Orion of light;
> Thy unchancelling poising palms were weighing
> the worth,
> Thou martyr-master: in thy sight
> Storm flakes were scroll-leaved flowers, lily
> showers – sweet heaven was astrew in them

His imagery was dramatic, and, despite his father's background, more given to poetic effect than accuracy, for example in the use of the word 'leeward'. Strictly speaking the vessel was driving to windward, before the force of the north-east storm, rather than to leeward, against the prevailing wind. Nevertheless, he accurately evokes an image of the travails of the ship bumping over the sandbank, paralleling the trials the nuns were about to undergo. According

to Hopkins, the nun's prayer was a symbol of a heroic choice, actively seeking the comfort of divine salvation: he contrasts the nuns' acceptance with those of the panic-stricken passengers scrabbling to cling on to any wreckage they could. However, the *New York Times* reversed his interpretation of the atmosphere aboard the wrecked vessel, as their correspondent praised the 'wonderfully cool, patient and self-possessed' behaviour of the stranded passengers, but censured the nuns' apparent panic:

> She to the black-about air, to the breaker, the thickly
> Falling flakes, to the throng that catches and
> quails,
> Was calling, 'Oh Christ, Christ, come quickly',
> The cross to her she calls Christ to her, christens
> her wild-worst Best.

There were five nuns on board who, by their terror-stricken conduct, seem to have added greatly to the weirdness of the scene. They were deaf to all entreaties to leave the saloon, and when, almost by main force, the stewardess (whose conduct throughout was plucky in the extreme) managed to get them on to the companion ladder, they sank down on the steps and stubbornly refused to go another step. They seem to have returned to the saloon again shortly, for somewhere in the dead of the night, when the greater part of the crew and passengers were in the rigging, one was seen with her body half through the skylight, crying aloud in a voice heard above the storm 'O, my God, make it quick, make it quick.'[37]

Questions were asked in the Reichstag in the immediate aftermath of the wreck, with a motion calling for the introduction of official inquiries into shipping casualties.[38] The German authorities were horrified that all aspects of the investigation had to be left to their British counterparts, who, since the 1850s, had compiled official statistics investigating accidents to shipping in an effort to mitigate the commercial and humanitarian impact of shipping disasters.[39] Bismarck's *Kulturkampf* might have driven the Franciscan nuns into exile, but the disaster compelled him to rush through new measures in 1877 to ensure the safety of German ships at sea.[40]

The wreck of the *Titanic* is often considered to be the wreck that has had the greatest cultural effect worldwide. At the time the scale and severity of the *Titanic* disaster had a global impact, with the loss touching the ports of Belfast, where *Titanic* was built; her ports of call at Southampton and Cobh; Halifax, Nova Scotia, where many victims were buried; and New York, her intended destination, which received the survivors landed from the *Carpathia*. Not only did it leave an indelible impression in the mind of the contemporary public, it also resulted in legislation enforcing the number of lifeboats aboard passenger liners which undoubtedly saved lives in the First World War. Yet other liner wrecks prior to the *Titanic* had a similar impact: the loss felt between different places, and with different cultural outcomes.

The diverse interpretations of the event as seen by New York hacks and the gentleman Jesuit poet coincide in the possible location for the wreck investigated on the Kentish Knock, with finds including broken crockery, bearing the Norddeutscher Lloyd crest, brought up from the wreck site.[41] The vessel's screw propeller was not found on or near the site, corroborating the captain's statement that the propeller came off as he attempted to reverse his ship off the Kentish Knock: 'The engine was backed imme-

diately, but after a few minutes the screw was lost, and the machinery stopped.'[42] Hopkins' poem, though dramatising the incident, never-theless accurately picked up on this point: 'the whorl [screw] and the wheel [helm]/ Idle for ever'

This missing screw prompted a wreck event which touched England, Germany and the United States alike. The grief felt in New York had specific ramifications in England and Germany: the physical establishment of an official lifeboat station at Harwich to respond to similar disasters; practical legislative measures in Germany to prevent further tragedies on German ships; and the writing of a poem which has entered the canon of English classic poetry, ensuring that the resonances of this other tragedy are still felt today, like those of the *Titanic*. Both losses were the product of their era, an age in which passenger traffic was higher than ever before, ships larger and technological achievements greater, but in which safety measures lagged behind (Fig 4.7).

Fig 4.7
This interior view of the reading room of the SS Suevic, *photographed in 1901 by Bedford Lemere, gives an idea of the attention to detail in the fitting out of passenger liners, as a skylight from the deck supplements the natural light from the portholes. The emphasis was on comfort rather than the safety considerations which would preoccupy modern ship architects: for example, the extensive timber panelling and wooden furniture would today be considered an unacceptable fire hazard. Nevertheless, all 524 crew and passengers were rescued from this White Star liner when she struck Maenheere Rocks, off the Lizard, in 1907, in contrast to the loss of the Titanic five years later. The* Suevic *rescue remains the RNLI's largest and most successful operation to date. (BL16481/003)*

In chase of cod: deep sea fishing

… on voyait au loin les eaux grises de la Manche où son père avait disparu autrefois dans un naufrage …

(… in the distance could be seen the grey waters of the Channel, in which his father had long ago lost his life in a shipwreck …)

(Pierre Loti, *Pêcheur d'Islande* [*A Fisherman of the Icelandic Fishing Grounds*], 1886)

The Age of Discovery initiated by European discovery of the Americas changed seafaring forever beyond the obvious ramifications of the transplantation of colonial settlers and slaves, the import into Europe of new foodstuffs from the New World and the creation of new trade routes and export markets between the Old World and the New, between settlers and indigenous peoples. It also provided an impetus for developments in ship design and technology, ships capable of supporting voyages lasting several years, transatlantic crossings and the natural consequence of European competition among the new American colonies: long-range warfare privateering on the Atlantic coasts of the Caribbean islands and Central America.

These developments, supporting larger crews, greater armament and a larger capacity to be self-supporting in victualling, also aided the development of long-range deep-sea fishing. This in turn was a result of the Age of Discovery as European explorers, from John Cabot in the late 1490s onwards, brought back word of abundant fish stocks in the area of the Grand Banks, an area of shoal water stretching over 200 miles east and south-east of the province of Newfoundland, where cod was particularly prevalent. Cabot's crew asserted that the seas in the area were 'swarming with fish'.[43] Those who followed in his wake were probably not the earliest Europeans to exploit these fishing grounds, but the systematic fishing of the Grand Banks certainly dates from this period, as these reports were enthusiastically followed up.

It would have been impossible to exploit these new transatlantic fishing grounds without several centuries' previous experience in processing and preserving the fish. Recent studies have suggested that fishing was largely confined to inshore waters until about AD 1000, when there was a change to deep-sea fishing.[44] The wreck of a vessel with 'ropes and nets' on board at Hunmanby (North Yorkshire) in 1318

suggests such exploitation of the North Sea. By 1333 North Sea fishing was sufficiently valuable for *La Eleyne*, an English fishing vessel which had caught £110 worth of fish after being at sea for a month, to be scuttled off Blakeney, Norfolk, and her fish stolen by German 'evildoers'. Most, if not all, of this fish must have been dried ('stockfish') for it to be worth anything to the pirates, who had come from as far afield as Rostock and Stralsund, on the eastern Baltic shores of Germany.[45]

Fishermen from the Atlantic ports of south-western Europe ventured out to Newfoundland, caught the cod and dried or salted it at sea for sale in European markets. This new source of fish was not only a welcome supplement to the European diet, but also vitally important for religious observance, which was particularly marked in those mainland European countries with an Atlantic seaboard, France, Spain and Portugal. Fish was eaten on fast days in lieu of meat, particularly during Lent – hence the interest among their fishing communities.[46]

The fertile Grand Banks were exploited first by the Portuguese from the early 1500s, then by the Basques of southern France and Spain from about 1525 onwards.[47] They were also economically important to the English, who were finding that they were increasingly frozen out of the traditional cod fishing grounds in the North Sea. The Grand Banks offered a means of circumventing the increasing restrictions laid on them in the 15th century by the Hanseatic League. The Hanse, the greatest of medieval trading alliances with a network of ports across the North and Baltic Seas, was becoming increasingly jealous of its share of the Icelandic and Scandinavian markets for fish. In a protectionist move, Henry V was persuaded by the Hanse in 1415 to prohibit English trade in Icelandic cod or stockfish, thereby preventing the English ports which were the League's trading partners from becoming their direct competitors. The English did flout the ban on occasion: on the west coast around 1450 *Le Cristofre* was wrecked on her 'return to the realm' from Iceland, 'contrary to statute'.[48]

From the first the Newfoundland fishing ships were characterised as *bankers* (*banquiers* in French), after the Grand Banks: although the shape and dimensions of the vessels involved in the Newfoundland cod fishery changed over time and the French terms *terre-neuva* or *terre-neuvier* ('Newfoundlander') were also used, *banker* remained the generic term

(Fig 4.8). As late as 1902 it was used of the French brig *Russie*, the pillage of which on the Isle of Wight caused great outrage in the French press.[49] Hard on the heels of these developments in deep-sea fishing came both a new type of wreck and new patterns of wreckage, with the first recorded losses of French fishing vessels along the southern and western coasts of England, on their way to or from the teeming Grand Banks.

The Penheleg manuscript[50] alludes to an incident involving two French bankers running aground near St Ives in the 36th year of Henry VIII's reign during 'war time between England and France', that is, around the time the *Mary Rose* was lost. One of these vessels was only 50 tons, the other 100:[51] reasonably large for the period, given that Southampton was considered pre-eminent in the import of preserved fish with around 500 tons' worth of catches in 1430.[52] The vessels were not wholly lost, the townsmen of St Ives bringing them 'within the key [quay]' while the survivors returned home under passport. The fish was impounded and a 'controversie' arose between local landowners, the Arundells and the Godolphins, over who had

the greater right to this wreck, the matter eventually being settled in favour of Sir John Arundell, who distributed both ships and fish among his supporters and friends.

The Penheleg manuscript also refers to the wreck of a similar vessel, this time English,[53] on the specific date of Candlemas in the 17th year of Elizabeth I's reign, that is, 2 February 1576, again in the vicinity of St Ives. Despite the manuscript's limitations, being largely based on recollections written for a specific legal purpose in a particular area of the country, they suggest not only the growing English involvement in the Banks fishery, but also that English and French bankers alike were routinely entering the Bristol Channel to find a market for their fish, to revictual, or to shelter from Atlantic and Channel storms, before returning to their respective home ports. By this time the Newfoundland fishery was well established in England, and lucrative: the wreck of the *John* at Exmouth through the carelessness of the pilot in 1573 led to the loss of 18,000 of the 70,000 'salt fish called Newfoundland fish' she had brought home, and a pecuniary loss of £200 (approximately £36,000 today). There was a greater loss

Fig 4.8
Return of the Terre-Neuvier, *Eugène Boudin, 1875. A stormy sky beyond hints at the hazards faced by the* terre-neuvier *or Newfoundland banker which has just returned to her home port in Brittany, as the men's belongings are unloaded onto the foreshore by their womenfolk in traditional Breton costume. Breton fishermen were at the forefront of the Newfoundland and Icelandic fisheries, and would have passed by English waters en route to both fishing grounds. Albeit safely drawn up on the shore, nevertheless the* terre-neuvier *gives an impression of how stranded vessels of this type might have looked.*
(Chester Dale collection. Image courtesy of the National Gallery of Art, Washington, DC)

on the cargo than the ship herself, valued at just over £66 (or the equivalent of £12,000).[54] These early records of English bankers prefigure the later development of the English Newfoundland trade naturally associated with the south-western coasts facing towards Newfoundland – in particular Bideford and Poole, which have left a legacy in the form of wrecks from the 18th century onwards.

By the late 1600s the market in Newfoundland cod was significant enough for French bankers to provide an attractive target for Dutch privateers, who were also doubtless motivated by the War of the Grand Alliance (1689–97). The English and Dutch were now allied against the French, instead of fighting one another as they had done within living memory. Echoing the capture of *La Eleyne* by German pirates over 300 years earlier, in 1697 a Dutch caper privateer captured a French banker[55] as a prize, which stranded on the Needles shortly after being taken. These captures underline how the humble fish was becoming an increasingly important resource.

The war also helps us to understand how and why the captured vessel came to grief where she did, at the western entrance to the Solent: suggesting first that, homeward bound for France, she had been intercepted somewhere in the English Channel (possibly fairly close to the Isle of Wight) and second, that her captors were therefore sending her for the nearest friendly port. As the capturing vessel was not English, this does not at first seem an obvious course of action. However, because of the alliance with the English, the Dutch could send their prizes towards England if that was more appropriate. Perhaps the captured vessel was also structurally weakened by her encounter with the privateer, which was not an uncommon fate with prize vessels. In this way, the odds were stacked against prizes surviving rough weather or accident, compounded by the partial swapping around of the crews and their replacement crew members' unfamiliarity both with the ship and the waters to which they were sent. In this case neither captors nor captives were habitués of English waters, and on this occasion the Dutch were deprived of a lucrative prize. In a way, the unfortunate French banker was as much a victim of the War of the Grand Alliance as the warships lost in the Battle of Beachy Head in 1690.[56]

The wrecks of bankers mirror the trajectory taken by the cod fishery over the centuries. The trade seems to have taken an upward curve

from the 1720s onwards, judging from the numbers of ships lost in English waters alone. A wreck in 1723 in Start Bay, south Devon, bears all the hallmarks of information literally being lost in translation. The testimony of the sole survivor of a 20-man crew was either transcribed phonetically or English eyes had great difficulty in reading his handwriting – as the vessel had gone to pieces there would have been no trace left of her name. Her departure from Newfoundland had somehow been made out, but little else was clear. The dead master had apparently rejoiced in the name of 'Umphiteer Louine Reir', his vessel being apparently the *John* (perhaps *Jean*, *Jéhan* or *Johan*).[57]

If the remaining information was garbled, how was the vessel's place of departure discovered? The cargo could provide a clue in such cases where none of the crew survived. In 1739 an anonymous ship was wrecked off Weymouth. It was deduced that she was a French banker from the 'mud-fish' (an alternative name for cod) 'slit after the French manner', which was washed ashore.[58] Similarly, when the *Commerce* was totally wrecked east of Cudden Point, Mount's Bay, Cornwall, in 1809, her 'register' was picked up, providing her name, but her voyage only became apparent from her cargo:

> no person whatever was saved from the wreck. She is supposed to be from Newfoundland, as the smell of oil was very prevalent and cod and other fish have been picked up by the wreckers.[59]

From the mid-18th century Poole came to dominate the Newfoundland trade in England (Fig 4.9), as can be seen from the ensuing wrecks, starting with the *Ranger* in Studland Bay, Dorset, in 1744. A regular 'wrecking point' for these Poole ships was the first English landfall in the Isles of Scilly, which accounted for the wrecks of the *Margaret* in 1771, the *Pheasant* in 1780 and the *Nymph* in 1809.[60] Dartmouth similarly rose to prominence in the Newfoundland fishery, also losing ships and lucrative cargoes among the Isles of Scilly, such as the brig *Courier* which foundered with all hands in 1808.[61] From the 1820s, numbers of both English and French vessels actively working the Grand Banks declined, particularly those of English vessels. There was a corresponding decline in the numbers of Newfoundland fishing vessels of both nationalities lost on the coast of England as they returned home with their fish. By now Canadian and American fishermen were beginning to exploit their 'local' resources on the Grand Banks, and were, of course, also returning their catches locally, rather than exporting them to Europe, so that they do not appear in English waters at this date.[62]

By the mid-19th century, Newfoundland commerce had diversified into the by-products of the cod trade and into export. The *Moira* of Ilfracombe foundered off the Lizard, Cornwall, while transhipping casks which had originated in Newfoundland from Poole for Bristol in 1830. 'Two casks of oil, supposed Newfoundland', were picked up off the Lizard, followed by other casks of 'cod blubber', which were sold shortly after the wreck, as well as the fishing gear. 'Blubber' is a term more usually associated with whale fat, but in the Newfoundland context 'cod blubber' was a product of its times, extolled by the Victorians for its health-giving properties, and exported to the 'mother country': cod livers rendered for oil.[63]

As the North American stake in the cod industry increased, by 1880 Canadian schooners were also exporting cod to England. This was the year that the Canadian *Gipsy*, like the *Moira*, was lost close to the Lizard near the Black Head while carrying cod to Poole, once the epicentre of the English Newfoundland fishery, thus closing the trade circle where it had begun.[64] Despite the exploitation of the Grand Banks by Canadian fishermen, the French interest continued up to and including the First World War, with a host of support industries, including the export of salt to preserve the fish and 'mother ships' carrying fishing gear: *Sainte Marie* or *Ste-Marie*, 1916 and *St-Pierre*, 1914, respectively, both lost off the Isles of Scilly. They were lost on the same day exactly 2 years apart, underlining the seasonal nature of fishing: both belonged to Fécamp, one of the centres of the French cod fishery. The *Russie*, mentioned above, which also belonged to Fécamp, was another such ship, carrying both salt and fishing gear.

Cod fishing is not only a seasonal occupation: its own history has been cyclical over several centuries. Cod is a migratory species, and over time 'migration patterns' of humanity chasing cod have also emerged, from Iceland to Newfoundland to the North Sea and back again with differing peaks and troughs in the history of each cycle. For example, the cod fishery flourished off Iceland during the Middle Ages, exploited by foreigners, and then again about 1880 to 1930, coinciding with a peak in the numbers of English and French trawlers and

other fishing vessels wrecked en route to or from Icelandic waters, including the Breton vessels for which Icelandic cod was a speciality.[65]

The story of cod remains topical: with the introduction of industrialised fishing the Grand Banks and elsewhere are now heavily overfished and a moratorium on cod fishing has been in place since 1995, with other species also severely restricted, except as bycatches.[66] Yet throughout history the numbers of shipwrecks of fishing vessels, English and foreign, have precisely mirrored the ebb and flow of fishing patterns.

Fig 4.9
The two main legacies of the Newfoundland trade are the lost ships and the remaining architecture. Poole's fine Georgian buildings, among them the Custom House, built in 1813 to replace an 18th-century custom house of similar design, were built on the Newfoundland trade. Eric de Maré collection. (AA98/04956)

Domestic traffic: local vessel types

Ocean liners sheltered from the storm
Ellan Vannin on the wave was borne
Her hold was full and battened down
As she sailed towards far Liverpool Town
Oh *Ellan Vannin*, of the Isle of Man Company
Oh *Ellan Vannin*, lost in the Irish Sea

(The Spinners, 'Ellan Vannin')

A significant minority of wrecks surrounding the English coastline are made up of local vessel types, specialised for particular functions and adapted to local cargoes, conditions and geography. They form small, but well-defined, groups, allied to the landscapes they served, tending naturally to cluster in distinct concentrations linked to their normal trade routes.

Fishing boats

Why are these groups so small? In part it is because the vessels themselves were usually small, and therefore were often overlooked in contemporary accounts (Fig 4.10). Their owners were often poor or of low social status and their vessels were numerous. As much because they were commonplace as because they were small, they were almost an invisible feature of everyday life. Because of this, it is difficult to build up an accurate picture of smaller victims of any given storm, as only the more significant vessels were named in any reports of shipping losses. Fishing vessels and collier brigs alike were routinely omitted from the documentary record. The losses of such vessels hit local communities hard in both human and financial terms, and the *George*, lost on the Essex coast in 1871, was typical:

> Loss of a Fishing Boat. The lugger GEORGE, the property of a fisherman named George, belonging to this port, was totally lost a few days since on the Kentish [sic] coast. It appears that George recently invested some of his hard-earned savings in the purchase of the craft, and at the time of the casualty was on his way home from Chatham, to which place he had taken a freight of herrings. It seems that the lugger was in charge of George and a lad, and soon after getting to sea encountered bad weather and was eventually driven on shore at Shoeburyness, where she became a wreck. The loss will fall heavily on George, who is a poor man.[67]

Another reason for the relatively small numbers of wrecks from regional vessel groups concerns their adaptation to particular environments, which, together with the local knowledge possessed by their crews, enabled them to survive in conditions where other vessels might well have perished. The local geography and the uses to which they were put naturally influenced the outcome of the wreck event. Each group had a distinctive feature of some kind, which, while often shared with other working vessels or wrecks, is particularly pertinent to that group.

For example, the well-known Cornish *gig* was a rowing-boat well adapted for inter-island travel in the Isles of Scilly, small and manoeuvrable, the stern high and narrow for the vessel's size, but it was also used elsewhere in Cornwall. It was built to be capable both of crossing open water and being easily beached. Its adaptation to local conditions made it a 'jack-of-all-trades', but most of these trades were themselves a product of the Scillonian topography. Since it was the first landfall in the Channel from the west, ships required pilots if they were fortunate, and rescue and salvage if less so, and the gig engaged in all of these. For this reason, gigs are generally footnotes to other wrecks: in 1816 a pilot gig was one of the vessels which put out to assist the distressed *Mary* arriving with mails from Rio de Janeiro. The gig was swamped by a large wave and sank, throwing all her 16 crew into the sea. Ironically the *Mary* remained intact, to be finished off by a gale some days later. Similarly, in 1839, the wreck of the *Solace* on Rosevear was followed the next day by the loss of a salvage gig from nearby St Agnes. In 1875 the *Hound*, a six-oared gig, capsized and foundered in a squall while returning from an inter-island cricket match.[68] More usually gigs played the role of rescuer rather than rescued, and very successfully, as in the rescue of the crew of the *Carvedras*, which foundered between Wolf Rock and the Longships in 1882. The crew took to their boat and were spotted off St Ives Head, having drifted to the coast of North Cornwall, whereupon a Cornish pilot gig launched to tow the crew inshore.[69]

Approximately 6 per cent of all wrecks recorded in English waters are those of fishing vessels, a surprisingly low figure given the historic importance of fish to the English diet and economy,[70] but all reflect each area's particular specialisms. Understandably, therefore, the wrecks of fishing vessels, largely, but not exclusively, coincide with their local coastlines

Fig 4.10 (opposite)
The Iveagh Seapiece. *The painting's alternative name,* Coast Scene of Fishermen Hauling a Boat Ashore, *perfectly describes its subject. Under the darkening sky of a looming storm, to the right one vessel has already been beached, while the fishing boat's crew struggle to haul her up the shore beyond the reach of the tide, as a precaution against the approaching storm. A broken spar in the foreground serves as a warning. At sea, another crew furl their sails among the surging waves as they wait their turn to wash in on the crest of a wave. Small, shallow-draught fishing vessels such as these were ideal for launching from, and beaching on, the shore. (J M W Turner, M960775 Kenwood House, the Iveagh Bequest)*

and regular fishing grounds. Off the coasts of Cornwall, for example, there are wrecks of Cornish *seine boats*, open rowing boats specialising in team fishing with a seine net shot from the largest of their number. Seine fishermen collaborated not only with one another, but also with observers on shore directing them towards shoals of fish visible on the surface. The seine net was usually a 'purse' net suspended from all the boats involved, drawn tight underneath the fish to prevent their escape, and dragged ashore by the group of boats.[71] The aptly named *Sprat*, 'dashed to pieces' at Porthleven Beach in 1880, was involved in mackerel fishing, while the more exotically named *Blucher*, which struck on the Doom Bar in 1827, was involved in the pilchard fishery synonymous with Cornwall.[72] The shore-to-boat *modus operandi* of the seine industry suggests that, like *Sprat* and *Blucher*, most of these boats will usually have been lost close to

shore, and indeed relatively close to their home ports: their range was a few miles east or west of their original port and approximately half a mile out to sea.[73]

Again, off the coast of Devon there are numerous wrecks of the famous sailing trawlers of Brixham, which developed from the late 18th century onwards (Fig 4.11). Trawling targets bottom-dwelling or -feeding species of fish through dragging deep-water nets upon the sea floor. As early as 1376 it was sufficiently established as a fishing practice to attract protests against the destruction of the bycatches.[74] It seems, however, to have been during the last years of the 18th century that trawl-fishing took hold on the Channel coast ports. Brixham fishermen early became specialists in trawling, beginning an enduring tradition of ranging further afield away from competition in the crowded English Channel. Brixham continued

Fig 4.11
A fisherman landing a catch
in the 1950s on the south
quay at Brixham from one
of the harbour's famous
sailing trawlers: the vessel's
mast is clearly seen to the
right. The photographer,
John Gay, was keen to
capture traditions which
were already all but obsolete
in the 1950s.
(AA087818)

to build sailing trawlers into the 20th century, in contrast to the trawler industry of Grimsby and Hull which went over to steam in the late 19th century and benefited from specialist steam trawler shipyards on the Humber. The south Devon coast is littered with the wrecks of Brixham's little wooden trawlers, characteristically ketch-rigged, though they also covered the western reaches of the English Channel and the Bristol Channel from an early date. A Plymouth trawler was noted in *The Times* as having foundered off Stoke's Bay, Hampshire, in 1802 – the earliest trawler wreck so far recorded in English waters, and probably noteworthy because systematic trawling was still in its infancy, for the loss of fishing vessels rarely made national news.[75]

A particular feature of the Brixham group emerged during the First World War: though large enough to venture out mid-Channel, they were too small to be torpedoed if sighted by enemy submarines and were usually captured and sunk by gunfire or scuttling charges.[76] However, the Brixham trawlers also illustrate

the recurrent theme of the fishing vessel acting as a rescue vessel at need. One Brixham crew cheerfully hailed the survivors of the Greek steamer *George M Embiricos*, sunk by gunfire off the Lizard on a stormy night in 1916, and stopped to pick them up after a passing liner had steamed on by, refusing to chance picking up the *Embiricos'* men in submarine-infested waters.[77]

Other groups of small British fishing boats were also targeted, accelerating the decline of the traditional sail fishing boat. On a single day in 1915, eight Lowestoft smacks were scuttled by gunfire approximately 30 miles off their home port; four of them appear to have belonged to the same fleet, a cruel blow to their owner and to the men who earned a hard living from these little boats. A survivor of this incident recounted that one smack out of the group was deliberately spared so that she could take on board the crews who had been ordered to abandon their vessels.[78] Similar incidents occurred elsewhere on the English coast, among others the numerous victims captured and picked off with scuttling charges by *U-57* in a sustained two-day campaign off the Yorkshire coast in 1916; the 5-ton *Mary Ann* and 6-ton *Success* sunk by *UB-39*, also off Yorkshire in 1916; and the 10 trawling smacks targeted off Trevose Head, north Cornwall, in March 1917.[79]

Wrecks of *cobles* are also localised to the waters of the north-east coast in which they operated, between the Humber to the south and the Tweed to the north.[80] The coble was a workhorse of this coast, used principally for fishing and pilotage: manoeuvrable and largely stable, the coble inspired the earliest lifeboats along the north-east coast, since above all lifeboats required a self-righting capability if lifeboatmen were to be able to save life in the worst of weather. Cobles sufficed as lifeboats at need, as in the *Forfarshire* tragedy in 1838.[81] It was usually, however, local fishermen who had knowledge of the local sea area sufficient to undertake rescues (up until the decline of the fishing industry in the late 20th century the majority of RNLI volunteers were fishermen).

Nevertheless, cobles had a propensity to capsize in sudden squalls and storms: at least 84 accounts of the sudden demise of a coble date to between 1788 and 1907.[82] Like the *keel* (below) it could be scaled up or down: either small enough to be a rowing boat, or large enough to take sail, or even both (Fig 4.12). The *five-man boat* was a variant of the coble, a specialist in offshore North Sea fishing: the name refers not

Fig 4.12
The Tyne lifeboat, built 1833 and therefore contemporary with Grace Darling's rescue of the crew from the Forfarshire in 1839, shows something of how the coble developed into a dedicated lifeboat as designed by William Greathead and others, and now stands under a commemorative Grade II listed canopy in Ocean Road, South Shields. She was involved in many famous rescues, not least on the night of 24 November 1864, when she was instrumental in the rescue of the survivors from the wrecks of the Stanley, Ardwell and Friendship (1364862, 1364863, and 1364859).
(© Mr A Hubbard. Source English Heritage)

to crew numbers, but to the five owners or shareholders who each had a stake in a vessel. The crew of one such boat, the *Brotherly Love's Increase*,[83] were saved by 'taking to their coble', suggesting that a larger sailing coble such as this carried a smaller rowing coble on board as a lifeboat.

There were exceptions to this general coincidence of types of fishing vessel and the local fishing area. Some vessels were capable of a greater range, a prime example being fishing vessels from the east coast of Scotland, which made seasonal visits to the Norfolk and Suffolk coasts to catch herring migrating south through the North Sea. Like mackerel and pilchards, herring congregate in large shoals which move and feed just below the water surface, so were suitable for drift fishing, using floating surface nets. The seas off Great Yarmouth had been famous for their herring catches for centuries, both for home consumption and as an export cargo.[84] From the late 1800s onwards, the Scottish fleet, already active in the summer season in their home waters, extended the season by following the herring south, joining the local fishing fleets off East Anglia. The 'herring girls', who gutted and prepared the fish for sale, in turn migrated to East Anglia with the herring and the drifters. In the late 19th century the Scottish vessels were small, as the loss of this little vessel makes clear:

> On Friday night a very heavy gale of wind pre-vailed at Yarmouth … the fishing boats were also most of them out at sea, and among them about 40 Scotch boats, which, from their size and the fact of their being open boats, are not fitted to stand rough weather … between 20 and 30 of them had put into Lowestoft, and were safe. In one instance, a Scotch boat belonging to Peter-head was lost, but the crew were happily saved.[85]

Unlike Brixham, however, the Scottish ports enthusiastically adopted the potential of the purpose-built steam drifter which was ideally suited to this annual migration (Fig 4.13). The heyday of the Scottish herring fishery based at Great Yarmouth and Lowestoft thus took place in the early years of the 20th century before the First World War, which naturally coincides with a spike in the number of Scottish drifters lost.[86]

Cargo vessels

In the 21st century domestic cargoes and passengers may be transported relatively cheaply and easily by road, rail and air. Until the advent of rail in the mid-19th century, poor roads meant that the quickest and easiest way to transport goods was, where possible, by river or sea, so local vessel types evolved to transport particular cargoes in particular areas.

The *Thames barge* with its visually distinctive spritsail was once a common sight in the Thames estuary: they had a very shallow draught equally at home among the Essex mudflats or the London docks (Fig 4.14). Operating as coasters bringing flour from Suffolk, hay from Essex and bricks from Kent, their sails could be stowed out of the way when unloading cargo. As with many

Fig 4.13
Scottish steam drifters enter the harbour at Great Yarmouth in 1947 with their cargoes of herring, a mainstay of the local economy, with Scarlet Thread leading the fleet. Her registration of KY 197 shows that she belongs to Kirkcaldy. Just behind, on her port side, is a Banff-registered drifter, probably BF 67 or BF 87, displaying both a steam funnel and a mizzen lugsail. The photographer, Hallam Ashley, was predominantly interested in recording a disappearing way of life. By 1947 the Scottish drifting industry was past its peak: as the numbers of vessels dwindled, so did the shipping losses associated with the industry. (AA98/10882)

Fig 4.14
A line of moored Thames sailing barges showing their characteristic rigging, a familiar sight on the river until the 1950s and 1960s, taken by S W Rawlings, an employee of the Port of London Authority (PLA). Their shallow draught, based on Dutch coastal barges, was ideal both for working the river and negotiating the sandbanks and shoals of the Thames Estuary, but they were also capable of coasting beyond the Thames to the neighbouring ports of Essex and Kent. Where they now survive as working vessels, they carry tourists instead of cargo: many were abandoned when road freight became more economic for smaller cargoes. Assemblages of hulked barges lie in the mud and ooze of the Thames Estuary. (AA001107)

once-common types of small vessel, supporting small-scale local businesses, once they had outlived their useful lives and were beyond economical repair, they were left to rot on the coastline they had once served. The advent of motorisation and containerisation finally drove the Thames barge out of commercial use, leaving even larger numbers to rot, though some survive for tourist charters. Thus it is that Thames barges remain in the mud on the coasts of Essex and Kent in very large numbers, reflecting how many there once were: around 1907 there were 2090 registered Thames barges (Fig 4.15).[87]

The self-descriptive *flat* was adapted for working the Mersey and the Dee, so that most flat wrecks are in the inshore waters of Merseyside and Cheshire. As the name implies, the flat was a barge with a flat hull suitable for navigating shallow estuarine and river waters, and thus suitable for working coastwise among the many saltmarshes peppering the coastline in that area. These saltmarshes in turn gave the flat a principal commodity: salt, which was also exported by ocean-going vessels. These ships illustrate the three main strands in the story of the Merseyside salt: the home export trade, in which the ship *Marion*, bound from Birkenhead for Bowling, in Scotland, was lost; trade with Ireland (*Ross*, for Newry, 1767); and across the Atlantic (*Nuncio*, bound to New Orleans, 1882).[88]

In its original form the flat was a sailing coaster, which worked the Welsh coasts as well as the rivers.[89] Those lost on Liverpool's principal hazard, the Burbo Bank, blocking the entrance to the Mersey to the west (Fig 4.16), provide a snapshot of their varied cargoes. The *Speculation* was inbound to Liverpool with limestone when she was lost in 1853; the limestone may have come from Wales, as in the case of another flat, the *Railway King*, which foundered on her passage from Bardsey to Liverpool in 1854.[90]

The flat was ideally suited to the many local extraction industries, including coal, iron ore, limestone, gravel, slate and sand, as well as industrial products or by-products such as worked or scrap iron, bricks and chemicals. Both the *Smelter* in 1892, laden with gravel from Piel in Cumbria for Runcorn, and the *Bessie* in 1909, laden with coal, also from Runcorn for Anglesey, were lost on the Burbo.[91] At nearly 60 years old, the *Smelter* was unable to withstand the force 9 conditions which compelled her to try unsuccessfully to seek shelter in the Mersey. Another flat was the *Red Jacket*, which foundered

in 1860 while performing lighterage duties, that is, taking on part of the cargo of a vessel which had not yet discharged in port.[92] In this case the cargo was arrowroot starch, regarded in Victorian times as highly digestible (and now seen as having little nutritional value). Flats were also ideal for working local canals such as the Sankey Canal. Indeed, aerial photographs from the 1940s record an assemblage of hulked flats in a canal dockside area at Runcorn, since filled in.[93]

The Severn *trow*, a type of flat-bottomed sailing barge, was similarly built on and worked both the English and the Welsh sides of the Severn. Like the Thames barge, the trow was adaptable, with a mast which could be taken down to pass under bridges – and worked both

Fig 4.15
Close-up view down the wreck of the Thames spritsail barge Rose, *built in 1880, from her prominent draught markings. She worked the Thames as a coaster until 1930, when she was converted to a lighter or towed barge and was abandoned by 1961 at Beaumont Quay at the inland end of Landermere Creek, Beaumont-cum-Moze, Essex. (AA96/05734)*

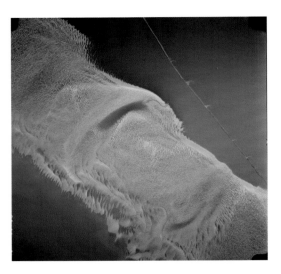

open water in the Bristol Channel and far upriver (Fig 4.17). Their remains thus appear on the Somerset coast, and in the River Severn and its estuary. They also sailed up the Severn's tributary rivers, where one was wrecked as far north as the River Lugg in Leominster; in Wales they also worked the River Wye,[94] proving their ability in non-tidal rivers. The trow worked equally varied, but equally local, cargoes, carrying timber products directly from the Forest of Dean, coal from the Gloucestershire coalfields and groceries to and from market in this predominantly agricultural area. As cargo- and as passage-boats they also crossed the Severn at its wider points, as did other forms of ferry boats to avoid a lengthy round trip inland. The trow is a cultural emblem of Severn trading: a pub remains in Bristol, just off the Welsh Back, called the *Llandoger Trow*.

As might be expected, trows built at various locations in the Bristol Channel and in the Severn have found a final resting place on the Severn at Purton in Gloucestershire. Among the hulks there are representatives of each of the three principal stretches of the Severn where they were built and where they generally plied their trade, among them the seagoing trow *Selina Jane* from the Bristol Channel port of Bridgwater, the Gloucester trow *Higre* and the *Britannia*, of Droitwich type, working the upper reaches of the Severn in Worcestershire. At Purton can also be found the remains of vessels which worked even more restricted areas, such as the distinctive lighters (barges built without any means of propulsion, and intended to be towed with their cargo) built to work the Stroudwater canal, for example, the Stroudwater barge *Rockby*.[95]

If the trow was a characteristic working feature of the Severn it was occasionally wrecked by another Severn feature, this time the natural tidal phenomenon known as the Severn bore, a large surge wave periodically ripping through the Estuary. As the wave surges inland, it is funnelled into an increasingly narrow and increasingly shallow channel which creates a tidal wave of great power. The bore occurs at regular periods throughout the year, and when it coincides with spring tides can be exceptionally powerful, creating a natural event which is a popular attraction. It would create an obvious environment for the loss of relatively small vessels otherwise well-suited to navigating the upper stretches of the Severn. Little, however, is currently known about the relationship between wrecks in the Severn and the tidal conditions under which they were wrecked, though two 19th-century incidents have come to light. The first, in 1809, saw the capsize and sinking of a passage boat crossing from the Arlingham to the Newnham side, attributed to a bore coming on top of a spring tide, and the two boatmen and their passenger were all drowned.[96] A later incident, in 1814, involving the loss of the sloop *Industry* of Minsterworth, appears to bear the hallmarks of a minor bore:

> she was lying to for the tide, when she was struck on the beam by a very heavy ground swell, which carried away the fore-scuttle, and filling with water, she immediately went down by the head.[97]

The picturesquely named East coast *billyboy*, like the Severn trow, was also capable of coasting as well as traversing the Humber and its estuary. In common with most coasters, whatever their type, the billyboy carried a variety of cargoes. It was more varied in appearance than most coasters, with several permutations of rig: the name 'billyboy' refers principally to the shape of the hull, but they could be ketch-, sloop- or schooner-rigged and were allied to the eponymous Humber keels and Humber sloops. Most were indeed built in, and belonged to, the Humber, but some wrecked billyboys had operated out of ports in the Wash or as far north as Glasgow before their demise. As East coast traders, their remains are therefore scattered along the eastern coastline of England or in the North Sea.

The *keels* of the Tyne and Wear were very different from the Humber vessels of the same name. They served the larger seagoing ships and gave their name to the Newcastle measurement of coal; the typical keel vessel was capable of carrying 21 tons, so that the keel came to denote 21 tons' measurement. Accounts of Tyneside colliers are readily identifiable without recourse to details of their home ports, precisely because their 'burthen' or 'burden' would be expressed in terms of keels rather than tons: 12 to 14 keels was common, approximately 250 to 290 tons. Keels and keelmen appear in the Latin of the *Tynemouth Chartulary* in 1322 and a century later in the Norman French of a statute of Henry V in 1421, tinged with a dash of Franglais:

Certeinz vesselx appellez Keles, par les queux tielx charbons sont caries de la terre jesques a les naefs en le dit port.[98]

Certain vessels called 'keels', by which such coals are carried from land to the ships in the said port.

This *modus operandi* changed very little over the following centuries and Tyneside newspaper reports of the 18th century show that colliers were still served by the smaller keels. Typically collier brigs would perhaps take on part of their lading at the quaysides or 'staiths' along the Tyne, then wait at anchor off Tynemouth and Shields in order to complete their lading, the little keels bringing the 'black diamonds' of coal to the larger vessels – yet even the larger ships were small to modern eyes. Some of them simply took on their all their cargo offshore from the keels, especially when the harbours were full.

Fig 4.17
View of the Gloucester Docks in the late 19th century, showing a mixture of vessel types, local and international, able to use the docks. In the right foreground a Severn trow belonging to Pill lies berthed with her mast folded down, with other trows mast up in the background. Elsewhere, a row of small barges lies in close proximity to the apparently foreign seagoing vessels Franz *and* Dr. Witte. *(CC53/00092)*

Passenger vessels

The Tyne and Wear were also full of ferries and 'passage boats', as they were frequently known (Fig 4.18), and furnish good examples of wrecks pertaining to these vessel types, though they were common to most rivers. They were the most localised of all vessel types in terms of their range, often taking people from one bank of the river to the other, or upstream or downstream between two points. It was often the easiest way for local farmers or their wives to take their produce to market. While women were often victims of shipwrecks as passengers in larger vessels,[99] the proportion of female passengers to male tends to be greater in these small passage boats. Typically carrying about 12 to 30 passengers at most, very often they were swamped if they were overloaded. Others were victims of collision, which was unsurprising, given that in crossing between banks of a river they might also cross the bows of larger vessels working up- or down-river. Sometimes it could be the combination of several circumstances, as in the case of the 'low ferry-boat' travelling from the Monkwearmouth shore to the southern shore of the Wear in 1795:

> The boatman, in crossing, pushing his boat-hook against the hawser of a ship, laying in the harbour, which was then much crouded [sic], the boat-hook broke, and the man fell into the river. The passengers, from an amiable desire to preserve his life, too precipitately pressed to the side over which the boatman fell, and the vessel unfortunately overset and sunk, by which accident, nearly 20 people were drowned.[100]

In 1759 one of these passage boats struck upon muddy ground en route from Poole to Ower Quay; realising the hopelessness of their situation, the boatman got out and encouraged his passengers to follow him across the mud to Furzey Island, where, inevitably, those lacking his local knowledge died in the mire. One man saved himself from their fate by the twin precautions of taking a diversion and using a butter basket.[101]

The earliest recorded loss of a ferry boat or *batella* was in the Thames in 1270, this time overladen with cargo: faggots (bundles of sticks used as firewood). There were only five passengers, including two women, Maud le Estreys and Alice de Grenewich. One of the dead was one William le Batiler 'of Grenewiz' whose surname suggests that he was the boatman.[102] That he and Alice both belonged to Greenwich suggests that the vessel was operating in that stretch of river: it may be circumstantial evidence of a ferry antedating one recorded at nearby 'Wulwych' (Woolwich) in 1308, normally cited as the earliest precursor of the Woolwich Free Ferry.[103] It seems that the stretch of river between Greenwich and Woolwich was a well-used crossing point in the Middle Ages, and remains so with the continued existence of Free Ferry (*see* Fig 1.6 for examples of such boats at a later date).

Further west, the loss of 17 lives aboard a trow in 1732 on the Noose Sands in the Severn suggests that she was being used as a passage vessel at a point where the Severn is wide, remains unbridged to this day, and meanders inland, forcing a detour of several miles by road in order to cross the river. Passage vessels could, of course, cross a wider span of the Severn Estuary. The Welsh ferry *Elizabeth* foundered in the Bristol Channel in 1831, while attempting to cross from Swansea to Bridgwater; she had been built at Chepstow just over 40 years earlier as a dedicated ferry boat.[104]

Fig 4.18
'Tail-piece' vignette from Quadrupeds, *vol. III. One of Thomas Bewick's charming and humorous vignettes inserted as chapter endings in his books, and grounded in the reality of everyday life. As two ferrymen punt the boat, two female passengers nervously eye the horse: if it becomes restive the vessel is likely to capsize. (Courtesy of the Natural History Society of Northumbria)*

In the north-west passengers embarked from Liverpool and other ports for Ireland. Many vessels lost on the Burbo Bank, off the Mersey, were passage vessels, such as the *Chichester*, outward-bound from Liverpool for Dublin shortly before Christmas 1773.[105] On the same route the *Earl of Moira* packet was lost in 1821, drowning half her 110 passengers.[106] The links between Liverpool and Dublin were strong, but there were also connections to other ports in Ireland: the *Manchester* and *Countess of Caithness* were wrecked on the Londonderry run in 1780 and 1799, respectively.[107] Passengers also regularly criss-crossed between the Isle of Man and the mainland: a packet service between Douglas and Whitehaven was established in 1767, but there were also links between the island and Liverpool. The *Union* was driven into the River Ribble in Lancashire with 14 passengers on just such a journey in 1814.[108]

The most notorious wreck on this route was, of course, the *Ellan Vannin*, lost off Liverpool Bar with all hands in 1909 and commemorated by the eponymous folk song sung by the Spinners.[109] The devastating loss of 33 lives was headline news; like the little inshore passage boats, ferries regularly carried livestock as well as human passengers, and the *Ellan Vannin* was no exception on this occasion. Investigations into the cause of the tragedy began at once, beginning with divers going down to the wreck. The results of their examinations suggested a collision, although there was also a prevalent view that the sea had finally overwhelmed her after a rough crossing. It was thought that she had 'broached to' (turned sideways into the wind) which led her to capsize. The wind was from the north-west and the weather said to be not unusual for December: under normal circumstances this would have been ideal for her crossing to Liverpool, but if driving before the wind in increasingly rough weather then the crew could rapidly lose control. The master of a passing steamer, the *Heroic*, reported that at about the same time, his vessel had also nearly 'broached to'.

Perhaps the age of the *Ellan Vannin* was a contributory factor, with 49 years in service, but she had generally been regarded as well-found and seaworthy. As with so many wrecks off the coast of Liverpool, the Mersey Docks and Harbours Board took the decision to blow her up to prevent obstruction to navigation: their assiduity extended well beyond the Burbo Bank and as a result even this distinctively tragic

wreck shares two features in common with other vessels in the area. Not only was it dispersed, like so many other wrecks nearby, but for this very reason, there is a far higher concentration of definitively identified wreck sites than elsewhere in the country.[110]

On the Dover–Calais crossing there were losses in both directions and of both nationalities: in 1771 an unnamed French passage vessel capsized in a sudden squall of wind as she approached Dover, while the *Flora* was lost just after setting out from Dover to Calais in 1820. Nor was it only English and French ships involved in the cross-Channel hop: the Dutch *Zorgvuldigheid* was another such vessel.[111] Arrival at Dover did not necessarily mean the dangers of the voyage were past: on 15 November 1802 the French packet *Flèche* misjudged the entrance to Dover harbour. The following week the *Rambler*, a French passage vessel, ran on shore nearby, while a further vessel, the *Two Friends*, 'also had a very narrow escape from being on shore'. As *The Times* noted:

> A party of our English boatmen station themselves ready on the spot every night to save the lives of any passengers who may want their assistance, as from the frequency of the accidents lately, they look for a stranded vessel every night.[112]

French passage boats were not the only regular cross-Channel visitors, for, during the 18th and 19th centuries, the French *chasse-marée* was a regular trader to and from the southern coasts of England. The name *chasse-marée*, occasionally spelt *chasse-marie*, means 'tide-chaser', an elegant description for her coasting function. Wrecks of *chasse-marées* are accordingly scattered along the Channel coasts, and could be regarded as a characteristic feature of the Channel landscape, common to both English and French waters. They were, however, wrecked as far north as the Bristol Channel and the coast of Norfolk since they had the capacity to make longer journeys.

Like many other coasters, they were principally involved in fetching coal from the Welsh and north-east coalfields for France, but inevitably they were also involved in the smuggling of wine and brandy. It is not always easy to tell whether alcoholic cargoes were illicit, since they were also exported quite legitimately from France to England. Sometimes the wine carried was in fact intended entirely for French domestic consumption, and French ships only ended up on the Channel coasts because they had had the misfortune to have been blown off course (or, as in one case, had been captured during war with France).[113]

The fate of the *Jeune Fanie* was a case in point: carrying salt and coins from Marennes and Camaret-sur-Mer for Dunkirk, the wind blew 'a hurricane' directly for the shore. The *Jeune Fanie* crashed into the rocks off Belle Tout, near Beachy Head, Sussex, drowning the master and his 11-year-old son immediately. The other four crew were thrown 'high and dry' by the 'irresistible force of the mighty surge', only to be confronted with the chalk cliff between Birling Gap and Cow Gap. They had almost resigned themselves to drowning as the tide came in, when a cliff fall and its attendant rubble was spotted. In this extremity, and in the dark in a foreign land, they scrambled upon the heap of rubble and huddled together to postpone the inevitable. One man then happened to grasp a bunch of sea kale, which reassured them that they were safe, 'proving the ocean was not accustomed to reaching the summit'.[114] All four were rescued at daylight, after the waters had receded.

This section can only give a flavour of all the various wrecks lost within the areas they worked. Generally speaking, most of the vessel types covered are reasonably well documented as working vessels, but their wrecking patterns are less so. Besides their obvious human interest, the wrecks of these regional vessel types clearly have close ties to community history beyond their economic importance to their respective communities. This is clearest in the case of fishing vessels.

Other local classes of vessel evolved specifically to take advantage of the sea's harvest in other ways, such as the Cornish gig; to cater for the particular industrial needs of a given community, such as the Tyne keel; some reveal aspects of local industries which have since disappeared or shrunk, such as on the banks of the Severn by the Forest of Dean; others became versatile workhorses carrying different forms of cargo as needed, as was the case with most riverine and estuarine vessels, so that, although they were not always confined to a characteristic cargo, they evolved a distinctive appearance.

Others will have undergone a characteristic wrecking process, such as the seine boats, close inshore, or have been wrecked on a voyage that reveals the scope or limitations of their physical range. Some were clearly very well adapted to both their function and local environment, so that, though widespread, they appear to be under-represented in the numbers of wrecks in their local area. The Deal luggers with fishing, pilotage and salvage streams of income, are a good example of these, yet they regularly went out to the wrecks of less fortunate ships on that most feared of all hazards, the Goodwin Sands.

Wrecks in canals are still very poorly understood: they were, more than most, confined to a particular waterway, since only vessels adapted to local conditions could navigate them, or they lacked sail and were drawn by horse or other means. Most will have been removed as navigational hazards but more attention has been paid to wrecks in rivers and at sea, so this appears to be a fruitful subject for the research of industrial history.[115] Most of these groups have historically been overlooked in local records for the more dramatic local tales of 'wreckers' and 'smugglers', but these are in fact a very small proportion numerically of all wrecks.

Finally, there are the groups of wrecks which were abandoned on the banks of the environments they served, along the Thames, Medway and on the Severn at Purton, for example: they were left to rot in increasing numbers after the Second World War when the use of sailing vessels to carry general or specific cargoes locally was no longer economical, perhaps the chief wrecking pattern for 20th-century representatives of particular vessel types such as the Thames barge. This group is an extreme example of a wrecking process which is characteristic of rivers and estuaries which were once alive with small working vessels, which were abandoned from the mid-20th-century onwards as they fell out of economic use, or when it was no longer worth the cost of repair against potential earnings. They 'held out' longer than ocean-going sailing vessels for their relatively small size enabled them to remain more adaptable and economical for longer, diversifying towards more modern cargoes, but for most of these vessels it was a losing battle. Representatives of some types survive as working vessels adapted to other uses, for example, tourism and diving, and it could be said that the Purton wrecks are among this group (Fig 4.19). They retain a 'working function' of sorts in shoring up the southern bank of the River Severn by forming an obstruction encouraging the formation of silt deposits along the river bank, preventing it being breached or

Fig 4.19
From coaster to part of a unique collection of local vessels united in abandonment: the melancholy appearance of the King *(1543147) as a giant spider with girders for legs is a result both of her past history and her final fate. Built of composite construction with a timber hull over iron framing, characteristic of the mid to late 19th century, she was formerly a schooner. During the Second World War she was cut down as a typical Severn towing barge, and ended her days in the post-war period beached and abandoned as part of the Purton hulk assemblage, where she was stripped of much of her salvageable material.*
(© Andrew Wyngard)

washed away where it lies very close to the parallel bank of the Gloucester and Sharpness Canal. Other hulks have been abandoned for similar purposes elsewhere. Interpreting this wide variety of wrecks in their respective environmental contexts is likely to become increasingly important in our characterisation of undersea landscapes and areas of maritime archaeological potential and provide a rich and relatively untapped source of investigation in community history. Each terrestrial landscape has its own corresponding wreck landscape; each has its own story to tell.

The story of the colliers

Dirty British coaster with a salt-caked smoke stack,
Butting through the Channel in the mad
March days,
With a cargo of Tyne coal …

(John Masefield, 'Cargoes')

The history of collier wrecks

The once-ubiquitous collier deserves a section all to itself. To date over 5,000 vessels, or over one-eighth of the wrecks recorded in English waters, are known to have been lost in the coal trade. The word 'collier' generally describes the function, not the form, of the ship: we have little idea of the appearance of early collier wrecks,

the earliest a Flemish ship wrecked on Filey Brigg in 1367, probably homeward-bound from Newcastle-upon-Tyne.[116] The circumstances of the wreck are consistent with Newcastle's early prominence in the coal trade: data for the Middle Ages indicate that 50 to 60 tons was the average export cargo from Newcastle,[117] so the Flemish ship was probably carrying a similar quantity, as well as a cargo of 'uncustomed' or 'duty-free' wool. The early – and continuous – dominance of Newcastle coal is reflected in the statistics for collier wrecks, and further evidenced by continuous demands for lighthouses on the east coast collier routes, which saw the erection of several 17th- and 18th-century lighthouses (not all of which were actually lit), clearly in response to collier losses.[118]

Though Welsh colliers in the pre-industrial period, like their Tyneside counterparts, regularly appear in the wreck record from the mid-17th century onwards, the numbers of colliers lost within English waters laden with coal from the Durham coalfield[119] outstrip the results for other ports and coalfields in England, Scotland and Wales combined. From the outset, London was Durham's principal market for coal, and remained so right up to the Second World War, but south coast ports were also significant buyers of Durham coal.

Around 1703, the year of the Great Storm, colliers began to be associated with specific vessel types: for example, the *pink*, a versatile narrow-sterned vessel flaring out at the sides, used for fishing and coasting. Coasting (carrying cargoes between two domestic ports) perfectly describes the 17th- and 18th-century coal trade. Virtually all the wrecked collier pinks of the early 18th century were involved in the east coast coal trade out of Newcastle-upon-Tyne; the only exception was the Norwegian *Providentia*, wrecked in 1763 at Monks House in Northumberland.[120] She was a victim of an all-too-common fate among the east coast colliers: the prevailing south-easterly wind in the North Sea could either blow a southbound ship leaving the Tyne off course to the northward, or force northward-bound vessels to overshoot the Tyne. In either case they would smash into the Farne Islands or elsewhere on the Northumberland coast.

Towards the end of the 18th and in the early 19th centuries, the collier brig became the principal form of vessel serving the east coast coal trade. Not all colliers were brigs, and brigs were renowned for their versatility, but on this route 'collier' and 'brig' were practically synonymous, wide, deep vessels with strong hulls intended to 'carry the maximum cargo with the minimum crew'.[121] Wreck reports confirm this by revealing a crew of between five and eight men as the norm.

The Seaton Carew designated wreck site[122] near Hartlepool is protected as a virtually unique example of a once-common sight on the east coast in the 18th century, the collier brig, embedded in the sands of the coastline which she once served (Fig 4.20). Strong candidates for the identity of this vessel emerge from the historical record, including the *Betty* or *Betsey*, lost in 1766. Another *Betsy* collier also came to grief here in 1814: she could well have been built in the 18th century,[123] as could any of the colliers wrecked near Seaton Carew in a gale of 1824: the *Wealands*, *Eliza*, *Dolphin* and *Suffolk*.[124]

Colliers were noted for their longevity, being repeatedly patched up and rebuilt over 50 or more years: a ship named the *Theodosia* called regularly at Newcastle from the 1750s to the

Fig 4.20
Low tides following storms exposed the wreck of this collier brig, still coherent after perhaps 175 years of burial under the sands at Seaton Carew. Her sturdy structure suggests that she was built nearer to the beginning than the end of the 19th century.
(© Tees Archaeology)

1830s before finally disappearing from the record.[125] The *Theodosia*, with some 80 years' service, gives some credence to the story of the well-known Tyneside collier *Betsy Cains*, whose long career was put to an end by a gale in 1827. The *Betsy Cains* 'put back' leaky to Shields as a gale blew up, and as it howled on she struck the Black Middens and went to pieces. Her origins are obscure and difficult to disentangle from a false association with bringing over William III from Holland in 1688, a legend well-established by the time she was lost. Just how old she was is uncertain: the Victorian historian Macaulay appears to have accepted her age but refuted her association with the 'Glorious Revolution' of 1688, which would have made her around 140 years old at the time of loss.[126] Eighty years' service, like *Theodosia*'s, is not impossible, but any ship over about 25 years old was potentially an accident waiting to happen, and the crew were fortunate be picked up off the rocks by the *Northumberland* lifeboat, rather than foundering at sea. Souvenir hunters came out in abundance, attracted by the legend:

> The *Betsy Cains*, noticed in our last as being on the rocks near Tynemouth, has since gone to pieces, the weather to the present, being very tempestuous. In relating the loss of this (supposed to be the oldest) British vessel, we cannot refrain from remarking the excitement of curiosity, not only to have a view of her, as she laid in a wrecked state, but to obtain some part of her, in token of the event for which she was most remarkable (the bringing over of William III). Individuals in Shields have received letters from Orange Lodges, requesting to procure them a piece of the vessel.[127]

The north-east collier brig evolved into two major localised variants, the *cat* from Whitby (of which Captain Cook's *Endeavour* was an example) and the *snow*, particularly associated with Sunderland. The cat was well suited for oceanic exploration despite its relatively small size, with capacious stowage and a flat bottom facilitating navigation of uncharted waters. The fact that no wreck so far recorded in English waters is explicitly described as a cat could be interpreted as a tribute to their sturdiness, but contemporary wreck reports may simply have glossed over the cat as they did so many colliers in general. Some wrecked Whitby colliers contemporary with the *Endeavour* were probably of cat type, such as the *Delight*, wrecked at Harwich after her maiden voyage in 1763.[128]

Like the brig, of which it was a variant,[129] the snow originated as a general cargo carrier,

judging by the variety of voyages, cargoes and nationalities of wrecked snows dotted around the country, but likewise became synonymous with the 19th-century coal trade. Two-thirds of all known snows wrecked in English waters belonged to north-east ports, one-third of these to Sunderland alone; others registered elsewhere can be directly linked with the coal trade.[130] Snow numbers rose in accordance with the growth in overseas markets for English coal, peaking in the 19th century, when Durham coal was exported worldwide. Snows and other colliers were lost off the English coast en route to places as far apart as Istanbul (1841), Penang (1854), Suez (1857), Bermuda (1860), Shanghai (1868), Alexandria (1871), Rio de Janeiro (1875), Java (1881) and Valparaiso (1891),[131] as well as to principal domestic and western European markets. These and other routes were also served by the collier brig and the *brigantine*, another brig variant.

The rise in the export market can be linked to the rise in steam as a locomotive power for trains, for ships, for engines, while European demand was primarily for heating and lighting. The losses of two snows and a barque, all from Shields, in the 1880s, reflect a sudden surge in demand from Motril, Spain. Orders from Hamburg peaked around 1800, then around 1855, but as German coal production in the Ruhr grew, the numbers of shipwrecks on the Tyne to Hamburg run correspondingly declined, though the trade picked up a little during the latter half of the 19th century. The *Iron Crown* was lost on the Spanish Battery inbound in ballast from Hamburg in 1881 (Fig 4.21), then the *Fenella* drove onto the Herd Sand in 1893.[132] Foreign ships also had a share of the export trade, either as regular North Sea traders based at their home ports in Germany, Norway and Russia, or as charter ships on one-off coal runs, such as the Finnish *Kiirus* wrecked off Great Yarmouth in 1871 en route from Hull for Marseille with coal and tar.[133]

Colliers in the physical and cultural landscape

Looking at wrecks in their wider landscape context, all colliers, whatever their form, reflected various aspects of the coal industry in which they were employed. As the mining industry developed, the names of Tyneside and Wearside colliers increasingly gave clues as to their ownership and the origin of the coal they were transporting when they were lost. The integrated nature of the process from extraction to transport

Fig 4.21
The Wreck of the *Iron Crown. The* Iron Crown *is shown shortly after the wreck by the local marine artist Robert Jobling in 1881. The seas and weather are so violent that it is difficult to discern that the vessel lies very close to the shore and that the artist must have been standing close to the rocks in order to compose this view. He shows the sea 'making a clean breach over her', in a common phrase of the time.*
(© Private collection, by courtesy of James Alder Fine Art)

to sale is seen in the way the cargo, port and ship were often in the same ownership, especially as significant colliery owners developed new ports or expanded existing ports in the 19th century – such as Seaham (Fig 4.22). Similarly their vessels belonged to Seaham, Sunderland, Shields or Blyth, as appropriate (rather than the southern ports which also specialised in running significant collier fleets, such as London or Whitstable). The names of the colliers reflect the origins of the coal, from those of the owners: *Blackett* (1770), *Tempest* (1777), *Boyne* (1820) and *Lambton* (1834); or their estates: *Wynyard* (1842); or those of the actual collieries themselves: the *Lumley* (1881), *Harraton* (1896) and *Cramlington* (1898); or the wider colliery area, such as the *Wearside* (1917).[134] These associations endured well into the 20th century, as shown by the *New Lambton*, torpedoed in 1940 en route from Hartlepool for London.[135] Recognition of the origins of the ship's names may narrow down the origins of the coal associated with the wrecks, and may have possible implications for the identification of wreck sites through the composition of their coal cargoes.

Other forms of name are associated with the destination or the use of the coal. For example, the Gas Light and Coke Co. evoked the properties of heat and light for their in-house colliers. One ship was named in the 1930s after their marketing character, *Mr Therm*, an animated gas flame.[136] Some were prosaic: *Torchbearer*, *Firelight*, *Flashlight* and *Fireglow*; some poetic: *Lampada* and *Lanterna*; and others scholarly, derived from Latin: *Lucent* and *Fulgens* (radiant), *Ignis* (fire), *Phare* (lighthouse).[137] All were attacked and sunk during either the First or the Second World Wars, bound from either Durham or South Wales ports for the Beckton works of the parent company in London or elsewhere (*Lucent* was lost supplying the battlefields of France). Ironically, as they were torpedoed, most of these ships would have gone down in a sudden blaze of light.[138]

The *New Lambton* was also typical in having a further association with the wider industrial landscape of the north-east coast, like most steam colliers of the late 19th and 20th centuries. She was built by two Wearside firms: the hull by S P Austin & Son Ltd in 1924, and her machinery by the N E Marine Engineering Co.

Ltd. Colliers were churned out by shipyards large and small on the banks of the Tyne, Tees and Wear, powered by the same coal that the ships they built were destined to carry: Swan Hunter, Wigham Richardson, Palmer's of Jarrow, Readhead's and Hawthorn Leslie of South Shields. Their reach extended far beyond the east coast coal trade: some were destined for the South Wales and other coalfields, as well as other shipping trades and routes.

The shipbuilding industry saw a decline parallel to that of coal, but one which began at an earlier stage. Similarly, at the end of their useful lives, steam colliers and other vessels associated with the coal trade were either abandoned near their home ports (Fig 4.23) or broken up at yards adjacent to those which had built them in the first place. *Mr Therm*, for example, was built on Wearside in 1936 and broken up on Tyneside in 1959, thus completing a circle comprising building, service and breaking.[139] There was a similar cycle for the colliers wrecked at the mouth of the Tyne during this industrial period: for example, the *Greenwood*, homeward-bound, in 1900, and the *Rotha*, outward-bound, in 1902.[140] Parts of these

vessels at the time would have been sold on and recycled as appropriate, but would eventually have passed out of use well before the present day. Ironically, therefore, wrecks of steam colliers are the most tangible links today to the Tyneside and Wearside shipping industries whence they came.

The phrase 'King Coal' refers to the centuries of dominance of coal as Britain's prime source of energy and a major employer in industrial districts. On a local level, however, coal was also king on Tyneside and Wearside: the supply of coal for export created the demand for ships belonging to, and operating from, the local rivers, where shipbuilding was literally fuelled by the easy availability of raw materials locally. Coal fired the furnaces and blasted the iron and steel which produced the colliers, which were simultaneously consumers of coal bunkered at their home ports, and exporters of coal for domestic, industrial and bunkering use at home and abroad. The entire loop from extraction to consumption was closed by King Coal, so that the steam collier in its turn became as ubiquitous as the sailing collier, and even more closely allied to the cargo it carried. The most important

Fig 4.22
Aerial view of Seaham harbour from the west. Seaham harbour was built by the third Marquess of Londonderry 1828–35 to ensure the seamless shipment of coal from his local mines to the consumer. Though there were some shipping casualties in the area before the construction of the harbour, most of the wrecks known in the vicinity postdate the opening of the harbour. (12299/17)

Fig 4.23
Wrecks off West Staiths, North Blyth, Northumberland. The staith or loading installation at background left was built to ship coal from the Ashington Colliery Co.'s pits. It was opened in 1928 and only ceased operation in 1989. The remains of two well broken wooden vessels can be seen in the foreground, probably coal barges abandoned as the trade declined; they were first recorded in this location by 1981 although they may have been abandoned earlier. Other vessel remains also lie scattered nearby, west of the staith (wreck record 907642). (AA039506)

advantage of the steam collier was its capacity over the collier brig, which in the 19th century averaged 250 to 400 tons, though larger vessels operated on the transatlantic routes: the *Chinchas*, lost en route from Liverpool for Rio in 1859, was 1,894 tons net, and laden with 3,000 tons of 'Runcorn coal'. The *Chinchas*, large for a sailing brig, was at the lower end of the average for a 20th-century steam collier (1,500 to 3,000 tons gross) though many were larger, 5,000–7,000 tons, and some were as small as 600 tons net (1,100 gross).[141]

Even during the two World Wars, which coincided with the heyday of steam freight by rail, coal for home consumption was still predominantly sent by sea to London and the south coast ports, and the entire infrastructure devoted to circulating domestic coal was geared towards transport by sea.[142] Ships enabled the easy transport of bunker coal for the domestic and export markets from port to port (just as petrol refineries are located on major rivers – Ellesmere Port on the Mersey, Immingham on the Humber and Shell Haven on the Thames).

King Coal dominated the east coast coal trade for so long and in such volume that other products originating in the same industrial area are easily overlooked, although they too were powered by coal. Their existence is revealed among the records of shipwrecks, paralleling the rise and fall of these trading patterns: in the late 18th and early 19th centuries, colliers laden with coal also carried glass, a typical Newcastle and Sunderland product. In the 17th century the north-east became a prime glass producer, taking over from the Sussex glass industry of the Weald, as deforestation enforced the adoption of coal as the primary fuel for glass manufacture. The rise of the glass industry therefore coincided with that of the collier brig, whose primary cargo provided a safe packing medium:

> These cases are brought to London in the coal ships, they being set on end in the Coles more than half its depth, by which means they are kept steady from falling and being broke by the motion and rowling of the ship.[143]

Like the coal within which it was normally packed, the glass was intended both for the domestic and the export markets. The *Boyne* was carrying coal when she was lost in 1820 en route to London with her dual cargo. The auction of the *Ranger*, whose recovery from her precarious position off Whitby forced her sale in 1797, reveals something of the proportions of glass to coal: two keels of glass wedged in among 18 of coal, that is, 42 tons of glass as against 378 tons of coal.[144] The Dutch *Vrow Margaretta* or *Juffrow Margarita* also came to grief at Whitby en route from Newcastle with coal and glass for

Amsterdam in 1781, while in 1755 the *Sukey* of Boston, Massachusetts, stranded on the Corton Sand off Suffolk returning to New England from Shields with the same dual cargo.[145] A transatlantic trade in glass seems scarcely credible, however tightly packed among coals, but the answer lies in the slow growth of the American glass industry and British encouragement of consumer demand, rather than competition, in her largest colony.[146] Perhaps some of the *Sukey*'s cargo was destined for the fashionable fanlights of 18th-century New England, for some examples of Massachusetts fanlights are contemporary with this ship.[147] Durham coal therefore may have had an unexpected impact on the landscape of the New World.

The east coast collier route had other impacts at home as well as abroad: it was a significant passenger route, since regular and frequent sailings by numerous vessels between the Tyne and the Thames made it the cheapest and most direct route before the advent of the railways (and indeed before the institution of regular packet services between two given ports) between Newcastle and London. Passenger demand on the collier route peaked in the late 18th century, but remained an important sideline for the mid-19th-century steam collier. Passenger numbers varied: a handful would be the norm, but 36 were reported aboard the *Countess Anne*, lost off Norfolk in 1754. Their social status also varied: the more important passengers of the 'middling sort' or above – clergy, gentlefolk and military officers – would be named: the rest remained anonymous. The survivors of the *Hawke Packet*, lost in 1803 while laden with £4,000 worth of coal and other goods, included a Mr Gibson, 'colour-manufacturer', of Gateshead, accompanying his consignment of paint to London: his lost cargo left him in 'deep distress' financially.

Travelling in this way during the 18th century exposed the passenger to wartime peril as well as to natural hazards. In 1747 a French privateer captured a collier, then marked out the English ship *Fanny* as his next victim. Her master, taking advantage of his familiarity with home waters, decoyed the privateer over the Goodwin Sands, where she duly came to grief. The *Fanny* magnanimously came to the assistance of her enemy, whereupon her captain is said to have discovered English prisoners from the captured collier, including his own wife, a passenger on board.[148] Some 50 years later, during the Napoleonic era,

a Sunderland collier, the *Honduras Packet*, returning to her home port in ballast with two 'North Country' ladies aboard, was intercepted in the English Channel by a French privateer and sent for Dieppe. The ladies 'persuaded and assisted the remaining crew to rise and retake the brig', but, despite their stalwart efforts, the weather intervened and the vessel was wrecked at Dungeness while escaping to England. The ladies wrote a spirited account of their adventures: 'In consequence of this last circumstance, each of us lost the whole of our cloaths (excepting what we had on) but have the greatest reason to thank Almighty God.'[149]

With a fair wind, and safely past sandbanks and privateers, it was possible to reach London from Newcastle-upon-Tyne within a few days, discharge the coal, and make a rapid return voyage using the prevailing south-easterly winds of the North Sea, aided by being 'light' or in ballast, the whole taking perhaps two weeks. Throughout its history, from the era of the pink to that of the steam collier, Tyneside's coal commerce was so profitable as to render a return cargo unnecessary, as evinced by the number of 'light' colliers lost, but passengers were a reliable source of additional revenue. The turnaround time between 'clearing out' for London and reappearing in the Tyne was generally two to three weeks, a little longer for the south coast ports. Under adverse conditions, the voyage in one direction only could take longer than a typical round trip: the artist Thomas Bewick recalled a voyage to London in 1776 involving three weeks 'beating about in good weather and bad'.[150]

The north-east collier was the product of its landscape: the coal which it exported to London, the people it ferried from Newcastle to London and back again, and the North Sea for whose rigours it was well adapted. The fate of the collier has also mirrored the decline of the once-dominant Tyneside shipyards and Durham coalfield, formerly pre-eminent features of the local terrestrial landscape. Of the latter few traces now remain, after the pit closures in the wake of the 1985 miners' strike. The landscape which once was pockmarked with pits whose wheels stood sentinel over their associated communities now shows few obvious scars of an industry which dominated the cultural landscape of the north and the news within living memory: all that remains may be a pit wheel, enclosing a village name sign. The pits have healed up just like an ear piercing on the

Fig 4.24
Brighton Beach, with colliers. *This little oil sketch, dated 19 July 1824, by John Constable, shows the* modus operandi *of the colliers which frequented the Sussex shore. They were beached to discharge their cargo, a safe proceeding on a sunny summer's day with little cloud, but extremely dangerous if a gale blew up from seaward. At least 13 colliers are known to have been wrecked on Brighton beach while delivering their coals between 1790 and 1850, as the wind suddenly backed and drove them higher up the beach or into each other with the incoming tide. For example, the Eagle (1393303), was owned and captained by the same man, 'by which misfortune his all was shipwrecked' in 1797. A similar accident occurred in 1822 as Brighton evolved into a resort, to the* Stockton *(1405633), beached 'under Williams' Baths', compounded by the neighbouring* Mary Ann *(1176491) being driven across her. Similar accidents were duplicated along the Sussex coast, for example the* Wynyard *(902848) in 1842.*
(Given by Isabel Constable © Victoria and Albert Museum, London)

removal of an earring. Likewise the sunken Tyneside colliers which litter the English North Sea coast form a hidden landscape with occasional clues to its presence on the seashore: the Seaton Carew brig is a survivor, preserved by stranding, of a trade once so pre-eminent that Daniel Defoe alluded to the loss of 'above 200 sail' in a single night's storm off the coast of Norfolk in 1695,[151] and the English coastline the last vestige of a seaborne trade that once spanned the world (Fig 4.24).

Between the wars: old and new

We greet the clippers wing-and-wing that race the Southern wool …
Beat up, beat in from Southerly, o gipsies of the Horn!

(Rudyard Kipling, 'The coastwise lights of England')

It would be generally true to say that the steel-hulled, screw-driven steamer became the 'typical' wreck for some 70 years between the late 19th century and the Second World War, so that they were largely contemporary with the period in which they were wrecked. At the same time, there was still a considerable hangover of wooden sailing vessels of mid- to late 19th-century build, for their seagoing career could continue for a surprisingly long period, from 50 to 80 years.[152] In straightforward numerical terms, sailing ships of all kinds, from small wooden fishing vessels and leisure craft to large

iron or steel liners, still dominated the seas until the First World War. For the period 1875 to 1900, for example, steamships comprised one-quarter of all wrecks, and sailing vessels the remaining three-quarters. Between 1901 and 1913 the proportions changed: steamers now accounted for one-third of wrecks, but sailing ships still accounted for the other two-thirds. The First World War was the 'tipping point' at which steamer losses outstripped sailing ships and led, largely, to the demise of the sailing vessel: by this time, approximately one sailing ship was lost for every three steamers. Between 1919 and 1938 sailing ships formed only one-third of wrecks as opposed to two-thirds steamers.[153] During this interwar period, there were also wrecks which did not fit the profile of the ubiquitous steel steamer. This section looks at two particular sectors of shipbuilding, which were relatively unusual: steel ships which were throwbacks to the days of sail, and the steam-powered craft which pushed the boundaries of technology.

As well-known sailing ships of their time, the *Preussen* and the *Herzogin Cecilie* were two of the most spectacular wrecks of the early 20th century in English waters and symbols of the last glories of the age of sail, represented by the massive steel sailing schooners and barques with three or more masts and 30 or more sails.[154] Their fates were intertwined in many ways, although they were wrecked a quarter of a century apart; they were built in the same year, 1902, and were each employed on one of the two long-distance routes which remained just about competitive for European ships – the *Preussen* to Chile for nitrates and the *Herzogin Cecilie* for Australian grain. These 'windjammers' as they were nicknamed, were able to take full advantage of the wind and were better suited to such long voyages than steamers: windjammers did not need to make landfall to bunker sufficient quantities of coal to traverse vast expanses of unpredictable ocean, and their routes were such that, in any case, bunker coal was unavailable until the ultimate destination. Either way, the Southern Ocean was still perilous (and remains so for those involved in round-the-world yacht races): the trade to Chile with nitrates as a return cargo involved rounding Cape Horn in both directions, outward-bound *against* the wind, while Australia-bound vessels went out via the Cape of Good Hope and returned via Cape Horn, virtually circumnavigating the Southern Ocean (Figs 4.25 and 4.26).

Both were built as German vessels: even though *Herzogin Cecilie* was sold out of German service to the Finnish owner Gustaf Erikson, she retained her German name. Erikson made a speciality out of buying up these old-fashioned windjammers, cornering the market in Australian grain for England. Thus it was that this specific route became a speciality of the port of Mariehamn in the Swedish-speaking Åland Islands, belonging to Finland, though a handful of other ships also participated in this trade. Many of the *Herzogin Cecilie*'s sisters in Erikson's fleet had originated with the German company Reederei F Laeisz, and their famous 'Flying P' liners (whose names all began with 'P'), for whom the *Preussen* had been built by Joh. C Tecklenborg. Nearly all of the surviving 'Flying-P' ships had, like *Preussen*, originally been involved in the Chilean nitrate trade and under Erikson's ownership transferred to the Australian grain trade.

Preussen, an unusual and unique five-masted schooner, and the largest sailing vessel in the world at the time, was the first of the two to be wrecked (Fig 4.27). She had taken in a general cargo, including pianos, at Hamburg in 1910 for Valparaiso and Iquique in Chile when she ran into heavy gales in the English Channel. Her run of bad luck continued as she emerged from the gales to hazy weather on the morning of 6 November, in which the steamer *Brighton* crossed her bows in mid-Channel and carried away her bowsprit and fore-rigging, by which she lost a great deal of her manoeuvrability.

Fig 4.25
The bowsprit and masts of the barque Pamir *as seen in the Royal Victoria Dock, London, after arriving with wool and tallow from Australia in December 1947, giving an impression of the beauty of a sailing barque. Like* Herzogin Cecilie, *she was an Erikson ship involved in the grain trade, and, like* Preussen, *she had also been one of the famous Laeisz 'Flying-P' liners. When photographed,* Pamir *was yet to claim the record for being the last commercial sailing vessel to round Cape Horn, in 1949: she sadly foundered in 1957 in a hurricane off the Azores. (AA001334)*

Fig 4.26
The four-masted barque Viking *seen moored in the West India Docks, probably in 1946 since the vessel had served as a grain store in Stockholm during the later years of the Second World War, after which Gustav Erikson, who also owned* Herzogin Cecilie *and* Pamir, *was able to reclaim his ship. Built in 1907 at the famous yard of Burmeister & Wain in Copenhagen, the* Viking *is one of the few surviving ships of the Grain Race era, now in use as a hotel in Gothenburg: others, like* Passat, Peking *and* Pommern, *have become floating museums. (AA001502)*

Fig 4.27
Photograph of Preussen,
one of a number taken
within a few days of her
stranding by a local
resident. At a cursory glance
the Preussen *appears to*
be anchored in calm
conditions, and little
appears amiss, but she is in
fact very close inshore, with
her foremast broken, and
listing to port. A number
of boats lie beside her,
presumably salvage vessels.
(Annette Evelyn Darwall
collection, BB052702)

The *Brighton* immediately offered assistance, in the form of a tow to Newhaven, but Captain Nissen, the *Preussen*'s master, refused and declined other offers of assistance from tugs and passing ships.

He was determined to 'put back' to Hamburg, and to that end decided to anchor east of Dungeness in the teeth of the increasing gale. His anchor chains burst and the anchors failed to hold, forcing his ship to run eastwards before the storm. At this stage Nissen was still hoping to arrange a tow back to Hamburg, but with the wind still increasing, it was felt that the safer option would be for three tugs to take her in tow towards Dover. Even this met with failure as her tow ropes parted and she began to drift ashore under the cliffs south-east of Fan Bay off the South Foreland. At first a recovery seemed likely, but two months later a gale ensured that she broke up where she now lies.

The end of the *Herzogin Cecilie* was similarly dramatic: her demise also came after initial hopes of her recovery and her loss made international headlines. It also deeply affected the crews belonging to Erikson's other ships as they came in to Falmouth and heard the news that the first of their number to arrive had been lost. Just as in the days of the *Cutty Sark*, when the tea clippers raced to be the first to bring home that year's consignment of tea, between the two World Wars the regular departure of the Finnish fleet for Australia and back to Britain with wheat developed into a media event known as the 'Grain Race'. The *Herzogin Cecilie* was a regular winner of this race, winning for the last time in 1936, arriving at Falmouth in 86 days from Wallaroo under Captain Sven Erikson.[155] Even as late as the 1930s, the first port of call for vessels bound for northern Europe was Falmouth, the westernmost major harbour in England, and therefore the principal landfall for those bound up-Channel. Frequently they called at Falmouth 'for orders'; that is, only upon arrival at Falmouth would they learn the onward final destination of their cargo, as did the *Herzogin Cecilie* with orders to continue to Ipswich. She left in rain which developed into a night fog; in these conditions she struck the Ham Stone in the early hours of the morning of 25 April 1939, and staggered towards Soar Mill Cove, where she went aground 'about 120 yards from shore'.[156]

The Salcombe lifeboat came to the rescue of the 21 crew and the solitary passenger, who had just embarked at Falmouth for the trip to Ipswich, being an old friend of the captain's wife. Erikson and his wife remained aboard for about 24 hours, eventually coming ashore in a breeches buoy run down from the cliff top to the ship, after an unfavourable report from two tugs unable to move the *Herzogin Cecilie* off the rocks. By now she was sitting with 'the sea washing over her bows, and with several bad holes in her side'.[157] In the opinion of a salvage officer who examined the vessel on the 28th the flooding had increased to 'high water level 20ft' and the foredeck was 'awash at high tide'; the 'vessel is unsalvable and should be discharged and stripped as soon as possible'.[158]

The *Herzogin Cecilie* remained in this position for several weeks, while attempts were made to salvage the grain, but most of it was already rotting, swelling up as it absorbed the water. It seems that the rotting grain helped in the disintegration of the ship, for almost immediately it began to 'start' the decking, that is, to push it outwards: the 'starting' was noticed in the salvage officer's report. After seven weeks the *Herzogin Cecilie* was, like the *Preussen*, towed away, this time to a more remote location at nearby Starehole Bay (Fig 4.28), where a clearance operation to remove her cargo could get under way, for by now the lingering odour of several thousand tons' worth of rotting grain was becoming a serious public nuisance. (Another Gustav Erikson ship, the *Moshulu*, like *Herzogin Cecilie* around 3,000 tons, was capable of carrying 5,000 tons or 60,000 sacks of wheat.[159]) There she began to settle into the sand. A number of gales over the ensuing months finally broke the ship up altogether, and in

September she was officially abandoned to be sold as scrap, as noted in the vessel's log-book. There was no benefit to be gained from attempting to refloat and repair the vessel, for the ship herself was uninsured, although the cargo was insured for £27,000.

The master, when examined by the Receiver of Wreck at Plymouth in May, gave his opinion that the cause of the wreck was 'the foggy weather, the tide setting the vessel off her course, and a possible magnetic disturbance'. This was largely corroborated by the disgruntled crew, although from their depositions it seemed that these issues need not necessarily have been fatal to the ship had the master been more experienced and morale higher in general throughout the long voyage. To this day the chain of events leading up to the wreck is not wholly clear, since the low morale may have skewed the evidence somewhat and led the crew to shift the blame onto Erikson.[160] It seems, from the reminiscences of two Englishmen who worked their passage aboard other Erikson ships in the 1930s, Eric Newby and Geoffrey Sykes Robertshaw,[161] that morale was perennially low aboard these ships, both from the natural hardships of the voyage itself and from the constant cost-cutting keeping these ships competitive against the odds. Driven by hunger,

Fig 4.28
The Herzogin Cecilie *was beached upright in Starehole Bay to facilitate the offloading of her rotting cargo. Although now well broken up, the classic outline of a sailing ship with a recognisable mast having gone 'by the board' amidships, is clearly visible below the surface of the water, at a maximum of 7m or 21ft depth: originally she had four masts. She lies in the inter-tidal zone since part of the bow section dries at low water.*
(Harold Wingham Collection HAW 9392/28)

wet and cold, it seems that tempers regularly frayed and led to poor decisions on board.

Not the least of the problems encountered by the Grain Race ships was the fact that their steel hulls were immersed in water for long periods without docking for repair and maintenance. As a result, maintenance was undertaken at sea, involving the notoriously arduous job of chipping rust within and without the hull.[162] As early as 1933 *Time* magazine noted that some of the ships involved were 'so old that the sailors could not chip the hull for fear the chipping hammers would go clean through the plates. Built from 16 to 45 years ago, sailed on a capital representing scrap value, the ships were uninsured.'[163] In other words, they were sailed to the extreme limit and were virtually uninsurable – hence the loss on the *Herzogin Cecilie*. In 1936 the stress told on the ex Flying-P *Parma* and *Ponape*: *Parma* was badly damaged in a docking accident at Glasgow and never again sailed commercially, being scrapped in 1938, while *Ponape* was so strained by heavy seas in rounding the Horn that she was immediately sold to shipbreakers. The *Abraham Rydberg*, one of the few ships in the trade not owned by Gustav Erikson, was also involved in a collision while coming up-Channel.[164]

In 1933 none of the ships featured in *Time* carried a wireless: Geoffrey Robertshaw recorded that every time they met a steamer they asked her to report them all well at Lloyd's. By this time the barques were in fact so obsolete, but such a sight as to be a marked attraction to steamers. In 1934 'a large American liner alters her course … and goes completely round us, actually stopping her engines … to give her passengers a chance of having a good look at our old ship the *Winterhude*.'[165] Located as they were in areas near popular coastal destinations, as wrecks both *Herzogin Cecilie* and *Preussen* immediately attracted many sightseers, both locals and tourists: according to *The Times*, 'thousands of people walked to Sewer [sic] Mill Cove', undeterred by the stench, to look at the *Herzogin Cecilie*.[166]

There could hardly have been a greater contrast between these two vessels and the contemporaries with whom they overlapped: not the steel-hulled steamers, but a number of other vessels which took advantage of innovations in design and technology – ships of ferro-concrete. If the windjammers represented the romance and the last glories of sail, in appearance and function the ferro-concrete ships were the complete opposite in every respect, designed and destined to be workhorses (Fig 4.29). Their construction material would appear to be at odds with their seagoing function, a contradiction in terms, since it was denser than water, but nevertheless, they worked, and they worked well. By the same token iron and steel hulls were an apparent contradiction in terms, since they were prone to rust, yet metal shipbuilding became the leading technology from the 19th century onwards. A number of shipyards specialising in ferro-concrete construction sprang up around the world from the 1890s onwards, but, although the technology was successful, this form of construction remained a specialist form of ship-building (Fig 4.30). However, the ferro-concrete vessels did receive a fillip with the continuing losses of more conventional vessels during the First World War. The shortage of metals and the time it took to build and rivet a standard steamer gave extra impetus to orders from the Admiralty for ferro-concrete craft, considered to be especially suitable for coastal, estuarine or river work, and thus freeing up steamers for sea passages. In other words, just like the steel barques, the specialist form of the ferro-concrete barges found a niche market in the early 20th century.

The technology used in the fabrication of these ships was acknowledged in their naming pattern – every single British vessel of this type at the time had a name beginning with the prefix *Crete-*, of which seven were wrecked in English waters: *Creteblock*, *Cretecable*, *Cretehawser*, *Creterock*, *Cretestem*, *Cretestile* and *Cretestreet*.[167] They were built for two specific purposes with completely opposite functions. Each yard was allocated a particular family of names beginning with the same letter in the second syllable, which not only gave them a 'house identity' but also indicated their function. The names of the *Cretecable* and the *Cretehawser*, which both refer to ropes or chains, identify them specifically as tugs for towing other vessels; most of the others were lighters or 'dumb' barges, which had no propulsion of their own, and could only be towed by other vessels, but were nevertheless useful as cargo carriers: their names reflect their lack of motive power, particularly that of the *Creterock*.[168]

Extraordinarily, in 1920, one representative of each type was lost in a single incident, as the tug *Cretecable* was towing the dumb barge *Creterock* from Shoreham-by-Sea to the Tyne.

Fig 4.29
The Cretemanor, *the first concrete vessel built by Hughes and Stirling at the Concrete Seacraft Co. in 1919, shortly after being launched in a traditional ceremony at the Albert Dock, Preston, Lancashire. She forms a stark contrast to the four-masted vessel moored beside her.*
(OP01210)

Fig 4.30
Construction work at the Concrete Seacraft Co., Fiddlers Ferry, in November 1918, showing the pre-cast concrete units for the Cretemanor *under construction. By this time the Admiralty's wartime order for concrete vessels was redundant. Most vessels were converted to peacetime usage.*
(BB96/00023)

The trawler *Lord Cecil* collided with the *Creterock* off the Humber; as the weaker link in the chain, without any other means of propulsion, the *Creterock* was badly damaged and had to be beached off Wheatall Point, near Sunderland, the *Cretecable* going ashore at the same time, and both vessels were lost as a result.

The *Cretehawser* was beached in 1935 in the River Wear at South Hylton, not far from where she was constructed by the Wear Concrete Building Co. of Southwick, to be broken up; however, she was never dismantled and stubbornly remains *in situ* in a bend in the river, opposite an industrial estate, despite her obvious attraction as a target for vandals. The *Creteblock* similarly remains ashore on the rocks near Whitby (Fig 4.31), while the remains of the *Cretestreet* were usefully incorporated into a pier wall in Kingston-upon-Hull in 1925. The only successful dismantling, albeit unintentional, of a concrete ship in English waters appears to have been that of the *Cretestem*, which fell victim to an air raid in 1943 in Hendon Dock, Sunderland.

As may be imagined, from the nature of their construction, the wrecks of the concrete vessels generally remain far more substantial than those of sailing ships of similar vintage with iron or steel hulls. They are certainly far more intact than the wrecks of the *Preussen* and the *Herzogin Cecilie* and can be compared to a particular group of terrestrial relics in their tenacity – the pillboxes of the Second World War – so that the destruction of the *Cretestem* is a particular irony. This quality of endurance has ensured their survival, so that it is no surprise that the seven ferro-concrete barges of the Second World War which have ended up among the Purton hulks in Gloucestershire are eminently suited to their second 'life' shoring up the embankment between the River Severn and the canal.[169] There is an all-pervading irony in the story of the steel barques and the concrete barges, from their construction and sailing careers to their final fates: the ambitious building of ever-larger sailing ships in the face of the growing dominance of steam, and the astonishing success of the ferro-concrete barges despite their unpromising materials. In fact the ferro-concrete vessels have now survived longer as wrecks than they did as sea-going vessels. The greatest irony is, perhaps, reserved for the *Herzogin Cecilie*: that she was ever wrecked in the relatively safe waters of the English Channel at all, having hauled thousands of tons of grain over thousands of miles through the world's most treacherous seas. Yet at the same time she is possibly the most accessible example of a steel barque wreck, for if these ships disappeared it tended to be in deep water in inaccessible regions, but her final resting place in the sheltered waters of Starehole Bay is now a popular novice dive.

Fig 4.31
Partial remains of the Creteblock, *Whitby Scar, North Yorkshire. Built on the orders of the Shipping Controller in 1919/20, by the Shoreham concrete ship specialist John ver Mehr, the* Creteblock *(909208) changed hands a number of times before becoming a Teesside tug. Her final use was as a fishermen's store at Whitby although, according to locals, she was retained for scuttling as a blockship in the event of invasion during the Second World War. Ignominiously for a tug, she was towed out of Whitby Harbour after the war, but had to be beached on Whitby Scar after taking in water and only scattered remains are now visible. (MF99/0790/05)*

5

Solving mysteries

Introduction

The story of a shipwreck is more than just the wreck event: it links into a number of different contexts. Even identifying a number of documentary references to the same ship can be a story in itself: a story of detective work, and of reading between the lines.

The number of reported wrecks in contemporary records can often seem overwhelming: this, and duplications in the same reports, distorts the true figures, particularly in the aftermath of specific weather events such as storms, gales and floods. Reports from different original sources – that is, from those who witnessed the wreck and reported it in their correspondence to the newspapers – can often focus on entirely different details of the same wreck, one naming or describing the vessel and her voyage, the other her master and cargo. These witnesses may have come from different locations in the vicinity, or seen or heard different details of the event. In the 18th century there was little or no sense of press editorship; wreck reports were printed, usually verbatim, as they came to hand, with no attempt to integrate or make coherent different narratives. The reporting of a Portuguese vessel from 1782 is absolutely typical of the way that information from first-hand sources is often 'split down the middle', with two separate accounts on different sides of a news sheet:

> A Portugueze [sic] brig, from Dublin to Oporto, drove on shore near St. Ives the 27th ult. Most of the cargo saved …

> The N S DEL CARMO, Abria, from Dublin to Oporto, is on shore on the northern coast of Cornwall; the ship totally lost, and most of the cargo.[1]

However, the salvage may have been in progress when the first witness saw the ship, and while it remained simply 'on shore', it could have then been deemed feasible to save the rest of the cargo. We may conjecture that by the time it was seen by, or reported to, the person who sent in the next report, the vessel was 'totally lost', and with her what remained of the cargo. It being January, and thus within the winter peak period for adverse and suddenly changeable weather, it seems likely that the weather may even have worsened, leading to the final wreck event.

We are on firmer ground with the lost ship's name. The destination of Oporto suggests some connection with the Iberian peninsula (not necessarily conclusive, since a vessel may trade between two nations unconnected with her home port); the abbreviation *N S* was standard press shorthand for the Spanish *Nuestra Señora*, Portuguese *Nossa Senhora* or Italian *Nuestra Signora*, all signifying *Our Lady*. There appears to be some garbling of languages since *del* is Spanish, but *Carmo* is Portuguese – typical of language confusion scattered throughout the wreck record, especially where, as in this case, the distinction between one language and another was not clearly understood. Other causes of confusion were words sounding similar to the English,[2] or where the original handwriting of foreign seamen could not be fully deciphered, as will be discussed further in this chapter. What is clear is that the name of the vessel is, effectively, a version of *Our Lady of Mount Carmel*. There is a case to be made for a Portuguese connection, and that the two accounts do indeed relate to the same vessel.

The *N S del Carmo* brings together a number of typical mysteries concerning wrecks: where and how where they lost; whether two different accounts with enough similarities relate to the same vessel; and how to decipher garbled versions of the name. Any or all of these may be solved by tracking the vessel across several editions of the reporting publication, or other sources. Later issues may confirm whether the vessel was lost, or whether it was 'got off' rocks or a sandbank, that is, recovered. Working backwards by using arrivals and departures lists in previous issues, often reaps dividends, although it is more likely to mention by name ocean-going and therefore more substantial vessels, than, say, colliers. Working back three issues from the wreck report,[3] we find that an *N S do Carmo*, in grammatically correct Portuguese, had arrived at Dublin on 18 January from Oporto, her master one 'D. Abue', close enough to the name of the master of the wrecked vessel to suggest that it refers to the same man. The variants of *Abue* and *Abria,* suggest that he is likely to have had the common Portuguese surname *Abreu,* giving us the tools to trace the stricken vessel further in English- and Portuguese-language archives and publications.

Deciphering contemporary records can involve not only foreign languages (or attempts at reproducing those languages by those unfamiliar with them!) but also historical or dialect English usages which can mislead a modern reader of standard English. For the years around 1800 a dialect term used in the counties of Lancashire and Cumbria can cause confusion: 'was put ashore/on shore' suggests to the modern reader that the vessel was deliberately beached. In fact it means 'was driven on shore' by the sea or the weather. The local version of events concerning the loss of the slave ship *Bee*, setting out from Liverpool in 1776, suggests that she was beached after losing her mast, in order to save life, whereas a London newspaper clarifies the situation:

> The *Bee*, Graham, from Liverpool for Africa, is put ashore on Heysham Sands, near Lancaster, after being dismasted; the crew are saved.

> Two vessels belonging to Liverpool were stranded in our Bay the 20th inst. in a hard gale of wind at SW ... The *Bee*, Greyham, from Liverpool for Africa, without any masts standing, is nearer the land, and dry about half ebb.[4]

In the same way the sloop *Peggy* was 'put ashore' near St Bees in 1776, and the *Providence* 'put on shore' at Beckfoot near Allonby in 1804, with 21 head of cattle still alive. In both cases this was after the crews had decided it was prudent to abandon their disintegrating ships, and were therefore not on board to deliberately beach them: indeed, another account of the *Providence* states that she 'was drifted upon the beach'.[5]

Date issues can also cause a great deal of confusion. Unlike other forms of monument, often constructed over a fairly substantial period, or revealing multiple building phases, a shipwreck is usually the work of a day or so (with a few exceptions where hopes of recovering the vessel were abandoned after some months). The lack of editorial control before the advent of serious professional journalism extended to what we would now regard as intellectual rights. Newspapers were posted out all over the country, with the result that items were commonly copied over verbatim from one regional print to another. Sometimes the date of loss was altered appropriately to reflect time elapsed since the initial report, so that 'Tuesday last' in one paper became 'on Tuesday se'ennight' (sevennight, ie 'a week last Tuesday') when it appeared elsewhere the following week. Frequently, however, in this process shipping news became detached from the original reporting date, so that an item about a shipwreck 'on Tuesday was a week' was reprinted word-for-word in one or more regional titles the following week, thus giving a more recent impression of the date of the wreck than was actually the case, and becoming increasingly erroneous with subsequent appearances.

This was partly because of dialect issues. Even today 'last Saturday' still causes confusion between individual English-speakers: does it refer to 'the Saturday just past', or 'Saturday last week' (even if there has been an intervening Saturday)? In 18th-century Norfolk, it was interpreted as 'on Saturday last week', but in Tyneside it was understood to be 'the Saturday just past'. With verbatim reprints lacking their original context, the date of a given shipwreck event was in as much danger of drifting as any loose wreckage.

A report of Newcastle colliers caught up in a gale at Lowestoft on 'Saturday and Sunday last' published in the *Newcastle Courant* on Saturday 28 October 1820, clearly illustrates the Tyneside understanding of the phrase and reveals that the gale occurred on 21–22 October. *Lloyd's List* corroborates this by a report of a 'severe gale of wind at south yesterday' clearly dated from Great Yarmouth on 23 October. However, a later edition of the *Newcastle Courant*, dated 11 November, incorporates a letter from Lowestoft:

> On Sunday morning last, a heavy gale of wind from SSW was experienced at this place ... About 12 o'clock, the inhabitants of the town had the pain of witnessing the distress of a vessel, which,

in attempting to gain the inner roads, through the Stamford Channel, struck upon a sand called Beacon Ridge, and in about the space of 7 minutes, went to pieces, and all on board perished.[6]

Clearly this was 'Sunday morning last', lifted from a newspaper local to Lowestoft, probably an edition printed exactly a week previously, on or around Saturday 4 November, by which time a further Sunday had passed; in other words, 'Sunday morning last' was understood quite differently on the Norfolk/Suffolk coast from the north-eastern coast.

Such difficulties are compounded by the discrepancies between the Julian and Gregorian calendars in England before 1752, when the Gregorian calendar was finally adopted in England.[7] Knowledge of both calendars is essential for the maritime history enthusiast, to discover not only the actual date of a wreck, but to accurately trace its history in contemporary sources. Motivated by xenophobia and anti-Catholic feeling against Papal approval of the adoption of the 'New Style' Gregorian calendar as early as 1582, the English held firmly to the Julian 'Old Style' calendar for another 170 years. By this time the English calendar was not only 11 days behind the rest of Europe (hence the campaign to 'give us back our eleven days'), but also with the additional local quirk of beginning the (civil) New Year on 25 March (the origin of the modern financial year), while 1 January was recognised as the traditional New Year.

This leads to a wide variation in English sources as well as a discrepancy with continental sources: *Lloyd's List*, as a mercantile publication, adheres rigidly to the beginning of the civil, legal and financial year in the dating of its issues, up to and including 1752, so that wrecks reported between 1 January and 25 March appear to be one year 'behind' the Gregorian year, (the modern reckoning). Some newspapers, however, even as early as the late 17th century, understood the year to begin on the customary date of 1 January, and dated their issues accordingly, while others, even in the same town, would date their issues using both years, thus, for example 'January 1, 1739/40'.

This can be no more than a brief introduction to some of the common issues facing the maritime historian, but other mysteries of interpreting documentary and archaeological evidence follow in this chapter. Documentary evidence is key to the identification and interpretation of archaeological materials, from the number of guns and the 'lines' or plans of a warship to the circumstances surrounding the wreck event and descriptions by eyewitnesses. All are important.

What happens to maritime archaeology remains? Logboats then and now

Ancient logboats, hollowed or burnt out of a single tree-trunk (monoxylous, from the Greek: *mono-*, single, *xylo-*, wood) are among the most intriguing of all wreck sites. They form an exceptional group of wrecks because of their construction and age, when and where they are found, and, not least, because they remain poorly understood. This is in part because the circumstances of discovery in the early days of archaeology omit salient facts – such as dates and locations.

There are two significant – and interlinked – questions: how old are they and how far can they be described as wrecks? These questions can only be answered by posing other questions. From the 16th century onwards antiquarianism took hold as 'gentlemen amateurs' began to challenge accepted views of British history, with the Society of Antiquaries being founded in 1707. These early antiquaries investigated, recorded and drew their discoveries, examined historical sources, and established collections of historical curiosities – becoming the foundation stone for the modern archaeological profession in providing a context, however limited, for their finds.

When, then, and where, were the first logboats uncovered in England, and what happened to them? Eleventh-century works in the River Ver associated with Abbot Ealdred of St Albans revealed a vessel, interpreted by the finders as ancient, having things which 'used to be used in ships' and 'evidence of the sea water which once bore the ship to Verulamium'.[8] The Abbot's sanctity ensured that the event was recorded, and the record survived: it is a rare hint of discoveries, including those of logboats, which must have occurred reasonably regularly. What happened when the Saxons uncovered an Iron Age logboat, for example, if they did do so? Was it seen as a remarkably preserved wonder, or was it simply regarded as an old example of a craft still in common use, and therefore not noteworthy? The continued use of logboats as a mode of transport in waterlogged landscapes up to the 19th century presumably made logboat wrecks less interesting, although this same familiarity must have led to widespread recognition of the nature of such finds. Judging by what happened to later logboat finds, medieval discoveries of logboats are likely to have been discarded, recycled as firewood, or otherwise destroyed or reused. The subsequent fate of the River Ver boat, which, unlike the discovery itself, was not recorded, also sets the tone for a common link between discoveries of ancient vessels, logboats and otherwise: to remain untraced after finding.

Early logboat finds were sometimes discussed in the context of ancient forests exposed on the shoreline. Because such finds tend not to have survived, it is difficult to ascertain whether their true nature was understood, including a distinction between worked timber and natural timber shaped by erosion. By contrast, the site of the Dutch East Indiaman *Amsterdam*, lost in 1749, is clearly a coherent wreck distinct from the submerged prehistoric forest it overlies. Both wreck and forest, known as the 'Moon Shore',[9] are regularly exposed under particular tidal conditions (*see* Fig 1.36a and b). Both may have undergone similar fates at different times, the one being, perhaps, overwhelmed in a storm in 1287 since a layer of 13th-century pottery was found on the site,[10] while the *Amsterdam*, outward-bound for the East Indies, struck Pevensey Bay during a gale. The effort of recovering the ship was beyond the wearied crew, already stricken with disease and death only two weeks into their voyage: they left her beached at Bulverhythe, in virtually the same location as the prehistoric forest. The environmental association of the two sites is accidental and coincidental but each provides clear evidence of the archaeological layering of the landscape. In a similar vein, four pieces of wood found on West Mary's Rocks in the Erme Estuary, near the Erme Ingot wreck site,[11] may be evidence of the tin trade during the late Bronze Age or early Roman period. These timbers were not, contrary to expectations, associated with a hull, but were far older, datable to around 6300 to 6200 BC, and were material remains of a flourishing Mesolithic forest.

Antiquaries noted other chance finds and clusters of logboat sites and attempted basic recording and interpretation. The earliest recorded 'modern' logboat find was around 1725 at Owthorne on an exposed area of the east coast, historically subject to repeated encroachment by the North Sea: longshore drift

of erosion material from this coastline is deposited to the south at Spurn Point (*see* Fig 1.1e). Typically for early logboat discoveries, the Owthorne find was published, albeit in 1841. Information was likely to have been second-hand at best, for the informant was 'an old man'.[12] The 1841 paper discussed the Owthorne find with a later discovery from the same area: an 'ancient British canoe' seen at Owthorne on 8 November 1785, following scouring of the sand layer in the inter-tidal zone by a series of unusually high tides.[13] This date does not coincide with any known wreck events on this coastline, so exposure would appear consistent with a sequence of high tides, rather than a single storm event. The site of this find was reported in 1841 as '50 yards south-east of the church', referring to the old church by then lost to the sea, the new church of St Peter having been erected some 2 miles inland in 1802. The 1785 find is therefore some measure of the sea's advance; by 1786 the sea was nibbling away at the churchyard itself. Later writers linked this 'ancient British canoe' with 'horns of the red deer and portions of trees' found 'not long ago', probably the forest revealed by the 1839 spring tides at about three-quarters ebb.[14]

The most interesting association of wreck material with a submerged forest is possibly that at Thurlestone Sands, where the remains of a forest were first noted in 1866, after being uncovered by a storm.[15] As with the chronology of the *Adventure*, revealed by the fate of the *Rooswijk*, other maritime casualties can provide a clue.[16] The best fit for meteorological conditions sufficient to reveal the submarine forest is presumably the 'hurricane' which swept through Torbay on 10 January that year, with the loss of 45 ships in harbour.[17] In 1923 similar storms (without damage to shipping this time) uncovered more of the site, including a number of fallen tree trunks and upright trunks which had been eroded level with the surface. All were still in the undisturbed subsoil of the forest bed, which had up until then been protected by a layer of sand (which shortly afterwards naturally re-covered the site). Most of the 1923 remains were either carried away either by souvenir hunters or by the tide.

When the debris was washed away from one of these timbers, it was revealed as a worked dugout canoe, with a flat top, shaped rounded sides and external marks made by human effort. Simple flint tools, possibly Mesolithic, found nearby suggested a potential 'boatbuilding' site, although the association with the remains of this logboat or those of any other craft remains unproven. Even so, the forest seems to have been the source of the canoe's timber, a convenient location for a form of early 'shipyard' close to both the raw materials and to a launch site, and possibly intended for travel nearby. If contemporary with the dugout, the tools form evidence of early industrial activity; if later, they may suggest clear phases of use or occupation (Fig 5.1).

As usual, however, with timber remains excavated in the 19th and early 20th centuries, without the application of modern conservation techniques, no trace now remains of this dugout. All that now remains is the documentary

Fig 5.1
It seems that the Thurlestone logboat was probably lost from a prehistoric 'boatyard', a very early example of a vessel being lost 'upon the stocks'. Four stages in producing a logboat are shown, from using wedges to split the logs open to fitting out the final vessel. That the Thurlestone find was recognised as a logboat when it was discovered suggests that it showed evidence of being a completed or nearly completed vessel.

evidence of publication.[18] In hindsight this was a missed opportunity, since the association of a wreck with the site of its manufacture is rare. At a later date ships on the stocks could be wrecked, vulnerable in their half-built state and waterside location to all sorts of accidents: a storm surge 'carried away' three new boats from shipwrights' yard at Polperro in 1817, and in 1763, a 'most dreadful fire' broke out in a local brewhouse at Shadwell, where a 'fine new ship which was just unmoored, and was to have sailed out of dock the same day, was also entirely consumed'. Storms also set back efforts to save ships which were being repaired *in situ*, such as when the *Calliope* West Indiaman stranded in 1807, which was 'building' in early 1808, was finished off by a severe gale.[19] Even so, the raw materials for newly built ships will normally have been sourced from elsewhere (even if 'local', they would not have come from the immediate vicinity of the building site) so that at present Thurlestone appears unique in enclosing the remains of a wreck of a possible 'new-build' or half-completed vessel in the environment from which the parent log originated.

The discovery of an 'ancient canoe' driven ashore at Tolcarne in Newquay in 1836 or 1837, was also specifically ascribed to a storm event, but where it came from and what subsequently happened to it are not recorded. A likely event was the storm of 27 March 1836, which also wrecked two ships in south Cornwall, when the wind was 'most tempestuous' and 'changed suddenly to a gale from SSE'.[20] In these circumstances, it would seem that this particular logboat, which has also since been lost, was possibly finally wrecked by being cast ashore, dislodged after several centuries or millennia from its previous resting place.

Partially answering one question in this way raises a further question about the fates of other logboats which have also disappeared from the record. We have very little understanding of the processes which have historically *uncovered* earlier wrecks at the same time as *causing* further losses to contemporary shipping: how many others were finally lost either before another weather event re-covered or destroyed the remains? The Owthorne, Thurlestone and Tolcarne logboats, as well as another example from Walton-on-the-Naze in Essex in 1936, make it difficult to be sure that other coastal logboats have not been lost to erosion or individual weather events in the past.[21]

The situation is, of course, exacerbated by the lack of written evidence when they were in use or lack of surviving documentary evidence during periods of erosion or climatological activity. Perhaps re-examining records of weather events in coastal regions may suggest particular events which might reveal further potential archaeology (the 'archaeology behind the archaeology').

If the recording efforts of early antiquarians left something to be desired, their preservation efforts were also somewhat inadequate. They did not appreciate that waterlogged wood, whether recovered from salt water, fresh water or peat, will warp and crack as it dries out, leading to partial or complete disintegration. Modern archaeological practice is completely different: the timbers of the *Mary Rose* were sprayed with water when she was raised in 1982, gradually replaced with a polyethylene glycol solution as a sealant coating. An Iron Age logboat, dredged from Poole harbour in 1964, was submerged in a tank for nearly 30 years before undergoing active conservation management using a sucrose solution, an excellent preservation medium for oak samples.[22] Understandably, if disappointingly, it seems that none of the 18th-century logboat finds have survived, all being untraced since discovery. This is the apparently the case even with a pair of logboats discovered in 1790 in a drainage ditch in Lincolnshire, said to have been donated to the British Museum, but untraced among their records or collections.[23]

Those logboats not revealed by storm events or inundations during the 18th and 19th centuries were typically located during dredging or drainage exercises, providing an easily understood context for their original function, that is, for fen- or marshland navigation. Cambridgeshire, Lincolnshire and Somerset are all rich in examples of this type (Fig 5.2).

Other dredged examples are associated with fishing activities and may date up to the medieval period. In 1930 a logboat was discovered in Staffordshire, in a layer of soil too shallow to signify the 'prehistoric', Bronze Age or Roman date beloved of early antiquarians and archaeologists, who were excited by these tangible links with the past but had an imperfect understanding of geological stratification or artefact context. Because these boats have rarely survived or been drawn, it is difficult to agree or disagree with the dates assigned to these artefacts. However, the medieval Hulton

Fishponds, close to the Staffordshire find, suggested both a plausible association with medieval fishing activity, and how it came to be lost.[24] A similar find in Knockin, Shropshire, was excavated before 1890 in deepening a weir brook in a location known as 'Fishponds Meadow'. The find sites for these two vessels are likely to be key to our understanding of their function: the Knockin vessel was, however, assigned a 'prehistoric or Roman' date when found and as the circumstances of discovery are obscure, the reasons for the dating are similarly unknown, perhaps based on an assumption that vessels of this particular type were confined to this 'primitive' period.[25] Certainly the Hulton logboat at least would appear to be evidence of the continuing use of logboats well beyond the Roman period.

Some logboat finds provide artefactual evidence of earlier bodies of water: for example, one was retrieved from a gravel pit along a former course of the River Lea, London. Although it disintegrated after recovery, it was

recovered in a context suggesting a settlement of Iron Age or Roman date beside the river.[26] A logboat which had originally sunk in a creek was recovered at Hasholme in a 'dry land' area of the River Foulness valley (Fig 5.3), north of the River Humber.[27] Similarly, a 14th-century logboat modified with additional planking was recovered from the old lake at Kentmere, Lake District.[28] Still others are found in riverine contexts or in marshes, often through peat-cutting activity, or in excavation activities relating to watercourses, whether navigable, flowing water not intended for navigation or standing water.[29]

The diversity of find sites points to a significant feature of logboat sites: that is, they have a greater inland spread than other maritime archaeology sites, being naturally better adapted to inland navigation, although we have also seen some evidence of coastal usage. Wrecks, of course, have always occurred in rivers and, later, during the industrialisation of Britain, in artificial waterways: but relatively little

Fig 5.2
In the marshy channels of the Somerset levels logboats were the most practical means of transport between the Iron Age Glastonbury Lake Village and other settlements. The shallow draught of the logboat was ideal for such fenland areas. They were most likely 'punted', with other crew members providing additional propulsion by means of paddles as required.

Fig 5.3
The remains of the 40ft-long logboat found at Hasholme, north of the Humber, under excavation, and thought to have been an Iron Age cargo vessel, carrying timbers and butchered meat. The logboat was possibly powered by up to 18 paddlers with steersmen.
(© Hull & East Riding Museum: Hull Museums)

evidence exists for industrial-period inland wrecks, compared to their contemporaries lost on the coastline. Our knowledge of the more ancient archaeology is in fact richer, even with its limited documentary evidence, than 'inland' wrecks such as those in canals belonging to a period much closer to the present day. The loss of minor river craft was less 'newsworthy'.

Additionally, though river navigation is not always less dangerous than the open sea (particularly in the Thames and Humber), the river environment tends to be more sheltered, with correspondingly fewer wrecks. Finally, in narrow waterways wrecks became navigational obstructions which were usually cleared quickly, leaving less of an archaeological footprint. We therefore know of more logboat archaeology from the highest reaches of the Severn in

Shropshire (seven or eight material finds) than we do of wrecks from the much more recent industrial period lower down the river, discovered only through documentary evidence.[30]

There is another significant question in considering the unique characteristics of logboat wrecks. How far can they be considered as wrecks? By definition they tend to be reasonably well preserved until discovery, at least well enough to be recognised albeit in a partial or damaged state. They may not have been wrecks at the time they were abandoned: abandonment itself does not form a wrecking event.[31] Thus the wrecking process is generally very different from conventional wrecks of a later date, and follows a long period of abandonment which may or may not have been intentional on the part of the original owner. Perhaps the boat was no longer serviceable or it was ritually abandoned, after the death of its owner, to be reclaimed by the elements. Such boats could also be used in funeral rites, as at the well-known Anglo-Saxon boat burial at Sutton Hoo, Suffolk or elsewhere.[32]

The vagaries of fate probably also militated against the survival of any logboats, intact or otherwise, since on discovery they were put to other purposes as firewood, as feeding troughs or as coffins, which can be interpreted either as 'recycling' or as the second phase of a 'wrecking process'.[33] Logboats generally appear to have remained in sufficiently good condition to have been recognisable as such: contemporary examples would have aided recognition. One logboat found in a tarn in the Lake District in 1888 was said to have been recognised by a local resident as having been in use some 40 or 50 years earlier.[34] Like so many others, it has since undergone a 'wrecking process' of being lost: possibly the finders lost interest on realising that it was not particularly old, but it seems to be a sad loss to posterity and our understanding of the social history of the Victorian Lake District.[35]

It would be interesting to know how and why the logboat found its way to the bottom of the tarn. Was its location on, rather than embedded in, the tarn bottom, merely an indicator of its recent date, or a clue to the manner of loss? Did it sink through structural damage or a weather event? Was it a simple accident, washed away from the shore in the turbulence of a storm? What condition was it in when it was lost? If it was structurally reasonably sound, was it, therefore, a wreck? Or, if it was unserviceable, why was it not turned into something else useful? It would have provided a good insight into the abandonment processes for earlier examples of the type.

The reasons for the abandonment process are often the most puzzling aspect of the logboat mystery. The Dover Bronze Age boat, despite being constructed of timbers lashed together, rather than fashioned out of a single log, provides a useful parallel. The Dover boat was found in a very good state of preservation, apparently pulled up in a safe place in a creek, suggesting it was not abandoned and remained seaworthy. It was of a type used for cross-Channel trade which could have ceased suddenly owing to its owner's age, infirmity, loss of partner trading vessels, the death of a trade contact or a general cessation in a particular traffic: these reasons are also likely to be applicable on the more localised trade routes which employed logboats. In this way the wreck process is comparable to their nearest modern equivalents, the abandoned sailing barges of Devon, the Thames, or Purton in Gloucestershire, relatively modern hulks of working vessels which have ceased to have a function. Modern transport methods (road, rail, air) have rendered them obsolete, and demand has shrunk for their traditional cargoes (for example, coal). These vessels have been abandoned in similar fashion to their ancient counterparts, to rot quietly upon the foreshore, although in the case of Purton they have effectively been recycled to form a core for the environmental development of an earthwork on the bank of the canal.[36]

It is arguable that the 'wreck process' of ancient logboats has historically tended to be suspended following the circumstances in which the vessel might have been abandoned or lost, whether as a result of 'wreck' damage or otherwise, to be preserved in a marine or peat environment, and to resume upon discovery: in other words, a multi-phase process. As we have seen, the intervention of modern conservation techniques has now made it possible to prevent a further wrecking process of inadvertent or deliberate destruction when such boats are found, a contrast with logboat finds in the 19th or early 20th centuries. Approximately 50 per cent of logboat finds have since disappeared or been compromised in various ways, including holes being drilled for museum display.[37] Others may have survived for some time before suffering environmental degradation: two logboats found in Cambridgeshire and Surrey, respectively, were removed to gardens, where they disintegrated naturally through exposure.[38] Likewise, in the mid-20th century a boat found during dredging for a sewer was abandoned to be taken by a local resident and converted to a piece of furniture.[39]

Extraordinarily, one Bronze Age boat located in 1886 on the banks of the River Ancholme was well treated by Victorian archaeological standards and preserved for exhibition at the Hull and East Riding Museum. Sadly, this boat was destroyed through an aerial attack in 1943 which caused extensive damage to the Hull and East Riding Museum, the culmination of a lengthy wrecking process interrupted over several millennia.[40] Uniquely, therefore, that logboat shared the same fate as modern steel steamers which came under similar attacks during the Second World War. Similarly, the Thurlestone environment led to the creation of two distinct monuments, of the same materials, lost under similar circumstances. The forest was covered with water as the sea crept inland over thousands of years, while the canoe, fashioned from local materials, became a *de facto* wreck through long abandonment. For other logboats, after this lengthy multi-phase process, the final manner of loss has ironically been their discovery and their disappearance in physical form and, often, from the documentary record.

Just how many Roman ships were wrecked off England?

We know very little about the activities of Roman shipping in English waters from the period of the first contact between the Romans and the ancient inhabitants of Britain to the departure of the last vessel as the Romans withdrew from Britain in AD 410. The literacy and bureaucracy brought by the Roman Empire to Britain has nevertheless left little trace of any of the vessels which came and went during the Roman occupation: naval vessels, auxiliaries, such as transports, and trading ships. There is no record, for example, of the names, types or roles of the numerous vessels of the *Classis Britannica*, the Roman fleet in Britain, which played a central role in the defence, occupation and provisioning of Britain, still less of the men who crewed them. As cogs in the imperial machine, the ships and their crews and navigators were of little importance individually, although vital to the successful Roman occupation of Britain. Few contemporary accounts have survived in official or vernacular written sources, such as the

Vindolanda tablets: this is not to say that there may not once have been versions of crew muster rolls, logbooks and cargo manifests, for example, or that forgotten or partial records may remain to be discovered. One tantalising glimpse is a funerary monument to a Roman soldier discovered in Chester in 1891 for which the inscription lacks the 'hic' for '[lies] here', suggesting that recovery of his body was expected, but it was never washed up. It may be indirect evidence for a Roman-period shipwreck off Cheshire.[41]

The only Roman shipwrecks for which we have direct documentary evidence in English waters are those recorded by Gaius Julius Caesar in his work *Commentariorum de Bello Gallico* (*On the Gallic Wars*), an account of his attempted invasions in 55 and 54 BC. Without Caesar's personal involvement in both invasions and the legacy of a written record associated with his name, posterity would lack even this information.

It appears that on both occasions a great storm arose which destroyed a good portion of his fleet. How far can we trust Caesar as a source? He was an eyewitness, but he was also a writer and a military leader. *De Bello Gallico* is thus both a literary work and a work of propaganda, justifying and glorifying his role in these failed invasion attempts at the fringes of the Roman Empire. He also fails to specify either the numbers involved or the precise location, which, however, is in keeping with a similar vagueness as to the departure ports and landing sites. Thus it becomes difficult to know or guess exactly where these ships were wrecked. The absence of evidence is not 'evidence of absence', as this vague approach is often true of Roman and medieval approaches to historical recording. Caesar does mention that the second attempt in 54 BC was launched from *Portus Itius* (generally, but not universally, accepted as Boulogne-sur-Mer) but whether he used the same departure port in 55 BC is unclear; similarly the harbour at Richborough (Latin *Rutupiae*) is thought to be the landing site of one, possibly both, invasion attempts.

What seems clear is that Caesar describes a storm arising after the arrival of the main fleet in 55 BC, at the same time that the remaining portion of his fleet was putting out from Gaul with a favourably 'soft' wind.[42] Just as they were approaching the English coast, near enough to be seen by those already encamped ashore, 'such a great storm suddenly arose, that none of them

could hold their course', driving some back eastwards to Gaul, others 'to the lower part of the island, nearer to the west' (Fig 5.4). The self-contradictory statement at first sight suggests an error on Caesar's part, or it may be that he wished to emphasise his fleet's difficulties to account for the failure of the invasion. However, this description does also suggest a sudden squally storm in which the wind backed from one quarter to another as suddenly as it arose. Those ships driven westwards by the storm were in danger of being swamped 'to their very great peril', but managed to beat back towards Gaul, another detail consistent with a squally storm, with the wind constantly shifting from one quarter to another, and with the location of the English Channel, where such storms are common.

Perhaps some of those ships driven westward were also wrecked, but Caesar does not record their fate, as he was not present. He concentrates on what he himself witnessed, which is a factor in favour of his reliability as a source. The storm coincided with the full moon and consequent high tides: those warships drawn up on the strand were swamped and wrecked, while the transport vessels (*onerarias*, 'vessels of burden') riding at anchor were lost through collision.[43] Altogether 'a great number of ships were broken', while those which escaped required repair, making it difficult for the crews to return to Gaul in time for the winter. The number of wrecks involved is tantalisingly vague, but they seem to have been visible by Caesar's forces, presumably encamped on the coast of Kent; if the landing site was indeed at or near Richborough, they may be close to the Roman shoreline, and therefore now up to 2 miles inland: part of the Roman-era beach and harbour was excavated in the vicinity of Richborough in 2008.[44]

A similar fate seems to have befallen Caesar's second invasion in 54 BC. If Boulogne was *Portus Itius*, then Richborough remains a strong candidate for the landing site (Dover, Deal and Walmer have also been suggested). Following the landing, he appears to have pursued the inhabitants, entertaining few fears for his fleet since they were at anchor facing towards a 'gentle and open shore'. En route, he was met by messengers who informed him that:

> a very great tempest had arisen, striking nearly all the ships, and throwing them upon the shore, since neither their anchors nor cables would hold, the sailors and ships' masters scarcely being able

Fig 5.4
Reconstruction giving an impression of the events which unfolded in the tempest described by Julius Caesar in 55 BC: dismasted vessels, wreckage, and survivors are cast ashore in the foreground; in the middle ground four vessels are in various stages of foundering, while in the distance two ships attempt to turn back for Gaul.

to survive the magnitude of the storm: thus it was that the [fleet] received great damage by that collision among the ships.[45]

Caesar returned to the coast to be confounded by what he saw. In his history he used the phrase *coram perspicit*, which can be interpreted in several ways. Rather than being deliberately ambiguous, it was perhaps meant as an expression of literary skill in combining different meanings into the same phrase. Literally it means, 'he saw in his presence': implying either that he saw 'before him' (that is, physically strewn before him) or 'with his own eyes', (that is, verifying the truth of what happened) that 'around 40 ships were lost'.[46] Thus he saw for himself the wreckage of 40 ships strewn over the shore, rather than deducing that 40 ships were missing by comparison with what remained of the fleet. We may surmise that, this being the case, the vessels were wrecked by an easterly gale, somewhere north of the cliffs of

Dover, which cannot be Caesar's 'gentle and open shore'.

In contrast to the surviving record preserved by association with one of the illustrious names of Roman history, the presence of other Roman wrecks in English waters can only be inferred by chance finds of surviving vessel or cargoes: sometimes the cargo is all that remains, as all traces of the hull have disappeared since the wreck event. They cannot be matched to any surviving documents, literary, administrative or otherwise. How, then, can we recognise them as Roman?

What do we mean by 'Roman', exactly? Do we mean 'Roman-era', or are we using 'Roman' to convey nationality as we do with later wrecks as 'English', 'French', 'Dutch' and so on? Given the extent of the Roman Empire, what was a 'Roman' ship? Caesar's account of the first invasion attempt suggests that he and his men were unfamiliar with the strength of the tides around Britain's coastline, particularly their response to the spring tides after the full moon: the tidal range of the Mediterranean is far less discernible to the point of being virtually non-existent. Caesar's surprise appears odd when at least some of the fleet must have braved both the Atlantic and the Channel en route from the Mediterranean for the northern waters around England; it seems equally odd when considering that other ships in the fleet had been built or requisitioned closer to the Channel and thus the principal embarkation point. We may speculate that among the crews were Romans making their first northward passage by sea, or their first Channel voyage following an overland march. Perhaps it was the capacity for destruction so close inshore which astonished them.

It seems that Caesar learnt from his experiences as he specifically mentions local craft from the Channel shores involved in the second attempt: 'private ships which each man had built to suit himself'. Additionally 40 ships of the fleet, built in the territory of the Meldi, around the Seine basin, had been pushed back by contrary winds before the main invasion attempt. These ships and their crews are likely to have been much more familiar with typical Channel tides and conditions. This all suggests a fairly diverse fleet which may also have included classical Roman triremes and biremes.[47] We cannot, therefore, say with any certainty that

any or all of the ships wrecked on either occasion, were 'Roman' in the sense of having been built in Italy and to a design suitable for Mediterranean warfare, although they may well have been built in territories more or less under Roman control, especially in 54 BC. Since these wrecked ships represented the failure of two incursions, and a successful Roman conquest of the territory they were to call *Britannia* did not occur until AD 43, the losses from Caesar's fleets cannot be said to represent the Roman period in Britain at this stage.

Like the failed invasion fleets, a number of wrecks of Continental origin, coinciding with the period of 'Roman history' in Europe, may well have occurred in English waters during the late Iron Age and represents a conflict between the cultural and chronological uses of the term 'Roman'. Some vessels may have been of classical Roman Mediterranean origin or construction; others from areas under Roman control or around the fringes of the Roman Empire; or Continental ships blown towards Britain in their trading voyages to Rome. Without greater certainty over their origins they can only be assigned an 'Iron Age' context. For example, the Poole harbour logboat mentioned earlier in this chapter has been carbon-14 dated to 345–245 BC, contemporary with Republican Rome: it was found close to Iron Age jetties. At some 10m long, it suggests indigenous involvement in cross-Channel trade.[48] There is no reason to suppose that ships originating in areas of Roman occupation or control were not similarly wrecked in English waters.

Wrecks in the Iron Age and Roman periods can therefore be classified according to seven distinct, but very basic, categories, of which the logboat represents the first: the period of first contact through trade. The second category corresponds to the period of regular, attempted, invasions, perhaps taking advantage of an existing Roman trading community with a military presence, beginning with Caesar's attempts as described above and ending with the successful invasion by Claudius in AD 43. Recent artefact finds at Fishbourne, near Chichester, suggest the presence of the Roman army between 10 BC and AD 10.[49]

There is also some evidence of trade between the Roman Empire and its newest outpost following the occupation, forming the third, and potentially the largest, category. The Erme Ingot site[50] yielded a number of tin ingots, which seem, by comparison with a number of French

Fig 5.5
Interior of a Samian ware bowl retrieved from the Pudding Pan wreck, intact and with relatively minor damage and abrasion still apparent after, perhaps, over a thousand years in the sea. The bowls retrieved from the wreck were of varying shapes and sizes, some broken or with severe marine incrustations. The finds from this wreck site are dispersed around various museums in the country.
(Image courtesy of Swansea Museum)

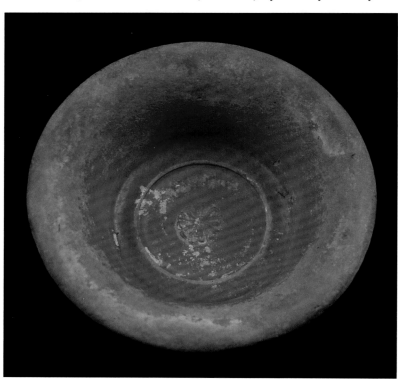

finds, to be datable to the late Roman period. The number of ingots found and the location of the wreck on the south-western coasts suggests that the wreck was involved in tin exporting activity, recorded by Greek and Roman writers. As the vessel had disintegrated, there was no hull context, which makes it difficult to determine whether this site represents the remains of a 'British' or 'Roman' vessel.

Since the 18th century fishermen have brought up a considerable quantity of Samian ware originating in France from a site in the Thames Estuary, known as the Pudding Pan Rock wreck, off Herne Bay (Fig 5.5), suggesting that this is also the site of a sizeable vessel with a cargo from Gallo-Roman sphere of influence, but it is impossible to tell whether the vessel was a 'British' one returning home, a 'Gallic' ship, a Gallo-Roman vessel or a purely Roman ship, and there may be more than one shipwreck.[51] In this category also falls the Gallo-Roman wreck found in Guernsey in 1982, dating to the 3rd century AD, and recognisable for what she was by the *amphorae* jars on board.[52] A Roman wine jar trawled up off the Longships, off Land's End, Cornwall, in the 1930s suggests that a Roman cargo vessel shared the fate of so many later ships by foundering after striking the Longships.[53] A late 3rd- to early 4th-century ship found at County Hall on the Thames in 1910, which was constructed in a Mediterranean style, may be evidence of trade between *Londinium* and Imperial Rome.[54] Again, rows of Roman tiles found off Hove suggest trading activity and a shipwreck, or cargo lost from a vessel in difficulties.[55]

A fourth group may be represented by vessels which were involved in domestic trade within Roman Britain. In 1962 a find at Blackfriars during the construction of a riverside wall brought to light a Roman-era shipwreck in the Thames, carbon-dated to about AD 150, which sank with her cargo of Kentish stone: this involvement in the home trade suggests the likelihood of the wrecked ship being an indigenous coaster.[56] A 2nd-century barge found at New Guy's House, Bermondsey, also on the Thames, seems to be of a local Romano-Celtic type, used for riverine trade.[57]

Other shipwrecks seem to fit into a fifth category, relating to the occupation and garrisoning of England. The Chester shipwreck memorial would seem to belong to this category. The Roman *pharos*[58] or lighthouse at Dover, datable to the 1st century AD, implies by its very presence that the Romans had experience of shipwreck in the English Channel, either by stranding on the Goodwin Sands or by failing to make the harbour, and were attempting to prevent others (Fig 5.6): it functioned as both warning and guiding light. It is also a testament to ongoing commercial, military and administrative links with the rest of the Roman Empire. Roman coins all dating to circa AD 180 have regularly been found at the northern edge of the Herd Sand, Tynemouth. All show little sign of being scoured by the sea, suggesting they have been protected by, and released from, a single site. This may be a Roman shipwreck perhaps lost in transporting troops to garrison Hadrian's Wall.[59] Like the Goodwin Sands to the south, the Herd Sand at Tynemouth has historically been a notorious shipping hazard, so that on location grounds alone, a shipwreck is a plausible explanation for the coins' presence there (although it has also been suggested they

Fig 5.6
Roman Pharos at Dover, seen from the south-east. (J870616)

have arrived in ballast material dumped at the mouth of the Tyne by later colliers).[60]

The natural corollary of the centralised administration of an empire with many far-flung outposts was that challenges to imperial authority could come from any area seeking greater autonomy. Coins of around AD 280 found off the Isle of Wight in the same site as that of the *Assurance* and *Pomone* suggest, perhaps, the final end of an invasion fleet sent to put down a rebellion by Carausius, who declared himself emperor in Britain. If true, this would be evidence of a sixth potential group, ships sent against insurrection in Britain and lost. In the words of a typically vague contemporary source, 'Neptune was indisposed towards the fleet' sent against Carausius, but this is a circumstantial explanation at best for the fate of the wreck suggested by these coins.[61] The County Hall wreck, rather than a trading ship, might be a member of this group. Coins found in the wreck dated to AD 296/7 have led to suggestions that she was lost in action either supporting or opposing the usurper Allectus (who in his turn assassinated Carausius and proclaimed himself emperor). The most that we can say, perhaps, is that the dating is contemporary with this turbulent period of the Roman occupation.

The seventh group may be the ships which bore the last of the Romans away from *Britannia* as the Roman Empire crumbled, or brought the first of the new settlers and raiders; the Roman withdrawal was accomplished by AD 410. No trace of this group has yet surfaced in either the contemporary record or the artefact evidence, but it would be logical to assume that this would mark the final phase of shipwrecks in English waters associated with 'Roman' activity. These events suggest a certain amount of potential archaeology which cannot yet be defined but which may offer a helpful framework for the context of Roman-era shipwrecks. The documentary facts pertaining to such incidents may no longer be recoverable – or were possibly never recorded if the throwaway comments in surviving records are anything to go by – but grouping the vessels in this way allows us to see the astonishing breadth and diversity of those few shipwrecks which have been recorded either from literature and inscriptions, or from archaeological remains. Matching the two is a challenge. Caesar's evidence, with its literary and military bias, permits us a glimpse of two numerically significant groups of vessels lost within a short space of time and a relatively restricted area, yet there have been no corresponding remains found. To date, the 'Carausius wreck' remains the only one in which a stray comment in surviving documentary evidence may potentially marry up with artefact evidence, a tantalising glimpse of what has been lost.

An ancient mystery: St Wilfrid on the coast of Sussex

> On sea and land my life seems to have been one long shipwreck.
>
> (Rudyard Kipling, 'The Conversion of St Wilfrid', *Rewards and Fairies*)

The remains of Bronze Age and Iron Age vessels are found with some regularity, but no records survive to tell us who the shipwrecked men were, what happened to cause the loss of their vessel, or the details of their journey. Sometimes the cargo and part of the vessel survive to suggest a context, but these wrecks remain, essentially, a mystery. This is also true of wrecks dating from the Roman era: with the exception of Julius Caesar's attempted invasions,[62] any Roman shipwreck records for the furthest outpost of their empire have gone the way of the lost ships. There is then a large gap between 54 BC and AD 666 when the records of another event have survived because of their association with a personage of some note: St Wilfrid cast upon the Sussex shore. During that time the Romans had conquered, occupied and left Britain, and the tribes from whom the Anglo-Saxons were descended had settled in their turn: but this particular wreck event throws up its own set of problems. Not the least intriguing issue is the fact that the vessel was recovered – so that it will have left little or no archaeological evidence – but its recovery helps to unlock the mystery of where, exactly, the saint came ashore.

St Wilfrid is a securely recorded historical personage, born approximately AD 633/4 into a Northumbrian family. From his youth he pursued a religious calling and is associated with the key event of the early English church, the Synod of Whitby in AD 664, which determined the course of Anglo-Saxon Christianity in following the customs of Rome rather than those of the Celtic church. Following the Whitby controversy, he was elevated to the see of York, but refused to be consecrated by any English bishop. Instead he travelled, *c* AD 665, to Compiègne, to be inducted by the West Saxon bishop Agilbert, neatly illustrating the international flavour of Anglo-Saxon Christianity. Christianity was a relatively new practice in Wilfrid's time, having been reintroduced in England in AD 597 following St Augustine's mission, but was not universal. Over the course of the following three centuries the Anglo-Saxons were to become indefatigable travellers in the name of Christianity and the intellectual life that went with it. They became missionaries to Europe (St Boniface, apostle of the Germans and St Willibrord, apostle to the Frisians), took up high office within the Church, became royal advisers and built up reputations in intellectual circles (all encapsulated in Alcuin of York's service to Charlemagne), made pilgrimages to Rome (as did Alfred the Great) – and, like St Wilfrid on three occasions, they went into exile.

The whereabouts of St Wilfrid's wreck was first discussed in detail over a hundred years ago,[63] taking for granted that he came ashore on the coastline regarded in modern times as that belonging to the county of Sussex, specifically in either Rye Bay or in the area to the west of Hastings. Upon re-examination of the evidence it is possible to arrive at a slightly different conclusion.

It appears that it was on his return home from France after his consecration that St Wilfrid's vessel went aground. Sawyer dates this event to the year AD 666.[64] Our principal source of information for the wreck event is the *Life of Wilfrid*, written by Eddius Stephanus, immediately after Wilfrid's death, and therefore approximately 35 years after the event. The biography itself is greatly exaggerated and credulous in tone, concentrating on the saint's miracles and attributing escape from shipwreck to supernatural causes. This particular incident was omitted from Bede's *History of the English Church and People*, completed in AD 731, our other principal near-contemporary source for the events of Wilfrid's life: Bede was a careful historian by the standards of the age. Conversely, Bede's omission may actually be a detail in favour of its authenticity, since the incident is not a common hagiographical feature shared by the lives and legends of several saints (unlike, for example, the closeness to animals common to different hermit saints).

In his favour Eddius Stephanus was close to Wilfrid himself, having been his chaplain; it is thus likely that the account originated from the saint himself. Bede may simply not have known the story. As is clear from his biography, Wilfrid is closely associated with the conversion of the

South Saxons of Sussex and with Selsey ('seal's island') in particular. Perhaps on his return to the county he recognised the scene of his earlier shipwreck: given a likely port of embarkation in Boulogne-sur-Mer, coming ashore in Sussex also seems likely. Yet the connection with Sussex appears suspiciously coincidental in the light of Wilfrid's later connection with the area. His biographer may have been keen to establish a symbolic connection prefiguring Wilfrid's later missionary work among the same people, supported by many Biblical allusions throughout (Fig 5.7):

As they were sailing from Gaul over the English sea with Wilfrith, the bishop of blessed memory … a fearful storm arose in mid-sea, and, as with the disciples of Jesus on the sea of Galilee, the winds were contrary. For a great gale blowing from the south-east, the swelling waves threw them on the unknown coast of the South Saxons. The sea too left the ship and men, and retreating from the land, leaving the shore uncovered, retired into the depths of the abyss.

And the heathen, coming with a great army, intended to seize the ship, to divide the spoil of money, to take them captives forthwith, and to put to the sword those who resisted. To whom our great bishop spoke gently and peaceably, offering much money, wishing to redeem their souls. But they with stern and cruel hearts like Pharaoh would not let the people of the Lord go, saying proudly that 'All that the sea threw on the land became as much theirs as their own property'.

… And so the comrades of our holy bishop, well-armed and brave, though few in number (they were 120 men, the number of years of Moses) determined and agreed that none should turn his back in flight from the other … thus these few Christians after thrice repulsing the fierce and untamed heathen, routed them with great slaughter, with a loss strange to say of only five on their side. And their great priest prayed to the Lord his God, who immediately ordered the sea to return a full hour before its wont. So that when the heathen, on the arrival of their kind, were preparing for a fourth attack with all their forces, the rising sea covered with its waves the whole of the shore, and floated the ship, which sailed into the deep. But greatly glorified by God, and returning Him thanks, with a south wind they reached Sandwich, a harbour of safety.

Sawyer appears to assume that the crossing is likely to have been from the neighbourhood of Boulogne-sur-Mer,[65] and that consequently

Fig 5.7
Reconstruction of the dramatic events as St Wilfrid and his monks defied the challenge of the pagan South Saxons before joining battle to save themselves and their ship. The refloating of the ship suggests she was little damaged, so that the 'miraculous' tide probably prevented an actual shipwreck from occurring: undoubtedly, had the pagans won they would have broken up the ship.

the south-east gale drove the vessel down the Channel and ashore either near Rye Bay, or further west along the coast between Hastings and Pevensey. Boulogne-sur-Mer lies on the French side of the shortest Channel crossing point, and is thus likely to have been a preferred embarkation port for England, but there may be other factors to consider. If the eventual destination of Sandwich was also the intended destination port (see below), departure from Boulogne-sur-Mer does indeed appear a reasonable assumption (Fig 5.8).

An alternative port might have been St-Valery-sur-Somme, the nearest port to Compiègne, where Wilfrid had been consecrated. St-Valery was also a Christian settlement and the port from which William the Conqueror was later to embark in 1066 for Pevensey. Against a departure from St-Valery-sur-Somme is the fact that a south-easterly gale, otherwise the most favourable wind for the St-Valery to England, crossing, blew the vessel off course, so that we return once more towards

the plausibility of Boulogne-sur-Mer as St Wilfrid's starting point.

The detail of an ebb tide uncovering the shore is consistent with the sandy beaches of Sussex, leaving the vessel 'high and dry'. The shallow draught of contemporary vessels,[66] enabling them to be easily refloated, and the survival of the crew corroborate this detail and the likelihood of the vessel's recovery. Such an event was historically typical of the area: prevailing southerly winds would drive vessels onshore, to be refloated if the wind changed, or wrecked if the wind remained in that quarter, with no possibility of getting the vessel off.[67]

It is difficult to see how a south-easterly wind swept the vessel as far west as the shoreline between Pevensey and Hastings as the vessel would have been forced northwards as well as westwards. The difficulty may be overcome by acknowledging the possible inexactitude of Wilfrid's recollections or of his biographer's account. A wind from a slightly different quarter, for example east-south-east, could quite possibly

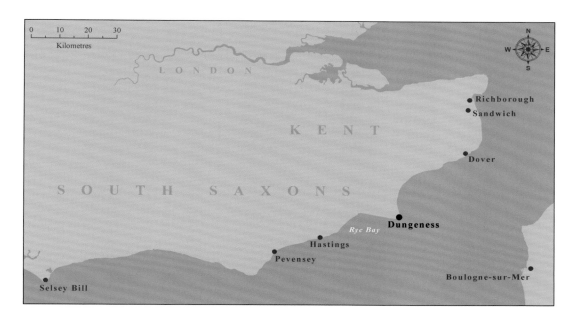

Fig 5.8
Location map of the principal sites discussed in relation to St Wilfrid's likely voyage and shipwreck.

have driven Wilfrid upon this particular stretch of coast. However, we then come to a more serious discrepancy in the direction of the wind which refloated the vessel, described as 'southerly'. On the southern coast of England a southerly wind would have forced the vessel to remain embayed – trapped on shore by the wind – since land lay to the north wherever she came ashore. Furthermore, it would then have been difficult for the vessel to round the prominence of Dungeness to the east and the 'corner' of the South Foreland to reach the safe haven of Sandwich to the north-east, although the oarsmen aboard may have made some difference in that respect.

Eddius Stephanus' account is therefore likely to be slightly incorrect, unsurprising when it records an event of 35 years earlier. We may summarise it as follows: based on the assumption that the vessel departed from Boulogne, an east-south-east wind would have made stranding in Rye Bay much less feasible, but the area between Pevensey and Hastings more likely, and consistent with landfall in the territory of the South Saxons.

But other possibilities should also be considered. Are the quarters from which the wind blew consistent with modern usage? Older writers often describe the wind as blowing *towards*, rather than *from* a quarter but this was neither consistent nor universal. It would certainly resolve the second issue: a wind blowing from the north to the south would certainly have blown the vessel off the southern shores of Sussex. However, a north-westerly

wind would have been *against* the intended voyage, whereas the south-easterly, as described, would have been ideal for any journey from north-western France to south-eastern England. Possibly it was the strength of the wind which was unexpected, rather than the quarter from which it blew. An initially favourable wind may have increased in strength such that the vessel was driven 'before the wind'. In such cases the wind is likely to veer one or more compass points, blowing the vessel off course or causing her to overshoot her intended port.

If the wind was from the south-east, the potential area of stranding would have been more likely to be east of Dungeness, perhaps between Dungeness and Folkestone. This area has historically been sparsely settled, although it is known to have been occupied in Saxon times.[68] Although in Kent, whence St Augustine's AD 597 mission had spread, the isolation of Dungeness and its environs, particularly to the east, and its proximity to the coastline of Sussex to the west, may make it a viable alternative candidate for the location of the shipwreck. Its sparse settlement seems at odds with the number of pagans ready to attack the men of God, but, as with Caesar's similar experiences, the danger may have been exaggerated rather than non-existent.[69]

Perhaps, then, it was the second gale leading to the recovery of the ship, rather than the first, which is slightly inaccurately described. Under a southerly wind, as we have seen, Rye Bay presents an apparently insurmountable problem for the recovery of St Wilfrid's vessel.

The two areas between Pevensey and Hastings further to the west, or around Dungeness, both have the advantage of solving the issue of the wind direction which enabled his ship to be refloated. Perhaps the southerly wind direction may be an approximation, rather than an exact description. A wind from the neighbouring compass point of south-south-west, for example, rather than due south, could conceivably have enabled a vessel on shore between Pevensey and Hastings to 'get off'. Despite the open water of Rye Bay to the east, however, assuming southerly conditions still prevailed, the local geography would have remained an insuperable obstacle. The ship would then remain embayed.

This leaves the third potential position in the vicinity of Dungeness, at the edge of the territory shared with the South Saxons, where a south-south-west wind would have been sufficient to allow the vessel to clear the land all the way to her final reported destination of Sandwich, the simplest navigational solution. Sandwich may in fact have been her destination all along, since in making for that port as a 'harbour of safety' after going aground in Sussex, she would have bypassed a number of ancient ports, any of which were known to welcome Christians. The most southerly of these, Folkestone, had had an established community of nuns since AD 630;[70] Dover also had a history as a well-established port since Roman times and probably earlier,[71] and must similarly have been a friendly port since it lay between known Christian communities at Folkestone to the south and Richborough (near Sandwich) to the north. For a party intending to make for Sandwich, under a strengthening south-easterly gale the isolated community of Dungeness would have been as unexpected and potentially hostile a landfall as Sussex to the west.

The miraculous arrival of the tide an hour earlier than expected may also be explained in the context of Sandwich as the intended destination throughout: this suggests that although the area in which the sailors found themselves was unknown to them, they may have realised their relative proximity to Sandwich and calculated their expectations of the tide accordingly. There are many variables involved in considering the effects of tidal ranges so far back in time, not least any subsequent physical alteration in the coastline. Modern tidal tables can therefore offer no more than a rough form of circumstantial evidence, but the tidal ranges displayed on sample dates in these tables may be able to shed some light on where St Wilfrid actually came ashore (Table 5.1).[72]

The greatest difference from Richborough (as the nearest port to Sandwich from which tidal data is now sampled) is Dungeness, the time being approximately 50 minutes earlier, the difference shrinking to 40 minutes earlier in the modern period. Hastings is slightly later than Dungeness, and Selsey Bill later still, always being closest to the time at Richborough despite also being further away from that port. Hastings could therefore, in terms of tide times, support the two earlier suggestions of Pevensey or Rye, but Dungeness tide times, being even earlier, would have taken Wilfrid and his companions by surprise if they were expecting to arrive in the vicinity of Sandwich.

It seems as if environmental factors may play their part in unravelling the mystery of a wreck event which occurred well over a thousand years ago. The actual 'lie of the land', the possibilities suggested by interpreting the second wind from intercardinal points close to southerly, and the tidal data may therefore come together, to place the site of St Wilfrid's temporary shipwreck nearer to Dungeness than to the coast of Sussex proper. The answer to the saint's prayers came not from divine intervention but from a well-established tidal phenomenon, in which high tide is earlier at Dungeness than it is to the east or west.

Table 5.1
Tide times contemporary with St Wilfrid's landing

Location	High Tide 21.07.666	High Tide 20.11.667	High Tide 28.11.2008 (for comparison)
Richborough	0825	0748	1149
Dungeness	0738	0640	1108
Hastings	0745	0646	1117
Selsey Bill	0804	0704	1119

A discussion of the Studland Bay wreck: problems and possible candidates

Two principal aims in researching wreck events through documentary sources are highlighting possible matches, enabling the identification of wreck remains as and when they are found, and defining areas of archaeological potential for undiscovered wrecks. These are opposite sides of the same coin.

As indicated previously, the date a wreck appears in the historical record may not necessarily be close to the date when the vessel was actually lost: correspondence and petitions by disgruntled masters and shipowners could continue for a number of years. Conversely, determining the date of a wreck site solely from the evidence of the wreck remains depends on a number of factors, generally tending to provide dating clues *after* which the vessel could have been lost. Examples are shipbuilding details datable either to their introduction or their obsolescence, using evidence such as dendro-chronology (tree-ring dating) and contemporary illustrations of ships (in manuscripts, on coins and in other media, such as pew ends).

Even if particular construction features went out of fashion, the ship was not necessarily withdrawn from service as a result. At best, perhaps, it is usually possible to say that the internal evidence of the ship's architecture suggests use during a certain decade or decades. How long she continued to sail thereafter is a matter for conjecture and would have been dependent on her function, maintenance and rebuilding, and the seas in which she operated. Two early 16th-century vessels illustrate this point: the *Mary Rose*[73] and the *Henry Grace à Dieu* or *Great Harry*. The *Mary Rose* was built in 1510: her rebuilding in 1536 permitted her to see 35 years' service before being wrecked in 1545, while the *Great Harry*, built in 1514, was rebuilt in 1539.[74] More typically, perhaps, English warships of this and later periods mostly saw service for 10 to 20 years to judge by their ages when wrecked.[75]

Associated artefacts from a wreck site may help to determine a more specific date of loss, but even then the date any coins were minted, or the armament or ship's bell were cast, can likewise do little more than point us towards a date after which the vessel could possibly have been lost. Distinctive cargoes are very useful in determining a wreck site's identity, although even this can be problematic. Other wrecks lost at the same location, stray material from nearby wrecks, items jettisoned from other craft over the years, or debris from later fishing activity, can all confuse the interpretation of vessel remains.

Generally, it is far easier to identify steamers, which are not only more recent, but built of different materials: their more recent date goes hand in hand with the creation and survival of greater documentary and internal evidence to support identification. They also have maker's plates for both hull and engines, which often have the name of the ship, her official number, and her number in the shipyard record books, all of which can be traced. No such information is available for wooden sailing vessels of the pre-official number era, although occasionally bells with names and/or dates are recovered.[76] The identity of warships is generally easier to establish, since details of such ships and their fates are more likely to be retained in the historical record, and can be matched with the number and pattern of their ordnance, such as the *Stirling Castle*[77] on the Goodwin Sands. Specific decorative features – carvings, stern decoration or figureheads – all have a symbolic function telling a three-dimensional story (for example, the Swedish *Våsa*, lost in Stockholm, 1628). All three features – distinctive cargo (Etruscan pottery), ordnance and decoration – identify the two parts in which HMS *Colossus*[78] now lies after sinking among the Isles of Scilly in 1798.[79]

Unsurprisingly, given these difficulties, many protected wreck sites of early vessels are named for their location, in the absence of any other specific identifying features, despite being designated for their intrinsic interest. The Studland Bay wreck (Fig 5.9) is an excellent example of such a site on the coast of Dorset.[80] It was originally identified as an Armada wreck, the Spanish *San Salvador*, recorded as having sunk in the area of Studland Bay later in 1588 while under tow.[81] Artefact evidence from the wreck site, associated with material from earlier in the 16th century, appears to rule out the *San Salvador*, although the nationality of the wrecked vessel is almost certainly correct. Her carvel construction (in which the frame is overlaid with timbers laid flush to one another, rather than overlapping, as in clinker-built vessels) is consistent with 16th-century southern European shipbuilding practice. The pottery

Fig 5.9
Diver from the
Archaeological Diving Unit
surveying an area of
coherent and well-
articulated planking on the
Studland Bay wreck in good
visibility: the dimensions of
the area under investigation
are shown by measuring
rods, and numbered survey
tags temporarily laid on
each plank enable position
fixing and identification of
timbers to assist with the
interpretation of the site.
(© Crown copyright.
Photograph taken by
Archaeological
Diving Unit)

found on board is an excellent example of a distinctive cargo, having been identified as Spanish lustreware and coarseware from the period 1450 to 1550, probably around 1500. Most notably, the close jointing of the futtock timbers (curved timbers used in the framing of the ship) is consistent with the instructions to build them 'well mortised' in the ordinances issued by Felipe IV in the second decade of the 16th century; similarly, approximately 55 per cent of the ballast stones recovered have also been identified as of Spanish origin, specifically from the Basque region.[82]

What of external evidence and the historical context? The dating of the associated artefacts towards the earlier 16th century is consistent with the state of trade between England and Spain before Henry VIII's divorce from Katherine of Aragon in 1533 strained Anglo-Spanish relations. This does not preclude the possibility that the vessel was perhaps blown off course at a later date, a fairly typical fate for ships in transit through the Channel with no specific intention of calling at any English port en route, and thus reasonably characteristic of wrecks all along England's Channel coastline. In terms of Spanish vessels alone, as early as 1302 the Navis Dei of San Sebastian,[83] from Flanders for Gascony, was wrecked at Slapton in Devon, while the Nuestra Senora de la Guarda foundered off Beachy Head en route from Cadiz for Le Havre in 1758.[84]

An interesting event around 1500 involves a different area of Dorset and a ship sailing to, rather than from, Spain, but is worth a digression as it reveals how little we know and how difficult it is to make a match for the wreck remains among surviving records, particularly when both contemporary records and the associated scholarship may be in various languages – French, German and Spanish, as well as English – making them less accessible. Even the artefacts associated with the wreck are of an ambiguous nature (Fig 5.10). Felipe I of Castile and his wife Juana la Loca ('Joanna the Mad') made an unscheduled stop at Melcombe Regis, when their ship, the Julienne, with two of her consorts, part of a fleet of 40 vessels bound from Zeeland for Spain, came ashore in a storm in January 1506. Henry VII subsequently received them graciously at Windsor Castle.[85]

Despite involving royal personages, and thus being better recorded than most contemporary shipping casualties, this incident remains poorly understood and sources also vary. Other locations, such as Poole Bay, have been suggested for the position of loss or landing. It is interesting that Melcombe Regis is specified, since it lies just north of Weymouth and the harbour itself. Did the Julienne come into harbour instead of being wrecked? Against this, Weymouth and Melcombe were distinct entities and rivals so it is possible that Melcombe itself was meant. In that case the ship missed

Weymouth harbour and was either deliberately beached or cast ashore by the sea at Melcombe. Contemporary observers naturally focused on the piety and fortitude of the regal passengers in the face of the storm, and the ensuing diplomatic hospitality: even so, it seems significant that a *Te Deum* was sung on arrival, and the travellers' reception suggests not only political initiative but also an enforced stay for repairs or for suitable replacements.

It is suggested that it took some time for Felipe I to hear of the fate of his scattered fleet, of which three were lost. Two crews were saved out of the three, suggesting that their ships had come ashore, which increased their chances of survival. Devon and Cornwall have been suggested for these wrecks, which would account for the time delay in informing Felipe I. Possibly, therefore, because the royal visitors survived, the *Julienne* was not necessarily counted among the lost vessels. However, without the involvement of royalty both domestic and foreign, it is possible that even these stories may have been lost to us.[86]

Discussing an obscure event in the wrong part of Dorset nevertheless provides useful context and suggests a potential line of enquiry, since it reveals much about the strength and grandeur of these diplomatic fleets. It may be that the Studland Bay wreck represents a similarly high-level mission carrying diplomats or royal personages. Similarly, up to four vessels carrying the retinue of the Duke of Najera miscarried on the southern coasts of England in 1544: the *Concepción*, possibly on the Isle of Wight, and three others on the Goodwin Sands.[87]

The lustreware found on the Studland wreck was a high-status product and as a small, but significant, proportion of the cargo, might have been for the use of an aristocratic retinue or as diplomatic gifts, explaining why there are apparently insufficient quantities to form an export cargo. In the same way, the cannon found at Studland, typical even then of mercantile vessels, would certainly have been appropriate protection for high-status personages on board.[88]

Examining documentary evidence for ships wrecked in the Studland Bay area reveals that another ship more certainly wrecked in this location was the *Santa Maria de Luce* 'of Lussheborne' (Lisbon), which first appears in existing records in February 1546.[89] The mayor of Poole was contacted by one 'John Baptist Sanvitores, Spaniard' to claim 'nine verses with their chambers and one oliphant's tooth'[90] which had been salvaged from the wreck, suggesting that they had been lost in the Poole area. The 'verses' are 'versos' or 'berçoes', breech-loading light artillery,[91] again consistent with the armed vessel whose remains now lie at Studland. The date of 1546 is within the date range for the pottery found at the site, but since salvage had clearly taken place, the wreck may have occurred at least some weeks or months earlier.

Nor need the Portuguese connection preclude identification with the 'Spanish' nature of the Studland Bay site, since the remains fit into the larger tradition of shipbuilding on the Atlantic coast of Iberia. 'John Baptist Sanvitores' at least was Spanish (although national distinctions were not always clearly understood by outsiders)

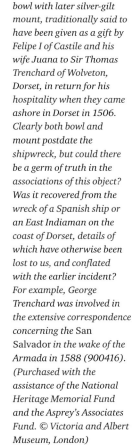

Fig 5.10
The Trenchard Bowl, a Chinese Jiajing period (1522–1566) porcelain bowl with later silver-gilt mount, traditionally said to have been given as a gift by Felipe I of Castile and his wife Juana to Sir Thomas Trenchard of Wolveton, Dorset, in return for his hospitality when they came ashore in Dorset in 1506. Clearly both bowl and mount postdate the shipwreck, but could there be a germ of truth in the associations of this object? Was it recovered from the wreck of a Spanish ship or an East Indiaman on the coast of Dorset, details of which have otherwise been lost to us, and conflated with the earlier incident? For example, George Trenchard was involved in the extensive correspondence concerning the San Salvador *in the wake of the Armada in 1588 (900416). (Purchased with the assistance of the National Heritage Memorial Fund and the Asprey's Associates Fund. © Victoria and Albert Museum, London)*

and Sevillian lustreware could conceivably have been picked up at Cadiz or elsewhere by a Portuguese ship (as at later periods, ships traded between ports unrelated to their home port). Diplomatic relations between the two countries were also then at their zenith: the king of Spain at the time was Carlos V, whose wife was Isabella of Portugal.

Both the 'Juana la Loca' and the *Santa Maria de Lussheborne* wrecks suggest directions for further research, or at least provide a contemporary context. It is also entirely possible that the wreck at Studland Bay represents another ship so far undiscovered from historical records. It may either never have been documented in the first place because there was nothing remarkable about it – unlike the *Julienne* and her passengers – nor subject to any salvage agreement – unlike the *Santa Maria de Lussheborne*. Any records made may, of course, have since been lost. Only four wrecks are documented on the coast of Dorset in the 16th century: yet the coastline can scarcely have been less dangerous than in the 14th century, when 10 wrecks were noted (a period from which far fewer records have survived; there was a single documented wreck in the 15th century), or later, from the 17th century, when 39 wrecks were chronicled. A similar increase between the 16th and 17th centuries can be discerned nationally, and may in part be due to increasing traffic, as well as attributable to the greater dissemination and survival of written and printed material from the late 16th century onwards.[92]

Significantly, three-quarters of known 16th-century wrecks around the coasts of England were recorded following the Dissolution of the Monasteries (1536–40), when numerous monastic documents, including those noting the rights of wreck held by individual monastic houses, were destroyed.[93] Many of these documents must have recorded the wreckage which came into the hands of the monks: with a few exceptions only the 'monastic' wrecks also documented in official records, such as the *Patent Rolls*, *Close Rolls* and *State Papers Domestic*, now remain for us to research. Among them were many wrecks pertaining to Dorset. One example is a document of 1275 ordering the Constable of Corfe to restore two tuns of wine to the Abbot of Cerne at Branksea, in the Poole area, thus uncovering the existence of a wreck of this date or earlier.[94] The Dissolution, occurring at around the time of, or shortly after, the Studland wreck, is therefore likely to

be a significant factor in the lack of surviving evidence which might give a clue as to its identity.

This 1275 wreck illustrates the reverse situation to the Studland Bay wreck site, in that the existence of a wreck appears in the historical record, but remains unmatched to any material evidence. For the period from 1200 to 1699 there are 58 Dorset wrecks recorded overall, only two of which have been derived from wreck remains (the Swash Channel wreck as well as the Studland Bay site).[95] The remainder are all derived from the official state sources mentioned above, since the wider dissemination of news through a public press would not happen until the end of the 17th century. Thereafter, the number of wrecks known to us from surviving reports therefore increases dramatically. Records for the Dorset coastline in the 18th century reveal 199 wrecks, but known wreck remains datable to the period remain few, with the exception of the *Halsewell*,[96] and another site suggested as the remains of the *Fanny*, lost in 1793.[97] There are, therefore, at least 197 other wrecks for the 18th century off Dorset whose remains are yet to be discovered, and an unknown number of 16th- and 17th-century wrecks. In that context, therefore, the Studland Bay wreck remains, unsurprisingly, an enigma, but nevertheless a valuable find.

Sir Christopher Wren and the missing 158 tons of Portland stone

Sometimes looking at less obvious sources is a very good way of revealing the archaeological potential of the seabed, and can provide a new perspective to monuments on land. The loss of a vessel and her cargo had an evident monetary impact which often works its way into records otherwise unconnected with ships and shipping. For example, in 1690, accounts reveal that half-way through rebuilding St Paul's Cathedral (Fig 5.11) after the Great Fire of London, Sir Christopher Wren lost a cargo of stone in the English Channel.[98] The losses sustained by the agents and ship's master were duly recorded by the Commissioners for the rebuilding of the cathedral:

5th March 1691 ... Mr Thomas Gilbert and Mr Thomas Wise, the Commissioners' Agents for the Quarries, in the Isle of Portland, do by their

Petition to ye Lords sett forth that in ye month of Aprill last past they had loaded and sent away a Vessell with 158 Tuns of Stone for the use of this Work, which Vessell overpressed with saile, endeavouring to keep Company with the fleet and convoy for fear of being taken by ye ffrench Privateer, foundered and sunk at sea, and pray a full allowance for the same, it happening in the time of a war …[99]

2nd April 1691 … the Petition of Mr Wall, Shipmaster, whose Vessell was lost at sea with 158 Tuns of Portland Stones for the use of this Building, praying to be allowed what Money he hath paid for taking in the said stones at ye Island.[100]

The situation was resolved three years later, in December 1694, when Gilbert and Wise were paid £40 as a 'compassionate case': there were clear concerns that such an allowance might otherwise set a precedent.[101]

These brief deliberations reveal a great deal of information: departure and destination, and, in a level of detail unusual for a 17th-century wreck report, the exact quantity and nature of the cargo, which is a direct result of the nature of the surviving evidence. (It appears much more revealing by contrast with the laconic entry 90 years later in *Lloyd's List* recording the fate of the *Charming Molly*, also laden with a Portland stone cargo for Dublin: 'lost at Scilly'.[102]) The little vessel appears to have capsized and sunk as a result of carrying too much sail for the prevailing wind conditions in attempting to match the speed of her convoy, becoming an indirect victim of the French privateer. We know neither her name nor the precise area where she was lost though the typical area of operation for French privateers in the English Channel and Straits of Dover suggests that she lies somewhere off the south coast.

Revealing the existence of cargoes of inorganic material, likely to remain *in situ* even as the organic remains of the hull degrade, is especially significant. Equally importantly, the wreck may be placed in the context of, and add another dimension to, the wider English landscape. It is linked to a historic quarrying industry on Portland (Fig 5.12) and also to the island's castle whose role by 1704 was to protect vessels laden with the stone from just such privateers,[103] and lastly, to the cathedral for which it was intended and which still stands today. It also hints at the possibility of further wrecks: the quantities of Portland stone consigned to rebuild London over 35 years were so vast[104] that this loss is unlikely to have been an isolated incident in the aftermath of the Great Fire of London. Privateers, weather events or even collisions in the Thames are all likely to have accounted for some Portland stone wrecks.

Fig 5.11
Elevated view of St Paul's Cathedral from the south-east, showing the extent not only of the Cathedral but also of the Portland stone used in its building. (N080597)

Fig 5.12
The Bill of Portland is seen from the landward end, with its distinctive quarries close to the cliffs for ease of transport. Stone quarried from Portland was exported by sea to Exeter and London in the 14th century. It is therefore possible that stone destined for the medieval building of Exeter Cathedral and the Palace of Westminster was lost en route, perhaps even off Portland itself, a notorious wrecking hazard. At the seaward end, the lighthouse is just visible. The Portland Race off the tip of Portland Bill (top left) is a distinctive area of turbulence where the tides meet as the seabed shelves, which has historically claimed a number of wrecks. Records for wrecks off Portland Bill are known from the 14th century onwards.
(NMR 23569/14)

If other documented losses and recorded wreck remains associated with other phases in the building of London are anything to go by, there must surely have been the potential for other wreck events connected with Wren's rebuilding of London. The *Exeter* was run ashore at Dover in 1764, 'being in a sinking condition' while carrying stone for the New Bridge at Blackfriars. It is known that this bridge was built of Portland stone so that the specific cargo and journey can be extrapolated from the otherwise missing details of the original report.[105] Similarly the loss of two vessels in 1804 and 1805 off the north-east coast en route from Dundee to London with stone for the 'new docks' tallies with the known use of Dundee stone for the new Import Dock at Wapping.[106] There is even documentary evidence for a further, very unusual, vessel within the City of Westminster itself, although nothing may now remain. In 1878 a cylindrical iron barge was broken up on the Embankment, discarded *in situ* following the fulfilment of its purpose, the safe conveyance from Alexandria to London of Cleopatra's Needle, which was a feat in itself. The barge broke its tow en route and both barge and Needle could well have foundered instead in the Bay of Biscay.[107]

From the perspective of actual wreck remains, a number of known wreck sites can also be associated with the same kind of historical context as the missing Portland stone. For example, at least two other wreck sites from a later date in the English Channel are known to contain a cargo of Portland Stone, one just off Portland itself (Fig 5.13).[108] Similar construction cargoes have been located elsewhere in London which may also be associated with a post-Fire context. One of the four wrecks excavated at Blackfriars in the 1960s and 1970s was the remains of a cargo vessel (known as Blackfriars Ship II),[109] dated by overlying rubbish and sherds of artefacts dumped into the river on top of the wreck, to have sunk in the third quarter of the 17th century, together with her cargo of bricks (Fig 5.14). Given the likely date of the wreck, the bricks may well have been part of a consignment also destined for the rebuilding of the City of London, particularly as the vessel seems to have been of barge or lighter-type construction, and would therefore only have operated locally. This in turn suggests that it is likely to have been loaded at many of the brickworks which sprang up along the banks of the Thames, dedicated to manufacturing bricks specifically for the post-Fire reconstruction.[110] The date is perhaps coincident with one of the Frost Fairs around that time and may suggest a reason why a vessel should sink relatively close to her destination.[111]

It could be that building accounts and reports as 'less traditional' sources for shipwreck reports, might well lead both to unusual perspectives on some of England's grandest monuments and to

Fig 5.13
A slab from the cargo of a 'Portland Stone' wreck dating from the latter half of the 19th century. The slabs remain stacked in the area of the former hold and are diagnostic features for the wreck in so much as they reveal the vessel's departure point and her manner of loss: angled to the starboard side of the vessel, they suggest that she capsized as she foundered, possibly due to a cargo shift in a storm.
(© Crown copyright. Photograph taken by Wessex Archaeology)

a wider context in the consideration of the national importance of shipwreck finds. The monks, who had England's earlier cathedrals built, often sourced stone from elsewhere: Caen stone from Normandy was extensively used, as at Canterbury Cathedral. Purbeck marble from Dorset was shipped on to many cathedrals easily accessible by sea: to Chichester and Exeter; via the River Thames to Westminster Abbey; and transhipped onwards by river to Norwich and Salisbury. Sir Christopher Wren's ship cannot have been the only one to have miscarried with such a heavy and awkward cargo which could, in itself, cause difficulties if not stowed correctly. Investigating Sir Christopher Wren's shipwreck, therefore, raises more questions than answers.

Fig 5.14
The brick cargo of the late 17th-century Blackfriars II river barge as originally excavated in 1969. The cargo remained neatly stacked, suggesting that the vessel was not lost in a violent wrecking event.
(© Peter Marsden)

How can we identify a ship involved in the slave trade?

It is often extremely difficult to prove that any particular wreck in English waters was involved in the slave trade, although the likelihood for 18th-century vessels is high. The nature of the so-called 'Triangular Trade', from Britain/Europe to Africa, and thence to the Americas before returning to European shores, poses its own particular challenges. The transport of a living human cargo took place principally on the notorious 'Middle Passage', the Atlantic route between Africa and the Americas, a trade in which most of the major European nations participated, to meet the demand for slave workers in the tobacco, cotton and sugar plantations of the New World. By definition, therefore, slavers wrecked in English waters were either outward-bound on the first leg, with trading goods and troops, or homeward-bound on the final leg of the triangle, with the fruits of slave labour, principally sugar, rum, cotton and tobacco, or even in ballast, their sole cargo bills of exchange,[112] making slaves highly unlikely to be their principal cargo.

Slaves were indeed brought over to Britain – often those already enslaved on the plantations. It appears that they were generally not transported to be traded, though there seem to have been exceptions where slaves were offered for sale in British port cities.[113] Of course they too suffered shipwreck in English waters, regardless of the type of ship in which they arrived: when the *Jolly Bacchus*, bound to London with rum from Jamaica, was lost near Dungeness in 1772, the sole survivor was 'the captain's slave' who was counted as one of the crew.[114] Many arrived in Britain as domestic and personal servants: Pero was the servant of John Pinney in Bristol, while Olaudah Equiano, a key figure in the abolition movement, was the servant of a naval lieutenant. Newspapers of the period occasionally carried advertisements appealing for the return of runaway slaves and black domestic servants.[115] Children born of relationships between slave women and white owners were also a facet of 18th-century black immigration into Britain, for example, Dido Elizabeth Belle, who grew up at Kenwood House, and Francis Barber, who was freed and entered regular employment as servant to Dr Johnson. Francis Barber was not alone: freed slaves and free black men settled in port cities as tradesmen and sailors in the Royal Navy.[116] With the American colonies of the European powers as well as the Caribbean being the principal destination for slaves, the presence of black slaves in Britain therefore seems to have been piecemeal, although inevitably a regular occurrence. There may have been as many as 15,000 black residents of varying status – slaves and free – in London by the end of the 18th century.[117] The trade in human beings was time-consuming, the voyages long and subject to delays of various kinds, and the ships themselves must have needed maintenance and repair. The wait for a return cargo for the final leg of the voyage could sometimes therefore eat into profits. The account of the wrecking of the Danish-Norwegian slave ship *Fredensborg*, off Tromøy, Norway, in 1768, appears to corroborate the less-than systematic arrival of slaves in Europe as well as the delays involved: there were only two slaves aboard when she struck, and they may have been acting as deck hands since nine slaves had been incorporated into the crew on the 'Middle Passage', because of death and disease on board, and were therefore seamen like Olaudah Equiano himself.[118]

The *Fredensborg* has been located, as have the *Henrietta Marie*, wrecked in 1700 off the coast of Florida and the *Adelaïde*, wrecked off Cuba in 1714. The *Henrietta Marie* carried signs of slaving activity, such as shackles, but some or all of her slaves had been disembarked in Jamaica by the time she was lost. Another known slaver post-dating the abolition of the trade in Britain was the *Guerrero*, a Spanish slave-runner also wrecked off Florida in 1827, which was searched for but not found in 2004–6.[119] If material remains are rare even on the Middle Passage, documentary evidence uncovering the slaving background of shipwrecks in England is rarer still, and actual shipwreck remains virtually unknown. There are only three possible exceptions so far discovered in English waters, and all are surprising and controversial. The earliest site, the so-called Salcombe Cannon site associated with 17th-century cannon and contemporary artefacts of both Dutch and Moorish origin, has already been discussed in Chapter 2 as representing the remains of a possible xebec, one of the far-famed 'Barbary corsairs' operating out of Islamic North Africa and which raided northern Europe for slaves. The Salcombe wreck may represent the failure of such an intended raid, but its nationality and the purpose of its voyage remain unconfirmed.[120]

A second wreck is that of the English snow *Douro*, which struck on the Round Rock among the Isles of Scilly in 1843 outward-bound from Liverpool for Oporto with textiles, bale goods, hemp, beads and flints (flintlock guns).[121] She was also laden with manillas or slave bangles (Fig 5.15), also known as slave tokens, many of which have been found scattered around the site and are extremely characteristic of this wreck. Textiles and bale goods were, of course, a principal Liverpool export, but they were historically a regular exchange cargo in Africa for slaves, as were beads and obsolete armament. What were they doing on an English ship in 1843, when in the British Empire the slave trade had been abolished in 1807 and slavery itself abolished in 1833? It would have been illegal for an English ship to be involved in the slave trade, but, perhaps, there was nothing to stop typical exchange cargoes being exported to Oporto for transfer to a ship trading between Portugal, Africa and Brazil, where the slave trade remained legal until 1888. In fact, Liverpool's trade with slave-owning Brazil was significant and grew in the aftermath of abolition, where the steady supply of slave labour to work the Brazilian cotton plantations kept down the prices of import cotton destined for the cotton mills of the English north-west, with the products of slave labour entering Britain quite legally. After 1810, shipments of cotton from Brazil were routed direct to England instead of via Lisbon and almost immediately the numbers of wrecks associated with the Brazilian trade started to rise, with three in quick succession. The *Piedade* and *União* were both lost in December 1810, followed by the *Thornton*, which stranded on the Burbo Bank after an arduous journey from Maranhão in Brazil, last from Galway. In turn the *Lascelles* was lost off Southport in 1822. All but the *Piedade*, lost on the coast of Kent, reveal that the trade was centred on Liverpool; and the two English and two Portuguese names of the ships suggest that the trade was equally pursued in England as well as in Portugal (or Brazil).[122]

This background may partly explain the mystery of the *Douro*, which seems to have been a regular trader to and from Oporto on the River Douro in Portugal, as her name implies. With such direct trading connections between Liverpool and Brazil, it would have been easy enough to land the cargo at Lisbon for transhipment to avoid detection but it is at great odds with the aggressive anti-slavery policy

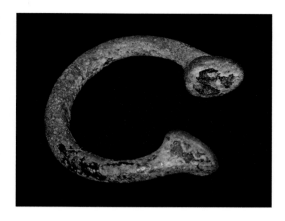

Fig 5.15
Manilla *or slave token from the wreck of the* Douro; *many such tokens have been recovered from this vessel.* (© Mark Dunkley)

pursued by the British and the Royal Navy at just this period, though it tallies with the known rise in the shipping of enslaved Africans to Brazil in the 1840s.[123] Just before the wreck event, the *Douro* had made a fast time from Oporto to England, leaving Oporto on 17 January 1843 and managing to strike the Burbo Bank before entering the Mersey, with a similarly fast turn-around at Liverpool, for she was wrecked while outward-bound again, either on the 26th or on the 28th. Her log book was found at sea after the wreck and it seems that the vessel sprang a leak, possibly because she had been insufficiently checked over after grounding on the Burbo. What was the hurry? Was the choice of a fast sailer for this particular consignment of goods for a reason? Did her status as a regular trader between Liverpool and Oporto give her a veneer of respectability? The enigma of this ship and her exact involvement in the slave trade remains unclear.[124]

The third wreck so far discovered is the *London*,[125] lost in a storm at Rapparee Cove near Ilfracombe in 1796. She was not an active slaver, but a transport ship bringing French prisoners of war from St Lucia (some contemporary sources say St Kitts) among them black prisoners. In this instance the *London* was performing the function of a 'cartel', a ship transporting prisoners-of-war for exchange, following the capitulation of the French in various islands of the West Indies, including St Lucia, St Vincent and Grenada, earlier that summer. A number of bones at the foot of Rapparee Cove have been located, and were initially identified as a mass grave of drowned black prisoners of war;[126] subsequent DNA testing of the bones was inconclusive, although the view was, and remains, that the bones were those of persons of white European origin. The wreck remains controversial, however, without full publication of the data relating to the remains.[127] Sufficient lives of all nationalities have been lost at Rapparee, including an Irish transport ship carrying Irish Jacobite soldiers, or 'rapparees', lost in 1691, and after whom the cove was named, and a Portuguese ship (*Nossa Senhora de) Bom Succeso*, 1780, to make any firm conclusion as to the origin of the human remains difficult.[128] The subsequent fate of the survivors has also been the subject of some controversy, since they were recorded as 'slaves', although under the Napoleonic code they were free men and served as such in the French army. Their transhipment from Devon in another cartel, the *Smallbridge*,[129] raises the question of their eventual fate. At this period the abolitionist movement in Britain was still gaining ground, and the onward despatch of the black prisoners raises the question of whether they were sold on as slaves. It would, however, seem odd to bring them over to Europe as prisoners only to return them as slaves to the Americas or Caribbean, a mystery which may only be solved by further testing and the publication of such testing.

The *Annual Register* for 1796 gave various accounts of the situation in the Caribbean, listing the articles of capitulation for St Lucia (the articles for other islands differ in some particulars), and providing some context for the treatment of the prisoners:

> Articles of Capitulation of the Island of St. Lucia:
>
> Article 4: The agent general, the commander in chief, and the forces of the republic, who have defended the island … shall be treated as prisoners of war and sent back to France as soon as possible. Answer: … the troops must remain prisoners of war until exchanged.[130]

The *Annual Register* also contains a contemporary account of the wreck, and the reference to 'blacks' as French prisoners rather than slaves stands out. Eyewitnesses showed no consciousness of a colour bar in their compassion for the victims lost by a sudden squall so close to a safe haven. We cannot then, at this stage, prove that the *London* was acting in the capacity of a *de facto* slave ship at the time of loss:

> October 16th: This evening a very melancholy accident happened at Ilfracombe: a ship called the *London*, from St. Kitts [sic] having on board a considerable number of blacks (French prisoners) was driven on the rocks, near the entrance of the pier, by a violent gale of wind, by which about 50 of the prisoners were drowned; those who got on shore exhibited a most wretched spectacle; and the scene altogether was too shocking for description. The wind was directly fair for the harbour.[131]

However, we can prove the identity of ships documented as wrecked in English waters as slavers, even if the presence of slaves or freed slaves on board at the time, or the identification of their remains, is currently difficult. The usual trajectory of a slave trade voyage in Britain involved departure from one of the ports usually associated with the slave trade (Bristol, Liverpool and London) for Africa with goods as exchange cargoes, like the *Johannah and Mary*, wrecked on Bideford Bar, outward-bound from Bristol, in 1735.[132] Contemporary reports show that soldiers were also embarked to repress any sign of slave rebellion. Consecutive issues of *Lloyd's List* in 1771 report first an action against the crew of the slave brigantine *George*[133] then the news that she had been wrecked on her return to England:

> The *George*, Bare, was cut off on the Windward Coast, and all the white people killed, except the captain, who is dangerously wounded. [134]

> The *George*, Bare, from Africa for Leverpool, foundered at the entrance of Leverpool harbour.[135]

The sequence and rapidity with which news of the *George* came tumbling out in the press suggests several things: first of all, that after having been 'cut off' (that is, the vessel was attacked from the shore and cut adrift while at anchor, a typical resistance tactic by local populations) all but one of her crew of 12 were killed (Fig 5.16). Under the circumstances, there was nothing for it but to leave the 'Windward Coast' immediately for Liverpool, probably with a scratch crew garnered from other Europeans in harbour; for the 'dangerously wounded' master could scarcely have sailed single-handed from Africa under normal circumstances, let alone with injuries. The second report following on so quickly after the first suggests that the news of the attack on the ship arrived with her in Liverpool Bay. Ironically, it is therefore likely that, after all that the ship and crew had undergone, the *George* was lost while waiting for a favourable wind to enter the Mersey.

That the press reports name Bare suggests that he remained in command and might have been the informant of the vessel's adventures

Fig 5.16
The Negro Revenged.
*Print engraved after
a painting by Henry Fuseli,
illustrating a stanza from
William Cowper's poem*
The Negro's Complaint
*(1788): 'Hark! He answers –
Wild tornadoes/ Strewing
yonder flood with wrecks/
Wasting Towns, Plantations,
Meadows/ Are the voice
with which he speaks.'
A bolt from above striking
a slaving ship and sending
her to the bottom depicts
divine wrath, while on the
shore, her intended victims
exult in their continuing
freedom. Abolitionists saw
wrecks of slave ships not
only as a sign of divine
displeasure but as
a step forward towards
abolition and this engraving
was published to coincide
with the abolition of slavery
in March 1807.
(© Victoria and Albert
Museum, London)*

and eventual loss, despite a journey of several weeks with severe injuries. Nevertheless, it seems likely that a sick master and a replacement crew, perhaps unfamiliar with the many sandbanks at the entrance to the Mersey, may have inadvertently played a part in the ultimate loss of their ship at journey's end. Bare must have been familiar with the Mersey approaches, as he had previously been in command of the *Denbia*, another Liverpudlian slaver, but he may not have been a particularly competent captain, for the *Denbia* had also been lost at the entrance to the Mersey some 18 months previously.[136]

The second leg of the typical slave trade voyage was the notorious 'Middle Passage' transhipping slaves from the coast of Africa, not only from the Windward Coast (modern Liberia and Côte d'Ivoire), but also from Cape Coast Castle (Ghana), Bonny (the Niger Delta) and Guinea (approximating to modern-day Guinea and Guinea-Bissau) to North America (the tobacco plantations of Virginia and elsewhere); South America, often lumped together as 'the Brazils' and 'the Honduras', and the Caribbean and West Indies. The third 'homeward-bound' leg of the voyage was to bring the products of slave labour to Europe, which were either desirable commodities in their own right (sugar, coffee, rum and tobacco) or were raw materials for the production of other goods (cotton for textiles, for example). These ships also acted as more conventional passage vessels to bring home governors, overseers, plantation owners and individual slaves. There is little to distinguish them in contemporary records from the 'West Indiamen' which plied between Europe and the West Indies or South America, bringing back the products of slave labour as a return cargo, but not themselves involved in voyages to Africa or to the Middle Passage.

There are other clues that a vessel's involvement with the slave colonies may go beyond that of the West Indiaman. Often, as described above, a slaver's voyage may be described in terms of the last leg of her journey, but she will retain some or all of an inanimate cargo indicating an earlier call in Africa: as the names 'Gold Coast' and 'Ivory Coast' indicate, Africa was rich in valuable trading commodities, and elephant ivory can only have come from Africa and not from the Americas. The presence of tusks aboard both the remains of the *Fredensborg* off Norway and the *Henrietta Marie* off Florida identified them both as slavers.[137] In the same way, the *Henrietta Marie*'s close contemporary, a Dutch 'homeward-bound vessel from Surinam', with her 'elephants' teeth', wrecked on the Dean Sand off Portsmouth in 1697 can be revealed as a slaver through documentary evidence, although her remains have never been found (she may, possibly, correspond with a Dutch ship, the *Brigdamme,* known to have been wrecked that year).[138] Similarly, initial reports in English reveal little about the *Juffrow Johanna Christi(a)na*, save that she was 'dashed to pieces' near Fowey in 1774, with the recovery of 'some wood, and a few pieces of Portugal gold'. Her true nature becomes apparent with greater detail emerging in more extensive reporting at home in the Netherlands: her departure point was specified as Curaçao in the Netherlands Antilles but with a cargo which included *Oliphants Tanden* ('elephants' teeth'); there was a similar clue to the real identity of the *Santa Maria de Luce* lost in 1546.[139] The same was true of English ships: the *Edward* was wrecked at Hoylake in 1782, homeward-bound to Liverpool from St Lucia. The ivory and 'camwood', a form of dyewood, transferred to her from the *Jason*, wrecked 'on the coast of Guinea', reveal the *Edward*'s earlier port of call at Gabon.[140]

The fates of the two Dutch vessels are a reminder of the multi-national involvement of most of the principal European powers in the slave trade: aside from the English and the Dutch, the Portuguese, Spanish, French, Danish and Swedish were also heavily involved in the trade in human cargo for their possessions in the New World. It is also a reminder that other slave trade wrecks may languish unrecognised in the documentary record: in many cases this may be partly because of the nature of the loss (since no one survived the wrecking of the *Juffrow Johanna Christi(a)na*, there was no one to tell her story to the English authorities). The 'Portugal gold' might have been a clue, but, given the international nature of contemporary trading currencies, cannot be definitive without more detail: only the Dutch-language reports from her country of origin have confirmed the exact nature of the ship.

The regular omission of one of the legs of the slave trade route should not, in itself, necessarily be seen as a sinister suppression of evidence, or as a sign of shame (though these two considerations may have applied in some instances) since there was a tendency for 18th-century sources to be 'split down the middle' and each supply partial details of a wrecking incident regardless of trade route or type of vessel. Most trade routes were well established and it was expected that the ultimate origination or destination ports and cargo would be understood by the contemporary reader. Spelling out the cargo of a vessel bound from Newcastle-upon-Tyne to London (coal) or from Setúbal ('St Ubes') for the Baltic (salt) was superfluous to contemporary readers. It is therefore desirable that more than one source should be traced for any given wreck event where possible, to uncover more about the trajectory of the voyage and to 'join up' the evidence. Only by combining details from different sources are we able to make a reasonable assumption that the vessel was involved in the slave trade (or any other trade for that matter), since wreck reports in contemporary sources are notable for their brevity. Details from newspapers for ships entering, leaving or 'clearing out' (clearing customs ready for departure) form a significant source for potential additional information, but comparative details of wrecks appearing in newspaper accounts may also be very revealing, especially in foreign-language sources, as we have seen with the *Juffrow Johanna Christi(a)na*.

Part of the difficulty in identifying vessels involved in the slave trade concerns their names: for the majority of ships engaged in any trade their names bear no relation to their usual cargo: as the *Juffrow Johanna Christi(a)na* ('Miss Johanna Christi(a)na') demonstrates, this was also true of the slave trade. However, there were exceptions, wherein a ship's name has a particular relationship to her trade: *Leviathan*, for example, is associated with whalers,[141] the whale generally being identified with the Biblical sea-monster of that name: 'There go the ships: there is that leviathan, whom thou hast made to play therein.'[142] In this way names such as *Denbia* (for Dembia) or *Juba* similarly also betray connections with slaving routes passing through the Congo and the Sudan, respectively.[143] Another ship in this category appears to be the *Traffick*, lost off Liverpool in 1775, for although the word was used of legitimate trade, by this period it had already acquired the connotations of trading in something that should not be made a commodity, as in the modern sense of trafficking drugs or women for the sex trade.[144]

There are other ways in which slave shipwrecks may be identified through profiling on the English Heritage database: for example, in looking at vessels with return voyages originating in Africa or the Americas, high-lighting vessels which might repay further research, and enabling a reasonably accurate estimate of the wrecked vessels involved to be made. A hierarchy of searchable terms is an extremely useful tool, given that contemporary sources are often very vague or partial, so that searching on a broad term such as 'Africa' brings up both vessels known vaguely to have departed from 'Africa' as well as those whose departure port was more precisely known, whether down to country, region or specific port. Wrecks laden with cargoes of gold or ivory may also, potentially, be identified as slave ships, and demonstrate that voyages ostensibly only from the Americas originated in Africa, particularly

in the case of ivory. Finally, suspect ships may, as we have seen above, be checked off against other databases, principally the Trans-Atlantic Slave Trade database, a seminal work in which over 36,000 slave voyages are recorded, which can provide final confirmation that these suspicions are correct.[145]

In some cases, ships have been identified which were not, at the time of writing, present in the Trans-Atlantic Slave Trade database: for other ships, such as the *Juffrow Johanna Christi(a)na*, further sources have been researched which have not been quoted, or which supplement information already in that database. For this reason, research undertaken for this book, and which remains ongoing, has in turn been shared with the Trans-Atlantic Slave Trade project so that it will benefit a wider audience beyond this book and beyond the English Heritage NHRE database. As a result of this research the number of wrecks in English waters known to have been involved in the slave trade has tripled, the first step towards identifying their remains on the seabed.[146] Tangible remains of shipwrecks involved in the slave trade may be difficult to locate, but information revealed through documentary evidence may not only bring us closer to discovering them, but also enable them to become virtual 'sites of memory' (Fig 5.17).

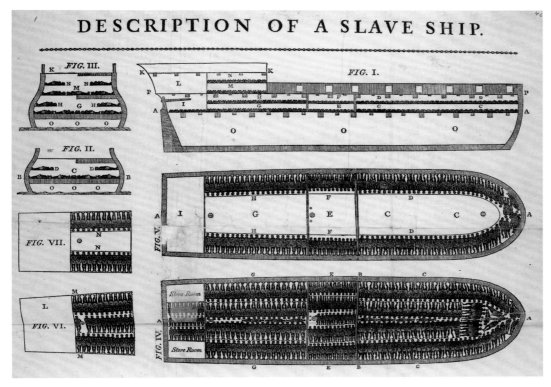

Fig 5.17
Description of a Slave Ship. *The famous image of the notorious* Brookes *slave ship, showing 454 slaves stowed together in appalling conditions, a powerful tool in the abolitionist armoury when published in 1787. Despite this adverse publicity, the* Brookes *continued in the slave trade until 1804 when she was condemned, presumably as unseaworthy. Less well-known is the fact that in 1799 she ran aground on the Cheshire coast, outward-bound from Liverpool, but was recovered (1338244). (By permission of the British Library Board)*

Salvaging ship names from the murky waters of the past

'It was a dark and stormy night … .' The old cliché has particular implications for maritime research. There are various ways in which vessel names can be misreported in original sources, commonly those of foreign origin. For example, nearby ships may not have been able to make out the name of a ship sinking with no survivors in heavy seas and driving rain, particularly if they were themselves in difficulties. Other factors may include the drowning of the master, perhaps the sole literate man aboard a small ship. Rescuers frequently relied on the oral testimony of traumatised foreign seamen unable to speak English, and if the rescuers were fishermen they themselves might have been illiterate. Thus officials could only write down what they thought they heard from the foreign sailors, or as filtered through local dialects, particularly distinctive local accents such as Tyneside or Norfolk, to produce a version of the name a long way from the original.

Even written accounts bring their own set of problems. It is difficult enough to decipher early English-language handwriting, but shipwreck accounts were frequently compromised in contemporary records by misunderstandings of both languages and foreign letter forms. The name of the ship may have been painted on its side in letter forms unfamiliar to English eyes – Greek, Cyrillic or *Fraktur* (German black letter Gothic), for example. Under these circumstances, it was difficult even for anyone literate or able to get by in another tongue to correlate what they heard from survivors with the name as seen on what was left of the ship. Unfamiliar Continental letter forms, even in the standard Latin alphabet, and letter groupings unknown in the English language, led contemporary observers astray, especially in conditions of poor visibility. This issue is, perhaps, most marked when the master survived and was able to write down the name of his vessel, only to be misread by the informant who provided the details to the

marine or regional press. However, the digitising of archives and other sources of data worldwide has provided solutions to these problems hitherto not readily available until relatively recently. A case in point is the following record, printed with a 'long s', ʃ, from *Lloyd's List*, 24 June 1760, no. 2,251 (Fig 5.18).

As the vessel had stranded upon a sandbank close to the coast, and in the busy approaches to Harwich from the Thames Estuary, it suggests that she was both easily seen by passing traffic and may have taken some time to settle into the sand (rather than breaking up quickly), so the authorities' principal sources were either direct sightings or a report from the master, who survived, or both. The difficult consonant cluster – *tmsd* – in his ship's name suggests some sort of distortion, but where to start?

The name *Boysen* is clearly of Scandinavian origin: the World Surname Profiler[147] shows that in modern times the name remains concentrated in populations around the Baltic, predominantly in Denmark. Voyage details alone cannot provide definitive information, since a vessel may trade between two ports unconnected with her home port, but if the vessel's last port of call coincides with the language of her name, it is likely to get us a step further. In this case we can make an informed guess that the ship's name is likely to be either Danish or Swedish. Proper nouns or similar name-words may prove a barrier to recovery of the vessel's name, but foreign-language dictionaries can be a first simple step towards reconstructing names based on common word forms.

Looking at a standard Danish dictionary online brings up a word, *sagtmodig,* whose physical resemblance to the original word appears promising.[148] Its definition is 'meek' and as such fits the profile of 17th- and 18th-century ship names from other Protestant countries, which emphasised virtues (such as English *Patience*, Dutch *Waaksamheid*, or its English equivalent, *Vigilant/Vigilance*). In this way vessels which have already been recorded on a database[149] can become a source of useful

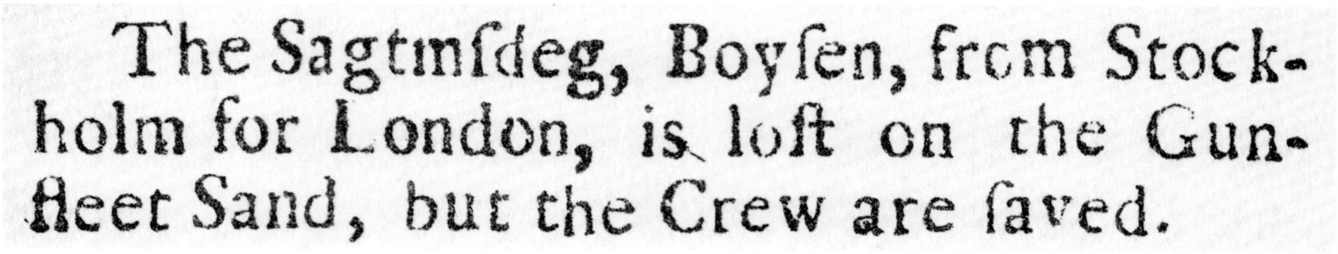

Fig 5.18
Detail of Lloyd's List *24 June 1760, no. 2,221, reporting the loss of the so-called* 'Sagtmsdeg'. *(By kind permission of* Lloyd's List*)*

The Sagtmſdeg, Boyſen, frcm Stock-holm for London, is loſt on the Gun-fleet Sand, but the Crew are ſaved.

comparative data and act as a control group for reconstruction purposes. Further research on a Swedish genealogical website recording vessels and crews[150] confirms that 25 Swedish ships with various spellings of the name *Sagtmodig* are known to have existed between the 17th and 19th centuries.

What went wrong in transcribing the name as *Sagtmsdeg*? Samples of 18th-century Danish handwriting from the Danish national archives' online guide[151] demonstrate that lower-case 'o' could resemble an English lower-case short *s* (long or 'leading' *s* and short *s* both being used in English), producing *Sagtmodeg*, while the *e* instead of *i* can be ascribed to orthographical variation (in the 18th century, spelling in most European languages was not fully standardised, differences being most marked in the vowels, but it should be stressed that these variants were not considered errors at the time): it is also possible to mistake an undotted *i* written with a flourish for an *e*.

Unfamiliarity with foreign handwriting and orthography also poses difficulties for modern readers, although this can be alleviated by making use of online and print resources, in order not to compound errors in the source material. One such case is that of a vessel omitted from contemporary *Lloyd's Lists* but recorded in a secondary source as *Zar Valdegbeid*,[152] a passage vessel from Calais which stranded east of the mole at Dover in 1799. Her name is clearly not, as might be expected, French, but its ending offers a clue: *-eid*. It is prefaced by a *b*, which is a common error made by English-language readers (then and now) faced with an *h* written in an unfamiliar, almost closed, form. Replacing *b* with *h* gives us the Dutch ending *-heid* (the equivalent of English – *ity*, *-ion*, *-ness*). The vessel is therefore likely to be Dutch, suggesting a target language for exploration. As with *Sagtmodig* above, *e* has been written for *i* in the syllable *eg*, in another typical example of 18th-century spelling variation, showing that fairly consistent rules can be applied across languages in terms of interchangeability of vowels.

Unexpected vowels are also one of the stumbling blocks to successful decipherment by the modern reader, but the ability to recognise common error patterns is key. Substituting one vowel for another can be a good technique: in this case, the substitution of *o* and *u* for *a* in *zar* and *val* respectively was successful (an *o* completed with a strong downstroke looping towards the next letter looks remarkably like English *a*; similarly, a cramped *u* written virtually closed up can also strongly resemble an *a*), for a first-stage reconstruction: *Zor Vuldigheid*. Recognising that the gap between syllables may represent one or more letters either omitted from the original source (a problem inherited from the original, 18th-century letter writer), or illegible in that source, but not marked up as such (a modern transcription error) the word or words can now be checked against an online Dutch dictionary.[153] This leads to a word defined in the dictionary, supplying the missing letter: *Zorgvuldigheid*, 'carefulness' or 'precision', and thus a plausible example, like *Sagtmodig*, of a contemporary ship name of northern European origin. Name reconstruction thus allows the ship to be traced in contemporary sources, in both *The Times* and the *Leeuwarder Courant*, as Z*orvuldigheid* and *Zorgvuldigheid* respectively.[154]

There is a point to this research: linguistic research reveals a shipwreck with a very individual tragedy. In this case identification as the *Zorgvuldigheid* opens up the details of the wreck, including the death of an English lady passenger living at Calais whose marital status is possibly deliberately unclear. According to the *Leeuwarder Courant*, she was bound for London to 'seek for her children', yet she is named as *Jufvrouw*, literally 'Miss', while in the English newspapers she is called 'Mrs' but her reason for returning home is unspecified. Thereby, perhaps, hangs a tale: at this period 'Mrs' was used indiscriminately for married and single women alike (akin to *Madame* in modern French usage),[155] though this was beginning to change. Why was she 'seeking' for her children, instead of 'returning for' them? Why was she returning alone? Why was she on the Continent at all? Had she fled the stigma of giving birth to illegitimate children, or was she a respectable widow who had moved abroad through penury, leaving her children in the care of relatives, perhaps now to be orphans altogether?

Deciphering German *Fraktur* was also fraught with difficulty. Like the supposed *Sagtmsdeg*, a wreck on the Goodwin Sands in 1870 was reported with a similar 'impossible' cluster of consonants, a German brigantine said to be the *Gelincnied* or *Gelinconied*[156] of Bremen. Both versions appear equally garbled to German and English speakers alike. The fact that the loss report coincides with another report on a different page of the same newspaper in almost

Fig 5.19
Reconstruction of the stricken Germania's *name in Fraktur, which means 'broken letters'. For someone unused to reading this script, these forms are difficult to interpret accurately or fluently, and easy to break up inappropriately, leading to* Germania *being read as 'Gelincnied' and 'Rickleffs' as Reckless. The latter is also perhaps influenced by the informant's opinion of the master's seamanship!*

GERMANIA

RICKLEFFS

Fig 5.20 (opposite)
Among the numerous nameboards, registration boards and figureheads in the collection of the Tynemouth Volunteer Life Brigade Watch House are two from the Jurneeks of Riga (1349493) lost during the severe storm of 13 November 1901: (a) one in Latvian Jurneks *(modern Latvian* Jurnieks, *which means 'sailor'); (b) the other in the German version* Juhrneek, *partly influenced by Cyrillic forms. These nameboards not only reflect the cosmopolitan nature of Riga in 1901 – then under Russian rule, with a Teutonic mercantile class and Latvian speakers – but are also the source of a variety of English spellings, particularly as only one crewman was rescued.* Juhrneeks *and* Jurneek *variously recombine the spellings from the nameboards, while* Jourhneeks *appears to be a phonetic spelling. (Photographs by courtesy of the Tynemouth Volunteer Life Brigade Museum)*

identical circumstances offers a fortuitous clue. Had both been posted in the Shipping News column, the coincidences would most likely have been spotted immediately, and merged, but coming from different sources and set in different columns, they are divorced from their context, and appear to tell the story of two different wrecks. When viewed in parallel the two accounts clearly go beyond coincidence:

> From Lloyd's. Posted on the Loss Book, March 24 … The *Germania* (Bremen brigantine) from St. Domingo for Hamburg, was totally wrecked last night on the Goodwin. Crew saved.

> Shipwrecks and Lifeboat Services – Broadstairs Thursday morning (By Telegraph). Captain Eljard reports that the lifeboat *Samuel Morrison Collins* belonging to the National Lifeboat Institution went out to a schooner, the Bremen brigantine *Gelincnied* (Reckless, master) which became a total wreck on the South Goodwin Sand. Her crew, however, were fortunately saved by the North Deal lifeboat *Vankoek*, which also belongs to the Lifeboat Society.[157]

Were they two vessels travelling in company from the same outward port? It is certainly possible and not unknown for wrecks on the Goodwin Sands, particularly given their close proximity to the Downs as an assembly point.[158] The coincidence of two names beginning with the same two letters makes this appear a little less likely. In the second report, the distortion of both vessel and master's names strongly suggests a transcription error of some kind, whether as seen by rescuers, or from statements or documents subsequently written out by survivors on landing. Both betray an effort to process

unfamiliar sequences of letters, assimilating them into a version approximating a familiar word. In other words, the brain makes sense of what the eye sees by relying on what it would normally expect to see following a certain pattern of letters, one of the building blocks of rapid reading, even now. In this case English readers clearly had difficulty deciphering German black letter forms, seeing *l* instead of *r*, *in* for *m* and *d* for *a* (Fig 5.19).

Further research confirms that only one vessel was involved in this incident, the master's name and the lifeboat being now attached to the *Germania* rather than the mythical *Gelincnied*:

> The Bremen brigantine *Germania*, Captain Rickleffs, from St. Domingo for Hamburg, laden with mahogany, got on the Goodwin Sands about 9pm on Wednesday 25th March. The crew left their own boat and were received on board the South Sand Head Lightship with every attention, and taken from thence, on the following morning, by the North Deal Lifeboat the *Van Kook*. The vessel has become a total wreck, but it is expected that the principal portion of her cargo will be saved.[159]

Similar difficulties in deciphering the handwriting of foreign nationals clearly led to the misidentification of a Norwegian barque lost on the Goodwin Sands in 1870 as the *Hony Sverne* in the original *Times* report:[160] the elaboration of *K* in Continental handwriting closely resembles English copperplate *H* and the typical rounded lower-case *r* with a long descender is easily mistaken for *n*. In this way the name of the vessel can be reconstructed as *Kong Sverre*, the name of a 12th-century ruler of Norway, King Sverre. That this is the correct form can be corroborated by other similarly named Norwegian ships lost in English waters in the late 19th and early 20th centuries.[161]

While being able to reconstruct ship names has obvious implications for retrieving further documentary evidence, there are other benefits, not least in raising awareness of the issue beyond the historical record. Unfamiliarity with foreign names and a lack of standardised spelling remain as issues for the reporting of finds today.[162] In terms of building a database of shipwrecks, it helps to eliminate duplication by reuniting separate accounts (which can artificially inflate the numbers of recorded shipwrecks), enabling a more accurate assessment of potential archaeology. In terms of archaeological remains, the discovery of the right name has obvious implications for identifying the iconography of any carvings or devices on wooden sailing vessels, while being able to trace the vessel in contemporary sources is a valuable tool for identifying the wrecking processes seen in vessel remains, and in helping to establish or eliminate possible identities for particular wrecks. Recognising a vessel's nationality will likewise suggest a possible baseline for analysing any hull timbers retrieved from remains. Finally, these few examples outline the potential offered by the increasing accessibility of archival resources online, particularly in foreign languages. Forensic linguistic research of this kind, not previously a tool in classical maritime archaeology, can therefore be used to illuminate and interpret both existing material and new finds (Fig 5.20).

Whatever happened to the *Elizabeth Jane*?

Background

What happens to wrecks following the wreck event, if they are not now lying at the bottom of the sea, or wedged in some impossible cove? Recording wrecks from documentary evidence is a good indicator of the archaeological potential of a particular area, showing a concentration of wrecks in particular areas or which wrecks are yet to be located, but the archaeological potential is not confined to the seabed or to the foreshore: it can also suggest where wreck materials are likely to be found ashore.

Typically wrecks lying in deep water could be 'weighed' (raised) or salvaged of valuable materials, especially cannon, and cargo where at all possible. This was a specialist task, and costly, leaving behind a partial or complete hull, and perhaps some or all of the cargo, depending on the difficulty of salvage. On the foreshore, where a wrecked vessel could be easily broken up – officially by the owners, insurance agents or their representatives, or unofficially by locals – it would appear unlikely at first glance that such vessels would leave much in the way of an archaeological footprint. Often what remained of a hull would be broken up and her materials sold by auction 'where she now lies', so that anything salvageable from the ships' materials and stores could be bought cheaply and reused in other ships as appropriate – her 'standing and running rigging', her capstans and other potentially useful parts. The materials thus recycled more or less disappear without trace, although given the high incidence of shipwreck and of grounding incidents, in which a ship could go ashore but be refloated with relatively little damage several times in her career, they may well have ended up in more than one wrecking incident and thus more than one such marine auction.

Where did they go? Whether broken up legally or otherwise, shipwreck materials stood a fair chance of being insinuated into the architecture and archaeology of a particular region. Ships' figureheads are perhaps the most obvious and easily recognisable form of ships' timbers to be incorporated into local

architecture. They may be added as exterior decoration to pubs and other buildings (Fig 5.21), although it is not always clear whether they came from shipwrecks or from shipbreaking activity – shipbreaking was not necessarily confined to wrecked ships since it was the natural fate of a vessel at the end of her useful life. Ships broken up at the end of their lifespan at dedicated breakers' yards are therefore distinct from those where the human activity of 'breaking up' simply finishes off a process begun by the sea.[163] Portable items, such as figureheads, may therefore end up at a location far from the original shipwreck or breakers' yards, obscuring their origins (Fig 5.22).

Figureheads were prone to the accretions of legend: one such example is the red lion figurehead associated with the Star Inn, Alfriston, East Sussex. The most specific story concerning this figurehead is that it came from

Fig 5.21
The figurehead over the Bosun's Locker, Falmouth, is from the Volant, an 1875 topsail schooner, bought by an Australian film-maker to beat the post-war shipping shortage, which left Belfast for a failed voyage to Australia in 1946.
By the time she arrived at Falmouth she was so unseaworthy she was refused permission to leave, and she was stripped down and left to rot.
Her figurehead was salvaged as an eye-catching sign for the chandlery, established in the same year.
John Gay collection.
(AA086608)

a Dutch ship wrecked nearby in 1675, but another version of the story has it that it came from a Dutch warship wrecked at some unspecified date, and it has also come within the orbit of the tales associated with a local gang of smugglers in the 19th century. In the same way the eponymous Red Lion at Martlesham in Suffolk is said to have come from a ship involved in the Battle of Solebay (1672), but there is little direct evidence for the connection.[164]

The origins of, and stories concerning, surviving figureheads are much clearer in dedicated collections – the Valhalla collection located in the Abbey Gardens at Tresco, Isles of Scilly, being the most famous, a symbol of the notoriously rocky Isles of Scilly. Figureheads

Fig 5.22
Castle's Shipbreaking Co., Baltic Wharf, Millbank, London as seen around 1900. Figureheads from HMS Colossus *(left) and* HMS Cressy *(right), both broken up in 1867, look out from the entrance towards Ponsonby Terrace, just north of Vauxhall Bridge: two further unidentified figureheads are seen in profile on the left.*
Over the lintel are inscribed the words of Nelson's famous Trafalgar signal: England expects that every man will this day do his duty. *The waggon outside advertises 'ship timber logs', showing that not even famed men-of-war could escape being broken up for firewood.*
(BB76/04423)

were picked up from the 1840s onwards with the express intention of including them in the collection, and thus ensuring that their links with the original vessel and original wrecking events were not broken. Another major collection of figureheads and ships' nameboards exists at Tynemouth Volunteer Life Brigade Station, commemorating the individual events in which the Life Brigade men were involved.[165] Other figureheads stand – or once stood – sentinel in churchyards, memorials to their dead crews (Fig 5.23).[166]

Less obviously, the materials from shipwrecks off Tynemouth could be easily sold to the collieries of the Durham coalfield, and were advertised for sale to these prospective customers in the regional press: their cargoes, as in the case of the *Burdon* in 1805, could

likewise be advertised as suitable for the mining trade: 'a quantity of new plank, fit for colliery and other uses'.[167] Similarly, Newcastle and Shields colliers wrecked elsewhere in the country, typically on the usual east coast run to London, or on the return trip, were usually broken up as soon as possible, and brought back on other colliers to be sold on at their home ports within 4 weeks, 6 weeks at the outside. In being broken up they retained their connection with the trade they had served, for wrecked colliers were often ultimately fated to be recycled as pit props or perhaps used in fashioning wagons or tramways:

> TO COLLIERY OWNERS: To be sold by auction, on the New Quay, North Shields, on Thursday February 6th: A large quantity of oak timber and plank, saved from the wreck of the brig *Ann*.

Fig 5.23
Appropriately, the kilted figurehead of the Caledonia *wrecked in 1842, complete with tam o'shanter, claymore and skean-dhu, watched over the grave of her crew in the churchyard of St Morwenna and St John the Baptist, Morwenstow (now replaced by a replica, the original having been removed to the church). (AA98/04739)*

The whole will be put up in lots, to suit purchasers. For particulars, apply at the office of Messrs Redhead and Dixon, South Shields.[168]

Materials from other wrecks are frequently said to be built into houses or churches, although evidence thereof is very hard to come by without intrusive analysis of structural timbers and confirmation by extensive research in documents contemporary with the date of building. For example, the church of St Peter and St Paul, Mottistone, Isle of Wight, was restored and reordered in 1863, the year after the nearby wreck of the *Cedarine* (a convict ship), from which the timbers are said to have been reused to furnish the chancel roof.[169] The church contains a stained glass window commemorating the *Cedarine*, but surviving documents appear to concentrate on the reseating of the church rather than repairing the roof, so it may be that the shipwreck timbers were used for the furnishings instead of the roof, a practice more securely associated with Flexbury Methodist Church, Bude, built as late as 1905. The 20-feet lengths of pitch pine at Flexbury were deck cargo jettisoned to avoid the loss of a vessel bound for one of the Welsh valley ports on the opposite side of the Bristol Channel. The salvaged timber was bought by the firm involved in building the church, and used for altar rails as well as pews.[170] Interestingly, Hawker's Hut at nearby Morwenstow is said to have been built by the Revd Robert Hawker from the timbers of the *Alonzo*, wrecked nearby in 1843;[171] it was Hawker who also had the grim duty of burying the victims of the *Caledonia* in 1842. He also raised her figurehead in the churchyard, so that there was a well-established local tradition of recycling ships' timbers for various purposes which are still visible in the built environment (Fig 5.24).

More tenuously, perhaps, the rood screen in the church of St Winwaloe, Gunwalloe, is said to be associated with, or made from timbers from, the wreck of the Portuguese carrack *St Anthony*, lost nearby in 1527 (Fig 5.25). There is nothing in surviving original sources to say that the screen was erected by grateful survivors of the shipwreck, as local tradition has it. They had little to be grateful for: their troubles did not end with their survival, for far from being given succour, they were hard pressed to keep their vessel from being pillaged even by the local gentry, for the wreck had merchandise worth £16,000 on board (nearly £6m today, based on

the retail price index, or almost £79m, in terms of average earnings), an attractive target for local looters.[172] The rood screen panels are no longer in their original location within the church but are now in two pieces beside the north and south doors, respectively, with four saints on each panel. At first sight the painted images are strongly reminiscent of Iberian Romanesque art – itself out of keeping both with the date of the wreck, being several centuries earlier, and its dating by one recent authority to the 15th century, again antedating the wreck.[173] The uniformity of each saint's appearance and the freshness of the paint suggest, first, that they were painted in an imitation of an earlier style and, second, that they have been compromised by at least two known restoration attempts, once in Victorian times and the second time as late as 1977, with two less restored images on the north side which may preserve something of the original appearance (which is not necessarily that of 1527).[174] The association between the

Fig 5.24
View of Hawker's Hut, Morwenstow, Cornwall. The Revd Hawker recycled the materials of the Alonzo *by building the hut overlooking the sea where she was lost, from which he used to look for other ships in danger. The hut served a commemorative, symbolic, and intensely personal function for this eccentric vicar, who found it increasingly painful to perform his grim duty of burying shipwreck victims. (© Andrew Wyngard)*

Fig 5.25
One half of the rood
screen at the Church of
St Winwaloe, Gunwalloe.
The carving appears
older than the very
conventionalized images.
(© Crown copyright.
Photograph taken by Wessex
Archaeology)

rood screen and the wreck may thus be of recent origin: the story is not mentioned, for example, in a history of 1838, which does, however, mention a local tradition of treasure buried in the dunes, associated with 'Captain Avery, the celebrated buccaneer' which may be a garbled folk memory of the *St Anthony*. If local traditions concerning treasure in the vicinity of the wreck are corrupted, then it is difficult to prove a more secure association between the screen and the wreck. Indeed some guidebooks fail to mention the screen's supposed origins.[175] Only dendro-chronological analysis will confirm the matter one way or another.[176]

There is therefore a handful of listed buildings scattered throughout the country said to contain structural shipwreck timbers: according to building inspectors and dendrochronologists, the presence of shipwreck timbers is regularly claimed by building owners, but these turn out on closer inspection to be other forms of worked timber, though the presence of ship timbers from the breakers' yards cannot always be ruled out entirely.[177] Most of these associations between shipwrecks and buildings therefore start with the wreck event which, whether well documented or otherwise, has come to be attached to the building.

The story of the *Elizabeth Jane*

The case of a house in Robin Hood's Bay, near Whitby, is different, and at the time of writing virtually unique in England. It began with the house and ended with the discovery of a hitherto unknown wreck. In 2003 some timbers were uncovered during the start of restoration works on the house, and were found to be carved with the words IPSWICH and ELIZABETH JAN..., which piqued the interest of the owner (Fig 5.26).[178] That these two timbers survived at all was fortuitous because they gave two names – a place name and a woman's name, which together indicated that the timbers came from the remains of a ship and that the female name was a ship's name. Other ships' timbers were also uncovered elsewhere in the cottage with treenail holes still present, further evidence that they had come from a ship:

> Investigation of the joists and rafters in the upper two floors of the cottage showed that they too had once belonged to a ship. Some are painted with tar and still have sand embedded in them; some are curved; and many 'furry' from being submerged in water. It is not surprising that they were concealed behind a plaster ceiling.[179]

As with all the best detective stories, the finding of one clue immediately raises more questions than answers. What was the rest of the name, likely to be *Jane* or *Janet*? What was her connection with Ipswich? How did she come to be in this cottage in Robin Hood's Bay? The proximity of the dwelling to the sea in an area well-known for accidents to shipping suggested the possibility of a wreck, but when, where, and how? Was it even a shipwreck? Could the wreck have occurred elsewhere?

Vessel names of the *Elizabeth Jane* type were popular in the English-speaking world in the 18th and 19th centuries and crop up regularly in contemporary publications and records. They appear principally to be the names of the master or owner's wife, mother, sister or daughter, in keeping with the English convention of referring to ships as 'she'. In the NRHE database there are 11 wrecks with similar names: another *Elizabeth Jane*, and also *Eliza Jane*; *Elizabeth and Jane*; and *Eliza and Jane*, all reflecting the widespread popularity of these two names during the 19th century.[180]

The owner had little to go on at first beyond the fact that the Ipswich board indicated the wrecked vessel's home port: she was the *Elizabeth Jan ...* of Ipswich. Investigations in Ipswich records turned up the cancellation of an *Elizabeth Jane* in the registers with the

Fig 5.26a
Elizabeth Jane *nameboard as displayed following the find. (By kind permission of the owner)*

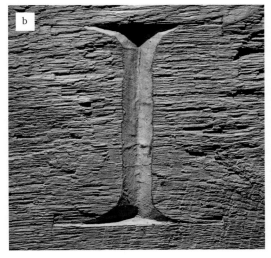

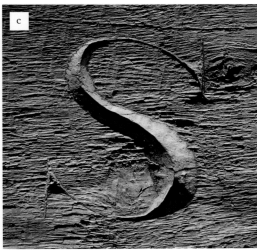

Figs. 5.26b and 5.26c Detail of letter I and letter S in 'Ipswich' port of registration board, showing the surviving yellow paint for visibility at sea, within the deeply carved letters. (By kind permission of the owner)

endorsement: 'Lost 9th July 1854 off the Coast of Yorkshire',[181] but this provided neither a specific association with Robin Hood's Bay nor any exact explanation of what actually happened to her or how she came to be in the cottage. There was a very small clue in the phrase 'off the coast of …' because this is misleading to the modern reader, and does not mean 'offshore' as we might expect. In 18th- and 19th-century accounts, 'off' instead signifies 'near' a place: but the Yorkshire coastline is a long one, and longer in 1854, extending north to the River Tees and south to the River Humber, than it is now. 'Off the Coast of Yorkshire' thus does little to narrow down the area, particularly as there are a number of notorious wrecking spots on the Yorkshire coast alone, but at least it does suggest that the vessel might well have come on shore.[182] The timbers' survival in the house suggests that interpreting 'off the Coast of Yorkshire' as a stranding is likely to be correct, for fewer serviceable timbers are likely to have been recovered from a sunken vessel.

Where, then, did the *Elizabeth Jane* come to rest (Fig 5.27)? A specific date is a seminal clue which leads naturally to contemporary newspaper accounts, in particular those from local newspapers, but she also made national news. Shipping news, as already explained in earlier chapters, was often garbled in the transmission from one newspaper to another. With the variety of newspapers available to the Victorian reading public, it is often very difficult to find the source report, which is often the most significant and contains details omitted by later reprints. The concept of acknowledging the original source of news was very slow to take off and makes this difficult job much harder. For example, though *Lloyd's List* contains two reports from consecutive issues, it was not the first to report the wreck:

Bridlington, 9th July. The Elizabeth & Jane, Archer, of and for Ipswich, from Sunderland, was abandoned last night leaky and with pumps choked: crew landed here.

Whitby, 10th July. The Elizabeth & Jane, of Ipswich, coal laden, came ashore yesterday at Peak, derelict, and in a sinking state. (See Bridlington paragraph in List of 10 July).[183]

The first thing which strikes the reader is the subtle variation in the ship's name – *Elizabeth and Jane* rather than *Elizabeth Jane*. The date is correct, but given the widespread nature of names of this kind, was she the right vessel?

However, errors of this kind were equally as commonplace – and understandable – when the first report might have been by word of mouth, following on from the chaos of wreck and rescue when the nameboard might have been difficult to read. The prevalence of the name formula 'X & Y' may also have led to a tendency to fill in the gaps by assuming an intrusive 'and' where the name had not been accurately read by those at the scene.[184] (It may well be that some of the other wrecks known to us as *Elizabeth and Jane* were also *Elizabeth Janes*.) Second, the two reports contain information 'split down the middle', suggesting two different witnesses and therefore sources, a typical feature of wrecks attracting more than one newspaper report: the one has the cargo, the other the voyage details; the one describes the abandonment of the vessel, the other her final fate.

In fact it turned out that the Bridlington paragraph was condensed for national dissemination via *Lloyd's*: tracing the quotation back through various local newspapers it appears with increasing levels of detail, some of it misspelt, such as 'North Creek' for North Cheek, Robin Hood's Bay. The most detailed version appears in the *Newcastle Courant*, which, because it was printed in the heartland of 'King Coal', made it its business to accurately report all marine accidents which could pertain to the coal trade and is one of the most reliable of all 19th-century sources. Characteristically, the *Courant* alone among the newspapers pinpoints the exact time at which the crew abandoned ship:

Bridlington Quay, July 9. The Elizabeth and Jane, Archer, of and for Ipswich from Sunderland, was abandoned off the North Cheek of Robin Hood's Bay at 9pm yesterday, leaky, and pumps choked; crew were picked up by the Samuel of Grimsby, and landed here this morning.[185]

How did the *Elizabeth Jane* come to spring a leak on a summer evening on a perfectly commonplace run south from Sunderland with coal? Was it sabotage? Her owner had had previous 'form' in 1840, being suspected of the sabotage of another collier brig also sunk in the North Sea for insurance purposes, but his acquittal on these charges was 'welcomed yesterday at Ipswich by the ringing of bells, the firing of cannon, the hoisting of flags on the different vessels in the dock, and by other demonstrations of satisfaction on the part of the population.'[186] When history repeated itself there appears to have been no follow-up by the authorities, but over 150 years later the circumstances still appeared very suspicious, until a second piece of information came to light.

It seems instead that the *Elizabeth Jane* may well have been fatally weakened by spending several months ashore at Newbiggin-by-the-Sea earlier that year:[187] under such circumstances it was fairly common for the affected vessels to get into further difficulties when they returned to service, typically foundering after springing a leak. In other words, the earlier incident was a secondary cause of the final loss of the vessel. In many cases repairs were botched, as in the case of the *Unicorn*, lost off Whitby in 1851 or 1857, attributed to 'imperfect repairs', while the 'extensive repairs and new copper sheathing' undertaken prior to sailing were not sufficient to save the *Kingston* from springing a leak off the Lizard in 1856. Similarly botched repairs prior to leaving South Shields for Shanghai meant that in 1868 the crew of the *Logan* were forced to abandon her off the Isles of Scilly: it was remarkable that they had made it that far, being forced to pump her out every watch.[188] The *Elizabeth Jane* remained on the rocks at Newbiggin for three months between January and April 1854, when she was refloated at 'high water springs', that is, the predicted higher than normal high tide, the usual saviour of a vessel otherwise stuck fast and 'high and dry'. She is next heard of at the end of what was probably her first voyage following the necessary repairs, when she arrived leaky at Ipswich from Blyth on 29 May 1854.[189] On that occasion she must once again have required repairs and set out again in ballast for Sunderland some time in June or July 1854. At least in ballast there was less strain to be put on the vessel: it was not for nothing that a vessel in ballast was said to be 'light', and she arrived safely to take on her southbound return cargo.

How did the timbers end up in the cottage? The site is visible to the south from the present building and it is likely to have attracted the interest of the locals. Having investigated possible nefarious dealings on the part of the ship's owner, it was easy to imagine that the house's owner was also acting illegally, for the Robin Hood's Bay area has also had a long history of associations with smuggling activities. The truth, however, was somewhat more prosaic. In the late 18th and 19th centuries the local coastguard was usually entrusted with securing the wreck and preventing looting of

timbers and cargo, particularly where alcohol was involved. Had the *Elizabeth Jane* struck just three months later, she would have come under the auspices of the newly formed post of Receiver of Wreck, but in this case it was the coastguard who, as usual, stepped in and took charge of the wreck. Members of the coastguard were usually Navy or ex-Navy men, building on earlier precedents: during the 17th and 18th centuries, the local militia regularly stepped in to prevent looting and to compel obedience, powers inherited by the Receiver of Wreck, who until 1995 retained the power to bear arms. It seems likely then, that there was little or no looting, but instead a sale of the wreck 'as she lay' on the South Cheek, was most likely forced by the

Fig 5.27
Robin Hood's Bay is bounded by the North Cheek where Elizabeth Jane *was abandoned and the South Cheek where she drifted ashore. She is likely to have come to rest on the rocks at Peak Steel on the north side of the South Cheek. At least five other wrecks have been lost on Peak Steel and another 13 are known to have stranded within Robin Hood's Bay over the centuries, with more in the immediate surroundings.*

Fig 5.28
Rocky Shore with
Dismantled Vessel. *Almost
contemporary with the
Elizabeth Jane, this
watercolour gives some idea
as to how she was broken up.
On a rocky shore on the
northern coast of England,
local men take advantage of
fair weather and low tide to
start breaking up a stranded
and dismasted vessel. Bright
red details on their clothing
draw the eye to the damage
on the vessel and to the cause
of loss: a boulder on the
foreshore. Some timbers have
already been levered
off and lie on the beach.
(George Chambers, 1838.
Dixon Bequest. © Victoria
and Albert Museum, London)*

insurers and probably advertised in local newspapers and by handbills. The sale would therefore have been properly supervised by the marine auctioneers as well as the coastguard and there would have been little opportunity for theft or smuggling of the wrecked timbers ashore (Fig 5.28).

However, despite this prosaic turn of events, a little romance remains to hang over the wreck site now in the cottage. It belonged to one Moses Bell, who also owned two other properties in the terrace. For him the timbers of the *Elizabeth Jane*, which were found in the upper two floors of the house, were an ideal opportunity to extend the house upwards (the layout of the site precluded building outwards) by taking advantage of a tall wall built a few years previously. An indenture from 1860 relating to the neighbouring property confirms one of 1848 in which 'Moses Bell his heirs and assigns may rest timber and any other materials in or upon

the East end of the said messuage' and suggests what may have happened next. Bell may have either bought the wreck to break her up on site over the winter commencing building operations, or acquired the timber in lots, in a similar fashion to the brig *Ann* (mentioned on p. 226). However he came by the timbers, he probably took advantage of the permissions laid out in the indentures and leant them against the neighbouring property awaiting suitable weather to begin building. They did not remain there for very long. Renovations were probably completed by 1856, since by then Bell was advertising his properties as holiday lets: 'Parties visiting the romantic scenery of Robin Hood's Bay can be accommodated with respectable lodgings at Mr M Bell's'.[190] One wonders whether he pointed out the site of the shipwreck to his lodgers as part of that 'romantic scenery' and told them the tale of how their 'respectable lodgings' came to be built.

How could the discovery of the *Elizabeth Jane* inform future recording of coastal houses?

The story of the *Elizabeth Jane* has ramifications for the assessment of maritime evidence, as the only known example of reused shipwreck timbers in a secure domestic context. It seems that wrecks known only from documentary evidence may not only illustrate the submarine archaeological potential but may also provide a basis on which to assess the origin of timbers built into houses in coastal communities. In fact, the *Elizabeth Jane* shows that documented wrecks may have no corresponding undersea remains, for the remains in fact survive elsewhere in a terrestrial context. She solves the issue of why shipwreck timbers appear generally to be over-reported as domestic (or other) structural features, since local legend plays a strong part, and 'romantic' associations with shipwrecks are much more appealing to home-owners and local historians for the origins of unusual timber features within buildings, than more prosaic explanations. As the case of the rood screen at Gunwalloe demonstrates, it is very difficult to prove an unbroken centuries-long association between a wreck and recycled timber, and it seems likely that those timbers which are genuinely the products of shipping or cargo losses are those which are *not* reported. It seems plausible that such features may be concentrated relatively locally within a few miles of the coastline, although wider dispersal into the neighbouring countryside cannot be ruled out. One such building fitting this profile may be Hartlaw Cottages, Newton-on-the-Moor, Northumberland, within 2–3 miles of the coast at Alnmouth. The original house is of late 17th-century origin and appears to retain its original roof and lintel timbers, which, like those belonging to the *Elizabeth Jane*, show evidence of treenails and would appear to be evidence at least for recycling from an original maritime context, if not from a wreck at least from a vessel at the end of its useful life. Some of the treenails inter-cut each other, suggesting repeated repair.[191]

It also raises the intriguing question of how many ships' timbers were incorporated into existing vernacular buildings and used for building new ones, and how they can be recognised. Generally exposed features such as cruck-framing, roof-beams or oak lintels become the focus of associations with a shipwreck,

but it may be that their shape or material is suggestive of curved ships' timbers or planking without any real basis in fact, not least the difficulty of obtaining timbers of sufficient size and soundness to take the structural burden of a roof: on these grounds alone the reuse of the timbers of the *Cedarine* at Mottistone seems less than plausible. Nevertheless, it is easy to see how the situation has arisen, for, after all, the similarity between shipbuilding and architecture is an ancient metaphor: the word for the 'nave' of a church ultimately derives from the Latin *navis*, 'ship'.

Thus, if the reuse of ship's timbers as structural elements in a building is virtually unknown despite being frequently suggested, it does not therefore follow that there was no reuse at all. Instead, the discovery of hidden features, as in the house containing the remains of the *Elizabeth Jane*, may indicate instead that it is the less visible structural features which are possibly those which have genuinely come from wrecks. It is very likely that, where wood from wrecked vessels was recycled for domestic architecture, it was probably incorporated for utilitarian purposes: floors rather than doors, joists, not wainscots, planks rather than exposed beams, and concealed beneath plaster, partitions and other surfaces, as in the case of the timbers from the *Elizabeth Jane*. Even where beams are exposed, as at Hartlaw, their relatively inaccessible location may make evidence of a primary maritime use difficult to spot.

The rediscovery of the *Elizabeth Jane* prompts a reassessment of how commonplace the practice of wreck recycling was, if up to now the focus has been on visible elements of the structure. The finding of hidden timbers is naturally an accidental process, so perhaps this approach is understandable enough. The *Elizabeth Jane* continues to prompt many questions beyond those arising out of the night on which she was lost. How many of these buildings have, like the vessels from which they were built, been destroyed? How many may have been revealed in the past, but their origin as vessel timbers unrecognised since an associated nameboard was not incorporated, or was obliterated or placed face-down? How many such features have been destroyed or covered up again? How can timbers from other shipwrecks known to us be recognised in the recording of buildings in coastal towns and villages or further afield? Is the *Elizabeth Jane* a unique case, as suggested by the lack of exact comparative examples, turning up as they do in other contexts, as parts (a rood screen, pews, seating in a greenhouse) or in other types of buildings (churches, huts, outbuildings) or a case which may stand as unique symbol for a once common practice?

The *Elizabeth Jane* is so much more than the sum of her broken parts: her very ordinariness, as a representative of the once-common collier brig, built into a vernacular cottage, suggests that she is unlikely to be an isolated example. By the same token, however, the nature of the use to which other timbers from wrecks like the *Elizabeth Jane* were put indicates that surviving genuine examples of reused wreck materials may be hard to detect except in restoration projects: investigations otherwise may be too intrusive. However, the *Elizabeth Jane* is an important case study showing what to look for: the maritime database could be used as a potential profiler to identify the sources of wreck materials in construction, either from hulls or salvaged timber cargo because phases of building activity could potentially be traceable in contemporary sources following wreck events, as in the case of the *Elizabeth Jane* herself.

There are so many seafront communities along the English coastline the question seems at first too large and the task too difficult, especially taking into account the way in which surviving written evidence becomes more and more difficult to trace the further back in time one goes. However, on the evidence of the nucleus of reused timbers in the area around Bude, it would seem logical that wreck timbers were, most naturally, reused in the immediate area of loss, and that examples of such recycling are more likely to occur in areas having high concentrations of wrecks. There are at least 119 recorded wrecks in and around Bude and a very similar number, 118, for the area around Robin Hood's Bay, both going back to at least the 17th century.[192] The profile of the two places is very similar in other respects: they both have long traditions of smuggling and the landing of contraband. Notwithstanding that Revd Hawker at Morwenstow and Moses Bell at Robin Hood's Bay clearly came by their 'recycled' timbers legitimately, it is plausible that many timbers quietly disappeared, taken by locals well used to moving contraband goods under cover of darkness. Finally, the secure contexts for these reused timbers date from a fairly narrow window, around the mid-19th to early 20th centuries. As a first step, therefore, in taking forward a new direction in maritime archaeology, the investigation of wreck materials in a shore context, it could well be fruitful to build in the routine querying of the maritime database to inform casework on 19th-century listed buildings in areas with notorious wrecking spots: for example, a known building date could be profiled against the date of wrecks in the vicinity. An upsurge in building activity would appear to be the natural consequence of a storm and may form a starting point for future investigations. Breaking open these hidden relationships would be a very exciting investigative direction to take, combining maritime archaeology and architectural history in a way never before attempted.

6

How does it all come together? What is left to find out?

THE *LONDON*: A CASE STUDY

ALISON JAMES, MARITIME ARCHAEOLOGIST, ENGLISH HERITAGE

The Protection of Wrecks Act 1973

Designated sites are identified as being likely to contain the remains of a vessel, or its contents, which are of historical, artistic or archaeological importance. The Protection of Wrecks Act 1973 (PWA) allows government to control access to sites in order to protect them from unauthorised activity. Access to the sites is controlled through four types of licence that are issued to a licensee; licences to visit, survey, recover surface artefacts and to excavate. Licences generally last a year and the licensee is expected to comply with the terms of the licence including the submission of site reports.

There are currently 47 sites in England designated under the PWA. The sites are diverse and represent the scattered remains of a Bronze Age 'cargo' through to the first Royal Naval submarine designed and built in Britain.[1] They represent only a fraction of the known historic shipwrecks on the English seabed and even fewer of the probable total number.

The *London*

The *London* first came to the attention of English Heritage in 2006 during investigative works preceding development (dredging) in the River Thames. Two adjacent wreck sites (known as the *London* and the *King*) were subject to archaeological assessment by the Port of London Authority ahead of dredging for the London Gateway project.[2] The name *King* is a sobriquet first applied to the second site only in 1979 and by which it remains known for convenience, though no ship of this name appears to have been lost in this area. However, it was not until October 2007 that English Heritage became aware of a threat to the site: reports were received that a diver had declared two bronze cannons to the receiver of wreck that had recently been recovered from the site of what was believed to be either the *London* or the *King*. At this time no position was provided to English Heritage and there were no reports of any other material being recovered from the site. Further threats to the site triggered its assessment of national importance for potential designation under Section 1 of the PWA .

The role of English Heritage

English Heritage is the UK government's advisor on all aspects of the historic environment in England and works closely with the government departments who make decisions about the historic environment. Since the passing of the National Heritage Act 2002, English Heritage's remit has been extended to include maritime archaeology out to the 12-nautical-mile limit around England. These responsibilities mean that English Heritage has the opportunity, subject to available resources and priorities, to support the conservation management of English sites already designated under Section 1 of the PWA, as well as being responsible for recommending others for designation in England.

Assessment for designation

Prior to recommending designation (where warranted) to the secretary of state, the Department of Culture, Media and Sport (DCMS), all sites are assessed against criteria that consider many things including the period, rarity, historical significance, survival and the diversity of the site; there are currently non-statutory frameworks for establishing the archaeological significance of underwater sites. Building on previous investigations, an archaeological assessment of the *London* and *King* sites was undertaken in October 2007 on behalf of the Port of London Authority. The results were then made available to English Heritage to assess the site for designation.

Importance of the *London*

The *London* was a Second Rate 'large ship' completed at Chatham in 1656 during the Interregnum. She is known to have participated in actions following the First Anglo-Dutch War (1652–4) and later formed part of an English squadron sent to collect Charles II from the Netherlands and restore him to his throne in an effort to end the anarchy which followed the death of Cromwell in 1658. The *London* was the flagship of Admiral Sir John Lawson and blew up on passage from Chatham to collect stores in March 1665.

It is important to consider the historic interest of a wreck and the period in which it was constructed and used. The *London* was built during a significant time of great political upheaval during the English Civil War. The Navy had sided with Parliament against the Crown, and the Commonwealth needed to build up a strong Navy to ensure its own survival. Ordnance and other finds have been identified on the *London* which, with the remains of the vessel, provide a unique insight into a ship built for the Commonwealth Navy under Cromwell.

There are some wreck categories which, in certain periods, are so scarce that all surviving examples that still retain some archaeological potential should be preserved. The age of a vessel is often closely linked to its rarity. The older a vessel is, for example, the fewer comparable vessels are likely to survive either in use or as wrecks, and the more likely it is to have historic interest. In 1652, during the First Anglo-Dutch War (1652–4), Parliament ordered the building of 10 new Second Rate ships. Only three of these ships were ever completed, the *London* being one. All were wrecked. The locations of the other two vessels, the *Richard* and the *Dunbar* are yet to be identified, although as both were also wrecked in the Thames, they are recorded as casualties in the NHRE database.[3] Therefore, the *London* was considered of extreme rarity suitable for designation.

The significance of a wreck may be enhanced by close historic association with documented important historical events or people, or by the supporting evidence of contemporary records or representations, including material already collated in the NHRE database, which plays a support role to the maritime archaeology team. In the case of the *London* there was a large range of historical information available to support the significance of the site in advance of designation. The loss of the *London* was recorded by Samuel Pepys in his diary entry for 9 March 1665:

> This morning is brought me to the office the sad newes of 'The London' in which Sir J. Lawson's men were all bringing her from Chatham to the Hope, and thence he was to go to sea in her; but a little a'this side the buoy of the Nower, she suddenly blew up. About 24 (men) and a woman that were in the round-house and coach saved; the rest, being above 300, drowned: the ship breaking all in pieces, with 80 pieces of brass ordnance. She lies sunk, with her round-house above water.

The contemporary Dutch artist, Willem van de Velde the Younger, also recorded the *London* in 1660 in two complementary ship portraits, now in London and Rotterdam (Fig 6.1).[4] Such recording was the more important, given the strained relations between England and the Netherlands at the time.

Site environment

The *London* is a relatively shallow site in just 10m of water. It is known from contemporary sources, such as Pepys' diary, that the ship blew up and it is likely that material lies scattered across the seabed. When a site is assessed for designation the degree of intactness of a wreck, the likelihood of the preservation of constructional and technological detail and the current condition of the remains is considered. Recent archaeological assessments have identified an abundance of loose material on the seabed in a remarkably well-preserved state. The two bronze guns reported to the receiver of wreck are particularly important. One of the guns is the only surviving piece by the noted London gunfounder Peter Gill, who appears in official records in 1594 and 1600,[5] it being fairly typical for guns to be reused at later periods. The other gun bears the crest of the Commonwealth and was cast specifically for the *London* in 1653/4. It is recorded the *London* had 76 guns fitted and historical sources reveal that nine of these were

Fig 6.1
The London,
a contemporary ship
'portrait' sketch by one
of the period's most noted
marine artists, Willem van
de Velde the Younger,
showing her elaborate
Baroque decorated counter-
stern, typical of the time,
and the disposition
of her guns.
(© Atlas van Stolk,
Rotterdam)

recovered prior to 1700. It is clear that further ordnance may remain at the site.

The nearby *King* site may represent a significant debris field scattered from the main wreck site by the force of the explosion, consistent with Pepys' description, and perhaps compromised by the remains of another vessel lost in the same position. This site is still under investigation to determine its true relationship to the main *London* site.

Importance of wrecked vessels

The importance of wrecked vessels can reflect the interest in their architectural design, decoration and craftsmanship, or their technological innovation or virtuosity, as well as how representative they are of contemporary ship types.[6] The *London* contains a combination of high-quality surviving features and technical elements. The site comprises an extensive range of structural elements, including fittings, armament and equipment, of a mid-17th-century warship. It offers the potential to provide important archaeological information in relation to the construction of Second Rate large ships.

Following this assessment English Heritage became aware that further uncontrolled salvage was planned on the site, possibly to target the remaining bronze guns. It was for this reason, as well as the clear importance of the site, that emergency designation was recommended to DCMS. The *London* represents a singular survivor of a ship from the Commonwealth Navy, a time when British naval power was emerging on the European stage; no other wreck

sites from this period have been identified. The *London* and *King* sites were designated by the Secretary of State, DCMS, in October 2008, and protected from the threat of salvage.

The future of the site

Designation is not the end of the process for the site. Once designation takes place it is a criminal offence to visit or work in a designated area without a licence granted by the appropriate secretary of state. The major threat posed by uncontrolled salvage is the removal of archaeological context, by which information is lost and cannot be recovered. Generally speaking licences from the secretary of state will only be issued to people who are considered to be competent and properly equipped to carry out operations appropriate to the historical and archaeological importance of a wreck and of any objects contained or formerly contained in a wreck (for example, site documentation and photography), so that the location and context of any artefacts seen or recovered are understood, and information is retained. A licensee for any site, not just the *London*, effectively takes on the role of a local steward for the site. Many licensees have built up relationships with sites and with English Heritage that span many years. Additionally, anyone may apply for a visitor licence to a designated wreck site since English Heritage policy is to encourage managed access rather than prohibit any access.

In addition English Heritage has commissioned further work to take place on the site by the contractor for archaeological services in relation to the PWA, currently Wessex Archaeology, to help us understand more about this fascinating and nationally important wreck, in particular to clarify its relationship to the *King* site. Each designated site is published in a report or series of reports, with information also being made available to the public through the NHRE records for each site (Fig 6.2).[7]

What is left to find out?

Full fathom five thy father lies,
Of his bones are coral made;
Those are pearls that were his eyes;
Nothing of him that doth fade,
But doth suffer a sea-change,
Into something rich and strange.

(William Shakespeare, *The Tempest*,
Act I, Scene II)

Fig 6.2

Clay pipe on the wreck of the London *in the Thames Estuary, just discernible in the typically silty conditions characteristic of the Thames. Poor visibility is just one of the challenges facing archaeological divers in UK waters, which are typically cold and murky. For example, the dynamic tides, currents and weather conditions which have historically contributed to wrecking events in the first place can also increase sand and silt mobility, making it difficult to see and photograph finds in context. (© Steve Ellis)*

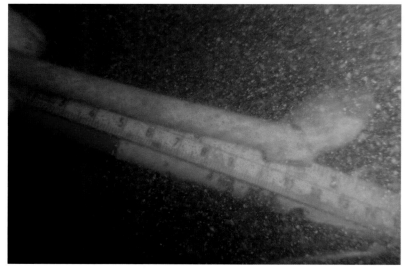

Where are we now?

The title of this book is *England's Shipwreck Heritage: from logboats to U-boats*, covering an enormous chronological sweep from the dawn of seafaring to the 20th century: it acts as a showcase for the achievements of the last 20 years of a unified maritime record for all of England, derived from a multitude of sources. It is not a 'stock-take' of the nation's wrecks, but a 'snapshot', for many individual stories have been omitted from the selection, particularly those which are well-known such as the story of the SS *Mendi*; likewise there remain more questions in gaining a greater understanding of maritime archaeology. Inclusion in this volume has been with the aim of demonstrating the varied links between shipwrecks and other forms of cultural heritage: monuments on land, historical figures and events, and works of literature and art, exploring the ways in which we can come to an understanding of the special interest and value of England's shipwreck heritage. Shipwrecks are integral to our understanding of our own archaeological, architectural and industrial heritage in ways that we have only just begun to understand, beyond the obvious connections with churchyard graves and monuments to those lost at sea in war and peace. The losses of specifically English types of vessel have been explored in relation to the terrestrial and maritime landscapes they served. However, shipwrecks in English waters cannot be seen in splendid isolation but as part of a common worldwide shipwreck heritage, part of which happens to lie within territorial waters, namely those of English and foreign ships engaged in international trade. Exploring the diversity of associations between maritime and terrestrial archaeology as well as using the data available on wrecks comparable in geographical location, type, manner of loss, cargo or other factors for profiling, permits the special interest and importance of any given shipwreck find to be assessed against a wide range of criteria, vital in the National Heritage Protection Plan.[8]

Any shipwreck find can be assessed for heritage protection under different kinds of legislation as appropriate: designation under the PWA; scheduling the buried remains of vessels under the Ancient Monuments Act 1979; or listing vessel structures permanently fixed to the ground or another structure. (Military aircraft and maritime graves are covered by non-heritage legislation that also has a heritage value in the Protection of Military Remains Act 1986.[9]) Designation practice for each piece of legislation has evolved its own set of criteria which contribute to the decisions by viewing the vessel in its wider context. Considerations of the special interest of vessel remains are, broadly speaking, governed by the vessel's age and rarity, which are closely interlinked, especially for those dating to before 1500, and for many vessels dating to between 1500 and 1815. Thereafter the survival of wreck remains increases exponentially so as to modify the criteria for determining special interest: rarity value is less of a consideration and associations concerning the vessel's relative historical importance in the national sense may take precedence, or considerations of representative value for vessels not otherwise represented as a preserved ship. For example, the period between 1815 and 1945 is characterised by rapid and frequent advances in ship technology, so that an early example of a particular technology might be of greater special interest than later examples; similarly, associations with particular historical events, not necessarily those of the two World Wars in which so many vessels were lost, may also increase the vessel's significance. By presenting a number of case studies in this book, it is hoped to enable a broader and deeper approach to the question of 'special interest'.

Shipwrecks form the cultural coral of the English coastal landscape: they may be seen as an organic part of that landscape, built to sail the seas and rivers into which they are now dissolving. This book can only be a 'snapshot' of the state of the national record at the time of writing. It is therefore useful to have a look at what where we are now, what we can do in the future, and what it means for England's shipwreck heritage.

Where do we go from here?

Undoubtedly, as more and more physical remains are exposed or located by divers the principal function of the national record increasingly becomes a mutually beneficial two-way flow of information: known data held by English Heritage is supplied to archaeologists, divers and local historians, while these and other interested parties supply English Heritage with further information about the wreck site, which then enters the public domain. The prime aim of this information flow is to make the data accessible to the public via published databases and print publication,[10] and the question of what constitutes 'special interest' is one that is becoming increasingly important.

One way of looking at it is to see the number of wrecks in the context of the number of other monuments. Standing at over 37,000 wrecks at the time of writing, the English Heritage National Record of the Historic Environment provides a superlative pool of matches and comparative examples from which to draw in the profiling of new finds. Shipwrecks in fact form the largest single category of recorded monuments: whether as documented casualties or as substantiated remains, they easily dwarf the 13,500 recorded churches of all denominations (including those no longer extant) included in the National Record of the Historic Environment.[11] This database remains dynamic with new additions as a result of internal research projects (for example, the Norwegian and Danish Wrecks Project, 2008), continuous formal data flows from external organisations (Receiver of Wreck droits, BMAPA reports) and externally funded projects (MEDIN Modern Wrecks Project, 2010).

The Modern Wrecks Project (Fig 6.3) brought the wreck record up-to-date in a 'history begins yesterday' approach, in line with other forms of historic monument recording: just as the criteria for listing have been extended to incorporate

buildings of post-1945 date, wreck recording has moved beyond the former cut-off point of the end of the Second World War (1945). As might be expected, losses since 1945 have dramatically declined, attributable not only to the end of the conflict but to the greater tonnage of modern vessels, capable of carrying more than their historic counterparts; the preference for air freighting (a trend which is now to some extent being reversed) and continuing advances in safety at sea. Nevertheless this project contributed over 500 new records to the wreck database and revealed new patterns in the distribution, manner and type of vessels lost: some of these patterns are already historical in themselves, for example, a peak in the numbers of trawlers from Eastern Europe in the 1970s and 1980s.[12]

The Modern Wrecks Project overlapped naturally with another recording programme in 2010, devoted to abandoned vessels on the foreshore, the National Hulks Assemblage Project undertaken by the Museum of London Archaeology for English Heritage.[13] Because of their relatively recent date, often left to rot in the post-war period when past economic repair or service, abandoned hulks have hitherto attracted little interest and are little understood. As recollections of such vessels and specific histories of individual craft are passing out of

Fig 6.3
The wreck of the fishing vessel Admiral van Tromp *(1525324), recorded during the Modern Wrecks Project in 2010, lies just east of the Black Nab on the North Yorkshire coast, near Whitby. Her remains are testament to the power of the sea, for she was lost as recently as 1976. She was still intact by the following year, but by 1989 was a mere skeleton of a ship, hard to find except at low water.*
(K020590)

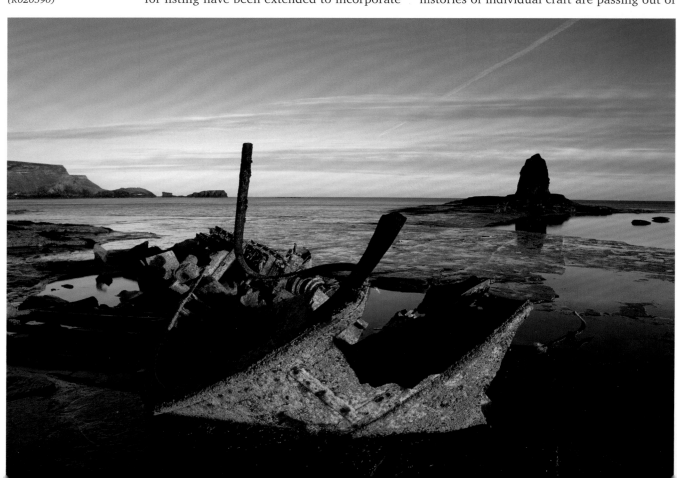

living memory, a section of recent industrial history is in danger of being lost very quickly, particularly given the threats to these sites from vandalism as well as environmental forces. These two projects alone illustrate that maritime archaeology is a subject which naturally still has enormous potential for growth, in terms of both the discovery of physical remains and the exploitation of documentary records (Fig 6.4).

What more can we find out?

If there is a certain urgency to the National Hulks Assemblage Project, part of the fascination of maritime archaeology is the breadth and diversity not only of what we know, but of what we do not yet know. As a single example, vessels lost in inland waterways, both natural (rivers, fens, lakes and the Norfolk Broads) and man-made (canals, cuts, docks and dykes) are poorly represented in the national record, yet these losses also emphasise the strong links between terrestrial and marine archaeology, and would readily fulfil the criteria of special interest in terms of the national narrative, the group value with the inland waterway itself, and of rarity, since we know of so few examples (yet they must once have been relatively common).

To take a handful of potential areas of exploration in terms of both documentary research and vessel remains: why have relatively few warship wrecks been found, despite this group being among the best-reported of all wrecks in English waters, and how can we use the absence of evidence as a measure of archaeological potential? To date, around 68 warship wreck sites have been definitively identified out of approximately 580 documented warship losses (excluding submarines and civilian ships requisitioned as auxiliaries) in English waters, representing some 12 per cent of the total: 480 currently remain confined to the written record. The remainder comprise sites either with corresponding documented records offering a strong, but unconfirmed, identity for the wreck; or seen to be warships but for which no identity has been put forward.[14] Warships provide the context for other forms of maritime archaeological material: the physical evidence for battlefields, which are, of course, monuments in their own right. Expended ammunition, from cannonballs to torpedoes and mines, are also archaeological material, but scattered and little understood or related to the wreckage they may have caused. Given the breadth and range of sustained actions over the centuries, notably the almost constant state of warfare with the French up to and including

Fig 6.4
An example of a mystery which has not yet been fully solved: the skeleton of an unidentified wreck on the foreshore at Cleethorpes, resembling the carcass of a great beast, seen from landward (1450012). The exposed 'backbone' of ribs and framing has been heavily colonised by bladder wrack, while some nails still remain embedded in the sternpost. This wreck may possibly be that of the Elfrida (1351931), a wooden schooner with iron bolts which matches her dimensions, although this wreck is said to have foundered offshore in this area in 1909. Was this a mistake, or was the vessel raised and beached here – a common question for similar unidentified hulks around the country? (Photograph reproduced by courtesy of Hugh Winfield, North East Lincolnshire Council)

the Napoleonic wars, maritime battlefield recording remains an area ripe for exploration and becomes significant in recording the tangible remains of events representing key narratives in our island's history. If this is the case for warships, our knowledge of privateers, for which sparse documentation survives, is even more partial.

We have also seen that our knowledge of maritime accidents in the distant past derives piecemeal from scant surviving evidence, both physical and documentary. As an example, even allowing for the post-medieval growth in trade, it seems barely credible that only 338 vessels have so far been retrieved from documents dated from 1150 to 1450. Closer examination of medieval data reveals clusters of wrecks for some years and none at all for others. The reigns of Edward II (1307–27) and Edward III (1327–77), kings avidly concerned with maritime matters, provide evidence for just over one-half the 338, with evidence of 50 and 128 wrecks, respectively. By contrast Edward III's successor, Richard II, seemed less concerned to intervene in wreck cases than his predecessors. Later records do not necessarily mean, therefore, that more documents have survived,[15] and, the further from centres of royal and administrative power, the less chance of surviving records, or even of any record ever having been made, of a wreck event: medieval wreck accounts are heavily biased towards population centres on the Channel and North Sea coast, which is also true in the early post-medieval period. There is a lower density of wrecks in the Bristol Channel and the Severn Estuary, as well as on the Cumbrian coastline, explained not by lack of navigational hazards or lower volumes of traffic, but by their distance from centres of power (Fig 6.5).[16]

Similarly wrecks from trades lower down the socio-economic scale, such as fish and coal (before the advent of large colliery owners) were overlooked in contemporary records in favour of more substantial vessels. There is also a small and easily overlooked group of wrecks of passage and fishing vessels chartered for leisure purposes from the mid-18th century onwards, principally for sightseeing at the burgeoning new resorts, such as Weymouth and Scarborough, but also for fishing trips, as at Berwick-upon-Tweed.[17] They make an interesting group and would do much to illuminate the development of the seaside resort as well as to provide context for other wrecks. The more documentary evidence

is collated, the more comparative data there is to draw on even if it cannot provide an exact identification for finds.

Understanding these limitations is a first step towards beginning to quantify how much data has been lost and how much archaeological potential there might be.

What questions can we ask in future?

What is the point of retrieving all these data from the past? A significant trend being developed in current research is *areas of marine archaeological potential* (AMAP), vital to English Heritage's National Heritage Protection Plan. There are several ways in which AMAPs can be predicted, but each method has its drawbacks and a more accurate model can only be produced by combining methodologies. Areas of known maritime hazards form the most obvious line of enquiry; the historical patterning of wreck reports from particular areas is another useful tool, since it may suggest a profile which may not coincide with that suggested by geophysical evidence (for example, at periods before the existence of the hazard, such as the silting up of the approaches to Liverpool). Some hazards encountered on major trade routes, such as the Goodwin Sands, cannot be bypassed, but others are easily avoided. For example, the many sandbanks in the Wash at first sight suggest significant potential for revealing shipwreck remains;[18] however, in practice, ships avoided this estuarine 'cul-de-sac' unless making directly for one of the Wash ports, such as Boston or King's Lynn, principally local fishing and cargo vessels. This knowledge is useful in profiling the archaeological potential of the Wash: the likelihood of particular vessel types rather than others, and that much of the archaeological material of interest is likely to come from Boston and King's Lynn, deriving from their medieval heyday as international trading ports tapping into the network of the mighty Hanseatic League. This material might include cogs and hulks of any nationality operating within the Hanseatic League, and thus be of intrinsic historic importance. Evidence for Hanse ships is scarce but is hinted at in some of the surviving wreck records from the Middle Ages, principally on the North Sea coasts.[19]

Throughout the book it has been stressed that partial data is a natural outcome of the survival patterns for written evidence of wrecks.

Fig 6.5
View of the Severn upstream from Frampton-on-Severn; the river remains tidal as far inland as Tewkesbury and represents a landscape whose wreck archaeology is relatively poorly understood, as is also true for the Severn Estuary and Bristol Channel in general, with many gaps in the documentary record which have yet to be filled. This section of the river, well silted with sandbanks, was difficult to navigate for larger vessels. Small medieval vessels found the Severn navigable, though not without difficulty: in 1284 two small cargo vessels were lost working from Bristol to Gloucester (1453990; 1453992) and in 1343 a Spanish ship driven ashore on the Forest of Dean side 'by the violence of the sea' was plundered by locals (1450476). In 1827 the Gloucester and Sharpness Canal, cutting off the loop of the river, was opened (visible in the photograph), enabling ocean-going vessels to reach Gloucester Docks in relative ease. This in turn led to a rise in ships lost in English waters bound into or from Gloucester.
(NMR 23587/24)

Likewise, historic wrecking patterns can only be useful for periods with enough existing data to be a sufficiently reliable predictor. The pursuit of documentary evidence thus remains a vital tool in predicting archaeological potential. It also suggests that important trading routes will be key indicators of archaeological potential: data for these is not so dependent on survival of documents, and is therefore useful in predicting the age, probable cargoes and likely nationalities of the vessels involved. In the same way analysis of historical patterns of wrecking caused by warfare and privateering looks likely to be helpful in demonstrating the predominant date ranges of wrecks within a particular geographical area.

So even as marine survey and archaeological techniques grow more sophisticated, they have not displaced research in primary sources. In fact the possibilities for documentary research are also increasingly sophisticated, so that the two more naturally converge. Both are driven by technology, at once complex yet simple: for documentary research, the ability to access online archives, official sources, and last but not least, user-generated content (photographs, volunteer transcription programmes and personal research projects) worldwide. Likewise, the increasing sophistication of imaging and survey tools, providing excellent 3D images of wrecks on the seabed (multibeam imaging, for example), has enhanced the ability to identify and interpret wrecks remotely, while technological advances permitting diving at greater depths and further offshore have increased the 'strike-rate' of reporting and identification. The question then is to pull all these things together to provide a 'one-stop shop' of information and to be able to assess and profile wrecks against one another and in terms of their historic environment, terrestrial as well as marine.

The themes discussed in this 'snapshot' are thus ripe for further exploration, and may serve as case studies in determining the special interest of vessels put forward for protected status. Equally importantly, it has enabled us to focus on identifying groups of wrecks which are little understood and are likely to be of exceptional interest in terms of their diversity and links with key narratives of national and international history: wrecks which are typically 'English' in type, cargo and trade, and those which have features in common with others of their type worldwide. In the latter category are wrecks of slavers, foreign warships, convict vessels and trading ships belonging to early international trading networks or companies, such as the Hanseatic League or the Hudson's Bay Company (as well as the English and Dutch East India companies). Likewise, the potential for exploring relationships with the wider archaeological landscape has only been hinted at in this book and remains immense, encompassing industrial heritage, commemorative monuments, dockyards and other elements of naval heritage, wrecks which occasioned the building of lighthouses and siting of lifeboat stations, wrecks which damaged new quayside installations and wrecks which took place in the same severe storms which also damaged terrestrial monuments. These themes also suggest the wide range of interests and disciplines which make maritime archaeology such a perennial source of fascination to those fortunate enough to be involved: not only history, naval history, archaeology, seabed survey and diving, but also social, military, industrial and local history, climatology, economics, languages and dialects, gun founding, literature, archival research, photography, mapping and aerial photography interpretation, marine biology, and a whole wealth of other subjects. Few areas of archaeology can attract so many contributors from so wide a range of fields, and you do not have to be an expert: a photograph of a recently exposed wreck, encountered at random while walking the dog, is as important a resource as

a highly technical maritime survey or the tracing of a long-hidden document, and may reveal the next candidate for designation.

Finally, in showcasing the diversity of England's shipwreck heritage, it is hoped to dispel the stereotype that shipwrecks are typically rare and generally ancient, being lost with untold treasure in dramatic circumstances and found under equally dramatic circumstances. Only a handful of wrecks fit this stereotype, such as, perhaps, the *Rooswijk*: in reality our shipwreck heritage is far more interesting and diverse. From the humble passage boat and coastal fishing vessel to the grand ocean liner maintaining a link between the Old World and the New, they have an everyday aspect to them far removed from the concept of the 'treasure wreck'. Yet in lacing a virtual dot-to-dot around England's coastline and beyond, these ruined ships have become treasures in their own right: a window into a common maritime heritage (Fig 6.6).

Fig 6.6
Little is known about the 'temporary wrecks' during and shortly after the Second World War, of which a good example is the Davaar *(1524836), shown beached for breaking up in September 1943. Originally built as a Clyde steam ferry in 1885, she was requisitioned to be sunk as a blockship at Newhaven in the event of invasion: instead the* Steady *(911965) inadvertently fulfilled that role when she was mined at the entrance to the harbour. Earlier photography reveals the* Davaar *moored at Newhaven in March 1942. Later that month she sustained minor damage during an air raid, after which it is unclear what subsequently happened to her, for she disappeared from photography by June 1942. The anti-invasion beach scaffolding is seen here neatly cut, to allow the* Davaar *to be beached: something which, perhaps, might not have happened earlier in the war when the threat of invasion was at its height.*
(RAF Photography TQ 4500/04, 05-SEP-1943)

APPENDIX
Contact details

http://www.english-heritage.org.uk

http://list.english-heritage.org.uk/:
National Heritage List for England (NHLE)

For details of existing wreck records

http://www.pastscape.org.uk:
National Record of the Historic Environment
(NRHE) records

To report a wreck

English Heritage Local Offices:

East Midlands:

English Heritage
44 Derngate
Northampton NN1 1UH
Telephone: 01604 735400
Email: eastmidlands@english-heritage.org.uk

East of England:

English Heritage
Brooklands
24 Brooklands Avenue
Cambridge CB2 8BU
Telephone: 01223 582700
Email: eastofengland@english-heritage.org.uk

London:

English Heritage
1 Waterhouse Square
138–142 Holborn
London EC1N 2ST
Telephone: 02079 733000
Email: london@english-heritage.org.uk

North East:

English Heritage
Bessie Surtees House
41–44 Sandhill
Newcastle-upon-Tyne NE1 3JF
Telephone: 01912 691200
Email: northeast@english-heritage.org.uk

North West:

English Heritage
3rd Floor Canada House
3 Chepstow Street
Manchester M1 5FW
Telephone: 01612 421400
Email: northwest@english-heritage.org.uk

South East:

English Heritage
Eastgate Court
195–205 High Street
Guildford GU1 3EH
Telephone: 01483 252000
Email: southeast@english-heritage.org.uk

South West:

English Heritage
29 Queen Square
Bristol BS1 4ND
Telephone: 01179 750700
Email: southwest@english-heritage.org.uk

West Midlands:

English Heritage
The Axis
10 Holliday Street
Birmingham B1 1TG
Telephone: 01216 256820
Email: westmidlands@english-heritage.org.uk

Yorkshire:

English Heritage
37 Tanner Row
York YO1 6WP
Telephone: 01904 601901
Email: yorkshire@english-heritage.org.uk

English Heritage Archive:

English Heritage
The Engine House
Fire Fly Avenue
Swindon SN2 2EH
Telephone: 01793 414700
Enquiry and research services: 01793 414600
Email: archive@english-heritage.org.uk

For applications to access England's Protected Wreck sites:

English Heritage
Fort Cumberland
Fort Cumberland Road
Eastney, Portsmouth PO4 9LD

Outside England

Northern Ireland:

Department of the Environment for Northern Ireland
Clarence Court
10–18 Adelaide Street
Belfast BT2 8GB
Telephone: 02890 540540
Email: enquiries@doeni.gov.uk
Web: http://www.doeni.gov.uk

Scotland:

Historic Scotland
The Scheduling Team
Historic Scotland
Longmore House
Salisbury Place
Edinburgh EH9 1SH
Telephone: 01316 688766
Email: hs.inspectorate@scotland.gsi.gov.uk
Web: http://www.historic-scotland.gov.uk/

Wales:

Cadw
Welsh Government
Plas Carew
Unit 5/7 Cefn Coed
Parc Nantgarw
Cardiff CF15 7QQ
Telephone: 01443 336000
Email: cadw@wales.gsi.gov.uk
Web: http://cadw.wales.gov.uk

Royal Commission on the Ancient and Historical
Monuments of Wales
Library and Enquiries Service
National Monuments Record of Wales
Plas Crug
Aberystwyth SY23 1NJ
Telephone: 01970 621200
Email: nmr.wales@rchamw.gov.uk
Web: http://www.rcahmw.gov.uk/

For further training

The Nautical Archaeology Society
Fort Cumberland
Fort Cumberland Road
Portsmouth PO4 9LD
Telephone: 01239 2818419
Web: http://www.nauticalarchaeologysociety.org/

To report material recovered from wreck sites

Receiver of Wreck
Spring Place
105 Commercial Road
Southampton S015 1EG
Telephone: 02380 329474
Email: row@mcga.gov.uk
Web: http://www.dft.gov.uk/mca/mcga07-home/
emergencyresponse/mcga-receiverofwreck.htm

NOTES

Unless otherwise stated, the date of latest accession of URLs is given as 16 October 2012.

Chapter 1 The hazards of the natural environment

1 The Channel Navigation Information Service, first instituted in 1972.
2 A distinguishing feature, not always necessarily dangerous in itself, may symbolise the threat posed by the hazard, as in the case of Wolf Rock. Popular etymology has it that the rock is named for the eerie howling noise formerly produced by the wind whistling through fissures in the rock, but it is now considered more likely to be an assimilation of Cornish *Gulfe*, still in use as the name of the rock in the 16th century, meaning 'bill' or 'beak' (the metaphor of teeth for rocks is an ancient one), towards an English word that sounded similar and equally represented a threat (Breeze 2005). Similarly, older spellings of *Eddystone* gradually settled into the version known today by analogy with the situation of stone itself, some miles out to sea with the waters swirling around it, and understood as such by 1724, when Daniel Defoe referred to this explanation of its name in *A Tour through the Whole Island of Great Britain: From London to Land's End*.
3 Haslett and Bryant (2004).
4 *1607. A true report of certain wonderfull ouerflowings of Waters, now lately in Summerset-shire, Norfolke and other places of England* … Edward White, printer, 1607.
5 Tentatively identified as Haisbro' or Haisborough Sand, possibly a transcription error; Haisborough remains one of the largest sandbanks off the coast of Norfolk, historically a regular shipwreck site.
6 One example being *A True and perfect relation of the great damages done by the late great tempest, and overflowing of the tyde upon the coasts of Lincolnshire and county of Norfolk: also an accompt of the ships cast away, houses beaten down, and men, women and children drowned by the late inundation*, printed at London in the year 1671.

7 *More strange nevves: of wonderfull accidents hapning by the late ouerflowings of waters, in Summerset-shire, Gloucestershire, Norfolke, and other places of England: with a true relation of the townes names that are lost, and the number of persons drowned, with other reports of accidents that were not before discouered: happening about Bristow and Barstable* printed at London: By W[illiam] I[aggard] for Edward White, 1607.
8 *See* note 6 above.
9 Risdon (1620, quoted in Haslett and Bryant 2004, 84–5).
10 'In January last [towards the end of the moneth], the sea at a flowing water meeting with Land-floudes, strove so violently together, that bearing down all things … a rupture made into Somerset-shire. No sooner was this furious invader entred, but he got up hie into the Land, and encountrin with the river Severn, they both boiled in such pride that many Miles [to the quantity of XX in length, and 4 or 5 at least in bredth] were in a short time swalowd up in this torrent'. *1607. A true report of certain wonderfull ouerflowings of Waters, now lately in Summerset-shire, Norfolke and other places of England* … Edward White, printer, 1607, accessed via http://eebo.chadwyck.com.
11 Indeed, such a pamphlet was rushed out in 1704: *An Exact Relation of The Late Dreadful Tempest: Or, A Faithful Account of The Most Remarkable Disaster Which Happened On That Occasion. Faithfully Collected By An Ingenious Hand, To Preserve The Memory Of So Terrible A Judgement*, 1704, accessed via http://eebo.chadwyck.com.
12 Recorded lives lost: 1,406 minimum, 1,819 maximum; this takes no account of any of the vessels where 'all hands' were lost without quoting any precise figures. A number of at least 2,000 appears plausible. Source: NRHE AMIE database 2009. Wheeler (2003) suggests that over 1,500 lives were lost.
13 Source for statistics: NRHE AMIE database 2009. *Canterbury*, wreck event, 1366318; *Eagle*, wreck event, 1164696, possible remains 911783; *Northumberland*, identified site, 1082118; *Resolution*,

wreck event, 902550; possible remains, (*Norman's Bay* wreck site) 1441075; *Restoration*, identified site, 1082116; and *Stirling Castle*, identified site, 1082115. *See also* the section '*Rooswijk* and *Stirling Castle*: Two Goodwin Sands Wrecks', in this chapter, for more on the *Stirling Castle*.
14 1432062.
15 Defoe (1704, 133–4).
16 London, Printed for F Thorn, near Fleet-street, 1705, accessed via http://eebo.chadwyck.com.
17 *Weazel*, 1494029; *Dainty Cruiser*, 1494038; *Happy Merchant*, 1494050; *Goodhope*, 1494051; *Swallow*, 1494052.
18 For 1309 *see* Reed (2002) and for 1408 Brazell (1968).
19 1709: 1481701; 1739–40: 1442925; 1443074; 1443076; 1443079; 1443080; 1456394; 1456395; 1456396.
20 1541475.
21 16 February 1709: *Out Letters (Customs)*, XV, 186–7, from 'Warrant Books: February 1709, 16–28', in *Calendar of Treasury Books, 1709*, vol. 23, 1949, 78–86, scanned and accessed via http://www.british-history.ac.uk/report.aspx?compid=90802.
22 1443074.
23 *Sherborne Mercury*, no. 151, 8 January 1739–40 [OS/NS, respectively]; 1456395/1456396.
24 1442925.
25 Officer (2009–11).
26 *Nouvelles d'Amsterdam*, 29 January 1740 [NS], 2.
27 *Kentish Post, or Canterbury News-letter*, no. 2,313, 5–9 January 1739–40 [OS/NS]; *Sherborne Mercury*, no. 151, 8 January 1739–40 [OS/NS].
28 *Newcastle Courant*, no. 6,904, 4 January 1809, 4; keel recorded at 1399051; *Hope* at 1399052; and the keel in Sunderland Roads at 1399488.
29 *Lloyd's List*, 31 January 1809, no. 4,323.
30 1406663.
31 *Durham County Advertiser*, no. 490, 24 January 1824, 3.
32 Richardson (1846, 233–6).

33 *Newby*, 1362127; representative record for the unconfirmed number of coal keels lost in the same incident, 1534592; representative record for the unknown number of harbour craft also lost, 1534593; *see* note 31 for source.

34 As a general term: variants on this name might be 'Ship News' or 'Marine Intelligence'.

35 Source: NRHE AMIE database 2009.

36 Source: NHRE AMIE database 2009. As might be expected, in the northern hemisphere greater numbers of wrecks occur during the autumn/winter season, from October to March, when bad weather is statistically more likely in English waters, than during the other six months of the year.

37 *Lloyd's List*, 15 October 1824, no. 5,951.

38 Source: NRHE AMIE database 2009.

39 *Lloyd's List*, 19 November 1824, no. 5,961; *Juno*, at Birling Gap, 902735; *Mary Ann* near Liverpool, 1360184.

40 1494484.

41 1352137.

42 *Lloyd's List*, 26 November 1824, no. 5,963.

43 *Lloyd's List*, 24 December 1824, no. 5,971.

44 973124.

45 *Leeuwarder Courant*, 7 December 1824, accessed via http://www.archiefleeuwardercourant.nl/. In fact, the issue ran for four pages, half of the front page being devoted to stocks.

46 Source: English Heritage NRHE AMIE database, 2010.

47 *Le Nicholas* of Bayonne, 1449187; *CPR*, Edward III, vol. XV, 1370–74, 176, membrane 27d; Larn and Larn (1977, 31), refers to a vessel lost 'near Sandwich', in the *CPR* for Edward I, in the year 1298, but this does not refer specifically to the Goodwin Sands. This 1298 wreck is recorded at 1178212.

48 For example, John Twyne, *De Rebus Albionicis, Britannicis, atque Anglicis commentariorum libri duo* (1590) referring to their supposed origin as an island overwhelmed to become a sandbank; William Lambarde, *A perambulation of Kent, conteining the description, hystorie, and customes of that shire; written in the yeere 1570, first published in the year 1576*; William Camden, *Britain, or, a Chorographicall Description of the most flourishing Kingdomes, England, Scotland, and Ireland, 1610, translated by R Gough, 1806*.

49 *CSP.Dom. Edward, Mary and Elizabeth*, 1547–80, no. 97.

50 *CSP.Dom. James I*, 1623–25, vol. 155, no. 28.

51 Source: English Heritage NRHE AMIE database, 2010.

52 *CSP.Dom. Charles II*, vol. 234, no. 111.

53 The *Red Lion*, 1178532; *Golden Lion*, 902036; Dutch vessel, 1502351; *Pegasus*, 881122. There may well have been more, but as has already been stated, the survival of documentary evidence owes a great deal to chance, while other wrecks are occasionally attributed to the Goodwins on tenuous grounds, for example two ships going to Moscow in 1598, recorded in the NRHE as 902046 and 1364517.

54 *Merchant of Venice*, Act III, Scene I.

55 *See* the discussion in this chapter of the *Stirling Castle* in section '*Rooswijk* and *Stirling Castle*'.

56 Attempts have also been made by the present author, independently of other researchers, to trace an origin for the story, but without success; *see also* Rhodes (2007). Even the date of 13 February 1748 attributed to the original wreck of the *Lady Luvibund* seems to be incorrect, for a storm was reported in the Deal area on 16 February 1748. Nevertheless, the NRHE holds a record for this ship (881145) for the sake of completeness, since, although acknowledged as legendary, it appears in many lists, eg Larn and Larn (1996).

57 Probable remains, 904880; account of wreck event, 1535509.

58 *See* this chapter '*Rooswijk* and *Stirling Castle*: Two Goodwin Sands wrecks', for more on the *Stirling Castle*.

59 The years 1756, 1759 and 1778 are skewed by the lack of extant *Lloyd's Lists* for those years, so any wrecks on the Goodwins or elsewhere will have been reported in other sources. In 1806 there were genuinely no losses on the Goodwin Sands reported in *Lloyd's List*, although it should still be said that there may have been wrecks of smaller fishing and coasting vessels which were generally not reported in *Lloyd's* (which, additionally, is true regardless of date).

60 Source: English Heritage NRHE AMIE data, 2010, based on 790 recorded casualties and 67 recorded sites associated with the Goodwin Sands, North Sand Head, South Sand Head, Kellett Gut and Gull Stream; Merritt *et al* (2007, 37).

61 *East Goodwin* Lightship, 904873; *South Goodwin* Lightship, 901832; charting information from the United Kingdom Hydrographic Office (UKHO).

62 1524144; *see* http://www.britishpathe.com/record.php?id=32935 for footage of this wreck site.

63 1616 wreck, 902064, *CSP.Dom. James I*, 1611–18, vol. 87, no. 2; 1621 wreck, 902060, *CSP.Dom. James I*, 1619–23, vol. 121, nos 47 and 47i; wreck of second ship of Hoorn, 902055, *CSP.Dom. James I*, 1619–123, vol. 111, no. 57, respectively.

64 895010; Thomas Trott, *Parliamentary Papers*, Vol. VII, Report of a Select Committee on the Cinque-Port Pilots, Minutes of Evidence, no. 41, quoted in Macfie (1984, 134).

65 896239; Craig (nd.).

66 Bower (nd).

67 *Gazelle*, 881205; Hill (2007, 451). In this source the tallow is described as of Russian origin, but the remainder of the *Gazelle*'s cargo appears to have been the product of the Australian stock-rearing industry, such as hides and wool, and there is no reason to suppose that the tallow, as animal fat, did not also originate from Australia. All these goods were non-perishable and well able to survive the long journey from Australia. Although Baltic Russia was also a principal source of tallow, Australia exported tallow for candles during the 19th century, and it remains an Australian export to the present day. St Augustine of England, Ramsgate, 469510.

68 1451382.

69 *Kentish Post, or Canterbury News-letter*, 29 December to 2nd January 1739/40 [NS], no. 2,311.

70 The French-language *Suite des Nouvelles d'Amsterdam*, 26 January 1740 [NS], 2.

71 According to Old Style in England; 11 January New Style as used on the Continent.

72 *See*, for example, Lamb and Frydendahl (1991, 170).

73 *Kentish Post, or Canterbury News-letter*, 5 to 9 January 1740 [NS], no. 2,313.

74 Officer (2009–11); *see* note 70 for source.

75 1443081.

76 1443086 and 1443087.

77 *See* note 72 for source.

78 Reed (2002); *see also* section 'Early Extreme Weather Events', in this chapter.

79 *Sherborne Mercury*, 8 January 1739/40 [OS/NS, respectively], no. 151; 1456395, 1456396.

80 Sample record: 442938.

81 *See* note 69.

82 *See* note 79. Hendrik Hop wrote: *Dat men des anderen daags enige stukken hout op het water had sien swemmen. En onder anderen een kist had opgenomen, behelsende verscheidenen brieven.* [Some pieces of wreck had been seen floating on the water the other day; some persons had taken up a chest, containing various letters.] Ex. inf. Andrea Otte, Rijksdienst voor het Cultureel Erfgoed, 13 August 2009.

83 *See*, for example, the loss of the *Halsewell* (904656) where the sailors 'furled their top-sails, but could not furl their courses, the snow falling thick, and freezing as it fell' ('Appendix to the Chronicle', *Annual Register*, 1786, 224).

84 *Loosdrecht*, 1451429; *Meermond*, 1376658; Wessex Archaeology (2006).
85 Lamb and Frydendahl (1991, 80).
86 *Swift*, 1339844. *Newcastle Courant*, 2 February 1805, no. 6,695, 4.
87 881150.
88 Dutch vessels continued to trade with the Dutch East Indies after the demise of the VOC in 1800, and likewise continued to be informally designated as 'East Indiamen'. Their trade routes and cargoes were similar, but they were no longer part of a state-sponsored enterprise. Such a ship was the *Jonkheer Meester van de Wall van Puttershoek* (918804) wrecked in Cornwall in 1867 and the last recorded Dutch 'East Indiaman' to be lost in English waters.
89 Source: NRHE database 2010. The situation appears to be largely reversed with English East Indiamen, but not quite to such a dramatic extent. Of those English East India ships whose voyage details are known, 17 were outward-bound while 24 were homeward-bound to London or, later, Liverpool.
90 2009–10; www.maritiemdigitaal.nl.
91 1082115. The *Stirling Castle* is the only one of the three known – and designated – wreck sites from that storm to have undergone comprehensive archaeological investigation.
92 Defoe (1704).
93 Perkins (1979).
94 Larn and Larn (1995); Dunkley (2005).
95 *See* note 62.
96 881141; *Nouvelles d'Amsterdam* du mardi 26 janvier 1740, 2.
97 Lambert Doomer, *Steilküsten und Klippen von Wight,* hand drawing from the Atlas Blaeu, XIX, 146, Österreichisches Nationalbibliothek, repr. in Isle of Wight History Centre, 'Earliest Known Scenes of the Isle of Wight', accessed via http://freespace.virgin.net/iw.history/iwscenes/dutch.htm.
98 Based on research in the NRHE AMIE database, 2009.
99 Source: NRHE AMIE database, 2009.
100 895874.
101 *Varvassi*, 1521915.
102 *Teamwork*, 1522568; Bruce (2008, 4); source: UK Hydrographic Office *SeaZone* database, 2007 refresh.
103 [NS], ie Dutch reckoning; *see* account of the *Rooswijk* elsewhere in this chapter for explanation of the discrepancies between English and Dutch dates at this period; note, however, that the discrepancy between the two was 10 days in the 17th century, rather than 11, as in the 18th century.
104 *Kampen*, 805298; *Vliegende Draak*, 896133.
105 [OS], ie English reckoning.
106 *CSP.Dom.* Charles I, 1627–8, vol. LXXXII, nos 6 and 18, respectively.
107 'The Dutch East India Company's Shipping between the Netherlands and Asia 1595–1795', Institute of Netherlands History, accessed via http://www.inghist.nl/Onderzoek/Projecten/DAS/search.
108 *CSP.Dom.* Charles I, 1627–8, vol. XCII, no. 36.
109 *CSP.Dom.* Charles I, 1627–8, vol. CXIII, no. 11 and 1628–9, vol. CXLII, nos 14 and 106.
110 *Moon*, 901997; Spanish ship from Sanlucar lost off the Lizard, 1318138.
111 Sources: NRHE AMIE database 2010; SeaZone, 2007 refresh data.
112 HMS *Assurance*, 1082105; HMS *Pomone*, designated area 1082106; part of site outside designated area 767332.
113 Tomalin *et al* (2000).
114 Bingeman (2001).
115 805314.
116 899479; as described in Tomalin *et al* (2000).
117 805319; *see also* note 111.
118 Amsterdam ship 1513791; French banker, 1228525.
119 Seventeenth-century site, 1121972; Bronze Age assemblage, 1439037.
120 Though rare, wreck-on-wreck collisions were reported with some regularity, often the result of an unreported or undiscovered recent wreck, although on occasion the collision could be with a much older or a known wreck. There were 16 reported wreck-on-wreck collisions out of 765 known collisions between 1700 and 1850. Source: NHRE AMIE database, 2010. More common, although usually less lethal to vessel or crew, was the snagging or loss of fishing gear on a submerged wreck or other feature, leading to the identification of 'fishermen's fasteners'. Some of these 'fasteners' have since been recognised as wrecks.
121 *Texaco Caribbean*, bow section, 1523168; stern section, 1523172; *Brandenburg*, 1523176; *Niki*, 1523184.
122 Source: NRHE AMIE data, 2011.
123 Reprinted in Kowaleski (2001).
124 Testimony of Harry Angwyne, reprinted in Pool (1959, 189–91).
125 1446462.
126 Source: NRHE AMIE data 2011.
127 1344/5 wreck, 1548883; *Adventure*, 1811, 905203.
128 905221.
129 Reprinted in Pool (1959, 163–228).
130 1463471; 1465921; 1466068; 1466071; 1466231.
131 1461840.
132 1461854.
133 1082127. For further discussion of the legacy of the *St Anthony* wreck, please *see* Chapter 5, 'Whatever Happened to Elizabeth Jane?'
134 1181945; *A full account of the late Shipwreck of the Ship called The PRESIDENT which was castaway in Mountz-Bay in Cornwal on the 4th of February last … by William Smith and John Harshfield, the only Persons that escaped in the said Wreck,* accessed via Early English Books Online at http://eebo.chadwyck.com.
135 919172.
136 *Tyne Mercury*, 12 January, 1808, no. 294, 4.
137 1496831; *CSP.Dom.* James I, vol. XI, 1623–25, vol. CLIX, no. 11, 24 February 1624, 159. In pre-decimal currency, pounds, shillings, and pence were often expressed in Latin form, thus *libri, sestercii, denarii*, abbreviated respectively to *l s d*.
138 *San Salvador*, 1449236; *Dollar Wreck*, 1449231.
139 1082108.
140 *Hercules*, 920388; *Neutralist*, 921065.
141 *Auguste Padre*, 1449240; *L'Union*, 1204382; *Arwenack*, 922194.
142 *Royal Cornwall Gazette*, 31 January 1862, no. 3058, 6.
143 *Royal Cornwall Gazette*, 19 December 1862, no. 3104, 4.
144 *See* note 134.
145 Luttrell (1857, 323).
146 1082128.
147 *London Gazette*, 25 to 28 November 1721, no. 6,011, 1–2.
148 *St. Andrew*, 1371532, as reported in *Lloyd's List*, 9 October 1840, no. 8,296, column 8; *Richard Montgomery*, 904735.
149 904773.
150 *See* the section 'A Dangerous Flat and Fatal', in this chapter.
151 1082118; Wessex Archaeology (2010b).
152 Seaton Carew wreck 1312495, discussed in Chapter 4, 'Colliers'; Littlehampton wreck, 1466504; Praa Sands, 1527009.
153 *See* 'Rooswijk and Stirling Castle: Two Goodwin Sands wrecks', in this chapter; *Royal George*, 805615.
154 1082114.
155 *Edam II*, 832248; *Ambassador*, 832158.
156 970892, *Durham County Advertiser*, 22 April 1815, no. 33, 3.
157 1387701, based on *Newcastle Courant*, 18 November 1780, no. 5,433, 4.
158 895010; *Lloyd's List*, 15 November 1825, no. 6,064.
159 894958; *Lloyd's List*, reports 16, 17 and 18 November, in issue no. 5,646, 20, 21, 22 and 23 November 1821 in issue no. 5,647.

160 *Royal Anne Galley*, 1082128; *John and Richard*, 1375462, quoted in *Tyne Mercury*, 11 February 1806, no. 194, 3; Wheel Wreck, 1453492; World Heritage Site listing, http://whc.unesco.org/en/list/1215.

161 *See* Fig 1.23.

162 389755.

163 Wessex Archaeology (2010b, 6).

164 *See* Chapter 4, 'Between the wars: old and new', for more on 'chipping rust' on long voyages.

165 A layer in which corrosion products are mixed with mineral and biological deposits attracted to metallic objects in seawater.

166 Arnaud (2007, 45–7).

167 *Marshall*, lost 1853 off the coast of the East Riding of Yorkshire, 907863; *Nile*, wrecked 1854 off Cornwall, 832091, her condition reported in UKHO, 2008, UKHO no. 16414; *Faith*, which foundered at sea 1855 off the Isle of Wight, 1397761.

168 1521994; *see* 'Introduction' in Chapter 2 for more detail on the *Lelia;* ADU 97/07, 1997.

169 Gull Rock cannon site, 1082112; Gull Stream cannon site, 1517639; Kingswear Cannon site, 832309; Salcombe cannon site, 1121972.

170 King (1779, 147–59).

171 Gull stream site, in King (1779, 147–59) and Redknap and Fleming (1985, 312–28); Blakeney cannon site, 1441696, in *Norwich Mercury*, 2 May 1835, no. 5,425, 3; *Harmony* privateer, 1388193.

172 Studland Bay wreck, 1082101; West Bay wreck, 1437873.

173 *See*: 'Just how many Roman shipwrecks were wrecked in England?' in Chapter 5 for further discussion of this wreck in the context of other Roman ships.

174 *Saucy Jack*, 1376888; *Ruby*, 1376920.

175 234 BMAPA finds reported and recorded at the time of writing in 2012: source NRHE AMIE database 2012.

176 1121974.

177 Chris Pater, EH Maritime Archaeology, pers. comm. 2010.

178 1401518.

179 http://www.wessexarch.co.uk/blogs/news/2012/04/11/wessex-archaeology-launches-fishing-protocol-archaeological-discoveries.

Chapter 2 Ships at war

1 Filey Bay site, 1366264; *Iona II*, 1082110; Seaton Carew wreck, 1312495; Wheel Wreck; 1453492. The *Richard Montgomery*, 904735, lost while carrying a wartime cargo, is designated under Section 2 of the Protection of Wrecks Act 1973 as a dangerous wreck, not as a historic wreck.

2 Wrecks of troopships from the American War of Independence: 'disabled soldiers' were lost from the *Golden Fleece* off Birling Gap, Sussex, in 1778, 902625; and Hessian troops from an unknown vessel in the Bristol Channel, homeward-bound from New York, 1784, 1326597. Peninsular Campaign wrecks: *Providence*, off the Bolt Head, Devon, in 1808, 877221, and *Dispatch*, off the Black Head, Cornwall, in 1809, 1087074, both homeward bound from Corunna, and the *Cameleon*, off the Manacles, Cornwall, in 1811, 920717.

3 *Guernsey Lily*, 927624; *Camellia*, 1338315; homeward-bound transport, 1338329; transport in ballast, probably outward-bound, 1542622.

4 HMS *Espion*, 881152; unknown troopship with 79th Regiment, 1398764, described in the *Tyne Mercury*, 28 April 1807, no. 257.

5 Hanoverian troops, 881156; troops of the German Legion, 878581 and 1315570.

6 453856.

7 900404.

8 1494605; 1494609.

9 1121974.

10 *Nympha Americana*, 1234801; reference *F. Farley's Bristol Journal*, 5 December 1747, no. 1592, 2; £100,000 was worth approximately £12.5m according to the retail price index, or 10 times that amount according to average earnings, in 2010 (Officer 2009–11). The French East Indiaman, 1387349, with a cargo of gold said to be twice that of the *Nympha Americana*, at £200,000; *Newcastle Courant*, 16 January 1779, no. 5,338; *Zeelilie*, 880060.

11 1379641; the vessel is being tested, among other things, for the presence of preserved organisms unique to the tropical waters in which *Beagle* once sailed.

12 899473.

13 1480987.

14 *Hussar*, 1252061; SMS *Baden*, 1163523.

15 Among them the torpedo boat destroyer *T-189*, 1528033, which sank en route from Cherbourg for Teignmouth, close to Roundham Head, Torbay, in 1920, or *UB 21*, 805579, which similarly broke tow and sank off Portsmouth in the same year.

16 *Augustine*, 902051; *Richard and John*, 1264355; *Play Prize*, 1264350.

17 1526504.

18 *L24*, 904582; *M2*, 904645; *M1*, 1393674; all of which are designated vessels under the Protection of Military Remains Act 1986.

19 1521994.

20 911513.

21 859017.

22 http://www.yavari.org.

23 *The Times*, 28 May 1903, no. 37,092, 13, column A; Officer (2009–11).

24 907870.

25 At least 10 vessels were lost after the cessation of hostilities between 1918 and 1920, and four between 1945 and 1950. Source data: NRHE AMIE database 2010, and *Lloyd's War Losses* (1990; 1991).

26 Source: NRHE AMIE database 2010.

27 Whitelock (1961, 42).

28 Ibid, 43.

29 Ibid, 57.

30 Ibid, 58.

31 *Chroniques*, iv. 91. Neither the *Cog Thomas* (1174960) nor the *Bylbawe* (1174964) were lost, but they were both very severely damaged. PRO E 101/24/14, Roll 3, Expenses of William Clewere, 18–32 Edward III, cited in Rose (2002, 65–6). *See also* Cushway (2011, 138, 140).

32 Cushway, (2011, 140).

33 Poem X in *The Poems of Laurence Minot 1333–1352*, reprinted in Osberg (1997).

34 1451036; a similar incident, without sinking the ship, is recorded between two English ships in Gardiner (1976, nos 45a–45d).

35 900416.

36 1062417.

37 *CSP.Dom.* Elizabeth I, vol 218, November 1588, accessed via http://www.british-history.ac.uk/report.aspx?compid=61092.

38 1179089; 1329644.

39 *CSP.Dom.* Charles I, vol. XV, 1639–40, 26–7, no. 74, 24–5, nos 66 and 68.

40 The Dutch Admiral Marten Harpertzoon Tromp attempted to involve him on the Dutch cause: ibid, 28–9, accessed via http://www.british-history.ac.uk/report.aspx?compid=52880.

41 *CSP.Dom.* Charles I, vol. XV, 1639–40, no. 66, 24–5; 1179051; 1329509; 1329519; 1329521; 1329525; 1329545.

42 1179083; 1179087.

43 The earliest recorded instance of this happening was in 1305, on the Bill of Portland; 900406.

44 The Fourth Anglo-Dutch war over a century later, 1780–1784, formed part of the wider conflict of the American War of Independence: its causes, motivations, and scope were quite different. However, this war also had impacts on shipping losses in terms of privateering activity on the English coast: for example, 1387778, 1387825, 1387855, and 1387859, Dutch privateers lost during this period, and 1325727, a victim of Dutch privateers.

45 *See*, for example, his discussions of the Four Days' Battle on Sunday 3 and Monday 4 June 1666, accessed via http://www.pepysdiary.com.

46 This claim first surfaced towards the 13th century during the reign of Edward II. Translated from the Norman French in which this claim was first made, English diplomats stated that the kingdom of England 'had from time immemorial retained peaceable possession of the sea of England and the islands therein' (Chaplais 1975, 206, quoted in Rodger 1997, 78, 525). Cromwell truncated the name of the *Sovereign of the Seas* to *Sovereign*, but she reverted to *Royal Sovereign* on the Restoration of Charles II in 1660. The *Royal Sovereign* was burnt at Chatham while awaiting repair in 1696, by which time she was nearly 60 years old; 1033732.

47 Reprinted in Sebborn (2000, 70).

48 1179114.

49 *Charity*, ex. *Charité*, 1228626.

50 1179111.

51 The Dutch had already adopted the Gregorian Calendar (New Style). In Dutch sources the battle took place on 10 December 1653, but according to the Julian Calendar then in use in England, the battle took place on 30 November.

52 Again a consequence of the difference between the Old Style and New Style calendars used by the English and the Dutch, respectively.

53 899237

54 Defoe (1722).

55 *Dolphin*, 1364465; *Fame*, 1364511.

56 *Prins Maurits*, 1364514; *(Stad) Utrecht*, 1364516; *Koevorden*, 1364512; *Ter Goes*, 1364484; *Zwanenburg*, 1364508; *Maarsseveen*, 1364479.

57 1364482.

58 1383153.

59 1441945 and 1494016, recorded from the BMAPA/EH Protocol.

60 *Duivenvoorde*, 1439297; *Hof van Zeeland*, 1439313.

61 1247565; as with all other captured Dutch ships taken into the Royal Navy, the new name was usually a direct translation of the vessel's original Dutch name. Alternatively, the name could be made more meaningful by a freer rendering: clearly for the Royal Navy Groeningen (now Groningen), was meaningless, but the city's coat of arms (which would have been a salient feature of the vessel's decoration) could be described instead, hence *Black Spread Eagle*. To this day a double-headed black eagle with wings outspread remains on the arms of Groningen.

62 1207005.

63 1247663.

64 *Diary*, 10 June 1667.

65 1033759.

66 *Diary*, 17 June 1667.

67 Some timbers and artefacts recovered during the extension works at Chatham Dockyard in the 1870s are attributed to one or another of the Dutch ships taken into English service, which were deliberately scuttled to form a chain of blockships. However, it is not known how the finders came to this conclusion. These timbers are now in the collections of the National Maritime Museum, London.

68 1536102; *London Gazette*, Thursday 6 June to Monday 10 June 10 1672, no. 684, 2.

69 *Alice and Francis*, 1383197, and *Katherine*, 1383204; unnamed Dutch vessel, 1383256, all expended; *Fountain*, ignited prematurely, 1383212; *Anne and Judith*, 1383206 and *Bantum*, 1383188, sunk by cannon fire.

70 1536053; *London Gazette*, Thursday 6 June to Monday 10 June 10 1672, no. 684, 2.

71 Account of wreck event, 1383252; sites representing possible remains, 912901 and 1533927; Wessex Archaeology (2010c).

72 908042; *see also* 'The London, from Find to Designation' in Chapter 6.

73 *London Gazette*, Thursday 13 June to Monday 17 June 1667, no. 165, 2; 1534250.

74 Many seem to be unsubstantiated, sourced to local tradition, or minor incidents blown out of proportion, thus making the Civil War appear even more obscure.

75 Compare also the Duart Point wreck in Scottish waters, dating from 1653; Scottish National Monuments Record NM73NW 8005.

76 Source: NRHE AMIE database 2011.

77 1215989; *CPR. Edward II*, vol. V, 1324–7, 143, membrane 12d.

78 Rodger (1997, 182).

79 For a fuller discussion of privateers, please *see* Rodger (1997, 199–200).

80 1121972; *CSP.Dom. Charles I*, 1625–6, vol. 1, nos 68–9, April 1625, and vol. 4, no. 35, July 1625, reprinted 1858.

81 Nichols (2011); Egilsson (2011).

82 *Newcastle Courant*, 11 October 1760, no. 4,385, 1.

83 1383212.

84 *See* discussion below, 'The Norman's Bay Wreck'.

85 Source: NRHE AMIE database 2009.

86 1225833; *Lloyd's News*, 19 December, 1696, no. 48.

87 1393291; *Newcastle Advertiser*, 22 July 1797, no. 458, 3.

88 1393475, *Newcastle Courant*, 17 November 1798, no. 6371, 4; broadside published *c* 1798, sold, Christie's, lot 196, sale 5603, 19 October 2005.

89 The casualty record for the *Resolution*, based on the documentary evidence only, is recorded at 902550; the Norman's Bay site, at 1441075. The separate records reflect the uncertainty over the identification.

90 Nayling (2008).

91 1082120.

92 *Nouvelles d'Amsterdam* du 17 juillet 1690 [NS]. Translation: author.

93 *VCH Sussex*, II, 159, referenced to the Kenyon MSS of the Historical Manuscripts Commission, 242.

94 Villette-Mursay (1991, 200); translation: author.

95 974985.

96 *Elswout*, 1167835; *Maagd van Enkhuizen*, 974986; *Tholen*, 1438083; and *Wapen van Utrecht*, 1167831. The known fates of the unidentified lost vessels, that is, 'burnt at Hastings', 'ashore at White Rocks' and 'burnt in Pevensey Bay' have been arbitrarily distributed among the named losses, to avoid artificially inflating the number of losses for the battle by having parallel records for unknown losses in particular locations and known losses in unspecified locations. It should be stressed that the identifications offered are arbitrary and subject to change as more information comes to light. I am also grateful to Alison Kentuck for her comments on guns carried as ballast (pers. comm. 20 September 2012).

97 National Archives, Kew, ADM 106/581.

98 Wessex Archaeology (2007a).

99 1264350.

100 Anderson (1996, 36).

101 1341132.

102 1033739; *see*, for example, a Dutch warship named the *Oranje*, wrecked in the Second Anglo-Dutch war, 1364482.

103 1247481; occasionally, where names referred to heraldic devices, a focus on their most significant feature, principally the heraldic beasts depicted, was preferred in rendering the name in English. In this way *Black Bull* was preferred as a translation for *Wapen van Edam*, over the literal *Arms of Edam*, which clearly signified little to the English; the black bull still forms part of the arms of the municipality of Edam-Volendam.

104 1480646.

105 *Calendar of Treasury Books*, December 1697, January 1698 and February 1698.

106 1480663.

107 902548; *CSP.Dom*, Charles II, 30 November 1667, no. 167.

108 *See*, for example, among these groups: the Loe Bar Wreck, thought to be the East Indiaman *President*, 1684, 1181945 in the first group; two Dunkirkers attacked by the Dutch in the Downs in 1624, 901996 and 1178886, are representative of the second group; among the third group, the *Kampen* and *Vliegende Draak*, 805298 and 896133, respectively (*see also* Chapter 1, 'Threading the Needles', where these wrecks are covered in more detail); and finally 1321584; this wreck strained relations between Henry VIII and James VI of Scotland, and involved the Bishop of Durham, Cuthbert Tunstall. *Letters and Papers Foreign and Domestic*, Henry VIII, 1534, no. 1,061.

109 *Calendar of State Papers: Foreign*, *Portugal*, Charles II, SP 89/6, Sir Richard Fanshaw to Secretary Bennet, 31 March 1663.

110 For example, *Resolution* was built in 1667 and rebuilt 1698, so this is not without the bounds of probability; however, the *Elswout* seems to have been built in 1677 and the *Tholen* in 1688, which would appear to rule out timbers from before 1659.

111 Forty guns or more seems to have been common among privateers in the 18th century, so it may be that privateer armament in the 17th century is poorly understood. Source: NRHE AMIE database 2010.

112 Nigel Nayling, pers. comm. 27 August 2009.

113 Source: NRHE AMIE database 2009.

114 Account of wreck event, 1534558; possible remains and designated wreck site, 1366264.

115 *Newcastle Courant*, 11 September 1779, no. 5,371, 4; *Lloyd's List*, 15 October 1799, no. 1,102.

116 Deposition of Thomas Berry, reprinted in *Newcastle Courant*, no. 5,374, 4; extract of letter from Scarborough printed in the same issue.

117 1324650; 1324655.

118 *Newcastle Courant*, 9 October 1779, no. 5,375, 4; Captain Pearson, letter to the Admiralty Office, 6 October 1799, in *London Gazette*, no. 12,021, 9 to 12 October 1779.

119 *Lloyd's List*, 28 September 1779, no. 1,097: 'the Merchant Ships separated during the Action; Part took Shelter on the Coast near Scarborough, and two are arrived at Hull'. In the same issue the arrival of four named ships, the *Content*, from Stockholm, the *Polly* and *Integrity* from Petersburg (ie St Petersburg), and the *Elizabeth* from Wyburgh, with '25 others' at Shields is noted: this is likely to be part of the same convoy. *Tyne Mercury*.

120 *Lloyd's List*, 28 September 1779, no. 1,097; *Newcastle Courant*, 2 October 1779, no. 5,374, 4; and *Tyne Mercury* serial, 28 September and 5 October 1802, nos 18 and 19, respectively; interestingly, it was probably a selling point for a new newspaper challenging the hitherto-dominant *Newcastle Courant*. The instalments were said to have come from a manuscript in French which had surfaced after Jones' death in 1792, having been translated into English for publication. However, it does not read like a translation, since the whole serialisation is completely at ease with English nautical idiom. It is therefore likely to have come from the original English of the *Memoires de Paul Jones, écrits par lui-même en anglais et traduits sous les jeux par le citoyen André*, Louis, Paris, 1798.

121 *Tyne Mercury* serial.

122 Ibid.

123 Letter to Benjamin Franklin, 3 October 1779, reprinted in Hart (1899, 587–90); *Tyne Mercury* serial.

124 Ibid.

125 Letter from Captain Pearson, 6 October 1779, to the Admiralty Office, *London Gazette*, 9 to 12 October 1779, no. 12,021.

126 66ft or 20.11m.

127 Fanning (1806–1808, 51–2).

128 *Lloyd's List*, 15 October, 1799, no. 1,102

129 Wessex Archaeology (2003a, ref. 53111.03.c).

130 Adams and Adams (2009) for the Filey Bay site; for other sites, *see* Cussler (1978; 1979) and Ocean Technology website.

131 Fanning (1806–1808, 42).

132 *Newcastle Courant*, 9 October 1779, no. 5,375, 4.

133 Goodall (2002); Port (1989).

134 Taffrail (1935, 98–9).

135 Casualty record, 1381010; possible remains, 909130.

136 Sailing times of cruise vessels between southern England and southern Norway were typically 36 hours as at 2009.

137 *Skuli Fógeti*, 1002311; *Barley Rig*, 1366064; *Gottfried*, 1473042; *Gaea*, 1002309; *Crathie*, 1002310; and *Thomas W Irvine*, 1366041.

138 *Rado*, 1916, possible remains, 978614, and casualty, 1375067; *Recepto*, identified remains, 908854; *Remarko*, 1916, casualty, 1340064; *Remindo*, 1918, casualty, 1234062; and *Resono*, possible remains, 908130, and casualty record, 1488828.

139 For example, in *Lloyd's War Losses* (1990), but this confusion is perfectly understandable given that an organisation devoted to mercantile shipping was compiling lists in which ex-civilian vessels were included.

140 Now held in the United Kingdom Hydrographic Office.

141 *Alberta*, 943131; *Orcades*, 943133.

142 Source: NRHE AMIE database 2010, with 32 identified First World War minesweeper-trawlers on the North Sea coasts, compared to 12 for the English Channel and 3 for the Thames. *Elise*, 1918, east of Blyth, Northumberland, casualty, 1001474, and possible remains, 1472010; *Lochiel*, 1918, off Scarborough, 1431936. Trawlers lost to collision: *Clyde*, 1917, off Sidmouth, 1071221; *City of Dundee*, 1915, off Folkestone, 1488813; *Swallow*, 1918, off Whitby, 1377077.

143 Off the modern coastline of Yorkshire 29 ships were mined (ie excluding the areas which administratively became Humberside and Cleveland in the 1970s but which were formerly part of the Yorkshire coastline) during 1914–18; 24 off the modern Humberside coastline, and 9 off Cleveland: 52 in total. Source: NRHE AMIE database 2010.

144 Source: NRHE AMIE database 2010.

145 The Great Western Railway (GWR), London, Midland and Scottish (LMS), London and North Eastern Railway (LNER) and Southern Railway (SR).

146 Supple (1987, 89–90).

147 For example, the tug *Bunty*, 978622, lost as an Admiralty collier en route from Hull with coal for the naval base at Rosyth on 21 October 1917.

148 *Moss Rose*, schooner, lost 10 September 1917, 906461; *Mary Seymour*, schooner, lost 10 September 1917, 906458; *Jane Williamson*, brigantine, 10 September 1917, 906459; *Agricola*, ketch, 12 September 1917, 1070034; *Gavenwood*, schooner, 7 November 1917, 924543; *Water Lily*, schooner, 10 September 1917, 1109048; and *Mary Orr*, ketch, 10 September 1917, 1109064.

149 Source: NRHE AMIE database 2010.

150 *Hurstwood*, 909225; *Brentwood*, 909216.

151 As at 2012.

152 Although the *Membland* identification has yet to be positively confirmed at the time of writing.

153 *Membland*, 909199; *Corsican Prince*, 909211; the identity displacement continues with the site now definitively assigned to the *Lanthorn*, which was formerly thought to be the *Sparrow* or *Spero*, at 1534327.

154 *London*, formerly thought to be the *Saint Ninian*: 909214. The site formerly attributed to the *London* was in turn identified as the *Brentwood*, and at the time of writing was considered to be the *Harrow*, 1308592.

155 *Moorlands*, possible remains, 909205; casualty record 1377305.

156 1375335.

157 Second Supplement to the *London Gazette* of Tuesday, 1 September 1914, published on Wednesday, 2 September 1914, no. 28,888, .6973; *The Times*, 22 January 1915, no. 40,758, 34.

158 1375342; possible remains 907922.

159 Messimer (2002, 274).

160 Gibson and Prendergast (1931, 150); 907921.

161 Term coined by the Norwegian historian Olav Riste for his 1965 book.

162 *See* Chapter 4, 'Between the wars: old and new'.

163 *New York Times*, 7 August 1918, 8. *Eglinton* was sunk in Heligoland Bight.

164 Coal reserves were known in the offshore Arctic archipelago of Svalbard to the north, belonging to Norway, but, among other things, Arctic conditions made transport difficult. In the 21st century deep sea coal has been located off the Norwegian coast, but its extraction is not necessarily feasible; Riste (1965, 170).

165 Halpern (1994, 378).

166 For example, the *Baron Stjernblad*, off Berwick-upon-Tweed, 1036074; *Markersdal*, south of Flamborough Head, 1375511; and *Rota*, south-east of Berry Head, 832212, all lost in 1917.

167 *Borgund I*, 1465978; *Barmston*, 900871.

168 These subsidiaries were A/S Bonheur and A/S Ganger Rolf (originally the names of two Norwegian lines taken over by Fred. Olsen): cf. the name of one of the lost ships, *Bonheur*, mentioned below. Both remain names associated with the cargo arm of the parent business. For the number of ships lost during the First World War, *see* http://www.fredolsen.com/?aid=9043556, based on Cooke (2007). Data on lost ships: source NRHE AMIE database 2009.

169 Bourne (2001, 189).

170 892105.

171 Source: NRHE AMIE database 2010; Riste (1965, 176).

172 *Borgå*, 1234091; *Bamse*, 1144837; and *Bretagne* 832221.

173 *Bob*, 1917, casualty, 1071224; *Bonheur*, 1918, casualty, 1472929; *Bør*, 1918, casualty, 1036077; *Borgny*, 1918, identified remains, 804989; *Borgsten*, 1917, casualty, 1472881; *Boston*, 1914, casualty, 1381010 and possible remains, 909130; *Brabant*, 1917, casualty, 1375251; *Brisk*, 1918: casualty, 1469333; and possible remains, 766922. (To this day the company's cruise vessels continue the tradition of names beginning with the letter B, a naming convention established in the late 19th century.)

174 *Lloyd's War Losses* (1990, 375–81); Taffrail (1935, 308–9).

175 *Lloyd's War Losses* (1990, 375), states her position as 23 miles off Coquet Island; von Munching (1968, 7) reduces this to 12 miles off Coquet Island.

176 1483842; *Lloyd's War Losses* (1990, 379).

177 Within English territorial waters alone the following ships from the same programme were also lost: *War Baron,* 1084811; *War Crocus*, 978634; *War Helmet*, 978634; *War Monarch*, 911964, and *War Tune*, 1554636. There was a similar naming programme during the Second World War with the prefix *Empire* – for ships built for, or under the control of, the Ministry of War Transport, including captured ships: one of the last vessels to be so named was the *Empire Windrush*, ex. German *Monte Rosa*, seized at Kiel in 1946.

178 ADM 137/3450, The National Archives, Kew; all quotations in this section from this source, unless otherwise stated.

179 *New York Times*, 18 April, 1918, 7.

180 805122.

181 Had she been carrying fuel oil, like the *War Knight* and *O B Jennings*, her fate might have been very different: she was to survive both World Wars, finally being broken up in 1949. Source: http://www.miramarshipindex.org.nz/ship/show/193133.

182 Original emphasis.

183 *New York Times*, 1 August 1919, 12.

184 908609; *The Times*, 26 June 1919, no. 42,136, 4; 28 April 1920, no. 42,396, 5.

185 *Warilda*, account of wreck event, 903629; two sites representing possible remains, 1482340 and 1482391. In fact the collision led to litigation: Judgment of the High Court of Justice, King's Bench Division, 14 February 1922, in *Adelaide Steamship Company Limited* v *The King*, *The Times*, 15 February 1922, no.42,956, 4.

186 Judgment of the High Court of Justice, Admiralty Division, 3 May 1917, in *Owners of Sailing Vessel* M Lloyd Morris v *Owners of steamship* Møhlenpris, *Lloyd's List*, 4 May 1917, no. 32,094, 4–5. For the *M Lloyd Morris*, *see* 924489; for the casualty record for the *Møhlenpris*, *see* 1174613; for her possible remains, *see* 911894.

187 1554675.

188 Intertitle, *Q-Ships*, New Era Productions Ltd, 1928.

189 Auten (1919, 19, 219).

190 With 29 Special Service Ships lost during the First World War (*BVLS*, Section I, 31) but the true number may have been masked given the nature of the service; other figures have been claimed elsewhere.

191 *Kent County*, 1916, 927610; *Penshurst*, 1917, 1382934; *Brown Mouse*, 1918, 1234072; *Stock Force*, casualty, 1483351. *See* note 196 for sites suggested as the *Stock Force*'s possible remains.

192 *See* Chapter 2, 'The battlefield of the North Sea: the sweepers, the colliers and the Scandinavians'.

193 Intertitle, *Q-Ships*, 1928.

194 Ibid.

195 Mordaunt Hall, Movie Review, *New York Times*, 17 September 1928, accessed via http://movies.nytimes.com/movie/review?res=9B04E1DA173FE33ABC4F52DFBF668383639EDE.

196 Auten (1919, 268).

197 Site now regarded as the probable remains of the *Stock Force*, 832265, UKHO wreck 18017. The two sites formerly regarded as the possible remains of the *Stock Force* are 832260, UKHO wreck 18010, and 832147, UKHO Wreck no. 18027.

198 Auten (1919, 259).

199 Akermann (1989, 254).

200 919757; McCartney (2003, 45–6); UKHO, Wreck no. 17584, 2008.

201 1086332.

202 Casualty 1534324, possible remains, 904603.

203 *The Times*, 26 March 1928, no. 44,851, 18.

204 National Historic Ships, founded 2006 in its present guise, the successor body to the National Historic Ships Committee, 1991.

205 Source: NRHE AMIE database 2011.

206 There is other footage of the demise of sailing vessels, for example the sinking of HMS *Implacable*, 1480987. Built in 1800 as the French warship *Duguay-Trouin*, she was captured after Trafalgar, taken into the service of the Royal Navy, and after a long history as a training ship, her upkeep and maintenance were considered too expensive in the austerity period following the Second World War. She was therefore scuttled in mid-Channel in 1949 with full ceremonial, flying both the White Ensign and the Tricolore to reflect her heritage, witnessed by representatives from both sides of the Channel. However, she was not under full sail at the time of loss but hulked (dismasted and cut down) and the film's purpose is clearly commemorative. 'Implacable to the End', http://www.britishpathe.com/record.php?id=27323

207 Holmes (2003).

208 *British Vessels Lost at Sea* (1988, sections III and IV).

209 Gardner (1949, 73); the exception was *Renown*, mined off the Sandettié Light Vessel in French coastal waters.

210 Gardner (1949); *Brighton Belle*, 904882; *Brendonia*, casualty, 882362 and possible remains, 904881; *Bravore*, casualty, 904405, and possible remains, 904884.

211 *Amulree*, 1199271. Dunkirk was not the only occasion on which yachts performed war service. Throughout the Second World War some 17 yachts were to be lost in English waters while operating as harbour defence craft, patrol vessels, dan layers and anti-submarine vessels (source: NHRE AMIE database, 2010). *Supplement to the London Gazette* of Tuesday, 15 July 1947, dated Thursday, 17 July 1947, no. 38,017, 3308 and Gardner (1949, 74).

212 HMS *Comfort*, 1199253; *British Vessels Lost at Sea* (1988, section III, 9); *Supplement to the London Gazette*, no. 38,017; http://www.warsailors.com/singleships/hird.html, based on Hegland (1976) and Norsk Sjøfartsmuseum (2003).

213 904914; Mordal (1968); http://www.auxmarins.com.

214 *N5065*, 1329420; *N9919*, 1329983; *L9481*, 1328538; *R3630*, 1323060; http://www.bbc.co.uk/ww2peopleswar/stories/35/a2764235.shtml.

215 1544031.

216 Tanks and bulldozers recorded at 911191; 'Whale Bridge' pontoon, 911187; *LCT(A)2428*, 1534450. I am grateful to Alison Mayor for allowing me to outline her story: all material from Mayor (2008).

217 RMASG file numbers ADM 202/304 ADM 202/305, ADM 202/306, National Archives, Kew, cited in Mayor (2008).

218 DEFE 2/418 Report by Naval Commander, Force 'J' (after action report) in Allied Naval Commander-in-Chief War Diary; ADM 199/1650, HM Ships and Vessels Lost: survivors' interrogation reports, entry 164/165, AB C Hunt of *LCT(A)2428*, both the National Archives, Kew, cited in Mayor (2008).

219 *LST507*, 1147663, casualty; 832476, possible remains; *LST531*, 1147639, casualty; 904600, possible remains.

220 *LST921*, 1534459; *LCI(L)99*, 1534460 ; for *LCM340*, 1534457; *LCM424*, 1534458.

221 British Library MS Arundel 263, http://www.bl.uk/onlinegallery/features/leonardo/leonardo.html.

222 A replica of the *Turtle* is on display at the Royal Naval Submarine Museum, Gosport.

223 *Maria*, 876571; *Annual Register* 1774, Chronicle, 245–8.

224 *Leeuwarder Courant*, 16 July 1774, no. 1,147.

225 Royal Commission on the Ancient and Historical Monuments of Wales 405760; http://www.coflein.gov.uk/en/site/405760/details/RESURGAM/.

226 *Holland No. 1* on display at the Royal Navy Submarine Museum, Gosport, http://www.submarine-museum.co.uk/; *Holland No. 5*, 1397999.

227 911782.

228 907529.

229 1393674.

230 http://www.english-heritage.org.uk/discover/maritime/map/hms-m-a-1/.

231 *U-48*, possible remains, 904880; account of wreck event, 1535509.

232 Source: uboat.net http://www.uboat.net/wwi/boats/successes/uc75.html *UC-75*; 907925; HMS *Fairy*, 907926.

233 McKee (1993, 45–58). Depth charges were also used as a preventive measure: for example, at Gibraltar depth charges were dropped at regular intervals to prevent submarines or even manned torpedoes slipping through the defences at the entrance to the harbour, a continuous and sickening noise for the men aboard troopships in harbour. Based on the comments of Corporal Cant, RAF, who called at Gibraltar in the troopship *Johan de Witt* en route Clyde to Freetown, November 1944.

234 Short Sunderland *DV972*, 1542779.

235 HM Trawler *Comet*, 919202.

236 *UC-19*: account of wreck event, 1542562; possible remains, 1542563.

237 I am grateful to Kate Brett, Naval Historical Branch, for this observation.

238 Source: NRHE AMIE data, 2011, and Ministry of Defence wrecks data to within 24 nautical miles of the English coast, 2011. No wrecks for 1941–3 are present in either set of data, although there are a number of unknown U-boats present which have not even been assigned either to the First or the Second World War.

239 21 ships identified as having been sunk by E-boat in English waters in 1942, and 9 in 1943, with one E-boat lost in 1942. Source: NRHE AMIE data, 2011. One well-known victim of the E-boats was the *Storaa*, now designated under the Protection of Military Remains Act (911934). *See* Chapter 2, 'Dunkirk and D-Day', for other E-boat victims.

240 Source for lack of U-boat sinkings: NRHE AMIE data, 2011 and confirmed by location maps for Allied ships lost published on http://www.uboat.net.

241 Almost half the recorded losses to U-boats in 1944–5 were off Cornwall and Devon: 16 out of 34 wrecks identified as sunk by U-boat during this period. Source: NRHE AMIE database, 2011.

242 *U-325*, account of wreck event, 1569892, possible remains, 919783, or possible remains, 1569888 (also suggested as *U-1021*); *U-400*, account of wreck event, 1570064, possible remains 1570063, or alternative possible site 1569876 (also suggested as *U-1021*); *U-1021*, account of wreck event, 1570055; possible remains formerly suggested as *U-1021*, 766920; possible remains, 1569876 (also suggested as *U-400*) and another possible site 1569888 (also suggested as *U-325*); based on the researches of Innes McCartney and Axel Niestlé, for which *see* Niestlé (2007)), and subsequent publication on individual U-boat records on www.uboat.net.

243 Niestlé (1998, 61, 102, 106).

244 *See* note 241. Illustrative of earlier confusion, 1569876 was formerly identified not as a U-boat, but as a steamer, possibly the *Warnow*, now identified at 1462202.

245 Log of HMS *Star*, ADM 53/61347; report of attack on supposed submarine by *R29*, RAF East Fortune, AIR1/259/15/226/92, both The National Archives, Kew; *UB-115*: Account of wreck event, 1543096; site of possible remains, 943542.

246 *The Times*, 5 December 1917, no. 41, 653, 6.

247 *L15*, 1515825; *L34*, 1515827, *L21*, 1515845, all in 1916; *L70*, 1515871, in 1918.

248 912878; *Lloyd's War Losses* (1990), p127; *The Times*, 3 May 1917, no. 41,468, 6.

249 Including those witnessed during the Battle of Britain and subsequently by the author's own parents.

250 Battle of Britain data source: NRHE AMIE database 2010; *5K + AR*, 1400389.

251 Lockheed Hudson *AM676*, 1433035; Short Stirling *EH960*, 1356979.

252 Source: NRHE AMIE database, 2011. The apparently high maritime figures reflect a current bias towards the recording of aircraft wrecks over the sea, rather than a simple majority having been lost over water. This is likely to change as more terrestrial aircraft losses are recorded.

253 Department of Information and Research Services, RAF Museum, Hendon, pers. comm., 10 August 2011.

254 Source: NRHE AMIE database, 2011.

255 *N238*, 1324762; *S1283*, 1324840.

256 Heinkel He 59 C2 *D-ASAM*, 1390808; Heinkel He 115 minelayer *M2+CL*, 1399933.

257 1540766.

258 911537.

259 904645.

260 Young (2001) suggests that the vessel was on her way to pick up a Hurricane; Carrott (2001) states that she was intended to deploy a Fulmar.

261 HMS *Patia*, 1001497; Heinkel, 1381894.

262 According to some sources, eg Carrott (2001), the aircraft made a second attack and two further bombs fell harmlessly; it was on the third attack that the bombs disabled the ship; Young (2001) states that there were two passes, which seems to have been the opinion of the survivors, eg David Pettit Davies, torpedoman. The confusion may, perhaps, be explained by the version of events from *1H+MH*,

apparently attracted to *Patia* by seeing her engaged in a gun battle with another aircraft, which may have overflown *Patia* once before the *Heinkel* did so twice. (Norman 2002).

263 Liddiard (2008).

264 Norman (2002).

Chapter 3 The vagaries of human nature

1 *Durham Packet*, 1046687; the *Durham Packet* was in fact recovered fairly shortly afterwards and is a perfect example of how those on board may be in mortal peril without material damage to their vessel. Conversely, it is often the case that a ship may 'go to pieces' without any loss of life.

2 Unknown fishing vessel, 1400517; *Helsingør*, 1254786.

3 Flower and Wynn-Jones (1974, 24, 40).

4 Guernseyman, 1434581; cutters in the Isle of Scilly, 1446657 and 1446658; the *Bell*, Porthleven, 1758, 920255; and the Lytham wreck, 1802, 1395136.

5 *Friendship*, 1391053, as reported in the *Newcastle Advertiser*, 22 January 1791, no. 119, 2; *see* also discussions in Bathurst (2006, *passim*, particularly 227). The crew of the *Abana*, 951908, were said to have mistaken the lights of Blackpool Tower for a lighthouse during a storm in 1894, but this may be a retrospective association of the wreck to the tower, which had recently opened, than circumstances related at the time.

6 The loss of the *Napoli*, BBC News, 22 January, 2007, accessed via http://news.bbc.co.uk/1/hi/uk/6288169.stm.

7 *Neptunus*, 1237521, *Norwich Mercury*, 20 February 1830, no. 5,148, 3.

8 *See* Chapter 3, 'Monuments to lifesaving'.

9 *See* http://www.bbc.co.uk/devon/content/articles/2007/07/16/napoli_timeline_feature.shtml.

10 Compton Mackenzie's 1947 novel and the subsequent Ealing film of 1949 were based on a real-life incident in the Hebrides in 1941, the wreck of the *Politician*.

11 899227.

12 Officer (2009–11).

13 Blackstone (1765). As late as 1803 the *Ariel* (1313975) was found adrift off Berwick-upon-Tweed, with a corpse and a live dog, the remainder of the crew having apparently already quitted the vessel.

14 1445503; 1119973; 1449125.

15 900412.

16 The medieval period is regarded as 1066 to 1540, the completion of the Dissolution of the Monasteries. The subsequent six decades therefore take us to 1599. Source: NRHE AMIE database 2010.

17 Source: NRHE AMIE database 2010.

18 *Fortune*, 1765, 1386105; *Ann & Mary*, 1780, 1387706; *Speedwell*, 1790, 1390915.

19 *Newcastle Courant*, 9 June 1804, no. 6,661, 1; 1339579.

20 *Tyne Mercury*, 1 January 1804, no. 136, 3.

21 1375536.

22 Fifty guineas was literally £52.50; although the relative value of the reward was approximately £3,700 according to the retail price index (Officer, 2009–11, 1).

23 1345763.

24 *Newcastle Advertiser*, 25 March 1809, no. 1,067, 4.

25 *Lloyd's Register of Shipping* and *Lloyd's List* are still published today, but are separate entities from one another and from the insurance market also bearing the name of Lloyd's.

26 Underwriters were originally those who were stakeholders in or subscribers to a maritime or commercial venture, and applied by extension to those who became stakeholders in the venture by providing insurance cover, and whose signatures would appear *under* the documents drawn up to that effect.

27 Officer (2012).

28 *Norwich Mercury*, 20 to 27 November 1725, 1; *Farley's Bristol News-Paper*, 20 November 1725, No. XXIX, 116 [printing error for page 119]; *Farley's Bristol News-Paper*, 30 April 1726, No. LII, 199; 1355381.

29 Dutch ship, 1438269; *Bristol Weekly Intelligencer*, 3 August 1751, No. 97, 3; *Nightingale*, account of wreck event, 1395142; possible remains, 920127.

30 920124.

31 *Bristol Weekly Intelligencer*, 23 December 1752, No. 168, 1.

32 Old Bailey Proceedings Online, http://www.oldbaileyonline.org, accessed on 14 May 2009. Moses Moravia first appeared in the records of the Old Bailey in 1744 for perjury (t17440113-33). In 1758 it emerged during the trial of John Carrier for fraud that he had been defrauded of £170 by Moses Moravia, 'since consined [sic] in Newgate, for the wilful loss of an insured ship', (OA 17581002).

33 Old Bailey Proceedings Online, http://www.oldbaileyonline.org: June 1752, trial of Moses Moravia, John Manoury and Solomon Carolina (t17520625-51), accessed on 14 May 2009.

34 *See*, for example, *Vittoria*, a Russian brig with a typically Baltic cargo of combustible hemp and tar, at Ramsgate in 1815; 894007.

35 *See* note 6.

36 *See* Chapter 5, 'Whatever happened to the Elizabeth Jane?'.

37 *See* note 10.

38 Source: NRHE AMIE database, 2012; and pers. comm. Ian Oxley, Mark Dunkley and Alison James, English Heritage, 2012.

39 1387321.

40 *Derby Mercury*, 28 February 1777.

41 1444450; *Ipswich Journal, or the Weekly Mercury*, 3 to 10 October 1730, no. 530; 10 to 17 October, no. 531.

42 Ibid.

43 Ridley (2004).

44 O'Regan (2002).

45 For example, the *Endeavour*, 893993, and *Shorn*, 893998, returning from Copenhagen with both men and troops, in 1807; *Somali*, 943559.

46 1385538; *Newcastle Courant*, 1 September 1759, no. 4,328, 2.

47 1375788; *Newcastle Courant*, 4 to 11 May 1745, no. 2,681, 2.

48 1084534; *London Journal*, 25 November 1720.

49 1047839.

50 HMS *Coquille*, 877156; *Endeavour*, 1565340; *The Times*, 18 December 1798, no. 4,360, 3.

51 1033735.

52 895821; *Victoria History of Hampshire and the Isle of Wight*, vol. V, 396, 1912.

53 919780; Gosset (1986, 10).

54 1393996; *Newcastle Courant*, 3 October 1801, no. 6,521.

55 1133153; *Sherborne Mercury*, 28 October 1799.

56 *Betsey*, 1338320.

57 900977; *Dorset County Chronicle*, 23 December 1847, no page given; *Lloyd's List*, 13 December 1847, no. 10,527, 3.

58 Source: NRHE AMIE database, 2011.

59 1082121.

60 *Dwina*, 1341324, *Newcastle Courant*, 18 August 1809, no. 6,932.

61 Source: NRHE AMIE database, 2011.

62 http://www.nmm.ac.uk/explore/sea-and-ships/facts/ships-and-seafarers/load-lines.

63 905942.

64 It is not necessary for a ship to be overloaded for her cargo to shift, since external factors, such as the security of ties and fixings used in stowing the freight, and violent sea conditions, can cause the cargo to break loose; nor does movement of the cargo necessarily imply that the vessel was carrying an excess.

65 Wreck event, 1070003; site now regarded as the possible remains of the *South Australian*, 1033938.

66 *The Times*, 15 February 1889, no. 32,623, 11; 16 February 1889, no. 32,624, 12; composite construction was a short-lived mid-19th-century phenomenon, an intermediate stage of ship construction as the age of the wooden sailing vessel yielded to that of the iron and then steel steamer, and wrecks of composite construction are accordingly relatively unusual.

67 1359912.

68 893757.

69 920396.

70 1320743.

71 1064890.

72 1067623.

73 *See* Chapter 2, 'The *War Knight*: a tragedy of war'.

74 1383001; *New York Times*, 3 March 1916; *Public Ledger (Philadelphia)*, 1 March 1916, vol. II, no. 145, 1.

75 1520001.

76 Casualty, 1230026; possible remains, 832177.

77 Pliny the Elder, *Natural History*, Book II, Section 234; Plutarch, *Natural Questions*, xii, in *The Morals*, vol.3; Venerable Bede, *Ecclesiastical History*, Book III, Chapter XV.

78 900881.

79 *Rose* of Amsterdam (not Hamburg), 970636; *CSP.Dom.* Charles I, vol. XI, 1637, vol. CCCLXIII, no. 3, 314.

80 *See also* Chapter 2, 'Under False Colours', for more on the buoyancy of timber cargoes.

81 Forty wrecks in the NRHE AMIE database with a cargo of cork are recorded; 32 were driven ashore by wind and weather. Where the remainder foundered, this was usually owing to collision or to war causes (mine, torpedo and aerial attack) against which the cork afforded little protection. In 1915, a lighter sank at the Blue Boar Wharf in the Medway (1209177): the cargo floated free, leaving the vessel without even the protective buoyancy of her cargo. The protective effect of cork was reduced, but not eliminated, with other timber cargoes: ships laden with deals or planks, for example, were commonly found stranded after being abandoned adrift at sea for days or weeks. For deal cargoes lost in English waters, stranding as a cause of loss outnumbered foundering by 2 to 1. Source: NRHE AMIE database 2010.

82 Unknown sloop, 1803, 1395009; *Autumn*, 1806, 1397680; *William and Isabella*, 1819, 971589.

83 *Newcastle Courant*, 18 October 1766, no. 4,700, 2.

84 1433286.

85 Thirty-two bushels; when applied to coal 36 bushels; Lewis (1848, 490–4).

86 *Newcastle*, 971420.

87 *Nautilus*, 938796; *Newcastle Advertiser*, 28 February 1795, 2 [issue number destroyed].

88 Weightman (2004).

89 Blain (2006).

90 Respectively, two English ships, *Lady Rowena*, 896354 and *Vicuna*, 1198073; one Guernseyman, *Éclair*, 923905; two Danish vessels, *Maren*, 1338935 and *Hamlet*, 1348430; and the Russian ship *Hesperus*, 897501 (source: NRHE database, 2009).

91 881464.

92 Blain (2006).

93 *See*, for example, *Hansard*, 25 February 1875, vol. 222 c.847; 28 June 1877, vol. 235, cc.398–9.

94 882255; 1873, *Board of Trade Casualty Returns*, Part III, 38.

95 1911, *Board of Trade Casualty Returns*, Appendix C, Table 3, 134; 925568.

96 For example, the Danish *Statistisk Oversigt over de i aaret 1893 for danske skibe i danske og fremmede farvande samt for fremmede skibe i danske farvande, indtrufne Søulykker*, published annually until 1996.

97 904735.

98 http://www.convoyweb.org.uk.

99 The problem is discussed more fully in Hamer (2004).

100 *Mary Rose*, 1121974; http://www.maryrose.org/; http://www.vasamuseet.se/en/.

101 Letter to Charles V of Spain, in *Letters and Papers Foreign and Domestic, Henry VIII*, July 1545, accessed via: http://www.british-history.ac.uk/report.aspx?compid=80407.

102 http://www.ucl.ac.uk/news/news-articles/0808/08080501.

103 *See* Newby (1999), Robertshaw (2008, *passim*).

104 *See* Chapter 4, 'Goods and People: Local Vessel Types', for a description of passenger behaviour; *Princess Alice*, 896332.

105 Brunel's SS *Great Western* of 1838 was paddle-driven but by 1843 his SS *Great Britain* was screw-driven (although she was not the first screw-driven steamer).

106 *Prince Arthur*, 952116; *Columbus*, 951847.

107 *The Times*, 5 September 1878, no. 29,352, 9.

108 *Ibex*, *Eastern Daily Press*, 5 September 1878, no. 2,469, 3–4; rowing boat, *New York Times*, 21 September 1878, 3.

109 *The Times*, 4 September 1878, no. 29,351, 7.

110 *New York Times*, 5 September 1878, 1.

111 Transcript of the Board of Trade Inquiry in *The Times*, 18 October 1878, no. 29,389, 6.

112 *New York Times*, 21 September 1878, 3.

113 *New York Times*, 4 September 1878, 1 and 5 September 1878, 1.

114 Report of the conclusion of the Board of Trade Inquiry, *The Times*, 1 November 1878, no. 29,401, 4.

115 *New York Times*, 21 September 1878, 3.

116 Merchant Shipping Act 1876.

117 *See* this chapter, 'Theft in medieval court cases'.

118 *Newcastle Courant*, 7 September 1782, no. 5,526, 3–4.

119 Rodger (2004, 375).

120 *Newcastle Courant*, 7 September 1782, no. 5,526, 3–4.

121 *Newcastle Courant*, 14 September 1782, no. 5,527, 3–4.

122 Ibid.

123 *Newcastle Courant*, 7 September 1782, no. 5,526, 3–4.

124 Ibid.

125 *Newcastle Courant*, 14 September 1782, no. 5,527, 3–4.

126 Equiano (1979); Francis Barber (Caretta 2003); Barlow Fielding (Rodger 2004, 394); Othello Sellours (Clayton 2007, 226).

127 *See* Chapter 1, 'Early extreme weather events' and '*Rooswijk* and *Stirling Castle*'.

128 Most of this fleet has been located among the Western Rocks of the Isles of Scilly: the *Association*, 880102 and the *Firebrand*, 880106, have definitively been identified. The *Romney* is likely to be the site recorded at 880103, with an accompanying casualty record at 1436004, and the Tearing Ledge designated site (1082123) may be the remains of the *Eagle*, whose wreck event is recorded at 1435979.

129 905407.

130 Chapter 5, 'Just how many Roman ships were wrecked off England?'.

131 1119117.

132 1456208, representative record for approximately 20 ships which were lost in the Solent.

133 *The Times*, 13 October 1836, no. 16,323.

134 1382945.

135 Also discussed in Chapter 5, 'What happens to maritime archaeology remains, part II: logboats then and now'.

136 1449053; *CPR*, Richard II, Vol. V, 1391–6, 233, membrane 17d.

137 1305015.

138 Source: NRHE AMIE database, 2010.

139 Grant to the barons of 'Winchilse' of the right to levy dues for the maintenance of a harbour light; *CPR*, Henry II, vol. 5, 140; *see* also Martin and Martin (2004, 4–17).

140 1250 wreck, 1455936; Three records in the mid to late 14th century for wrecks in the vicinity of Winchelsea: *La George*, 1346, 1445792; *Seynte Marie*, 1356, 1445786; *La Cristofre*, 1387, 1450471.

141 Martin and Martin (2004, 4, 15–17).

142 *Snowdrop*, 1390681; *Constant*, 1390682.

143 My grateful thanks to Dr Paul Cavill, University of Nottingham and Dr Oliver Padel, for alerting me to the existence of the 1405 citation, and thus the wreck of that date, derived from *Ministers' Accounts for the Duchy of Cornwall*, SC6/819/15, The National Archives, Kew; NRHE AMIE record 1548631. For the 1589 wreck, please *see* 1496845, from text reprinted in Arber (1880, 394).

144 Manner of loss sourced from NRHE AMIE data 2011.

145 1376394.

146 *See* Chapter 1, 'Early extreme weather events'.

147 905157; *Royal Cornwall Gazette*, 16 November 1811, no. 438.

148 905437; *Royal Cornwall Gazette*, 25 July 1845, no. 4,162, 2.

149 905544.

150 1110480; source NRHE AMIE database, 2011.

151 Analysis of NRHE AMIE database, 2011. See also Bathurst (2006, 10, 227, *passim*); few prosecutions were actively brought for the deliberate showing of false lights suggesting that this was less common than generally thought.

152 *OED*, September 2011; http://www.oed.com/viewdictionaryentry/Entry/230603, accessed on 25 November, 2011; Portuguese ship, 1633, 896118, *CSP.Dom*, Charles I, vol. VI, 1633–4, vol. CCXLIV, 172, no. 21.

153 *Royal Cornwall Gazette*, 22 December 1827, no. 1,278; *Jane*, 921089.

154 Naish (1985, 107).

155 *William*, 1343396; *Beulah*, 927701.

156 *See* Chapter 1, 'A dangerous flat and fatal'.

157 Earliest known wreck recorded in relation to the Dudgeon Lightship, the *Mayflower*, 1785, 1326992.

158 1898 Dudgeon incident, 1351919; 1902 incident, 928726; 1940 incident, 1539589.

159 1217507.

160 927661.

161 971446; *Newcastle Advertiser*, 6 February 1790, no. 69, 2.

162 937835; *Newcastle Courant*, 11 December 1802, no. 6,583, 4.

163 *Ardwell*, 1364863; *Escort*, 1548412; *Friendship*, 1364859; *Stanley*, 1364862; and *Martin Luther*, lost the following day, 1366705.

164 *See* also Fig III in the Introduction, as fishermen approach the survivors' boats with caution.

165 *Eliza Fernley*, 1379256; *Laura Janet*, 1379270; *Mexico*, 951889.

166 1548542.

167 1001526; *Newcastle Courant*, 22 November, 1806, no. 6,789.

168 1001507; *British Gazette and Berwick Advertiser*, 15 March 1817, no. 481.

169 *The Times*, 19 September 1838, no. 16,838, 6.

170 Ibid.

171 For example, the *Johns*, 1845, 1367628; *Lady Ross*, 1847, 1001530; *Success*, 1853, 1368010; and *Trio*, 1860, 1370713.

Chapter 4 The transport of goods and people around the world

1 As preserved in quotations by later writers; *see* Cunliffe (2002).

2 Erme Estuary site, 1082113; information from the site designation.

3 Moor Sand site, 1082109; Salcombe Cannon site Bronze Age assemblage, 1439037; Salcombe Cannon site 17th-century wreck, 1121972. *See also* Chapter 1, 'Threading the Needles', for further discussion of the Moor Sand and Salcombe sites.

4 367061.

5 63898; Hull Museums.

6 *Indian Chief*, 895185; *Somali*, 943559.

7 1674 wreck, 1145385; *Paulina*, 1397601.

8 *Cambrian Princess*, 1902, 1162459, which foundered after a collision in the English Channel; *Dovenby*, 1914, lying in two parts after a very severe collision, reflected in the two records for the two distinct parts of the site, 908038 and 908039.

9 *Albany*, 1887, 1137614.

10 876549.

11 Source: NRHE AMIE database, 2010.

12 1327013.

13 Source: NRHE AMIE database, 2010. Twenty-one outward-bound Dutch East Indiamen have been recorded, as opposed to four homeward-bound (this excludes wrecks taken as prizes or involved in the Anglo-Dutch wars); the discrepancy is less marked among English East Indiamen, favouring homeward-bound in an approximate ratio of 3:2 (17 as against 27 wrecks, again excluding vessels on other voyages).

14 *Reference Book VIII*, 340, published in 'Warrant Books: December 1708, 11–20', *Calendar of Treasury Books: 1708*, vol. 22 (1952), 461, accessed via: http://www.british-history.ac.uk/report.aspx?compid=90639.

15 Institute of Netherlands History, *The Dutch East India Company's Shipping between the Netherlands and Asia, 1595–1795*, accessed via: http://www.inghist.nl/Onderzoek/Projecten/DAS/detailVoyage/91055.

16 *Maan*, 1364518. Larn and Larn (1977, 1996) quotes the loss of two ships named the *Red Lion* of London and the *Golden Lion* of Middelburg in 1592, respectively 1178532 and 902036, calling them East Indiamen, but this appears to be extrapolated from the long lists of cargo salvaged from these vessels, indicating richly laden ships. However, no ships of these names appear in standard works of East India ships from either country.

17 1383043.

18 901997. An illustration of the fashion in ships' names in the 17th century, part of a shared culture of Protestantism in the Netherlands and England that largely, but not wholly, turned away from naming conventions derived from Christian culture, and towards secular names. It is also a tribute to the high status of East Indiamen, since they received names also bestowed upon contemporary warships: Dutch *Wassende Maan* (*Waxing Moon*), 1626, *Halve Maan* (*Half Moon*), 1653.

19 *CSP.Dom. Charles I*, vol. VII, no. 110.

20 Jacob Johnson, the diver, was involved in recovering goods from this wreck (*see also* Chapter 1, 'Threading the Needles').

21 As late as 1867, nearly 70 years after the official dissolution of the VOC, the *Jonkheer Meester van der Wall van Puttershoek* had been a regular trader to the Dutch East Indies for a number of years when she was wrecked at Angrouse Cliffs, Cornwall, 918804.

22 *Alexander*, 1144791; *Abercrombie*, 1046694, based on 'Chronological Table for the Year 1815', *Lancaster Gazette*, 13 January 1816.

23 The identification of the lady as Persian appears in Larn and Larn (1995); *Lancaster Gazette*, 1 April 1815, col. 5.

24 *Halsewell*, 904656; *Earl of Abergavenny*, 904659.

25 'An Abstract of the Narrative of the Loss of the *Halsewell* East-Indiaman, Capt. R. Pierce, which was unfortunately wrecked at Seacombe in the Isle of Purbeck, on the coast of Dorsetshire, on the Morning of Friday the 6th of January, 1786. Compiled from the Communications, and under the Authorities of, Mr. Henry Meriton and Mr. John Rogers, the two chief Officers who happily escaped the dreadful catastrophe', *Annual Register*, 1786, Appendix to the Chronicle, 224–3. All quotations concerning the *Halsewell* from this source unless otherwise stated.

26 Cabin for officers and passengers 'abaft and under the round-house' (*OED*), although later in the text it seems to be used as a synonym for the round-house itself.

27 Trial of Stephen Newman for burglary, 25 October, 1786, accessed through Old Bailey Online: http://www.oldbaileyonline.org/browse.jsp?ref=t17861025–33.

28 At the time of writing (2010) these were the *Admiral Gardner*, 1082122; *Amsterdam*, 1082114; *Kennemerland*, accessed via: http://www.historic-scotland.gov.uk/kennemerlandsitedescription.pdf; Loe Bar wreck (thought to be the remains of the *President*), 1181945; *Rooswijk*, 1451382; and *Schiedam*, 1082108.

29 *Sophia Magdalena*, 893818; French East India or private 'country' ships: *Modeste* (1748), 1233981; unidentified French Indiaman (1779), 1387349; *Duchesse de Chartres* (1781), 1325266; and *Sans Pareil* (1793), 920372.

30 Account of wreck event, 1197074; possible remains 801951.

31 *Schiller*, 858537; *Pomerania*, 883110; *Mosel*, 918702.

32 The only known vessel remotely associated with this traffic in English waters is the *Jura* which stranded near Liverpool homeward-bound from Ireland following a passage from Quebec in 1864. Wreck event, 1033646; boiler remains, 906829.

33 *New York Times*, 8 December 1875.

34 HMS *Eurydice*, 899473.

35 *The Loss of the Eurydice, Foundered March 24, 1878*, and *The Wreck of the Deutschland: to the happy memory of five Franciscan Nuns, exiles by the Falk Laws, drowned between midnight and morning, Dec. 7th, 1875*, both posthumously published 1918.

36 *New York Times*, 9 December 1875.

37 *New York Times*, 22 December 1875.

38 *New York Times*, 11 December 1875.

39 *Parliamentary Papers: Board of Trade Casualty Returns*.

40 ZDF: *Fahrten ins Ungewisse: 31 Stunden Hölle auf der Deutschland*, broadcast on 13 April 2008 with supporting webpages on http://www.zdf.de/ZDFde/inhalt/13/0,1872,7186221,00.html?dr=1, accessed on 23 September 2008 (not archived) and seq.

41 *See* note 40.

42 *New York Times*, 9 December 1875.

43 Quoted in Wilson (1996), original source not traced.

44 On the evidence of the Medieval Origins of Commercial Sea Fishing Project, *see* Barrett *et al* (2008).

45 Hunmanby ship, 1456066; *La Eleyne*, 1446404. The latter's cargo was worth approximately £40,500 as at 2007 according to the retail price index, or £881,500 according to average wages (Officer 2009–11).

46 For example, Fernando (Ferdinand) II of Aragon and Isabella I of Castile (1451–1504) were known as *los Reyes Catolicos*, 'the Catholic kings'; Pritchard (2004, 140); Freedman (1995, 424).

47 Pritchard (2004, 140).

48 1451081.

49 895806.

50 *See* Chapter 1, 'Cornwall's rocky coves'.

51 *Mary Rose*, 1121974; Newfoundland bankers,1462062 and 1462074 respectively; in the original manuscript a tonnage of 400 was written for the larger vessel, but this is thought to be a transcription error by the 18th-century copyist; the manuscript no longer exists in any version earlier than the 18th-century copy.

52 Cutting (1955), Hutchinson (1994).

53 1466120.

54 Officer (2009–11), in terms of the retail price index.

55 For *La Eleyne*, *see* note 45 above; for the French banker intercepted by the Dutch caper, *see* 1228525.

56 *See*, for example, the *Anne*, an English Third Rate fired in Rye Bay, to prevent capture by the French, 1082120, for further discussion of which *see also* Chapter 2, 'Privateering' and 'The Norman's Bay wreck: evidence of an English or a Dutch warship – or of something else?'

57 1366137. The information may be more garbled than this. It seems clear that the two last elements of the master's name are those most easily reconstructed. Most wreck records give the name of the ship first, followed by that of the master, following universal convention in transmitting the movements of ships. It would therefore seem plausible that the master's name was Louis Reine or something similar. 'Umphiteer', instead of being part of his name, may instead be the name of the vessel, possibly a version of *Amphitrite* (cf French Third Rate warship *Amphitrite*, built 1700) or *Amphiptère* (a heraldic winged serpent). In this case *John* may, in fact, be the name of the informant, a quite typical example of the way in which salient details can be garbled.

58 1456257; *Sherborne Mercury*, 4 December 1739, no. 146, 1.

59 1087369; *Sherborne Mercury*, 29 December 1806, 4.

60 *Ranger*, 1145375; *Margaret*, 880219; *Pheasant*, 880195; and *Nymph*, 878593.

61 878588.

62 Smith Homans and Smith Homans (1858, 333–4); NRHE AMIE database, 2010.

63 921105; *Lloyd's List*, 12 February 1830, no. 6,507; *West Briton*, 9 April 1830. Cod blubber is attested from 1792 onwards: *Dictionary of Newfoundland English*.

64 1087141.

65 Þór (nd); the *Mouette* of Pontrieux was one of the Breton ships lost on such a voyage, off the Isles of Scilly in 1896, 859003.

66 Fisheries and Oceans Canada (2009).

67 1517730; *Ipswich Journal*, 28 January 1871, no. 6,872.

68 *Mary*, 878614; and gig associated with the *Mary*, 1509719; *Solace*, 878680; and gig associated with the *Solace*, 1509723; *Hound*, 1392949.

69 905957.

70 *See* Chapter 5, 'In chase of cod: deep sea fishing'.

71 Tregellas Pope (1983), accessed via: http://www.st-keverne.com/history/Misc/Seine-fishing.html.

72 *Sprat*, 923978; *Royal Cornwall Gazette*, 17 September 1880, 6; *Blucher*, 905258; in 1827 the exploits of Blücher, German Field Marshal, as one of the allies against Napoleon at Waterloo, was still within living memory.

73 Pollard (2007, 52).

74 Alward (1932).

75 1517182.

76 Eighteen of these Brixham trawlers were sunk by scuttling charges, and five by gunfire or shelling in the First World War: source NRHE AMIE database, 2009.

77 924495.

78 *Achieve*, 914562; *Quest*, 1490862; *Strive*, 1490872; *Venture*, 914565; and *Athena*, 914568; *Coriander*, 914560; *Fitzgerald*, 914561; and *Prospector*, 1490870; Wood (nd, 116–18).

79 *See*, for example, the steam trawler, *Nil Desperandum*, one of *U-57*'s victims off Scarborough, 938281; *Mary Ann*, 1374982; *Success*, 1374997; for the 10 sailing smacks lost off Trevose Head, *see*: *Ena*, 906309; *Proverb*, 906312; *C A S*, 906313; *Rivina*, 906314; *Nellie*, 906316; *Lent Lily*, 906317; *Jessamine*, 906318; *Inter-Nos*, 906319; *Hyacinth*, 906320; and *Gracia*, 1109332.

80 For the wrecks of cobles, English or Scottish, in Scottish waters, *see* RCAHMS database *Canmore*: http://canmore. rcahms.gov.uk/.

81 *Forfarshire*, 1548542; *see also* Chapter 3, 'Monuments to lifesaving'.

82 Source: NRHE AMIE database, 2010.

83 1404107.

84 *See*, for example, 1484722, a wreck near Shoeburyness of a vessel taking herring from Great Yarmouth for London; while 1383305, a Flemish vessel, was wrecked in the export trade in 1666.

85 *Eastern Daily Press*, 11 November 1878, no. 2,526; the lost vessel is 1321567.

86 Coull (nd); *see*, for example, *Marie Roze*, of Peterhead, lost off Great Yarmouth in 1907, 1224677 and *Frigate Bird*, of Banff, lost on the Scroby Sand, also off Great Yarmouth, 930154.

87 Thames Sailing Barge Trust, *see* http://www.bargetrust.org/shorthist.html.

88 *Marion*, 906884; *Ross*, 1320311; *Nuncio*, 906904.

89 I am grateful to Deanna Groom, Royal Commission on the Ancient and Historical Monuments of Wales (RCAHMW), for shedding light on the flats of the North Welsh coast.

90 *Speculation*, 1033635; *Railway King*, 1372636.

91 *Smelter*, 1380367; *Bessie*, 906812.

92 1035861.

93 1527046.

94 1437170; flats and trows also came ashore on the Welsh banks of the Dee and Severn respectively, but these wrecks are outside the scope of this book. For these and other Welsh wrecks, *see* the RCAHMW database *Coflein*: http://www.coflein.gov.uk , which records 25 trows.

95 Barnett (2008, 4); *Selina Jane*, 1535446; *Higre*, 1535454; *Britannia*, 1535429; *Rockby*, 1535434.

96 1526317.

97 1509981; *Gloucester Journal*, 30 May 1814, no. 4,809, 3.

98 Act 9 Henry V c.10, quoted in *OED;* translation author's.

99 *See* elsewhere in this chapter, for example, 'East Indiamen'.

100 1392341; *Newcastle Courant*, 25 April 1795, no. 6, 185, 4.

101 1046573.

102 1496196.

103 Kent Fines, No. 16, I Edward II, in Greenstreet (1877, 314).

104 Trow, 1485812; *Elizabeth*, 1383056.

105 1037530; *Lloyd's List*, 21 December 1773, no. 495.

106 1033627; *Lloyd's List*, 14 August 1821, no. 5,618.

107 *Manchester*, 1324996; *Countess of Caithness*, 952253.

108 952360.

109 906979.

110 Source: NRHE AMIE data, 2010.

111 French passage vessel, 1185792; *Flora*, 894040; *Zorgvuldigheid*, 882719. For more on the *Zorgvuldigheid*, *see* Chapter 5, 'Salvaging ship names from the murky waters of the past.'

112 *Flèche*, 1395555; the *Rambler* and *Two Friends* do not seem to have been lost and are, therefore, not recorded on the NRHE AMIE database. *The Times*, 23 November 1802, no. 5,573, 3.

113 For sample wrecks, *see* the *Pelagie de Means*, off St Ives in 1821, 904973; and the *Pékin* off Norfolk in 1853, 927857; for the captured *chasse-marée*, *see* 1338066.

114 Still a characteristic species in the Beachy Head landscape; Land Use Consultants (2005, 398).

115 *See*, for example, the wreck of the *Active* coaster in the Sharpness Canal, 1831, 1357513; or of a barge at her moorings in the Manchester Ship Canal, 1907, 1382524.

116 1456037.

117 Hatcher (1993).

118 Woodman and Wilson (2002, 106, 108).

119 The Durham coalfield comprised modern-day County Durham, Tyneside and Northumberland, with Newcastle and Shields as its chief outlets.

120 1385986.

121 Hatcher (1993, 475).

122 Seaton Carew wreck, 1312495.

123 *Betty*, 1766, 1386122; *Betsy*, 1814, 1315771.

124 *Wealands*, 937720; *Eliza*, 937724; *Dolphin*, 937727; *Suffolk*, 937728.

125 The *Theodosia* was traced by the present author in the arrivals and departures lists at approximately fortnightly intervals in the shipping columns of the *Newcastle Courant* from the 1750s to the 1830s; she occasionally disappeared for a time, suggesting that she was laid up for repairs, but always reappeared before she vanished from the record for good in the 1830s. Over the course of her history she was clearly a much-loved vessel, for she had only five masters, but by the time she disappeared from the record scarcely any of the original *Theodosia* can have remained. No account of her loss has to date been located, so she was in all likelihood simply broken up when no longer fit for service.

126 Letter from Thomas Babington Macaulay, dated from the Albany, London, 31 January 1856, said to have originally been published in the *Newcastle Weekly Chronicle*; reprinted in *The Monthly Chronicle of North Country Lore and Legend* (Anon. 1887, 32). Royal associations with shipping under dramatic circumstances were fiercely conserved: on his restoration to the throne in 1660, Charles II himself bought the fishing smack *Surprise*, which had served him well in escaping to France in 1651, renaming this particularly poignant souvenir of his exile the *Royal Escape*.

127 *Betsy Cains* (there are numerous variant spellings), 1031974; *Newcastle Courant*, 3 March 1827, no. 7,847, 4.

128 *Delight*, 926708; other possible cats may be the *Nightingale*, also wrecked 1763, 971303; a collier of unknown name, wrecked 1772, 1311850; the *Royal Briton*, lost 1784, 1388306; and the *Flora*, wrecked 1786, 1327195.

129 The main difference is in the provision of a small mast abaft the mainmast.

130 One hundred and seventy-six snows associated with north-east ports out of 264 known snows; 58 of these were registered at Sunderland. Source: NRHE AMIE database, 2009.

131 Respectively, *Elton*, 928921; *London*, 927871; *Ontario*, 1300955; *Cresswell*, 1251027; *Logan*, 858275; *Lizzie Anne*, 913842; *Catherine Griffiths*, 858538; *North Wales*, 928062; and *Dryad*, account of wreck event, 1067099, and possible remains, 832173.

132 *Iron Crown*, 878418; *Fenella*, 1365476.

133 *Lumley*, 1881, 1307986; *Messenger*, 1882, 913883; and *Olive Branch*, 1883, 928405, all bound for Motril; *Kiirus*, 1517734. The *Kiirus* belonged to the Finnish port of Nykarleby, now Uusikaarlepyy, but was called 'Russian' in contemporary sources, since at the time of loss Finland was a Grand Duchy of Russia.

134 *Blackett*, 1386562, cf Blackett Street in Newcastle-upon-Tyne; *Tempest*, 1207486, from the family name of the Marquis of Londonderry, Vane-Tempest-Stewart; *Boyne*,1347399, derived from the title of the eldest son of the Marquis of Londonderry, Lord Boyne, who is also commemorated in the pub of that name at Langley Moor, Co. Durham; *Lambton*, 936633, from the family of that name with extensive interests in the Durham coalfields; *Wynyard*, 902848, from Wynyard Park, formerly the Vane-Tempest-Stewart estate; for *Lumley*, *see* note 133 above, derived from the eponymous colliery; *Harraton*, 908845, and *Cramlington*, 1260931, from the collieries of those names; *Wearside*, 901537, wreck event, 908120, possible remains.

135 1349605.

136 Designed in 1932 by Eric Fraser for the Gas, Light and Coke Co.

137 *Torchbearer*, 1939, 912678; *Firelight*, 1917, casualty, 1500249, with two sites claimed as her possible remains 908643 and 908754; *Flashlight*, 1941, casualty, 1352139, possible remains 1534302; *Fireglow*, 1941, casualty, 1349703, with two sites being claimed as her possible remains, at 1456746 and 1456747; *Lanterna*, 1916, casualty, 927605 and possible remains, 907515; *Lampada*, 1917, casualty 1376943, possible remains 909231; *Lucent*, 1917, casualty 1517814, possible remains 918705; *Fulgens*, 1915, 927588, possible remains, 907465; *Ignis*,1915, casualty 914564, possible remains 912875; *Phare*, 1917, casualty 1376872, possible remains 909157.

138 A small schooner collier, which failed to make Tynemouth Pier, has an extraordinary name for the prudish Victorian period: part reference to light, part literary allusion, she was called the *Light of the Harem*, lost in 1870, her name deriving from the poetic tale of that name incorporated in Thomas Moore's *Lalla-Rookh*; 1375394 (*Lalla Rookh* was also a popular name and belonged to three wrecks, lost in 1850, 1854 and 1873: 902855, 927862 and 1174833, respectively).

139 Source: *Miramar Ship Index* 2009: http:// www.miramarshipindex.org.nz/.

140 *Greenwood*, 1365976; *Rotha*, 1313495.

141 Source of average tonnage for collier brigs and steam colliers: NRHE AMIE database, 2010; *Chinchas*, 922147, wrecked off Cornwall.

142 *See* Chapter 2, 'The battlefield of the North Sea', for more detail on the specific losses of colliers in the First World War.

143 1703 – original source unknown, quoted in Pilbin (1937).

144 *Boyne*: see note 134. *Ranger*, 1304586; *Newcastle Advertiser*, 4 February 1797, no. 434, 3.

145 *Vrow Margaretta*, 973248; *Sukey*, 1300227.

146 Spillman (n.d).

147 Birks-Hay (1990, 131–4).

148 *Hawke Packet*, 1209714; *Countess Anne*, 926665; privateer, 881146: *See* further, Chapter 2, 'Privateering', for more information on the Tyneside resistance to privateering.

149 1339827; *Tyne Mercury*, 20 November 1804, no. 130, 3).

150 Bewick (1862, 94).

151 Defoe (1724, 94–5); *see* representative records for the northbound, 1470004, and southbound, 1470015, colliers, respectively; Lamb and Frydendahl (1991, 55–6).

152 Based on examples in the NRHE AMIE database, 2010.

153 Source: NRHE AMIE database, 2010.

154 *Preussen*, 901826; *Herzogin Cecilie*, 832170.

155 Greenhill and Hackman (1991).

156 *The Times*, 27 April 1936, no. 47,359, 11.

157 *See* note 156 above.

158 Evidence of T Shotton, reprinted in Greenhill and Hackman (1991).

159 Newby (1999, 12).

160 Greenhill and Hackman (1991).

161 Eric Newby in the *Moshulu*, 1939; Geoffrey Sykes Robertshaw in the *Olivebank*, 1932, *Winterhude*, 1933–4, *Ponape*, 1935–6, and *Olivebank*, 1938–9. *See* Newby (1999) and Robertshaw (2008).

162 *See* Newby (1999, 137) and Robertshaw (2008, 85, *passim*).

163 *Time* (1933).

164 Newby (1999, 22); Robertshaw (2008, 238–9).

165 Robertshaw (2008, 133).

166 *The Times*, 27 April 1936, no. 47,359, 11.

167 *Creteblock*, 909208; *Cretecable*, 1367148; *Cretehawser* 1367408; *Creterock* 1367144; *Cretestem* 1367404; *Cretestile* 1340241; *Cretestreet*, 907881.

168 Although the *Creteblock* has overtones of 'a block of concrete', in nautical terms a 'block' is a pulley system.

169 *See*, for example, *FCB 76*, 1535215; *FCB 68*, 1535216; and *FCB 78*, 1535217.

Chapter 5 Solving mysteries

1 *Lloyd's List*, 5 February 1782, no. 1,333.

2 For example, the three Dutch ships reported in 1815, 1816 and 1818 as *Good Hoop*, conflating English *Good* and Dutch *Hoop*, for *Goede Hoop* (ie *Good Hope*), 1343984, 1344757, 1345957.

3 *Lloyd's List*, 25 January 1782, no. 1,330.

4 *Cumberland Pacquet*, 26 October 1775, no. 54, 2; *Lloyd's List*, 27 October 1775, no. 688; 1324287.

5 *Peggy*: *Cumberland Pacquet*, 28 November 1776, no. 111, 2, 1396647; *Providence*: *Newcastle Courant*, 13 October 1804, no. 6679, 4, and *Newcastle Advertiser*, 20 October 1804, 4,1396438.

6 *Newcastle Courant*, 28 October 1820, no. 7,516, 4; *Lloyd's List*, 24 October 1820, no. 5,536; *Newcastle Courant*, 11 November 1820, no. 7,518, 3; 1404770.

7 This has been discussed briefly in Chapter 1: '*Rooswijk* and *Stirling Castle*: Two Goodwin Sands wrecks'.

8 Sections in bold correspond to the quotes in the text: 'Quod cum fecissent fossores, juxta ripam asseres quernos cum clavis infixis, pice navali delinitos **(quales solent esse in carinis)** invenerunt. Necnon et quaedam navalia armamenta, utpote anchores rubigine semirosas, et remos habienos, in certum et manifestum signum aquae marinae, **quae quondam Warlamcestense vexit navigium, repererunt**' (*Acts of the Abbots*, Cotton MS Claudius E.iv, fol. 101r, (2), quoted in T Wright (1844, , 439–57); Ellmers (1973, 177–9); 1534860.

9 *Amsterdam*, 1082114; 'Moon Shore' 414371.

10 Ray (1930, 264).

11 1439158.

12 910909; recorded in McGrail (1978) as *c* 1715 but dated in Poulson (1841) as approximately 60 years prior to 1785, thus around 1725. As so often, it remains untraced.

13 910673: Wilson (1870–2), accessed via: http://www.visionofbritain.org.uk/place/ place_page.jsp?p_id=13882 ; Poulson (1841); Trollope (1872); and McGrail (1978, 251).

14 Probably 'Noah's Wood'; Poulson (1841); Trollope (1872); and Bulmer (1892), accessed via http://www.genuki.org.uk/ big/eng/YKS/ERY/Owthorne/ Owthorne92.html.

15 441056.

16 *See* Chapter 1, '*Rooswijk* and *Stirling Castle*: two Goodwin Sands wrecks'.

17 *See*, for example, the *Cambria*, 1060378, which was lost during this gale.

18 Keeper of Human History, Plymouth City Museum and Art Gallery, pers. comm. 14 July 2009.

19 1817 wreck at Polperro, 921023, *West Briton*, 24 January 1817, reprinted in Larn and Larn (1995); 1763 wreck, 1385989; *Newcastle Courant*, 16 July 1763, no. 4,530, 2; *Calliope*, 1402239, *British Gazette and Berwick Advertiser*, 23 January 1808, no. 4, 4.

20 Tolcarne logboat; 422012; losses on 27 March 1836 were the *Traveller*, 922243, and *Susan*, 922244; *Royal Cornwall Gazette*, 1 April 1836.

21 Walton-on-the-Naze logboat, 925071.

22 *Mary Rose*, 1121974; 'The Mary Rose Ashore', page 5 of 6, accessed via: http://www.maryrose.org/project/ashore6.htm; Poole Iron Age logboat, 457515. The logboat is now on display in Poole Museum.

23 349451; McGrail (1978, 243–4).

24 77717; McGrail (1978, 215–6).

25 66748; McGrail (1978, 229–30).

26 405481; McGrail (1978, 280–1).

27 1534903.

28 10916; McGrail (1987, 75).

29 74973 and 75031, found in works for Manchester Ship Canal in 1889 and 1890 respectively; 468269, in excavating for a sewer, Sandwich, Kent; 65925, cattle pond; 39393, well; 40972, reservoir.

30 Wrecks of a barge lost near Worcester in 1728, 1435205, and of a Severn trow which sank on the River Lugg near Leominster in 1751 are known, 1437170.

31 I am grateful to Alison Kentuck, Receiver of Wreck, for clarifying the legal status of such vessels (pers. comm., 2012). Abandonment through no longer being useful does not equate to wrecking.

32 389755.

33 Council for British Archaeology (2002, 6); Bob Mowat, RCAHMS, pers. comm., 2009.

34 43143.

35 By contrast, reports of the *Swan* and *Teal* sinking at their moorings on Lake Windermere during a storm, as reported in *The Times*, 20 November 1893, no. 34,113, 10, reflected the Lakes' popularity as a Victorian holiday destination. Both were recovered.

36 Example of abandoned Torridge barge, 1518416; example of abandoned Thames barge, the *New World*, 1025294; Purton wrecks: overall record for site, 1389847.

37 McGrail (1978); NRHE AMIE database, 2010.

38 372099; 394310.

39 417358.

40 63307. I am grateful to Paula Gentil, Curator of Archaeology, Hull and East Riding Museum, for more information on this wreck.

41 The monument is broken, lacking the dedicatee's name. He was … *opt[i]onis ad spem ordinis c[enturia] Lucili Ingenui, qui naufragio perit s[itus] e[st]* … 'An optio, serving in the century of Lucilius Ingenuus, who perished in a shipwreck. He is buried …['here' missing]'; Henig (2004, 20). An alternative interpretation might, of course, be that the vessel was lost in transit and the stone erected on arrival, 1563796.

42 *De Bello Gallico*, Book IV, Chapters 28 and 29; translation author's.

43 Representative record for the warships, 1508029; representative record for the lost transport vessels, 1508031.

44 Wilmott and Tibber (2009, 22).

45 *De Bello Gallico*, Book V, Chapters 9–11; translation author's.

46 Representative record for these ships, 1508006 'circiter XL navibus', or 'about 40 ships' so that perhaps, more or fewer ships were actually wrecked in the storm. It sounds fairly specific, and as 5 per cent of a fleet of 800 may be a credible figure for the number of wrecked vessels – or reveal the exaggerated size of Caesar's fleet. Compare the numbers involved in the D-Day operation (*see* Chapter 2).

47 *De Bello Gallico* Book V, Chapter 5: 'Ibi cognoscit LX naves, quae in Meldis factae erant'.

48 457515; on display in Poole Museum.

49 Russell (2005).

50 1082113; ingots now in the possession of the Royal Albert Memorial Museum, Exeter.

51 1544457.

52 Rule and Monaghan (1993).

53 421225.

54 County Hall hulk, 1544107.

55 1359528; for this reason alone it is difficult to quantify isolated finds of a single amphora, for example, as representing the remains of a wreck site. The fact that cargo was washed overboard or jettisoned – or even accidentally lost – did not necessarily mean that the wreck of the vessel then ensued, or even if it did, that it was lost in the same vicinity. Losing some or all of the cargo often meant saving the ship. *See* Dean (1984).

56 405065. Unsurprisingly, perhaps, a greater concentration and a greater diversity of Roman-era ship finds have been located from *Londinium* than elsewhere in the country; for example, 408189, a logboat from Newham. *See also* note 52 above.

57 New Guy's House hulk, 1489830; now a scheduled monument.

58 467772.

59 1341949.

60 At least 240 shipwrecks have been recorded upon the Herd Sand, most of which were colliers. As has been mentioned earlier (Chapter 4, 'The story of the colliers'), the trade in coal was so profitable that most colliers ran 'light' (in ballast) on the return leg to Newcastle-upon-Tyne so that a considerable quantity of ballast was dumped at Tynemouth over the centuries. For most other vessels a full or partial return cargo was required to cover costs. Source: NRHE AMIE database, 2009. *See also* Chapter 1, 'What happens after the wreck event?', for further discussion of ballast dumping.

61 805319; *see also* Chapter 1, 'Threading the Needles', for further discussion of wrecks in the area.

62 *See also* Chapter 5, 'Just how many Roman wrecks are there off England?'.

63 Sawyer (1883); 974975

64 *See* note 63 above, and also still accepted today: see eg Lapidge *et al* (1999, 474).

65 Boulogne-sur-Mer was known as a port from Roman times, possibly as Portus Itius, or Bononia, or both.

66 *See* the almost contemporary Sutton Hoo ship burial, which has been calculated as 1.5m depth (Friel, 2003, 24).

67 *See also* Chapter 4, 'The story of the colliers', for historical records of colliers left 'high and dry' on the coast of Sussex.

68 http://www.liv.ac.uk/geography/RomneyMarsh/RM&20Timeline/Timeline.htm [accessed 28 November 2008: no longer live].

69 *See* Chapter 5, 'Just how many Roman ships were wrecked of England?'.

70 Eanswith, abbess of Folkestone, was the daughter of the King of Kent, Eanbald: she died c 640.

71 *See* the Pharos, Dover.

72 Admiralty Easytide (2009).

73 1121974.

74 Rodger (1997, 476).

75 Source: NRHE AMIE database, 2011. See also Chapter 4, note 125, for the often greater longevity of colliers, however.

76 1372701 possible wreck site of the *Pearle*, lost after 1717, the date inscribed on her bell; 1312211, record for a *Pearl* lost in the area in 1741.

77 1082115.

78 Bow section, 880070; stern section, 1343769.

79 The gun carriage with the name *Colossus* inscribed on it was not found until 1999.

80 1082101.

81 900416.

82 Thomsen (2000, 69–86).

83 1445671.

84 902595.

85 1544402.

86 For example, *Bournemouth Guardian*, 13 January 1912. The storm and its consequences are extensively discussed in Fleming (2010, 409–410, in Spanish), which synthesises material from contemporary commentators as well as later scholars in a variety of languages.

87 *Concepción*, 1119176; the other three vessels, 1119409, 1178372 and 1178431.

88 Thomsen (2000); Gutiérrez (2003).

89 1480411.

90 Henry VIII, *Letters and Papers, Foreign and Domestic*, vol. 21, Part I, January–August 1546, 2 February 1546, no. 154, eds James Gairdner and R H Brodie, 1908; the presence of the 'oliphant's tooth' suggests a possible voyage to Africa and connection to the slave trade. One *Santa Maria da Luz* is recorded in 1532 as being involved in the slave trade, but it is difficult to be certain that it involves the same vessel given the time lag between 1532 and 1546. http://www.slavevoyages.org/tast/database/search.faces. *See also* the discussion later in Chapter 5, 'How can we identify a ship involved in the slave trade?'.

91 With thanks to Nicholas Hall, Royal Armouries.

92 Source: NRHE AMIE database, 2010.

93 Source: NRHE AMIE database, 2010.

94 *CPR* Edward I, 1272–81, membrane 24d; *CCR* Edward I, 1272–79, membrane 3, and 1279–88, membrane 2; 1445812.

95 Source: NRHE AMIE database, 2010.

96 *See* Chapter 4, 'East Indiamen'.

97 Source: NRHE AMIE database, 2010; *Halsewell*, 904656; *Fanny*, documentary evidence, 900557; possible remains, 904663.

98 1463278.

99 *Minute Book*, Wren Society (1939, 67–8).

100 Ibid.

101 Wren Society (1939, 78).

102 *Charming Molly*, 880198; *Lloyd's List*, 19 December, 1780, no. 1,225.

103 English Heritage (2000, 21).

104 Secondary sources: 6m tonnes overall, http://www.thetemplebar.info/portland_stone/index.html; 1m cubic feet http://en.wikipedia.org/wiki/Portland_stone.

105 1185077.

106 *Peggy*, 1804, 1339568; *Commerce*, 1805, 970953; Porter and Hobhouse (1994, 577).

107 Wreck of cylindrical barge, 1379848.

108 For example, 911222, which refers to a barge laden with Portland stone, thought to have sunk during the second half of the 19th century; approximately a mile east of Portland is 832514.

109 1541475.

110 Marsden (1996, 145–59).

111 *See* Chapter 1, 'Early extreme weather events', in which this context is suggested for the loss of Blackfriars II.

112 Tibbles (2000, no pagination).

113 Tibbles (2000, no pagination); National Archives introductory text, nd, *Arriving in Britain*, http://www.nationalarchives.gov.uk/pathways/blackhistory/intro/intro.htm.

114 883650; *Lloyd's List*, 27 November, 1772, no. 3,828.

115 To set this into context, throughout the 18th century there were also newspaper appeals for the return of runaway white apprentices, or of wives who had left their husbands alleging ill treatment: part of a culture regarding human beings as chattels.

116 *See*, for example, Clayton (2007); Willis (2009); Tibbles (2000).

117 Tibbles (2000).

118 Svalesen (1995, 455).

119 *Fredensborg* http://unesco.no/component/content/article/147 and http://unesco.no/component/content/article/145; *Henrietta Marie* http://www.melfisher.org/henriettamarie.htm; *Adelaïde*, http://www.underwaterdiscovery.org/Sitemap/Homepage/aboutus/News.aspx?&XmlDocument=0002.xml; *Guerrero*, http://www.melfisher.org/turtleharbor.htm.

120 1121972; *see* Chapter 2, 'Privateering'.

121 878697; I am grateful to Michael Smith, University of Newcastle, for sharing his knowledge of slave exchange cargoes.

122 *Piedade*, lost on Christmas Day 1810 on the Mouse Sand, Kent, 893914; *União*, on Longton Sands, Lancashire, also in December 1810, 1046710; *Thornton*, 1046721; *Lascelles*, 952030.

123 *See*, for example, Horne (2007, *passim*).

124 *Liverpool Mercury*, 27 January, 1843, no. 1,655; *The Times*, 27 January, 1843, no. 18,204, 6; *Morning Post*, 3 February 1843, no. 22,479, 8.

125 878080.

126 Now in Barnstaple Museum: pers. comm. Alison Mills, Community Heritage Officer, 16 September 2009.

127 BBC News, 7 February 2001: http://news.bbc.co.uk/1/hi/uk/1157768.stm. No data have to date been published stating the grounds for the ethnic identification of the remains; information from Dr Horton via Louisa Pittman, pers. comm., 25 December 2010, suggests that the remains are of white ethnic origin and are likely to be the remains of local fishermen or from the other wrecks at Rapparee.

128 Unidentified ship from Ireland, 877410; the name Rapparee Cove was not applied until much later, however; *(Nossa Senhora de) Bom Succeso*, 1318501.

129 TNA ADM 103/41.

130 *Annual Register*, 1796: Appendix to Chronicle, 74–5.

131 *Annual Register*, 1796: Chronicle, 39.

132 877411.

133 952197.

134 *Lloyd's List*, 31 May 1771, no. 228.

135 *Lloyd's List*, 4 June 1771, no. 229.

136 1320812.

137 Malcolm (2002, 12).

138 1228512: *Flying Post, or the Postmaster*, 20 to 23 February 1697 [NS], no. 278; *Lloyd's News*, 23 February 1696 [OS], no. 76; http://www.slavevoyages.org/tast/databases/search.faces, voyage 10064.

139 920308; *Lloyd's List*, 13 December 1774, no. 597; *Leeuwarder Courant*, 24 December 1774, no. 1170, 1–2; *see also* the discussion concerning a similar clue in the status of the *Santa Maria de Luce* in Chapter 5, 'Two possible candidates for the Studland Bay wreck'.

140 1325608; *Lloyd's List*, 29 October 1782, no. 1,409.

141 1198393, wrecked after arriving at Deptford with 'four fish'. Sometimes the name is a connection with the sea, rather than with whaling, specifically: the name in these cases is in the same class as ships named after other 'marvels of the deep' such as *Mermaid*, *Sea Horse*, *Siren* and the like.

142 Psalm 104, 26; authorized version.

143 *Denbia*, 1320812; *Juba*, 878058.

144 1324304; *OED*.

145 http://www.slavevoyages.org.

146 Source: NRHE AMIE database, 2010–12. Prior to embarking on the book only nine vessels were indexed with the term 'slave ship'; 53 others have since been identified as being slavers and the number is likely to grow with further research.

147 http://www.publicprofiler.org/worldnames/.

148 http://www.websters-online-dictionary.org/definition/Danish-english/.

149 Such as the NRHE AMIE database.

150 http://www.gstromberg.nu/forsres.asp?hrnr=22093&orand=+OR.

151 http://www.sa.dk/content/us/genealogy/styles_of_handwriting.

152 Larn and Larn (1996); 882719.

153 http://www.websters-online-dictionary.org/definition/Dutch-english/.

154 *The Times*, 30 December 1799, no. 4,679, 2 and 31 December 1799, no. 4,680, 3; *Leeuwarder Courant*, 22 January 1800, no. 2,228, 1.

155 *See*, for example, *The Expedition of Humphry Clinker* (1771), in which one character, Mrs Tabitha Beale, is a maiden aunt.

156 881286.

157 *The Times*, 25 March 1870, no. 26,707, 10 and 12, respectively.

158 For example, the story of the *Oostereem*: *see* Chapter 1, '*Rooswijk* and *Stirling Castle*: Two Goodwin Sands wrecks'.

159 *Deal, Walmer, Dover and Kentish Telegram*, 26 March 1870, accessed via: http://www.kent-opc.org/Parishes/News/Deal%20Wrecks%201870s.html.

160 881292; *The Times*, 13 October 1870, no. 26,880, 9. An earlier posting on the loss-book in *The Times* of the previous day, 12 October 1870, no. 26,879, 7, has the name as *Kongs Sverre*.

161 1338566, 1882; 859004, 1896; 1259016, 1913.

162 I am grateful to Alison Kentuck, Receiver of Wreck, for pointing out that this phenomenon continues to occur today.

163 For this reason, the NRHE does not normally record ships which have been sent for 'breaking up'. They are not wrecks in any classical sense, although this does not preclude artefacts or timbers finding their way from the breaker's yard into the fabric of a building or being included in collections. Chesapeake Mill in Hampshire is a rare recorded example of a building containing such timbers, named for the USS *Chesapeake*, an American frigate captured during the Anglo-American war of 1812, 234720. Another example would be the timbers from HMS *Hindustan* and HMS *Impregnable*, incorporated into the Tudorbethan part of the Liberty of London building, Regent Street.

164 Dutch vessel wrecked 1675, 974964. The brewers who owned the Red Lion at Martlesham in the 1950s reiterated the connection with a 'Dutch frigate' lost in Solebay. I am grateful to Sarah Kmosena, National Maritime Museum, for bringing references to the Red Lion in the Museum's acquisition materials to my attention.

165 See below for a specific example: the *Caledonia* figurehead.

166 905407; now removed to the church where it is mounted on display. A replica now stands in its place over the graves of the shipwrecked sailors.

167 1339891; *Newcastle Courant*, 16 February 1805, no. 6,670, 1.

168 971567; *Newcastle Courant*, 1 February 1817, no. 7,321, 4.

169 Wharton-Lloyd and Pevsner (2006, 183); *Cedarine*, 1505845; I am grateful to Matti Watton, Assistant Archivist, Lambeth Palace Library, for this information.

170 With thanks to Mr and Mrs John and Diana Smeeth, pers. comm., 23 August 2010. Pitch pine and pit props came ashore at Millook and Cancleave from the jettisoned cargo. From the latter place salvagers scrambled down the cliff to push the wood out to sea, whence it was towed back to Millook by rowing boats, and thence pulled up the shore by horse. Mr Smeeth's grandfather was one of those involved in salvaging the cargo.

171 905422.

172 *St Anthony*, 1082127; Officer (2009–11); Commission to Sir John Arundell and others, and Petition of Francis Person [sic], factor to the King of Portugal, in *Letters and Papers, Foreign and Domestic*, IV, Henry VIII, 1524–30, accessed via: http://www.british-history.ac.uk/report.aspx?compid=91276.

173 Pevsner (1970, 78).

174 Cant, pers. comm. following visit to the church, July 2010.

175 Gilbert (1838, 128).

176 Preliminary assessment of the rood screen doors in 2012 for English Heritage suggested that only the painted panels of these doors appear to be of any age: the surrounding screenwork is likely to be later. With thanks to Peter Marshall, English Heritage, for his assistance.

177 Source: National Heritage List for England, 2011; Martin Roberts, Historic Building Inspector, English Heritage; Nigel Nayling, University of Lampeter, both pers. comm., 2009.

178 I am grateful to the owner for allowing me to see the remains of the *Elizabeth Jane in situ* and to tell her story. His further researches can be followed at http://www.lostbrig.net.

179 Gavin (unpublished).

180 *Elizabeth Jane*, 1854, 1485826 and 1865, 905688; *Eliza Jane*, 1881, 1210952; *Elizabeth and Jane*, 1726, 1434612, 1826, 1242147 and 1833, 878121; *Eliza and Jane*, 1818, 905202; 1826, 895024; 1837, 1047735; 1870, 893568; and 1892, 1370608.

181 Suffolk Records Office, Ipswich: IG 2/2/4.

182 Since then new administrative authorities have come into being. Following 1974 administrative area reform new administrative counties of Humberside to the south and Cleveland to the north of the Yorkshire coastline were created. Following further reform in 1996 the affected areas are, respectively, East Riding of Yorkshire and Redcar and Cleveland.

183 *Lloyd's List*, 10 July 1854, no. 12,570, 7; 12 July 1854, no. 12,572, 2.

184 The reporting of any wreck may turn up variant forms of the vessel's name, as with *Elizabeth Jane* herself: other than the intrusive 'and', transposed names were also common, eg *Jane (and) Elizabeth*. For example, compare the ship *Ann & Mary* in 1804, which was also reported as the *Mary Ann*, 1339579, while a *Mary Ann* of 1822 also turns up as *Ann and Mary*, 1176491. Equally, if not more common, were variant spellings, thus *Ann(e), Betty/Betsy/Betsey*. Additionally, rescuers and rescued alike were often too traumatised to give coherent or accurate accounts of the ship involved, precise details additionally being obscured by crew deaths or by the inability of any survivors to make themselves understood in English.

185 *Newcastle Courant*, 14 July 1854, no. 9,371, 3; the *Hull Packet and East Riding Times*, 14th July 1854, no. 3,628, 3, has an intermediate version: 'Bridlington Quay, July 9. The *Elizabeth & Jane*, Archer, of and for Ipswich from Sunderland, was abandoned off the North Creek of Robin Hood's Bay yesterday, leaky, and pumps choked; crew were picked up by the *Samuel* of Grimsby, and landed here this morning.'

186 *Ipswich Journal*, 20 April 1844, no. 5,479.

187 *Newcastle Courant*, 13 January 1854, no. 9,345, 2; 21 April 1854, no.9,359, 6.

188 *Unicorn*, 1307460, Larn and Larn (1997, no pagination, section 5, Yorkshire [CE]), based on *Board of Trade Wreck Returns* 1851 but indexed in Larn and Larn (1997) under 1857, and hitherto untraced by author in contemporary newspapers under either date; *Kingston*, 922062, *Royal Cornwall Gazette*, 4 July 1856, 5; *Logan*, 858275, Larn and Larn (1995).

189 *Ipswich Journal*, 3 June 1854, no. 6,004.

190 *Ipswich Journal*, 15 July 1854, no. 6,010; Gavin (unpublished); reference indentures; *Whitby Gazette*, 4 September 1856.

191 Arnold and Howard (2010).

192 Source: NRHE AMIE database, 2010.

Chapter 6 How does it all come together? What is left to find out?

1 Erme Ingot site, 1082113, and National Heritage List for England, 1000054; *HMSM A1*, 911782, and National Heritage List for England, 1000043.

2 *London*, 908042; *King*, 908041; National Heritage List for England, 1000088.

3 *Richard*, lost as the renamed *Royal James*, during the Raid on the Medway in the Second Anglo-Dutch War, when she was scuttled as a blockship, 1179931; *Dunbar*, renamed *Henry*, burnt by accident in Chatham Dockyard in 1682, 1033735.

4   National Maritime Museum, Royal Museums Greenwich; Atlas van Stolk, Rotterdam.

5   Peter Gill or Gyll is listed in the Ordnance Office Registers of 1594 as an active gunfounder. See also *Acts of the Privy Council*, vol. 30, 9 May, 293, 4 June, 355.

6   English Heritage, *Ships and Boats, Prehistory to Present: Designation Selection Guide* (2011a), and *Ships and Boats: Prehistory to 1840: Introduction to Heritage Assets* (2012).

7   *See*, for example, Wessex Archaeology (2010a; 2012).

8   English Heritage 2011b.

9   Dunkley (2011); *Ships and Boats: Prehistory to Present: Selection Guide* (English Heritage February 2011).

10 Accessed via http://www.pastscape.org.uk.

11 Source: NRHE AMIE record, 2011.

12 Source: NRHE AMIE record, 2011; Komar (2010).

13 Davies (2011).

14 Source: NRHE AMIE record, 2011.

15 Source: NRHE AMIE record, 2011, which reveals that 40 wrecks were found in the reign of Richard II. He reigned two years longer than his great-grandfather, Edward II, but records of 10 fewer wrecks survive; data for wrecks in all three reigns retrieved from the *Calendar of Close Rolls* and *Calendar of Patent Rolls*. It is also possible that other factors were at work: the wrecks which did occur in Richard II's reign may simply have been less contentious, but this in itself reveals just how little we know about medieval wrecks.

16 Source: NRHE AMIE database, 2011.

17 Weymouth wreck, 1733, 1375343; Scarborough wrecks, 1798, 1393453 and 1393455; Berwick-upon-Tweed wreck, 1460827.

18 Merritt *et al* (2007, 34).

19 The year 1377 saw the loss of the Hanse ships *Le Cristofre*, 1450218; *Goddesknyght*, 1450253; *Marioncogge*, 1450233; *Maydagh,* 1450257; and *Palmedan*, 1450247; 1381, unknown Hanseatic vessel, 1450863; 1387, *La Cristofre* of Stralsund, 1450471; 1389, unknown Hanseatic vessel, 1449486; 1395, *La Cristofre* of Dantzig (Gdansk) 1447754; 1432, unknown Hanseatic vessel, 1450018. Others may possibly be inferred from the presence of ships plying to and from Hanse ports: Hamburg, Dantzig (Gdansk) and Bergen, among others.

BIBLIOGRAPHY

Unless otherwise stated, the date of latest accession of URLs is given as 16 October 2012.

Adams, J and Adams, M 2009 'Filey Bay wreck licensees report'. Unpublished report for English Heritage

Adams, M 2002 'Burbo offshore wind farm: archaeological report'. Unpublished report for National Museums and Galleries on Merseyside

Adams, M and Harthen, D 2007 'An archaeological assessment of the Sefton Coast, Merseyside, part 2'. Unpublished report for National Museums Liverpool Field Archaeology Unit, <http://www.sefton.gov.uk/pdf/TS_cdef_archaeology2.pdf>

Akermann, P 1989 *Encyclopedia of British Submarines, 1901–1955*, self-published

Alward, G L 1932 *The Sea Fisheries of Great Britain and Ireland*. Grimsby: Albert Gait

Anderson, R C 1966 'Lists of men of war 1650–1700: part I, English ships 1649–1702'. *Society of Nautical Research Occasional Publications* No. 5, 2nd edn, London

Anon, 1844 'The loss of the brig *Colina*'. *Nautical Magazine* 298–300

Anon, 1887 'The monthly chronicle of north-country lore and legend', Vol. 1. published for the *Newcastle Weekly Chronicle*, Newcastle-upon-Tyne: Walter Scott

Arber, E 1880 *An English Garner: Ingatherings From Our History and Literature*, vol. III. Birmingham: Edward Arber

Archaeological Diving Unit, 1997 '*Lelia*, Mersey Channel, Merseyside, England'. Unpublished report, Report No. ADU97/07

Arnaud, C H 2007 'Saving shipwrecks'. *Chemical and Engineering News* **85**, 2, 8 January, 45–87

Arnold, A and Howard, R 2010 'Hartlaw Cottages, Newton-on-the-Moor, Shilbottle, Northumberland: tree-ring analysis of timbers.' Unpublished report for English Heritage

Auten, Lt. Commander Harold, 1919 *Q-boat Adventures*. London: Herbert Jenkins Ltd. Reprinted 2003. Penzance: Periscope Publishing

Barnett, L P 2008 *The Purton Hulks: The Story of the Purton Ships Graveyard*. Self-published

Barrett, J, Johnstone, C, Harland, J, Van Neers, W, Ervynck, A, Makowiecki, D, *et al* 2008 'Detecting the medieval cod trade'. *Journal of Archaeological Science* **35**, 4, 850–61

Barrow, P 1998 *Slaves of Rapparee: The Wreck of the* London. Bideford: Edward Gaskell Publishers

Bathurst, B 2006 *The Wreckers: A Story of Killing Seas, False Lights and Plundered Ships*. London: Harper Perennial

Bede, the Venerable 1991 *Ecclesiastical History of the English People*, trans. L Sherley-Price, rev edn. London: Penguin

Bethmann-Hollweg, Theobald von 1917 'Speech to the Reichstag', 31 January, <http://www.firstworldwar.com/source/uboat_bethmann.htm>

Bewick, T 1862 *A Memoir of Thomas Bewick: By Himself*. London: Robert Ward, Newcastle-on-Tyne and Longman, Green, Longman and Roberts

Bidwell, P 2001 'A probable Roman shipwreck on the Herd Sand at South Shields'. *Arbeia Journal* **6–7** (1997–8), 1–21

Bingeman, John 2001 'Historic Wreck Sites of the Solent', Hampshire and Wight Trust for Maritime Archaeology, <http://www.hwtma.org.uk/uploads/documents/Annual%20 Lectures/10_2001_Historic%20Wreck%20Sites%20of%20 the%20Solent%20-%20John%20Bingeman.pdf>

Blackstone, Sir William 1765 *Commentaries on the Laws of England*, vol. I, Oxford: Clarendon Press

Blain, B B 2006 'Melting markets: the rise and decline of the Anglo-Norwegian ice trade 1850–1920'. Working Papers of the Global Economic History Network No. 20/06, London School of Economics, <http://eprints.lse.ac.uk/22471/>

BMAPA & English Heritage 2003 *Marine Aggregate Dredging and the Historic Environment: Guidance Note*. London: British Marine Aggregate Producers Association and English Heritage

Bourne, J M 2001 *Who's Who in World War One*. London: Routledge

Bower, Jacqueline, nd, 'The Deal boatmen – heroes or villains?'. Kent Archaeology paper No. 9, <http://www.kentarchaeology.ac/authors/009.pdf>

Brazell, J H 1968 *London Weather*. London: HMSO

Breeze, A 2005 'Wolf Rock, off Land's End'. *English Place-Name Society Journal* **37**, 59–60

British Vessels Lost at Sea 1914–1918 and 1939–1945, 1988 (collated facsim edn of the original HMSO publications). London: Patrick Stephens

Bruce, P 2008 *Solent Hazards*, 5th edn, 2nd rev. Lymington: Boldre Marine

Bulmer, T and Co. 1892 *History, Topography and Directory of East Yorkshire*. Self-published

Caesar, Gaius Julius 1914 *Commentariorum de Bello Gallico: C. Iuli Caesaris Commentarii Rerum in Gallia Gestarum VII A. Hirti Commentarius VIII*, ed. R Rice Holmes. Oxford: Oxford University Press

Caesar, Gaius Julius 1917 *Commentariorum de Bello Gallico: The Gallic War*, parallel English and Latin text, trans H J Edwards (Loeb Classical Library No. 72). Cambridge, MA: Heinemann and Harvard University Press

Camden, W 1610 1806 *Britain, or, a Chorographical Description of the flourishing Kingdoms of England, Scotland, and Ireland and the islands adjacent, from the earliest antiquity*, trans R Gough, printed for John Stockdale, Piccadilly, by T Bensley, Bolt Court, Fleet Street, London

Caretta, V 2003 'Naval records and eighteenth-century black biography'. *Journal for Maritime Research* November, http://www.jmr.nmm.ac.uk/server/show/conJmrArticle.102 [subscription-only site]

Carrott, G 2001 'The loss of the fighter catapult ship HMS *Patia*, April 1941'. *Air North* **41**, April, 189–91

Chaudhuri, K N 2006 *The Trading World of Asia and the English East India Company 1660–1760*. Cambridge: Cambridge University Press

Clayton, T 2007 *Tars: The Men who Made Britain Rule the Waves*. London: Hodder and Stoughton

Coad, J 2011 *Dover Castle: A Frontline Fortress and Its Wartime Tunnels*. London: English Heritage

Cooke, A 2007 *The Fred. Olsen Line and its Passenger Ships*. London: Carmania Press

Coull, J R, nd, *Herring Fishing in Scotland*, <http://sites.scran.ac.uk/secf_final/silver/coull.php>

Council for British Archaeology 2002 'Log boat from Tay estuary dated to the later Bronze Age'. *British Archaeology* **63**, February, 6

Craig, R nd 'Pugin's *Caroline*'. *True Principles* **1**, 3

Cunliffe, B 2002 *The Extraordinary Voyage of Pytheas the Greek: The Man Who Discovered Britain*. London: Penguin

Cushway, G 2011 *Edward III and the War at Sea: The English Navy 1327–1377*. London: Boydell Press

Cussler, C 1978–9 *Search for the* Bonhomme Richard <http://www.numa.net/expeditions/bonhomme-richard/>

Cutting, C L 1955 *Fish Saving: A History of Fish Processing from Ancient to Modern Times*. London: Leonard Hill

Dasent, J R ed 1905 *Acts of the Privy Council*, vol. 30. London: HMSO

Davies, L 2011 *Hulk Assemblages: Assessing the National Context: Final Report: English Heritage Project No.5919*. London: Museum of London Archaeology

Dean, M 1984 'Evidence for possible prehistoric and Roman wrecks in British waters'. *International Journal of Nautical Archaeology*, **13**, 78–80

Defoe, D 1704 *The Storm: or, a Collection of the most remarkable casualties and disasters which happen'd in the late dreadful tempest, both by sea and land* (Reprinted 2005). London: Penguin

Defoe, D 1719 *Robinson Crusoe* (Reprinted 2007). London: Penguin

Defoe, D 1722 *A Journal of the Plague Year*, reprinted 2003. London: Penguin

Defoe, D 1724–6 *A Tour through the Whole Island of Great Britain: From London to Land's End, divided into circuits or journies* (facsim Frank Cass & Co. Ltd 1968)

DeWitt, J 2002 *Early Globalization and the Economic Development of the United States and Brazil*. Westport, CT: Greenwood Publishing

Dunkley, M 2005 'A shipwreck on the Goodwin Sands: local maritime archaeological stewardship', *Conservation Bulletin* **48**, Spring, 28–9

Dunkley, M 2008 '*Rooswijk*, Goodwin Sands, off Kent: Conservation Statement & Management Plan'. Unpublished document, English Heritage, London

Dunkley, M 2011 'Valuing our heritage: conservation principles and heritage protection, *Nautical Archaeology Newsletter*, Spring, 3

Eddius Stephanus, 1927 *The Life of Bishop Wilfrid*, ed and trans B Colgrave. Cambridge: Cambridge University Press

Egilsson, Rev Ólafur 2011 *Reisubók Séra Ólafs Egilssonar*, ed and trans as *The Travels of Reverend Ólafur Egilsson* Karl Smári Hreinsson and Adam Nichols, <www.reisubok.net/default.aspx>

Ellmers, D 1973 'The earliest report on an excavated ship in Europe', *International Journal of Nautical Archaeology* **2**, 1, 177–9

English Heritage 2000 *Portland Castle*. London: English Heritage

English Heritage 2011a *Ships and Boats: Prehistory to Present: Selection Guide* (February 2011, reprinted May 2012). London: English Heritage

English Heritage 2011b *National Heritage Protection Plan*, <http://www.english-heritage.org.uk/professional/protection/national-heritage-protection-plan/>

English Heritage 2012 *Ships and Boats: Prehistory to 1840: Introduction to Heritage Assets*. London: English Heritage

Equiano, O 1789 *The Interesting Narrative of the Life of Olaudah Equiano, or, Gustavus Vassa, the African* (reprinted 2007). Harmondsworth: Penguin

Everard, S 1949 *The History of the Gas Light and Coke Company 1812–1949*. London: Ernest Benn Ltd (facsim edn A&C Black 1992)

Fanning, N 1806–8 *Nathaniel Fanning: An Officer of the American Navy, 1778–1783, by Himself*. New York (reprinted William Abbatt, New York, 1913; facsim edn, Applewood Press 2009)

Fenn, J 1823 *Original Letters written during the reigns of Henry VI, Edward IV and Richard III By Various Persons of Rank or Consequence*, vol. V. London: G G J and J Robinson

Fisheries and Oceans Canada, 2009 'The Grand Banks and the Flemish Cap', <http://www.dfo-mpo.gc.ca/international/media/bk_grandbanks-eng.htm>

Fleming, G B 2010 'La visita a Inglaterra de Juana I (enero-abril de 1506)'. *Juana I en Tordesillas: su mundo, su entorno*, ed M À Zalama. Valladolid: Grupo Pagina

Flower, R and Wynn-Jones, P 1974 *Lloyd's of London: An Illustrated History*. London: Lloyd's of London Press Ltd

Fontana, D nd 'The Cowdray engravings and the Loss of the *Mary Rose*', <http://www.myoldmap.com/dominic/maryrose/>

Freedman, B 1995 *Environmental Ecology: The Ecological Effects of Pollution, Disturbance, and Other Stresses*, 2nd edn. San Diego, CA: Academic Press

Friel, I 1995 *The Good Ship: Ships, Shipbuilding and Technology in England 1200–1520*. London: British Museum Press

Friel, I 2003 *A Maritime History of Britain and Ireland*. London: British Museum Press

Froissart, J 1369–1400 *Chronicles*, trans G Brereton (reprinted 2004). Harmondsworth: Penguin

Gardiner, D M 1976 'A calendar of early Chancery proceedings relating to West Country shipping 1388–1493'. Devon and Cornwall Record Society Publications, No. 21

Gardner, W J R 1949 *The Evacuation from Dunkirk: Operation Dynamo, 26 May–4 June 1940*. London: Admiralty Historical Section

Gavin, S 2010 'The ship in the cottage', Unpublished article

Gibson, R H and Prendergast, M 1931 *The German Submarine War 1914–1918*. London: Constable & Co. Ltd. (reprinted Periscope Publishing 2002)

Gilbert, D 1838 *The Parochial History of Cornwall, Founded on the Manuscript Histories of Mr Hals and Mr Tonkin*, vol. II. London: J B Nichols and Son

Goodall, J 2002 *Whitby Abbey*. London: English Heritage

Goodburn, D, with Tyers, I and Goodburn-Brown, D 1993 'Fragments of a 10th century timber arcade from Vintner's Place on the London waterfront'. *Medieval Archaeology* **37**, 78–92

Gosset, W P 1986 *Lost Ships of the Royal Navy, 1793–1900*. London: Mansell

Gray, A S, Sambrook, J and Birks-Hay, T 1990 *Fanlights: A Visual Architectural History*. London: Alphabooks (A&C Black)

Gregory, D 2006 'Mapping navigational hazards as areas of maritime archaeological potential: the effects of sediment type on the presence of archaeological material'. Unpublished report, No. 13808-0001-01, Nationalmuseet (Denmark)

Greenhill, B and Hackman, J 1991 Herzogin Cecilie: *The Life and Times of a Four-Masted Barque*. London: Conway Maritime Press

Greenstreet, J 1877 'Abstract of Kent Fines anno 1 to anno 6 of Edward III'. *Archaeologia Cantiana* **XI**, 305–58

Gutiérrez, A 2003 'A shipwreck cargo of Sevillian pottery from the Studland Bay Wreck, Dorset'. *International Journal of Nautical Archaeology*, **32**, 1, 24–41

Halpern, P G 1994 *A Naval History of World War I*. Annapolis, MD: Naval Institute Press

Hamer, M 2004 'The Doomsday wreck'. *New Scientist* 21 August, 36–9

Hart, A B ed 1899 *American History Told by Contemporaries, Vol. II, The Building of the Republic*. New York: Macmillan

Hart-Davis, A and Troscianko, E 2002 *Henry Winstanley and the Eddystone Lighthouse*. Stroud: Sutton Publishing

Haslett, S K and Bryant, E A 2004 'The AD 1607 coastal flood in the Bristol Channel and Severn Estuary: historical records from Devon and Cornwall (UK)'. *Archaeology in the Severn Estuary* **15**, 81–9

Hatcher, J 1993 *The History of the British Coal Industry, Vol. 1: Before 1700: Towards the Age of Coal*. Oxford: Clarendon Press

Hegland, J R 1976 *Krigsseilasen Under den Allierte Offensiv,* vols 1 and 2. Oslo: Dreyer

Henig, M 2004 *Corpus Signorum Imperii Romani: Great Britain, Vol. 1, fascicule 9: Roman sculpture from the north-west Midlands*. London: Oxford University Press

Henwood, W J 1872 'Remarks in relation to paper read by H Michell Whitley, 14th November 1871'. Fifty-Fourth Annual Report of the Royal Institution of Cornwall, Truro

Hill, R 2007 *God's Architect: Pugin and the Building of Romantic Britain*. Harmondsworth: Penguin

Hiscock, K 2009 'Revealing the reef: marine life settling on ex-HMS *Scylla*', <www.marlin.ac.uk/learningzone/scylla>

Holmes, R ed 2003 *The Oxford Companion to Military History*. Oxford: Oxford University Press

Hopkins, G M 1953a 'The wreck of the *Deutschland*: to the happy memory of five Franciscan Nuns, exiles by the Falk Laws, drowned between midnight and morning, Dec. 7th, 1875', *Gerard Manley Hopkins: Poems and Prose*, ed W H Gardner. London: Penguin Classics

Hopkins, G M 1953b 'The wreck of the *Eurydice*, Foundered March 24, 1878', *Gerard Manley Hopkins: Poems and Prose*, ed W H Gardner. London: Penguin Classics

Horne, G 2007 *The Deepest South: The United States, Brazil, and the African Slave Trade*. New York: New York University

Hutchinson, G 1994 *Medieval Ships and Shipping*. London: Leicester University Press

Hyde, F E 1971 *Liverpool and the Mersey: The Development of a Port, 1700–1970*. Newton Abbot: David and Charles

International Slavery Museum, nd 'Liverpool and the slave trade', <http://www.liverpoolmuseums.org.uk/ism/slavery/europe/liverpool.aspx>

Institute of Netherlands History, nd 'The Dutch East India Company's shipping between the Netherlands and Asia 1595–1795', <http://www.inghist.nl/Onderzoek/Projecten/DAS/search>

Isle of Wight History Centre, nd 'Earliest known scenes of the Isle of Wight', <http://freespace.virgin.net/iw.history/iwscenes/dutch.htm>

Jenkinson, D 2010 'The ship carving of All Saints' Church, East Budleigh, C16', <http://www.ovapedia.org.uk/index.php?page=The-Ship-Carving-of-All-Saints-Church-East-Budleigh-C16>

Kemp, P ed 1988 *Oxford Companion to Ships and the Sea*, rev edn. Oxford: Oxford University Press

King, E 1779 'An account of an old piece of ordnance, which some fishermen dragged out of the sea near the Goodwin Sands, in 1775'. *Archaeologia* **V**, 147–59

Komar, A 2010 'End of project report: Modern Wrecks Project – creation of AMIE records for post 1945 shipwrecks in English territorial waters'. Unpublished report, English Heritage

Kowaleski, M ed 2001 *The Havener's Accounts of the Earldom & Duchy of Cornwall, 1287–1356*. Exeter: Devon and Cornwall Record Society, New Series, vol. 44

Ladle, L 1993 *The Studland Bay Wreck: A Spanish Shipwreck off the Dorset Coast*. Poole: Poole Museum Heritage Series, vol. 1

Lamb, H H 1977 *Climate: Present, Past and Future: Vol. 2, Climatic History and the Future*. London: Methuen & Co

Lamb, H H and Frydendahl, K 1991 *Historic Storms of the North Sea, British Isles and Northwest Europe*. Cambridge: Cambridge University Press

Land Use Consultants 2005 'South Downs integrated landscape character assessment, < http://www.southdowns.gov.uk/planning/integrated-landscape-character-assessment>

Lapidge, M, Blair, J, Keynes, S and Scragg, D eds 1999 *Blackwell's Encyclopedia of Anglo-Saxon England*. Oxford: Oxford University Press

Larn, R and Larn, B 1977 *Goodwin Sands Shipwrecks*. Newton Abbot: David and Charles

Larn, R and Larn, B 1995 *Shipwreck Index of the British Isles, Vol. 1 The West Country*. London: Lloyd's Register of Shipping

Larn, R and Larn, B 1996 *Shipwreck Index of the British Isles, Vol. 2 The South Coast*. London: Lloyd's Register of Shipping

Larn, R and Larn, B 1997 *Shipwreck Index of the British Isles, Vol. 3 The East Coast*. London: Lloyd's Register of Shipping

Larn, R and Larn, B 1998 *Shipwreck Index of the British Isles, Vol. 4 Scotland*. London: Lloyd's Register of Shipping

Larn, R and Larn, B 2000 *Shipwreck Index of the British Isles, Vol. 5 Wales and the West Coast*. London: Lloyd's Register of Shipping

Lewis, B 1973 'Corsairs in Iceland'. *Revue de l'Occident Musulman et de la Mediteranée* **15**, 15–16, 139–44

Lewis, S 1848 *A Topographical Dictionary of England*. London: Samuel Lewis & Co.

Liddiard, J 2008 'HMS *Patia*'. *Diver* January, 74–6

Lloyd's Register of Shipping, 1764 London: Lloyd's Register Group

Lloyd's War Losses: The First World War: Casualties to Shipping Through Enemy Causes, 1914–1918 (facsim reprint, Lloyd's of London Press Ltd 1990)

Lloyd's War Losses: The Second World War: Casualties to Shipping Through Enemy Causes, 19391945, 2 vols (facsim reprint, Lloyd's of London Press Ltd 1991)

Looseley, R 2006 'Paradise after hell'. *History Today* **56**, June, 32–8

Luttrell, N 1857 *A Brief Historical Relation of State Affairs from September 1678 to April 1714*, vol. 3. Oxford: Oxford University Press

Macdonald, L 1980 *The Roses of No-Man's Land*. London: Michael Joseph

Macfie, A L 1984 'The report of the House of Commons Select Committee on the Cinque-Port pilots, 1833'. *Archaeologia Cantiana* **101**, 131–6

Malcolm, C 2002 'A collection of artifacts recovered from the shipwreck *Henrietta Marie*', <http://www.melfisher.org/pdf/HM-Artifacts-2002-NOAA-Report.pdf>

Mariners' Museum 2000 *A Dictionary of the World's Watercraft: from Aaak to Zumbra*. London: Chatham Publishing

Marsden, P 1994 *Ships of the Port of London: First to 11th centuries AD*. London: English Heritage Archaeological Report 3

Marsden, P 1996 *Ships of the Port of London: 12th to 17th Centuries AD*. London: English Heritage Archaeological Report 5

Martin, D and Martin, B 2004 *New Winchelsea, Sussex: A Medieval Port Town* (Field Archaeological Unit Monograph No. 2). London: Institute of Archaeology, University College

Mayor, A 2008 *Tanks and Bulldozers Project*. Southsea: Southsea Sub-Aqua Club

McCartney, I 2003 *Lost Patrols: Submarine Wrecks of the English Channel*. Penzance: Periscope Publishing

McCombie, G 2008 *Tynemouth Priory*. London: English Heritage

McDonald, K 1999 *Dive Sussex*. Teddington: Underwater World Publications

McGrail, S 1978 'Logboats of England and Wales with comparative material from European and other countries: Part I: discussion and catalogue'. *BAR British Series* 51 (i)

McGrail, S 1987 *Ancient Boats in N W Europe: The Archaeology of Water Transport to AD 1500*. London: Longman

McKee, F M 1993 'An explosive story: the rise and fall of the common depth charge'. *The Northern Mariner* **III**, 45–58

Merritt, O, Parham, D and McElvogue, D M 2007 'Enhancing our understanding of the marine historic environment: navigational hazards project: final report'. Unpublished report, Bournemouth University

Merritt, O 2008 'Refining areas of maritime archaeological potential for shipwrecks – AMAP 1'. Unpublished project report 1.2

Messimer, D R 2002 *Verschollen: World War I U-boat Losses*. Annapolis, MD: Naval Institute Press

Metropolitan Borough of Wirral, Environment, Transportation and Planning Strategy Select Committee, 2002 'Report of the Deputy Chief Executive/Direct of Planning and Economic Development', 22nd October 2002, http://www.wirral.gov.uk/Minute/public/envped021022rep01_6912.pdf [accessed 10 August 2009, link no longer live]

Middlewood, R and Ashdown, J 1972 'The Mewstone Ledge site'. *International Journal of Nautical Archaeology* **1**, 1

Mordal, J (Hervé Cras) 1968 *Dunkerque*. Paris: Éditions France Empire

Munching, L L von 1968 'Merchant shipping losses of Allied, Neutral and Central powers during and shortly after World War I'. Unpublished typescript

Naish, J M 1985 *Seamarks: Their History and Development*. London: Stanford Maritime

National Maritime Museum 2004 'Ships, seafarers, and life at sea: load lines', <http://www.rmg.co.uk/explore/sea-and-ships/facts/ships-and-seafarers/load-lines>

Nayling, N 2008 *The Norman's Bay Wreck, East Sussex: Tree Ring Analysis of Ship Timbers: Scientific Dating Report* (Research Department Report Series No. 25-2008). London: English Heritage

Newby, E 1999 *Learning the Ropes: An Apprentice in the Last of the Windjammers*. London: John Murray

Newman, M 2009 'A record of England's underwater past that's fit for the future'. Unpublished conference paper

Nichols, A 2011 'Kidnapped in Iceland'. *BBC History* **12**, 2 February, 56–9

Niestlé, A 1998 *German U-Boat Losses During World War II: Details of Destruction*. Annapolis, MD: Naval Institute Press

Niestlé, A 2007 'The loss of *U 325*, *U 400* and *U 1021* (published online 11 May 2007), <http://www.uboat.net/articles/index.html?article=69>

Norman, B 2002 *Broken Eagles 2: Luftwaffe Losses over Northumberland and Durham 1939–1945*. Barnsley: Pen and Sword Books

Norsk Sjøfartsmuseum 2003 *Sjøforklaringer fra 2. Verdenskrig*. Oslo: Norsk Sjøfartsmuseum

Officer, L H 2009–11 'Purchasing power of British pounds from 1264 to present', Measuring Worth, <http://www.measuringworth.com/ppoweruk/>

O'Regan, H 2002 'From bear pit to zoo'. *British Archaeology* **68**, December, 12–19

Osberg, R H ed 1997 *The Poems of Laurence Minot 1333–1352*. Kalamazoo, MI: Medieval Institute Publications, online edition <http://www.lib.rochester.edu/Camelot/teams/minot.htm>

Page, W ed 1912 *The Victoria County History of Hampshire and the Isle of Wight*, vol. 5. London: Constable

Page, W ed 1926 *The Victoria County History of Kent*, vol. 2. London: St Catherine Press

Palmer, M 1998 *Eddystone 300: The Finger of Light*. Torpoint: Palmridge Publishing

Peacock, B 2009 'In situ neglect'. *Nautical Archaeology Newsletter,* Summer, 3

Pepys, S 1983–9 *Diaries*, ed P Gyford, <http://www.pepysdiary.com> (based on *The Diary of Samuel Pepys*, ed H B Wheatley, George Bell & Sons, London)

Perkins, D R J 1979 'Wreck of a British man-of-war discovered on the Goodwin Sands'. Interim report, The Isle of Thanet Archaeological Unit

Pevsner, N and Radcliffe, E 1970 *Buildings of England: Cornwall*. Harmondsworth: Penguin

Pilbin, P 1937 'External relations of the Tyneside glass industry'. *Economic Geography* **13**, 3 July, 301–14

Platt, C 1988 *Dover Castle*. London: English Heritage

Pliny, the Elder 1938 *Natural History, Books I–II*, trans H Rackham (Loeb Classical Library No. 330). Cambridge, MA: Heinemann and Harvard University Press

Plutarch 1878 *The Morals vol. 3*, trans W Goodwin. Boston, MA: Little, Brown & Co.

Pollard, C 2007 *The Book of St Mawes: Pilots, Pilchards and Politics*. Wellington: Halsgrove

Pool, P A S 1959 'The Penheleg MS'. *Journal of the Royal Institution of Cornwall* **III**, 3, 163–228

Port, G 1989 *Scarborough Castle*. London: English Heritage

Porter, S and Hobhouse, H eds 1994 *Survey of London, Vol. XLIV, Poplar, Blackwall and the Isle of Dogs*, vol. 2, London: Athlone Press for the Royal Commission on the Historical Monuments of England

Poulson, G 1841 *The History and Antiquities of the Seigniory of Holderness in the East Riding of the County of Yorkshire*, vol. 2, Hull: Robert Brown

Pritchard, J 2004 *In Search of Empire: The French in the Americas, 1670–1730*. Cambridge: Cambridge University Press.

Quartermaine, J and Raynor, C 2009 'The old dock: how Liverpool grew to greatness'. *Current Archaeology* **233**, August, 12–21

Ray, J E 1930 'Reports of local secretaries: Hastings'. *Sussex Archaeological Collections* **71**, 263–4

Redknap, M and Fleming, M 1985 'The Goodwins archaeological survey: towards a regional marine site register in Britain', *World Archaeology*, **16**, 3, 312–28

Reed, N 2002 *Frost Fairs on the Frozen Thames*. Folkestone: Lilburne Press

Rhodes, E L 2007 'The legend of the Lady *Luvibund*', <http://www.emmalouiserhodes.com/articles/legend-of-lady-luviband.php> [accessed 12 November 2007, link no longer live]

Richards, J 2008 'Dunkirk revisited', <www.dunkirk-revisited.co.uk>

Richardson, M A 1846 *Local Historian's Table-Book of Remarkable Occurrences, Historical Facts, Traditions, Legendary and Descriptive Ballads, &c. &c. Connected with the Counties of Newcastle-upon-Tyne, Northumberland, and Durham*, vol. V, Newcastle-upon-Tyne

Ridley, G 2004 *Clara's Grand Tour: Travels with a Rhinoceros in Eighteenth-Century Europe*. London: Atlantic Books

Risdon, T 1620 *The Chorographical Description or Survey of the County of Devon with the City and County of Exeter* (facsim 1811 edn, Barnstaple 1970)

Riste, O 1965 *The Neutral Ally: Norway's Relations with Belligerent Powers in the First World War*. London: Universitetsforlaget, Oslo/Allen & Unwin

Robertshaw, E S, and Carter, E (ed) 2008 *Before the Mast: In the Grain Races of the 1930s*. Truro: Blue Elvan Books

Roddie, A 'Jacob, the diver'. *Mariner's Mirror*, **62**, 3, 253–69. Society for Nautical Research, London

Rodger, N A M 1997 *The Safeguard of the Sea: A Naval History of Britain, Vol. I, 660–1649*. London: HarperCollins

Rodger, N A M 2004 *The Command of the Ocean: A Naval History of Britain, Vol. II, 1649–1815*. London: HarperCollins

Rodríguez García, J M 1998 'Los enfrentamientos bélicos con Inglaterra y sus gentes: la visión Castellana, 1250–1515', *Revista de Historia Militar* **84**, 2, 1–45, <http://usuarios.multimania.es/historiador1969/revhmil.htm>

Rose, S 2002 *Medieval Naval Warfare 1000–1500*. New York: Routledge

Rule, M 1982 *The Mary Rose: The Excavation and Raising of Henry VIII's Flagship*. London: Conway Maritime Press

Rule, M and Monaghan, J 1993 *A Gallo-Roman Trading Vessel from Guernsey: The Excavation and Recovery of a Third Century Shipwreck*. Guernsey Museums Monograph No. 5. Guernsey: Guernsey Museums and Galleries

Russell, M 2005 'Ruling Britannia'. *History Today* **55**, 8, 5

Salzman, L F ed 1937 *The Victoria County History of Sussex, Vol. IX, The Rape of Hastings*. London: Oxford University Press

Sawyer, F E 1883 'St. Wilfrith's life in Sussex and the introduction of Christianity'. *Sussex Archaeological Society, Sussex Archaeological Collections: Relating to the History and Antiquities of the Counties of East and West Sussex* **33**, 100–128

Schäuffelen, O 2005 *Chapman Great Sailing Ships of the World*. New York: Hearst Books

Sebborn, D J 2000 *Your Faithful Servant: Insights Into the Life of the Cromwellian Navy from the Letters, Despatches, and Orders of Robert Blake General at Sea*. Whitstable: Pryor Publications

Seal, J 2002 *The Wreck at Sharpnose Point: A Victorian Mystery*. London: Picador

Shadwell, T 1675/2005 'The libertine', in Deborah P F (ed) *Four Restoration Libertine Plays*. Oxford: Oxford World's Classics, 1–84

Shakespeare, W 1596–8 *The Merchant of Venice*, ed W Moelwyn Merchant. London: Penguin

Sicking, L and Arbreu-Ferreira, D eds 2009 *Beyond the Catch: Fisheries of the North Atlantic, the North Sea and the Baltic, 900–1850*. Leiden: Brill

Smith H J and Smith H J Jr 1858 *Cyclopedia of Commerce, 1858*, vol. 1. New York: Harper and Bros (facsim edn 1970)

Smollett, T 1771 *The Expedition of Humphry Clinker* (2005 edn). London: Penguin

Sobel, D 1998 *Longitude: The True Story of a Lone Genius who Solved the Greatest Scientific Problem of His Time*. London: Fourth Estate

Spiers, T J 2004 'Shot Down over Dunkirk: 28th May 1940', *BBC People's War*, <http://www.bbc.co.uk/ww2peopleswar/stories/35/a2764235.shtml>

Spillman, J nd 'Glassmaking, America's first industry', <http://www.antiquesandfineart.com/articles/article.cfm?request=929>

Stafford, R 2009 *The Ellan Vannin Story: An Account of the Loss of the SS Ellan Vannin*. Douglas: Manx Heritage Foundation

Stanger, C 2002 'Burbo offshore wind farm, Vol. 4: technical report No. 4: seascape and visual assessment, July

Statens Arkiver, Denmark nd 'Styles of handwriting', <http://www.sa.dk/content/us/genealogy/styles_of_handwriting>

Stromberg, O G nd Båtsmansdatabasen (Database of Seamen), <http://www.gstromberg.nu/index.htm>

Studer, P ed 1913 *The Port Books of Southampton, or (Anglo-French) Accounts of Robert Florys, Water Bailiff and Receiver of Petty Customs, AD 1427–1430* (Southampton Record Society No. 15). Southampton: Cox and Sharland

Supple, B 1987 *The History of the British Coal Industry, Vol. 4: 1913–1946: The Political Economy of Decline*. Oxford: Clarendon Press

Svalesen, L 1995 'The slave ship *Fredensborg*: history, shipwreck, and find'. *History in Africa* **22**, 455–8

Swinburne, A C 1904 'Grace Darling'. *The Collected Works of Algernon Charles Swinburne*, vol. VI. London: William Heinemann

Taffrail (Captain Taprell Dorling, DSO, FRHistS, RN) 1935 *Swept Channels: Being an Account of the Work of the Minesweepers in the Great War*. London: Hodder and Stoughton

Taylor, H 1861 *Instructions for Mariners Respecting the Management of Ships at Single Anchor, and General Rules for Sailing, Also Directions for Crossing the North Sea, the Cattegat, &c., With an Address to Seamen: To Which is Prefixed a Memoir of the Author's Life*, 7th edn. London: James Imray & Son

Tennent, A J 1990 *British Merchant Ships Sunk by U-boats in the 1914–1918 War*. self-published

Thomsen, M 2000 'The Studland Bay wreck, Dorset: hull analysis'. *International Journal of Nautical Archaeology* **29**, 1, 69–85

Þór, J Þ nd 'Shark and cod fisheries: pioneering period', Icelandic Fisheries, <http://www.fisheries.is/history/the-age-of-sail/shark-and-cod-fisheries/>

Tibbles, A 2000 'Ports of the Transatlantic slave trade', TextPorts conference paper, Liverpool Hope University College, <http://www.liverpoolmuseums.org.uk/ism/resources/slave_trade_ports.aspx>

Tomalin, D, Simpson, P and Bingeman, J 2000 'Excavation versus sustainability in situ: a conclusion on 25 years of archaeological investigations at Goose Rock, a designated historic wreck site at the Needles, Isle of Wight'. *International Journal of Nautical Archaeology*, **29**, 1, 3–42

Toulmin Smith, L ed 1872 *The Maire of Bristowe is Kalendar, by Robert Ricart, Town Clerk of Bristol, 18 Edward IV*. Camden Society Second Series

Tregellas P R ed 1983 *Down to the Sea in Ships: The Memoirs of James Henry Treloar Cliff*. Redruth: Dyllansow Truran

Trollope, E 1872 *Sleaford and the Wapentakes of Flaxwell and Ashwardhurn in the County of Lincoln* London: William Kent

Tucker, J 2008 *Ferries of Gloucestershire*. Stroud: Tempus

UNESCO, nd 'The slave ship *Fredensborg*', <http://unesco.no/component/content/article/145>, <http://unesco.no/component/content/article/147>

Villette-Mursay, P de 1991 *Mes campagnes de mer sous Louis XIV*, ed Michel Vergé-Franceschi. Paris: Editions Tallandier

Weightman, G 2004 *London's Thames* London: John Murray

Wendes, D 2006 *South Coast Shipwrecks off East Dorset and Wight 1870–1979*. Self-published

Wessex Archaeology 2003a '*Bonhomme Richard*, Filey Bay, North Yorkshire: designated site assessment: full report'. Unpublished report for English Heritage

Wessex Archaeology 2003b '*Stirling Castle*: designated wreck site: desk-based assessment'. Unpublished report for English Heritage

Wessex Archaeology 2005 'Protocol for reporting finds of archaeological interest'. British Marine Aggregate Producers Association and English Heritage

Wessex Archaeology 2006 '*Rooswijk*, Goodwin Sands: undesignated site assessment'. Unpublished report for English Heritage

Wessex Archaeology 2007a 'Norman's Bay Wreck: designated site assessment'. Unpublished report for English Heritage

Wessex Archaeology 2007b '*Stirling Castle*, Goodwin Sands: designated site assessment'. Unpublished report for English Heritage

Wessex Archaeology 2008 'Marine class descriptions and principles of selection in aggregate areas'. English Heritage Project No. 5383

Wessex Archaeology 2010a 'HMS *London*, Southend, Thames Estuary: designated site assessment', Archaeological report

Wessex Archaeology 2010b '*Northumberland*, Goodwin Sands, Kent: designated site assessment'. Unpublished report for English Heritage

Wessex Archaeology 2010c 'The *Royal James*, Southwold, Suffolk: undesignated site assessment'. Unpublished report for English Heritage

Wessex Archaeology 2012 'HMS *London*, Southend, Thames Estuary: designated site assessment'. Archaeological report

Wharton-Lloyd, D and Pevsner, N 2006 *The Buildings of England: The Isle of Wight*. London: Yale University Press

Wheeler, D 2003 'The great storm of November 1703: a new look at seamen's records'. *Weather* **58**, 11, 419–27

Whitelock, D ed with Douglas, D C and Tucker, S I 1961 *The Anglo-Saxon Chronicle*. London: Eyre and Spottiswoode

Willis, S 2009 *The Fighting Temeraire*. London: Quercus

Wilmott, T and Tibber, J 2009 'Richborough, a Roman and medieval port!'. *Research News*: *Newsletter of the English Heritage Research Department* **12**, Summer 20–2

Wilson, I 1996 *John Cabot and the* Matthew. Bristol: Redcliffe Press

Wilson, J M 1870–2 *Imperial Gazetteer of England and Wales*. London and Edinburgh: A Fullarton & Co

Wright, T 1844 'On antiquarian excavations and researches in the Middle Ages'. *Archaeologia* **30**, 439–57

Wood, W nd *Fishermen in War Time*. London: Sampson, Low, Marston & Co

Woodman, R and Wilson, J 2002 *The Lighthouses of Trinity House*. Bradford-on-Avon: Thomas Reed Publications

Woods Hole Oceanographic Institute 1952 *Marine Fouling and Its Prevention*. Annapolis, MD: US Naval Institute

Wordsworth, W 1843 'Grace Darling', <www.bartleby.com>

Wordsworth, W 1805 'To the daisy', <www.bartleby.com>

Wren Society 1939 *Drawings and models of the construction of St Paul's Cathedral, measured drawings of the old choir by F C Penrose, Thomas Malton's drawings 1797–1800. Part 1: the contract book, part 2: the minute book, part 3: the 'frauds and abuses' controversy, and part 4: building accounts 1668–1675*, vol. 16. Oxford: Oxford University Press

Young, R 2000 *The Comprehensive Guide to Shipwrecks of the North East Coast, Volume 1 (1740–1917)*. Stroud: Tempus

Young, R 2001 *The Comprehensive Guide to Shipwrecks of the North East Coast, Volume 2 (1918–2000)*. Stroud: Tempus

ZDF 2008 *Fahrten ins Ungewisse: 31 Stunden Hölle auf der Deutschland*, microsite associated with programme broadcast by ZDF, <http://www.zdf.de/ZDFde/inhalt/13/0,1872,7186221,00.html?dr=1> accessed 23 September 2008 [not archived/no longer live]

Contemporary sources

Annual Register

Board of Trade Casualty Returns

Bristol Weekly Intelligencer

British Gazette and Berwick Advertiser

Bury and Norwich Post, and Suffolk Herald

Calendar of Close Rolls (CCR)

Calendar of Patent Rolls (CPR)

Calendar of State Papers Domestic (CSP.Dom)

Calendar of State Papers Foreign

Calendar of Treasury Books

Cumberland Pacquet

Deal, Walmer, Dover and Kentish Telegram

Dordrechtse Courant

Durham County Advertiser

Farley's Bristol News-Paper

F. Farley's Bristol Journal

Felix Farley's Bristol Journal

Hansard

Hull Packet and East Riding Times

Ipswich Journal

Kentish Post, or Canterbury News-letter

Lancaster Gazette

Leeuwarder Courant

Letters and Papers, Foreign and Domestic

Liverpool Mercury

Lloyd's List

Lloyd's Register of Shipping

London Gazette

Morning Post

New York Times

Newcastle Courant

Norwich Mercury

Nouvelles d'Amsterdam

Public Ledger (Philadelphia)

Royal Cornwall Gazette

Sherborne Mercury

Statistisk Oversigt over de i aaret 1914 [1915/1916/1917/1918] for danske skibe i danske og fremmede farvande samt for fremmede skibe i danske farvande, indtrufne Søulykker, Copenhagen, 1915/1916/1917/1918/1919

Suffolk Chronicle

Sunderland and Durham Shipping Gazette and Mercantile Advertiser

The Times

Tyne Mercury

West Briton

An Exact Relation of The Late Dreadful Tempest: Or, A Faithful Account of The Most Remarkable Disaster Which Happened On That Occasion. Faithfully Collected By An Ingenious Hand, To Preserve The Memory Of So Terrible A Judgement, 1704, <http://books.google.com/books?id=mD0LAQAAIAAJ>

1607. A true report of certain wonderfull ouerflowings of Waters, now lately in Summerset-shire, Norfolke and other places of England … Edward White, printer, 1607, <http://www.eebo.chadwyck.com>

More strange nevves: of wonderfull accidents hapning by the late ouerflowings of waters, in Summerset-shire, Gloucestershire, Norfolke, and other places of England: with a true relation of the townes names that are lost, and the number of persons drowned, with other reports of accidents that were not before discouered: happening about Bristow and Barstable printed at London: By W[illiam] I[aggard] for Edward White, 1607, <http://www.eebo.chadwyck.com>

A True and perfect relation of the great damages done by the late great tempest, and overflowing of the tyde upon the coasts of Lincolnshire and county of Norfolk: also an accompt of the ships cast away, houses beaten down, and men, women and children drowned by the late inundation. Printed at London in the year 1671, <http://www.eebo.chadwyck.com>

A full account of the late Ship-wreck of the Ship called The PRESIDENT which was castaway in Mountz-Bay in Cornwal on the 4th of February last … by William Smith and John Harshfield, the only Persons that escaped in the said Wreck … Printed for Randal Taylor, London, 1684, <http://www.eebo.chadwyck.com>

England's Second Warning: Being a further and more particular Account of the great Damage done both by Sea and Land, by the late amazing Storm and Tempest that happened on Saturday the 11th of August 1705 London, Printed for F Thorn, near Fleet-street, 1705 <http://eebo.chadwyck.com>

The National Archives (TNA) ADM 103/41, 106/581, 199/1650, 202/304, 202/305, 202/306, ADM 53/61347, AIR1/259/15/226/92, DEFE 2/418

Filmography:

British Pathe, 1954, 'Implacable to the end', http://www.britishpathe.com/record.php?id=27323

British Pathe, 1954, 'Storm havoc', http://www.britishpathe.com/record.php?id=32935

New Era Productions Ltd. 1928 *Q-Ships*. British Film Institute

ZDF, 2008. *Fahrten ins Ungewisse: 31 Stunden Hölle auf der Deutschland*

Reference works

Oxford English Dictionary (OED)

Websites and web publications

Admiralty EasyTide, <http://easytide.ukho.gov.uk/EASYTIDE/EasyTide/index.aspx>

BBC news website, <http://www.bbc.co.uk/news/>

British History Online, <www.british-history.ac.uk>

British Library, Online Gallery, 'Leonardo da Vinci', <http://www.bl.uk/onlinegallery/features/leonardo/leonardo.html>

British Pathé, <http://www.britishpathe.com>

Channel Navigation Information Service, <http://www.dft.gov.uk/mca/mcga07-home/emergencyresponse/mcga-searchandrescue/mcga-theroleofhmcoasguard/mcga-_hm_coastguard_-_the_dover_strait.htm>

Civil Hydrography Programme, < http://www.dft.gov.uk/mca/mcga-safety_information/nav-com/mcga-dqs-hmp-hydrography/civil_hydrography_programme_results.htm >

ConvoyWeb, <http://www.convoyweb.org.uk>

Dictionary of Newfoundland English Online, <http://www.heritage.nf.ca/dictionary/>

Diver Magazine online, <http://www.divernet.com/>

Encyclopedia Titanica, <http://www.encyclopedia-titanica.org>

Eskside, the search for the Bonhomme Richard, http://www.eskside.co.uk/clive_cussler1.htm

http://www.eskside.co.uk/clive_cussler2.htm

http://www.eskside.co.uk/clive_cussler3.htm

Ferro-Concrete Ships, <http://www.mareud.com>

First World War, a multimedia history, <http://www.firstworldwar.com>

Flight International, Supplement, <http://www.flightglobal.com/pdfarchive/index.html>

Fred. Olsen & Co., History, <http://www.fredolsen.com/?aid=9043556>

Great Books Online, <www.bartleby.com>

Kent Online Parish Clerks, Deal and Walmer Newspaper Extracts, <http://www.kent-opc.org/Parishes/News/Deal%20Wrecks%201870s.html>

Les épaves au large de Dunkerque, <http://dkepaves.free.fr>

Lost Brig Elizabeth Jane, <http://www.lostbrig.net/>

Mary Rose Trust, <http://www.maryrose.org/>

Medieval Origins of Commercial Sea Fishing Project, <http://www.mcdonald.cam.ac.uk/projects/Medieval_Fishing/coll.html> and <https://www.onroerenderfgoed.be/projecten/the-medieval-origins-of-commercial-sea-fishing-project/>

Mel Fisher Maritime Museum, http://www.melfisher.org/henriettamarie.htm>, <http://www.melfisher.org/turtleharbor.htm>

Mémorial des marins morts pour la France, <http://auxmarins.net/accueil>

Miramar Ship Index, <http://www.miramarshipindex.org.nz>

National Archives, 'Arriving in Britain', <http://www.nationalarchives.gov.uk/pathways/blackhistory/intro/intro.htm>

Ocean Technology, <http://www.oceantechnology.org/BHR.htm>

Old Bailey Online: The Proceedings of the Old Bailey 1675–1913, <http://www.oldbaileyonline.org/>

Oxford Dictionary of National Biography, http://www.oxforddnb.com

Royal Commission on the Ancient and Historical Monuments of Scotland, Canmore database <http://www.rcahms.gov.uk/canmore.html>

Royal Commission on the Ancient and Historical Monuments of Wales, Coflein database, <www.coflein.gov.uk>

Royal Navy Submarine Museum, Gosport, <http://www.submarine-museum.co.uk/>

Thames Sailing Barge Trust, <http://www.bargetrust.org/shorthist.html>

The Ships List, http://www.theshipslist.com/

The U-boat wars 1939–45 (Kriegsmarine) and 1914–18 (Kaiserliche Marine) <http://www.uboat.net>

Timeline for Romney Marsh, http://www.liv.ac.uk/geography/RomneyMarsh/RM%20Timeline/Timeline.htm [accessed 28 November 2008: no longer live]

Trans-Atlantic Slave Trade Database, http://www.slavevoyages.org/tast/database/search.faces

Vasa Museum <http://www.vasamuseet.se/en/>

Warsailors, <http://www.warsailors.com>

World Surname Profiler, <http://www.publicprofiler.org/worldnames/>

Wrecksite, <http://www.wrecksite.eu>

Yavari Project, <http://www.yavari.org/>

ACKNOWLEDGEMENTS

With very grateful thanks to Gillian Grayson, Neil Guiden, David Hilton and Martin Newman, all Heritage Data Management, Designation Department, English Heritage, Swindon, for all their very kind help, encouragement, support and comments, and to all my other colleagues within English Heritage at large and at the NRHE in particular. Especial thanks to my maritime specialist colleagues in Designation and elsewhere in English Heritage, namely Mark Dunkley, Alison James, Ian Oxley and Chris Pater for a great deal of informative insight and suggestions along the way, particularly Alison for her contribution; and to Judith Dobie for her illustrations.

Within English Heritage I also owe an enormous debt to René Rodgers, Sarah Enticknap and Robin Taylor for their editorial guidance; Kieran Byrne for his technical assistance and for many helpful insights and comments; Edward Carpenter for alerting me to many vital aerial shots; Tom Duane for the maps; Michael Evans for comments on the *Preussen*; Jo Freeman for assistance with running data searches; Anna Komar, Modern Wrecks Project Officer; Tanja Watson, for her help with Swedish and other Scandinavian documents and contacts; Anne Wiggans for help with picture research; and all the staff at the English Heritage Library, Swindon, namely Nicky Cryer, Claire Field, Felicity Gilmour, Helen Jurga, Diana Sims, Caroline Steele and Elly Thornton for patiently answering questions and tracking down sources and materials of all kinds. Rod FitzGerald, Neil Guiden, Emma Jordan, Julie Lancley, Sarah MacLean and Tanja Watson most kindly checked all the NRHE AMIE numbers, for which I owe them enormous thanks.

Special thanks are due to Alison Kentuck, Receiver of Wreck, for her very helpful comments and suggestions. Very special thanks must go to Stephen and Vicky Gavin for allowing me to tell their story, and to our mutual friend Bernard Thomason who put me in touch with them. I am immensely grateful for the specific assistance and kindness provided by Dr Mark Adams, Liverpool Museums; Kitty Brandon, Wessex Archaeology; Kate Brett, Naval Historical Branch; Paul Cavill, Institute of Place Name Studies, University of Nottingham; Jonathan and Macarena Davies; Martin Davies; Ian Emmerson, James Alder Fine Art, and the present owner of the *Iron Crown*; Hazel Forsyth, Museum of London; Paula Gentil, Curator of Archaeology, Hull and East Riding Museum; Paul Goulder; drs Karen Gelijns, Ministerie van Defensie, Netherlands; Dee Groom, RCAHMW; Guy Hannaford, UKHO; June Holmes, Natural History Society of Northumbria; Knut Klippenberg, Fred. Olsen; Sarah Kmosena, National Maritime Museum, Royal Museums Greenwich; Ian Marshall, Museum of London; Alison Mayor; Nelson Mceachan and his team, UKHO; Alison Mills, Museum of Barnstaple and North Devon; Bob Mowat, RCAHMS; Peter Murphy, English Heritage; Nigel Nayling, University of Wales, Lampeter; Andrea Otte, Rijksdienst voor Cultureel Erfgoed, Netherlands; Louisa Pittman, University of Bristol; Justin Reay, Bodleian Library, Oxford; Graham Scott, Wessex Archaeology; Matt Skelhorn, MoD; Michael Smith, University of Newcastle; Matti Watton, Lambeth Palace Library; drs Willem Weber, Zeeuws Maritiem MuZEEum; Dave Wendes; Peter Williams, English Heritage; and Hugh Winfield, North East Lincolnshire Council.

Finally, more personal thanks must go to my long-suffering husband, Andrew Wyngard, for putting up with the continuous 'wreck talk' and for his moral support during the writing of this book.

INDEX

Page numbers in **bold** refer to figures and tables.

A

A1, HMSM *48*, 108–9, **109**
Abbie Perkins 128
Abraham Rydberg 186
Adelaïde 214
Admiral Gardner 41
Admiral van Tromp **240**
'Admirals All' (Newbold) 61
Admiralty Wreck Register 130
Adventure 28
aggregate extraction 49
air-sea rescue 113
aircraft
    First World War **111**, 111–12, **112**
    interwar years 113
    Second World War 105, 109, **112**, 112–13, **113**, 114
airships **111**, 111–12, **112**
Albatros 83
Albemarle 151
Alberta 85
Alexander 153–4
Alfred, King of Wessex 52, 57–8
Algarve 90
Alliance 77, 78, 79
Alonzo **227**, 227
Alum Bay 29, **30**, 31
Ambassador 42
Amboyna Massacre 152–3
Amphion, HMS (lost 1914) 82–3
Amphion (lost 1796) 123
Amsterdam x, 42, **43**, 152, 192
Amulree, HMS 104
Amy 101

Ancholme River log boat 197
Ancient Monuments Act 1979 239
Anglia **56**
Anglo-Dutch wars 53, **61**, 61–7, **63**, **64**, **65**, **66**, 152
Anglo-Saxon 32
Anglo-Saxon Chronicle 52, **53**, 57–8
Anglo-Saxon period 57–8, 202–6, **204**, **205**, **206**
Angwyne, Harry 37
animals 122–3
Ankh 104
Ann and Mary 119
Anne 71
Annual Register 216
Anson, HMS 38
Appledore **5**, 5–6
aqua fortis 126
Aquitania **xi**
Ardgantock 95
areas of marine archaeological potential (AMAP) 242
Ariel, HMS 109
Arinia 41
Arms of Rotterdam 74
artefacts viii, 27, 28, 47–8, 116, 207–10, 218
artworks 66, 152, **153**
Arwenack 39
Ashley, Hallam **168**
Association 138–9
Assurance, HMS 31–2
August Herman Francke 130
Auguste Padre 39
Augustine 54
Aungban 93
Auten, Lt Commander Harold, VC 99, 100, 101

B

Baden, SMS 54
Badzunra, Aurea 157–8
ballast material 48–9, 73, 208
Bamse **90**, 91
bankers 160–3, **161**
Baralong 99
Barbary Corsairs 68–9
Barber, Francis 137, 214
Barley Rig 83, 84
Barmston 90
barratry 120–2
Battle of Britain 112
battles
    Atlantic 114
    Beachy Head 71, 73, 76, 162
    Britain 112
    Downs 59–60, **60**
    Dungeness 62–3
    Four Days' 64
    'Glorious First of June' 123
    Goodwin Sands 62
    Jutland 81, 91
    Kentish Knock 62
    Les Espagnols sur Mer 58–9
    Lowestoft **63**, 63–4, **64**
    Maldon 57
    Portland 63
    Raid on the Medway 64
    Solebay **64**, 64, **65**, **66**
    Solent **132**, 132–3
    St James's Day 64
    Three Days' 63
    Winchelsea 58–9
bawleys 103
Beachy Head 71, 73, 75, 76, 162, 174, 208
Beagle, HMS 54
Bede 203
Bee 190
Bell 115

Bell, Moses 232
Belle, Dido Elizabeth 214
benzine 92, 94, 128
Berry, Thomas 80
Berwick Castle 109
Bessie 169
Betsey (lost 1799) 124
Betsey (lost 1859) 126
Betsy 176
Betsy Cains 177
Betty 176
Beulah 143
Beverly, James 27
Bewick, Thomas **172**, 181
Bideford Bar 216
Big Harcar Rock 146, 147
Bill of Portland 57, 101, 113, 124, 128, **212**
billyboys 170
biological colonisation 45–6
Bismarck, Otto von 158
Black Middens 1, **3**, 10, **145**, 177
Black Spread Eagle 64
Blackburn Iris *N238* 113
Blackfriars Ship II 9, **10**, **213**, 213
Blackwood, Commander 92, 94
Blake, Admiral Robert 62
Blanche et Marie 130
Bleak House (Dickens) 118
Blesk 128
blockships 62, 65, **244**
Blucher 165
Board of Trade Casualty Returns 130
Bom Succeso 216
Bonhomme Richard 77–81, **78**
Borgå 91
Borgund I 90
Boston 82
Boswell, William 74

Boudin, Eugène **161**
Boyne 180
Brandenburg 33
Brazil 215
breach of the sea 42–3
breeches buoy 145, 184
Brentwood 87
Bretagne 91
brigantines 177, 216, 221, 222
Brighton 183–4
Brighton Beach, with colliers (Constable) **182**
Brighton Belle 103–4
brigs 14, 44, 115–16, 124, 142, 161, 162, 182, 226
    colliers 11, 119–20, 123, 164, 171, **176**, 176–7, 180, 230
Bristol Channel 40, **56**, 111, 170, 172, 227, 242
Britannia 170
British Vessels Lost at Sea 1914–18 91
Brixham 165–6, **166**
Bronze Age wrecks viii, 33, 149, **149**, 197, 235
Brookes **219**
Brotherly Love's Increase 167
Brown Mouse 99
Brownsman Island lighthouse 146
Buck, Samuel and Nathaniel **11**, **141**
Buis 24
Burbo Bank 169, **170**, 173, 215
Burdon 226
Burgh van Alkmaar 62
Bylbawe 58–9
Bywell Castle 134–5, **135**

C

C11, HMSM 109
Cabot, John 160
Cadw 247
Caesar, Gaius Julius 198–200, 202
Caledonia 139, **226**, 227
calendars xii, 21, 191
Calshot lighship **143**
Cambrian Princess 150

Canada 56
canals 10, 127, 169, 174, 196
cannons and cannonballs 48, 64, **64**, 68, **70**
Canterbury 7
Carausius 202
careening 32, **136**, 136–7
Carew, Vice-Admiral Sir George 133
cargo vessels **11**, 51, **52**, 68, 69–70, 105, 167–71
cargoes, dangerous 125–31, **126**, **127**, **128**
'Cargoes' (Masefield) 175
Carolina, Solomon 120–1
Carrick Roads **36**, 36
Carvedras 164
cats **98**, 100, 122
cats (colliers) 177
Cedarine 227
Cerf 77
Charles I 61
Charles II 66, 236
Charming Molly 211
chasse-marées 173–4
Chatham 65, 123
Chattahoochee 92
Cheshire 86, 169, 198
    Traffick 219
Chesil Beach 154
Chichester 173
Chinchas 180
Christina 14
Church of St Peter and St Paul, Mottistone 227
Church of St Winwaloe, Gunwalloe 227–8, **228**
Churchill, Sir Winston 101
Clapham 129
Clarendon 139–40
Classis Britannica 197
Clokeman, Jordan 67
coal 85–6, 88–9, 130, 150, 179–80
    see also colliers
coastguard 54, 231–2
coastline variability **1**, 1
'The coastwise lights of England' (Kipling) 139, 182
cobles 166–7, **167**
cod 160–3
coffee trade 156

Cog Thomas **58**, 58–9
Coke, Sir John 15, 152–3
colliers 150, 171, **176**, **178**
    First World War targets 85–8
    glass trade 180–1
    names 178
    passengers 181
    in physical and cultural landscape 177–82, **182**
    privateering targets 69–70, 77
    spontaneous combustion 130
    types 175–7
Collina 127–8
collisions 94–5, **96**, 108–9, 118–20, 134, **134**, **135**, 172
Colossus, HMS (lost 1798) 207
Colossus, HMS (lost 1867) **225**
Columbus 134
Comet 109
Comfort, HMS 104
Commentariorum de Bello Gallico (Caesar) 198–200
Commerce 162
Commonwealth Navy 236, 238
Concepción 209
Constable, John **182**
Constant 141
contact details 245–7
contamination of sites 32
'The Conversion of St Wilfrid' (Kipling) 202
convict ships 151, 227
convoys 89–90, 92–7, **93**
copper sheathing 136
Coquille 123
Cornelia 14
Cornwall **34**, 34–40, **35**, **36**, **37**, **38**, **39**
    Albemarle 151
    Alonzo **227**, 227
    Anson, HMS 38
    Arwenack 39
    Auguste Padre 39
    Bell 115
    Betsey 124
    Blucher 165
    Caledonia 139, **226**, 227
    Carvedras 164
    Chinchas 180
    Collina 127–8
    Comet 109

Commerce 162
Constant 141
Le Cristofre 160
Elizabeth (lost 1745) 123
Emile Marie 142
Falls of Afton 101
First World War 166
fishing vessels 162, 163, 164–5, 166
Gabriell 35
George M Embiricos 166
Gipsy 163
Glenart Castle **56**
H52, HMS 54, 100–1
Hercules 39
Indian Chief (lost 1797) 126–7
Industry 170
Juffrow Johanna Christi(a)na 218
Kingston 231
Manly 142
Moira 163
Mosel 157
N S del Carmo 189–90
Narrow Escape 36
Neutralist 39
Nile 48
Olive Branch 123
Penshurst 99
President 38, 39–40
Roman wrecks 201
Royal Anne Galley 40, 44
sand effects 41, **42**
Sarah (lost 1802) 142, 145
Scarborough 69, **70**
Schiedam 39
Scylla, HMS 54
Second World War 111
Snowdrop 141
Sprat 165
St Anthony 37–8, **39**, 227–8
Star 142
storms 7–8
L'Union 39
Volant **224**
Washington Packet 123–4
Yanikale 125
Ymer 130
corrosion 46–8, **49**
Corsican Prince 87

Countess Anne 181
Countess of Caithness 173
Countess of Scarborough 77, 78
County Durham 75, 175, 177, 181
　Betsy 176
　Betty 176
　Dolphin (lost 1824) 176
　Eliza 176
Courageux 70
Courier 162
Cowper, William **217**
Cras, Hervé 104–5, 107
Crathie 83, 84
Creagh, Martin 120
Cressy, HMS **225**
Creteblock 188, **188**
Cretecable 186, 188
Cretemanor **187**
Creterock 186, 188
Cretestem 188
Le Cristofre 160
Cromwell, Oliver 61, 62, 236
Cumbria 113, 169, 190, 242
　George (lost 1771) 216–17
　Hannah 10

D

D-Day landings 105–7, **106**
Dainty Cruiser 8
Damhorst, Brigita 157–8
Darkdale **128**
Darling, Grace 146, 147–8, **148**
Darling, Robert 146, 147–8
Darro 96
Dartmouth 162
dates 190–1
Davaar **244**
Day, Mr 108, 114
de Bek, Martin 116–18
Deal Castle **60**, 60
Dean Sand 218
debris fields 43–4
Defoe, Daniel viii, 6–7, 7–8, 43, 63–4, 68, 182
dendrochronology 71, 74, 76
Denmark 52, **53**, 57–8, 81, 88–9, 90–1, 220–1

Department of the Environment for Northern Ireland 246
depth charges 109–10, **110**, 111
Derfflinger 82
designation of wreck sites 235–9
Deutschland 156–9
Devon
　Abbie Perkins 128
　Ambassador 42
　Amphion (lost 1796) 123
　Appledore storm **5**, 5–6
　Blackburn Iris *N238* 113
　Blesk 128
　Bom Succeso 216
　Bretagne 91
　Bronze Age wrecks **149**, 149
　cannon and cannonballs 48
　Coquille 123
　Edam II 42
　Endeavour 123, 177
　fishing vessels 162, 165–6, **166**
　hazardous cargoes 128
　Herzogin Cecilie 182–3, 184–6, **185**, 188
　Iona II 55
　John 161, 162
　Kleine Hendrick 150
　Lady Elizabeth 128
　London (lost 1796) 215–16
　M1, HMSM 109
　Maria 108
　medieval sailing ships **52**
　Navis Dei 208
　Nightingale 120
　San Pedro Mayor 59
　Smeaton's Tower **142**
　South Australian 125
　Spanish Armada 59
　Stock Force, HMS 97–8, **98**, 99–100
　submarines 109
　vessels collapsed 42
　World Wars 91, 111
Dickens, Charles 118, 130
Dissolution of the Monasteries 210
distribution of shipwrecks **viii**, **ix**
dogs **98**, 115
Dollar Wreck 39

Dolphin (lost 1665) 63
Dolphin (lost 1824) 176
Donegal **56**
Dorset 48, 49, 207–10, **208**
　Alexander 153–4
　Algarve 90
　Amy 101
　Bamse **90**, 91
　Barmston 90
　Borgå 91
　Borgund I 90
　Brown Mouse 99
　Christina 14
　Earl of Abergavenny **x**, 154
　Elizabeth (lost 1761) 141–2
　Fanny 181, 210
　Halsewell 154–6, **155**, 210
　M2, HMSM 113–14
　Ranger 162, 180
　Robert Shaw 124–5
　San Salvador 38–9, 59, 207
　Santa Maria de Luce 209–10, 218
　La Welfare 118
Douro **215**, 215
Dovenby 150
Dover 15, 102, **102**, 139, 197, 201, **201**, 206
Drake, Sir Francis 67, 75
Dream 32
dredgers and dredging 49, 194, 197, 235
Duc de Duras 77
Dudgeon lightship 144
Duivenvoorde 64
Dunbar 236
Dungeness 62–3, 75, 181, 205, 206
Dunkirk evacuation 102–5, **103**, 107
Dunkirkers 69, 70
Durham Packet 115
Dutch East India Company (VOC) 21, 24, **24**, 152–3
Dutch East Indiamen **151**, 151
　Amsterdam x, 152, 192
　Anglo-Dutch wars 51, 64
　Bonhomme Richard 77–81, **78**
　Goodwin Sands wrecks **21**, 21–6, **23**, **24**, **25**
　Kampen 30–1
　Loosdrecht 24

Maan 152
Maarsseveen 64
Meermond 24
Nassau 30–1
Needles wrecks 30–1
Oostereem 24–5
Oranje 64
Prins Willem 30–1
Rooswijk **21**, 21–6, **23**, **24**, **25**
Terschelling 30–1
Vliegende Draak 30–1
Vlieland 30–1
Wieringen 30–1
Dwina 125

E

E-boats 110
Eagle (lost 1703) 7
Eagle (lost 1707) 138
Earl of Abergavenny **x**, 154
Earl of Moira 173
East Indiamen *see* Dutch East Indiamen; English East Indiamen
ecological disasters 128
Edam II 42
Eddius Stephanus 203, 205
Eddystone 109
Eddystone lighthouses 141–2, **142**
Eddystone Rock 1, 35, 141–2
Edward 218
Edward II 242
Edward III 58, 59, 242
Edward, the Black Prince 58, 59
Eendracht 64
Eglinton 89
Eighty Years War 59, 61
La Eleyne 160
Elfrida **241**
Elise 85
Eliza 176
Eliza Fernley 146
Elizabeth and Martha 120–2
Elizabeth I 67
Elizabeth Jane 228–33, **229**
Elizabeth (lost 1745) 123
Elizabeth (lost 1761) 141–2

Elizabeth (lost 1808) 145
Elizabeth (lost 1831) 172
Ellan Vannin 164, 173
'Ellan Vannin' (The Spinners) 164, 173
Elliot 9–10
Elswout 73
Emile Deschamps 104–5
Emile Marie 142
Endeavour 123, 177
Endurance 9, 129
Engel Gabriel 63
England's Second Warning pamphlet 8
English Channel 1
  colliers 86, 91
  collisions 55, 183–4
  Dunkirk and D-Day 101–7, **103**
  passenger vessels 173
  Portland stone wreck 210–13
  Romans 200–1
  St Wilfrid 204
  storms 12, 29, 30
  U-boats **56**
  War Knight 92–7, **95**, 128
  see also Anglo-Dutch wars
English Civil War 53, 61, 67, 236
English East Indiamen 31–2, 38, 44, 151, **151**, 152–3, 153–4
English Heritage
  contact details 245–6
  Fishing Protocol for Archaeological Discoveries 50
  London case study 235–8, **237**, **238**
  Modern Wrecks Project 240–1
  National Heritage Protection Plan 242
  National Hulks Assemblage Project 240–1
  NRHE database xii, 229, 236, 240, 245
  reattribution of sites 88
  role 235
  sharing information 219, 239–40
  site assessment 235–6
Enseign Roux 92–3
Equiano, Olaudah 137, 214

Erikson, Captain Sven 184
Erikson, Gustaf 183
Erme Ingot site 149, 192, 200–1
Espion, HMS 52
Essex 194
  Arinia 41
  Boyne 180
  Deutschland 156–9
  Dovenby 150
  George (lost 1871) 164
  Hawke Packet 181
  Hussar, HMS 54
  Marlborough (lost 1739) 22, 23
  Play Prize 54, 74
  Richard and John 54
  Rose **169**
  Ruby 49
  Sagtmodig 220–1
  Saucy Jack 49
Eurydice, HMS 54, 157
Evelyn, John 53, 65, 66
Exeter 212
extreme weather events 4
  1607 Severn flood 4, 4–6, **5**
  freezes and thaws 8–11, **9**, **10**
  Great Storm of 1703 **6**, 6–8
  Great Storm of 1901 15
  storm of 1705 8
  storms of 1824 12–15

F

Fairfax 62
Fairy, HMS 109
Faith 48
Falcon **126**
Falls of Afton 101
Falmouth 36, 123, 127, 184
Fame 63
Fanning, Nathaniel 79–80, 81
Fanny 181, 210
Fassbender, Henrika 157–8
Fegan, Lt 92, 93, 94
Felipe I of Castile 208–9
Fenella 177
ferries *172*, 172
ferro-concrete ships 186, **187**, **188**, 188

fertilizer trade 150
figureheads **224**, 224–6, **225**, **226**
Filey Bay site 80
Finland 177, 181, 184
fire and explosions 122–5, **124**, **126**, 126–31, **127**
Firebrand 138
fireships 53, 59, 60, 62, 64, 65, 75
First World War 81–2
  aircraft **111**, 111–12
  anti-submarine technology 111
  auxiliary vessels 81–2, 83–5, 91
  Battle of Jutland 81, 91
  colliers 85–8
  collisions 94–5, **96**
  convoys 89–90, 92–7, **93**
  depth charges 111
  fishing vessels 166
  hospital ships **56**
  losses **97**
  mines and minefields 56, 82–3, **84**, **85**, 92
  minesweepers 82, 83–5
  post-war fate of German fleet 54
  Scandinavian aid **89**, 89–91
  shelling terrestrial targets 82, **83**
  U-boats **110**, 110
  War Knight 92–7, **95**
Fisher, Commander R L 104
fishing and fishing vessels 49–50, 160–3, **161**, 164–7, **165**, **166**
Fishing Protocol for Archaeological Discoveries 50
five-man boats 166–7
flats 169
Flèche 173
Flexbury Methodist Church, Bude 227
floods 4, 4–6, 10–11, 21
Flora 173
flying boats 113
  see also seaplanes
'Flying P' liners 183, **183**, **184**, 186
foodstuffs, trade in 150

forests, submerged 192
Forfarshire 146–7, 166
Fortune 119
Fountain 69
Four Days' Battle 64
France
  Battle of Beachy Head 71, 73, 76, 162
  chasse-marées 173–4
  fishing vessels **161**, 161, 162, 163
  privateering 69–70, 181, 211
  Revolutionary War 69
  War of the Grand Alliance 162
  World Wars 86, 105–7, **106**
Franklin, Benjamin 77
Frau Metta 140
Fred. Olsen line **90**, 90, 91
Fredensborg 214, 218
friendly fire 79, 88, 104, 131
Friendship (lost 1759) 123
Friendship (lost 1775) 120
Friendship (lost 1791) 115–16
Froissart, Jean 58–9
Frost Fairs 8–10, **9**, 22
Furious, HMS **111**
Fuseli, Henry **217**
future research **241**, 241–2

G

Gabriell 35
Gaea 83, 89
Garland, HMS 92, 93
Garret, Revd George 108
Gas Light and Coke Co. 86, 178
Gay, John **166**, 224
Gazelle 20
Gena 112
George (lost 1771) 216–17
George (lost 1871) 164
George M Embiricos 166
Germania 221–2, **222**
Germany 39
  Beachy Head wreck 75
  coal 177
  Deutschland wreck 156–9

Goodwin Sands wrecks 44, 52, 221–2, **222**
High Seas Fleet 54
liners 156–9
secularisation 158
U-boats *see* U-boats
windjammers **183**, 183–6, **184**
see also First World War; Second World War
gigs 164
Gilbert, Thomas 210–11
Gill, Peter 236
Gipsy 163
Glasgow Packet 146
glass trade 180–1
Glenart Castle **56**
Gloucester Castle **56**
Gloucestershire **171**, 188, 197
Britannia 170
Higre 170
King **175**
Rockby 170
Selina Jane 170
Golden Lion 16
Goodhope 8
Goodwin Sands **1**, 8, 15–20, **20**
Adventure 28
August Herman Francke 130
Battle of 62
Burgh van Alkmaar 62
charts **18**, 18
comparison of wrecks 26–8
Dunkirk evacuation 102
Espion, HMS 52
Gazelle 20
geography 17
Germania 221–2, **222**
Golden Lion 16
Hoffnung 44
Kong Sverre 222
Lady Luvibund 17
Le Nicholas **16**
life saving 19
in literature 16–17
Loosdrecht 24, 28
Mary (lost 1703) **6**, 8
Meermond 24, 28
mobility 17–18
Northumberland 7, 8, 41
number of wrecks 18–19

Ogle Castle 19, 44
Oostereem 24–5
Pugin's association with **19**, 19–20
Red Lion 16
Restoration 7, 8
Rooswijk **21**, 21–6, **23**, **24**, **25**
Royal Adelaide 19
Sagtmodig **220**, 221–2, **222**
salvagers 19, 20
South Goodwin lightship 19, 28
Stirling Castle 26–8, **27**
U-48 17, 109
Gossamer 82
Gottfried 83, 89
Grace Dieu 125
Grafton, HMS 104
Grain Race ships 183–6, **184**, **185**
Grand Banks 160, 162, 163
Great Harry **132**, 207
Great Storm of 1703 viii, **6**, 6–8, 26–8
Great Yarmouth 52, 143, 145, 167, **168**, 177
Greathead, H 145
Greenwood 179
Guernsey 201
Guerrero 214
Gull Stream site 48
Gyon, Stephen 121

H

H52, HMS 54, 100–1
Hals, Frans **153**
Halsewell 154–6, **155**, 210
Hamburg 177, 183–4
Hampshire 29, 166
Grace Dieu 125
Impétueux 123
Mary Rose x, 41, **41**, 49, 53, **132**, 132–3, 194, 207
Royal George 42, 136–7, **137**
see also Isle of Wight
Hanna Larsen 88
Hannah 10
Hans Kinck 88

Hanseatic League 160, 242
Happy Merchant 8
Hartlaw Cottages, Newton-on-the-Moor 233
Harwich 49, 52, 54, 99, 159, 177
Hasholme logboat 195, **196**
Hawke Packet 181
Hawker, Revd Robert 227, **227**
Hawker's Hut **227**, 227
Heinkel *1H+MH* 114
Helford River 7–8
Helsingør 115
Henrietta Marie 214, 218
Henry 123
Henry V 160
Henry VIII 133
Hercules 39
Herd Sand 10, 177, 201–2
Hero 146
herring 167, **168**
herring girls 167
Herzogin Cecilie 182–3, 184–6, **185**, 188
Highland Warrior **150**
Higre 170
Hird, SS 104
Historic Scotland 246
History of the English Church and People (Bede) 203
hit-and-run accidents 118–20, **119**
Hof van Zeeland 64
Hoffnung 44
Holland submarines 108
Hondius, Abraham 9, **9**
Honduras Packet 181
Hop, Hendrik 22
Hope (lost 1771) 10
Hope (lost 1808) 119–20
Hopkins, Gerard Manley 157–8
Hornsey 88
hospital ships **56**, 59, 138
Hound 164
Howard, Theophilus, 2nd Earl of Suffolk 59, 60
hue and cry 118–20, **119**
Hultenschmidt, Barbara 157–8
Hulton logboat 194–5
human error 115, 131–9, **132**, **135**
human nature 115–16

Humber and Humberside 77, 166, 170
Alberta 85
Frau Metta 140
Marie Knyght 140
Orcades 85
Hurstwood 87
Hussar, HMS 54
hydrophones 99, 111

I

Ibex 134
ice as cargo 129–30
ice damage 9–10, 10–11, 22
Iceland 69, 82, 160, 163
Ida 88, 89
Impétueux 123
Implacable, HMS 54
Indian Chief (lost 1797) 126–7
Indian Chief (lost 1881) 150
Industry 170
information, sources of viii–x, 14–15, 210, 242
inland trade routes 149
insurance fraud 115, 120–2
inter-war period 182–8, **183**, **184**, **185**, **187**, **188**
Iona II 55
Iron Age 191, 194–5, **195**, **196**, 200
Iron Crown 177, **178**
Isabella 14
Isle of Man 173
Isle of Wight
A1, HMSM **48**, 108–9, **109**
Anglo-Saxon 32
Assurance, HMS 31–2
Baden, SMS 54
Cambrian Princess 150
Cedarine 227
Clarendon 139–40
Concepción 209
Donegal **56**
Dream 32
Engel Gabriel 63
Eurydice, HMS 54, 157
Faith 48
Kampen 151

lifesaving 139–40, **140**
materials from wrecks 227
Mendi 96
Navis de Jehsu Christi de Portu
116–18, **117**
New Dawn, HMS 92
Pomone, HMS **30**, 31–2
Roman finds 202
Russie 161
storms 7–8, 157
Teamwork 30
theft 116–17
Varvassi, SS 29–30
Vliegende Draak 30–1, 151
War Knight 92–7, **95**, 128
war vs. peacetime losses
96, **97**
warships 54, 92–3
see also the Needles
Isles of Scilly **1**, 115, 152
Association 138–9
Charming Molly 211
Colossus, HMS 207, **225**
Courier 162
Douro 215, **215**
Eagle (lost 1707) 138
Firebrand 138
Hound 164
Logan 231
Loreto 55–6
Margaret **34**, 162
Mary (lost 1816) 164
Nymph 162
Pheasant 162
Romney 138
Sainte Marie 163
Schiller 157
Solace 164
St-Pierre 163
Torrey Canyon 128
Zeelilie 54
Iveagh Seapiece (Turner) **165**
ivory 218, 219

J

Jager, Robert **18**
Jaguar 104
Janszoon, Jan 68

Jaunty, HM Tug 107
Jeune Fanie 174
Jobling, Robert **178**
Johannah and Mary 216
John 161, 162
John and Sarah 65
John L Manson 107
Johns 77, 80
Johnson, Jacob 31
Johnson, John 27
Jolly Bacchus 214
Jones, John Paul 77–81, **78**
Joseph and Hannah 70–1
Josua 65, **66**
journalism viii, 6, 12, 53, 66–7
see also newspapers
Juana la Loca 208–9
Juffrow Johanna Christi(a)na
218
Julienne 208–9
Jurneeks **223**
Jutland 81, 91

K

Kampen 30–1, 151
keels 10, 11, 166, 170–1
Kellett Gut 17, 27–8
Kennemerland 151
Kent 15, **55**, **60**, 76, 169
Admiral Gardner 41
Amulree, HMS 104
Anglia **56**
Black Spread Eagle 64
Brandenburg 33
Brighton Belle 103–4
Comfort, HMS 104
Duivenvoorde 64
Emile Deschamps 104–5
Exeter 212
Falcon **126**
Flèche 173
Flora 173
Friendship (lost 1759) 123
Helsingør 115
Henry 123
Hof van Zeeland 64
Indian Chief (lost 1881) 150

John and Sarah 65
Jolly Bacchus 214
Maan 152
Moon 31, 152–3
Niki 33
Piedade 215
Pomerania 157
Preussen 182–4, **184**, 186
Richard Montgomery 41, 130–
1, **131**
Royal Charles 64, 65
Royal James 66, **66**
Sambut 105
Sisters 130
Sophia Magdalena 156
Stirling Castle 7, 8, 17, 26–8,
27, 41, 207
Texaco Caribbean 33
Tholen 73
Zorgvuldigheid 173, 221
see also Dover; Goodwin
Sands; Straits of Dover
Kent County 99
Kentish Knock 62, 115, **157**,
157–9
Kia Ora 93
Kiirus 177
King **175**
Kingston 231
Kipling, Rudyard vii, 139, 156,
182, 202
Kleine Hendrick 150
Knivestone 1, 146
Knockin logboat 195
Koevorden 64
Kolberg 82
Kong Sverre 222–3

L

Lady Elizabeth 128
Lady Luvibund 17
Lancashire 173, 190
Columbus 134
Eliza Fernley 146
Laura Janet **146**
Mexico 146
Prince Arthur 134
Spiraea 128
União 215

Land's End **2**, **34**, 34–5,
124, 201
Langebark 152
language and dialect 190, **220**,
220–2, **222**, **223**
Lanthorn 87–8
Lascelles 215
Laura Janet 146, **146**
Lawrence of Arabia 113
Lawson, Admiral John 236
Lawson, Captain 62
Leeuwarder Courant 221
legacy wrecks 130–1, **131**
legislation, protection 239
Lelia 48, 55
The Libertine (Shadwell) 75
Liberty Ships 130
licences, diving 238, 246
Life of Wilfrid (Eddius
Stephanus) 203, 205
lifeboat stations 139, 145, **145**,
148, 159
lifeboats **144**, 145–6, **167**, 184
lifesaving 19, 116, 139–48, **144**,
145, **146**, **148**, 166
lighthouses
Brownsman Island 146
Eddystone 35, 141–2
the Lizard 38
Longstone 146–8, **147**
the Needles **29**
Roman pharos 15, 20, 139,
201, **201**
Smeaton's Tower **142**
St. Catherine's Point 139, **140**
Trevose Head 142
Winchelsea 140–1
lightning strikes 124–5
lightships 143–4
Calshot **143**
Dudgeon 144
Goodwin Sands 15, 19,
28, 144
Long Sand 115
Newarp 119
lime trade 129
Lincolnshire 194
Hanna Larsen 88
'The liner she's a lady' (Kipling)
156
liners 156–9, **159**, 182–6, **183**,
184, **185**

Litchfield Prize 7

Liverpool 41, 48, 55, 169, 173, 215, 219

Lizard peninsula 31, **35**, 38, 40, 163, 166

Lloyd's insurer 120

Lloyd's List ix, 4, 216
   1771 floods 10
   1824 storms and wrecks 12, **13**, 14
   dates 190–1
   language and dialect **220**, 230
   privateering 69
   World Wars x, 56, 91

local vessel types 164–75, **165**, **166**, **167**, **168**, **169**, **171**, **172**, **175**

Lochiel 85

Loe Bar 37–8, 40

Logan 231

logboats 191–7, **193**, **195**, **196**

London
   Elliot 9–10
   Marlborough (lost 1730) 122
   Minerva 126
   Princess Alice 133, 134–6, **135**
   Tilbury **127**

London and *King* sites 235, 236, 238

London Gazette 4, 6, 8, **65**, 66, 67

London (lost 1665) 66, 125, 235–8, **237**, **238**

London (lost 1796) 215–16

London (lost 1918) 88

longshore drift **3**, 192

Longstone lighthouse 146–8, **147**

Loosdrecht 24

looting 116–18, 142–3

Lord Cecil 188

Loreto 55–6

'Loss of the *Eurydice*' (Hopkins) 157

Loti, Pierre 160

Lowestoft **63**, 63–4, **64**, 167

Lowestoft smacks 166

Lundin, James 120

Luttrell, Narcissus 40

Luxborough Galley **124**

Lydd, HMS 104

Lytham St Anne's **146**

M

M Lloyd Morris 96

M1, HMSM 109

M2, HMSM 113–14

Maagd van Enkhuizen 73

Maan 152

Maarsseveen 64

Madame Midas 92

Manby apparatus **144**, 145

Manchester 173

Manly 142

Manoury, John 120–1

Margaret **34**, 162

Maria 108

Marie Knyght 140

Marion 169

Marlborough (lost 1730) 122

Marlborough (lost 1739) 22, 23

marque, letters of 53, 67–8

Mars 119–20

Marshall 48

Mary Ann (lost 1804) 119–20

Mary Ann (lost 1916) 166

Mary (lost 1703) **6**, 8

Mary (lost 1816) 164

Mary Rose x, 41, **41**, 49, 53, **132**, 132–3, 194, 207

Masefield, John 175

Massey Shaw 102, 104

materials from wrecks 223–36, **224**, **225**, **229**

Mayor, Alison 106

McDougall, Captain Alex 80

Medway, raid on 64–5, **65**

Meermond 24

Membland 87

Mendi 96

Merchant of Venice (Shakespeare) 16–17

Mersey and Merseyside 54
   Bessie 169
   Chichester 173
   Countess of Caithness 173

Earl of Moira 173

Edward 218

Ellan Vannin 164, 173

Lascelles 215

Lelia 48, 55

Manchester 173

Marion 169

Railway King 169

Red Jacket 169

Smelter 169

Speculation 169

St Andrew 41

Thornton 215

Union 173

Metis 134

Mexico 146

Middle Ages viii–ix, 52, 57–9, **58**, 67, 116–18, **117**, 139

Middleton, Admiral Sir Charles 136

Minerva 126

mines and minefields 56, 82–3, **84**, **85**, 91, 92, 109, **110**, 111

minesweepers 82, 83–5

Minot, Laurence 58–9

Mirlo 92, 93

Misson, John 120, 121

Mitera Marigo **36**

Modern Wrecks Project 240, **240**

Møhlenpris 96

Moira 163

Moon 31, 152–3

Moon Shore site 192

Moor Sand site 33, **33**, 149

Moorlands 88

Moravia, Moses 120–1

Mosel 157

Mr Therm 178, 179

mutually assured destruction (MAD) 114

N

N S del Carmo 189–90

nameboards **222**, 226, **229**

names
   colliers 177–8
   deciphering **220**, 220–3, **222**, **223**

ferro-concrete ships 186
   slavers 218–19

naphtha 92, 94, 127, 128

Napoleonic Wars 52, 69

Napoli, MSC 116

Narrow Escape 36

Nassau 30, 31

National Heritage Protection Plan 239, 242

National Record for the Historic Environment (NRHE) database xii, 229, 236, 240, 245

Nautical Archaeology Society 247

Nautilus 129

Navis de Jehsu Christi de Portu 116–18, **117**

Navis Dei 208

the Needles 1, 28–32, **29**, **30**, **31**, 162

The Negro Revenged (Fuseli) **217**

'The Negro's Complaint' (Cowper) **217**

The Netherlands
   artworks **8**, 8, 152, **153**
   global trade 152
   Goodwin Sands, concern about 15, 19
   language and dialect 220–1
   privateering 69, 162
   Seventy Years' War 152
   slave trade 218
   spice trade 152
   War of the Grand Alliance 76, 162
   see also Anglo-Dutch wars; Dutch East Indiamen

Neutralist 39

New Dawn, HMS 92

New Lambton 178–9

New York Times viii, 89, 94, 157

Newbolt, Henry 61

Newby 11

Newby, Eric 185

Newcastle 129

Newcastle Courant 4, 190–1, 230

Newcastle-upon-Tyne 85, 87, 175, 180–1

Newfoundland cod fishery 160–3, **161**

newspapers ix
   'hue and cry' 118–19, **119**
   slave trade 216
   war journalism 53
   weather events 4, 6, 12,
      14–15, 21
   wreck news 28, 39, 154, 157,
      190, 230
   see also journalism
Le Nicholas 15, **16**
Nightingale 120
Niki 33
Nile 48
Nine Years' War 71, 76
Norfolk 5, 48, 50, 167, 182
   Beulah 143
   Blanche et Marie 130
   C11, HMSM 109
   Countess Anne 181
   Courageux 70
   Dolphin (lost 1665) 63
   Durham Packet 115
   La Eleyne 160
   Elizabeth (lost 1808) 145
   Fame 63
   Fortune 119
   Friendship (lost 1775) 120
   Kent County 99
   Kiirus 177
   Koevorden 64
   Maarsseveen 64
   Mary Ann (lost 1804) 119–20
   New Lambton 178–9
   Oranje 64
   Prins Maurits 64
   Snipe, HMS 145
   Swift 24
   Ter Goes 64
   Utrecht 64
   William 143
   Zwanenburg 64
Norman's Bay wreck 71–6, **72**
Nornen **42**
North Sea
   Bonhomme Richard 77–81, **78**
   First World War 50, 81–91,
      83, **84**, **89**
   fishing vessels 160, 166–7
   storms 12, 14

   wreck numbers 91, **92**
   see also Anglo-Dutch wars
Northumberland 91, **180**, 233
   Bywell Castle 134–5, **135**
   Elise 85
   Forfarshire 146–7, 166
   Glasgow Packet 146
   Heinkel *1H+MH* 114
   Hero 146
   Isabella 14
   Johns 77, 80
   Patia, HMS 114
   Providentia 176
   Somali 123, 150
   Suffolk 176
   Wealands 176
Northumberland 7, 8, 41
Nortraships 91
Norway **89**, 89–91, 129–30, 176
Norwich Merchant 123
Nouvelles d'Amsterdam 71, 73
Nuestra Senora de la Guarda
    208
number of shipwrecks vii, 86,
   91, **92**, **97**, 210, 240
Nymph 162
Nympha Americana 54

O

O B Jennings 92, 93–4
Oberon, HMS 94
Ogle Castle 19, 44
oil 94, 126–9, **127**, **128**
Olive Branch 123
Oostereem 24–5
Operation Dynamo 102–5, **103**
Operation Neptune 105–7, **106**
Operation Tiger 107
Orange Tree 75
Oranje 64
Orcades 85
Ostenders 75–6
Ouse, HMS 111
overloading 115, 125, 135
Owthorne Church 140
Owthorne logboat 192

P

paddle steamers 133–4
Pallas 77, 78, **78**
Pamir **183**
pamphlets 4–6, 8
Paracas 33
Parma 186
Pasley, HMS 92, 94
passenger vessels 150–1, 153–9,
   155, **159**, 172–5, 181
PastScape website xii, 245
Patia, HMS 114
Paulina 150
Pearson, Captain Richard 77,
   78, 79, 80, 81
Pêcheur d'Islande (Loti) 160
Pegasus 16
Peggy 190
Pendennis 36, **36**
Penheleg manuscript 36–7, 161
Pennington, Sir John 59–60
Penshurst 99
Pepys, Samuel 53, 62, 65, 66,
   236
Peru 55, 150
Petingaudet 96
Pheasant 162
Phoenix 138
Piedade 215
La Pilegrym 67
pinks 175–6
Play Prize 54, 74
Plimsoll line 125
Plinlimmon **103**
Plymouth **35**, 69, 121, 123,
   141, **142**
Plymouth 69
Pomerania 157
Pomone, HMS **30**, 31–2
Ponape 186
Poole 162, 163, **163**, 200, 209
Poole harbour logboat 200
porcelain trade 156
Portland stone wreck 210–13,
   213
Portsmouth 123, 137, 218
Portugal 75, 117, 152, 215
post-wreck events 40
   biological colonisation 45–6,
     47, **49**
   concretion 48, **49**

   corrosion 46–8
   debris fields 43–4
   human activities **48**, 48–50
   migration **50**
   sand effects 40–2, **41**, **42**, **43**
   undersea action 44–6, **46**, **47**
   wave effects 42–3
Poyntz, Captain John 15
Praa Sands 41–2, **42**, 113
preservation methods 194
President 38, 39–40
press *see* newspapers
press gangs 123–4
Preussen 182–3, **183**–4,
   184, 186
Prince Arthur 134
Princess Alice 133, 134–6, **135**
Prins Maurits 64
Prins Willem 30, 31
prisoners 65, 79, 88, 181,
   215, 216
privateering 53–4, 67–71,
   68, **70**
   Bonhomme Richard 77–81, **78**
   Norman's Bay wreck 71–6, **72**
Protection of Military Remains
   Act 1986 108, 114, 239
Protection of Wrecks Act 1973
   108, 109, 130, 235, 239
Providence 70, 190
Providentia 176
Pudding Pan Rock wreck
   200, 201
Pugin, Augustus Welby
   Northmore **19**, 19–20
Pytheas the Greek 149

Q

Q-ships **97**, 97–101, **98**, **99**
Q-ships film 99–101

R

Railway King 169
railways 86, 125, 167
Raleigh, Sir Walter 67

Rambler 173
ramming 58, 58–9, 109
Ramsay, Admiral Sir Bertram 101
Ranger 162, 180
Rapparee Cove 215–16
Rawlings, S W **168**
reattribution of wreck sites 88
Receiver of Wreck 25, 49, 88, 231, 247
Reculver towers 140, **141**
Red Jacket 169
Red Lion 16
Redcar 145
Reinagle, George Philip **138**
Reinkobe, Norbeta 157–8
reporting a wreck 245–6
reporting material from wrecks 247
researching wrecks vii–viii, 189–91
  Bonhomme Richard 80–1
  dates 190–1, 207
  death toll vs. vessels lost 7
  future research 241–4
  identification clues 207
  information sources viii–x, 14–15, 210, 242
  language and dialect 190, **220**, 220–2, **222**, **223**
  names **220**, 220–3, **222**
  Norman's Bay wreck 71–6, **72**
Resolution x, 7, 64, 74, 76
Restoration 7, 8
Resurgam 108
Return of the Terre-Neuvier (Boudin) **161**
Rewa **56**
Richard 236
Richard and John 54
Richard II (Shakespeare) 107
Richard Montgomery 41, 130–1, **131**
Robert Shaw 124–5
Robertshaw, Geoffrey Sykes 185, 186
Robin Hood's Bay 218, 228–34, **229**, *231*
Robinson Crusoe (Defoe) 43, 68
Rockby 170
Rocky Shore with Dismantled Vessel (Chambers) **232**

Roman wrecks 32, 197–202, **199**, **200**, 201
Romney 138
Ronzieres, Daniel 22, 24
Rooswijk **21**, 21–6, **23**, **24**, **25**, 26, 27, 28, 43–4
Rose **169**
Rotha 179
Royal Adelaide 19
Royal Anne Galley 40, 44
Royal Charles 64, 65
Royal Commission on the Ancient and Historical Monuments of Wales 247
Royal George 42, 136–7, **137**
Royal James 66, **66**
Royal Marines Armoured Support Group 106–7
Royal National Lifeboat Institution (RNLI) 145, 166
Royal Tar 122–3
Ruby 49
Russie 161

S

Sagtmodig **220**, 220–1
Saint Ninian 87, 88
Sainte Marie 163
Salcombe Cannon site **33**, 33, 44, **68**, 68–9, 149, 214
Sallee Rovers 68–9
Salmon 101
salt 37, 163, 169
salvagers 19, 20, 31, 74, 223–4
Sambut 105
Samian ware **200**, 201
San Pedro Mayor 59
San Salvador 38–9, 59, 207
sand effects on wrecks 41–2, **42**, **43**
Sandown Castle **60**
Santa Maria de Luce 209–10, 218
Sanvitores, John Baptist 209–10
Sarah (lost 1709) 75
Sarah (lost 1802) 142, 145
Saucy Jack 49
Sawyer, F E 203

Scandinavia 128–9
Scandinavian vessels 81–91, **89**, **90**
Scarborough 69, **70**
Scarborough Castle 78, 82
Scarborough minefield 84–5
Scarlet Thread **168**
scavenging of cargo 116
Schiedam 39
Schiller 157
Scottish herring fishery 167, **168**
Scratchells Bay 29, **30**
scuttling 54
Scylla, HMS 54
Seaham 86, 178, **179**
Seal, Jeremy 139
seamarks 139, 140, **141**, 148
seaplanes 111–12, 113
  see also flying boats
Seaton Carew wreck site 51, **176**, 176, 182
Second World War 101–2
  aircraft 105, 109, **112**, 112–13, **113**, 114
  Anti-Aircraft Operations Room **102**
  D-Day landings 105–7, **106**
  depth charges 109
  Dunkirk evacuation 102–5, **103**, 107
  mines and minefields 56
  submarines 109
  U-boats 110–11
seine boats 165
Seinte Marie 139
Selina Jane 170
Sequoya 92
Serapis, HMS 77–8, **78**
Severn 4–6, 169–70, 172, 174, 242, **243**
Severn bore 5, 170
Shadwell, Thomas 75
Shakespeare, William 16–17, 107, 238
Shaw, Aircraftsman (T E) 113
Shields 2, 8, 10, 177
shifting of cargo 125–6
shipbuilding 55, 59, 179, 186, 193–4
Shipping Controller 90
The Shipwreck (Turner) x

Shovell, Admiral Sir Cloudesley 138
Sint Maria 62
Sister Kirkes, Humberside 140, **141**
Sisters 130
site assessment 235–6, 239
Skipjack 82
Skuli Fógeti 83
slave trade 150, 214–19, **215**, **217**, **219**
Sleight fleet 84
Smallbridge 216
Smeaton's Tower, Plymouth **142**
Smelter 169
Smith, Gawen 15
smuggling 115, 173, 231
Snipe, HMS 145
Snowdrop 141
snows (colliers) 177
Solace 164
Solent x, 33, 42, **132**, 132–3, 162
Somali 123, 150
Somerset 52, 170, **195**
  Elizabeth (lost 1831) 172
  Nornen 42
'The song of the dead' (Kipling) vii
Sophia Magdalena 156
South Australian 125
South Goodwin lightship 19, 28, 144
South View of the Tower of London (Buck and Buck) **11**
Southampton 32, 161
Southsea Sub-Aqua Club 106
Sovereign of the Seas 62
Spain 59–60, 76, 152, 207–8
Spanish Armada 53, 59, 207
Speculation 169
spice trade 152–3, 156
the Spinners 164, 173
Spiraea 128
spontaneous combustion 130
Sprat 165
Spurn Point **3**, 192
St Andrew 41
St Anthony 37–8, **39**, 227–8
St Catherine's Point 96, 139–40, **140**
St Christopher 75

St George 138

St James's Day Battle 64

St Lucia 215, 216, 218

St Mawes castle 36

St Paul's Cathedral 210–13, **211**

St-Pierre 163

St Wilfrid 202–6, **204, 205, 206**

Star 142

Star, HMS 111

steam drifters 167, **168**

steamships 125, 133–4, **134,** 144, 182, 207

Stirling Castle 7, 8, 17, 26–8, **27,** 41, 207

Stock Force, HMS 97–8, **98,** 99–100

The Storm (Defoe) 6–7, 7–8

storms 2, 4

 1703 viii, **6,** 6–8

 1705 8

 1739 **21,** 21–3

 1824 12–15

 1901 15

 55 and 54 BC 198–9, **199**

 see also extreme weather events

Straits of Dover 17, 33, 105

Strathord 91

stress 96–7

Strymon **85**

Studland Bay wreck 207–10, **208, 209**

Style, Captain Thomas 152–3

submarines 100–1, 107–11, **109,** 113–14

 see also U-boats

Success 166

Suevic, SS **159**

Suffolk 70, 196

 Augustine 54

 Eendracht 64

 Fountain 69

 Gena 112

 Jozua **65**

 La Pilegrym 67

 Sukey 181

 Suffolk 176

 Sukey 181

Sunderland 10, 11, 113, 129, 177, 188

Sussex

 Amsterdam x, 42, **43,** 152, 192

 Anne 71

 Bylbawe 58–9

 Cog Thomas **58,** 58–9

 colliers 2, **182**

 Davaar **244**

 Eagle (lost 1703) 7

 Elswout 73

 Jeune Fanie 174

 lighthouses 140

 Maagd van Enkhuizen 73

 Norman's Bay wreck 71–6, **72**

 Nuestra Senora de la Guarda 208

 Nympha Americana 54

 Orange Tree 75

 privateering 54

 Resolution x, 7, 64, 74, 76

 Sarah (lost 1709) 75

 St Christopher 75

 St Wilfrid 202–6, **204, 205, 206**

 submarines 108

 Thomas Lawrence 55

 Vikings 52, 57

 Vriesland 73

 Wapen van Utrecht 73

 Warilda **56,** 96

 World Wars 105

Sutton Hoo ship burial 44

Swallow 8

Sweden 156

Swift 24

Syringa, HMS 92, 93

T

tanks 105–7, **106**

Tartar, HMS 95

tea trade 156

Teamwork 30

Tees and Teesside

 Betsy (lost 1814) 176

 Betty 176

 Betsey (lost 1766) 176

 Dolphin 176

 Eliza 176

 Hartlepool 14, 82, 176

 Seaton Carew wreck site 51, **176,** 176, 182

 Suffolk 176

 Wealands 176

The Tempest (Shakespeare) 238

temporary wrecks **244**

Ter Goes 64

Terschelling 30, 31

Texaco Caribbean 33

textiles trade 156

Thames **11**

 barges 167, **168,** 169, **169**

 collisions 134–5

 ferries 172

 Frost Fairs 8–10, **9**

 pleasure craft 133

 Roman wrecks 201

Thames Estuary 21, 22, 131, **157,** 157

theft 116–18

Theodosia 176–7

Tholen 73

Thomas 43

Thomas Lawrence 55

Thomas W Irvine 83, 84

Thompson, Isaac **3**

Thornton 215

Thrasher, HMS 88

Thurlestone Sands logboat 192–3, **193**

Tilbury **127**

timber cargoes 129

Time magazine 186

The Times 112, 134, 147, 157, 173, 186

Titanic **xi,** 129, 132, 136, 157, 158–9

'To the daisy' (Wordsworth) 151

tobacco 123, 150

Tolcarne logboat 194

Tonnage Agreement 90

Torrey Canyon 128

trade 149–51

Traffick 219

Trans-Atlantic Slave Trade project 219

transports 51–2

trawlers 50, 51, 83–5, 163, 165–6, **166**

trawling 49–50

Trenchard Bowl **209**

Trenchard, Sir Thomas 208–9

Trevose Head lighthouse 142

trows 169–70, **171,** 172

Turner, J M W **x, 144, 165**

Two Friends 173

Tyne **167**

Tyne and Tyneside **3,** 201, 226–7

 Ann and Mary 119

 armed cargo vessels 69–70

 Betsy Cains 177

 Burdon 226

 colliers 175–82

 Crathie 83, 84

 Cretecable 186, 188

 Creterock 186, 188

 Cretestem 188

 Dainty Cruiser 8

 Fenella 177

 ferries 172

 freezing and flooding 10

 Friendship (lost 1791) 115–16

 Goodhope 8

 Greenwood 179

 Happy Merchant 8

 Hope (lost 1771) 10

 Hope (lost 1808) 119–20

 'hue and cry' **119,** 119–20

 Iron Crown 177, **178**

 Jurneeks **223**

 keels 170–1

 lifesaving 145, **145, 167**

 Newby 11

 Paulina 150

 Roman coins 48

 Rotha 179

 Swallow 8

 Weazel 8

Tynemouth Chartulary 171

U

U-boats

 First World War **55, 82, 85,** 86–8, **87,** 92–7, 109–10, **110**

 Q-ships, hunted by **97,** 97–101, **98, 99**

Second World War 110–11
U-1021 111
U-106 **110**
U-325 111
U-400 111
U-48 17, 109
U-57 166
U-98 100
UB-115 111
UB-34 87
UB-39 166
UB-80 91, 100
UC-19 109–10
UC-39 88
UC-75 109
UK Hydrographic Office
  (UKHO) 19, 88
União 215
Unicorn 231
L'Union 39
Union 173
United States
  Civil War 51, 55, 108
  emigration to 157
  fishing 162–3
  ice trade 129
  Liberty Ships 130
  privateering 77–80, **78**
  slave trade 150, 214–19
  submarines 108
  War of Independence 51–2
  World Wars 91, 107
Utrecht 64

V

Valacia 93
Valhalla collection 225–6
van de Velde the Elder, Willem
  63, 66
van de Velde the Younger,
  Willem 66, 236, **237**
van den Broecke, Pieter **153**
vandalism **48**, 50, 241
Vanland **126**
Varvassi, SS 29–30
Vasa 132
Vengeance 77, **78**
Ver River logboat 191–2

Vereenigde Oost-Indische
  Compagnie (VOC) 21, **24**,
  24, 152–3
  see also Dutch East Indiamen
Verney, Francis 68
Viking **183**
Vikings 57–8
Villette-Mursay, Philippe de 73
Vimy, HMS 104
Vitality, HMS **85**
Vliegende Draak 30–1, 151
Vlieland 30, 31
Volant **224**
Von der Tann 82
Vriesland 73
Vrow Margaretta 180

W

Wakeful, HMS 104
Walmer Castle 60, **60**
Walsingham 123–4
Wapen van Rotterdam 74
Wapen van Utrecht 73
War Knight 92–7, **95**, 128
War of the Grand Alliance 76,
  162
War of the Spanish Succession
  76, 138
Warilda **56**, 96
wars
  American Civil War 51,
    55, 108
  American War of
    Independence 51–2
  Anglo-Dutch wars 53, **61**,
    61–7, **63**, **64**, **65**, **66**, 152
  Eighty Years War 59, 61
  English Civil War 53, 61,
    67, 236
  First World War *see* First
    World War
  French Revolutionary War 69
  Napoleonic Wars 52
  Nine Years' War 71, 76
  Second World War *see* Second
    World War
  Seventy Years' War 152
  War of the Grand Alliance
    76, 162

War of the Spanish
  Succession 76, 138
warships
  Anglo-Saxon period **52**, 57–8
  changing use 52–3
  civilian vessels 51–2, 81–2,
    83–5, 85–8, **87**, 88–91,
    89, **90**
  crews 53
  decommissioning process 54
  early history 52, **53**
  fireships 59, 60
  friendly fire 104
  future research 241–4
  Great Storm of 1703 7, 8,
    26–8, **27**
  Needles wrecks 31–2
  ramming **58**, 58–9
  records of losses 51
  scuttling 54
  Spanish Armada 59
  technological advancements
    54
  transports 51–2
  War Knight 92–7
  War prefix 92
  see also Anglo-Dutch wars;
    battles; First World War;
    privateering; Second
    World War
the Wash 70, 113, 242
Washington Packet 123–4
wave effects on wrecks 42–3
Wealands 176
Wear and Wearside 10, 11, 170–
  1, 172, 177–8, 179, 188
Wearside, HMS **85**
weather *see* extreme weather
  events; storms
Weazel 8
Webb, George 135
La Welfare 118
Wentworth 134
Weymouth 59, 208–9
whalers 129
Wheel Wreck 44, **45**
Wheeler, John 120
Whitaker Spit 22
Whitby Abbey 82, **83**
Wieringen 30, 31
William 143

Winchelsea 58–9, 140–1
windjammers **183**, 183–6,
  184, **185**
winds, prevailing 2, 40,
  181, 205
Winstanley, Henry 141
wireless 186
Wise, Thomas 210–11
Withernsea Church 140
Wolf Rock 1, 34–5
Wordsworth, John 154
Wordsworth, William 147, 151
The Wreck at Sharpnose Point
  (Seal) 139
wreck mounds 41, **41**, 42
'wreck of sea' 116–17
'The wreck of the *Deutschland*'
  (Hopkins) 157–8
Wreck of the Iron Crown
  (Jobling) **178**
wreck sites vii, **viii**, **ix**, x
wreckers 142–3
wrecking, deliberate 115–16,
  142–3
wrecks as shipping hazards 30,
  33, 103–4
Wren, Sir Christopher 210

Y

Yanikale 125
Yapura 55
Yavari 55
Ymer 130
Yorkshire
  Admiral van Tromp **240**
  Alliance 77, 78, 79
  Betsey 126
  Bonhomme Richard vs. *Serapis*
    77–81, **78**
  Boston 82
  Brentwood 87
  Bronze Age wrecks 149
  Canada 56
  colliers 180–1
  Corsican Prince 87
  Creteblock 188, **188**
  Dwina 125
  Elizabeth Jane 228–34, **229**

Fairy, HMS 109

ferro-concrete ships **188**

First World War 82, **83**, 84–5, 87, 88, 91, 166

fishing vessels 160, 166

Gossamer 82

Gottfried 83, 89

Hurstwood 87

Ida 88, 89

Lanthorn 87–8

Lochiel 85

Marshall 48

Mary Ann (lost 1916) 166

Membland 87

Moorlands 88

Nautilus 129

Saint Ninian 87, 88

Sister Kirkes, Humberside 140, **141**

Skipjack 82

Strathord 91

Success 166

Thomas 43

Unicorn 231

Vanland **126**

Vrow Margaretta 180

Z

Zeelilie 54

Zeppelins 112, **112**

Zon 152

Zorgvuldigheid 173, 221

Zwanenburg 64

Time-Saver Standards for Building Types

Other McGraw-Hill Handbooks of Interest

Baumeister and Marks · Standard Handbook for Mechanical Engineers
Brady · Materials Handbook
Callender · Time-Saver Standards for Architectural Design Data
Conover · Grounds Maintenance Handbook
Considine · Energy Technology Handbook
Crocker and King · Piping Handbook
Croft, Carr, and Watt · American Electricians' Handbook
Foster · Handbook of Municipal Administration and Engineering
Gaylord and Gaylord · Structural Engineering Handbook
Harris · Dictionary of Architecture and Construction
Harris · Handbook of Noise Control
Harris · Historic Architecture Sourcebook
Hicks · Standard Handbook of Engineering Calculations
Karassik, Krutzsch, Fraser, and Messina · Pump Handbook
LaLonde and Janes · Concrete Engineering Handbook
McPartland · McGraw-Hill's National Electrical Code Handbook
Merritt · Building Construction Handbook
Merritt · Standard Handbook for Civil Engineers
Morrow · Maintenance Engineering Handbook
O'Brien · Scheduling Handbook
Perry · Engineering Manual
Rau and Wooten · Environmental Impact Analysis Handbook
Stubbs · Handbook of Heavy Construction
Tuma · Engineering Mathematics Handbook
Urquhart · Civil Engineering Handbook
Woods · Highway Engineering Handbook

Time-Saver Standards for Building Types

Second Edition

Edited by

JOSEPH De CHIARA

and

JOHN HANCOCK CALLENDER

McGRAW-HILL BOOK COMPANY

New York   St. Louis   San Francisco   Auckland
Bogotá   Singapore   Johannesburg   London
Madrid   Mexico   Montreal   New Delhi
Panama   Paris   São Paulo   Hamburg
Sydney   Tokyo
Toronto

Library of Congress Cataloging in Publication Data

De Chiara, Joseph, date
   Time–saver standards for building types.

   Includes index.
   1.   Modular coordination (Architecture)
2.   Building materials—Standards. I. Callender,
John Hancock, joint author. II. Title.
NA2760.D42   1980   729'.2   80-13229
ISBN 0-07-016265-4

4567890KPKP898765432

The editors for this book were Harold B. Crawford
and Ruth L. Weine, and the production supervisor was
Paul A. Malchow. It was set in Technica Medium by
The Kingsport Press.

Printed and bound by The Kingsport Press.

Contents

Contributors   xi

Organizations   xiii

Preface to the Second Edition   xv

Preface to the First Edition   xvii

1. RESIDENTIAL 1

Dimensions of the Human Figure   3
Living Areas   5
Living Rooms   6
     Furniture   6
     Furniture Sizes   7
     Furniture Arrangements   8
     Furniture Sizes and Clearances   14
Dining Areas   15
Combined Living-Dining Spaces   20
Combined Dining Area–Kitchen   21
Bedrooms   22
Combined Living-Sleeping Areas   27
Kitchens   29
Laundry Rooms   41
Bathrooms   48
Closets   58
Apartments   70
Housing Densities   82
Housing for the Elderly   87
Housing for the Handicapped   102
Parking for the Handicapped   117
Group Homes   119
Senior Citizens' Center   122
Mobile Homes and Parks   129
Youth Hostels   140
Site Planning   146

2. EDUCATIONAL 161

Nursery Schools   163
Children's Center   167
Child Care Centers   168
Elementary and Secondary Schools   169
     General   169
     Site Selection   173
     Busing, Parking   174
     Recreation Facilities   175

Contents

Safety   176
Kinds of Schools   178
Administration Suites   185
Learning Resource Centers   188
Classrooms   190
Multipurpose Rooms   195
Student Lockers   197
Language Laboratory   200
Science Facilities   200
Arts   205
Music   206
Industrial and Vocational Facilities   210
Home Arts   211
Food Service   212
Physical Education   218
Auditoriums   229
Guidance Services   231
College and University Facilities   233
Classrooms   233
Lecture Rooms   234
Gymnasiums   236
Physical Education and Sports Facilities   240
Field House   241
Dormitories   242
Handicapped Students   255
Libraries, Academic and Research   257
Individual Study Carrels   274
Student Unions   285
Computation Centers   293
Communications Centers   296
Regional Education Center (Supplementary)   298
Resource Facilities (Library)   300
Large-Group Facilities   303
Audiovisual   314
Theater-Arts-Laboratory Teaching Station   320
Programs and Programming   323

3. CULTURAL.   327

Museums   329
Small Museums   336
Gallery Design   339
Libraries   341
Branch Libraries   343
Space Requirements   344
Service and Space Relationships   347
Library Location   348
Branch Buildings   350
Bookmobiles   350
Bookstack Data   351
Theaters   352
Sight Lines   362
Stage Space   365
Community Theaters   371
Amphitheaters   377
Music Facilities   380

4. HEALTH   393

Hospitals   395
Surgical Suite   403

Contents

Nursery 405
Pediatric Nursing Units 409
Diagnostic X-Ray Suite 412
Pharmacy 418
Teletherapy Units 420
Electroencephalographic Suite 424
Physical Therapy Department 425
Occupational Therapy Department 428
Laboratory 431
Labor-Delivery Suite 437
Radioisotope Facility 439
Outpatient Activity 441
Emergency Activity 456
EDP Unit 458
Rehabilitation Centers 461
Mental Health Centers 476
Nursing Homes 482
Child Health Station 489
Medical Schools 490
Dental Schools 511
Nursing Schools 528
Youth Treatment Centers 544
Multiphasic Health-Screening Centers 550

5. RELIGIOUS 557

Churches, General 559
Churches, Lutheran 564
Churches, United Methodist 570
Temples and Synagogues 582
Chapels 589
Church Schools 592

6. GOVERNMENTAL AND PUBLIC 601

City and Town Halls 603
Courthouses 608
Fire Stations 628
Firehouses 631
Police Stations 636
Police Facility 646
Jails and Prisons 653
Incinerator Plants 669
YMCA Buildings 676
YWCA Buildings 677
Boy's Clubs 690
Recreation Centers 696
Neighborhood Service Centers 702
Embassies 704
Post Offices 708
Access Ramps for the Handicapped 709
Public Toilet Rooms for the Handicapped 710

7. COMMERCIAL 711

Regional Shopping Centers 713
Retail Shops 730
Show Windows 735
Women's Wear 736

Contents

Men's Wear 739
Bookshops 740
Gift Shops 740
Jewelry Shops 741
Barber Shop 743
Tailor and Cleaner 743
Beauty Shop 744
Shoe-Repair Shop 744
Florist Shops 744
Drugstores 745
Liquor Stores 746
Shoe Stores 748
Supermarkets 751
Banks 753
Bank Vaults 754
Restaurants and Eating Places 755
Restaurant Seating 759
Food Bars 763
Serving Units 764
Liquor Bars 765
Nondining Spaces 766
Kitchens 768
Offices, General 780
Work Stations 782
Private and Semiprivate 788
Conference Rooms 790
Layout 791
Space 792
Planning 793
Clearances for Private Offices 798
Clearances for General Offices 798
Insurance Companies 800
Medical Offices 801
Radiological Offices 806
Dental Offices 807
Law Offices 810
Ophthalmological Offices 814
Parking 817
Automobile Dimensions 817
Car Classification 822
Parking Garages 824
Parking Lots 835
Automobile Service Stations 839
Automotive Shop 843
Gas Filling and Service Stations 844
Automobile Dealer Centers 845
Truck Dealer and Service Facilities 854
Radio Stations 858
TV Stations 865
Hotels 870
Motels 899
Computer (EDP) Facilities 912
Photographic Laboratories 915
Funeral Homes 916

8. TRANSPORTATION 919

Airports and Terminals 921
Airport Cargo Facilities 953
Air Cargo Terminals 957